Seventeenth-Century
Roman Palaces

Seventeenth-Century Roman Palaces

USE AND THE ART OF THE PLAN

PATRICIA WADDY

THE ARCHITECTURAL HISTORY FOUNDATION
New York, New York

THE MIT PRESS
Cambridge, Massachusetts, and London, England

Library of Congress Cataloging-in-Publication Data

Waddy, Patricia.
    Seventeenth-century Roman palaces: use and the
art of the plan/Patricia Waddy.
        p.   cm.
    Includes bibliographical references.
    ISBN 0-262-23156-5
    1. Rome   (Italy)—History—1420–1798.
2. Palaces—Italy—Rome.   3. Rome (Italy)—
Social life and customs. 4. Barberini family. 5. Architecture, Baroque—Italy—Rome. I. Title.
DG797.9.W33 1990
945—dc20   90-31131
                                  CIP

Patricia Waddy is Associate Professor of Architecture
at Syracuse University.

Designed by William Rueter

FOR RICHARD KRAUTHEIMER

Contents

Acknowledgments

THE HISTORY of this book seems to me rather like the history of the "Casa Grande," the Barberini family palace in via dei Giubbonari. It began modestly enough in 1977, when I thought I would write a short article setting forth what an anonymous advisor to the Barberini had to say about the workings of a seventeenth-century Roman palace. Bit by bit it grew, as one discovery led to another question. Countless individuals, institutions, and circumstances affected that growth; some intervened for only a critical moment, and others maintained their involvement for longer periods of time. For a while, the large and ungainly form of this study resembled that of the "Casa Grande" in the 1630s, before Taddeo Barberini's major project for reforming the structure. I hope it may be spared the hard times on which that palace fell, but I would be pleased if this work eventually should be as completely absorbed in the fabric of the discipline of architectural history as is the "Casa Grande" in the life of the city of Rome today.

It is my pleasure to thank some of the persons and institutions that have made this book possible.

In 1976–77, Howard Saalman focused my rambling attention on the question of use. The earliest phases of the research were supported by a Summer Stipend from the National Endowment for the Humanities (1977) and a Fellowship from the American Council of Learned Societies (1978). The Senate Research and Equipment Fund of Syracuse University contributed to my studies in the summer of 1980. Irving Lavin showed me the biography of Taddeo Barberini (ABarb., Ind. IV, no. 1254, published here as Appendix 3) when he realized its relevance for my interpretation of Palazzo Barberini; and Joseph Connors generously gave me his draft of a transcription of the etiquette followed by the ambassador of the grand duke of Tuscany in Rome (ASF, Medici del Principato, vol. 2658, published here as Appendix 1) and encouraged me to include it in this book. Tod Marder crystallized for me the importance of the moment at which something happens, for the interpretation of documents. In 1984–85 a sabbatical leave from Syracuse University and a Fellowship from the National Humanities Center enabled me to begin to give shape to this study and to write about half of it; I am especially grateful to the administration, staff, and other fellows of the National Humanities Center for providing a setting that was both supportive and stimulating. Several people gave invaluable help in my pursuit of drawings of the "Casa Grande" now in the Archivio Storico of the Cassa di Risparmio di Roma and then of photographs of the drawings: Jack Freiberg; Professor Russell T. Scott, Signora Bianca Passeri, and Signora Karin Bull-Simonsen Einaudi of the American Academy in Rome;

Signor D'Anchise, archivist of the Archivio Storico, Cassa di Risparmio di Roma; and Signor Roberto Del Signore of the Centro di studi sulla cultura e l'immagine di Roma. David DiMarco shared his expertise in graphic presentation and made several of the reconstruction drawings. Countless friends, colleagues, students, and complete strangers generously listened to parts of this study in various conversations and public presentations; they offered their suggestions and criticisms and buoyed my enthusiasm.

The Biblioteca Apostolica Vaticana, the Archivio Segreto Vaticano, the Bibliotheca Hertziana, and the Library of the American Academy in Rome have provided not only their incomparable resources but also their hospitality and support of my work over the years.

I offer special thanks to John Beldon Scott. For several years we have worked in tandem on our respective topics, sharing information, documents, flashes of discovery, and gossip about the seventeenth century. The specific references to his work in the notes are but a partial indication of his sustained contribution to this book.

Richard Krautheimer is absolved of all responsibility for the contents of this book, for we were barely in contact during the crucial years of research and writing. His teaching and example, however, were always before me. I have valued his exacting scholarship, his sense of the vitality of his subject, and his awareness that whatever we write as historians is only a "post station" in our pursuit of our subject. It is with affection and respect that I dedicate this book to him.

Introduction

BUILDINGS have lives in time, and those lives are intimately connected with the lives of the people who use them. Buildings come into being at particular moments and in particular circumstances. They change and perhaps grow as the lives of their users change. Eventually — when, for whatever reason, people no longer find them useful — they die. The artistry of the designers of buildings is exercised in the context of that life, as well as in the context of a life that art itself may have.

Rome in the seventeenth century was distinctive in ways that affected the lives of its buildings. It was dominated by the institution of the papacy, a powerful if carefully balanced synthesis of temporal and spiritual power. A major European capital, its head of state and principal courtiers were celibate churchmen; the getting and spending of both money and power — and concomitantly the occasion for the building of palaces — were therefore not to be predicted according to a continuous line of succession. The legacy of antiquity was more than an idea; it was a physical reality in terms of noble ancient structures, ravishing colored marbles and finely carved architectural ornament, and the sheer intractable mass of Roman masonry. This physical substance of the city reverberated in buildings through the centuries. Terrain and climate inevitably came into play. Artistic traditions were im-portant, for seventeenth-century architects could look back to the assured accomplishments of two centuries of postmedieval designers: there were models, whether to guide their work in reliable channels or to be transcended. There were, finally, remarkable individuals — patrons, amateurs, and architects who probably would have achieved architectural distinction of some form or other even if they had lived and worked elsewhere. Analogies may be drawn between developments in seventeenth-century Rome and those in other times and places, and similar lines of investigation may be pursued elsewhere; still, the conclusions and hypotheses presented in this book cannot be assumed to apply to other times and places, and indeed they can often be demonstrated to be inapplicable. Seventeenth-century Romans themselves were aware of the differences between their buildings and, for example, those of their fifteenth-century countrymen or those of contemporary Parisians.

Romans were especially enthusiastic builders of palaces. More than simple shelters, their palaces were both public statements of the position of their families and stages within which the important business of diplomacy and representation could be played out. They were major expenditures (along with lavish carriages and substantial dowries for daughters or nieces) in a city devoted to ecclesiastical and diplomatic decorum.[1] Construction industries prospered: in 1622, when the population of the city numbered about 110,000, there were 415 carpenters' shops, 388 masons' shops, and 78 stonecutters' shops.[2] Both patrons and architects devoted considerable energy to the design and construction of palaces. If today those secular structures seem eclipsed by the enduring splendors of Roman churches, it is perhaps because, committed from the beginning to the flexible accommodation of complex patterns of activities, they have adapted so well to the exigencies of modern life.

The first part of this book is an attempt to reconstruct the general program for any large palace in seventeenth-century Rome — the basic patterns of aristocratic life and building that were accepted as normal, right, and proper, and that did not have to be explained to any Roman architect. The complex organism of the household is here dissected into its several functional components, with as little violence as possible to the connecting fibers and tissues. The focus is first of all on the activities accommodated by the house, and then on the forms that that accommodation assumed in some buildings. Wonderfully fruitful for this research has been a group of handbooks on etiquette and household management, the product of an age of order and regularity, from which one can learn how to carve a chicken, how to address a letter to the king of Poland or to an "ordinary gentleman," what are the duties of the palace janitor, how to keep financial accounts, how to receive a cardinal or the ambassador of the grand duke of Tuscany, when to take down tapestries and put up other wall hangings for summer, what activities and behavior are appropriate for the anteroom, and much more. Further evidence can be found in theoretical works, contemporary accounts, household records and other documents, and the buildings themselves. As with any living thing, there is inevitably variation and change in the organism of the household, and I have tried to indicate both the range of possibilities and the developments

within even the limited time span of this study. Finally, I have characterized the life within the palace in terms of movement, which is embodied especially in the three-dimensional plan of the building. I have further speculated on the art of the plan — that abstract aspect of the design of a palace which is nevertheless as much subject to the artistry of the designer as is the façade or the courtyard elevation. Use in a building is rather like subject matter in a painting: a given group of functions can be accommodated in any number of ways, and with varying degrees of artistry.[3]

In the second part of the book, five palaces are considered in detail. They are palaces of the brothers or nephews of popes — that is, persons at the pinnacle of Roman society, with the financial and persuasive resources of the papacy at their disposal. The need of these patrons is not the result of generations of prominence; rather, it comes into being suddenly, with the elevation of their kinsman to the papacy. With the architects of their choice, they can devise palaces that directly address their requirements and aspirations. Their undertakings therefore provide fixed points on a scale of sorts, according to which changes over time can be estimated, and against which the palaces of lesser persons can be measured. The palaces are characteristically Roman in that not one of them is constructed entirely *ex novo*. The palace at Palestrina is built into the remains of the ancient sanctuary of Fortuna Primigenia, and the Palazzo Barberini alle Quattro Fontane is founded partly on ancient Roman masonry. All five incorporate sixteenth-century construction. Their small adjustments and major rebuildings occur in response to the exigencies of the lives of their owners. The owners select architects who are congenial to their aspirations and collaborate with them in one way or another. The architects include some of the most prominent in Rome (Carlo Maderno, Gianlorenzo Bernini), as well as minor masters (Paolo Maruscelli, Francesco Contini) and others who are barely remembered today (Giovanni Maria Bonazzini, Angelo Torrone). The specific forms of the buildings, in plan, elevation, and detail, are due to the artistry of these architects. There are historical relationships among the several architects, and within and among the five buildings. The several histories of growth and change are typically Roman. Although I have focused on just one century of their development, the lives of the five buildings have continued to the present day.

For these studies it has been essential to determine exactly what was built at any given moment. Documents of construction *(misura e stima)* have been invaluable, for they record in detail what was actually built for the purpose of calculating payments to the craftsmen. When read in their entirety, these long documents (a few hundred pages for a major building or remodeling) yield up a remarkably convincing picture of the work, with precise measurements of walls, vaults, pavements, openings, stucco moldings, and every other part of the fabric. While their virtue lies in the thoroughness and consistency of the record, their length precludes their complete transcription. Instead, I have included only relevant excerpts (along with complete citations) in the notes. Inventories of furnishings can be very evocative of the quality of palaces and can also give some specific information about the uses of rooms, or the outfitting of certain types of rooms, or even architectural features of the rooms. Descriptions and drawings help too. My plans and descriptions are therefore presented with a certain confidence, coupled, however, with modesty: they are reconstructions and not archaeological surveys.

Having reconstructed what was done at precise moments in a building's life, and having understood how those acts of building are related to the needs and purposes of the owners, we are then in a position to consider the artistry of what was done, its authorship, its relationship to the designs of other buildings, and its significance for our understanding of architectural activity in seventeenth-century Rome. I have interwoven questions of historical evaluation with reconstruction and explanation, since what was built is at once the product of various causes and the means to the artistic result.

Beyond having made an empirical contribution by reconstructing segments of the lives of these buildings, I hope to have accorded planning some of the importance that it has always held for architects and clients alike, to have presented a view of some buildings that is more than simply pictorial, to have clarified our understanding of the respective roles of architect and patron, to have probed the processes of design, and to have observed the essential unity between architecture and life.

NOTE ON MEASUREMENTS

Dimensions usually are given in *palmi romani,* the unit of measure employed in the *misure e stime* and other documents of seventeenth-century Rome: 1 *palmo* = 0.2234 meter, or about 9 inches; 10 *palmi* = 1 *canna.*

Part I: Anatomy of a Palace

CHAPTER ONE

The Apartment

THE BASIC UNIT of planning in a Roman palace was the apartment, a set of rooms for the use of a single important resident, and the model resident was a cardinal.[1]

In the ecclesiastical society of seventeenth-century Rome, the leaders of society, who set the patterns of behavior and standards to be approximated by others, were cardinals — that is, single celibate men of high rank. (The pope, although exalted from the cardinalate, was unique in his spiritual and temporal dignity and therefore did not offer an appropriate model for others' behavior.) Cardinals, however heterogeneous in their wealth and individual distinction, nevertheless formed a distinct class, headed by the cardinal nephew of the reigning pope and the dean, or oldest member, of the College of Cardinals. Lesser churchmen lived in more modest circumstances, and secular leaders had to include accommodations for their wives and other family members in their palaces; yet their manners and dwellings were but modifications of the patterns set by cardinals.

The cardinal ate and slept in his apartment, but its use went far beyond those private functions. In the papal capital, thronged with ambassadors and courtiers intent on diplomatic commerce, the paying of calls, whether of courtesy or of substance, was a major activity; and this activity took place not at some separate place of business but in apartments within palaces, according to an elaborate etiquette which was itself an important vehicle of diplomacy.[2] The design of the apartment was therefore intimately bound to that etiquette: living quarters that would not accommodate the ceremony of receiving callers were useless.

Roman etiquette was important enough to require handbooks setting forth its principles and details. The most prominent of these was *Il maestro di camera*, by Francesco Sestini da Bibbiena, first published in 1621 and then republished in 1639, with several later editions.[3] The etiquette was further distinctive enough to require explication for foreigners. Tantouche's *Traicte de tout ce qui s'observe en la cour de Rome . . .* (Paris, 1623) was written on the occasion of the departure of the Cardinal de la Valette for Rome, not to discuss French usages, with which the cardinal and his entourage would already be familiar, but to set forth those of Rome, to which "his dignity would require him to conform as closely as possible." The etiquette is the same as that described by Sestini, but with occasional notes to clarify points for the new French cardinal.[4] Conversely, Roman travelers abroad noted the differences between foreign usages and those to which they were accustomed at home.[5] The etiquette was enough of a curiosity that the Protestant convert Gregorio Leti detailed it in his description of Roman institutions in 1675.[6] It was fundamental enough that other contemporary handbooks on household management referred to details of etiquette while describing duties of the several members of the household staff.[7] It was subtle enough that individual cases were set down in special memoranda — for example, a note on the etiquette that Don Taddeo Barberini (not yet prince or prefect) observed in calling on and then receiving the Duke of Mantua; the practices of Costanza Magalotti Barberini, a woman and sister-in-law of Urban VIII, in receiving guests; and a detailed account of the etiquette to be used by the ambassador of the grand duke of Tuscany with respect to every person with whom he would be likely to deal in Rome.[8]

A fundamental issue in Roman etiquette was the recognition of the respective ranks of the participants. Rank itself was established by several considerations: the distinction between ecclesiastical (higher) and secular (lower) status; particular offices held; the distinction of one's family or, in the case of ambassadors, the prince or nation served; one's position within that family; and one's age. Signs of rank included the number and quality of carriages in the guest's train; the clothing worn for a visit; the announcement of the guest's arrival by the ringing of a bell in the stair; the points in the guest's progress toward the audience room at which he would be met, first by gentlemen attendants and then by the host; forms of address used; compliments paid; the offering of the left or right hand by the host; the arrangement of chairs in the audience room; the lowering of the *portiera*, or door hanging, during the interview (for guests of higher rank); and, on departure, the points in the suite at which the guest was bade farewell, first by the host and then by his gentlemen attendants. Infractions of etiquette were noted and sometimes had serious consequences, as in the Conestabile Colonna's affront to his visitor the Cardinal of Lyon in accompanying the cardinal to a point *near* his carriage and then quickly returning to his ground-floor apartment without waiting for the cardinal to mount his carriage and depart — an incident that affected relations between the French community in Rome and the Romans in 1636.[9] If there was any uncertainty as to how to receive a guest, the best advice was to put the guest off for a few hours, making some excuse, until inquiries could be made as to the details of his rank. Some persons were praised for their ingenuity in dealing with problematic situations, as the cardinal who took to his bed, pretending to be sick, receiving his guest there, so that the usual requirements for advancing to meet the guest at some particular point in the suite would not have to be observed; and the cardinal who nodded toward two guests arriving at the same time in such a way that it was left to the guests to decide which of them should have precedence.[10] Situations intolerable to one party or the other simply were avoided: Taddeo Barberini withdrew from public ceremonies to avoid confrontations with the secular ambassadors who would not yield precedence to him as Prefect of Rome, and the ambassadors exercised similar restraint;[11] the ambassadors of Tuscany declined to visit the Cardinal Colonna, because of uncertainties of forms of address to be used.[12]

The etiquette as described in handbooks of the late sixteenth and seventeenth centuries assumes a particular architectural setting (Fig. 1). The apartments in which guests were received were normally (but not always) on the *piano nobile,* and the stair was therefore an essential feature of the path to the audience. Beyond the landing of the stair was the large *sala,* or "sala dei palafrenieri," succeeded by perhaps two anterooms and, finally, the audience room. Beyond the audience room and not normally accessible to guests were the cardinal's bedroom and a service room. The number of anterooms could vary, according to the prestige of the resident; and the private rooms could be augmented by a study, gallery, or other room. The chapel opened from one of the anterooms. Additional nearby rooms might also be useful.

The ceremony of receiving guests was per-

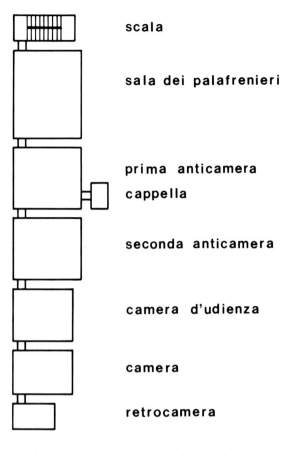

scala

sala dei palafrenieri

prima anticamera

cappella

seconda anticamera

camera d'udienza

camera

retrocamera

1 The apartment in seventeenth-century Rome (author)

fectly in accord with the linear sequence of rooms of the apartment. The guest arrived at the foot of the stair, delivered there by his carriage. If of high rank—a cardinal, a grand duke, an ambassador of a king, or possibly an ambassador of Tuscany or Savoy—his arrival was announced at this point by the ringing of a bell.[13] The guest ascended the stair and advanced through the *sala* and anterooms to the audience room. He was met, first by attendant gentlemen and then by the host, at a point commensurate with his rank, with respect to that of his host. For example, a visiting cardinal would be greeted by gentlemen

at the foot of the stair and then by the cardinal host in the *sala,* or (as a sign of greater respect) possibly beyond the door of the *sala,* but surely no farther than the top of the stair. For the ambassador of the grand duke of Tuscany, the cardinal host would come forward one and one-half rooms (to the middle of the outer anteroom, if there were the standard two anterooms), the gentlemen having greeted the visitor one room earlier. Ambassadors of Malta, Bologna, and Ferrara would be met by the gentlemen in the outer anteroom and by the cardinal in the middle of the inner anteroom, although the ambassador of Malta was to be treated a little better than the other two. The points at which guests of other ranks were to be met were similarly specified. Compliments were exchanged, the guest was offered the left or right hand of the host, and host and guest continued to the audience room.[14]

In the audience room further signs of rank were revealed. For guests of high rank, the *portiera* was lowered over the doorway, ensuring privacy during the interview (but for a woman guest the *portiera* was normally left raised).[15] The chairs in the room were positioned according to the respective ranks of host and guest, whether facing the door (the favored position), with the back to the door, with the side toward the door, or some subtle variation of the basic positions.[16] The sensitivity of this matter is shown by Cassiano dal Pozzo's description of the visit of the grand duke of Tuscany to Cardinal Francesco Barberini: the chairs had been positioned so that their sides were equally toward the door, but the grand duke, "through an excess of goodness and modesty," twice adjusted his chair to show greater deference to the cardinal, who then twice adjusted his own chair to restore the balance between the two.[17] Lunadoro notes the great difficulty of determining the proper arrangement of seats, in his opinion a skill learned more from practice than from theory.[18] The cardinal nephew of the reigning pope would never offer a seat to a lesser prelate or to the ambassador of Bologna or Ferrara, or to secular persons of lower rank, although other cardinals would do so.[19] At last the interview began, and once again rank came into play, as the person of higher status initiated the conversation.[20]

At the conclusion of the interview, on signal from the host, the *portiera* was raised and the guest accompanied to points once again commensurate with his rank, to be bade farewell first by the host and then by the gentlemen attendants; and these points were different from those at which he had been greeted. The cardinal would accompany his cardinal guest to his coach; and, as soon as it would have begun to move, he would turn away. The ambassador of the grand duke of Tuscany would be escorted to the coach, but the cardinal would turn to leave before the coach would have begun to move. The ambassadors of Malta, Bologna, and Ferrara would be accompanied the length of the two anterooms by the cardinal and one room farther by his gentlemen attendants. Persons of other ranks would be treated similarly, the gentlemen always going about one room farther than the cardinal host with the departing guest.[21] Virtually every possibility was foreseen, and procedures were set forth—for example, for the arrival of a second guest while the first guest was taking his leave, or for the departure of several guests at once.[22]

If ritual was prescribed and the apartment was specifically defined, there still was room for some variation in both etiquette and architecture. The host could show subtle favor by advancing a step or two beyond the prescribed point in greeting a guest, or by devising well-calculated combinations of position, words of greeting, and the extension of the left or right hand. It was Duke Cesarini's "choice" to exercise an "excess of courtesy" toward the Tuscan ambassador by waiting at the top of the stair until the departing ambassador had reached the first landing.[23] The apartment could have more or fewer anterooms, according to the rank or pretentions of the host, and the pattern of points of greeting and farewell would be stretched or

compressed accordingly.[24] The private chamber of the cardinal could be complemented by a study, gallery, or other room for private use. Additional rooms near the *sala* or outer anteroom, but outside the basic suite, would be useful if a distinguished guest was required to wait while the cardinal was busy with someone else (but lacking such a withdrawing room, the *maestro di camera* would simply empty an anteroom of other persons so that the distinguished guest could wait there with appropriate comfort and dignity).[25]

The ceremony of dining complemented that of the reception of guests and enjoyed a similar relationship between a fixed architectural framework and flexibility of action. Meals were served in the apartment, but the location and particular arrangements of the service might vary according to circumstances. Although no room was set aside exclusively for dining, meals often were served in the outer anteroom (which is even called "the room where the Prince will eat" in Evitascandalo's handbook).[26] The season or particular day's weather might suggest that a meal should be served "in a cool place, a garden, a loggia, or a cool room, or, on the other hand, a warm room, with or without a fire."[27] Banquets might be arranged in the *sala*. In any case, tables of the appropriate size were brought and set up for the meal and were taken away when the meal was over. Tables for the service of both food and wine were similarly brought and set up, usually in an adjacent room. A permanent *credenza,* or serving table, was arranged in the *sala* for use when meals would be served in the first anteroom,[28] or some other convenient room might be pressed into service.[29] It was also possible to arrange the serving table in the same room, but in that case it had to be out of sight of the dining cardinal.[30] As for an audience with the cardinal, so too with a meal, one's position at table was determined by rank, with respect to the entrance to the room, the position of the carver, and one's right hand.[31] Food was brought in courses (alternating between hot courses from the distant

2   The service of the *trinciante* (left) and the cook
(right) (Scappi, *Dell'arte del cucinare,* 1610, frontispiece) (Biblioteca Apostolica Vaticana)

kitchen and cold plates from the *credenza*), art-
fully sliced by the carver (Fig. 2),[32] and placed
before the cardinal and his guests. The gentlemen and other staff members stood in attendance, removing their hats whenever the cardinal lifted his cup to drink. The meal over, all was
removed and the room was once again available
for the reception of guests or any other appropriate use. It was also possible to eat privately, in
one's own chamber, but that was not the custom
among persons of rank and was worthy of comment: the Venetian ambassador Angelo Contarini included in his characterization of the Capuchin Antonio Barberini, brother of Urban VIII
and Cardinal of S. Onofrio, the remark that he
ate very simply, alone, without ceremony, and
with his table turned toward the wall.[33]

A private room beyond the audience room was
set aside for the cardinal's sleeping and toilette.
It did not figure in the etiquette of receiving
guests. Chamber attendants entered the room
only in the absence of the cardinal to perform
such services as cleaning, making the bed, bringing water for washing, removing wastes, and
bringing the clothes to be worn that day.[34] The
room was locked at night, with an attendant
sleeping outside the door to hear his master's call
during the night.[35] Cardinal Francesco Barbe-

rini's personal attendant, the priest Luciano Fabriani, described Francesco's daily routine on
waking, presumably in his apartment at the Cancelleria: the cardinal would rise two hours before
daybreak and ring for Fabriani, whose room was
connected with Francesco's by a "scala secretis-
sima"; Fabriani would come to light candles,
help the cardinal dress, and prepare his private
chapel for mass; the cardinal would make his
private devotions and say mass; later Fabriani
would open the door, and chamber attendants
would come in to help the cardinal finish dressing in preparation for hearing a public mass said
by a chaplain in the main chapel.[36]

The chapel was an essential element of a major
apartment. It was a small separate room, kept
locked when not in use.[37] It opened to one of the
anterooms, where the household could gather to
hear mass, and it had a window to an inner room
of the apartment, from which the cardinal could
hear mass privately.[38]

Preceded by public spaces—the stairs and
loggias—the apartment was recognized as private territory, controlled by its resident. A resident or house guest in another's palace commanded the apartment only up to the door of the
outer anteroom; that is, the *sala* was beyond the
limit of his apartment. Accordingly, a cardinal
resident in the Vatican palace did not exercise
the usual signs of jurisdiction (including the
ringing of a bell) and accompanied departing
guests only as far as the door of his own apartment.[39] If a cardinal was staying as a guest in the
house of the grand duke in Florence, he would
escort his own callers only as far as the door of his
apartment, "but not beyond, because his jurisdiction does not go farther."[40] Hosts similarly
respected the limits of their guests' apartments.

Within the apartment, the several members of
the cardinal's household frequented only those
rooms to which they were entitled by their position. *Palafrenieri* were to stay in the *sala,* except
when they would be sent into the anterooms for
a specific task, for example, the bringing of firewood.[41] Gentlemen (*gentilhuomini* or *camerieri*),

chamber assistants *(aiutanti di camera),* and pages stayed in the anterooms, especially during the hours of audience, and were not to spend time in the *sala.* The gentlemen's duties were to show honor to the cardinal by their presence, to assist in the reception of guests, and to make conversation with guests who were obliged to wait a while in the anteroom. While not otherwise occupied, they might play a board game like chess or read a spiritual or historical book; chamber assistants were especially encouraged to read, that they might learn something while at the same time dispelling the boredom of standing on duty.[42] Assistants were to enter the bedroom only in the cardinal's absence, unless they were to help him dress or otherwise perform some specific service.[43] Even the task of cleaning was divided according to the nature of the rooms: the public spaces were swept by the *scopatore* (literally, "sweeper"); the *sala* was kept clean by the *palafrenieri;* and the private rooms were cleaned by the *scopatore segreto* or by the chamber assistants.[44]

The several rooms of the apartment were characterized not only by their occupants but also by their furnishings. The sparsely furnished *sala* of a person of high rank was dominated by a baldacchino beneath which stood the *credenza* with its plate rack, ready for service during meals. Benches stood along the walls, and chests containing bedding were for the use of the *palafrenieri* on duty during the night. Large candleholders for evening light were permanent fixtures of the room. A fire would be built in the fireplace during the winter months, but *palafrenieri* and others were not to be allowed to sit around the fire; rather, they were to be made to stand and move about to keep warm.[45] If the resident was a cardinal of high birth he displayed a second baldacchino in the outer anteroom, a chair beneath it turned toward the wall.[46] Both anterooms contained chairs and stools, a table on which lights would be set in the evening, and board games for the gentlemen's amusement.[47] Tables for dining were brought in only at meal-

time. The audience room was furnished according to the pleasure of the cardinal, with chairs to be arranged for visits, a table, and a small table for the bell, to be placed near the person of highest rank during an interview.[48] Seventeenth-century inventories reveal the sparse sumptuousness of the rooms, with richly upholstered sets of chairs, inlaid tables and little chests, and wall hangings of fabric or leather.[49]

The architecture of the apartment thus provides not only places for eating and sleeping but also a stable framework within which the flexible drama of the reception of guests can be played out. The setting is linear and sequential, with clearly marked points of reference in the stair, the rooms, and their doorways. The sequence is long enough to accommodate the many gradations of rank that must be distinguished. The several rooms (*sala,* anterooms, audience room, bedroom) have their separate characters and are frequented and served by specific members of the household. The audience room itself is a neutral space within which furniture and persons can be arranged with respect to its one fixed point, the door.

The two interdependent systems—an etiquette based on hierarchical distinctions with respect to an architectural framework, and the particular form of that architectural framework—seem fully developed by the early decades of the seventeenth century. Sestini (1621), Tantouche (1623), and Lunadoro (1635, but first composed ca. 1617) all describe essentially the same etiquette, and they assume an architectural sequence of stair, *sala,* two anterooms, and audience room, with a private bedroom beyond. Outside the realm of theory, the descriptions of the practices of the ambassador of Tuscany and of Costanza Barberini, along with other documentary evidence, show the firm establishment of both etiquette and apartment. The buildings studied in the second part of this book show several concrete realizations of the abstractions described in the texts.

When Cardinal Francesco Barberini traveled

3 Paris, Notre Dame and the Archbishop's Palace (no. 2) (Pérelle, *Veues des plus beaux bâtimens de France*, Pl. 27, detail)

abroad in the 1620s, he was unavoidably aware of the contrast between Roman apartments and those of France and Spain, and between Roman usages and those of other nations. In Paris in 1625, he was lodged in splendidly furnished rooms in the archibishop's palace, near the Cathedral of Notre Dame (Fig. 3, no. 2), but his apartment had only three main rooms, "camera, anticamera e sala," according to his cupbearer, Cassiano dal Pozzo. Richly outfitted beds were

in both "anticamera" and "camera," in the second of which Francesco apparently was to sleep. A *retrocamera*, chapel, and small "gabinetto" were private rooms, beyond the "camera." In other words, Francesco had a typical (if splendid) French *appartement* of *antichambre, chambre, cabinet,* and *garderobe* (only the first two for the reception of guests), preceded by a *salle.* A loggia had to be called into service to extend the suite for the observance of Roman etiquette, and the cardinal ate according to his usual style, but in the *sala.*[50] On his visit to Louis XIII at the Louvre, he passed through the Tuileries palace, the length of the Grande Galerie, and the Petite Galerie to find the king in his "camera," in a red damask bed surrounded by a balustrade[51] — not at all like a Roman audience room. Further peculiarities of planning, decor, and ceremony awaited him on his trip to Spain in 1626 — all to be recorded by Cassiano dal Pozzo.[52]

The well-defined apartment of early seventeenth-century Rome was distinct not only from contemporary apartments in France and elsewhere but also from Roman apartments of only a century earlier.

The ideal palace for a Renaissance cardinal in Rome is described by Paolo Cortesi in his *De Cardinalatu,* published in 1510, shortly after his death.[53] The basic palace type was the same as that still current in the seventeenth century — a three-story block with an interior courtyard. The cardinal's apartment lay on the *piano nobile* and was gained by a stair from the loggia of the courtyard. Its first room was a large *sala (aula),* at first glance similar to the *sala* of a seventeenth-century apartment but different in its uses and relation to other rooms. The chapel was to be open to the *sala* (not to an anteroom) for the hearing of mass by everyone gathered there. The audience room was in or immediately adjacent to the *sala,* without intervening anterooms. Paintings that might adorn the walls of the audience chamber would show that audience might be given in a number of ways: the prince seated, or walking about, or standing with his back to the light, in the *sala* or in a garden loggia, but not according to the formal scheme described by Sestini and other later authors. The dining room, adjacent to the *sala* and overlooking a garden, was to be coupled with the silver closet *(cella argentaria),* where visitors could see the display of silver vessels — an arrangement unlike the secure *credenza,* or butler's pantry, of the seventeenth-century palace. The bedroom was to be paired with the night study, "in the inner parts of the house." In other words, the apartment is described not as a linear suite of rooms but, rather, as three clusters of rooms; there is no sense of an articulated framework within which hierarchical distinctions among persons can be measured; and there are not the distinctive, precisely named and characterized rooms of the seventeenth-century apartment.

Frommel organized his careful investigation of the uses of rooms in sixteenth-century Roman palaces according to the names given the rooms in contemporary documents and plans;[54] in this way he revealed both the imprecision of naming rooms with respect to function and the lack of a coherent linear sequence in the earlier buildings. The "sala grande" was the most important interior space, where ceremonies and audiences might be held in addition to such special events as banquets, theatrical productions, and dancing; the chapel was adjacent (as in Cortesi's ideal scheme but not in the seventeenth century); the *sala* might be furnished with musical instruments, rugs, and works of art, but not with tables and chairs, except during banquets; and *palafrenieri* were not associated with it. The smaller "salotto," or "sala seconda," was directly adjacent to the *sala grande;* it functioned as a waiting room for audience and as a serving room for banquets in the *sala.* The "saletta" was another, smaller, representational room of imprecise function. The "anticamera," so important a room for the seventeenth-century apartment, was used in the sixteenth century for various functions, in various relations to other rooms.

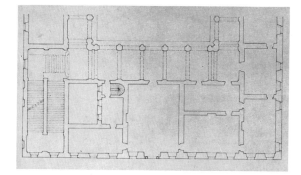

4   Palazzo Farnese, *piano nobile,* reconstruction of façade wing of project of 1516 (C. L. Frommel, *Der römische Palastbau der Hochrenaissance,* III, Pl. 55a)

The "camera" was a smaller room to be used both for sleeping and for receiving guests, without the distinction between public and private functions that developed later. Even as late as 1596, when Evitascandalo published the revised version of his *Maestro di casa,* and when he described the uses of the rooms as Sestini and others were to do later, the association of specific names with specific functions had not become fixed: he describes the "sala," the "stanza dove il Principe mangiarà" (that is, the outer anteroom), the "anticamera" (the inner anteroom), and the "Camera del Principe, o dell'audienza," and elsewhere he writes of "le camere," without distinguishing between audience room and bedroom.[55]

The change from the compact princely apartment of the early sixteenth century to the extended linear suite of the seventeenth century can be traced in Palazzo Farnese.[56] Begun in 1514, the palace was built in sections, as finances permitted. The rooms behind the five easternmost bays of the façade were built first; with the stair and the light court behind the third and fourth bays, they formed a palace in miniature, in which the cardinal could live while construction proceeded. The next phase, begun in 1515, included the colonnaded vestibule, the "salotto dipinto" above, and the rooms to the north (Fig. 4) — a fragment of what Frommel has recon-

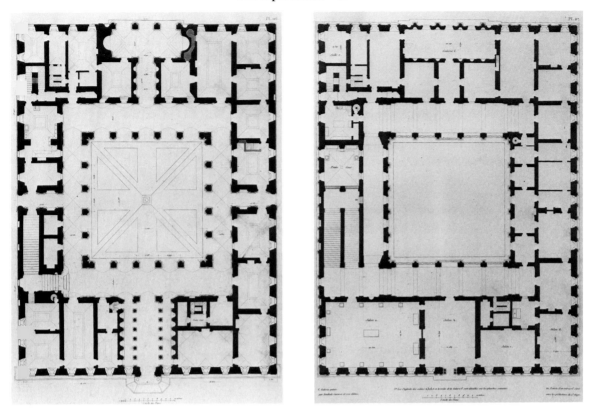

5   Palazzo Farnese, (left) ground floor and (right) *piano nobile* (Letarouilly, *Edifices de Rome moderne*, II, Pls. 116, 117)

structed as a double palace for the residence of the cardinal's two sons, but nevertheless a complete dwelling for one distinguished resident, with its stair in the east angle of the block, the "salotto dipinto" as the "sala grande," the next room to the north as "camera seconda" or "salotto," and the north corner room as "camera," both bedroom and audience room. A similar apartment of a few grand rooms would have been projected to the southwest for the second resident. Work stopped, to be taken up again only in 1540–41, according to a revised plan (Fig. 5). In the interval, the cardinal had become Pope Paul III, his son Ranuccio had died, and his son Pier Luigi had become Duke of Castro. The design for a double palace, if ever conceived, was no longer appropriate; but at the same time the status of the family had greatly changed. A single major apartment, enlarged in both scale and number of rooms, was developed from the nucleus of rooms begun in 1515: the stair was moved from the east angle of the building to a position along the southeast side of the courtyard; the former site of the stair and the cluster of small rooms in the east angle gave way to a new grand *salone* five bays long; the "salotto dipinto" and the following room became anterooms; a chapel was opened to the second of the anterooms (at least by 1547); the north corner room became the "camera a paramento in sul cantone overo tertio salotto"; and the suite continued around to the northwest side of the palace. Now an urban residence for the duke, son of the pope, the palace had taken on the plan of the papal residences—

the Vatican palace (Fig. 6) and Palazzo Venezia
—in the extended linear suite and especially in
the naming of the fourth room in the suite as the
"sala dei paramenti." [57] The formal similarity to
noble apartments of the seventeenth century is
clear.

Still, the duke's palace was not a papal palace.
It had assumed the dignity and the pretention of
a papal palace in its plan, and the pope might
indeed come and use the palace on occasion; but
the fact remained that the duke and his sons did
not have the same activities or ceremonies that
the pope had. Although rules of precedence had
long been intrinsic to the papal court, its ceremonies remained rather static with respect to its
architectural setting. Persons positioned themselves in relation to one another according to
their respective ranks, but all were clearly subordinate to the pope. They approached him with
due respect as he sat on his throne; he did not
advance to meet them.[58] The relationship of
papal ceremony to its architectural setting in seventeenth-century Rome remained distinct from
that of the etiquette of cardinals and other
Romans to their apartments. If the plan of the
apartment may be sought in papal planning, the
uses to which the apartment is put have their own
development.

By the time of Montaigne's visit to Rome in
1580–81, the apartment of a suite of many rooms
leading to the audience room was not confined
to palaces of papal families but was generally well
established.[59] By the end of the century, older
palaces once inhabited by persons of quality were
deemed inadequate if their apartments had too
few rooms.[60]

The form of the apartment was no more inert
or fixed than any other aspect of Roman life, and
it continued to change in the course of the seventeenth century. The suites of rooms became still
longer. Anterooms in excess of Sestini's standard
of two were introduced. There might be two audience rooms, for guests of different rank. In
1687–88 Tessin observed two audience rooms in
the south wing of Palazzo Barberini alle Quattro

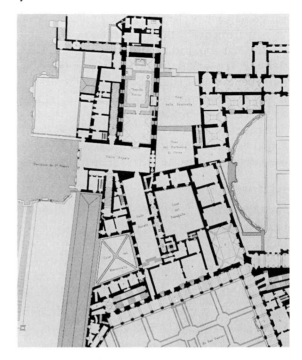

6   Palazzo Vaticano, plan (Letarouilly, *Le Vatican
et la basilique de Saint-Pierre*, II, Pl. 6)

Fontane (see Fig. 102, C5 and C6), the first for
"knights and prelates" and the second for unspecified persons; and in Palazzo Chigi in piazza
SS. Apostoli he also noted two audience rooms
(see Fig. 204, C11 and C14), the second for
"women and particular knights." [61] The baldacchino, previously restricted to the *sala* (where it
hung over the *credenza*) and the outer anteroom,
appeared in the audience room. The inventory of
the "Casa Grande" ai Giubbonari in 1648 lists a
number of baldacchinos, one of them specifically in the "Stanza dell'Audienza" of Taddeo
Barberini's apartment.[62] Palazzo Chigi's two audience rooms had baldacchinos when Tessin visited, as did room C2 in the apartment for paintings in 1667; Palazzo Barberini had a baldacchino
in the second of the cardinal's audience rooms
and also in the audience rooms of the prince and
princess in the north wing, when their apartments were remodeled in the 1670s; in Palazzo

Borghese, each of the two audience rooms of the twin apartments of the ground floor, as remodeled in 1671–76, had a baldacchino (see Fig. 42, A8b and A11–12). A portrait of the reigning pope hung beneath the baldacchino.[63] Another elaboration was the introduction of the representational bed, or *zampanaro,* in a room after the audience room but before the noble inhabitant's actual private sleeping room. Romans may have been influenced by the splendid beds they saw in reception rooms in France, even as they insisted on the privacy of sleep. The *zampanaro* is present as early as 1648 in the Barberini "Casa Grande" ai Giubbonari. In Palazzo Borghese in 1671–76, both prince and princess had a room with a *zampanaro* in their twin ground-floor apartments (see Fig. 42, A9 and A13). Tessin paused long in admiration of Cardinal Chigi's splendid bed in a richly decorated alcove in Palazzo Chigi, completed in 1668 (see Fig. 204, C16).[64]

CHAPTER TWO

Comfort

IS ROME COLD in the winter and hot in the summer? Were seventeenth-century Romans concerned about comfort? Did Roman palaces provide any comfort against the assaults of climate? Many a modern visitor to the city would quickly assent to the first question while doubting the other two.

Nathaniel Hawthorne visited the city in the winter and spring of 1858 and wrote poignantly of his discomfort, not only in the Palazzo Larazani in via di Porta Pinciana, where he found his rooms "very uncomfortable, it being impossible to warm them by means of the deep, old-fashioned, inartificial fireplaces"; but also in palaces where he visited collections of paintings, and almost everywhere else he went: "I have only once been warm enough even in the sunshine, and out of the sun never at any time." In the painting gallery of Palazzo Borghese, on 25 February 1858, "it was very comfortless—indeed I suppose nobody ever thought of being comfortable there, since the house was built—but especially uncomfortable on a chill, damp day like this. My fingers were quite numb before I got half way through the suite of apartments, in spite of a brazier of charcoal which was smouldering into ashes in two or three of the rooms. There was not, so far as I remember, a single fireplace in the suite." In Palazzo Doria, on 10 March, he viewed the paintings displayed in the rooms around the courtyard and observed that "all the rooms are colder and more comfortless than can be imagined without having been in them. . . . In the whole immense range of rooms I saw but a single fireplace." At Villa Borghese, on 18 April, "on this almost summer-day, I was quite chilled in passing through these glorious halls; no fireplace anywhere; no possibility of comfort; and in the hot season, when their coolness might be agreeable, it would be death to inhabit them." [1] Johann Wolfgang von Goethe, although more cheerful than the American visitor, similarly observed on 13 January 1787, "The days are getting chilly and one is better off anywhere than indoors when the rooms have neither stoves nor fireplaces and are only good for feeling uncomfortable in." [2]

If Hawthorne avoided Rome's summer heat, Goethe did not. On 5 July 1787 he succinctly reported, "The heat is terrific." Still, he was sanguine about the weather, writing on 27 July, "My room is a pleasant place to live during the hot weather," and, on 11 August, "The sky is always cloudless and at noon the heat is ferocious, but I escape the worst of it by staying in my cool studio." [3]

Although Hawthorne did not realize it, he had the advantage of visiting Rome during a relatively warm climatic period. In the seventeenth century, Italy, along with the rest of the Northern Hemisphere, was in the grip of what has come to be called the "Little Ice Age," a period within the present interglacial era characterized by lower temperatures and advances of glaciers in the Alps, Scandinavia, and Iceland. Scholars disagree about the precise limits of the period, but its main phase for most parts of the world falls between 1550 and 1700.[4] In Europe, several kinds of historical evidence allow the identification of variations within the period: cool summers in 1560–1600, warm or average spring-summers in 1601–16, "outstanding cold episodes" in 1617–50, a heat wave in 1635–39, and warmer weather in 1651–86. Although the average mean surface air temperature was probably only about 1°C. lower than that of the relatively warm twentieth century, it was enough to cause a shorter growing season, later wine harvests, and significant glacial movements.[5]

The length and conditions of winter in seventeenth-century Rome are suggested in contemporary books on household management, and they are confirmed by Giacinto Gigli's record of several specific meteorological episodes in his *Diario romano (1608–1670)*. Liberati states that clothing appropriate to the season should be issued to members of the *famiglia* twice a year, on the first of November for winter and on the first of June for summer (although, he adds, many households wait until St. Peter's Day for the change to summer clothing).[6] Evitascandalo gives the dates for the seasonal changing of wall hangings in palaces: in November tapestries are to be hung for winter, and at Pentecost (that is, May or early June) they are to be replaced by silk or leather hangings.[7] He specifies that a fire is to be laid in the *salone* beginning on the first of November, or whenever it becomes cold.[8] Gigli notes the arrival of cold weather, sometimes accompanied by rain or even freezing rain, just prior to that date in five years.[9] Evitascandalo indicates that rain rather than snow is to be expected in winter, when he writes of the necessity of protecting horses and carriages from winter rain and summer sun; but snow is a possibility, in his experience, even as late as April.[10] Gigli's experience verifies those notes. Sustained rainfall,

especially in December, frequently led to the swelling of the Tiber and flooding in the lower parts of the city. (Gigli records Tiber floods between October and February in ten years; by contrast, he notes spring and summer floods only three times.)[11] Yet reports of frost, snow, and ice are not uncommon in Gigli's diary, from late October even until the beginning of May. He writes of unaccustomed cold, sustained snow, and ice in January 1621, "such that one could hardly leave the house." Carnival Tuesday in 1654 was calm and beautiful "but cruelly cold"; and a few days later, on 22 February, snow fell and remained one and a half *palmi* deep for three days. Frost is reported as late as 7–10 May in 1644.[12] Even June and July might be cold and rainy, as in 1647 when "for the whole month of July one never felt warm," or in 1652 when Innocent X went to Frascati for the first time for a month's stay but had to return to Rome after only nine days because of the midsummer cold.[13] Gigli notes much sickness associated with the cold weather, and damage to vines and other crops because of late spring frosts.

While there might be mild days in the winter, as in February 1652 when people put on their lighter clothing, or in February 1655, "warm as if it were March,"[14] Gigli's occasional reports of remarkable heat were reserved for the summer months. On 6 July 1611, a huge fire lasting for more than eight days was "caused by nothing other than the insufferable heat, much greater than ordinary for the season." The whole month of June and the beginning of September 1645 were times of extraordinary heat. There were hot days in the summer of 1646 too: Gigli's aunt died on 25 June, and he comments that her unburied body remained incorrupt even in the very hot weather; and more days of heat and sickness followed in August. In May 1650 heat was combined with dryness. Only once is "unbearable sunshine" reported out of season, in November 1650.[15]

Clearly, architectural protection from the rigors of both heat and cold was desirable in

Rome, and the need for warmth in the winter was even greater than that which Nathaniel Hawthorne or a twentieth-century visitor might feel. Alberti, writing in the relative warmth of the mid-fifteenth century, advised particular attention to comfort in the summer, "for indeed in my opinion, a wise man should build rather for summer than for winter. We may easily arm ourselves against the cold by making all close, and keeping good fires; but many more things are requisite against heat, and even all will sometimes be no great relief."[16] If one can judge from the preponderance of Gigli's reports of cold weather, compared to only a few episodes of remarkable heat, the seventeenth-century Roman might disagree with Alberti.

However pleasant appropriate warmth or coolness might be, there was another important reason to seek thermal comfort: health. Vitruvius wrote of the unhealthiness of excessive heat or cold.[17] Alvise Cornaro, seventy-five years old when he wrote his treatise on architecture, attributed his longevity to the moderate temperatures maintained in his well-designed house, which protected him from extremes of heat and cold, "mortal enemies of old age."[18] Scamozzi enumerates the many ailments brought on by bad winds and cautions against the unhealthy use of stoves.[19]

Writings on architecture show that seventeenth-century Roman architects had at their disposal a number of means to achieve thermal comfort, and the evidence of both documents and buildings shows that they consistently employed many of those means.

The most important means for furnishing comfort in palaces was the provision of separate rooms or apartments for use in the different seasons. The practice extended back to antiquity, for Vitruvius assumed the existence of separate rooms for use in summer, winter, and the intermediate seasons of spring and autumn.[20] Theorists from Alberti onward either recommend or assume the use of separate rooms or entire apartments for summer and winter.[21] Descriptions and guides to prominent palaces in Rome identify apartments as for summer, winter, and even intermediate seasons.[22] Seasonal apartments were characterized by their location within the palace, by details of their design, and by their fittings.

First and foremost was the matter of orientation with respect to the sun. Summer rooms were to face north for protection from the summer sun. These rooms will seem melancholy in winter, however, and rooms for that season are to be open to the low warm rays of the winter sun from the south and, to a lesser degree, the west. Rooms with an eastern exposure are generally good for spring and autumn, and even for summer, but they do not receive much sunlight during the winter. Rooms to be used at particular times of the day might vary the pattern: libraries, for morning use, might enjoy eastern light; rooms for bathing, an afternoon activity for which warmth was desirable, would profit from a western orientation; and dining rooms, used late in the day, might be toward the west for winter, the east for spring and autumn, and the north for summer. Vitruvius gives such advice; writers of the fifteenth, sixteenth, and seventeenth centuries concur;[23] and the practice of architects and inhabitants alike conforms to the pattern.

Coupled with orientation according to sunlight, but subordinate to it, is orientation according to winds. Cool breezes may be desirable in the summer,[24] but their value is not stressed. Much more important is protection from the winter wind — as fierce an enemy as the summer sun.[25]

An important architectural strategy for controlling the exposure of rooms in seventeenth-century palaces was the use of *appartamenti doppij,* or double apartments. A wing of the palace would be two rooms thick, so that the two parallel files of rooms, sheltering one another, would offer alternative orientations. Scamozzi, writing in 1615, notes the double apartment as characteristic of Roman palaces.[26] The author of Barb. lat. 4360 lists this feature of planning among the

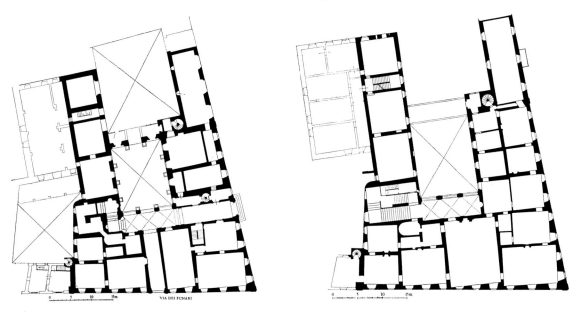

7 Palazzo Mattei, (left) ground floor and (right) *piano nobile* (Howard Hibbard, *Carlo Maderno and Roman Architecture 1580–1630*, A. Zwemmer Ltd., 1971, Figs. 2, 3)

amenities that he would include in the Barberini palace to be built, precisely because it would offer protection from heat, cold, and winds.[27] The advantage of double apartments seems to have been recognized only in the late sixteenth century. A classic example of an older palace planned without double apartments is the rambling Vatican palace (see Fig. 6). The Palazzo Colonna-Barberini in Palestrina, enlarged in 1498, similarly deploys long single apartments (see Fig. 181). The older (eastern) portion of the Sforza palace, which was to form part of the north wing of Palazzo Barberini alle Quattro Fontane, was constructed in 1583 as an apartment only one room deep; its westward extension was added probably in 1612, as a double apartment with two large rooms turned to the cool north and two smaller rooms enjoying a southern exposure (see Fig. 96).[28] The author of Barb. lat. 4360, writing ca. 1625 and taking his cue from the Sforza palace, planned that double apartments would open from the four *sale* of his design (see Fig. 133).[29] In the sixteenth century the future Palazzo Chigi in piazza SS. Apostoli was a U-shaped structure with wings only one room thick; the *appartamento nuovo* added between 1596 and 1606 was a double apartment of six rooms, the larger three turned to the northeast and the smaller three to the southwest (Figs. 191, 192).[30] The westward extension of Palazzo Borghese, built between 1606 and 1610 and incorporating an older house on the site, took the form of a double apartment, in contrast to the single flight of rooms earlier built around the palace courtyard (see Figs. 20–23; but it seems that here the double apartments on the mezzanine and *terzo piano* were divided between husband and wife rather than summer and winter use).[31] Maderno's Palazzo Mattei, constructed between 1598 and 1613, featured a double

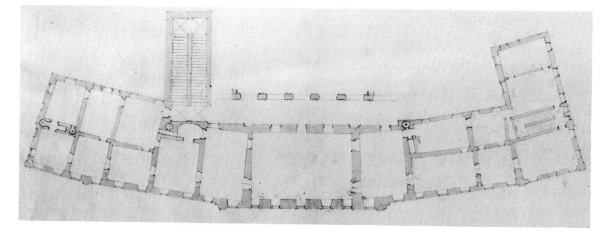

8 Palazzo Ludovisi-Montecitorio, plan (Windsor Castle, Royal Library. ©1989 Her Majesty Queen Elizabeth II)

apartment with a suite of larger rooms turned to the east and smaller rooms to the west (Fig. 7). Bernini's 1653 plan for the Palazzo Ludovisi-Montecitorio, only partially built, had a pair of double apartments extending left and right of the central *sala* (Fig. 8).

The anonymous author of Barb. lat. 4360 notes an advantage, similar to that of the double apartment, to be gained by sheltering rooms with a loggia.[32] Yet loggias were employed on all sides of Roman courtyards, regardless of orientation, because they served functions other than comfort. They provided shelter for the arrival of a guest to the foot of the stair, for circulation of persons and carriages, and for the waiting members of a guest's entourage. By the same token, loggias did not normally appear on façades, where those functions were absent, even when protection from the sun might be desired. Only a two-dimensional image of a loggia appears on the two upper stories of the west façade of Palazzo Barberini (see Fig. 92), even though a true loggia might have made the central *salone* cooler in the summer.

Similar to the double apartment, with regard to thermal advantage, is the room with no exposure at all. Rooms in the middle of the house, sheltered on all sides, are protected from extremes of heat and cold, as Palladio noted with reference to the central *sala* of his Villa Cornaro at Piombino Dese.[33] The author of Barb. lat. 4360 saw such dual protection as an advantage of a bedroom set into the angle of the courtyard of his proposal, "comfortable for sleeping in all seasons," and another room, "covered on all sides, and cool, although somewhat dark."[34] In Palazzo Barberini the cardinal's great anteroom is an internal room, lit only by clerestory windows to the east; it serves his summer and winter apartments alike (see Fig. 102, C2).[35]

Another aspect of the location of seasonal apartments within the palace is the level of the rooms. Manetti says that Nicholas V's palace at the Vatican was to have had three stories, for use at different seasons of the year: the ground floor for summer, the middle floor for winter, and the uppermost floor for spring and autumn, all with identical floor plans. Although in fact the popes seem not to have moved from floor to floor with the changing of the seasons, Manetti's report nevertheless suggests that he believed in the advantage of doing so.[36] The west wing of Palazzo

Borghese was occupied in this way in the early seventeenth century: above the ground-floor sculpture gallery and service rooms were mezzanine rooms without fireplaces — that is, summer apartments — for both Giovanni Battista Borghese and his wife, Virginia; rooms on the *piano nobile,* with fireplaces, were apparently for Giovanni Battista alone; those on the third floor followed the same plan and orientation as the mezzanines below but contained fireplaces and therefore would have been suitable for winter use.[37] Scamozzi explains that a similar distinction of seasonal quarters according to elevation is provided in palaces of Florence and Genoa, with summer quarters on the ground floor and winter rooms above; and in Spain, an especially warm country, the lower rooms ("because they are more comfortable, and cooler in the summer") are given to the men, while women must inhabit the upper story.[38] The ground floor may benefit from the coolness of the earth,[39] from a lessened exposure to the sun when buildings stand close to one another, and from adjacent shaded and fountain-filled gardens. Middle floors would receive somewhat more sunshine but would be spared the stronger winds of the highest level, while being insulated by the spaces above and below.

The rebuilding of the Palazzo Chigi in the 1660s included a ground-floor summer apartment (see Fig. 203, B1 – B6); the extensive remodeling of Palazzo Borghese's west wing in 1671 – 76 included ground-floor summer apartments for both prince and princess (see Fig. 42, A4 – A20); and the ground-floor rooms of the south wing of Palazzo Barberini alle Quattro Fontane were finished as a summer apartment in 1673 – 79 (see Fig. 165, B3 – B12).[40] In all three cases the rooms were used for the display of works of art — sculpture in the Palazzi Chigi and Barberini, and paintings in the Palazzo Borghese. Also, in all three cases the apartments were not used for sleeping. Each of Palazzo Borghese's two summer apartments contained a bedroom furnished with a *zampanaro* (a splendid representational

bed) but with none of the fittings expected in a room actually used for sleeping, according to an inventory of 1693.[41] The summer apartments of the other two palaces lacked even these representational beds.[42] The dampness earlier noted in the ground-floor rooms of Palazzo Chigi before its remodeling was such that they could not be used for sleeping. While stone sculptures might inhabit these ground-floor rooms continuously, humans would be able to enjoy their coolness only during the day.

The size and proportions of rooms could vary according to the season in which they were to be used. Alberti prescribes small and low rooms for winter use and large and spacious rooms for summer, for "a great quantity of air inclosed in a large room is like a great quantity of water, not easily heated."[43] In winter Cardinal Bernardino Spada enjoyed the use of four "camerini" with low ceilings, formed by the subdivision of a "camerone" on the south side of his palace: "In winter the low ceilings are not stifling but pleasurable, since they defend the more against the rigors of the season."[44] Rooms for spring and autumn might logically be medium-sized.[45]

Features of construction might also affect the warmth or coolness of rooms. According to Alberti, a vaulted ceiling is both warmer in the winter and cooler in the summer, but Francesco di Giorgio recommends vaults specifically only for winter rooms.[46] Alberti further advises dry, well-drained soil under the house and, especially for coolness in the summer, an air space under the floor.[47] Dampness was a chronic problem in ground-floor rooms in Rome, making the ground floor of the Palazzo Colonna (later Chigi) unsuitable for apartments, and prompting the installation of a wood floor in the rooms for the *palafrenieri* on the ground floor of Palazzo Borghese in 1619.[48] Mezzanines are recommended above winter apartments by Scamozzi,[49] whether to provide an insulation space or simply to fill the area above the low-ceilinged winter rooms. In Barb. lat. 4360, the anonymous proposal for a new Barberini palace, a double ceiling over the library is recommended to protect against heat and cold as well as against leaks.[50] In general, thickness of walls seems to have been determined for reasons of structure rather than comfort; but Francesco di Giorgio (following Aristotle, who identified heat and moisture as active qualities and coldness and dryness as passive) felt that thin walls could adequately resist cold while thick walls were required to resist heat.[51] The author of Barb. lat. 4360 acknowledges the value of thick walls in maintaining a cool temperature in the wine cellar,[52] but he never calls on them in support of human comfort.

Window openings should be of an optimum size, in relation to the size of the room, so that they will admit enough light and not too much heat or cold, writes Palladio, and he suggests proportions that will achieve this end.[53] He adds that lining up windows and doors *en filade* has, among other advantages, the effect of making the house cooler in the summer; but windows and doors are aligned in both winter and summer apartments, in apparent disregard for the presumed advantage of comfort. Alberti simply advises small windows for winter rooms.[54] Scamozzi notes that Florentine palaces have only a few windows, specifically in order to resist the coldness of the winter air and the suffocating heat of the summer.[55] A glance at any prominent Roman palace reveals windows of uniform size on all its faces. Clearly the aesthetic ideal of regularity has overridden any thought of variation for the sake of thermal comfort. Still, the ratio of window area to wall area (rather low when compared to that of palaces in northern Europe) may have been arrived at through a practice that involved the balancing and optimizing of competing requirements, including comfort.

Rooms for winter, writes Alberti, "must be warm and have good fireplaces," but excessive fires should be avoided, for reasons of health.[56] Cornaro's house, carefully designed to fend off excessive cold and heat, still requires "a little fire," not a stove *(stufa)*.[57] Scamozzi condemns

the Germans' "universal, and so dangerous use of stoves [*stufe*]."[58] He describes several types of fireplaces, characteristic of different regions, including the fireplace set entirely into the thickness of the wall, "alla romana."[59] The evidence of documents and surviving fireplaces confirms Scamozzi's observation that Romans rejected the more vigorous heat of stoves and projecting fireplaces in favor of the recessed fireplace — the occasion for special marbles and possibly an elaborate design (as in the *sala* of Palazzo Barberini alle Quattro Fontane, see Fig. 141) but never the grand focus of a room as in France and other northern countries.[60] The unhealthy stoves were not used.

In Rome, fireplaces regularly were built in winter apartments and rooms intended to serve in all seasons (including the *sala*). In contrast, they were regularly omitted from rooms for summer use. It was the duty of the *scopatore, palafrenieri,* and chamber assistants to bring wood and lay fires in the *sala*, anterooms, and audience room.[61] Although a fire was kept in the *sala*, there must have been no thought of warming the entire vast room. In the *sala, palafrenieri* and others were not to loiter around the fire but were to keep warm while walking about.[62] The anterooms would have been warm enough to encourage the gentlemen to attend to their posts of duty instead of lingering in their own fireless rooms.[63] The gallery of the palace proposed in Barb. lat. 4360 (see Fig. 133, H), which might also be used as an anteroom, was to have a fireplace; but the author imagined that the room might be warm enough in the winter without a fire, because of its southern exposure.[64] Firescreens would provide protection against the strongest heat of the fire in the audience room.[65] Bedrooms were frequently fireless; these were not rooms for daytime activities, and sleepers could stay warm with the help of warming pans and wool blankets.[66] Ashes from the kitchen fire were reserved first for the prince's warming pan, and then for others.[67] Cardinal Flavio Chigi seems to have had an aversion to fireplaces, for in the remodeling of his palace in the 1660s he had many removed, even from rooms likely to have been used in the winter.[68] All in all, Romans seem to have remained a bit skeptical about abundant heat from fires, whether because of concerns about health or industry or simply because of a preference for cooler air.

Palladio knew that ancient Romans had warmed their buildings with hypocausts; but Scamozzi, who had seen them, believed hypocausts to have been special delights and not ordinary heating.[69] The anonymous author of Barb. lat. 4344 also knew of the system and considered it much superior to fireplaces, braziers, and German stoves.[70] Its heat was much more salubrious, he believed, for it was less violent, could be tempered by opening and closing vents, and warmed a space from the perimeter inward. He recommended the inclusion of hypocausts in the Barberini palace to be built, but in vain. Neither the Barberini nor other seventeenth-century Romans employed hypocausts.

For summer apartments, adjacency to a garden was desirable. "Parlours for summer require water and the verdure of gardens," according to Alberti.[71] Scamozzi too recognized the cooling effect of "branches of verdure and sprays of cool water."[72] Palladio recommended that spring and autumn rooms overlook a garden.[73] The author of Barb. lat. 4360 proposed a design for the Barberini palace to be built that would include a garden on the south side of the palace, with trees to shade rooms to be used frequently in the summer; an enclosed garden to the east would complement an elliptical salon which would have been especially pleasant in the summer.[74] As finally built, the Barberini palace included an enclosed garden adjacent to Donna Anna Barberini's summer apartment and larger gardens to the east and south, accessible from the Barberini cardinal's summer apartment.[75]

The choice of wall coverings for a room or apartment would be determined by the season of its occupancy. Alberti advised that wool wall hangings would make a room warmer, while linen hangings would make it cooler.[76] Scamozzi too would cover the walls with hangings (*panni,* of unspecified fiber content) to warm an apartment.[77] Hooks were regularly installed during construction for the hanging of fabric or leather revetments in the principal apartments.[78] In Palazzo Barberini alle Quattro Fontane, tapestries (of wool) hung in the cardinal's winter apartment, while his summer apartment was characterized by its red damask hangings.[79] The feigned tapestries painted on the walls of the Sala dei Fasti Farnesiani of the Palazzo Farnese at Caprarola are in the summer apartment and must be seen as a more comfortable alternative to wool tapestries.[80] For rooms that would be used in both summer and winter, it was the *guardaroba's* duty to change the hangings according to the change of the seasons.[81] Sometimes an independent tradesman, a *festarolo,* would be hired to do this seasonal work.[82]

Fountains were sometimes features of summer rooms — whether for actual cooling or for their association with gardens. In 1671–76, in the ground-floor (summer) apartments of Palazzo Borghese (see Fig. 42), a silver fountain was installed in the prince's audience room A11–12, a pair of alabaster fountains enhanced the princess's audience room A8b, and more fountains were in A5 and A14.[83] A fountain was in a room of the Sforza palace adjacent to the *giardino segreto* in 1626, before the structure was incorporated as the north wing of Palazzo Barberini.[84] A fountain was placed in the center of Taddeo's ground-floor anteroom B29 in the construction of Palazzo Barberini in 1628–32 (see Fig. 101).[85] By the time of Tessin's visit in 1687–88, a fountain surmounted by a statue of Bacchus had been installed in room B36, in what Tessin identified as the prince's summer apartment (see Figs. 165, 171), and in the middle of oval room C17, opening to the gardens, was a fountain incorporating an antique bronze statue of Venus or Galatea.[86] Tessin also saw a fountain in the ground-floor "summer rooms" of Palazzo Chigi, in corner room B1 (see Fig. 203).[87]

Other assorted devices might promote comfort in the summer. An *avviso* of 22 July 1615 reports that the Cardinal Zappata sought respite from the summer heat by suspending an awning over the courtyard of his house in Parione, at the level of his rooms, and spraying water over it to create a cooling and refreshing "rain."[88] Cool air from the cellar might be conducted to the summer rooms through air shafts, according to Scamozzi; Palladio notes that in Costozza, near Vicenza, such shafts draw naturally cool air from caves to houses.[89] In Rome, an air shaft indicated on a plan for the house of Antonio da Sangallo the Younger may be for this purpose.[90] The arched openings of a loggia might be glazed and then opened or closed according to the season.[91]

Louvered shutters, seemingly essential for summer comfort in present-day Rome, were not used for that purpose in the seventeenth century. The very few instances of *gelosie*, or slatted shutters, are not for shade and ventilation but rather for visual privacy. *Gelosie* installed in the Ripetta balcony of Palazzo Borghese, built in 1676, can be seen closed in Specchi's view of the palace in 1699 and open in his view of ca. 1704 (see Figs. 35, 46).[92] *Gelosie* were useful for the discreet observation of public activities. According to Lunadoro and Leti, cardinals might do well to follow the example of the Medici cardinal, later Pope Leo XI, who watched theatrical performances from behind *gelosie*.[93] When Paul V wanted to observe activities in piazza Scossacavalli in the Borgo, he watched from behind *gelosie* at his nephew's palace.[94] *Gelosie* were proposed for the projecting balcony of a casino to front on strada Pia by the author of Barb. lat. 4360, "so that one could hardly have a finer view of the streets of the city, without being seen."[95] At the same time, *gelosie* provided protection from casual observation from outside; for example, in the description of the women's apartment in Barb. lat. 4360, *gelosie* are prescribed for the windows that can be seen from the garden.[96] In Palazzo Chigi, *gelosie* in the lower part of windows in rooms E16 and E18 gave privacy to these exposed

positions; the exit from room C9 to the garden was similarly protected; and in 1683, when an arch was built over the vicolo del Piombo to connect room C4 with the carriage house, the passage was shielded from glances from the piazza by *gelosie* (see Fig. 210, extreme left).[97] In 1609, four *saliceni* were installed in the windows of Giovanni Battista Borghese's bedroom;[98] whether or not these were identical with the *gelosie* reported in other documents and shown in engravings, they were surely employed for privacy. The evidence of contemporary views of Roman palaces suggests that the general use of louvered shutters was not introduced until the middle of the eighteenth century. Piranesi's *Vedute di Roma* of 1756, for example, shows shutters on only a few buildings (on plates 29, 34, and 35).

Still, there might be movable shades at the windows to protect from the heat of the summer sun. At Palazzo Chigi in piazza Colonna, as drawn by Lieven Cruyl in 1664, shades are hung before all the windows of the south façade— some neatly furled and others extended to shade the rooms within (Fig. 9). Such *stuoie (store, stuore)* were part of the original building, not later makeshift additions. Among the preparatory contracts for the construction of Palazzo Barberini is a list of prices for ironwork, including "tinned bars to hold the *stuore* at the windows."[99] In the course of construction, fifty brass rings (that is, two per window) were installed at the windows of the apartment on the *piano nobile* of the south wing, "for drawing the *store*."[100] *Store* were attached to all forty-five windows of Palazzo Chigi in piazza SS. Apostoli, in May 1668.[101] That the shades were hung only in the summer is shown by Taddeo Barberini's payment to a *festarolo* for the autumnal changing of wall hangings in fifteen rooms in the "Casa Grande" ai Giubbonari in 1629, including the removal of thirty-five *store* from the windows.[102] At Palazzo Chigi in piazza SS. Apostoli, in addition to the *stuoie,* an inventory lists large curtains for protection against the sun inside the two west-facing arches of the gallery C17 (see Fig.

9   Piazza Colonna, drawing by Lieven Cruyl (reversed), August 1664 (The Cleveland Museum of Art, Dudley P. Allen Fund)

204), and a large awning used in the courtyard of the palace in the summer.[103]

However many devices might be available to make a room more comfortable, the Romans' basic method seems to have been to recognize that different places are inherently warmer or cooler, because of orientation, elevation, or construction, and then to move themselves and their activities to those more comfortable locations. The notion of the palace as a framework within which an aristocratic life can be arranged accord-

ing to circumstances, as seen in Chapter 1 in the design of the apartment, also pertains when comfort is taken into account. The designer provides both warm and cool rooms, and then the prince occupies them according to the season or even the time of day. His sleeping place may change from month to month, as indicated in a document for a bit of work in "the room where His Eminence S.r Cardinal Antonio [Barberini] is sleeping in this month of July."[104] He might eat in a warmer or cooler room, in a loggia, or even in a garden casino.[105] He might seek out an underground room or cryptoporticus, like that under the entrance terrace of the Villa Aldobrandini, noted in a contemporary description as a cool and shaded place even in the afternoon.[106] He might even leave his house entirely. Montaigne remarked that Romans differentiated not only among rooms in their houses but also among neighborhoods in the city, sometimes even renting two or three palaces in different parts of town at great expense, for the sake of seasonal well-being.[107] Contemporary accounts are replete with notices of the seasonal movements of the pope and cardinals from their city palaces to suburban villas or country estates. Alberti had earlier noted that a distinction between country houses and city houses for the rich was that "they use their country house chiefly for a habitation in the summer, and their town house as a convenient place of shelter in the winter"; and Palladio too had observed that "we are, for the most part, in the country during the summer season."[108]

"Nothing can be said relating to the sun and winds but what must alter according to the difference of the climate, since the north wind is not light and the south unhealthy in all places," wrote Alberti; and other writers agreed that different climates required different architectural responses for comfort.[109] One might add that cultural preferences also affected those architectural responses. The several types of fireplaces presented by Scamozzi correspond to the requirements and preferences of people in different regions. Scamozzi's review of palaces of many cities and nations similarly shows an array of local practices. Sources show that seventeenth-century Romans knew of many means for achieving thermal comfort, but they selected only those that suited them. From about 1600 the double apartment was favored in Rome (but not, for example, in France). In the sizing and placement of windows and doors, an aesthetic ideal of regularity tempered a desire for comfort. Excessive heat was avoided in the winter, even when it might have been attained. Ground-floor dampness meant that the coolness of that story could be exploited only in a limited way. The principle of movement within an articulated framework naturally informed all aspects of Roman life, for reasons of comfort as well as social behavior.

Surely a large part of Nathaniel Hawthorne's discomfort in Rome in the winter and spring of 1858 was that he was visiting works of art displayed in summer apartments: the ground-floor rooms of the western wing of Palazzo Borghese, the gallery of Palazzo Doria, the wonderfully cool Villa Borghese. In the midst of his chilly Roman February, Hawthorne visited the family of the American sculptor W. W. Story in their apartment on the *secondo piano* of the north wing of Palazzo Barberini (see Figs. 99, 103) and wrote of the pleasant and cheerful rooms, which "afford a very fine outlook over Rome, and have the sun in them through most of the day."[110] In the small, low-ceiled rooms, equipped with fireplaces,[111] oriented to the west and south, he had no occasion to complain of the cold.

CHAPTER THREE

Noblewomen

SEVENTEENTH-CENTURY Rome was populated by a significantly larger number of men than of women: at the beginning of the century, in 1600, there were 109,729 persons, 63,133 men and only 46,596 women; and the predominance of men prevailed through the fluctuations of population over the years.[1] Concomitantly, the presence of the papal court in Rome meant both a large number of temporary residents in Rome, intent on diplomacy, and a large number of ecclesiastics (in 1600, almost 6,000 bishops, priests, monks, and nuns). The leaders of this society were the pope's chief courtiers, the cardinals. In such a society, the lives of noblewomen and the architectural provisions for those lives hold special interest.

Noblewomen's Lives

Giovanni Battista de Luca's *Il cavaliere e la dama* gives a picture of the proper life of a Roman noblewoman.[2] In relation to her husband, the woman should be subject, dependent, submissive, humble, obsequious, and patient. Appropriate activities for women are handwork with linen, wool, and silk; taking care of the house; attending to the good education of the children (although wet nurses may often be employed, and girls destined for marriage may be educated in a convent rather than at home); being obse-quious to the husband; and cultivating the fear of God. As for literature, sciences, liberal arts, spirited and gracious conversation, games, dancing, playing instruments, singing, and similar activities—women are advised not to involve themselves in these; for, while in men it is praiseworthy to cultivate both gifts of the body and gifts of the mind, in women such development rarely works out well, leading instead to greater exposure and license and a loss of modesty. Women most certainly should not attempt to study theology; this would only lead to errors. In social contacts between men and women, great prudence and circumspection should be exercised: meetings should always be in public, in full light, and not too frequent; and no letters or notes should be exchanged. This picture is in marked contrast to that of noblewomen at the court of Urbino in the early sixteenth century, as presented by Castiglione in *Il cortegiano,*[3] or the active lives of such sixteenth-century women as Isabella d'Este. Women in seventeenth-century France were much more involved in affairs of the world than were their Roman contemporaries, according to Christopher Wren's estimation of them when he visited Paris in 1665: ". . . the Women, as they make here the Language and Fashions, and meddle with Politicks and Philosophy, so they sway also in Architecture . . ."[4] Italian men traveling in the train of Francesco Barberini, papal legate to France in 1625, were surprised by the openness, lively conversation, and freely obtained kisses of French women — favors which led to no "conclusion." In his journal of the cardinal's voyage, Cesare Magalotti relates the tale of a young Italian man's encounter with a spirited woman of Avignon and his eventual acute embarrassment at his misinterpretation of her behavior, then ponders the profound differences between the social conduct of French women and that of Roman women.[5] The dedication of *Il cavaliere e la dama* to the extraordinary Christina of Sweden, who, as the author declares, brings together the characteristics of *cavaliere* and *dama,* seems not to have been influenced by de Luca's picture of an admirable noblewoman.[6]

Contemporary accounts of public occasions in Rome confirm de Luca's ideal of a modest and circumscribed life for women, in the Roman atmosphere of religious celibacy and male dominance. At the formal, ceremonial entry of the French ambassador to Rome on 25 November 1608, according to an observer's account, the streets were full of carriages and people, while princesses and other women watched from the shelter of windows and doorways.[7] On 11 February 1651, Gigli noted that the princess of Rossano had had a special wood loggia built in the façade of her palace in via del Corso, with windows and proper furnishings, from which ladies could watch the Carnival festivities in the street below.[8] (In contrast, a century earlier, in 1545, women enjoying Carnival festivities from the balcony of Palazzo Farnese had been joined by men, including many cardinals and even the pope.)[9] When theatrical performances were given at the Palazzo Barberini, the women attended on a single night, escorted by their husbands; and cardinals, prelates, and other men saw the production on another night.[10] The pious Donna Costanza Barberini chose not to attend performances of the comedies at all and did not allow her women attendants to do so either.[11] At banquets women sat at tables apart from men, or at least the seating arrangements and service were carefully contrived so as to protect men and women from one another. Cardinals in particular were cautioned not to sit between two women.[12] At the banquet following the marriage of Taddeo Barberini and Anna Colonna, fourteen secular members of the two families were arranged on the right side of the table, the three women guests grouped together after the bridal couple; and fourteen cardinals were arranged according to rank on the left side.[13]

In the family palaces as well as in public, the scrupulous separation of the sexes was maintained, and separate apartments were arranged for the women. The women's daily lives were not generally involved with those of their husbands; rather, they were surrounded by women companions, some of noble families and some of lesser rank, perhaps ten in number, who resided in secluded apartments in the palace.[14] They also had their own staff of male servants, apart from those of their husbands: *palafrenieri,* chamber attendants *(camerieri),* coachmen, stewards, chaplains, and others.[15] Expenditures in support of their companions and servants were recorded distinct from those of the men of the family.[16] Separate kitchens for the women were maintained, and separate accounts were kept for the provisioning of their tables.[17] Women had their own horses and carriages.[18]

In contrast to the partitioning of the women from the rest of the household, there was also a certain kind of participation of women in the diplomatic business of Rome. In spite of the extreme dominance of men in Rome, and celibate churchmen at that, it was nevertheless seen as necessary that prominent men should have female counterparts, at least for the playing out of the serious business of visiting. Wives fulfilled this role for the secular nobility, and churchmen enlisted close female relatives. There were several occasions on which noblewomen would receive formal visits. Newly created cardinals paid visits of courtesy not to Roman barons but to their wives, on some occasion for celebration or congratulation.[19] The ambassador of Tuscany was advised that prominent women newly arrived in Rome were to be sent messages of welcome and then be called on.[20] Cardinal legates called on the wives of the important men in whatever province they were visiting; and a cardinal who traveled to a city governed by a grand duke — for example, Florence — called on the grand duchess (and the dowager grand duchess, if there was one) immediately after his first visit to the grand duke.[21] Women called on other women, both guest and hostess acting on behalf of men of their family, as in the case described by Maffeo Barberini (the future Urban VIII) in a letter written from Paris to his sister-in-law Costanza Barberini: newly elevated to the cardinalate in 1606, he reminded Costanza to pay respects to the two sisters-in-law of his benefactor Pope Paul V (Virginia and Ortensia Borghese).[22] Groups of women, along with their companions and serving women, might visit a noblewoman especially on a holiday or other special occasion.[23] Women might also go to the papal palace for an audience with the pope,[24] and they might have occasion to call on a cardinal.[25]

Costanza Magalotti Barberini provides a most impressive example of the obligation of a Roman noblewoman to participate in diplomatic society.[26] She was a modest and pious woman of a Florentine mercantile family who in her youth had hoped to become a nun; but her parents thought it better that she marry Carlo Barberini. This she did, in 1595. A dutiful wife and devoted mother, according to contemporary accounts, she continued in her modest ways. When her brother-in-law Maffeo Barberini was elevated to the papacy as Urban VIII in 1623, she found herself thrust into a prominence that she did not want. Urban obliged her to use the title "Eccellenza," customary for relatives of a pope, and to hold court. Even after her husband's death in 1630 the pope denied her petition to be allowed to enter a convent as *conversa,* and she could only retire to the family palace, whether the "Casa Grande" ai Giubbonari or (from 1632 until 1634) the Palazzo Barberini alle Quattro Fontane, to

live as in a cloister. This secluded secular life was possible to her only because her son Taddeo had married Anna Colonna in 1627 and the younger woman was then available to assume the public duties of a female relative of the pope.[27] At last, in 1640, she was able to enter the newly founded convent of the SS. Incarnazione, where her two daughters were nuns. Although she retained secular garb and remained free to come and go, she rarely went out. Feeling herself unworthy of a nun's habit, she lived as a novice; only twenty-four hours before her death on 15 August 1644, she finally received the habit and made her profession as a nun.[28]

An account of the etiquette observed by Costanza as first female relative of the pope, presumably in her apartment in the "Casa Grande" ai Giubbonari, has survived.[29] It followed in principle the etiquette prescribed for men of the period, but it was more condensed. For example, she greeted guests who were cardinals at the door of the anteroom immediately preceding the audience room, inside or outside the door, depending on the rank of the particular cardinal, and bade them farewell in the outer anteroom before the outermost room of her apartment, the *sala dei palafrenieri.* (A cardinal would greet another cardinal in the *sala dei palafrenieri* or at the top of the stairs and then accompany him to his coach after the visit.)[30] Other male visitors were shown respect in proportion to their rank. Since Costanza apparently had only two anterooms and eschewed the use of the *sala* and stairs, she had to depend heavily on compliments and gradations of deference in her manner to show distinctions among the ranks of her many callers. Donna Costanza's women callers — wives of ambassadors, princesses, duchesses, marchionesses, relatives of cardinals, and so forth — were shown greater deference, according to the conventions of the system, than were men of comparable rank. To bid farewell to women who bore the title "Eccellentissima," Costanza would go to the limit of her apartment (never done for a man), to the outer door of the *sala dei palafre-*

nieri, or even beyond, to the top of the stair.

As women's etiquette was an adaptation of that used by men, men also made certain adjustments in their normal etiquette with respect to women. Men gave precedence to women on visits, in encounters with their carriages in the streets, and at banquets; but if there were more than two or three women, a cardinal need yield only to the woman of highest rank.[31] Following the good example of Cardinal Aldobrandini, later Clement VIII, cardinals gave audience to women of whatever rank with the *portiera* raised (although it might be lowered if the woman guest was the cardinal's mother or sister).[32] At papal audiences women were allowed to sit on a stack of three or four cushions (instead of standing or sitting on stools or other specified chairs, as men would do); and, again following the example of Clement VIII, they were offered refreshments in another room at the conclusion of the audience.[33]

Noblewomen's Apartments

Women who fulfilled responsibilities of receiving and paying calls in the diplomatic society of Rome required apartments similar to those of men.

In Palazzo Borghese, after the remodeling of 1671–76, Prince Giovanni Battista (grandson of Marcantonio) and Princess Eleonora had two pairs of apartments in the west wing of the palace: parallel suites on both the ground floor and the *piano nobile,* with the prince's rooms toward the street and his wife's toward the garden (see Figs. 42, 47).[34] On the ground floor they shared the first three large rooms to the left of the entrance from piazza Borghese (A4, A5, A6), and then each had an anteroom (A10, A8a), an audience room (A11–12, A8b), and a room containing a *zampanaro,* a large and elaborate bed (A13, A9); smaller rooms and a chapel followed in the extension toward the Ripetta. Upstairs, after the grand *sala* and its adjacent chapel C7, there followed two anterooms (C8, C9), an audience room (C10), two more rooms (C11, C27), and a

chapel (C30) for the prince; and three anterooms (C12, C13, C14), an audience room (C15), a smaller room (C28), and a gallery (C35) on the princess's side. The walls of the ground-floor rooms were covered with paintings from the famous Borghese collection (instead of the usual fabric or leather hangings), and the furnishings and hangings at the doors and windows were similar in kind and in richness in the two apartments, the only differentiation being that the first three rooms and the prince's suite were done in red and the princess's rooms had green hangings and upholstery. Each of the two audience rooms had a baldacchino in the appropriate color.[35] The equivalent and parallel suites corresponded to the similar and parallel forms of etiquette by which both prince and princess would have received guests. They also provided for easy connections between the more private rooms of the husband's and wife's suites, and the princess's two suites were placed toward the garden, conveniently below the apartment of her women attendants.

The few notices of noblewomen's suites in Palazzo Borghese before 1671 suggest that they too were comparable to those of the men (though always separate from them) — richly furnished and suitable for the playing out of Roman etiquette.[36] In particular, an apartment that included a chapel, in the northeastern wing of the palace, was at one time used by Donna Virginia, wife of Giovanni Battista Borghese and sister-in-law of the pope. This apartment was later taken over by Cardinal Pier Maria Borghese, who lived there until his death in 1642,[37] and the cardinal's residence there demonstrates the suitability of the apartment for a prominent unmarried man as well as for a widowed noblewoman.

Like Palazzo Borghese, Palazzo Barberini was also to house women relatives of a pope. Donna Anna Colonna Barberini had a large and richly furnished suite in a most prominent location, on the *piano nobile,* in the north wing (see Fig. 102).[38] Its chapel C30 was the site of the baptism of her daughter Lucrezia on 8 September 1632.[39] Her rooms were entered from the grand central salone, and four anterooms (the vault of the third, C29, bearing Andrea Sacchi's splendid fresco of the "Divina Sapienza")[40] preceded the audience room C27. The large number of anterooms was appropriate to Anna's high rank and also surely useful in allowing her to express many gradations of respect to her varied visitors without going beyond the door of her apartment to the sala or stairs (inappropriate for a woman) and without having to depend on compliments and other nonarchitectural signs, as had her mother-in-law in an apartment with only two anterooms. A small spiral service stair S8 descended from the inner rooms of the apartment to the basement and ascended to the attic and the quarters of her women attendants; and a separate private stair S7 communicated with the apartment of her husband Taddeo below. Like Virginia Borghese's apartment, Anna's rooms could readily be converted to the use of a cardinal: Antonio Barberini, recognizing the natural coolness of the northward-oriented rooms, arranged his summer apartment here when he took over the entire palace in 1635.[41]

Later, widowed and alienated from the Barberini family, Anna continued to live in a style befitting a woman of her rank. In 1651 and 1652 she bought houses near SS. Apostoli and the palace of her Colonna relatives, forming from them a single complex called Palazzo dell'Olmo, or dei Colonnesi, where she lived until her death on 31 October 1658. The inventory of her possessions in the palace reveals a suitably prestigious apartment, including a sala dei palafrenieri, anteroom, chapel, audience room, and so forth.[42]

In contrast, the widowed Costanza Barberini eschewed splendor and ceremony and lived modestly in two rooms in a remote part of the Palazzo Barberini alle Quattro Fontane, on the "secondo piano nobile" (see Fig. 103, D25 and D26).[43] According to a contemporary account, her rooms, though warmed by a fireplace, were very modestly furnished: without the rich wall hangings customary for a person of her rank, the walls held only simple devotional pictures; there were no jewels, gold, or silver; and there were

only a few old chairs, some of black leather with black fabric covers and some with seats of straw.[44] She slept on a straw pad, without the usual more comfortable mattress atop it; and when she moved to the convent in 1640 she gave up the straw as well, to sleep directly on the boards of the bed.[45] Costanza's private chapel D49 was on the same floor of the palace as her rooms but somewhat removed from them. Adjacent to Costanza's rooms, to the north, were the kitchen D28 (with a turnbox, or rota) and dining room D27 of her women attendants, and their bedrooms were in the attic of the north wing.

Pietro Cataneo remarked that noblewomen rarely went out but customarily spent much more time at home than their husbands did, and that accordingly they had a special need for airy and attractive quarters.[46] The limitations of noblewomen's lives made it especially desirable that they have places for enjoying the informal companionship of their women attendants within the palace and in enclosed gardens. The anonymous Barberini advisor, the author of Barb. lat. 4360, proposed a garden accessible from the women's apartment, enclosed, planted with an ellipse of trees, and centered on a fountain: ". . . the women could come here from their apartment, and remain here at their ease, alone, without being able to be seen by anyone."[47] In the Palazzo Barberini alle Quattro Fontane the designer contrived a six-room "casino" in the north wing, opening to an enclosed garden, which Anna and her companions could enjoy in warm weather (see Fig. 110).[48] At the Palazzo Colonna-Barberini in Palestrina, the apartment occupied by the princess in 1629 was adjoined by a little garden, with a house for the "signorini," probably in the area now occupied by the church of S. Rosalia. The three-bay loggia and its fountain, a part of the princess's apartment, may also have been an attempt to provide the women with a pleasurable place within the confines of the palace (see Fig. 181, A9).[49] At Palazzo Borghese after 1671, the princess's ground-floor apartment opened to the enclosed garden.

It was essential that a woman's apartment be

accompanied by the apartment of her women attendants—normally located in an attic or mezzanine, convenient to the noblewoman's apartment and at the same time secluded and isolated from the rest of the palace. The women had individual rooms, a common kitchen and dining room, and a turnbox (rota) that permitted them to receive food and other supplies without coming into contact with the temptations of the rest of the palace. In Palazzo Borghese, the marriage of the young prince Marcantonio Borghese to Camilla Orsini on 20 October 1619 was the occasion for arranging rooms for the bride's attendants. Four attic rooms E1–E4, which had been constructed and finished with plastered walls and simple brick pavements in 1607, on the southwest side of the courtyard, were subdivided and joined to the corner rooms (see Fig. 34). Each small room had a window, a sloping wood ceiling, and a door opening to a corridor. A latrine was installed in the small spiral stair S4 serving this apartment. Rooms E8 and E9 were probably the women's pantry and kitchen; the corner room E9 was fitted with a wood ceiling and two lavatories, and a turnbox was made and installed.[50] The major remodeling of the palace in 1671 included another apartment for women in the attic of the west wing, which followed exactly the same pattern (Fig. 49, E7, E12–E22).[51] The simple furnishings of the individual women's rooms were listed in an inventory made in 1693: for each room, a plain bed, an armchair, a straw-seated chair, possibly a small table with a single drawer, a devotional picture on the wall, a chamber pot, and a close-stool.[52] This was quite in contrast to the opulence of the many-roomed apartments of the princess whom the women served.

At Palazzo Barberini the situation was similar. The women attendants of Donna Anna Colonna Barberini were accommodated in the west end of the upper floors of the north wing, just above Anna's apartment (see Fig. 103). Their small private rooms were complemented by three larger vaulted rooms, each with a window to the west: the kitchen D24; the dining room D23, with a fireplace; and D22, a storeroom, which was also the location of the required turnbox.[53] The attendants of Anna's mother-in-law, Costanza, had a separate but similar set of rooms.[54]

The remodeling of Palazzo Chigi for the occupancy of Cardinal Flavio Chigi was the occasion for removing a women's apartment and its old turnbox, which would not be necessary in the all-male household of a cardinal.[55]

However separate the lives of men and women in seventeenth-century Roman society, it was nevertheless important that there be easy access between the private rooms of apartments of husband and wife. Since both suites were linear, extending outward from the sala, a few basic solutions naturally emerged. Suites of husband and wife might be parallel, as for Eleonora and Giovanni Battista Borghese after 1671; they might be located one above the other, as for Anna and Taddeo Barberini in their palace at the Quattro Fontane or at Palestrina; or they might stretch in opposite directions around a courtyard, thereby sharing both public entrance and private access, as in the Palazzo del Bufalo-Ferraioli.[56]

Beyond these functional relationships, the design of women's apartments might or might not affect the planning or appearance of the whole palace. Women's apartments can readily be used by men, as both Pier Maria Borghese and Antonio Barberini demonstrated, but men's apartments cannot be used by women without the additional provision of quarters for their women attendants and, optimally, some informal rooms and an enclosed garden. Probably the most common point of view is exemplified by the Palazzo Borghese, in which the whole building is seen as a three-dimensional plastic matrix within which women's apartments (as well as any other person's quarters) can be arranged according to the needs of any particular time. Palazzo Barberini seems exceptional in that the clear logic of its internal and external organization is apparent only if one understands the particular relationships among men and women and the role each resident played in the Barberini family and in Roman society.[57]

CHAPTER FOUR

The *Famiglia*

ROVIDED with many-roomed apartments for summer and winter use, the cardinal or secular prince in seventeenth-century Rome would further require a *famiglia,* or household staff, of perhaps one hundred persons in support of his dignity and daily needs. The necessity of ordering and managing a household of such size led to the writing of handbooks for individual officers[1] and the keeping of records,[2] and these in turn reveal to us the structure and operation of the household in the context of the architecture of the palace.

The Organization and Development of the *Famiglia*

As in the larger diplomatic society, so too in the palace: relationships among members of the household were controlled by a clear hierarchy of authority and responsibility.[3] The *maggiordomo,* "companion to his lord, and not a servant," stood second only to the prince and oversaw everything.[4] The affairs of the household were then divided into two realms: those concerning the person and activities of the prince, administered by the *maestro di camera;* and those concerning the maintenance and operation of the palace and its staff, directed by the *maestro di casa.* Each major division had its further subdivisions and internal hierarchical relationships. The *maestro di camera,* expert in the usages of court, com-

manded the dean of the *palafrenieri,*[5] who supervised the *palafrenieri;* he commanded also the gentlemen (*camerieri*), who were superior to the assistants (*aiutanti di camera*) and pages; and he directed the chaplains, among whom were distributed certain specific duties. The *maestro di casa* directed the steward (*scalco*), who in turn oversaw the work of the cook, butler (*credenziero*), carver (*trinciante*), purchaser (*spenditore*), and quartermaster (*dispensiero*); he similarly directed the stable master, who oversaw the grooms, coachmen, and stable boys; he supervised the wardrobe master (*guardaroba*), who had his own assistants. There were, further, assistant cooks, scullery boys, assistant butlers, porters, cleaning men, and so forth. According to the descriptions in handbooks of household management, duties were laid out clearly. Places within the palace in which specified officers would exercise authority were similarly defined. For example, as we have already seen, the *palafrenieri* stayed on duty in the *sala,* and the gentlemen attended in the anterooms. The chief cook exercised authority in the kitchen, where only the steward was allowed to enter.[6] The butler was responsible for the contents of the *credenza,* including the silver; no one else was allowed in the room, or even near enough to put his hand through its gate.[7] The quartermaster kept records of the contents of the storeroom; he did not allow other people to enter but dispensed supplies through a window or gate.[8]

The highly articulated household was seen as an organic whole. Liberati compared it to the heavens, in which each star moves in its own path and sphere but without conflict with a superior force, such that the harmony and mechanism of nature are preserved. In a second analogy, he writes, "The entire court moves like a body composed of many members, animated by a single mind in the good service of the Prince."[9]

Members of a household were distinguished not only by duties but also by social rank. The gentlemen attendants, chaplains, and many of the officers were "gentlemen," themselves entitled to personal servants. They were set apart by their dress and manners, and they were entitled to eat together, enjoying better food than persons of lower rank, possibly even in a special dining hall, if the prince provided them with meals in the palace.[10] Other responsible officers might not yet be "gentlemen." Still lower on the social scale were "servitori bassi," the lower servants. These social strata extended across the two realms administered by the *maestro di casa* and the *maestro di camera*.

The *famiglia* was composed almost entirely of men, and a churchman's household was entirely male. In his description of the *infermiero,* or nurse, Evitascandalo noted the inappropriateness of women's caring for the sick in an ecclesiastical household and the consequent necessity that this office be filled by a man.[11] In households of married men—for example, that of Taddeo Barberini—women are included only as laundresses, nurses for children, and companions to the noblewomen.[12]

The size of the household could vary considerably, according to the wealth and position of the prince. Certain offices could be combined: for example, the *maggiordomo* could also serve as *maestro di casa* and bookkeeper; the *auditore,* or legal advisor, could also be the theologian; a single person could supervise the storeroom *(dispensa),* wine cellar, supply of wood, and fodder for the horses; the steward could also be the carver; the cleaning man could double as

porter.[13] Categories of attendants could vary in size: *palafrenieri* might number four, six, nine, or twelve, so that two, three, or four might stand guard in the *sala* in a given shift;[14] a cardinal should have at least two chaplains, but he might have more;[15] the door of the cardinal's chamber was to be attended by two, three, or four gentlemen *(camerieri).*[16] A smaller household would require fewer persons for its own maintenance—for example, fewer assistants to the cooks and workers in the staff dining room. The wife of a secular prince would require women attendants, and his children would necessitate first nurses and then tutors.[17] A prince's special interests might entail corresponding members of the household: Cardinal Antonio Barberini employed six musicians; his brother Francesco included two library assistants in his household; Marcantonio Borghese required an attendant for his ball court.[18] Evitascandalo recommends that a minimum of twenty-three offices are necessary to the household,[19] but that might mean as many as thirty-five persons. In 1599, Clement VIII, worried about the poverty of four of his newly created cardinals, gave the four annual pensions to support twenty attendants, apparently a strict minimum for the dignity expected of a cardinal.[20] Maffeo Barberini, on the eve of his election to the papacy, had a *famiglia* of moderate size— forty-six persons, including eighteen gentlemen and chaplains and nine *palafrenieri.*[21] The households attached to the palaces included in the second half of this book were considerably larger than the minimum. In 1621 Prince Marcantonio Borghese supported a household of 142 persons and his older cousin Cardinal Scipione Borghese's household numbered 224.[22] Taddeo Barberini, living at the Palazzo Barberini alle Quattro Fontane, supported 143 persons, including twenty-six women, in 1633 and 163 persons in 1634.[23] Cardinal Francesco Barberini's household increased from sixty-two to ninety-four in November 1626, and by March 1637 he counted 134 persons in his employ.[24] His brother, Cardinal Antonio, had a household numbering 128 members in April 1642. In comparison, Cardinal Flavio Chigi's household of only ninety-four in 1666 seems rather modest.[25]

The household of the pope was like that of a cardinal or a secular prince insofar as its organization in support of attendance on the person of the pope and maintenance of his palace and staff. It was, however, larger (a reflection of the pope's exalted status), and it included a few peculiar variations. Since it was customary that each cardinal and ambassador resident in Rome send the dean of his *palafrenieri* to serve a newly elected pope, the pope's corps of *palafrenieri* was accordingly larger than the others' — more than forty men.[26] The court of Clement VIII included six chaplains and about thirty gentlemen attendants *(camerieri segreti)* — more than a cardinal would have; and they were further complemented by other categories of gentlemen attendants: *camerieri della bussola, camerieri extra muros, camerieri scudieri,* each with specific duties; and *camerieri d'honore,* distinguished by birth or accomplishments, but not required to be in attendance at the palace.[27] A few other officers included in the list of the papal *famiglia* in 1650 were peculiar to the papal court.[28]

There was a long tradition of large households for both pope and cardinals, stretching back to the early centuries of the Church. According to Leti, there had developed a mutual obligation between secular princes and princes of the Church: the zeal and generosity of secular princes enriched the Church; and the Church, not wishing to appear ungrateful, introduced ecclesiastical ceremony *(il decoro Ecclesiastico)* in Rome, so that the Church as father should be appropriately magnificent and be able to give greater glory to the princes as sons.[29] Through the centuries, periods of austerity alternated with periods of splendor, but by the early sixteenth century the institution of a large *famiglia* for the pope was well established.[30] Leo X maintained a household of 683 persons.[31] Paul IV lived modestly while a cardinal, but as pope he wanted to maintain the splendor that seemed due the pa-

pacy: his papal *famiglia* included 734 persons.[32] Some cardinals had to be admonished to maintain the decorum befitting the dignity to which they had risen, but others required no urging. Cardinal Pietro Riario, nephew of Sixtus IV, had a court of 500 persons; and Cardinal Thomas Wolsey, prime minister of Henry VIII, had a court of more than one thousand.[33] In 1526–27 (when 700 people lived at the papal palace), Cardinal Farnese supported 306 persons, Cardinal Cesarini counted 275 persons among his household, and Cardinals Orsini and del Monte had households of 200 persons each.[34]

By the beginning of the seventeenth century there were some changes in both the size and the constitution of cardinals' households. In the course of the sixteenth century the number of cardinals had risen from thirty-five to seventy, and many were without personal fortunes. In general, cardinals in 1571 were less rich than those in 1500, according to figures published by Delumeau. Yet even very wealthy cardinals had smaller households: Carlo Borromeo, papal nephew of Pius IV and among the richest cardinals, had a *famiglia* of only 150 when the Vatican had 1,500; and in 1598 Cardinal Pietro Aldobrandini, also a cardinal nephew, supported only 140 persons. Both ecclesiastics and laymen had fewer servants in 1600 than they did in 1500, possibly because of the abolition of slavery in the course of the sixteenth century and the consequent reduction in the supply of labor. Although luxury increased toward 1600, its display no longer took the form of a very large *famiglia.*[35]

Along with the reduction in the size of the *famiglia* of a cardinal or secular prince, there were changes in its constitution which clarified and strengthened the part concerned with the "camera." Francesco Priscianese's outline of a household for a Roman nobleman in 1543 lists 107 persons, but the *maestro di camera* is not among them. By the time of Evitascandalo's account of a household in the closing years of the sixteenth century, the *maestro di camera* is one of two important supervisors of the life of the palace, especially concerned with the ceremonies of paying and receiving calls.[36] Priscianese specifies six *palafrenieri,* while Evitascandalo expects twelve in a house of quality.[37] Priscianese names two prelates or gentlemen worthy of eating with the prince, and four *letterati* in various fields; but Evitascandalo replaces them with several gentlemen attendants *(camerieri)* whose main duty is to attend the prince in the anteroom, and who stand while the prince eats.[38] The duties of the six "camerieri" called for by Priscianese are those of the "aiutanti di camera" in Evitascandalo's manual (that is, caring for the rooms, beds, wall hangings, and so forth);[39] and the earlier writer does not mention pages, whom Evitascandalo sees as gentlemen-in-training.[40] Priscianese notes thirty-six persons of the rank of "gentleman" and specifies the number of personal servants that each is to have (ranging from three for each of the two prelates to five to be shared by the ten *scudieri*);[41] Evitascandalo is less consistent in indicating the status of the attendants and officers and does not grant them personal servants—a shift in emphasis toward service with respect to the prince. The elaboration of the *famiglia* of the "camera" in the second half of the sixteenth century would seem to be consonant with the development of the linear apartment and the ceremonies of the reception of guests, as described in Chapter 1. At the same time, the ceremony of eating might be slightly less emphasized, as Priscianese's ten *scudieri,* charged with serving at meals, are eliminated, their service assumed by gentlemen *(camerieri)* and pages in Evitascandalo's scheme.[42] The shift in emphasis in the history of the publication of handbooks corresponds to the change in the composition of the *famiglia:* handbooks having to do primarily with eating were published between 1570 and 1610; those giving special attention to the "camera" are ca. 1620 to 1635; general books of household management occur throughout the period.[43]

The introduction of coaches in Rome in the mid-sixteenth century and Romans' great enthusiasm for the new mode of transportation and display meant the introduction of a new category of servants: coachmen. Priscianese specifies a stable of forty horses and mules, with a stable master (with his personal servant) and ten assistants; Evitascandalo gives new prominence to coachmen.[44]

Above everyone else and second only to the prince, in Evitascandalo's household, is the *maggiordomo*—an office absent in Priscianese's list. Instead, the earlier writer recommends the *riveditore generale,* an officer usually lacking in Italian courts, and especially in Rome. According to Priscianese, the *riveditore* is common in Naples and throughout the kingdom, and he has equivalents in France (the *contralvor*) and Spain (the *vededor*). More than a careful bookkeeper, he is charged with periodic visits to the entire estate of the prince and intimate familiarity with all its parts and operations. Such a paragon, advises Priscianese, is not impossible to find. A gentleman, he would be entitled to two servants; and his salary would amount to 120 scudi per year (the same as that of the *maestro di casa*), plus bonuses.[45] The kind of oversight offered by Priscianese's *riveditore* must have become necessary in Roman households by the end of the century, for Evitascandalo's *maggiordomo* provides it, along with bookkeeping skills and gentleman's status.[46] The *maggiordomo* therefore caps the clarified and balanced hierarchy of the *famiglia.*

The development of the Roman *famiglia* did not rest with the equilibrated pyramid of Evitascandalo. By 1658, Liberati could report two further developments. Since the office of *maggiordomo* was frequently given to a person of distinguished birth rather than to someone with practical experience, the need for sure oversight of the affairs of the prince called for yet another officer. Paolo Giordano Orsini, Duke of Bracciano, accordingly invented a new office in the Court of Rome, that of the *sopraintendente generale.* Liberati further states that the *maestro di casa,* although subordinate to the *maggiordomo,* can perform the duties of the *sopraintendente generale* should the household not include that officer.[47] A second development concerned the *camerieri*—chamber assistants for Priscianese but gentlemen attendants for Evitascandalo. According to Liberati, while all the courts had previously had *camerieri* who were entitled "gentlemen" (following Evitascandalo's outline), only those of the greatest princes were maintaining them by the time of his writing in 1658; the *camerieri* of the lesser courts had come to be more like chamber assistants (*aiutanti di camera*).[48] That a major court in the later part of the century would have a large number of "gentlemen" *camerieri* (more than the two, three, or four suggested by Evitascandalo) is shown by the roll of the household of Cardinal Flavio Chigi in 1666: of the ninety-four persons listed, seventeen are grouped together as gentlemen (*signori*) and four are chaplains; they are followed by a list of seven *aiutanti di camera,* without title.[49]

The sixteenth and seventeenth centuries saw development in the institution of service, at all levels of the domestic hierarchy. In the 1580s Torquato Tasso wrote of a change in Italian society such that the modern courtier had become the successor to the citizen of earlier years. The honor of commanding had been abandoned for the honor of serving. *Prudenza civile* gave way to *prudenza cortigiana,* dedicated to preserving the honor of the prince, from which would derive one's own honor.[50] Introductions and dedications of the several handbooks on etiquette and household management published during the period provide further evidence of the honor found in service: the authors of the books are proud to be distinguished officers in the households of distinguished cardinals or noblemen. Fierce allegiance to the prince whom one served extended through the ranks and accounted for several street conflicts and brawls recorded in contemporary accounts.[51]

Professional identity found in service led to the formation of various confraternities in these decades. Cooks and pastry makers formed a confraternity in 1513, with the pope's private cook as its prior. Coachmen organized a confraternity during the papacy of Paul III, when coaches were still quite new in Rome. Butlers (*credenzieri*) established a confraternity under Paul IV in 1557. Trainbearers (*caudatari*) and chaplains of cardinals were similarly organized.[52] Finally, in 1624, the Congregazione Urbana was founded for gentlemen attached to the courts of cardinals, princes, ambassadors, and other dignitaries. Their patron saints were SS. Giovanni e Paolo, who had been courtiers under Constantine; and the first protector of the congregation was Cardinal Francesco Barberini, nephew of the pope. Membership was reserved for those who had served for at least fourteen years. There were 170 charter members.[53]

Accommodations for the *Famiglia*

If a large *famiglia* made possible the life of the prince in his palace, it also made necessary some architectural arrangements for its proper functioning and its own maintenance.

WORKPLACES

The prince's apartment was the workplace of those who assisted in the reception of guests and attended the person of the prince. *Palafrenieri* were in the *sala;* gentlemen, assistants, and pages were in the anterooms; and assistants and the cleaning person (*scopatore segreto*) were admitted to the prince's private rooms for specific duties, as discussed in Chapter 1.

The *palafrenieri* might require an additional room outside the apartment. As Evitascandalo explains, the group of twelve men was divided into three shifts of four each, to serve in the *sala* in turn. The four who had been on duty the previous day formed a second guard: although they might not be in the *sala,* they were not to leave the palace, in case they might be needed.[54] For these men a special room in the palace would be welcome. Palazzo Borghese had such a room in 1607–8: on the ground floor of the west wing, room A10, formerly a carriage room, was remodeled for the *palafrenieri,* and in 1619 they used rooms A11 and A12 (see Fig. 20).[55]

In support of the prince's dining in his apartment, two special offices were required: the butler's pantry *(credenza)* and the wine steward's room *(bottiglieria).* These are distinct from the similarly named tables arranged for service during meals.

The butler's pantry was to be as near the *sala* as possible, dry, airy, and spacious. Foods that would not spoil (oranges, lemons, fennel, and the like) were to be kept there, as well as the silver for the service of the prince's table. The room had to be secure, to protect both the food and the silver of the prince; accordingly, it was to have a gate that could be kept locked, and the butler or his assistant was to sleep there.[56] *Credenze* in Palazzo Borghese cannot be located specifically, but records of their remodeling in 1619–22, for Cardinal Scipione Borghese and the young Prince Marcantonio Borghese, give a picture of the furnishings and uses of the office. The cardinal's *credenza,* adjacent to the kitchen for his staff and the rooms of Giovanni Battista Petroni (his butler?), were outfitted with a cupboard for silver, another cupboard, a shelf for other storage, and a lavatory.[57] The prince's *credenza* was next to his bookkeeping office and had a fireplace, shelves, a counter for cleaning silver, a large press for folding linens, a smaller portable press for napkins, a lavatory, and a table for use in the *sala.*[58] Running water and drainage for the sink were important requirements, documented in the *credenze* of Palazzo Barberini in both 1638 (see Fig. 101, B3) and 1676 (see Fig. 164, A21)[59] and Palazzo Chigi (see Fig. 202, A9).[60] These *credenze* were relatively convenient to the *sala* and anterooms above, thanks to well-placed service stairs; in 1557, in the still-unfinished Palazzo Farnese, the *credenza* was in the west corner of the ground floor (see Fig. 5a)[61] — rather removed from the main apartment toward the piazza.

The *bottiglieria,* or wine-steward's room, should be convenient to the prince's apartment and also to the wine cellar. Like the *credenza,* it should be secure against tampering and theft. One of the *palafrenieri* was selected to serve as wine steward *(bottigliere),* and he was supervised by the cupbearer *(coppiero);* in other words, the *bottiglieria* was within the "camera" part of the household. Working from his office, the wine steward set up a small table in or near the room where the prince was to eat, provided the wine and glasses, and returned the glasses to the *bottiglieria* after the meal.[62] The *bottiglieria* planned for Palazzo Farnese in 1540–46 was on the ground floor, just to the right of the entrance vestibule and connected with the anterooms of the apartment above by a small stair; it included basins for cooling the wine in water.[63] The *bottiglieria* in Palazzo Chigi in piazza SS. Apostoli was room B13 on the ground floor (see Fig. 203), connected by private stairs with both the cardinal's apartment on the *piano nobile* and the wine cellar (probably A10) below. It had shelves, a large cupboard, two beds (for the *bottigliere* and his young assistant), and water piped in from the fountain in the garden.[64] In Palazzo Barberini alle Quattro Fontane the *bottiglierie* were similarly situated and equipped: ground-floor room B7 until its removal to make way for a new kitchen in 1646 (see Fig. 101), and basement room A23 after 1675 (see Fig. 164).[65]

While the *credenza* and *bottiglieria* should be somewhat convenient to the prince's apartment, other offices should be kept at a distance.

The heat, noise, and smells associated with the preparation of food in the kitchen were quite apart from the ceremony of serving and eating in the apartment. Kitchens might be 150 paces removed from the apartment[66] and were properly on the ground floor, with easy access to a courtyard or street.[67] The best arrangement was to have two kitchens, the first for the food of the prince *(cucina segreta)* and the second for that of the numerous household staff *(cucina comune).* If only one was possible, the cook would have to keep a special watch on the prince's food. The

10 The palace kitchen (Scappi, *Dell'arte del cucinare,* 1610) (Biblioteca Apostolica Vaticana)

first cook *(cuoco segreto),* superintended by the steward, presided over the kitchen. The second cook *(aiutante di cucina,* or *cuoco comune)* cooked for the staff and helped the first cook in the preparation of banquets. Both were assisted by boys who were not themselves cooks.[68] Security was important: windows to the street were to be barred, and unauthorized persons were not allowed to enter the kitchen.[69] Individuals sharing a single palace would have separate kitchens and separate cooking staffs.[70]

Evitascandalo describes a well-equipped kitchen: "It would be supplied with all the necessary copper, iron, and earthenware utensils; with a couple of pots that can be locked, full of water, for use with the prince's foods; with a table for

working doughs, and everything else needed for that work; with a table for arranging the plates, a large cupboard, and chests with latches, for holding cold foods and the day's supplies; and also with a big fly-trap or fly-shoo, because of the many flies in this city. There would be a bed for the kitchen boy, so that he would not stay by the fire all night. Near the hearth (which ought to be low, and not high like that of an inn), there should be a waist-high counter [*poggio*], for the convenient cooking of many sorts of foods with coals, with three or four chambers for the coals, for pots and saucepans, which would save much wood and charcoal; and this cooking counter would be separate from that for the *famiglia*."[71]

The view published with Scappi's cookbook shows such a kitchen, with a fireplace, spits for roasting meats, racks and shelves for storage, a cooking counter with five chambers for coals, a large basin supplied with running water, and tables for preparing foods, working doughs, and arranging the serving plates; a small room for the kitchen boys ("camerino per garzoni") is beyond the doorway to the right; only the precaution against flies is missing (Fig. 10).[72] The several functions shown in Scappi's view could be divided among several rooms: the main kitchen, the baking room, the scullery, and storerooms for foods, wood, charcoal, and grains.[73]

In actual practice, kitchens in the palaces considered in detail in the second part of this book conform closely to the standards of Evitascandalo and Scappi, in both architectural features and furnishings.[74] A ground-floor location is the norm, surely because of the ease of access for deliveries and the requirements of running water and drains, but the multiroom kitchen of Palazzo Chigi and that built at Palazzo Barberini in the 1670s were in newly excavated basements (see Fig. 164, A21–A27; Fig. 202, A1–A4, A13–A14). At Palazzo Chigi a ramped stair eased the problem of deliveries (see Figs. 202, 203, S6). It is also clear that separate kitchens were maintained for separate households within a single palace, as in the case of Giovanni Battista and Francesco

Borghese or, later, Marcantonio and Scipione Borghese in Palazzo Borghese.[75] So too was the *cucina segreta* separate from the *cucina comune*. Even in the modest "Casa Grande" ai Giubbonari in 1609–12, there were two small but separate kitchens, for the Barberini and for their staff.[76] The staff kitchen could even be well outside the palace, as at Palazzo Barberini in the 1630s and Palazzo Chigi in the 1660s.[77]

Only kitchens for the women attendants of a noblewoman departed from the norms of Evitascandalo and Scappi. They were upstairs, as part of the women's secluded apartments, equipped with fireplaces and lavatories but not ovens.[78] The requirement of isolating women and their activities within the palace overrode any inconveniences of location.

The *dispensa,* or dispensing storeroom, served the household staff rather than the prince himself. Supplies were bought by the purchasing agent *(spenditore),* according to the instructions of the steward *(scalco);* the porter *(sportarolo)* delivered them to the *dispensa,* where the quartermaster *(dispensiere)* stored them, kept records, and dispensed provisions to the kitchen and the household in an orderly manner. In addition to supplies for the cook, foodstuffs, candles, torches, brooms, and everything else given as allotments of provisions to the *famiglia* were kept here. The office had to be dry, airy, and spacious; it had to be secure, with bars on windows to the street; it had to be convenient to both the porter and the *famiglia* but completely separate from the quarters of the prince.[79] It was paired naturally with the kitchens and the staff dining hall *(tinello,* below, pp. 44–45) and was normally on the ground floor of the palace.

Cardinal Scipione Borghese's *dispensa* had at least two rooms, and its furnishings are characteristic of the office: shelves, a rack for salami, cupboards, and so forth, a wooden inner door *(bussola)* with a window for dispensing allotments, and a loft over the door where an assistant could sleep.[80] A lavatory (documented in Palazzo Barberini's *dispensa*)[81] would also be use-

ful. A convenient ground-floor location, near the *tinello* and kitchens and often just next to a major entrance, was chosen in the palaces considered in Part II. At Palazzo Borghese, Giovanni Battista Borghese's *dispensa* was in room A2 (see Fig. 20); later, the *dispensa* of his son Marcantonio seems to have been in the northeastern part of the palace, on the ground floor, near the staff kitchen.[82] At the "Casa Grande" ai Giubbonari in 1609–12, the *dispensa* was room A17, in the low wing at the rear of the courtyard, next to the *tinello* (see Fig. 57).[83] At the Palazzo Barberini alle Quattro Fontane, Taddeo Barberini's two-room *dispensa* A5–A6 opened from north *entrone* A8 (see Fig. 100).[84] In 1674 the Barberini *dispensa* was moved to a building apart from the palace, along with the *tinello,* bakery, and bookkeeping office[85]—a clear sign that it served the household staff and not the prince himself. Palazzo Chigi's *dispensa* B8 (also grouped with the bookkeeping office) was just next to the main entrance (Fig. 203).[86]

The bookkeeper *(computista)* did not actually handle money, but he kept the accounts necessary for the management of the large household.[87] His office *(computisteria)* was furnished with a writing desk and cupboards for the many volumes of records that he produced.[88] A ground-floor room B9, with abundant light and easy access, was chosen for this office in Palazzo Chigi in piazza SS. Apostoli (see Fig. 203).[89] The *computisteria* at Palazzo Barberini alle Quattro Fontane was in room B6 in 1641–43 but was moved to a more advantageous location in rooms B9–B10 in 1644–45 (see Fig. 101); in the 1670s it was moved once again, to a building outside the main palace, to make way for the new ground-floor apartment of the south wing.[90]

A cardinal's all-male household could not include a laundress, and so laundry normally was sent out.[91] Adami complains of problems with Roman laundries and notes that many households would send their laundry to Marino or Frascati.[92] Noblewomen and their attendants, however, required laundries. The household of

Prince Taddeo Barberini included two laundresses in 1643, listed among the "women" of his wife Anna.[93] Donna Anna's laundry was in the north wing of the palace, in A2, complete with basins, a water heater, and a door to the spiral stair S8 leading to the attic rooms of her women attendants (see Fig. 100); Donna Costanza Barberini had a similar laundry in the eastward extension of the north wing.[94] There was another laundry, for linens, in the northeast part of the site, in a house formerly belonging to one Accorambono or Corambono.[95] Cardinal Antonio Barberini did not need a laundry and felt free to convert Anna's laundry into a bath in 1641, when he was resident in the palace.[96]

The apartments of the prince were richly but sparely furnished. Personal and household goods of all sorts were stored in the *guardaroba* and then consigned to authorized officers or brought out for use when required. Household inventories show the distinctive pattern of distribution of goods within the palace. The apartments contained wall hangings, sets of chairs, tables, and so forth, but they did not have chests or cupboards for the storage of clothing and other objects for daily or occasional use. These things were kept together, "in guardarobba." This practice is in contrast to that of the fifteenth century, as revealed, for example, by an inventory of the Palazzo Medici in Florence in 1492: in rooms called "camera" there were chests and trunks containing clothes, costly utensils, and rugs; in the "anticamera" or "soffitto" were linens and clothes; the office or study was a treasury as well as a library.[97] The *cassone,* so characteristic of Florentine fifteenth-century dwellings and common even in the sixteenth century, is almost entirely absent from inventories of seventeenth-century Roman household furnishings.[98]

The general requirements for a *guardaroba* are set out by Evitascandalo and the anonymous author of Barb. lat. 4360. It should be high in the house, where it will not interrupt the suite of apartments, and where the noise of the beating of fabrics and other activities will not be bothersome; and it should be in the interior of the house, not on a public street. It should be secure from fire and thieves, oriented toward good winds, and not damp but airy. It should be large and spacious, furnished with cupboards and a big table for brushing and folding things. There should be more than one room, so that goods can be grouped according to kind or value; and there should be a loggia for airing things in the shade. A stair by which large and bulky objects may be brought easily to the *guardaroba* should be complemented by a private stair for the prince's discreet movements.[99] The author of Barb. lat. 4360 proposes a *guardaroba* on the fifth level of his design for Palazzo Barberini (see Fig. 133e, L): above the oval hall, it would have been an ample rectangular room adjoined by two smaller rooms; a loggia would have opened to the east (with an open terrace above), and a secure mezzanine chamber below would have held especially valuable goods. According to the author's prescription, the convenient straight stair to the main room of the *guardaroba* would have been complemented by a spiral stair ascending from the principal apartment to the secure mezzanine, the main room, the loggia, and the upper terrace.[100]

Within this office, the *guardaroba,* or wardrobe-master, exercised control. Assisted by the *aiutante di guardaroba,* he was in charge of all the movable possessions of the prince—furnishings, wall hangings, linens, clothing, silver and other precious objects, pots and utensils for the kitchen, and so forth.[101] He sewed, mended, aired, brushed, and folded. He had mattresses remade once a year. He sent soiled things to the laundry. He kept careful records of everything, including consignments of silver to the butler (*credenziero*) and copper vessels and other equipment to the cook. He saw to the seasonal and occasional hanging of tapestries and other revetments. In the evening he came to the anteroom to learn what clothes the prince would want to wear the following day, so that he could ready them. The *guardaroba* was therefore not only a place for storage but also the site of the servicing, tending, and recording of the prince's possessions.

The loggia that normally accompanied a *guardaroba* might have other uses than the airing of clothing and other goods. The author of Barb. lat. 4360 notes that from the upper terrace of the loggia of his proposed *guardaroba* one can enjoy distant views.[102] In July 1610 Paul V visited Palazzo Borghese and took a meal "at the summit of the house," presumably in the loggia E7 adjacent to the *guardaroba* (see Fig. 24), facing the coolness and view of the Pincio to the northeast.[103] Yet these must be seen as extra advantages rather than as primary uses of the *guardaroba* loggia.

The close functional relationship between *guardaroba* and rooftop loggia explains the peculiarities of form and location noticed by scholars who have considered the loggia first as a belvedere.[104] Set back from the façade of the building (in accord with the advice of Barb. lat. 4360, fol. 31), hard to see from the narrow street below, possibly enclosed toward the street, and even turned from what might be considered the most desirable view, the loggia was primarily a workplace. The Villa Aldobrandini in Frascati, called the "Villa Belvedere," shows the clear ordering of function. The uppermost level of the building contains but a single large room, the *guardaroba*, and its adjacent loggia forms part of the three-tiered structure facing the hillside against which the villa is arranged. The remarkable view is in the other direction, to the north. A contemporary account describes the view and mentions specific points from which it is to be enjoyed: the three-bay loggia opening to the circus-shaped terrace, the upper terrace before the entrance to the house, and the rooms on the *secondo piano*, but *not* the central room on the uppermost level (the *guardaroba*) or its adjacent loggia.[105]

The palaces considered in the second half of this study consistently follow the recommendations of Evitascandalo and Barb. lat. 4360 for the *guardaroba*. The office is frequently found above the *salone* and is regularly linked with a loggia. Further, as with other offices, a separate *guardaroba* is maintained for each major resident of the palace.

Even in its most modest form, the "Casa Grande" ai Giubbonari in 1581–86 had a *guardaroba* on the top story, with a loggia for hanging things out to air (see Fig. 53).[106] Through subsequent enlargements and rearrangements of the building, the *guardaroba*-loggia combination remained in the upper part of the house.[107] The conspicuous arcaded rooftop loggia finished in 1625 (see Figs. 72, 84) was associated with the *guardaroba*, according to an inventory of the "Casa Grande" in 1648.[108] By 1671, the enlarged palace had only one major resident, Cardinal Antonio Barberini, but he needed many rooms for his numerous possessions: a "Stanza n° 35 della Guardarobba," apparently on the main floor; a "Guardarobba da basso" of three rooms, for wall hangings, fabrics, linens, and clothes, in particular; and a "Guardarobba à Tetto" of about seventeen rooms.[109]

In Palazzo Borghese the *guardaroba* for Giovanni Battista Borghese was E5, over the new *salone*, and its loggia was E7 (see Fig. 24).[110] Francesco Borghese's *guardaroba*, equipped with nine large cupboards, was in his half of the palace, not quite at rooftop but on the third floor, above the "sala vecchia" (see Fig. 23, D29; seen in section, Fig. 26).[111] By 1620 a third *guardaroba*, the "guardarobba nuova," was established for Prince Marcantonio in rooms D26–D28 (see Fig. 31).[112]

There were multiple *guardarobe* at the Palazzo Barberini alle Quattro Fontane too. The prince's *guardaroba* was the tall attic constructed over the central *salone*, joined to a U-shaped corridor-like room F5 over the cove of the *salone* vault and a one-story loggia F6 with an unroofed terrace G2 above (see Figs. 105–6, 115; cf. Figs. 99, 162). The princess's *guardaroba* was separate from that of her husband, in an attic just to the north of the main *guardaroba*.[113] The "old guardaroba" surviving from the Sforza palace was still to be identified in the upper part of the east end of the north wing of the palace.[114] A fourth *guardaroba* was for Francesco — the vaulted room D1, below his library (see Fig. 103); but a record of payment for woodwork "in our *guardaroba* or rather library" suggests that the library had usurped what was acknowledged as the *guardaroba*'s rightful place at the top of the house.[115]

Palazzo Chigi's ample *guardaroba* F17 was also at the top of the palace (see Fig. 207). There was originally no loggia, but its many clerestory windows may have made the room itself open enough for the airing of clothing and other goods. Before long, however, an open loggia was built above the second *guardaroba* F19, between 1672 and 1675.[116]

HOUSING

For each person the prince provided a small monthly salary and provisions of one kind or another for housing and food. The anonymous author of a description of the court of Urbino ca. 1500 declared that the whole *famiglia* should live in the palace, as far as possible, in places convenient to their duties and appropriate for their rank — the major officers in private rooms (shared only with their personal servants) and others two, three, or four to a room. The room would be furnished simply with a bed and bedding, a small table, a bench, and a lamp. Only officers would keep modest fires; the others' rooms would be unheated so as not to discourage their occupants' attendance at court.[117] In 1587 Baldi located gentlemen's rooms in the west wing of the ground floor of the Palazzo Ducale.[118] In sixteenth-century Rome, quarters for gentlemen and servants were often in mezzanines, the third floor, or attics.[119] Priscianese (1543) speaks of a single small room for a gentleman, and Evitascandalo indicates that the gentleman had no need for firewood, since his meals would be prepared in the kitchen and he would keep warm at his post of duty, the anteroom.[120]

The Palazzo Condulmer-Orsini-Pio in Campo dei Fiori (see Figs. 73, 74, 75, no. 636), built ca. 1450 and inhabited by a succession of distinguished residents, including cardinals, through the sixteenth century, was described in 1601 as having only two major apartments, the rest of the building being given over to services and the *famiglia*.[121] In contrast, the large seventeenth-century palaces considered in the second half of this study were filled with large apartments and special rooms for the use of the major inhabitants. There were very few spaces available for servants. The absence of servants in Palazzo Chigi in piazza SS. Apostoli is confirmed by parish census records, which show only a handful of people in the palace and many others in several houses in the neighborhood.[122]

Of the large *famiglia*, persons with special responsibilities toward the person or possessions of the prince lived within the palace. First among these was the personal attendant to the prince, who should be housed as close as possible to his master, in case he should be needed during the night. In addition, a subordinate assistant might sleep by the door, to hear the prince's call and go quickly to summon the attendant from his room.[123] Cardinal Francesco Barberini's personal attendant, the priest Luciano Fabriani, described his room as being connected with that of the cardinal by a "most private stair," by which he would descend when summoned by the ringing of a bell.[124] Cardinal Antonio Barberini seems to have slept in room C8 in Palazzo Barberini in April 1644; and the adjacent room C9, with access to the service stair, seems to have been used by his attendant (see Fig. 102).[125] Other officers with special responsibilities in the palace slept near their posts: the butler in the butler's pantry, to guard the silver,[126] and the cook or his assistant in the kitchen.[127] Woodwork done in Palazzo Borghese in 1619 records such facilities: in the kitchen of the prince, a loft "for the cook to sleep"; in the *dispensa*, a screened-off corner "for sleeping."[128] Stable boys slept in the stable. Evitascandalo cautions that they should be provided with beds, for, if they sleep on the hay, the horses won't eat it.[129] The anonymous author of Barb. lat. 4360 describes a dormitory, a loft about 30 × 90 *palmi,* for fourteen or sixteen beds for stable hands.[130] At least two *palafrenieri* were to remain in the *sala* during the night, resting on chests from which bedding could be withdrawn *(letti da credenza);* but this was considered a post of duty and not a residence: the inclination of *palafrenieri* to have either wives or mistresses made it necessary that they live outside the palace, at least in the case of a cardinal's palace.[131]

A noblewoman's female attendants also lived within the palace, in the secure apartment described above in Chapter 3. They thereby were able to serve their mistress better, and at the same time they were shielded from the risks of life outside the palace.

Except for these special cases — persons with special responsibilities to the person or possessions of the prince, and women attendants — the numerous members of the *famiglia* lived outside the palace, but in its neighborhood, and in places provided by the prince.

A direct if possibly cumbersome solution to the problem of housing the *famiglia* outside the palace was simply to rent whatever houses might be available for them in the neighborhood — a not uncommon practice, according to an anonymous Barberini advisor.[132] Many notices in the Archivio Borghese refer to the maintenance of such houses for Borghese *famiglie;*[133] Carlo Barberini rented many houses in the vicinity of the "Casa Grande" ai Giubbonari for his *famiglia;*[134] and Cardinal Flavio Chigi followed this practice, according to parish census records.[135]

Taddeo Barberini recognized the suitability of a single, readily administered building as a residence for his *famiglia.* While his portion of the Palazzo Barberini alle Quattro Fontane was being constructed, Taddeo lived in the "Casa Grande" ai Giubbonari and rented the nearby Orsini palace, called the "Palazzo dell'Orologio," located at the east end of Campo dei Fiori,

for his *famiglia* (see Figs. 73, 74, 75 [no. 636]).[136] Although built by Cardinal Francesco Condulmer, nephew of Pope Eugene IV, a description from around 1601 shows its formal inadequacies: it had no proper façade because of its foundation on the ruins of the Theater of Pompey; a portal from the Campo dei Fiori led to a large but malformed courtyard with a loggia "as ugly as it could be," and an unroofed stair led up to the *sala;* there were only two large apartments, and the rest of the building was for servants.[137] However inadequate for a princely dwelling in the seventeenth century, the palace, built in the first place to house many servants, must have seemed ideal for Taddeo's large *famiglia* (143 persons in 1633).[138] From the time of his marriage in late 1627 until his move to the Quattro Fontane in the spring of 1632, he rented the "Palazzo dell'Orologio" from its owner Paolo Giordano Orsini; when he returned to live permanently at the Giubbonari in October 1634, he once again rented it for his *famiglia.*[139]

Cardinal Scipione Borghese too had decided to house his large *famiglia* in a single unified palace — not a normal palace with large rooms and suites but one especially designed for the *famiglia.* The Palazzo della Famiglia Borghese (see Figs. 37, 38) was built across the piazza to the south of the Palazzo Borghese between 1624 and 1627.[140] Its broad façade, while not especially distinguished, fits comfortably among early-seventeenth-century palaces in Rome. It presents an image of the usual three stories, with the addition of mezzanine and attic windows (as on the main palace across the way). Three-bay sections at the ends are framed by graded rustication; the ground-floor stucco imitates drafted masonry, and the three arched portals are framed in strong rustication. The plans, however, reveal an organization that has nothing to do with that of noble palaces. Stables are included at one end of the ground floor, and the rest of the building is divided into apartments, usually of two rooms.

We can glimpse the life within one of the apartments through an inventory made on 21

April 1643, at the death of its occupant, one Don Francesco Ceccarelli, who lived there with his mother, Prudentia.[141] His apartment had three rooms—larger than most. The first room seemed centered on the fireplace, where we can imagine that food was prepared, for the inventory lists fireplace equipment (including a grill, a tripod, and a spit), several copper vessels, forty majolica and plain plates, other pots and dishes, simple worn chairs, a *credenza,* and so forth. The second room contained two beds of unequal quality, one of walnut with red fabric hangings, and the other of simpler form and fittings. There were a prie-dieu and a big cupboard filled with clothes, but no other furniture—just pictures, towels, clothes, a basket of old books, and so forth. In the third room, "in the room where the above-named Francesco used to sleep, on the side toward the kitchen," we find his walnut bed, some modest chairs, a little desk, about twenty paintings, various personal effects, and clothing. A fireplace is indicated in this room, too, by fireplace equipment and a box of ashes. This three-room apartment of a gentleman, with fireplaces, was surely more generous than the single unheated room specified for courtiers in the household of the Duke of Urbino ca. 1500;[142] yet it bears no comparison to the apartments of the Borghese prince whom he served. Small and sparsely and modestly furnished, its three rooms contained everything that supported Don Francesco's life. Here he ate, slept, studied, and conversed with his mother. It was surely entirely private, without the ceremonial aspects of a prince's apartment; and at the same time it was not his alone, since his mother was there and (if the second bed in the second room is an indication) possibly a serving girl as well.

When the Barberini were planning their new palace at the Quattro Fontane, in the 1620s, an anonymous advisor proposed a design that would cover the large site and would include (in addition to major apartments) many accommodations for the *famiglia.* He notes that no palace nowadays, however large, seems to have enough rooms for the *famiglia,* and that the residents of the major Roman palaces have to rent many houses for their staffs.[143] Perhaps taking his cue from the contemporary Palazzo della Famiglia Borghese, the author proposes a building for members of the Barberini *famiglia* with two main stories separated by a mezzanine, each level having two rows of rooms flanking a central corridor (see Fig. 133, U). Fifteen rooms per floor would, according to his calculation, yield apartments for fifteen major courtiers, each with two rooms and a mezzanine for possessions and servants. In addition, the palace itself would offer a number of apartments for courtiers, particularly on the second and fourth levels in the corners of the main block, and behind the hemicycle; these apartments were usually of two rooms but sometimes of three or even four. Stable boys, *palafrenieri,* and coachmen would be put in dormitories over the carriage rooms; women would be in the long apartment north of the enclosed garden; the gardeners would have a house at the northeast corner of the site; and other servants could be tucked into mezzanines. All told, a *famiglia* of about 125 persons would be accommodated.[144]

The comprehensive plan of the anonymous advisor was not adopted. Instead, the Palazzo Barberini was designed to house almost no one besides the four principal residents (Taddeo Barberini, his wife Anna, his mother Costanza, and his brother Cardinal Francesco), and the women attendants. Taddeo then rented a group of about twenty houses in the neighborhood, from a number of landlords. They were ordinary Roman row houses, about 20 *palmi* wide, as shown in the Maggi map of 1625 (see Fig. 117), in Lieven Cruyl's drawing (see Fig. 91), and in a plan of houses at the southeast corner of the piazza (see Fig. 116). Taddeo remodeled the houses at his own expense, converting most of the ground-floor shops into housing and opening passages between adjacent courtyards; and he installed his *famiglia* in them.[145] But Taddeo's selection of houses was not random. Together with similar houses that he bought and converted into stables and carriage houses, the rental houses clustered about the base of the great palace and provided a controlled contrast which supported the designer's idea of the palace's position in a larger context.[146]

In 1635 Taddeo's brother, Cardinal Antonio, rented Taddeo's portion of the Palazzo Barberini alle Quattro Fontane and also, apparently, the same group of houses for the *famiglia;* a list of Antonio's rentals for his *famiglia* in 1644[147] corresponds closely to the list of Taddeo's rentals a decade earlier. When his own use of the Palazzo Barberini eventually extended through the three apartments originally designed for Taddeo, Anna, and Francesco, Antonio could find room for a few of his *famiglia* within the palace;[148] but most of his household lived in the rented houses.

EATING

The prince was responsible not only for housing but also for feeding his staff. While the prince ate with great ceremony (see Fig. 2), his attendants watched respectfully, removing their hats whenever he lifted his cup. The *famiglia* ate later, elsewhere.

The writer from Urbino ca. 1500 recommended not one but two *tinelli,* or staff dining rooms, for the separate dining of staff members of different ranks — an arrangement followed a century and a half later at the Palazzo Colonna-Barberini at Palestrina.[149] Other writers suggested separate sittings in a single *tinello.*[150] Whatever the arrangement, the room was capacious, located near the kitchens and pantry (that is, normally on the ground floor of the palace), provided with a fireplace, and outfitted with tables and benches. In a plan drawing for Palazzo Farnese, ca. 1549, the *tinello* is shown, labeled, in the south corner of the ground floor, adjacent to the *dispensa* and kitchens.[151] In Palazzo Borghese in 1606–10 it seems to have been ground-floor

room A1 (see Fig. 20). By 1619–20 Marcantonio Borghese's *tinello* seems to have been moved along with his *dispensa* to the northeast part of the palace.[152]

In the course of the sixteenth and seventeenth centuries the *tinello* gradually fell into disuse. Priscianese writes that it used to be a great honor to eat in the *tinello* but that now (1543) it is considered a vile and horrible thing, and a dishonor. Even so, he continues, there are many advantages to the *tinello.* It is more economical, more equitable, and more flexible. Further, if everyone had the "liberty" to eat in his own room (still a single room and not the two- or three-room apartments of the Palazzo della Famiglia Borghese or the Barberini's remodeled houses), it would be more a burden than a liberty: one's small room would have to be both bedroom and kitchen; the whole palace would smell like a *tinello,* and the dirtiness of that way of life would be objectionable.[153] In spite of these arguments, the institution of the *tinello* continued to decline. Rossetti in 1584 wrote that some servants would eat in the house, and that others would receive money instead, to provide their own meals.[154] At the turn of the century Evitascandalo stated without prejudice that there were two ways of feeding the staff: (1) the *tinello* or (2) *parte,* that is, the distribution of provisions to the staff, who then can fix their own meals.[155] At about this time, Palazzo Borghese still had the *tinello.* Slightly later, in the 1620s, the Barberini's anonymous advisor included *tinelli* on the lowest floor of his proposal for the new Palazzo Barberini.[156] Yet there is none in the palace as built, begun in 1628. An old staff kitchen was removed from the lowest level of the north wing and a new one built outside the palace; in addition, the remodeled houses rented for *famiglia* were fitted with fireplaces to be used for cooking by their individual occupants.[157] Adami in 1636 describes the second of Rossetti's alternatives: many courts, he says, now give money instead of provisions, or along with only bread and wine, since it is less work for the quartermaster (*dispensiere*). The *tinello* is relegated to history, as he says that "in former times" meals were served there.[158] By 1658 Liberati can write that hardly anyone uses the *tinello,* provisions or money having replaced it.[159] In Palazzo Chigi (1664–67) there is no *tinello,* although a kitchen for the *famiglia* was maintained outside the main palace (see Fig. 208, G); Cardinal Chigi's list of comparatively high monthly payments to his *famiglia* suggests that he had chosen the alternative of cash payments in lieu of food, and many of the apartments he provided for members of his household were equipped with fireplaces or even kitchens.[160]

The *tinello* seems to have survived only in special cases. In country residences away from Rome, where staff members are removed from their usual dwellings, a *tinello* would be desirable.[161] In the Barberini palace at Palestrina, staff dining rooms are noted in a description of 1630 and an inventory of 1638.[162] The expectation of a *tinello* in the country was clear in courtiers' dismay when Innocent X announced that on his forthcoming sojourn in Frascati in the summer of 1652 there would be none — in contrast to the generosity of Urban VIII on his twice-yearly trips to Castelgandolfo.[163] A second exception survived in women's apartments, which remained firmly in the palace even while men courtiers and servants moved out. The demise of the *tinello* corresponds to the increasing independence of housing for the *famiglia,* outside the main palace and provided with cooking facilities.

CONSEQUENCES FOR DESIGN

The high degree of organization and clear allocation of responsibilities within the *famiglia* had its counterpart in the planning of areas assigned for the work of specified staff members. The constant concern for security meant that each office was isolable. The perennial needs of receiving, recording, and dispensing supplies were reasonably accommodated in ground-floor offices. Kitchens consumed many of those goods and further required much water; they too were consistently located on the ground floor or in a well-lit basement, in spite of the requirement of chimneys rising the full height of the palace. As long as the *tinello* was maintained, it formed a natural partner with the kitchen and the *dispensa.* Cortesi describes the constellation of kitchen, *dispensa,* and *tinello* in his account of the ideal cardinal's palace in the early sixteenth century;[164] it continues through the sixteenth century (for example, Palazzo Farnese) into the seventeenth. The *guardaroba*'s dissociation from the street and its need for light and air meant that its development occurred in the uppermost part of the palace; its raised volume and loggia enlivened the roofscape with little regard for the view from below. The resulting stratified plan — the activity of services associated with the street, the expanse of noble apartments above, and the security of possessions (along with women attendants) in the uppermost part of the building — then had to be laced together with service stairs for the appropriate connections among levels.

The removal from the palace of facilities for housing and feeding the *famiglia* had important consequences for the design of palaces in the seventeenth century. First, the elimination of the *tinello* meant that the architect's planning problems were simplified: he did not have to provide that large ground-story room or the corresponding kitchen for the staff. The ground floor became available for other uses — perhaps a sculpture gallery. Likewise, since most of the *famiglia* lived outside the palace, the architect did not have to provide many small rooms for them within the palace, with passages and service stairs for their discreet movement. In other words, the ratio of service rooms to major apartments was adjusted in favor of the latter. Palaces like the old Orsini palace in Campo dei Fiori, with only two apartments and the rest given to services, were eclipsed by palaces like that of Cardinal Chigi, filled with grand rooms. Yet apartments for women attendants, with their requirements of small rooms, kitchen and *tinello* (usually on an upper floor), turnbox, and access to the princess's apartments, remained.

The continuing necessity of providing housing for the *famiglia,* even if outside the palace, presented certain opportunities to the designer. If the many members of the *famiglia* were not simply absorbed into the neighborhood in scattered houses, the designer could use their dwellings to complement whatever ideas he may have

had about the relation of the main palace to the city. The Palazzo della Famiglia Borghese complemented the Palazzo Borghese; together the two palaces defined the large piazza between them, so that the Borghese presence was ever more forcefully asserted in the neighborhood and therefore in the city (see Fig. 40). The housing for the Barberini's *famiglia* at the Quattro Fontane reinforced the contrast of their palace with its immediate neighborhood and allowed the new Palazzo Barberini to assert its relationship to a larger context (see Fig. 91).

CHAPTER FIVE

Personal Cleanliness

O N RISING in the morning, a cardinal washed his hands, combed his hair, and dressed in the clothing ordered from the *guardaroba* the night before. He was assisted in dressing by his gentleman attendant or a chamber assistant *(aiutante di camera)*, or he dressed himself, according to his own preference.[1] The privacy of his toilette was in marked contrast to the French ceremony of the *lever*. Luciano Fabriani's account of his master Cardinal Francesco Barberini's morning routine delicately refrains from any mention of washing and speaks only of the cardinal's dressing and performing private devotions.[2]

The water used for morning ablutions was brought to the cardinal's private chambers not by pipes but by a chamber assistant.[3] Because the assistant normally was to enter the cardinal's room only in his absence, the water must have been delivered the previous evening or, alternatively, must have been carried only as far as the adjacent service room. A gentleman attendant then prepared the water, towels, clean linens, a comb, and whatever else was required.[4] In the bedroom there was normally a washstand on which a bowl and pitcher of water could be set. There is no indication that the water was heated. Evitascandalo and Liberati speak only of the washing of hands in the morning; if this is but a euphemism for more extensive washing, it nevertheless suggests only limited cleansing. The at-

tendance of a barber every morning was not needed. Cardinal Antonio Barberini's shaving bowl was found in room C22 of Palazzo Barberini alle Quattro Fontane, far from his bedroom C8 but near his bath and other rooms for informal pleasures (see Fig. 102).[5]

The washing of hands was also part of the ceremony of dining. Before the cardinal and his guests went to table, the cupbearer presented water to his master. Bowing, he offered the basin in his left hand and the pitcher in his right. The steward *(scalco)* presented a towel. Chamber assistants offered water and gentlemen provided towels for prelates or other gentlemen eating with the cardinal, each guest using a separate basin and towel. The washing completed, the cupbearer bowed again, removed the utensils, and gave them to a *palafreniere* to return to the *credenza*.[6] The ceremony was worthy of Montaigne's notice, on his visit to Rome in 1580.[7] Palace inventories list numerous basins and pitchers. A matched set of four small majolica pitchers and four basins, adorned with the arms of Cardinal Antonio Barberini, "for presenting water for the washing of hands," must have been for this service at meals.[8]

Gentlemen attendants and other members of the household might wash in their own rooms. At Palazzo Barberini, the rooms of the theologian Padre Ignazio Mignozzi contained a modest washstand.[9] At the Palazzo Barberini in Palestrina, in 1637, the simple furnishings of several bedrooms for members of the *famiglia* included washstands, basins, and pitchers.[10] Don Francesco Ceccarelli had a washstand with a pitcher in the bedroom of his apartment in the Palazzo della Famiglia Borghese, but his mother had none in her room.[11]

Bathing was not a common activity in seventeenth-century Rome. It was known that ancient Romans had bathed daily, for reasons of cleanliness; but, according to Alessandro Petronio in 1592, the much more convenient modern custom of wearing undershirts had caused the practice of bathing virtually to disappear.[12] There were surely other reasons for the change in custom — concerns about health, and Counter-Reformation injunctions against sensual pleasures. Around 1625, the anonymous author of Barb. lat. 4344, recalling both Roman baths and the resurgence of bathing, especially "all'antica," in the fifteenth and sixteenth centuries,[13] advised that the Barberini include a bath in their new palace: "The use of baths and hot baths has been virtually discontinued; nevertheless they can still be seen today in a few palaces; and certainly, if we consider the usefulness that can be derived from them, in terms of salubrity, cleanliness, and pleasure, it seems to me that the effort and expense would not be badly employed, especially where there is a good supply of water, as there is in Rome."[14] Yet his recommendation includes the acknowledgment that baths were hardly used at that time. Another anonymous advisor, the author of Barb. lat. 4360, presented a very detailed proposal for a new Barberini palace that included no bath. The palace as constructed in 1628–38 had no bath.

The exclusion of bathing from Roman aristocratic life by the late sixteenth century makes all the more surprising the construction of an elaborate bathing suite on the ground floor and mezzanine of the westward extension of Palazzo Borghese in 1612–14 (see Figs. 28, 29). The construction of 1606–10 had included no bath. On the southwest side of the palace, the new bath enjoyed the orientation to the sun recommended by Vitruvius and Alberti.[15] The bathing room (*stufa*) itself, A17, was a vaulted room 18 × 18¾ *palmi* in plan, on the ground floor, with a single window to the street.[16] There were faucets and a drain that emptied the tub,[17] but the tub itself was presumably portable: documents of construction give no evidence of a built-in tub, and a wooden bathtub is listed in an inventory of 1615.[18] The bathing room was complemented by other small chambers arranged around the vertical axis of a small spiral stair S9.[19] To the east of the bathing room and stair was A16, the "stanzia del' sciaquatore cioè la stanzia per servitio della stufa," 26½ × 15 *palmi*, vaulted, with a small door to the street and a window; it contained a stove for heating water.[20] Above these two ground-floor rooms were two corresponding mezzanine rooms ("mezzaninetto") with low, vaulted ceilings; and above these, at the level of the mezzanine rooms of the rest of this wing of the palace, were two more vaulted rooms — B14 over the bathing room corresponding to it in size, and larger B13 (31¼ × 26½ *palmi*) extending over both the "stanzia per servitio della stufa" and its ground-floor neighbor A15. A toilet was nearby. These rooms, connected with one another by the stair and passages, could be entered from the ground-floor or mezzanine corridors or from the mezzanine apartments; but their circulation was kept separate from that of the service rooms below and the main apartments above. There were fireplaces in the rooms above the *stufa*.[21] Documents do not reveal the decoration of the bathing room itself, but it surely was in harmony with that of the mezzanine rooms: the walls of B14 were finely plastered and hung with revetments, and its vault (in contrast to the wood ceilings of the apartments at this level) bore a rich stucco decoration including four eagles and four dragons.[22] A document of 1619 mentions a newly made daybed for these rooms.[23] This compact apartment of small, warm, richly decorated rooms, focused on the bath, would have been a special feature of the new addition of 1612–14, offering more than simple sanitation. Suffused by the warmth of his steamy bath, the user could ascend to the intimate mezzanines to dry, rest, and contemplate his sense of well-being.

In the 1670s, the remodeling of the ground floor of the palace, with a vista through a continuous suite of rooms, necessitated the removal of the "stanzia per servitio della stufa" A16 and its small intermediate mezzanine; but the *stufa* itself remained in place, along with the other mezzanine rooms of the suite (see Figs. 42, 44). The *stufa* was now heated by a "fornacella" in a basement corridor at street level, and the old spiral staircase S9 was enlarged and extended downward to this corridor.[24]

In 1641 Cardinal Antonio Barberini installed a bath in the previously bathless Palazzo Barberini alle Quattro Fontane.[25] The bath is sketched as a later insertion to a plan drawing of 1628 and labeled "stufa" (see Fig. 149, A).[26] A water supply and drains were already in place, because a laundry had earlier occupied this corner of the building.[27] The new bath was about the same size as that at Palazzo Borghese, about 19 *palmi* square. A copper vent ("sportello di rame nella volta") was set into its vault "a schifo," presumably to help control the temperature in the room. (Vitruvius, followed by Francesco di Giorgio, had recommended a similar device employing a bronze disk for controlling the temperature in sweating baths.)[28] The built-in elliptical tub contained two seats, and around the perimeter of the room was a stone bench. A new stove heated water in a caldron. Antonio's inventory of 1644 included eight copper basins, two copper kettles, and a shovel and pan of iron, all "for the *stufa*";[29] it would seem then that hot water was transferred from the caldron to the tub by means of these vessels, or that Antonio soaked selected portions of his body in the basins.

At first glance, this single room, however richly it may have been decorated, seems modest compared with the intricate cluster of rooms in the bathing apartment of Palazzo Borghese; however, the easy access provided by stair S8 to Antonio's comfortable private rooms above meant that Antonio might enjoy the same leisurely postlude to the bath as did his Borghese compatriots. Room B24 contained a daybed ("letto di riposo"), and B23 and B25, with musical instruments and games, were warmed by fireplaces (see Fig. 101).[30]

Antonio later installed a *stufa* in the "Casa Grande" ai Giubbonari, when he was living in that palace, but we know neither the specific location nor the form of the bath. A professional attendant was paid for coming to the palace and operating the *stufa* for the cardinal's benefit for ten days in 1666[31] — an incident that shows that bathing was not a customary activity but that nevertheless it was still common enough at that date to support an independent tradesman. Antonio may have used the *stufa* in 1666 for therapeutic purposes, for he seems to have been in ill health: a barber was paid for bloodletting only three days after the payment to the *stufarolo*.[32]

Except for these three instances, the palaces considered in detail in the second part of this book did not have baths. Nor did their residents bathe in portable tubs, for none (other than the Borghese tub of 1615) is listed in any of the inventories of the palaces. More baths may yet be discovered in other seventeenth-century palaces. For now, however, one can only wonder at the motivation of the Borghese family in constructing the elaborate little bathing suite in 1612–14 and then maintaining it in altered form in the remodeling of 1671–76, and the motivation of Antonio Barberini in inserting a bath into his palace in 1641 and again in 1666. The special requirements of supplying, heating, and draining water for bathing, best accomplished on the ground floor of a palace, were simply not an issue in the customary planning of palaces. Instead, the most important architectural feature in support of personal cleanliness was the service stair, with access to the private chambers of the apartment. By such stairs the chamber assistant could discreetly supply small quantities of water for washing, probably at room temperature, and later remove the waste.

Alberti ardently advised that elimination and human wastes be kept far from dwelling rooms, except that sick people might use close-stools; but contemporary practice was otherwise, as he indicated when he wrote, ". . . in our own houses, in our best chambers (where we ourselves are to rest) and as it were at our very bolsters, we are so unpolite as to make secret privies, or rather store-rooms of stink."[33] Nor was his advice heeded in seventeenth-century palaces, where close-stools and chamber pots were regularly included among the furnishings of gentlemen's and ladies' bedrooms. They were to be kept clean by chamber assistants or the *scopatore segreto,* who would enter the room only in the absence of the resident.[34] In Palazzo Barberini Cardinal Antonio Barberini's close-stool (with a majolica bowl) and chamber pot were in his bedroom, room C8 (see Fig. 102). Another close-stool was in the rooms of Padre Ignazio Mignozzi, and several others were stored in the *guardaroba.*[35] At Palestrina in 1648 bedrooms A6, A10, A11, B10, B11, and B16 were equipped with close-stools and chamber pots (see Fig. 181).[36] Each of five small bedrooms in the women's apartment of Palazzo Borghese contained a close-stool and a chamber pot in 1693 (see Fig. 49).[37] Each of twelve small bedrooms for members of the *famiglia* at Palestrina had one or both pieces of equipment; their occupants may have been either men or women.[38]

Facilities might also be arranged in convenient locations for guests at the palace. Evitascandalo and Rossetti advise that rooms near a hall in which a banquet is to be given be equipped with chamber pots, beds, and other amenities.[39] A sketch plan in the Archivio Chigi (Fig. 11) shows the arrangement of a cardinal's apartment, with two small rooms for the convenience of visiting

cardinals; adjacent to room C, where congregations were held, a "stanza per fare acqua li Em^{mi} Card^{li}" (room D); and between the *sala dei palafrenieri* and the first anteroom, a "busseletta per fare acqua sue Em^{me}" (room G).[40] The close-stool in A13, the representational bedroom of the ground-floor apartment of Prince Giovanni Battista Borghese, may have served visitors, since the room was not a private sleeping room; the pendant bedroom A9 of the princess on this level had no similar furnishing (see Fig. 42).[41]

Francesco di Giorgio had recommended that toilets *(necessarii)* be built separate from the dwelling rooms but still handy, in convenient locations, comfortable, and odorless, so that people would be encouraged to use them, to the benefit of their health. They should be vented. They should not be constructed over sewers; rather, there should be a pit underneath, containing twenty-five or thirty loads of coarse gravel, so that liquid wastes would drain away and solids would dry up, leaving no odor.[42] In the first half of the sixteenth century toilets had been proposed or constructed in the principal apartments of some palaces: small private chambers with built-in seats, whose shafts were embedded in the wall and flushed by rain water. Frommel notes such facilities in the proposed Palazzo dei Tribunali, Palazzo Baldassini (although the rooms adjacent to the ground-floor toilets may have been for services), Raphael's palace project Uffizi A311, and Sangallo's design for the palace of Agnolo da Castro.[43] Frommel reasonably distinguishes these from "row toilets," multiple facilities located in other parts of the palace, for members of the staff. Whatever the extent of its usage in the sixteenth century, the permanent facility seems to have been rejected by persons of high rank in the seventeenth century. Palazzo Borghese seems exceptional in having a toilet and lavatory in room B5 in Giovanni Battista's mezzanine apartment, and apparently another toilet in room D15 of his wife Virginia's apartment, both installed in the construction campaign of 1607–10 (see Figs. 21,

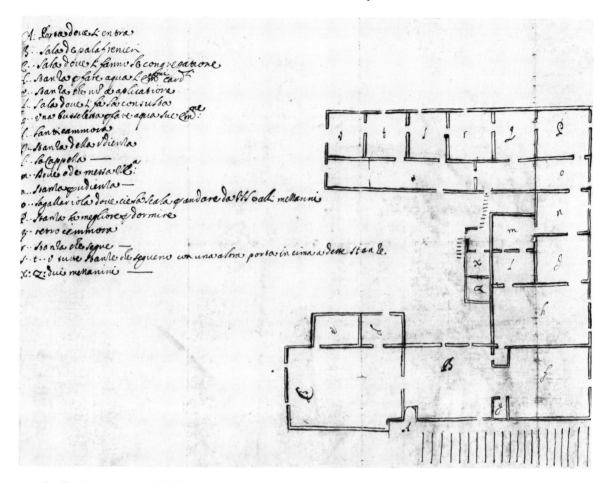

11   Cardinal's apartment (Biblioteca Apostolica Vaticana, Chigi P.VII.10, fol. 42r)

23).[44] Except for these, there were no permanently constructed toilets in the major apartments of any of the palaces considered in detail in Chapters 9 through 15, according to the documents of their construction.

Portable facilities in convenient locations seem to have been the prerogative of gentlemen and some women; others must have used the *luoghi comuni* or *necessarii* of the palace — privies usually located in or adjacent to a stair.

The anonymous author of Barb. lat. 4360 declined to locate privies in his otherwise very detailed proposal for the Barberini palace to be built, but he stated that they would be "numerous, and convenient, and in places where they would not give offense to the rest of the house."[45] In the palace as eventually built, the facilities are indeed isolated from the major apartments, but they are not numerous. Borromini's partial plan of Taddeo Barberini's half of the palace, prepared shortly before construction began, shows two niches in the rounded corners of a small chamber opening from the landing of service stair S7 (see Fig. 147).[46] In the course of construction this area of the palace was redesigned,[47] so that no facilities remained on the levels of the principal apartments; but their association with service stairs was maintained. A privy with two places is found on the uppermost floor of the palace, in E49, next to stair S10 (see Fig. 104);[48] its location suggests that it was to be used by Costanza's women attendants. More centrally located was the privy on the *secondo piano*, D29a, accessible from service stair S7 (see Fig. 103).[49] Another was at the lowest level, at the foot of service stair S7 (see Fig. 100);[50] this and the privy D29a could share the *cantera* under the stair landing.[51] Another privy was carved into the corner of the ground-floor room next to Anna's laundry.[52] Large pipes installed in the wall drained the toilets. In the south half of the palace, only one privy, E11, was constructed (see Fig. 104; cf. Fig. 152). It was between the large oval stair and service stair S3, at the level of the upper mezzanines, and its drain extended downward in the wall a distance of 111 *palmi* to the base of the oval stair. Its vaulted *cantera* was constructed in an excavation outside the palace, in the forecourt.[53] These facilities ignored Francesco di Giorgio's recommendation of a gravel-filled drainage pit. They required periodic cleaning, and payments for this service are recorded in the Archivio Barberini.[54]

The other palaces considered in detail in the second half of this book were similarly equipped. In 1612 the "Casa Grande" ai Giubbonari had a single "luogo comune," E9, a tiny room at attic level next to the service stair (see Fig. 61).[55] The western wing of Palazzo Borghese in 1610 had one privy for servants, in passage D6, adjacent to stair S6 (see Fig. 23), and others were beyond the north corner of the courtyard, at the level of the *piano nobile*.[56] The compact addition of 1612–14 included four more, all associated with stairs.[57] When an apartment for women was built in the attic rooms south of the courtyard in 1620, a privy was installed in its spiral service stair S4 (see Fig. 34);[58] and the women's apartment built in the attic of the west wing in 1671–76 included a privy in E23 (see Fig. 49).[59] In Palazzo Chigi, attic room EE2, accessible from the service stair

S5 through room EE1, contained a privy; another was in a small chamber C23 on the *piano nobile;* and a third was in a tiny chamber F20 at the summit of spiral stair S4 (see Figs. 206, 204, 207).[60]

It would seem that a noblewoman's attendants might use either close-stools or built-in privies. Some of the *luoghi comuni* were constructed in conjunction with women's apartments and clearly were intended for the use of women attendants. Companions of the austere Donna Costanza Barberini had a built-in privy near their rooms, but those of Anna Barberini had none in their apartment in the west end of the north wing of Palazzo Barberini. No inventory survives from the years of Taddeo and Anna's occupancy of the palace, and we cannot know for sure that Anna's women's rooms were furnished with close-stools; yet the rooms of the attendants of Eleonora Boncompagni Borghese had those portable facilities in 1693, along with a privy built in 1671–76.

The small houses inhabited by members of a prince's or cardinal's *famiglia* had built-in privies much like those of the palaces — tiny chambers with single seats and pipes to conduct the wastes to a catch basin. Several are noted in accounts of the remodeling of houses for the Barberini and Chigi *famiglie*.[61] Three can be seen in plan in Figure 116: in Madonna Agata Rosa's house, one in a narrow chamber behind the stair; and in the neighboring house, one in a niche at the foot of the stair and another in a rectangular wall niche in the front room. In the plans of the Palazzo della Famiglia Borghese, conduits for privies are shown in the stairs and in the small triangular chamber at the west corner of the courtyard (see Fig. 37), but Don Francesco Ceccarelli, who lived in that building, had the additional luxury of a chamber pot in his bedroom.[62]

For the design of palaces, then, the requirements of personal hygiene were dealt with so simply that the author of Barb. lat. 4360 felt no need to exercise his ingenuity in planning facilities. There was a fundamental class distinction in that the principal residents of a palace and their guests used furnishings (close-stools and chamber pots), and the servants shared built-in privies. For the former, those same service stairs and private entrances to bedrooms by which water was brought for washing were also most important for the movements of servants who kept the fittings clean. For servants as well, stairs were crucial architectural elements, because they provided not only convenient access for users but also unbroken vertical passage for wastes through the house to basement or underground collection basins. The actual toilets were small and simple masonry constructions, with wooden seats and no moving parts, and their waste pipes and vents were simply embedded in the thick masonry walls. Like close-stools, the built-in privies required periodic cleaning.

The planning problems of the early sixteenth century, involving hot baths and built-in toilets for principal residents, are dismissed by the seventeenth century. The principle of human movement within an articulated architectural framework is applicable instead.

CHAPTER SIX

Pleasure and Special Interests

HE APARTMENT of a Roman palace, while intended for the serious business of receiving guests, was also a place for leisure activities. Games like chess and backgammon were played in the anteroom (but playing for large amounts of money was a vice to be avoided). Even more vigorous exercise was possible: the billiard-like game of *trucchi* was considered good for exercise, but Evitascandalo advised that the activity be kept far from the prince's *camera*.[1] In Palazzo Barberini in 1644, Antonio Barberini and his attendants could enjoy *trucchi* in room C11, and three tables for *trucchi* in room C10 transformed that vestibule into a veritable game room. Earlier, they had played in C34 (see Fig. 102).[2] Music could be enjoyed in the apartments. Antonio grouped most of his collection of musical instruments in room B27 in Palazzo Barberini (see Fig. 101), and additional cembali were in rooms B23, B28, C23, C29, and C39.[3] Meanwhile, in the "Casa Grande" ai Giubbonari, a cembalo was in the "room before the chapel" in the apartment toward the via dei Giubbonari, and two were in the room between Taddeo's audience room and his bedroom.[4] Works of art could be enjoyed and books read in almost any room. Still, individual owners of palaces might have particular enthusiasms that would require specially designed spaces outside the normal apartments.

Ball Courts

In his treatise of 1555, Antonio Scaino da Salò praised the ball game as an "exercise so noble and rare, so pleasurable to both body and spirit," and the author of Barb. lat. 4360 recommended that large palaces have ball courts "for the exercise and entertainment of courtiers, and also sometimes of the patrons."[5]

Barb. lat. 4360 outlines the architectural requirements: an easily accessible location ("quasi publico") that is nevertheless private, not too near the patron's rooms (because of the noise) yet at the same time convenient to them; a vaulted court 30 *palmi* high, 30 *palmi* wide, and about 86 *palmi* long; and an adjacent room where the court attendant can keep his supplies and where players can "dry off, change, and rest" after a vigorous game (see Fig. 133, K).[6] Just such a court was built at Palazzo Borghese in 1611–14: on the ground floor of the Ripetta wing, vaulted room A21, measuring 81¼ × 28½ *palmi,* was accompanied by a changing room A20 and, overlooking the court through a grilled window, a spectators' room B17 (see Figs. 28, 29). It was easily reached from the garden or from the Ripetta entrance, and it was directly below the private rooms of the major apartments.[7] The athletic facility may have been constructed especially with the young prince Marcantonio

Borghese in mind; it was he who paid the court attendant in 1626, even though his older cousin Scipione Borghese was then living in that wing of the palace.[8]

Scaino's treatise describes four kinds of ball games (two with rackets and two without) and specifies the equipment and court for each. The dimensions given by Barb. lat. 4360 and those of the ball court at Palazzo Borghese correspond to Scaino's small court for the game with rackets (66 × 22 "piedi antichi Romani," or about 88 × 29 *palmi*). The enclosed and roofed court was divided by a cord (hence *pallacorda*) at a height of 3½ feet (5 *palmi*), from which was suspended a net about 1 *palmo* wide. Each of two teams had three players.[9]

There was a ball court at Palazzo Barberini, but, unlike the proposal in Barb. lat. 4360, it was not an integral part of the palace. Instead, it was located in the garden, next to a laundry, in the northeast corner of the site, on property once owned by Accorambono or Corambono.[10] In the production of the opera *Chi soffre speri* in the Barberini theater in 1639, one of the scenes impressed the audience with a view of the palace garden including the ball court[11] — whether an enclosed structure like that at Palazzo Borghese or an open court. The ball court was still there in 1669–73, when a carriage drive was constructed under it.[12] Although its exact design is not known, it is clearly not to be confused with the "sferisterio" shown in Letarouilly's nineteenth-century plan, along via Pia (the present via XX Settembre), a stadium for a different kind of ball game.[13]

The Barberini "Casa Grande" in via dei Giubbonari had no ball court, but the nearby Palazzo Condulmer-Orsini-Pio (see Fig. 75, no. 636), rented by the Barberini for their *famiglia* beginning in 1627, included one; presumably it was somehow distinct from the body of that disorderly palace, since it was specified separately in the record of the rental.[14] When the Barberini bought Palestrina in 1630, they found an area for

playing ball in a small courtyard behind the east wing of the palace, where players would be shielded from the summer sun.[15] This outdoor court must have been for a different game, or at least a more informal game, than that played at Palazzo Borghese.

Whatever the advantages of the game, and whatever the Borghese and Barberini enthusiasms for it, the ball court remained optional in seventeenth-century palaces; for example, there was none at Palazzo Chigi in piazza SS. Apostoli.

Libraries

A few books might be kept and read in almost any room of the palace. Even sizable collections might simply fill bookcases in one or two rooms of an apartment. For example, when Cardinal Scipione Borghese moved to the Palazzo Borghese in 1621, he had bookcases moved from his palace in the Borgo and installed in his study, room D23 (see Fig. 31).[16] Taddeo Barberini had enough books to fill seven bookcases and thirty-four pages of an inventory of his possessions (including many books on agriculture, military subjects, and history), yet all were kept in a single room, his study on the *secondo piano* of the "Casa Grande."[17] In 1644 his brother Cardinal Antonio seems to have used the last room in his ground-floor apartment in Palazzo Barberini, room B36, as a library (see Fig. 101); Antonio's holdings had grown by the time of his death in 1671, but still he was able to contain his library in three rooms of his private apartment on the *secondo piano* of the "Casa Grande."[18] Only his brother Cardinal Francesco was so assiduous a collector of books as to require a library of distinct architectural identity.

Francesco's library, larger than any other room in Palazzo Barberini except the grand *salone,* rose above the roof of the south wing of the palace (see Fig. 105, F1; cf. Figs. 121, 163, and 173).[19] It was vaulted *a schifo,* and its windows opened toward the east (following Alberti's injunction) and south. The scholars who would come to study there[20] could reach it directly, without passing through any of the apartments, by the large elliptical stair. Nearby was a smaller room F2 for manuscripts and medals. Small rooms in the attic of the southwest wing seem to have been Francesco's study, in conjunction with his library (see Fig. 104, E5–E10),[21] and similar rooms just below could have included his librarian's apartment (see Fig. 103, D5–D10). The library was distinguished by its carved walnut shelving, the work of Giovanni Battista Soria; more than simple pieces of furniture (as had, apparently, held Scipione Borghese's and Taddeo Barberini's books), the shelving was architectural in scale and conception (see Fig. 122). The bays of its two stories were marked by Ionic pilasters and (on the lower story) freestanding columns, and spiral stairs in the corners led to the upper level. The library merited a special note in Totti's brief description of the palace in 1638, and in 1665 Carlo Cartari judged it second in Rome only to the Vatican library in both beauty and the richness of its holdings.[22] Although in a private palace, Francesco's library transcended any domestic function and became a model for institutional libraries—for example, Borromini's Biblioteca Vallicelliana in the Casa dei Filippini.[23]

The proposal for a library in the new Barberini palace, as described in Barb. lat. 4360, must have been prepared with Francesco in mind.[24] The author considers a library both a great ornament and a useful facility in a palace. He describes a multiroom library on the *secondo piano* of the palace: a long hall, 200 × 28 *palmi,* to which are appended three rooms each 40 × 28 *palmi* for restricted books, manuscripts, and various natural and artificial curiosities; a reading room with a catalogue; and two rooms for the librarian (see Fig. 133, I, J). Like the actual Barberini library, this one would be open to the qualified public and therefore would be easily accessible without passage through an apartment, but at the same time it would be convenient to the private rooms

of its owner. Its light vault would be carefully constructed so as to protect the room from cold, heat, and rain. Unlike Francesco's library, the proposed facility did not reveal itself in the outer form of the building.

The great built precedent for Francesco's library was surely that at Palazzo Farnese. It was mentioned already in an inventory of 1568 (that is, while the building was still under construction), but its wood-coffered ceiling was being made only in 1578. It was on the *secondo piano,* its main room in the center of the façade wing, directly over the *salotto dipinto,* and its second room immediately to the north. The library was easily accessible to visiting scholars by means of the main stair and corridor toward the courtyard; and librarian Fulvio Orsini's rooms were nearby in the northwest wing of the palace.[25] It was not architecturally distinct but was contained within the rectangular block of the palace.

The library in Palazzo Chigi was very much like that of Palazzo Farnese, in its location and configuration within the palace. Its two large rooms were on the *secondo piano,* immediately behind the façade (see Fig. 206, E6, E7). Visiting scholars could reach the library easily by means of the main stair, and the cardinal could enter from his private rooms nearby. Its shelving was designed by the architect Bernini and made by the distinguished joiner Antonio Chiccheri (who also carved its wood-coffered ceiling); like that at Palazzo Barberini, the shelving was architectural in scale, with a wood spiral stair leading to its upper level.[26]

The library of a palace, then, would seem to be an architectural problem only when the owner has an especially large collection of books that might be open to the qualified public. In that case, control of access is a major issue involving contrasting requirements: outside users need to reach the library with as little involvement as possible with the rest of the palace, and the owner himself wants to enjoy the library from the private rooms of his apartment. A second issue is the design of shelving for proper storage of the books. The choice of a vaulted or beamed ceiling, the provision of good lighting, and accommodations for the librarian all have to be attended to, but these requirements are less demanding than that of access.

Theaters

Ceremony and spectacle were an integral part of Roman aristocratic life, so that the line between theater and daily life is imprecisely drawn.[27] Processions of carriages through the streets were watched, and the reception of guests in a palace was carefully choreographed. At mealtime, the gentlemen attendants stood and watched the elaborate service, ready to remove their hats whenever the prince should drink, and the performance of the carver *(trinciante)* was a special attraction.[28] For a banquet, such crowds of spectators might come to admire the elaborate displays and service of food that special measures would have to be taken to control them.[29] The troupe of players in the foreground of Cruyl's view of Piazza Barberini during Carnival 1665 (see Fig. 91) have their stage on wheels as they take their performance through the streets of Rome. Musicians, commedia dell'arte troupes, or more formal groups could almost as easily enter into palaces to perform in *sale* or anterooms. Ademollo has counted 130 comedies that took place in private houses in Rome during Carnival 1678. The audiences might be small—a maximum of about one hundred persons in Ameyden's house in the 1640s—or considerably larger.[30]

Lunadoro (1635) wrote that cardinals should not attend theatrical performances, or at least should conduct themselves properly, following the good example of the Medici cardinal (later Leo XI) by watching from a withdrawn place behind a screen.[31] In 1675 Leti wrote that "in earlier times" cardinals had not attended comedies and that even now those aspiring to the papacy should not do so; and he repeated Lunadoro's advice that those who do attend should

remain behind a screen so as not to be seen.[32] The ascetic Costanza Barberini eschewed this worldly activity altogether, nor did she allow her women companions to attend theatrical presentations.[33] Such reserve, however, seems not to have affected her sons.

From 1632 until 1637, operas were presented in Palazzo Barberini, in Francesco's first anteroom, later remembered as the "*salotto* where the comedies used to be given" (see Fig. 102, C2; Figs. 119, 120).[34] The three Barberini brothers shared the honor of host: for example, in 1636 on the first night Cardinal Antonio invited cardinals, prelates, and other members of the papal court; on the second night Taddeo and Anna received women with their husbands; and on the third night Cardinal Francesco was host to the ambassador of Spain with his wife, the bishop of Cordova, and other persons especially of the Spanish faction in Rome.[35]

The spacious, vaulted anteroom was two stories high and received light from clerestory windows to the east. It was easy of access, so that guests could enter from the central *salone* or (after the construction of elliptical stair S2, begun only in April 1633)[36] directly from vestibule C10. It had no special architectural features that would distinguish it as a theater. Figure 120 shows the room arranged for a musical performance; there must have been room for an audience of only a few hundred people. *Guardaroba* D1 served as dressing room for the performers.[37] That part of the palace was still under construction at the time, and the anteroom provided the occasion for a double spectacle: the invited guests filled the room itself, and an additional mass of onlookers crowded the masons' scaffolding for a glimpse through the windows.[38] Even the businesslike *avvisi* convey the splendor of the music, the costumes, and the changes of scenery, all within the rectangular volume of the anteroom.[39]

The rooms to which the anteroom eventually would lead were not yet ready for occupancy (although Taddeo and his family were already living in the north wing of the palace); the ante-room's use as a theater during Carnival, therefore, in no way interfered with the daily operations of the palace. The situation changed when the south half of the palace was finished, by which time the Barberini's aspirations for their theatrical productions had increased beyond those of their fellow Romans. A separate theater, adjacent to but apart from the palace, was called for.[40] It was ready for the presentation of a revised production of *Chi soffre speri* during Carnival 1639. Just to the north of the palace, it incorporated the wall and portal designed earlier by Pietro da Cortona (see Fig. 162, no. 4, "Teatro da Comedie"). Carriages could deliver the guests directly to the door of the theater and then wait on the terrace to the north of the palace or in the piazza below. It was considerably larger than the anteroom in the palace, measuring about 136 × 118 *palmi* and accommodating 3,000 to 4,000 persons, according to contemporary accounts. Still, it seems to have had no special architectural features beyond its size and ready access. Benches were used for seating, and the screens from behind which cardinals might discreetly observe the proceedings must also have been movable furnishings.[41]

In July 1669, when the ambassador of Spain visited the prince and princess at Palestrina, he was entertained by a musical drama presented in the "sala della commedia," a large ground-floor room of the Barberini palace permanently kept as a theater.[42] This was apart from another large hall where a ball was held. It was presumably in one of the old *cantine* of the palace and must have been limited in both size and natural lighting by the ancient walls and vaults.

The Barberini seem to have been exceptional in constructing a theater at their palace in Rome and later designating a room at Palestrina for use solely as a theater. Otherwise, that same flexibility that characterizes the use of the palace in other respects seems to have served Romans' theatrical interests as well.

Collections of Art

Collections of paintings and sculptures were not only for the private delectation of their owners; they were also part of their public reputations. Visitors had seen and studied the sculptures assembled in the statue court of the Belvedere in the Vatican in the early sixteenth century and had entered the courtyards of Palazzo della Valle, Palazzo Farnese, and others to admire the sculptures displayed there. In the seventeenth century, not only sculptures but also paintings were assembled in special apartments of palaces and made increasingly accessible to artists, travelers, and other interested persons.[43]

In Palazzo Borghese in 1610, the "galleria delle statue" was the enclosed loggia A8, on the ground floor, facing the garden. It was joined to three adjacent rooms A4, A5, and A6 (see Fig. 20). Sculptures were displayed here until 1625, when they were transferred to the Villa Pinciana. Twenty statues remained as ornaments to the courtyard, but the rooms in the palace were given over primarily to the growing Borghese painting collection — described by Totti in 1638 as "the finest paintings of our times."[44]

Cardinal Antonio Barberini concentrated his works of art in the two apartments of the north wing of the Palazzo Barberini, apart from his principal apartment for the reception of guests in the south wing. An inventory of furnishings in 1644 refers to the lower of the two apartments specifically as the "apartment of paintings and sculptures."[45] The paintings covering the walls were sometimes arranged thematically — for example, thirty-six portraits in anteroom B28, twenty-eight additional portraits and nine muses in B26, and many landscapes in B32. Most of the sculptures were small pieces — statuettes and busts.[46] These apartments had formerly been occupied by Taddeo and Anna Colonna Barberini; and furnishings, games, and fireplace equipment in an inventory of 1644 indicate that Antonio too was spending time here, surrounded by his collections.[47]

In the 1660s and 1670s, apartments for works of art achieved greater autonomy. They were so located within the palace that visitors could enter them without passing through other rooms of the palace. While retaining the form of normal aristocratic apartments, they seem not to have accommodated their full range of activities. In Palazzo Chigi (1664–67), sculptures were arranged in the ground-floor "summer" apartment, immediately to the left of the entrance (see Fig. 203). Its airy painted decoration recalled the outdoor setting of such earlier collections as the statue court of the Belvedere.[48] Paintings were upstairs, in the "Appartamento nobile de quadri"—rooms C1–C4 (see Fig. 204); 406 paintings covered the walls, from the ceiling downward. Room C4 was called "Anticamera," and room C2 had a baldacchino; but, like the sculpture apartment on the *pian terreno,* there was no bedroom or other provision for sustained occupancy.[49]

At almost the same time (1663–66) Antonio Barberini remodeled twelve rooms of the ground floor of the "Casa Grande" ai Giubbonari as an apartment for paintings—again like a normal apartment in that there were a *sala,* a chapel, two audience rooms (with baldacchinos), and a room with a *zampanaro* (but here that elaborate furnishing hung over only a daybed). While the cardinal might enjoy spending time with his paintings, he lived upstairs.[50] So too in the Palazzo Borghese in 1671–76, the twin apartments of prince and princess on the ground floor were arranged in suites with anterooms, audience rooms, and representational bedrooms, but the lack of private facilities made it clear that neither prince nor princess was to live here.[51] In the remodeling of Palazzo Barberini in 1673–79, all apartments for residence were removed to the upper floors, while the ground floor was given over to works of art—sculptures in the south wing and paintings in the north wing. Tessin

remarked on the absence of furnishings in these rooms, beyond the display of the works of art;[52] they were clearly not intended to be lived in.

All of these apartments (except for the Chigi painting apartment) are on the ground floor of the palace, where they doubled as summer apartments for daytime use.[53] The ground-floor location might be thought especially appropriate for sculptures, because of their substantial weight and their resistance to the dampness often associated with ground-floor rooms in Rome; yet all lie above vaulted basements, thus negating the advantage of solid ground while at the same time mitigating the disadvantage of dampness. Indeed, paintings were displayed on the ground floors of Palazzo Borghese and the two Barberini palaces. Ready accessibility to the outside visitor seems the most important criterion for location of the collections—happily accommodated by the growing availability of ground-floor space due to the decrease in demand for staff kitchen, *tinello,* and related spaces for the increasingly independent *famiglia.* All employ the form of a major apartment, with a sequential arrangement of *sala,* anterooms, audience room, and sometimes even a representational bedroom, so that the illusion is maintained of a visit to a private person's collection; yet the reality is that the prince or cardinal would himself be something of a visitor to his collection. The intimacy of association between works of art and personal leisure, so noticeable in the arrangement of Cardinal Antonio Barberini's apartments in the north wing of Palazzo Barberini in 1644, has been severed in favor of greater accessibility to visitors like Nicodemus Tessin and the readers of Rossini's and Panciroli's guidebooks.

Galleries

Borghese sculptures were displayed in the "galleria delle statue" in 1610; yet the distinctive long, narrow room called "gallery" was typically a private room, richly adorned according to a comprehensive design rather than housing a collection of individual works of art.[54]

The anonymous author of Barb. lat. 4360 recommends that every palace have a gallery (with no reference whatever to works of art), and the gallery that he proposes for the Barberini participates in both the public and the private realms of the palace.[55] At 28 × 320 *palmi,* it would be exceptionally large (even longer than that at Villa Mondragone, the author notes), and it might be used as a *sala* or anteroom, attended by guards, preceding three rooms at its east end (see Fig. 133, H). At the same time, it is described as a place to which the patron can withdraw from his major apartment, especially in the winter. The gallery at Palestrina was also capable of doubling as an anteroom, in 1669.[56] The same ambiguity of position within the palace can be seen in the extraordinarily long gallery of Palazzo Pamphili (its vault splendidly decorated by Pietro da Cortona in 1651–55): although three anterooms removed from the *sala,* it was hardly an intimate chamber and indeed was the site of such lavish entertainments as a banquet given by the ambassador of James II for Innocent XI in 1685.[57]

These, however, seem to be exceptions. Other galleries in seventeenth-century Rome follow the example of the gallery in the Palazzo Capodiferro (later Spada) of the 1550s—a relatively small (13 × 2.5 meters/58 × 11 *palmi*), richly decorated, intimate room connected with the private rooms of Cardinal Girolamo Capodiferro.[58] The gallery that Carlo Maderno added to Palazzo Mattei in 1613–17 is attached to the end of the main apartment on the *piano nobile* (see Fig. 7). In his extension of Palazzo Borghese in 1611–14, Maderno included a "galerietta ò studio" measuring 57 × 28¼ *palmi* on both the *piano nobile* and the *terzo piano,* both extensions of the private rooms of their respective apartments (see Fig. 30, C35, and Fig. 31, D23). Scipione Borghese installed his study in the "galer-

ietta ò studio" on the *terzo piano* when he moved to the palace in 1621.[59] In Palazzo Barberini, in spite of the advice of the author of Barb. lat. 4360, the only gallery is the "gallarietta" in Anna's intimate garden apartment, where the vault and upper walls were painted by Pietro da Cortona's assistants in 1631 (see Fig. 102, C35; Figs. 111–114).[60] Cardinal Chigi's small galleries are similarly connected with the private rooms of his several apartments (see Fig. 203, B14; Fig. 204, C17; Fig. 206, E18).[61] In the splendidly remodeled ground-floor apartments for the display of works of art in Palazzo Borghese, the gallery, of modest dimensions, occurs in its expected place, after the representational bedrooms (see Fig. 42, A14; Fig. 43).[62]

To the group of long, rectangular rooms properly called "gallery" might be added the exceptional elliptical salon on the *piano nobile* of Palazzo Barberini (see Fig. 102, C17; Fig. 144). Like the several galleries, it is not part of a regular suite of rooms in an apartment. It is at the end of the cardinal's summer apartment if that apartment is entered from anterooms C2 and C3; or, it might double as an anteroom leading from the central *salone* to that apartment if the apartment's sequence should begin with C15.[63] It has a special permanent decor of pilasters and niches for sculptures rather than the changeable fabric revetment of the apartment. It is even loggia-like in its relation to the garden to the east—a recollection of the probable origin of the rectangular gallery form in loggias.

Uses of these several galleries varied considerably—from the "literary exercises" that Teti says were held in the oval salon of Palazzo Barberini[64] to the pastimes of Donna Anna Barberini and her women attendants in the *gallarietta* of her apartment. In every case, however, the gallery is somehow extra, outside the course of a normal apartment not only in its use but also in its position and decor.

CHAPTER SEVEN

Coaches

BY THE SEVENTEENTH CENTURY, coaches were an important fact of Roman life.[1] Although Isabella d'Este had brought a carriage to Rome in 1525, it was only around the middle of the sixteenth century that the popularity of carriages began to spread. They very quickly became essential for every person of quality. In 1564 Pius IV was enough concerned about the new fashion that he felt called upon to direct the cardinals to ride horses instead of going about in coaches, which he considered more suitable for women; but his admonition was to no avail.[2] In 1581 Montaigne could report that distinguished persons went about only in carriages, and that only lesser persons and youths rode horses.[3] At St. Peter's in 1644, John Evelyn noticed that a carriage "belonging to Card. Medicis had all the metall worke of Massie Silver, *viz,* the bow behind and other places; and indeede the Coaches at Rome, as well as Covered Wagons, which are also much in use, are generally the richest and largest that I ever saw."[4] Splendid carriages became a major sign of the wealth and status of their owners and a major occasion for expenditures. They quickly found their place in the elaborate etiquette of the day, and they correspondingly required physical space in the palaces and in the city.

As rules of precedence determined one's place within an audience room or at a dinner table, so too the interior of a coach became ordered by similar rules. The six places were ranked so that the two rear seats (facing forward) were the most desirable, the seats by the two doors next in order, and the two seats in the front, facing backward, the least prestigious; and of each pair, the seat to the right was preferred.[5] Once settled, the passengers also consulted rank to determine their behavior: for example, if more than one cardinal was in the coach, the older cardinal would give commands to start and stop, even if the coach was not his. Rules of precedence likewise applied in the encounters of coaches in the city streets — often as much a matter of necessity as of courtesy, because of the narrowness of streets. In ecclesiastical Rome, others would stop and yield to a cardinal's coach, but there were nevertheless exceptions: after stopping, a cardinal would let a woman's coach be the first to start again, and he might also let the coach of a *letterato* proceed first, as a sign of his respect for letters.[6]

The etiquette of receiving guests took carriages into account. For very distinguished guests, the finer distinctions of rank were acknowledged in the host's accompanying the guest to the foot of the stair, to his waiting carriage, and then turning to leave either before or after the coach began to move.[7] Another sign of rank was simply the number of carriages that accompanied a person on his visit. A single carriage would suffice for a routine visit, but for more important ceremonial calls a train of carriages would be required. Persons might lend their carriages to one another for such occasions. Taddeo Barberini was out with seventy or eighty carriages and many servants, *palafrenieri,* and pages when he encountered the Venetian ambassador in an incident of precedence that would have serious diplomatic repercussions.[8] The anonymous author of Barb. lat. 4360 was pleased to note that his proposal for the new Barberini palace provided a piazza that would accommodate a hundred carriages while still leaving unimpeded a path down the center to the south entrance to the palace (see Fig. 133).[9] Some cortèges would include even more than a hundred coaches. On 13 September 1647 the French ambassador, going to a papal audience at the Quirinal Palace with five carriages and many liveried attendants, was accompanied by a cortège of more than one thousand persons in 202 coaches; and the same train escorted him on his visits to cardinals in the following days.[10] An especially splendid cortège occurred in 1650, when the ambassador of Spain went to his first audience with three hundred carriages, of which one hundred were sent by Prince Ludovisi, eighty by the Conestabile Colonna, sixty by Prince Gallicano, and twenty-five by the Princess of Botera.[11]

It is only to be expected that such large and splendid objects, the use of which had become so integral a part of Roman life, would come to affect the design of palaces. A person of rank had to accommodate not only his own carriages but also those of his distinguished visitors. We have already noted that the carriage entered into the etiquette of paying visits, and to do this it literally entered the palace, passing through the main portal, taking the visitor to the foot of the main staircase, moving through the loggias of the courtyard, waiting there for the duration of the visit, and receiving its passenger once again at the foot of the stair. The author of Barb. lat. 4360 proposes dimensions for the Barberini palace that specifically take visitors' coaches into ac-

count: an arched portal would be 14 *palmi* wide and 28 *palmi* high, and the arches of a courtyard loggia would have the same dimensions. The loggia on the side of the courtyard adjacent to the entrance would be 33 or 34 *palmi* wide, to allow for the turning of carriages that would take passengers to the foot of the stair and then wait in the loggia; the loggias on the other three sides of the square courtyard could be narrower, only 22 or 23 *palmi,* but still wide enough for two coaches.[12] Palaces that did not provide passages free of steps and wide enough for carriages, even if relatively new and otherwise well designed, would nevertheless be inadequate. The elegant Palazzo Baldassini, built in the early sixteenth century, before the Roman craze for carriages, has four steps up from the street to the entrance passage and another three steps up to the level of the courtyard, precluding the admission of carriages to the foot of the stair. The Palazzo Farnese, the construction of which stretched through the years of the sixteenth century, fortunately was begun on a grand enough scale, and with a courtyard at a low enough level, that it was not rendered obsolete by the new carriages; even so, its dimensions are smaller than those proposed in Barb. lat. 4360, with a portal of 2.9 meters / 13 *palmi,* a first loggia of 6.230 meters / 28 *palmi,* and side loggias of 4.334 meters / 19 *palmi* (see Fig. 5).

Outside, visitors' carriages also made demands on the palace and its site. When Maffeo Barberini, newly created cardinal, returned from a diplomatic mission in France in 1607, his anticipation of guests in carriages (corresponding to his new rank as well as to theirs) meant that he could not take up residence in his palace in via dei Giubbonari, which at that time opened onto only a very narrow street (see Figs. 52, 62); instead, he stayed at the Palazzo Salviati in piazza di Collegio Romano.[13] Barb. lat. 4360 also makes clear the necessity of ample parking space for visitors' carriages outside the palace. It is surely no accident that the great Roman palaces of the later sixteenth and seventeenth centuries rise on piazzas instead of in narrow streets. The space of the piazza not only enhances the monumentality of the great building; it also satisfies a most important function. At the Barberini palace in via dei Giubbonari, it was not until around 1640 that Maffeo's nephew Taddeo had a chance to improve the situation: the nearby piazza del Monte di Pietà was enlarged, and Taddeo was able to bring the entrance to his palace forward to share in the amplitude of that piazza.[14]

At the same time Taddeo proposed to widen a narrow side street leading to his stables: the text and notes on a chirograph of August 1642 (see Fig. 81) show that the vicolo along the southwest side of his property was to be widened 3 *palmi* at its south end and 1½ *palmi* at its west end, so that "it will be wide enough that carriages can pass, which they cannot now do." The proposed enlargement would make the street 14 *palmi* wide at its south end and 11½ *palmi* wide at the west end — still considerably narrower than Palazzo Farnese's courtyard loggias.[15]

Not only guests but also residents of palaces would arrive and depart by carriage. For public movements, the main portal served well, but other occasions required carriage access to a private entrance. Barb. lat. 4360 describes a carriage drive around the south and east sides of the proposed building, to give light and air to the lower rooms on those sides, to isolate the whole block of the building, and also, specifically, to deliver the residents by carriage to private entrances and stairs (see Fig. 133, Q).[16] In the palace as built, stair S9 provided a private exit for Taddeo Barberini (see Figs. 99, 100, 101).[17] At Palestrina, carriages could go up a ramp and around the west end of the palace into a private courtyard to receive the residents (see Fig. 181, B12).[18] At Palazzo Borghese, a carriage could wait at a door at the foot of spiral stair S4 or stair S7 (see Fig. 20).[19] At the "Casa Grande" ai Giubbonari passage A5 was newly made in 1610, specifically to connect Cardinal Maffeo's apartment and private stair S2 with the street (see Fig. 57).[20] At Palazzo Chigi a private exit opened from

ground-floor room B1 to the narrow vicolo del Piombo along the southeast flank of the palace (see Fig. 203).[21]

The growth in the prestige of the Barberini family in the seventeenth century is paralleled by an increase in their need for carriage rooms. In 1594 Maffeo Barberini had two carriages,[22] but his "Casa Grande" had no carriage rooms; only in 1609–12 were rooms A10 and A16 built for that purpose (see Fig. 57).[23] In 1621, when Maffeo was paying wages to three coachmen, carriage rooms were part of the new construction at the "Casa Grande."[24] Carriage rooms were included in the rental of the Palazzo Condulmer-Orsini-Pio for Taddeo Barberini's *famiglia,* beginning in 1627.[25] At the Palazzo Barberini alle Quattro Fontane, eleven carriage rooms of various sizes would accommodate twenty-five to thirty coaches in 1632–34.[26] Twelve carriages were listed in the inventory of Taddeo's goods in 1648, after his death in Paris.[27] Even his modest uncle, the Capuchin Cardinal Antonio di S. Onofrio, had four carriages.[28]

Coach rooms were of necessity on the ground floor and had wide doorways, but they did not have to be in the palace itself. The small house occupied by Enea Orlandini, absorbed into Palazzo Borghese in 1607–10, had two coach rooms.[29] Orlandini may have rented them out to the various tenants of the neighboring Palazzo del Giglio-Deza; it is unlikely that the resident of so modest a house would himself need two coach rooms. The Borghese remodeled room A10 as the *palafrenieri*'s room, and A13 remained a coach room for a few years longer, until the Ripetta extension of 1611–14 (see Fig. 20).[30] Borghese coaches were later kept in the large entry hall below A18,[31] finally designated "rimessone" in the remodeling of 1671–76 (see Fig. 42).[32] The Borghese also had coach rooms outside the palace, in nearby buildings — for example, four *rimesse* "toward the piazza," new in 1619,[33] and carriage rooms in neighboring houses for Cardinal Scipione Borghese's coaches in 1621.[34]

PALAZZO DELL'ECC^{MO} SIG^R PRENCIPE CHIGI IN PIAZZA COLONNA
Architettura di Giacomo della Porta, è seguitato da Carlo Maderni, è terminato da Felice della Greca
1. Facciata del Palazzo sù la via del Corso · 2. Altra Facciata nella Piazza Colonna. 3. Fontana nella Piazza. 4. Palazzo della Curia Romana.
Dato in Luce da Domenico de Rossi dalle sue Stampe in Roma alla Pace con Priuil. del S. P., e Licenza de Sup.

12   Palazzo Chigi in piazza Colonna, engraving by Specchi (Biblioteca Apostolica Vaticana)

The old Palazzo Sforza had coach rooms on its lowest level, but those rooms were taken over by other functions when it was remodeled as Palazzo Barberini alle Quattro Fontane (see Fig. 100, A2 and A5),[35] and Barberini coaches were kept outside the palace. The smallest of the eleven Barberini *rimesse* held only a single coach. Some were the ground-floor rooms of houses to the north of the palace, and others were built anew. The only requirement was a portal wide enough to admit a coach (that is, about 11 *palmi*), and for this the shop opening characteristic of Roman row houses often served well.[36] In Specchi's view of Palazzo Chigi in piazza Colonna (Fig. 12), a two-horse coach is emerging through such a portal with little room to spare.

An ideal stable is described by the anonymous author of Barb. lat. 4360 (see Fig. 133, S).[37] For him, the modern paragon was the stable at the Villa Aldobrandini in Frascati, 280 *palmi* in length, its long central aisle flanked by stalls for seventy-two horses.[38] The available space at the site of the Palazzo Barberini to be built suggested to the author a more compact arrangement of two vaulted halls, each with a central aisle flanked by stalls, also for seventy-two horses. It was to be built at the northwest corner of the sloping site, under a broad terrace, its two aisles opening to the drive ascending to the terrace and west portal of the palace. Its open siting, away from the main part of the palace, meant that its noises and odors would not reach the apartments on the *piano nobile*. Two additional vaulted halls, also under the terrace, would complement the stable. That nearer the stable would contain the daily supply of straw and hay for the horses on its lower level; and above would be a dormitory with beds for fourteen or sixteen stable hands. (Evitascandalo had advised just this separation of sleeping boys from hay, for the sake of the freshness of the hay.)[39] The second vaulted chamber, with its entrance higher along the drive bordering the raised terrace, would have been for coaches. On a spare corner of the site, there would have been room for a little apartment for the stable master *(maestro di stalla)*. While the quarters of both the stable master and his hands would have windows to the stable, there might also be one or two lofts over the doors in the stable, where someone might sleep, to be able to respond quickly to any disturbance in the stable during the night. Another room, to have been constructed under the terrace north of the palace and east of the stable, would have held the day's supply of grain and equipment for the stable. Barns for long-term storage of grain and hay would have been at some distance from the stable, and saddles and tack would have been kept with the coaches. A fountain on the north terrace and another at the northwest corner of the site would have provided water for the horses. Perhaps aware of Taddeo Barberini's special interest in his horses, the author of the proposal provides a stair by which the patron can descend privately from the palace directly to the stable, as well as a door directly from the lowest level of the palace to the coach room.

The actual situation at the Palazzo Barberini was considerably less formal. As for quarters for many members of the *famiglia* and the coaches, so too the small houses in the neighborhood were remodeled to accommodate the horses.[40] The typical Roman row house lent itself well to conversion as a stable. The ground floor, measuring perhaps 23 × 55 *palmi,* could be outfitted with a row of seven or eight stalls, each about 7 × 14 *palmi,* with a passage running the length

of the stable. A pavement of bricks in the stalls and the more sturdy cobblestones in the passage, a channel for drainage for the horses' wastes, and a long manger would complete the remodeling. A fountain was in the courtyard behind the stables. With this arrangement, horses could be grouped according to type or customary employment—for example, country horses, mules, saddle horses, horses for the carriage of "His Excellency," horses for the coach driven by the coachman Andrea. There were nine such stables, each accommodating three to ten horses or mules, and a large stable, its new roof measuring 170 × 46 *palmi;* in all, there was room for about a hundred horses. Hay and grain were kept in barns to the northeast—also apparently remodeled row houses.[41]

The resident of a small house might stable his horses very near his own quarters. For example, Monsignor Francesco Barberini's "Casa Grande" had a stable on the northwest side of the courtyard in 1581; but it is surely no accident that, as the house grew in size and prestige, the stables were removed.[42] The Sforza palace had stables on the lowest level, opening to the north, but these too were removed by the Barberini.[43] The noises and smells of stables were better kept away from the apartments of distinguished persons. Carriages, however, made good neighbors.

Cardinal Chigi made a clear distinction between stables and coach rooms in his palace in the 1660s. Five coach rooms lined the courtyard (see Fig. 203, B19, B20, B21, B22, and B27),[44] but a new stable was built as far away as possible, beyond the garden, toward the present via SS. Apostoli (see Fig. 208, D). Previous residents had seen the desirability of the remote location and had built a stable in that area, labeled "stalle che si serve al Presente" on the site plan of 1664 (see Fig. 189). In 1666–68 the new stable was built, its dimensions and proportions suggesting the model of the stable at Villa Aldobrandini. It was just the right size for about sixty horses arranged in two files of stalls flanking a central passage.[45] Bernini's quick sketches show his ideas for the stable—its vaulted hall surmounted by an arcaded loggia or rooms, and a "corridor or gallery" connecting the palace with the stable (see Figs. 214, 215, 216). The arrangement provided an unencumbered courtyard, a remote location for the stable, a convenient passage to the stable for the cardinal, and the containment and regularization of the garden, shielded from the view of the monastery of S. Marcello across the street, by means of the long, narrow structures.[46] Falda's map of 1676 (see Fig. 209) shows the controlled composition. The inconvenience of bringing horses around from the stable to the courtyard to hitch them to the coaches would be minor, in light of the formal and functional advantages.

CHAPTER EIGHT

Use and the Art of the Plan

IFE in seventeenth-century Roman palaces is characterized by movement — in contrast to the seeming stolidity and immutability of their grand exterior forms. Walls and floors provide a framework for the coming and going of guests and the finely tuned movements of host and gentlemen in receiving those guests; the movable ritual of dining, itself performed with a parade of food from the distant kitchen; transferral from apartment to apartment according to the season of year, along with the taking down and putting up of wall hangings and window shades; discreet movements of servants through hidden stairs and passages to bring water and carry away wastes; noisier movements of horses and carriages as they enter and maneuver in the courtyard; the arrival of the quantities of food and other supplies, and their distribution; the daily passage of the numerous *famiglia* through the portals of the palace to their workplaces and perhaps to their meals in the *tinello;* movements of scholars to libraries at the top of the house or other visitors to the ever-growing collections of art.

Yet nothing was left to chance. The framework for both public and private movement was articulated so as to order and control it.

The heart of a palace was the apartment of the noble person housed therein, with its articulate linear sequence of public and private rooms.

Each important resident had his or her own apartment, and alternate rooms or even complete apartments were provided for comfort in winter or summer. The apartments were supported from below by all the services requiring ready access from the outside, whether for supplies, persons, horses and carriages, or water. Above were those parts of the palace to which access should be restricted — private quarters, women attendants' apartments, the *guardaroba.* The apartments were connected with their many subordinate parts and to the city beyond by stairs — grand and expansive for ceremonial entry, and small, hidden, and efficient for private movements. The apartments were amplified by loggias, galleries, ball courts, libraries, and rooms for art collections. They extended outward to gardens, piazzas, and vistas. Even beyond the limits of the property, they found support in stables, carriage houses, and quarters for the *famiglia.* Each part of the palace had its own identity, and access to it was carefully controlled. While the framework of the palace was very generous and admitted of much flexibility, that flexibility was always qualified. A noble apartment might be used by a man or a woman, by a cardinal or a secular prince, but it would not double as an apartment for women attendants. A theater might be arranged temporarily in a *sala* or anteroom, but not in a *guardaroba* or *tinello.* A bathing room would not be installed in the attic, nor women's quarters on the ground floor. Liberati's metaphor for the *famiglia* could well be extended as a description for the architectural framework within which the household lived and functioned: "one body composed of many members, informed by a single spirit, in service of the prince."[1]

How shall this generic description be translated into actual buildings? The several activities that take place within a Roman palace—the subject of the first several chapters of this book—are but part of the raw material of a building. To them must be added materials, constructional technology, the size and configuration of the site, civil laws (whether restrictive or enabling), finances, time, personal preferences, current fashions, cultural traditions, architectural theory. These many factors are brought together and given form through design, a process as much in evidence in the plan of a building as in its façade. The plan of a building has to do with organization and movement: organization of parts and of the whole; and movement between outside and inside, within a room or other part of a building, and from part to part. It is therefore an especially significant aspect of the design of a Roman palace, in which organization and movement are crucial. Design involves choices, and several designers confronted with a single set of circumstances are likely to develop as many different formal solutions. The failure to choose may be just as distinctive a characteristic as a decisive, even idiosyncratic, choice. Artistic personalities may be in evidence as much in plan as in elevation.

The plan has always been of primary importance to architects. Yet it is an abstraction in the sense that visitors never actually see the plan of a palace as they would see its façade or a wall of one of its rooms; rather, they comprehend it through the intellect aided by movement through the building. The *drawing* of a plan is a representation of that abstraction, and the abstraction is itself as truly subject to the operations of design as any façade. Church planning is especially concerned with the shaping of a single large space, often in relation to its vaulting or other covering; in palaces, while single rooms may receive special attention, the ordering and interrelationship of many spaces on several levels is important.

The designers whose work is explored in the second part of this book confronted a number of choices—aspects of their respective styles. The organization of an individual part of a plan involves its shape, its proportions (whether general or specific), the nature of its boundary (open or closed, continuous or discontinuous, smooth or plastic), and its articulation to reinforce or alter the fundamental properties of its shape. The organization of the whole palace involves relationships of various sorts among the parts. There may be some underlying organizing armature, or each connection may be seen as an isolated incident. Axes of organization may or may not be the same as axes of vision or movement. Symmetry may be present with respect to a wall (a picture-like field) or with respect to a spatial axis. The three-dimensional organization of a palace may involve vertically continuous walls or other supports, or it may involve transformations from level to level. Interior order and exterior order may or may not coincide, at such critical points as doors and windows, loggias, and major formal divisions. Similarly, interior shapes and exterior shapes may or may not correspond, for the walls between the two may be conceived of as controlling or yielding: the designer's conception of the relationship between space and substance comes into play.

Organization and movement go hand in hand, for one way of understanding organization is through movement through the building, and one result of organization is control of that movement. The very act of entry can be sharp and decisive, or gradual and modulated. The visitor is propelled or impeded, directed or diverted, according to the shaping of the plan. There may or may not be extended sequences of rooms or spaces. Stairs can be important explorations of the three-dimensionality of the building.

Visual access can encourage physical access or can imply that access even when it is not actually possible.

The drawing is the architect's medium, through which he organizes and quantifies structure, substance, spaces, and paths of movement. In the drawing, he can *see* the organization of a space or group of spaces, which will not be seen in the building but rather understood through movement, memory, anticipation, and ordering of experiences in the mind. As long as the three-dimensional organization of the building is simple — that is, as long as it is essentially a two-dimensional design projected vertically — the conventions of plan drawing readily convey the design: continuous line = edge, surface; dark = solid; light = void (see Fig. 184). When the designer conceives a complex three-dimensional scheme, then the medium of drawing is stretched to its limits. It is not just a matter of perspective drawing (showing the three-dimensional configuration that the eye sees from any given position), for the plan remains abstract and insists on relationships that are not visual. Maderno and Borromini in particular were faced with the problem of representing three-dimensional plans in the two-dimensional medium of drawing (see Figs. 146, 147).

However abstract, the drawing is still seen and manipulated by the designer, with some visual value in addition to its abstract value. The inevitably linear nature of the medium and the individual's way of manipulating it (a dynamic gesture, a slow and sensuous line, a ruled line) have something to do with the results. Patterns are developed. Forms that are visually satisfying are taken to be physically satisfying as well.

In the detailed studies of palaces that follow, the general uses discussed in the first seven chapters are joined by particular uses of the owners or residents of the palaces. The lives of persons are interwoven with the lives of their buildings. Designers are thrust into the history of those persons and buildings, and much of their effort is directed toward planning — that is, designing for the organization and movement that characterize the lives of the palaces. At successive moments in the lives of those buildings, the design problems shift and new interpretations emerge. Plan and image may sometimes go hand in hand, but at other times they seem to ignore one another, with only the substance of the wall as a mediator between the two. In the end, a whole building results, and the artistry of the designer, working within the inevitable circumstances of the commission, emerges.

Part II: Some Palaces in Seventeenth-Century Rome

CHAPTER NINE

Palazzo Borghese

THE Palazzo Borghese rises in the Campo Marzio district of Rome, near the Porto di Ripetta on the Tiber. The size of the cembalo-shaped palace block was such that it seemed to Totti in 1638[1] more a "castello" than a palace. Toward the piazza Fontanella di Borghese, its elegant southeast façade, ordered by a stucco representation of drafted masonry and pilaster strips, is about 185 *palmi* long (Fig. 13); its plainer southwest façade, open to the piazza Borghese, extends almost 550 *palmi* in length (Figs. 14, 15). To the north and east the bulk of the palace confronts the fabric of the city across narrow streets. To the west its narrow two-story loggia and hanging garden reach out to the Tiber (Fig. 16). Within is "the most beautiful courtyard of baroque Rome,"[2] enframed by a two-story loggia of arches springing from paired columns. However imposing, the palace represents no stylistic or typological innovation. Rather, it seems characteristically Roman, not only in its form but also in its story of growth and change in response to physical and historical circumstances. The early seventeenth-century construction accepted and incorporated the outline of the site as well as an old building in the western part of the property and a sixteenth-century fragment of a larger design. Subsequent alterations in response to changes in the life of the Borghese family were carried out within the accommodating matrix of the structure. Some-times the patron showed special interest in the design and was actively involved in its progress. Sometimes distinguished architects were at work, and sometimes minor practitioners saw to the fabric. Sometimes it was a matter of small adjustments and rearrangements; sometimes, however, a distinctive architectural form was discovered within the given conditions.

Howard Hibbard has reconstructed the history of the construction of Palazzo Borghese and also has attributed the several phases of the design to specific architects (Fig. 17).[3] Monsignor Tommaso del Giglio bought the property near the Ripetta in 1560. He ignored the small Palazzo Farnese-Poggio in the western part of the site and instead began construction of a new palace facing the piazza Fontanella di Borghese, a broad extension of the recently cut via dei Condotti. The building was to be oriented not to the river but to the heart of the city. By the time of his death eighteen years later, there stood only that southeast wing, not yet roofed.[4] Hibbard attributed its façade (see Fig. 13) to Vignola (died 1573) but was less certain about the design of the courtyard, whose loggia had barely been begun;[5] and he did not comment on the design or the authorship of the plan. In 1586 the large fragment was bought by Cardinal Pedro Deza, who employed Martino Longhi the Elder to continue the work on the eastern wing, toward the via di Monte d'Oro. In addition to the grand staircase and the

13   Palazzo Borghese, southeast (Alinari/Art Resource, N.Y.)

rooms of that wing, Longhi and his successor, probably Flaminio Ponzio, completed the northeast and southeast loggias of a courtyard, then clearly intended to be five bays square, and a single bay of its southwest loggia.[6] The extent of the building by 1593 is shown in Tempesta's map of that date (Fig. 18).

This fragment of some larger design provided all the essential elements of a dwelling for a single distinguished resident, and it was in fact inhabited by a succession of tenants in the years following Deza's death in 1600. It presented an elegant façade to the city as a prelude to the vestibule, entrance loggia, and large double-ramp staircase. On the *piano nobile,* the *sala* (called the "sala vecchia" in later Borghese documents) stretched behind four bays of the façade. The rooms to the right of the *sala* were too few to form a complete apartment; but to the left, extending around the eastern corner, between the staircase and the via di Monte d'Oro, was an apartment of several rooms suitable for the reception of guests. A second story and attic were above the *piano nobile.* Kitchens were located to

14 Palazzo Borghese, southwest (author)

the north of the stairs, and the ground floor and mezzanines were adequate for other services and some staff members who might live in the palace.[7] Its obviously fragmentary state — in a city filled with torsos of both ancient buildings and modern constructions — was no impediment to its inhabitation: Cardinal Alessandro Farnese (later Paul III) had lived in his Palazzo Farnese while it was under construction, and Taddeo Barberini would later live in the half-finished Palazzo Barberini alle Quattro Fontane.[8]

The last of the several tenants, Cardinal Camillo Borghese, finally purchased the property on 14 February 1605 for 42,000 scudi.[9] Only three months later, on 16 May 1605, he was elevated to the papacy as Paul V; and with this unexpected event the course of the life of the palace was greatly altered.

Paul V and His Brothers Build, 1605–10

Camillo Borghese was the eldest of the seven children of Flaminia Astalli and Marcantonio I Borghese (Fig. 19).[10] Two brothers and a sister had died before Camillo's election to the papacy. A second sister, Ortensia, had married Francesco Caffarelli; their son Scipione, born in 1576, was later to assume the Borghese name and be created cardinal by his uncle in 1605. As papal nephew, Scipione was able to indulge his passion for art through both active patronage and ruthless confiscations.[11] While Camillo was pursuing

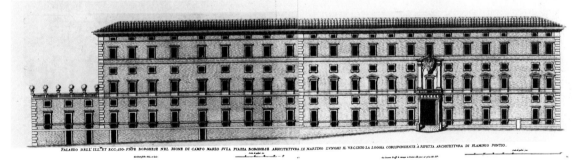

PALAZZO DELL' ILL'·ET ECC·SIO· FN'PE BORGHESE NEL RIONE DI CAMPO MARZO SVLA PIAZZA BORONESE ARHCITETTVRA DI MARTINO LVNGHI IL VECCHIO LA LOGGIA CORISPONDENTE À RIPETTA ARCHITETTVRA DI FLAMINIO PONTIO.

15 Palazzo Borghese, southwest elevation, engraving by Falda (Biblioteca Apostolica Vaticana)

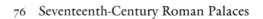

16   Palazzo Borghese, west façade and hanging
garden (I.C.C.D., Rome, ser. C, no. 8926)

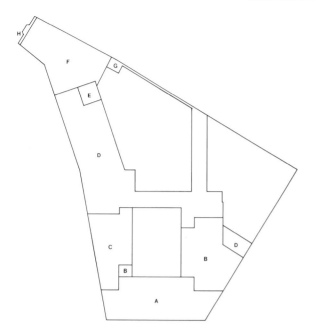

17 Palazzo Borghese, building phases (author)
A: Del Giglio, 1560–78; B: Deza, 1586–1600;
C: Borghese, 1605–7; D: Borghese, 1607–10;
E: Borghese, 1608–10; F: Borghese, 1611–14;
G: Borghese, 1626; H: Borghese, 1676

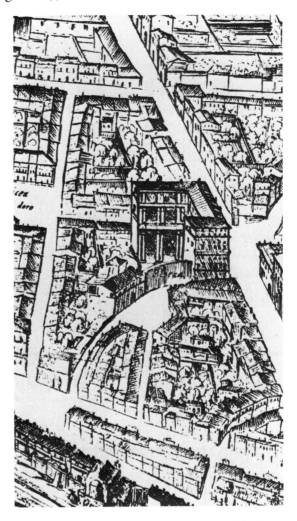

18 Tempesta Map of Rome, 1593, detail with
Palazzo Deza (later Borghese)

an ecclesiastical career, his brothers Giovanni Battista and Francesco were advancing the family fortunes through law and business. Giovanni Battista had already been named *sollecitatore apostolico* by Gregory XIII in 1584; on Camillo's accession to the papacy, both Giovanni Battista and Francesco received military appointments. Francesco married Ortensia Santacroce but the pair remained childless. Giovanni Battista married Virginia Lante in 1588, and on 3 July 1601 their union produced the only Borghese of his generation and the focus of the family's hopes, Marcantonio II. In 1610 the pope bought for his young nephew the fief of Sulmona, in the Kingdom of Naples, with its title of prince. Such were the aspirations of the family that attempts were made to arrange a marriage for Marcantonio with a daughter of Henry IV, King of France.

Eventually, in 1612, an advantageous Roman marriage was arranged with Camilla Orsini, daughter of the Duke of Bracciano and a grandniece of Sixtus V, her dowry set at an exorbitant 100,000 ducats; the wedding took place in the new chapel of the Quirinal palace, celebrated by the pope, on 20 October 1619.

After his election to the papacy, Paul V had the papal palaces at the Vatican, the Quirinal, and elsewhere at his disposal. He intended that the

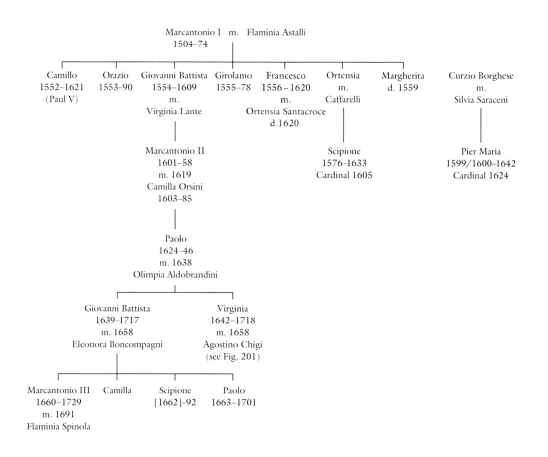

Marcantonio I m. Flaminia Astalli
1504–74

Camillo
1552–1621
(Paul V)

Orazio
1553–90

Giovanni Battista
1554–1609
m.
Virginia Lante

Girolamo
1555–78

Francesco
1556–1620
m.
Ortensia Santacroce
d.1620

Ortensia
m.
Caffarelli

Margherita
d. 1559

Curzio Borghese
m.
Silvia Saraceni

Marcantonio II
1601–58
m. 1619
Camilla Orsini
1603–85

Scipione
1576–1633
Cardinal 1605

Pier Maria
1599/1600–1642
Cardinal 1624

Paolo
1624–46
m. 1638
Olimpia Aldobrandini

Giovanni Battista
1639–1717
m. 1658
Eleonora Boncompagni

Virginia
1642–1718
m. 1658
Agostino Chigi
(see Fig. 201)

Marcantonio III
1660–1729
m. 1691
Flaminia Spinola

Camilla

Scipione
[1662]–92

Paolo
1663–1701

19 Borghese family

Palazzo del Giglio-Deza-Borghese accommo-date his two brothers and their households (al-though he might spend an afternoon or a few days there, possibly displacing his kinsmen for the duration of his stay).[12] According to Roman practice, each brother would maintain his own household and occupy clearly delimited quarters within the shared palace. Francesco Borghese and his wife, Ortensia, were able to move into the already existing palace, using the entrance, grand stair, and *salone* C19 to the southeast. Giovanni Battista rented the Palazzo Giraud-Torlonia in the Borgo in the winter of 1608–9, while await-ing completion of new apartments along the southwest side of the still-unfinished courtyard for himself, his wife Virginia, and their young child Marcantonio.[13] Under Flaminio Ponzio's direction, a second entrance A3, for Giovanni Battista, was made on the southwest side of the palace, from the new piazza Borghese; a new *salone* C5 and the elliptical stair leading to it were placed at the west corner of the courtyard; and apartments were extended outward from that nucleus (Figs. 20–24).

Work proceeded in two distinct phases. The first anticipated the second,[14] and some changes were introduced in both design and use of the rooms while construction was under way. The

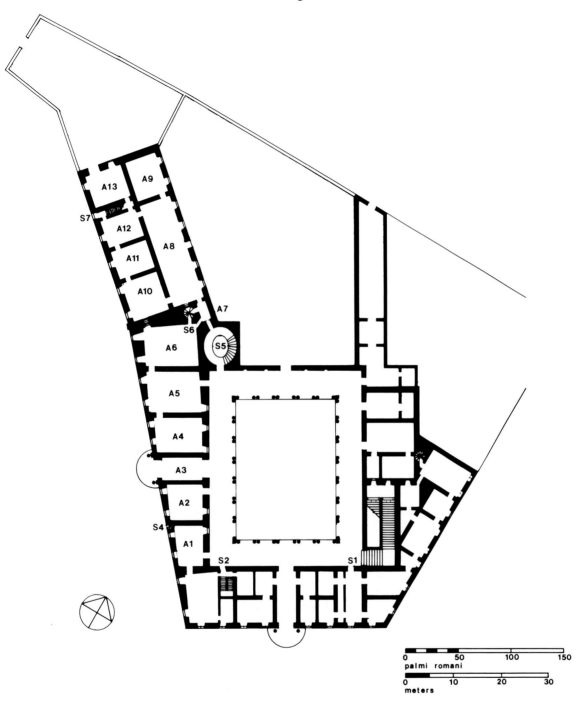

20   Palazzo Borghese, 1606–10, ground floor, reconstruction (author)

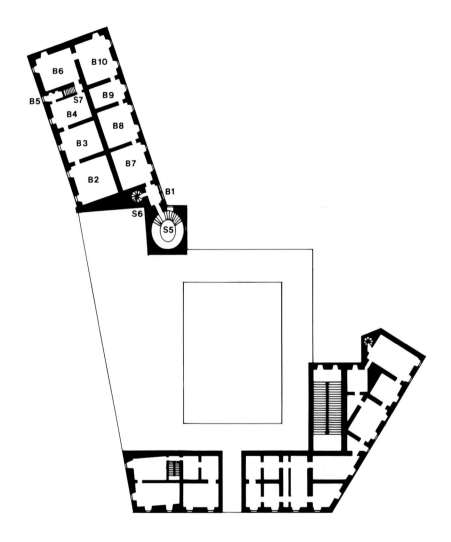

21   Palazzo Borghese, 1606–10, ground-floor mezzanines, reconstruction (author)

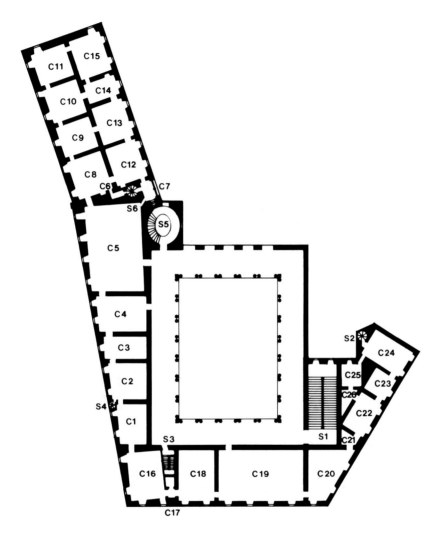

22   Palazzo Borghese, 1606–10, *piano nobile,* reconstruction (author)

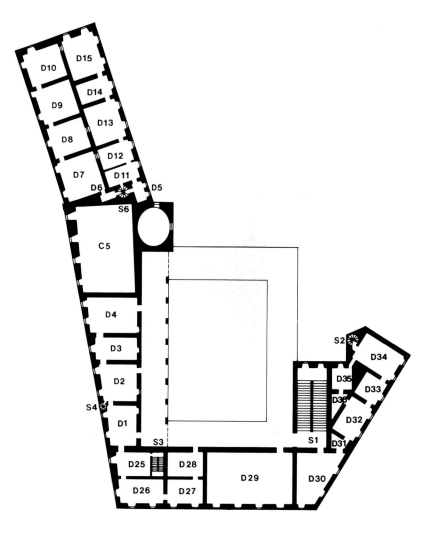

23   Palazzo Borghese, 1606–10, *terzo piano,* reconstruction (author)

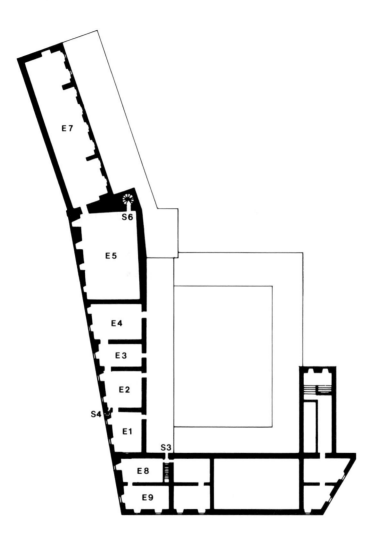

24   Palazzo Borghese, 1606–10, attic, reconstruction (author)

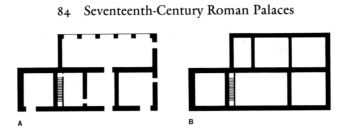

25　House of Enea Orlandini, reconstruction: (A) ground floor, (B) mezzanine and *primo piano* (author)

first campaign saw construction of the seven bays extending westward from the Deza construction, including the entrance A3 and three large ground-floor rooms A1, A2, A4; corresponding rooms on the *piano nobile,* "terzo piano,"[15] and attic; and six bays of the southwest side of the courtyard (see Fig. 17). Its masonry is recorded in five *misure* dating from 22 June 1606 to 23 July 1607.[16] The second campaign continued the building westward and incorporated the small Palazzo Farnese-Poggio, where one Enea Orlandini had been living (Fig. 25; shown in Tempesta's view, Fig. 18). The ground floor of this modest house had a row of four rooms along the street (the two end rooms for carriages) and a loggia of five arcaded bays toward the garden. Above were a ground-floor mezzanine and a *primo piano,* each with a large central room toward the street and five smaller rooms, and an attic over the range of rooms toward the street.[17] Between the construction of 1606–7 and Orlandini's house, two additional ground-floor rooms A5 and A6 were built and surmounted by *salone* C5 and, above, a *guardaroba* E5. The small house was extensively remodeled and raised the full height of the rest of the palace. A multitiered *loggetta* C7 and spiral service stair S6 were tucked between the *salone* and the west wing. The grand elliptical stair S5 was built at the southwest corner of the courtyard, which was closed from the garden to the west by the five-bay, two-story loggia. Various adjustments were made throughout the palace. During the course of the work, it was decided to fill out the corner of

Orlandini's house by the addition of rooms A9, B10, C15, and D15; masonry for this second phase was measured from 18 September 1607 to 2 September 1610.[18]

The location of the new entrance in the seventh bay of the southwest façade, opposite the fourth bay of the courtyard, signaled a change and expansion of the design of the del Giglio-Deza palace. The courtyard, originally to have been five bays square, became a rectangle of five by seven bays.[19] Perhaps the smaller design would have ignored Orlandini's house, but the enlarged design engaged it. The reuse of the old structure yielded some economies, but in exchange its modest cellular structure, orientation, and irregularities were imposed on the plan of the palace.[20]

The planning was schematically simple. The spacing of the paired columns of the courtyard loggia determined the location of parallel walls dividing rooms A1–A6. The thickness of the segments of wall forming their southwest boundary was adjusted so as to minimize their distortion from perfect rectangles.[21] The walls were continued without interruptions from the foundations to the roof. In Orlandini's house a new wall was inserted between rooms B3 and B4, and between rooms C9 and C10;[22] and the northwest corner of the house was filled out with rooms A9, B10, C15, and D15[23]—both operations reinforcing the cellular structure of the house and increasing its contrast to the larger rooms of the new construction to the southeast.

Within this simple three-dimensional matrix

the quarters of Giovanni Battista Borghese and his wife, Virginia, were arranged.

On the *piano nobile* (see Fig. 22), *sala* C5 was hung with new leather revetments of blue and gold, decorated with the dragons and eagles of the Borghese arms; its two *portiere* bore the personal arms of Giovanni Battista.[24] New furnishings were made, including twenty-one *scabelloni* with backs for the *sala,* and seventy-two unusually large *scabelli* and ten *buffetti* to be shared with other rooms on this floor.[25] Seven statues and nine busts were moved into position,[26] and a tall baldacchino was hung over the *credenza.*[27] More blue and gold leather hung the walls of rooms C8, C9, and C11, and room C10 was embellished with damask hangings.[28] There were fireplaces in six of the eight rooms on the *piano nobile* of the west wing, only rooms C9 and C10 being without them.[29] In the course of construction, with the addition of room C15 beginning in September 1608, C14 became identified as a chapel and was fitted with a window for hearing mass from the new corner room and with a walnut *cancellata* marked with Giovanni Battista's arms.[30] Matching blue and gold revetments were hung here too.[31] The four rooms C8–C11, extending en suite from the *sala,* whose *portiere* bore his arms, must have been Giovanni Battista's main apartment for the reception of guests.[32] It is likely that he used C8–C10 as anterooms (the chapel opening from the third anteroom) and C11 as audience room, for all had rich wall hangings; C12 and C13 could have been useful as rooms ancillary to the anterooms and C15 as a private withdrawing room. There is no indication that any room on this level was a bedroom.

Both Giovanni Battista and his wife, Virginia, had rooms in the mezzanines below the *piano nobile* (see Fig. 21; the only mezzanines in Giovanni Battista's part of the palace in these years,[33] according to records of work there). Ten shutters (that is, enough for five windows) were made for windows "in the mezzanine apartment where

His Excellency [Giovanni Battista] sleeps" in October 1609.[34] Another document speaks of ordinary shutters "for the mezzanine rooms where the Signore stays," and four louvered or pierced shades *(saliceni)* "for use at the windows and in the rooms where the Signore sleeps."[35] Virginia's rooms are noted in an account of whitewashing in "the mezzanines where Her Excellency the wife of Sig.ʳ Giovanni Battista lives."[36] The small stair S7 led from room B4 to the ground-floor room A12 (where *palafrenieri* stayed, at least by 1619);[37] and in the tiny room B5 over the stair, opening from B4, was a toilet with a lavatory.[38] These facilities must have served Giovanni Battista, for it would hardly have been appropriate for his wife's rooms to have been connected with the *palafrenieri*'s rooms below; Virginia would have used the rooms toward the garden. The rooms were nicely finished, with painted wood ceilings.[39] There was a fireplace only in the corner room B10, and old fireplaces were removed from rooms B2, B3, B4, and B6.[40] It would seem, therefore, that the entire *appartamento doppio* was intended for summer inhabitation, in spite of the unfavorable orientation of rooms B2–B6 (but they may have been adequately shaded by buildings across the narrow street). The rooms are no better served than the apartment on the *piano nobile,* since there are no private stairs (except S7) at the western end of the double suite, and the only entrance is through room B7.

Giovanni Battista and Virginia seem to have shared the *terzo piano* of the west wing too (see Fig. 23). Four of the rooms (D7, D9, D10, and D15) had fireplaces and would have been comfortable when the mezzanine rooms would have been cold.[41] The four rooms toward the street, D7–D10, were both taller and higher in elevation than those toward the garden: they were built over the taller suite of rooms on the *piano nobile,* and they rose to support the new loggia E7, while a sloping roof covered rooms D11–D15.[42] Virginia must have used the rooms toward the garden, for a document describes her apartment as being under a roof.[43] The four rooms toward the street are described consistently as a set in the documents of construction. They had wood ceilings, and the walls of the first three (D7–D9), "where Signor Giovanni Battista lives," were hung with revetments below a painted frieze 3 *palmi* in height.[44] As in the lower apartments, circulation would have been less than ideal.

Giovanni Battista, then, seems to have been well housed, with an ample major apartment for the reception of guests on the *piano nobile* and both summer and winter rooms for sleeping and private use. Virginia was less well provided. As sister-in-law of the pope, she would have had to receive guests — for example, Costanza Barberini, who called to pay her respects on behalf of her own brother-in-law, Maffeo Barberini, after he had been created cardinal by Paul V.[45] Yet no suite of reception rooms or important furnishings can be identified as hers. Perhaps she used rooms C4–C1, opening to the south of the *salone.* Her women attendants required rooms, yet there was no space left for them in the western wing of the palace, convenient to her mezzanine and third-floor rooms. Attic rooms E1–E4 (see Fig. 24) might have been outfitted for them, but the documents of construction give no evidence of this. That women were housed somewhere in the palace is attested by two references: a bit of metalwork for two windows in the "women's chapel in the new rooms" (those on the southwest side of the *cortile*) was recorded on 9 March 1609;[46] and another bit was done for a room "on the way to the women."[47] Even Virginia's winter apartment in rooms D12–D15 must have been less fine than that of her husband — lower, colder (with windows to the northeast and a fireplace documented only in D15), and lacking the painted frieze and revetments of Giovanni Battista's rooms.

A person conspicuously absent from the palace is Marcantonio Borghese, child of Giovanni Battista and Virginia and the papal nephew on whom the hopes of the family were concentrated. Born in 1601, he was but four years old when his uncle became Paul V. He was reared not at home but at the papal court, under the tutelage of his cousin Cardinal Scipione Borghese.[48]

On the ground floor, to the left of the entrance, the three new rooms A4–A6 were joined to the refurbished loggia A8 of Orlandini's house to form a sculpture gallery (see Fig. 20).[49] Rooms A4–A6 had vaulted ceilings with stucco decorations surrounding central painted panels, and travertine fireplaces.[50] At first the "loggia vecchia" was open to the garden through five arches, but in the course of construction the openings were filled in with four windows framed in travertine and a door. The dual identification of the room was felt in March 1609, when the carpenter submitted a bill for work in "the loggia, that is, the gallery."[51]

The other ground-floor rooms were for services. To the right of the new entrance, the *dispensa* was located in A2,[52] and the *tinello* may have been in A1.[53] Room A10, the first of the ground-floor rooms of Orlandini's house — five steps lower than the newly constructed rooms and formerly a carriage room — became a room for *palafrenieri.*[54] At least by 1619 the two neighboring rooms A11 and A12 were also used by the *palafrenieri*; at that time they were improved with wood floors as protection against dampness and with other woodwork including a dining table.[55] Stair S7 connected A12 with the mezzanine above. Room A13, opening toward the courtyard to the west, was for carriages.[56] The new corner room A9 was connected with the gallery A8 by a doorway, but its use is uncertain.

At the top of the house stood the *guardaroba* E5, in its customary location over the *sala,* and its loggia E7 (see Fig. 24). Service stair S6 rose from the ground to the *guardaroba* with 125 steps.[57] The newly constructed loggia, the "loggia nova," was at first open to the northeast, with eight broad arches in its low pilaster-framed façade.[58] By September 1608 it was being transformed into the "room with big windows," or the "rooftop loggia with big windows next to the *guardaroba*," by the installation of masonry and large windows in its arched openings.[59] Perhaps it was here, "at the top of the house," that Paul V dined when he visited the palace in July 1610.[60]

The new oval stair at the western corner of the courtyard provided splendid access to the *salone* on the *piano nobile*,[61] but means of private circulation were in short supply. A spiral service stair S4 was set into the thickness of the wall between the first two new rooms, A1 and A2. It was lit by tiny windows still visible in the façade of the palace (see Fig. 14). At the base of the stair was a door to the piazza, and other doors gave access to rooms A1, C2, and D2.[62] Another spiral stair connected room D4 with the attic.[63] For the entire western wing, the only service stair was S6, extending 108 *palmi* from the ground floor to the attic. This stair was the core of a complicated system of passages on four levels. At ground level, the stair opened to the vaulted passage A7, which connected loggia/gallery A8, the large oval stair, and room A6. It was also possible to pass through the small stair from A6 directly to A8; four steps in the thickness of the wall led down to the lower level of the gallery. At mezzanine level the stair joined the open "loggietta" B1, which connected the large stair and mezzanine room B7. At the *piano nobile* passage C6 branched out from the spiral stair to room C8 toward the street, and *loggetta* C7 opened toward the garden. In what was apparently the richest of the passages, a balustrade and granite column framed the view of the garden, the central rectangle of the little vault was framed by stucco ornamentation, and a small window gave light to the spiral stair. C7 joined the *salone* C5, the large oval stair (via a straight flight of six steps), room C12 toward the garden, and the spiral stair. On the *terzo piano* passages similarly branched out from the spiral stair: D6 to room D7; a door directly from the stair to D11; and chamber D5 (closed, with two small windows toward the garden) to room D11. Finally, stair S6 rose to the

door of the *guardaroba*.[64] The ingenious structure of stairs and passages was the only means by which services could be brought to the apartments in the west wing, and unfortunately it occurred at the public end of the suite instead of at the private end. Further, servants coming to the stairs and passages would have to traverse the courtyard and pass through the oval stair or enter through the sculpture gallery or even the *salone*.

Toilets, customarily associated with stairs, were also in short supply. Pipes for toilets were installed in passage D6, adjacent to service stair S6, and in room D15.[65] The latter must not have been for servants, since it was so far removed from the stairs. No privies were associated with the stairs in the rooms to the southwest of the courtyard. Instead, they were located beyond the north corner of the courtyard, at the level of the *piano nobile*.[66]

Documentation for the quarters of Francesco and Ortensia Borghese is sparse. Francesco's guests would enter through the façade on the piazza Fontanella di Borghese and turn right to ascend the large double-ramp stair S1 constructed in the 1580s. Francesco's apartments were centered on the "sala vecchia," C19, four bays long, with mezzanine windows above its four large windows (see Fig. 22; seen in section, Fig. 26). Its wood ceiling was refurbished in 1617 with twenty paintings on canvas (each 10 × 6½ *palmi*).[67] There was a fireplace, and the walls of the *sala* were hung with red leather.[68] The "second room," for which Spanish leather hangings were provided, must have been the corner room C20, for the hangings included three overwindows.[69] An inventory of 1620 lists damask hangings in this "Anticamera falza" and also in the following room, C22, the "room before the chapel [C26]."[70] The suite must have extended on to C23 and C24. According to a plan of ca. 1608 (Fig. 27),[71] all of these rooms had fireplaces; they therefore must have been intended for winter use in spite of their eastward orientation. Francesco also had rooms on the *terzo piano* (see

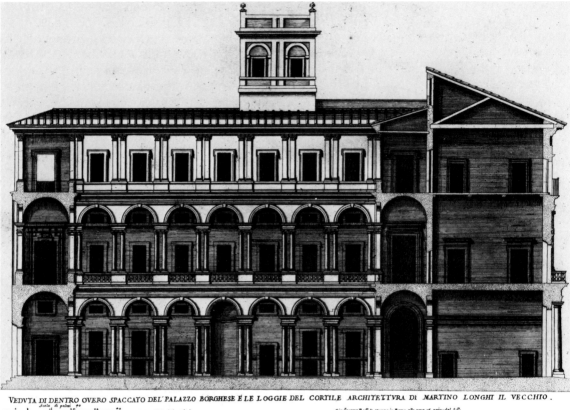

VEDVTA DI DENTRO OVERO SPACCATO DEL PALAZZO BORGHESE É LE LOGGIE DEL CORTILE ARCHITETTVRA DI MARTINO LONGHI IL VECCHIO.

26   Palazzo Borghese, section through courtyard and southeast wing, engraving by Falda (Biblioteca Apostolica Vaticana)

Fig. 23); the inventory of their leather revetments in 1610 suggests that they were rooms D25–D28, with a fireplace in at least the second room.[72] By the time of his death in 1620 he had extended his apartment from these four rooms (now beginning with D28) through rooms D1–D4 along the southwest side of the courtyard; in June, at the time of the inventory, the eight rooms were hung with damask and other fabric revetments.[73] Indeed, already in 1607 Francesco had absorbed some of the newly constructed rooms into his apartments, according to an account for hardware for a door between old and new rooms, and for doors and windows "in the new rooms of the old palace where Signor Francesco lives"; but the account does not indicate which story the rooms were on.[74]

Ortensia's rooms are more difficult to locate. She had a suite of reception rooms, for an inventory of 1610 lists leather table covers for her "anticamera dell'audienza" and "camera dell'audienza," without specifying their location.[75] These might have been C18 and C16, to the southwest of the *sala vecchia,* and the apartment might even have extended into the newly constructed C1 and beyond. If her sister-in-law Virginia was indeed using rooms C4–C1, this arrangement would have provided an interesting concentration of women's quarters in the palace. Alternatively, Ortensia might have received

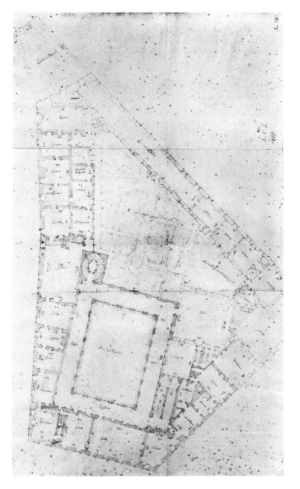

27   Girolamo Rainaldi, project for completion of
Palazzo Borghese, ca. 1608 (Albertina, It.AZ 1001)

guests in the suite of rooms above that of her
husband, in the apartment D30–D36, opening
from the upper landing of the grand stair. A single room for Ortensia, D28, seems isolated
among those of Francesco's upper apartment in
1610.[76] The documents are silent as to the location of her women attendants' quarters.

The mezzanine rooms in Francesco's half of
the palace seem to have been not for major residents but rather for officers and services. The
credenza was in a mezzanine.[77] The *scalco* lived in

vaulted mezzanine rooms extending from the
southeast façade through to the loggia of the
courtyard, under Francesco's apartment.[78] The
trinciante had a mezzanine room toward the
piazza.[79] The *maestro di casa* had rooms on the
ground floor, with a window to the loggia on the
southeast side of the courtyard.[80] The rooms of
several other members of the household staff are
mentioned in documents, but they cannot be
located precisely.[81]

A kitchen for Giovanni Battista was to have
been in the basement under room A10, but this
plan was abandoned by May 1608.[82] Instead,
kitchens for both Giovanni Battista and Francesco were in the area toward Monte d'Oro, to
the north of the courtyard. Apparently taking
advantage of older houses along the vicolo bordering the property to the east (see Fig. 18), the
kitchens were only one story high; there were
windows and a door toward the street. The
kitchens were entered from the north corner of
the palace courtyard, through a small courtyard.
They had the usual fittings—hearth, sinks,
counters, food warmers *(scaldavivandi),* and a
partitioned-off corner, probably for the bed of
the cook or his assistant. Drains carried waste
water to the garden, the courtyard of a neighboring house, and the sewer in the street.[83]

A laundry was installed in a basement room of
the palace, toward a piazza (whether to the
southeast or to the southwest). It had built-in
tubs and furnaces for heating water in cal-
drons.[84] Prior to 1605, when cardinals had lived
in the palace, there would have been no need for
a laundry. The residence of the Borghese women
introduced this requirement.

An *avviso* of 23 April 1608 names the praiseworthy features of the new palace: the oval stair,
as yet unfinished; rich wall hangings; and "nineteen most beautiful rooms on one floor and almost in a single suite," which the pope could
enjoy on his visits.[85] Yet other *avvisi* are critical of
the design, and the pope is reported to have been
dissatisfied with the distortions of the façade and
many of the rooms.[86] He may have been thinking

of such rooms in the old house as C11, whose walls had to be lined with brick to bring them into square;[87] or of the rooms on the ground floor whose walls were not straightened until 1671;[88] or of the unevenness of levels, so that five steps had to be introduced between rooms A6 and A10,[89] and two steps between the third-floor rooms toward the street and those toward the garden.[90] He may also have been dissatisfied with irregularities in rooms designed and built anew — most conspicuous among them the new *sala*, whose four sides measured 48½, 78, 51½, and 82 *palmi*,[91] and indeed all the rooms along the southwest side of the courtyard, in spite of the shaping of the exterior wall. A resident might have remarked that the nineteen rooms "almost in a single suite" could not be used in that way because of the location of the two *saloni* and chapel C3; rooms C4, C3, C2, C1, C16, and C18 were too few to be divided between the two apartments and were not logically related to only one of the *saloni*; suites could not even develop to the length customary for a person of status, and Giovanni Battista had to sleep either above or below his main apartment on the *piano nobile*. The planning device of the *appartamento doppio* was not used for the advantage of thermal comfort. Fireplaces had to be used in rooms facing north and east, because those rooms were not reserved for summer use. Private circulation left much to be desired, especially in the west wing, whose only service stair S6 stood near the entrance to the suites instead of near their innermost rooms. Apartments of husband and wife stood in no clear relationship to one another, and arrangements for the women attendants of the two papal sisters-in-law remain obscure.

Building Continues, 1611–14

In December 1609, mortally ill, Giovanni Battista Borghese lamented the coincidence of his impending death with the completion of the palace.[92] Yet it might have been more appropriate to speak of a pause in the work rather than its completion. Larger plans were afoot both before and immediately after Giovanni Battista's death, and a major building campaign was under way within two years. Perhaps some of the inadequacies of planning in the palace of 1610 were understood as only temporary, pending some further construction; or perhaps they were the stimulus to further additions. Surely changes in the life of the family and the constellation of inhabitants also provoked changes and additions to the palace.

A plan of the *piano nobile* of the palace (Fig. 27), by Girolamo Rainaldi,[93] shows a project for additions that would fill the entire cembalo-shaped block. Hibbard dated this plan 1610–12 — that is, between two major phases of construction — but it might be even earlier. It shows in dark poché the del Giglio-Deza palace purchased by Cardinal Camillo Borghese in 1605, the courtyard and rooms along its southwest side, and the remodeled Orlandini house incorporated in the palace; and Rainaldi's proposed additions are shown in outline. Room C15, constructed beginning in September 1608 to fill out the corner of Orlandini's house, is drawn in outline. This suggests that Rainaldi may have prepared his plan before room C15 had been added — that is, before September 1608.

Girolamo Rainaldi's plan shows three large *saloni*: the *sala vecchia* in the southeast wing, the newly constructed *sala* toward Piazza Borghese, and a proposed *sala* — measuring 65 × 75 *palmi*, decidedly the largest of the three — opening from the north corner of the courtyard. The palace was apparently to be not merely a double but a triple residence. Perhaps Cardinal Scipione Borghese was to join his two uncles in the palace; or perhaps the family was looking forward to the eventual marriage of young Marcantonio and the establishment of his household. Only two major stairs are shown, so that the third resident would have to share a stair (and presumably an entrance portal) with one of the others. Directly opposite its entrance, the new *sala* would open to a "salotto," 55 *palmi* square, with three windows toward the narrow vicolo to the east. A large chapel with an elliptical vault would open from the *salotto,* and a pair of apartments would extend in opposite directions. The larger of the two developed along the northern boundary of the site and included an "anticameretto," a "cameretto," and two rooms labeled "camera," followed by a "studio" and a "galleria" 225 *palmi* in length. The gallery led to a garden terrace overlooking the Ripetta at the westernmost corner of the site. Service stairs were included adjacent to the "cameretto" and near the western end of the gallery. The smaller apartment was composed of a new "anticamera" south of the *salotto,* an ample rectangular service stair, and probably two rooms, C24 and C25, labeled "camera," with a small spiral stair, in the old part of the palace. This apartment confronted the old apartment to the north of the *sala vecchia,* also composed of "salotto," "anticamera," and two "camere," along with the triangular chapel C26 (cf. Fig. 22).

Rainaldi reveals the difficulty in assigning rooms C18, C16, C1, C2, C3, and C4 to apartments opening from either of the two already existing *sale:* from *sala* C19 extend "salotto," "anticamera," "camera" C1, and "camera" C2, a reasonable if short apartment; but, opening from sala C5, "salotto" C4 and "capella" C3 are too few unless the rooms of the other apartment are invaded. To the west of the new *sala* C5, Rainaldi shows the "salotto" C8, "anticamera" C9, "camera" C10, and "camera" C11 of what we have identified as Giovanni Battista's apartment. C12 is called "anticamerá" and C13 "camera," suggesting the beginning of a parallel apartment toward the garden, but C14 reveals a contradiction in its label "camerino ò capella": does it belong with the garden suite as a small chamber of unspecified use or to Giovanni Battista's apartment as chapel? The yet-to-be-constructed C15 is a "retrocamera," with respect to the chapel or C11. Beyond, Rainaldi proposes a "studio," the service stair shared with the long gallery, and an "oratorio" before the "giardino pensile"

overlooking the Ripetta. To the northwest of the courtyard, within the borders created by old and new construction, are a garden and a small "giardin di melangoli."

The large scale of Rainaldi's proposed additions is striking, in contrast to the older construction; but in other respects the plan seems rather old-fashioned. The names he assigns to rooms suggest a sixteenth-century construction of apartments. By the beginning of the seventeenth century, the "salotto" had been designated the first of a sequence of anterooms and a distinction had been made between the audience room and the "camera" where a prince or cardinal would sleep. Further, except for the new apartment along the north edge of the property, with its curiously named "anticameretta" and "cameretto" (actually larger than the following "camere"), the apartments are all rather short. It is possible that private rooms were intended to be separated from the suite, in a mezzanine or upper floor; the several proposed stairs might lead to such rooms. Rainaldi shows a fireplace in almost every room, regardless of its orientation, so that he did not envision seasonal occupancy of the apartments. Further, he ignores the modern planning device of the *appartamento doppio* (except where it already existed, in Orlandini's old house), in spite of ample open space for his additions. The "giardino pensile" to the west surely anticipates the construction of 1612–14, but the unhappy collision of gallery, oratorio, and studio, with their separate doors to the terrace, contrasts with the felicitous arrangement that Carlo Maderno was soon to construct there.

Rainaldi's scheme for additions to the palace was set aside, but there nevertheless survived the notion that more was to be built. According to an *avviso* of 14 July 1610, Paul V visited the palace, admired the work that had been done there, and gave some orders for its completion. The report of three days later was more explicit as to the pope's directions: he ordered that rooms for a new library be made in the part of the palace toward the Monte d'Oro; he ordered that the setting of the palace in the city be improved by cutting a street toward the Corso and by purchasing a group of houses opposite the palace and replacing them with "some fine structure"; he ordered that a room be added toward the Ripetta, that the stables be extended to the via di Ripetta, and that a neighboring palace and house be bought so that a small palace could be built for the use of Francesco and Ortensia when the pope should wish to stay in the main palace for a few days.[94]

Paul V's interest in extending the palace toward the Ripetta, already adumbrated in Rainaldi's design, was developed in a major addition of 1612–14 (Figs. 28–31). This work was in the area of the "cortile della legna," enclosed by walls and a portal toward the Ripetta in 1608.[95] From the street this extension seems one with the earlier building (see Figs. 14, 15), but its plan and the attitudes that inform that plan are entirely different from the work to which it attaches. Although several architects were involved — Hibbard discusses the contributions of Ponzio, Maderno, and Van Zanten[96] — it seems that the planning is Maderno's. Ponzio died in 1613, but an even more important reason for assuming that he did not plan the extension is the extreme difference between his earlier planning at the Palazzo Borghese and the work of 1612–14. Van Zanten "was not an altogether competent technician,"[97] a qualification which, as we shall see, was important for the conception and execution of the new building. The plan can be shown to fit well with Maderno's other work and can shed light on the matter of his own artistic personality.

In its irregularly shaped and limited volume, the new addition contained rooms that varied greatly in size and character.[98] Beginning with the alleviation of the inadequacies of Ponzio's apartments, Maderno added one room for each of the apartments on each of the three levels. Rooms B11, B12, C28, C27, D16, and D17 inconspicuously adjoin the old rooms. They are rectangular, appropriately a bit smaller than their predecessors; and they follow immediately in suite, making more generously sized apartments. The suite on the *piano nobile* toward the street terminates in a trapezoidal chapel C30, with lavish stucco decoration,[99] so that it was possible to return C14, formerly a chapel, to the suite of rooms toward the garden. Yet in this unusual position the new chapel must not have been intended to function in the customary manner, with the *famiglia* gathered outside the door to hear mass. It might have been conceived as a private oratory, or as a garden chapel (like the chapel of S. Sebastiano at the Villa Aldobrandini) in conjunction with the hanging garden beyond. Either chapel C3 on the other side of the *sala* or soon-to-be-remodeled C7[100] would have been the public chapel. The apartments on the *piano nobile* and *terzo piano* were amplified by special rooms for the private enjoyment of the residents and their guests: on each floor were a gallery or study[101] (C35 and D23) and an open loggia with a richly stuccoed vault (C31 and D20).[102] The pleasurable loggias looked out to a hanging garden and, beyond the river, a panorama including Castel Sant'Angelo, St. Peter's, and the landscape of Prati. These rooms contrasted in size and shape to the private rooms of their apartments, from which they were easily accessible. The innermost rooms of the apartments are served by spiral stairs: toward the garden, a stair S11 rises from the *piano nobile* to the attic; a second stair S10 connects the apartments on the *piano nobile* and upper floor toward the street; a third, S9, moves downward from the mezzanine on that side to the ground-floor rooms; and a fourth stair, S8, rises through the center of the entire cluster of rooms.[103] Latrines, in short supply in 1610, were added in the new construction: at the foot of stair S11, at the top of stair S8, in a mezzanine above the chapel C30 (accessible from stair S10), and in a "stanzino del necessario" near stair S9.[104]

The improved apartments and the hanging garden stood above a group of new rooms of specialized uses. On the ground floor, toward

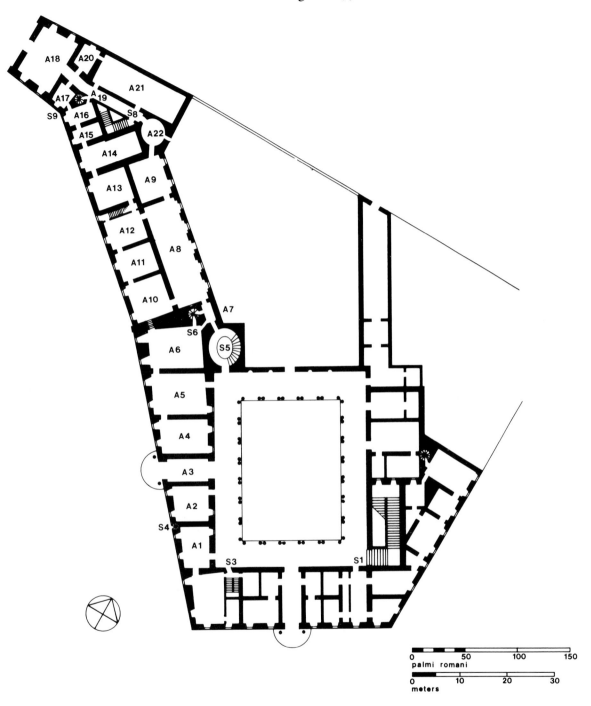

28   Palazzo Borghese, 1611–14, ground floor, reconstruction (author)

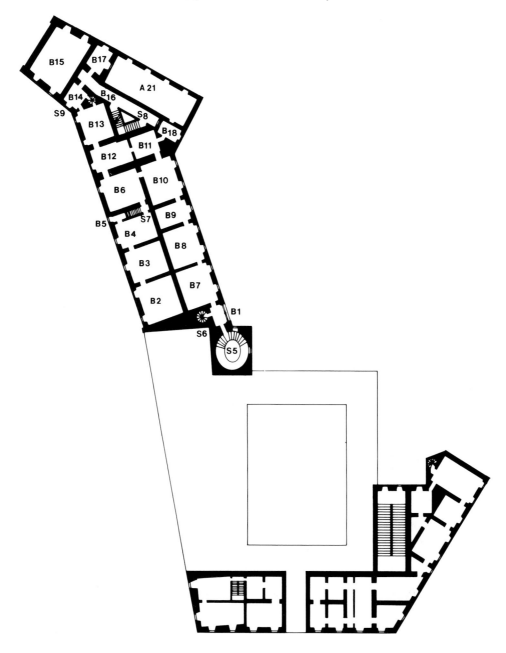

29 Palazzo Borghese, 1611–14, ground-floor mezzanines, reconstruction (author)

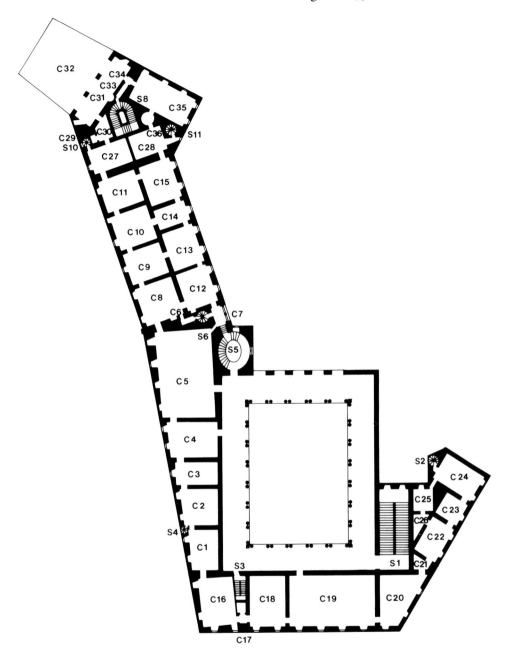

30   Palazzo Borghese, 1611–14, *piano nobile,* reconstruction (author)

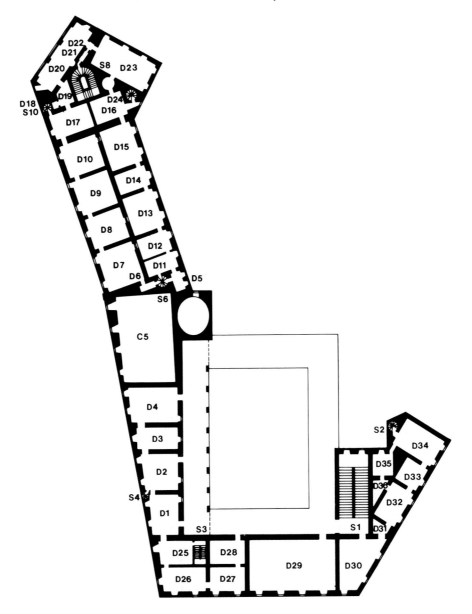

31   Palazzo Borghese, 1611–14, *terzo piano,* reconstruction (author)

the via dell'Arancio, was the large rectangular volume of the ball court, A21, measuring 81¼ × 28½ *palmi* and rising through the mezzanine.[105] It was readily accessible from street or garden, not too far from the apartments, but adequately separated from those private rooms so that noise would not give offense.[106] It was adjoined by a dressing room A20 on the ground floor and above by a room B17 for spectators, who could view the game through a grilled window.[107] Across the central corridor, opposite the dressing room, was a small apartment for bathing—an uncommon facility in a seventeenth-century palace.[108] The vaulted bathing room A17 received hot water from A16, where there was a stove for heating the water. Spiral stair S9 led up to a cluster of intimate, richly decorated rooms associated with the bath: intermediate mezzanines above A17 and A16, with low vaulted ceilings, and, at the level of the normal mezzanines in this wing, B14 and B13. A new kitchen was installed in rooms A14 and A15—the larger room called the "cucina comune" and the smaller the "cucina segreta ò stanza del sciacquatore."[109] Both had fireplaces. An oven was included in A14 and a *sciacquatore* or sink measuring 13¾ × 4¼ *palmi* was built in A15. The large entrance hall A18 provided a service entrance from the busy via di Ripetta to the kitchens.[110] It also housed carriages, since the former carriage room A13 could no longer be used in that way.[111]

In his shaping of paths of circulation, Maderno's artistry is especially apparent. The service entrance is direct and unimpeded. Goods can be brought directly into the ground-floor corridor and thence into the kitchens. Entry from the garden or from the old ground-floor gallery A8 and garden room A9 is entirely different in character. The colliding geometries of the plan are reconciled in a domed elliptical hall A22. Its six doors and feigned doors must have alternated with the six landscapes with gilt stucco frames painted here by Annibale Du-

rante.[112] This gracious chamber is a pivot which allows the visitor to reorient himself and to enter the corridor, perhaps to proceed to the ball court, or perhaps to ascend the L-shaped stair S8 to the mezzanine corridor. The kitchens are held away from this path and are not accessible from the elliptical vestibule. At the mezzanine one can look down into the ball court. A door opposite the spectators' room leads into the intimate mezzanines above the bath and thence into the mezzanine apartment toward the street. At the other end of the corridor, one can pass through a doorway, up a few steps, to a rectangular "ricetto," or vestibule, B18, opening into the other mezzanine apartment.[113] Perhaps more appealing than any of these doorways is the opening to the stair. Reentering the triangular stair S8 (Fig. 32), one finds its second leg curving and transforming itself into a U, at the apex of which is a landing opening on the *piano nobile* to a passage C33 to a small square chamber C34, which in turn opens to the left to the loggia C31 and to the right to the gallery C35[114]—rooms similar in shape and appeal, the one open to the hanging garden, and the other its closed counterpart. These rooms are worthy destinations of the path beginning at the garden door, and one would go no farther unbidden. Small doors and passages lead on to the private rooms of the *piano nobile* apartments, but the path is broken so that privacy is maintained. Persons emerging from the apartments pivot in the circular chamber C36 ("transito tondo") before the gallery[115] or pass through the trapezoidal passage or chapel C30[116] to the loggia, and only from these special rooms do they begin their descent to the garden or ground-floor gallery. The small spiral stairs S10 and S11 that serve these apartments are for internal communication only; the U-shaped stair ignores the apartments and connects those other spaces—intimate yet communally enjoyed.

Just as Maderno controls and separates the paths of movement through this little section of the palace, he also makes a clear break between

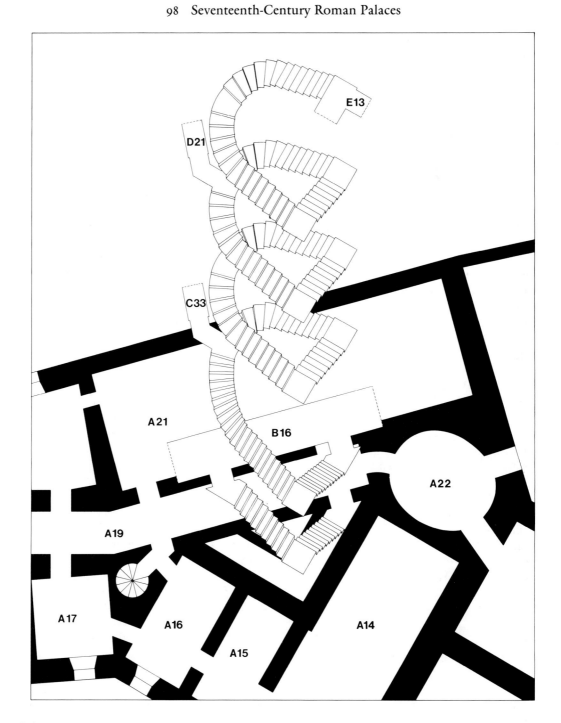

32   Palazzo Borghese, stair S8, analytical drawing (David DiMarco)

two levels. The stairs are already an indication of the break. Spiral stairs S10 and S11 do not descend below the *piano nobile,* and S9 connects only the ground floor and the mezzanine. The central stair S8 continues from ground to attic, but significantly it changes in form just at that division between the upper and lower parts of the palace. To the lower part belong the activities of ball court, hot bath, kitchen, and service entrance; to the upper part, the places for privacy and quiet enjoyment. The break in use is signaled by the break in form, for within the uniform perimeter walls almost no form, volume or solid, continues throughout the height of the building. The large rectangular kitchen A14 supports two mezzanine rooms, B11 and B12, of unequal size, and at the *piano nobile* the smaller of these rooms is succeeded by C28, several *palmi* wider. The small kitchen A15 and its neighbor A16 are surmounted by a large squarish mezzanine B13, which then is cut back at the *piano nobile* to the sequence of spiral stair, rectangle, and trapezoid. The ball court, rising through the mezzanine level, supports the wall of the gallery C35 and loggia C31 above its vault. The elliptical entrance A22 from the garden quickly gives way to the rectangular chamber B18 at mezzanine level, which in turn is succeeded at the *piano nobile* by the triangle of masonry cut by a window passage from room C28 and spiral stair S11. Even in small ways it seems that Maderno gratuitously introduces differences where it would have been easy enough to repeat a form: for example, on the *piano nobile* the tiny chamber C29 adjoining the trapezoidal chapel measures 5 × 8 *palmi;* the corresponding chamber D18 on the upper floor is 6¾ × 6 *palmi.*[117] The whole figure of the plan changes, from the thrust of colliding orthogonal patterns toward the Ripetta on the ground floor and mezzanine, to the nudging and nestling of isolated units into a snug cluster in the upper stories.

Along with the variety in plans from level to level, there is also a great variety in shapes. Compared to the near uniformity of the rooms of the old house remodeled as the garden wing of Ponzio's building, Maderno uses a cacophony of rectangles, squares, trapezoids, triangles, circles, the ellipse, and the U-shape.

The planning of such a three-dimensional structure is difficult in terms of both solid and void. We have already considered the intricacies of Maderno's paths and the arrangement of volumes. Masonry walls, with their great weight, are not lightly stood upon vaults or openings. Most important are Maderno's structural preparations for the reception of the walls of the two-story loggia, which could more easily have sat forward over the bath A17 and dressing room A20. Shifting this large rectangle back entailed building broad arches of tile in the vaults of the ball court and corridor.[118] A similar reinforcing arch was thrown across the kitchen A14 to support the partition between B11 and B12.[119] Other relieving arches of tile were built in the walls themselves, spanning openings below.[120] Such techniques were not unknown earlier; for example, walls rose above the vault of the garden loggia A8 in the old house incorporated in the palace in 1607–10. An anonymous advisor to the Barberini, writing ca. 1625, describes the method of placing a thin wall over a reinforcing arch in a vault.[121] Maderno boldly places massive walls over spaces below, displaying a technical skill that Ponzio's earlier work did not require.

The spatial and structural virtuosity of the interior are as completely masked on the southwest façade as is the break in construction (Fig. 33; cf. Figs. 14, 15). Maderno simply continues the pattern of windows and horizontal string courses already established in 1607–10; he even regularizes the uneven spacing of the first six bays by his addition of three closely spaced bays. A formal break comes only at the angle of the property line, where quoins terminate the three-story bulk of the palace and a balustrade edges the hanging garden; but even here the forms of the ground floor and mezzanine are continued. Characteristically, Maderno distinguishes between the surface pattern and the interior volumes of the plastic mass of masonry.[122] Only on the narrow Ripetta façade is the two-story loggia revealed, its detailing apparently worked out by Giovanni Van Zanten within Maderno's framework (see Fig. 16).[123]

This small but intricate work cost more than all the previous building, according to a memorandum summarizing the expenditures for the palace. Paul V spend 6,500.00 scudi for various statues, columns, and other pieces of stone. From 1605 through 1610, Giovanni Battista and Francesco Borghese spent a total of 55,371.49 scudi. From 1611 through 1622 (including smaller works executed after the completion of the Ripetta extension in 1614), Marcantonio spent 72,219.69 scudi for the "seconda fabrica"; in 1613 alone he spent 17,461.24 scudi for masonry and 6,600.00 scudi for stonework. Cardinal Scipione Borghese spent 3,000.00 scudi for a stair (S12) attached to the garden façade of the Ripetta extension in 1626, ceilings in the apartment on the upper floor, and paintings.[124] Marcantonio paid for the Ripetta extension,[125] and he is always named as client in the *misure* of the work.[126] Some aspects of the design may have been due to his special requirements; for example, the inclusion of the ball court may reasonably have been for the youth rather than for his aged uncle Francesco or even his cousin Scipione (thirty-six years old in 1612). The planning may have anticipated his marriage to Camilla Orsini; the marriage agreement had been signed on 5 August 1612, more than seven years in advance of the wedding.[127] Still, because of his youth, we cannot expect Marcantonio to have been an active patron, informing the design. One document shows Francesco to have been acting as supervising client in 1614.[128]

Nor is it clear who was intended to live in the newly extended apartments and enjoy the amenities of the Ripetta wing. The documents of construction in 1612–14 give no indication whatever.

33   Palazzo Borghese, southwest façade, from west (author)

Marcantonio Marries and Francesco Dies

Although major construction came to a conclusion in 1614, the interior of the palace continued to be shaped and revised. Then, in the short period of only fifteen months, three major events in the life of the family either provoked changes or made them possible: the marriage of Marcantonio to Camilla Orsini on 20 October 1619; the death of Francesco on 20 June 1620; and the death of Paul V on 28 January 1621 and Cardinal Scipione Borghese's subsequent move to the palace.

With the lengthening of the Ripetta wing came the redefinition of apartments and the relocation of chapels (see Fig. 30). In the summer of 1615 work continued on the new trapezoidal chapel C30 with its adjacent tiny sacristy: a wood screen of four panels was installed to enclose the chapel proper from the passage from room C27 to loggia C31; an altar and its base were placed in the chapel; and a cabinet was made for the sacristy.[129] In the same year the *loggetta* C7 lost its earlier function of connecting the large elliptical stair with the rooms toward the garden when it was converted into a chapel.[130] Room C14, made into a chapel in 1609,[131] was relieved of that function and returned to the suite of rooms toward the garden.[132] The group of ten rooms could now reasonably be divided into two parallel suites of five rooms, each with a chapel, access from spiral service stair S6, and access to the loggia and terrace overlooking the Ripetta.

Although the new *salone* and other rooms in that part of the palace had been splendidly outfitted in 1610 with leather revetments, special furnishings, and sculptures, a new campaign of decoration was undertaken in 1614. Fra' Cosimo Piazza painted broad friezes below the carved and gilded wood ceilings of *salone* C5 and neighboring room C4, and possibly in C1 as well, in 1614–15.[133] The paintings in the *salone* included scenes from the story of the ancient Roman Marc Anthony and Cleopatra[134]—an obvious reference to the young prince Marcantonio Borghese. On a visit to the palace on 16 July 1614, Paul V admired the work already done, noting that it was proceeding quickly, but with sureness and spirit, and in an innovative technique of oil on wet plaster.[135] Giovan Francesco Guerrieri and several assistants painted in the palace from November 1615 until September 1618.[136] He concentrated on painting friezes at the top of the walls of rooms C12, C13, and C14. The monochromatic frieze in the first room contained trophies and arms framed by putti. In the second room, C13, was an ambitious allegorical cycle, the four walls bearing the respective Triumphs of the Liberal Arts (Parnassus), Religion, the Sciences, and Virtue, set in landscapes. The third room, the former chapel, featured landscapes flanked by emblematic figures. The first two rooms had been neglected in 1610, falling outside the sequence of Giovanni Battista's anterooms; and

C14 had earlier been outfitted as a chapel. Now the three were seen as the first three rooms of a major apartment toward the garden.

The work of refurbishing continued in other rooms of the *piano nobile,* on the southeast and southwest sides of the courtyard. The ceiling of *sala vecchia* C19 was entirely redone, with twenty paintings on canvas, each measuring 10 × 6½ *palmi,* set into its newly gilded framework. Four mezzanine windows were filled in (cf. Falda's section, Fig. 26), and painters worked on scaffolding below the ceiling, presumably painting a frieze.[137] Two mezzanine windows were closed and twenty rosettes were carved for the coffers of the beamed ceiling in neighboring C18.[138] Corner room C16 received a frieze painted on canvas by Guerrieri; the ceilings of this room and adjacent C17 were gilded and fitted with twenty-four wood rosettes.[139] The ceilings of rooms C1, C2, and C3 were similarly gilded, and C3 also was painted.[140] Finally, a new, exceptionally large *credenza* and baldacchino were made for the *salone* C5, and the enclosing railing was enlarged to accommodate them.[141] In the summer of 1618 the pope stopped by the palace and was pleased to see the new paintings and fittings.[142]

While all this work was in progress, the palace seems to have been inhabited only by Francesco and Ortensia Borghese and their servants.[143] Marcantonio was still in residence in the Borgo. The widowed Virginia, suffering the displeasure of Paul V, had retired to the Clarissan convent at S. Lorenzo in Panisperna.[144] One of Guerrieri's assistants, the landscape painter Abelle, was living in room C13 while painting there.[145] Still, rooms free of scaffolding might be used for special occasions: in July 1614 Paul V had lunch in the palace, "in the new rooms," perhaps in the loggia overlooking the Ripetta, while Scipione, Francesco, and Marcantonio ate "in the ground-floor rooms," the rooms of the sculpture gallery A4, A5, A6, A8.[146]

As the time of the long-anticipated marriage grew near, specific preparations had to be made.

For the day of the wedding feast, additional furnishings were required: long tables and shelves for the *credenza* and *bottiglieria,* and extra tables for the *famiglia* in the *tinelli.*[147] For the permanent accommodation of the bride's women attendants, a new women's apartment was needed. Attic rooms E1–E4, constructed and modestly finished in 1607, were subdivided and remodeled for Princess Camilla's women (Fig. 34).[148] Seven small rooms with sloping wood ceilings and small windows to the northeast opened to a segmented corridor. A pantry and kitchen for the women were probably in the two corner rooms E8 and E9; the latter was fitted with lavatories.[149] A door was made to the women's apartment, and next to it was installed a wooden turnbox *(rota)* for passing food to the women.[150] A niche for a latrine was made in the spiral stair S4.[151]

At the same time an apartment was prepared for the women attendants of Marcantonio's mother, Virginia. Mezzanine rooms B2–B10 (see Fig. 29), nicely finished and used by Giovanni Battista and Virginia just a few years earlier, were in need of repair by 1615, when many cracks were patched and other work done.[152] In 1619 these rooms were divided between the women and the pages by the filling in of three doorways in the partition between the two suites of rooms. A partition was made to contain the turnbox, and a toilet (with pipes going down to the cellar) and lavatory were installed. A window to the ball court was walled up (suggesting that the women's rooms extended along the garden as far as vestibule B18), as was a door at the top of a stair to the mezzanines. The women's apartment was further secluded by a gate in the passage preceding it — presumably vestibule B18.[153]

The mezzanine rooms where the pages lived received twelve new window leaves — that is, enough for six mezzanine windows. The lavatory was removed (presumably that installed in the tiny room B5 in 1608), but a new dining table and *credenza* for the pages' meals were provided.[154] In 1626 there were ten pages, overseen by their master Don Giovanni Battista Baratti and served by one Horatio Grassi.[155]

The *palafrenieri*'s rooms were just below those of the pages, on the ground floor toward the street. Because of the dampness of those ground-floor rooms, A11 and A12 received wood floors raised 1½ *palmi* above the pavement. There was a door at the foot of the stair S7 that exited directly to the street. Their rooms were equipped with a toilet, a lavatory, and a fountain, the drain of which passed through the wall to the street. The long dining table, 13½ × 4 *palmi,* would have accommodated the twenty-five *palafrenieri* in the prince's service in 1626.[156] These were apparently not lodgings but day rooms for the use of the *palafrenieri* while they were away from their posts of duty in the *sala;* their actual place of residence was a house on the piazza.[157]

Their pages, *palafrenieri,* and women attendants settled on the ground floor, in the mezzanine apartments, and in the attic, Marcantonio, Camilla, and Virginia, along with Francesco and Ortensia, found their apartments on the *piano nobile* and *terzo piano.*

The prince's main apartment, on the *piano nobile,* must have included the newly decorated rooms on the southwest side of the courtyard — among them the chapel C3, for which new fittings were made in 1620, including a wooden balustered enclosure 15 *palmi* high and 21 *palmi* broad, two grilled windows, and a baldacchino whose frame measured 10 × 7 *palmi.*[158] The new enclosure would allow passage through the chapel to anterooms and eventually an audience room. The cornice of the coffered ceiling of the prince's bedroom required repair in 1620; it was probably one of the rooms in the south angle of the palace, which had ceilings of this type.[159] Meanwhile his uncle Francesco was using the rooms on the *piano nobile* opening from the northeast end of the *sala vecchia;* his revetments hung in the *sala vecchia,* the "Anticamera Falza" C20, the "room before the chapel" C22, and chapel C26.[160]

At the time of his death on 20 June 1620, Francesco was also using a suite of eight rooms on the

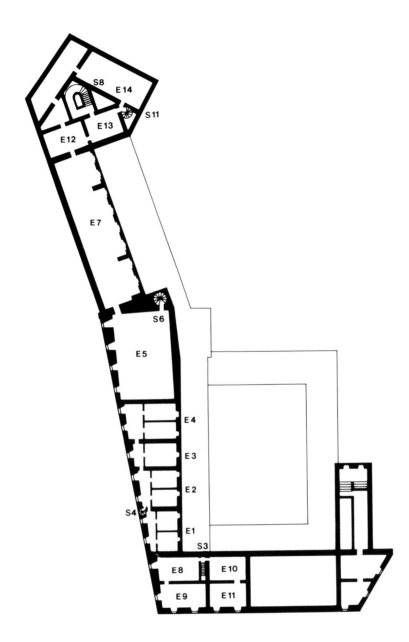

34   Palazzo Borghese, 1620, attic, reconstruction (author)

terzo piano, above those of Marcantonio.[161] Marcantonio quickly took these for himself: by August 1620 he had had the plaster repaired.[162] By October 1620 he had had reassembled in one of the rooms a large cabinet for the storage of clothing, removed from his wife's rooms. Thirteen *palmi* high, 9 *palmi* deep, and 19 *palmi* wide, it was fitted with extensions of 1½ *palmi* on each side so that it would fill the northeast end of room D25. Not surprisingly, this monumental piece of furniture gave its name to the "Antica-mera . . . dove è l'Armario" or "stantia dell'Armaria."[163] The "guardarobba nuova" was then formed in the three neighboring rooms, D26, D27, D28.[164]

Camilla used the rooms on the third floor toward the garden, D11–D16, where Virginia had earlier lived; the large cabinet later moved to her husband's rooms was installed here early in 1620.[165] The rooms were equipped with a toilet (probably that installed in D15 in 1609) and were served by two spiral stairs S6 and S11.[166]

Virginia Borghese seems to have recovered from the pope's displeasure, for by 1620 she had resumed her place in the palace. She must have had rooms on the *piano nobile* or *terzo piano* toward the street in 1620, for two new window frames for "the rooms where she sleeps," with both glazed leaves and shutters, measured 10½ × 5½ *palmi*—dimensions appropriate for those parts of the palace.[167] At the same time she must have had other rooms, for a wood ceiling 27½ × 23 *palmi* and a window frame of 5¼ × 4½ *palmi* were made for her rooms "sotto tetto"; that description and the window size suggest the third-floor rooms toward the garden, but the ceiling size does not fit any of those rooms.[168]

In 1619 and 1620 much work was done to prepare the offices for Marcantonio's service, for they had been neglected and unused since his father's death in December 1609. The private kitchen and staff kitchen, with their connecting passage and adjacent loggia, were refurbished with new window frames, doors, furnishings (including a cupboard for keeping meat cool), a loft for the cooks in the *cucina segreta,* and a room in

the *cucina comune* for the kitchen boys. Partitions were built, and the roof was remade.[169] Marcantonio's kitchens remained separate from those of his uncle Francesco.[170] Adjustments were made to the *tinello* and its *loggetta,* 29½ *palmi* long; they stood next to the kitchens and opened to the kitchen courtyard.[171] The roof of Francesco's *tinello,* separate from that of Marcantonio, was repaired.[172] The *dispensa,* in the same area, was remodeled, with new partitions, an enlarged window, and walled-up doors (including one that had exited to the street); and it was fitted with racks for meats, a corner partition behind which the quartermaster could sleep, and other woodwork.[173] In the palace proper, the *credenza* received a fireplace, brought from a room on an upper floor, and a sink *(sciacquatore)* with its drain; doors and shelves were installed; many new furnishings were made, including tables for use in the *sala,* tables at which the carvers would perform their service, and presses for napkins and other linens.[174] A table was made for the use of the *bottiglieria* in the *sala.*[175] Furnishings were made for the bookkeeping office.[176] Work was done around the latrines, presumably those beyond the north corner of the courtyard; and windows were fitted with bars in the janitor's room opposite the latrines.[177]

Before the establishment of the "guardarobba nuova," there were two separate *guardarobe* for Marcantonio and Francesco. In September 1619 various furnishings and six large window frames, 10⅙ × 5¼ *palmi,* were made for the *guarda-roba;*[178] the number and size of the windows suggest Francesco's *guardaroba* D29, over the *sala vecchia.* After Francesco's death, nine large storage cabinets, each 9 × 9 × 3 *palmi,* were taken from Francesco's *guardaroba* and installed in that of Marcantonio, above his *sala,* arranged in two rows.[179]

Rooms for many gentlemen and officers of Marcantonio's princely household were found within the palace, in attic rooms and elsewhere; and others were placed in houses in the neighborhood.[180]

These several provisions for the operation of

35   Palazzo Borghese, from west, detail of Specchi engraving (I.C.C.D., Rome, ser. N, no. 935)

Marcantonio's household were made within the confines of the palace as already constructed by 1614. It was a matter of shifting, shaping, and furnishing the matrix of rooms already established.

Scipione Moves In

Yet another major rearrangement within the palace was occasioned by the death of Paul V in 1621 and Cardinal Scipione Borghese's consequent decision to move to the palace. He had been living in the Palazzo Giraud-Torlonia, Giovanni Battista's one-time residence in the Borgo, which he had bought when Giovanni Battista had moved to the new palace in 1609.[181] He now took over the entire wing toward the Ripetta, displacing Camilla and Virginia, as well as Virginia's women attendants, who had been living there. A first requirement for his reception of guests was a bell to be rung on the arrival of persons of high rank, and this was installed within a month of Paul V's death.[182]

With the removal of women from the Ripetta wing, Scipione could remove the women's mezzanine apartment and its characteristic turnbox; the *rota* was gone by August.[183] Instead, the mezzanine rooms toward the garden were remodeled for the cardinal's *maestro di camera,* and those toward the street (where Marcantonio's pages had only recently been housed) accommodated the *maestro di casa.*[184]

Scipione himself had rooms on all the other levels of the wing (see Figs. 28, 30, 31). He used the *salone* C5 (for the entrance to the palace from via di Ripetta was only a service entrance), installing there a new balustrade around the *credenza.*[185] Nine new mezzanine windows were installed above the windows of his apartment on the *piano nobile* — that is, in the suite of five rooms toward the street and the spiral stair and loggia beyond.[186] The "capelletta nuova" of his apartment, C7, was redecorated with painting and gilding.[187] The cardinal slept upstairs, toward the street; his new bedroom window had four glass leaves and four opaque leaves.[188] Also on the *terzo piano,* he outfitted room D23 as his study, with shelves brought from the palace in the Borgo; and he had it redecorated with paintings and gilding.[189] Loggia D20 was enclosed; the window frames, each with eight glazed leaves, filled the entire width of the openings (14 *palmi*), and additional panels fit beneath the semicircular arches and behind the balustrades below.[190] The westward-facing loggia would have been a veritable sun-room in the winter — quite different from the arrangement shown in Specchi's engraving of ca. 1704 (Fig. 35), which has three normal windows set in opaque surrounds under the arches. The lower loggia C31 was left open to the hanging garden but was supplied with a wooden slatted shutter.[191] Scipione also enjoyed the ground-floor apartment — that is, the sculpture gallery,[192] which he transformed into a painting gallery in 1625 when he transported much of the statuary to the Villa Pinciana.[193] By 1638, when he published a guide to Rome, Totti could write of "the finest paintings of our times," and of "a most famous gallery" at the Palazzo Borghese.[194]

When he moved to the palace at the Ripetta, Scipione Borghese brought with him his *famiglia* — 224 persons in 1621, considerably more than the 142 persons in the service of Marc-antonio.[195] They needed places to work and places to live. The cardinal had to outfit the full range of offices, because those already existing in the palace were being used by Marcantonio and his household. These included *credenza, botti-glieria,* kitchen, cellar for charcoal, *dispensa, ti-nello,* bookkeeping office, archive, *guardaroba,* and stables.[196] The stables were clearly outside his part of the palace: one was in the part of the palace "toward Monte d'Oro"; another, for mules, was in "the house on the corner toward S. Lorenzo"; there was a new stable "in the house where the Ripetta dogana is [*or* was]"; another "stalla vecchia" was noted as in the palace, with a door toward a courtyard; another was "in Bal-duino's house."[197] A carriage room was in a house at piazza Nicosia.[198] The *credenza* and bookkeeping office were "in the palace," oppo-site one another, and a door from the *credenza* led to the staff kitchen,[199] probably A14, which had been constructed for this function in 1612–14. There was also a private kitchen,[200] reason-ably A15. Basements were put to use for the stor-age of charcoal and also for a *dispensa.*[201] A document speaks of the storage and dispensing of wine in the ball court,[202] but perhaps this dis-pensing *tinello* was in a basement under the ball court, since Marcantonio seems to have contin-ued to use that athletic facility: he retained an attendant for it in his *famiglia.*[203] Marcantonio also maintained an interest in the bathing apart-ment in Scipione's wing of the palace, for it was he who paid for repairs around the water heater of the *stufa* in 1623.[204]

While the *maestro di casa* and *maestro di ca-mera* had mezzanine apartments in the palace, other officers lived in nearby houses. The *mag-giordomo* lived in "the house on the corner," and the Cavaliere Ansidei lived in a house toward the river.[205] Other gentlemen lived in a house in pi-azza Nicosia.[206] Rooms were prepared for several

other persons, but their locations, whether in the palace or in nearby houses, are uncertain. As usual, there were lofts for stable hands and rooms for coachmen in the stables.[207]

Scipione continued to improve his apart-ments. In 1622 and 1623 friezes were painted in his rooms, and in 1631 there was more painting and gilding in four rooms of his third-floor apartment.[208] In 1626 he built a stair S12 leading from the garden up to the third floor (shown in Figs. 42, 47, 48), thereby providing a more direct path from garden to studies C35 and D23 and the two loggias than had Maderno's articulated se-quence of passages and stairs.[209]

Meanwhile, Marcantonio, his wife, and his mother were restricted to those parts of the pal-ace that framed the courtyard.

In 1623 the loggia on the third floor, on the southwest side of the courtyard, was enclosed to make four additional rooms, D37–D40 (Fig. 36).[210] They would have been approached from stair S1 and the open loggias, for stair S5 was then the domain of Cardinal Scipione. The rectangu-lar rooms fit within the regular bay system of the loggia. With the old rooms toward the piazza, with which they were connected, they formed an *appartamento doppio.* They had no fireplaces and, with windows to the northeast, would have been comfortable only in the summer; in contrast, the four rooms to the southwest had been equipped with fireplaces from the beginning. *Sala* D40 was the largest of the new rooms; its wall 60½ *palmi* in length required plastering after the re-moval of the old large windows, and a large opening was replaced by a pipe for the rope of the bell installed in the stair by Cardinal Scipione in 1621.[211] Rooms D39, D38, and D37 were called simply the first, second, and third rooms, respec-tively; but, when friezes were painted, room D38 was more precisely identified as a study.[212] Room D2 was "the room where he sleeps in the winter," presumably for Marcantonio.[213] A new small door was made to stair S3, so that the rooms could be served from that stair as well as from S4. Three hundred forty-six hooks were installed for

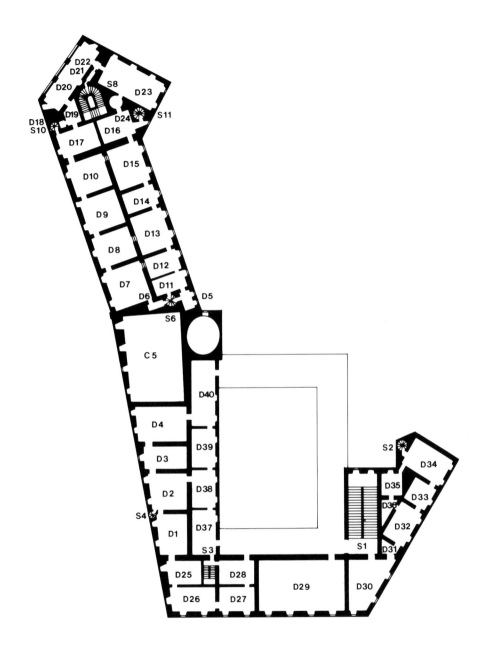

36   Palazzo Borghese, 1623, *terzo piano,* reconstruction (author)

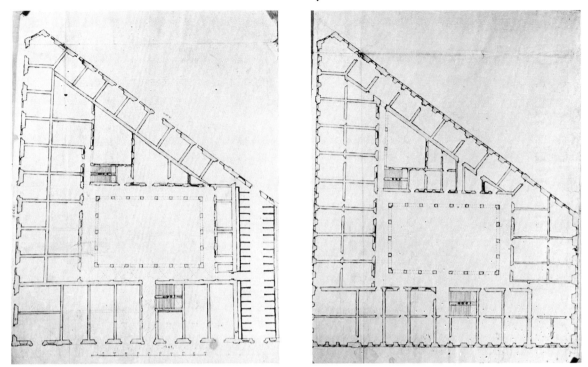

37   Palazzo della Famiglia Borghese, (left) ground floor and (right) apartment level (Joseph Connors)

revetments, and Giovanni Serodine painted friezes 2½ *palmi* high in rooms D37, D38, and D39.[214] These rooms were surely for Marcantonio. The document of construction makes it clear that the new rooms are an addition to the apartment toward the piazza, where the prince slept — the apartment that Marcantonio had taken over on the death of his uncle Francesco in June 1620. The set of eight rooms would have provided him comfortable and well-appointed quarters for both summer and winter.

Marcantonio maintained an apartment on the *piano nobile,* where three fireplaces were repaired in 1623, in addition to his apartment on the *terzo piano.*[215] This was presumably the apartment prepared for him in 1619, the rooms between the two *saloni* (see Fig. 30). In January 1622 the travertine frames of three doors in this apartment were removed and turned around[216] — presumably to reorient them to the *sala vecchia*

C19, which the young prince might use now that his cousin Cardinal Scipione was using *sala* C5. He could ascend easily to his private rooms on the *terzo piano* by means of stairs S3 and S4.

Virginia had an apartment of at least three rooms, which were plastered in 1623.[217] These must have had a prominent location in the palace, for in that same year she was attended by pages, *palafrenieri,* chamber assistants, porters, and coachmen, as well as by women companions.[218] Perhaps she lived in the rooms to the north of the *sala vecchia,* which were renovated in January 1622.[219] There is almost no sign of Camilla in the documents. Ortensia died in 1620.[220] The women attendants were still in the attic apartment on the southwest side of the courtyard.

The arrival of Scipione's household in the palace may have prompted some work for the accommodation of Marcantonio's staff. The *bot-*

PALAZZO DELLA FAMIGLIA DELL' EC.S.PNE BORGHESE SV LA PIAZZA INCONTRO IL PALAZZO DI SEC.ARCH.DI ANT. DE BATTISTIS.

38   Palazzo della Famiglia Borghese, façade, engraving by Falda (Biblioteca Apostolica Vaticana)

tiglieria was moved to a new location, perhaps to make way for Scipione's needs.[221] A new partition separated the *credenza* and the bookkeeping office, apparently on the ground floor of the palace, toward the courtyard.[222] A new *tinello* was built near the kitchens.[223] Many houses in the neighborhood were repaired for members of Marcantonio's *famiglia,* who seem to have lived there in apartments of one, two, or three rooms.[224]

Scipione, Marcantonio, Camilla, and Virginia had hardly settled themselves into their newly remodeled and refurbished apartments when their cousin Pier Maria arrived in Rome to receive the cardinal's hat and live with them in Palazzo Borghese. Born in Siena in 1599 or 1600, the son of Curzio Borghese and Silvia Saraceni, he was only a year or two older than Prince Marcantonio. He was made cardinal by Urban VIII on 7 October 1624, along with Antonio Barberini and Lorenzo Magalotti. His residence and that of his *famiglia* are recorded in the palace in parish census records,[225] but it is hard to imagine where the young cardinal might have been

housed, with proper decorum, in the already full palace. Perhaps he was able to share the parallel suites in the Ripetta wing with Cardinal Scipione. At some time he had an apartment including a chapel "toward the piazza nova" — a designation indicating the rooms on the southwest side of the courtyard, where Marcantonio had been living in 1623. Later he moved to an apartment that had previously been occupied by Virginia, also including a chapel, "toward the street that goes toward Monte d'Oro" — that is, the rooms north of the *sala vecchia.*[226] It was in this well-furnished apartment, complete with wall hangings, that he died on 15 June 1642.

The very large number of staff members (142 for Marcantonio and 224 for Scipione in 1621) must have strained the resources of rental housing in the neighborhood and presented problems of management. In 1624 Scipione undertook to build a new palace — actually an apartment building — for his *famiglia.* Houses had been bought in the area to the southwest of the recently cleared piazza Borghese in 1611–14, and Scipione made further purchases here in 1626 and 1627. The land was cleared, and the new "Palazzo della Famiglia Borghese" was built in 1624–26, with an extension to the rear in 1627 (Figs. 37, 38).[227] Stables were on the ground floor, and four stories of apartments, most of two rooms, were arranged around the central courtyard. A picture of a modest but comfortable life in one of the apartments is given by an inventory of the goods of Don Francesco Ceccarelli, who lived in three rooms with his mother, Prudentia, and died there in April 1643.[228] Although totally unlike its parent palace in plan and internal arrangement, the new palace was rather similar to the older in appearance (cf. Fig. 15). It presented a broad and unified face to the piazza, reflecting that of the palace on the other side. Together, the two controlled the large volume of the piazza Borghese, or piazza Sterrata, magnifying the presence of the Borghese family in the neighborhood (Figs. 39, 40).

The frequent rearrangements within the palace between 1618 and 1624, to accommodate changing constellations of inhabitants, did not affect the building's outward appearance. Changes took place within the almost neutral matrix of its walls and floors, behind the reserved mask of its façades. Cardinals' and princes' apartments were interchangeable, as were those of men and women (except that a noblewoman's attendants must be provided with a turnbox). Mezzanine rooms for principal residents could be turned to offices or quarters for staff members. Rooms could be improved by the addition of paintings or other decoration. Chapels could be inserted or removed. Services could be rearranged. Open spaces could be enclosed. Circulation could be rerouted. There seems to be almost no formal necessity or controlling design for the architectural work in the palace in these years. Rather, the general scheme of strings of rooms opening out from large *saloni,* arranged in four or five stories, provided a hospitable if inarticulate setting for the life of the noble family.

The architects who oversaw the work in these years are not well-known figures. Hibbard noted

39   Palazzo della Famiglia Borghese, Palazzo Borghese, and piazza Borghese (Totti, 1638) (Biblioteca Apostolica Vaticana)

that Scipione's revisions to the west wing were undertaken first by Giovanni Van Zanten, who was both papal architect and Scipione's architect until his death in 1621; he was succeeded by Antonio Battisti, who in turn was replaced by Sergio Venturi.[229] Meanwhile, Gasparo de' Vecchi worked for Marcantonio: he signed a *misura* for Marcantonio on 18 July 1620,[230] and he was listed as "Architect" in the roll of Marcantonio's household in 1626.[231] Battisti also worked for Marcantonio, for he signed *misure* for the construction and decoration of the prince's new rooms on the *terzo piano* in 1623.[232] Venturi was apparently in charge of the construction of the Palazzo della Famiglia Borghese.[233] The docu-

PALAZZO DELL ECC.ᵐᵒ SIG. PRENCIPE BORGHESE.
Architettura di Martino Lunghi il vecchio.
1. *Facciata principale uerso la Piazza.* 2. *Altra Facciata uerso la strada deCondotti.* 3. *Loggia uerso Ripetta.* 4. *Palazzo della Famiglia di sua Ecc.ᵃ*
Datò in Luce da Domenico deRossi dalle sue Stampe in Roma alla Pace con Priuil. del S.P. e Licenza de Superiori.

40   Piazza Borghese and Palazzo Borghese, engraving by Specchi (Biblioteca Apostolica Vaticana)

mentation does not allow us to clarify the artistic personality of any of these architects, and it may be that the tasks at hand called more for technical competence than for an architectural imagination. In spite of the almost constant flux of inhabitants and architectural activity in 1618–24, the palace remained curiously stagnant with respect to architectural control.

Of all the architectural rearrangements in the wake of Marcantonio's marriage and Scipione's move to the palace, none affected the image of the family in the city more than the construction of accommodations for their household staff—the Palazzo della Famiglia Borghese. Totti recognized this in 1638, when in his guide to Rome he illustrated not the elegant southeast façade of the palace but the piazza framed by the south-west façade, the Palazzo della Famiglia Borghese, and the line of bollards with chains (see Fig. 39).[234] Paul V had wanted to improve the setting of the palace and strengthen its relation to the via del Corso;[235] with the construction of the new building and the consequent definition of the piazza, that relationship was discarded in favor of an autonomous Borghese arena. The source of this momentous idea remains lost.

Giovanni Battista and Eleonora Remodel

By the 1670s the only principal residents of the Palazzo Borghese were Prince Giovanni Battista (grandson of Marcantonio, born in 1639; see Fig. 19), his wife Eleonora Boncompagni, and their three young sons.[236] Giovanni Battista's father

Paolo had died on 24 June 1646, only twenty-two years old; and his widowed mother, Olimpia Aldobrandini, had married Camillo Pamphili on 10 February 1647. His grandfather died in January 1658. His sister Virginia became the wife of Agostino Chigi, nephew of Pope Alexander VII, in July 1658; and Giovanni Battista married Eleonora the same year, 22 October 1658.

Giovanni Battista undertook a major remodeling of the palace in 1671. He concentrated on the parts to the south and west. His architect was Carlo Rainaldi, son of Girolamo, who decades earlier had prepared the plan shown in Figure 27. The masonry matrix yielded to Rainaldi's designs, and a coherence and homogeneity lacking in the earlier palace at last emerged.

Although no drawings survive to reveal Rainaldi's thinking in graphic terms, the document of masonry construction from 1671 to 1676 is wonderfully detailed and indicates something of motivation and process as well as results.[237]

The ground floor to the west of entrance A3 was remodeled to provide major apartments for prince and princess (Fig. 41). Service functions — kitchens and rooms for *palafrenieri* — were removed. The floor level of rooms in the west wing was raised to the level of rooms A4, A5, and A6, and full basements were excavated below, thereby surely alleviating the problem of moisture that had prompted the installation of wood floors in A11 and A12 in 1619. The ground-floor mezzanines were removed (except for B13 and B14),[238] so that the rooms were appropriately lofty in spite of their raised floors; and vaults *a schifo* were installed. The wall between A11 and A12 was removed, as was the now useless stair S7, to make one large room A11–12 toward the street; and a new wall was inserted in A8 to form squarish A8a and long A8b. Everywhere walls were augmented or shaved back to regularize the volumes of the rooms and correct those deformities that had displeased Paul V in 1608.[239]

This work provided the nucleus of two similar and parallel apartments — that toward the street for the prince and that toward the garden for the princess. Without fireplaces and on the ground floor, adjacent to the garden, they were naturally summer apartments. Although not so designated in the document of construction, they are called summer apartments in guidebooks of the early eighteenth century; and it was here that Nathaniel Hawthorne so chilled on 25 February 1858.[240] The couple shared the first three rooms, A4, A5, and A6. The prince's anteroom A10 was followed by "His Excellency's large audience room" A11–12 and the "last room where the *zampanaro* is," A13 — a representational bedroom with a splendidly equipped bed. Toward the garden were the princess's anteroom A8a, the "Signora Principessa's large audience room" A8b, and A9, the room containing the princess's *zampanaro*. A flight of nine semielliptical steps descended from the door of the princess's audience room to the garden.[241] As summer rooms, the apartments had fountains and other appropriate furnishings: in A5, a fountain and large table of porphyry; in A11–12, a silver fountain; in A8a, an oval porphyry table; in A8b, two fountains, two tables, and two vases, all of alabaster. The central painted rectangular panels of the vaults were enframed with stucco ornaments. The walls were neither painted nor provided with hooks for revetment, for they were to be covered with paintings from the family's extensive collection. Doorways were shifted, one by one, so that the prince's apartment would be unified by an unbroken vista from the old *dispensa* A2 to the right of the entrance through his suite of rooms; and doorways in the princess's rooms were similarly shifted to allow a shorter vista from the newly opened passage A7 through her three rooms.[242]

Beyond the parallel suites, room A14, formerly the kitchen, was remodeled as a short gallery, and a stair of three flights was built to connect the gallery with a mezzanine at first preserved above it. The old kitchen A15 was converted into a chapel as a terminus for the prince's suite, with A16 beyond as a room for hearing mass privately. Then plans changed, and the idea

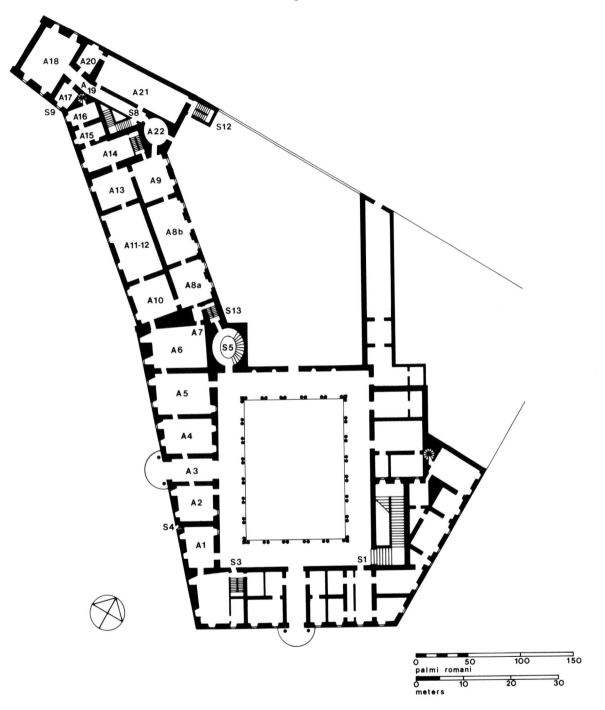

41   Palazzo Borghese, 1671, ground floor, first plan, reconstruction (author)

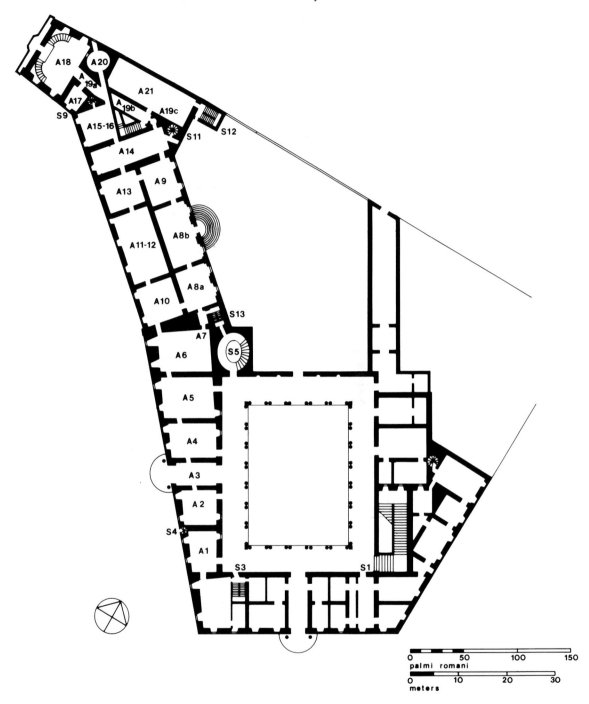

42   Palazzo Borghese, 1671–76, ground floor, reconstruction (author)

43   Palazzo Borghese, gallery A14 (I.C.C.D., Rome, ser. E, no. 42206)

of extending an infinite vista through the apartment swept all before it (Fig. 42). The newly constructed stair S14 and the mezzanine above the gallery were torn out,[243] oval vestibule A22 was destroyed, and gallery A14 was extended to a length of 72½ *palmi* and splendidly decorated (Fig. 43). The new chapel A15 was demolished and thrown together with A16 to form the nearly square "stanza dipinta."[244] Passages were cut to allow the vista to continue across the old corridor A19, channeled by a new diagonal wall bisecting the corridor. The old changing room A20 for the ball court was reshaped into an elliptical chapel; and a new window was cut in its exterior wall, so that the visual axis continued beyond the confines of the palace, through the neighboring "palazzetto" owned by the Borghese, across the Tiber, and on to the horizon.[245] The princess's enfilade was extended too, albeit not so dramatically as that of her husband, through the enlarged gallery A14 to a tiny elliptical chamber A19c, its vault measuring but 7 × 6 *palmi*. The southeast wall of the gallery A14 took account of the eccentric location of the two doorways that allowed the two vistas (see Fig. 43), and two feigned doorways were added to establish a balanced composition.

The importance of clear passage and uninterrupted vista is shown in the design and construction of the new passage A7 connecting room A6 with the princess's anteroom A8a. Previously, one had had to pass from the corner of A6 through the rectangular passage connected with the main elliptical stair and then to the loggia/gallery A8; or one entered the spiral stair S6 and then descended four steps to A8 (see Fig. 28). Now the lowest nineteen of the 125 steps of stair S6 were removed and a beam inserted to support the rest of the stair so that a passage could be opened from A6, with its jamb "aligned with the door that passes into the audience hall [A8b]."[246] Then a double-ramp stair was made in the old passage A7, rising to the mezzanine level, where a connection was made with the spiral stair S6

(Fig. 44, see Fig. 42). The way from the anterooms to the princess's apartment was now clear, but anyone wanting to ascend the service stair had to begin in rectangular S13 and then transfer to spiral stair S6 at mezzanine level.

Giovanni Battista was so pleased with the long vista through his apartment that he frequently brought guests to see it, even during construction. Scaffolding had to be taken down for each visit and then reerected, and the prince was charged for the loss of masons' time.[247]

Nicodemus Tessin recorded the splendid fittings of the apartment, its walls covered with 660 paintings; and an inventory of 1693 confirms his account.[248] The first three rooms and those of Giovanni Battista's apartment had red damask *portiere* and matching upholstery, while the princess's rooms were done in green. Each audience room had a baldacchino of appropriate color, and each bedroom (A13, A9), a splendid *zampanaro*. Alabaster doorframes complemented the fountains, tables, and vases of alabaster, silver, and porphyry in several of the rooms. The vaulted ceilings were enriched by stucco enframements, gilding, and painting. The gallery A14 contained twelve porphyry and alabaster busts of emperors and four busts of consuls, two alabaster fountains, and two small tables also of alabaster, along with eight large mirrors painted with putti by Ciro Ferri and flowers by Stanchi. Giovan Francesco Grimaldi directed the work here and designed the elaborate stucco decorations (see Fig. 43).[249] The chapel was also richly stuccoed, and three feigned doors joined with the entrance, the window of the "prospettiva," and the window for hearing mass to complete the symmetrical arrangement around the altar.

These fine rooms seem to have been used for daytime activities but not for sleeping and related personal needs.[250] The beds in A13 and A9 were too splendid for actual sleeping, and they were not supplied with sheets or blankets at the time of the inventory of 1693. There was only one close-stool, in A13. There were no *retrocamere* for

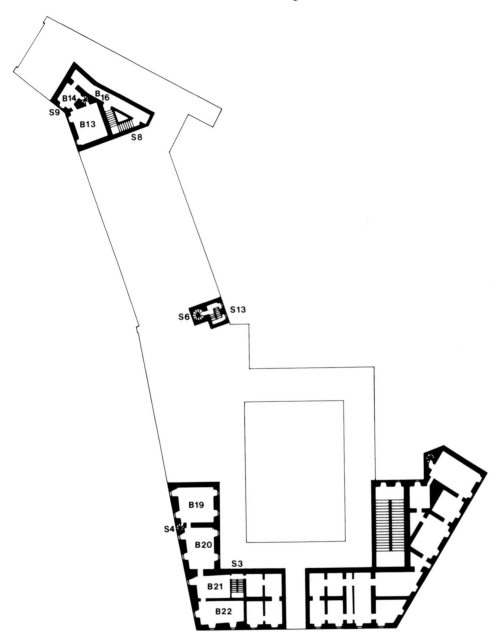

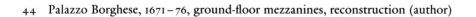

44   Palazzo Borghese, 1671–76, ground-floor mezzanines, reconstruction (author)

service to the bedrooms. Most telling, the all-important vistas penetrated the bedrooms to the rooms beyond—an unthinkable breach of privacy if these were to have been rooms for sleeping, but reasonable enough if the beds remained symbolic. Just a few years earlier Cardinal Flavio Chigi had installed a splendid *zampanaro*, in which he did not sleep, in a richly decorated alcove at the end of his suite of reception rooms (see Fig. 204, C16);[251] the Borghese now joined him in this elaboration of the apartment.

Outside the twin apartments, the bathing room A17 of 1612 still survived, but its facilities for heating water had to be moved from old A16 (now part of the "stanza dipinta") to a basement room below the bath. The spiral stair S9 was extended downward with seven new steps to a basement corridor with access to the water heater; and six steps led to the bathing room, now lower than its remodeled neighbors on the *pian terreno*.[252] Mezzanine rooms B13 and B14 were also retained as part of the bathing suite (Fig. 44): a fireplace was rebuilt in B13, and in 1693 B14 was furnished with a few chairs and a bed, along with "old paintings by Tempesta."[253] On the other side of the bisected corridor, the ball court A21 also survived, but it lost its changing room and spectators' room to the new chapel; it seems to have been used simply for storage. The old *entrone* was divided vertically, with a room for carriages at street level and a richly painted room at the newly established level of the ground-floor apartments (see Fig. 42, A18).[254] Tessin called this upper room an "essahl,"[255] surely not a permanent dining room but—with its painted decoration of landscapes enframed by architectural elements and bas-reliefs and its two corner fountains (Fig. 45)—a place for a pleasant afternoon lunch. Symmetrical curving flights of steps led up to the entrance to the new balcony built out toward the Ripetta; slatted shutters provided privacy for those watching the activity of the busy river port or the landscape beyond from within the covered balcony (Fig. 46; see also Figs. 16,

35). The balcony was not built until spring 1676, and revisions in the corner fountains were made at about the same time.[256]

Rainaldi's reforming completely changed the character of the ground floor (see Fig. 42). In place of the disjointed assemblage of art gallery and assorted service rooms (see Fig. 28), there was now a unified apartment. The axis on which the unity depended was the visual axis from entry A3 through the oval chapel to the view beyond; and it was complemented by a shorter but similarly assertive axis from passage A7 to the "cuppolino" A19c. The rooms now had a uniform floor level, and all were regularized rectangles (except for the regularized ellipses of the two termini, the chapel A20 and the tiny chamber A19c). They were further unified in the sequence of their volumes: the expanding sequence of A4, A5, A6 was drawn in at A10 but released again in the newly enlarged A11–A12, the prince's audience room, then contracted in A13 in preparation for the last rooms leading to the chapel. Reformed A15–A16 was made comparable in volume to A13. Toward the garden, the opening of passage A7 and the insertion of a wall to form A8a and A8b created a similar dynamic sequence of related volumes. The disjunction of new construction of 1610 and the small cells of the old house of Enea Orlandini, previously so apparent, had been erased.

Rainaldi's work on the *piano nobile* was similar in character (Fig. 47). Here too doorways were shifted and rebuilt so that the rooms would be unified by long visual axes—that toward the street extending almost the full length of the building, from the *salone* westward through five rooms to the trapezoidal chapel C30 and eastward through the rooms along the southwest side of the courtyard to corner room C16, and that toward the garden extending from chapel C7 to gallery C35.[257] A telling detail is the revision of the doorways in the circular passage C36: for Maderno, this was an articulating joint, a hinge between the suite of the apartment toward

45   Palazzo Borghese, room A18, west corner (I.C.C.D., Rome, ser. E, no. 42195)

ALTRA VEDVTA DEL PALAZZO DELL'ECC.^o SIG.^r PRENCIPE BORGHESE
Architettura di Martino Lunchi il Vecchio
1 Facciata principale nella Piazza, 2. Loggia uerso Ripetta, Architettura di Flaminio Pontio. 3.Porta con loggia sopra fatta di nuouo che corisponde alla Galleria, Architett. del Caŭ Rainaldi. 4.Fianco uerso la Piazza di Monte d'Oro, 5.Piazza Borghese. 6. Strada de Condotti .

46 Palazzo Borghese, from west, engraving by Specchi (Biblioteca Apostolica Vaticana)

the garden and the gallery, and it separated as much as it connected; for Rainaldi the tiny rotunda is quintessentially a passage, and he shifts the doorway to the gallery to align it with the other. Similarly, doors between rooms C27 and C28 and between C11 and C15 are rebuilt to align them with the windows in those rooms.[258] Again similarly, Maderno's vertical articulation of circulation was undone as Rainaldi extended the spiral service stair S11 downward to the ground floor, into the area of the now demolished elliptical vestibule, with twenty-eight new steps (see Figs. 28, 42).[259]

The rooms of the *piano nobile* were generally refurbished, with the cleaning and restoration of painted friezes in eight rooms with wood ceilings

and the restoration of stuccoes in the three vaulted rooms C27, C28, C35 and the vaulted loggia C31. Pavements were redone and fireplaces were replaced. Eight hundred fifty hooks were installed for revetments.

As on the ground floor, so too on the *piano nobile* the rooms toward the street are assigned to Giovanni Battista and those toward the garden to his wife, Eleonora. Room C8 is called "anticamera," and room C10 is "His Excellency's audience room." Room C12 is Eleonora's first "anticamera," but the "Signora Principessa's audience room" is shifted farther back in her suite, to room C15—probably because C14 was deemed too small for that function. Eleonora's chapel would be C7, accessible from the *sala* as

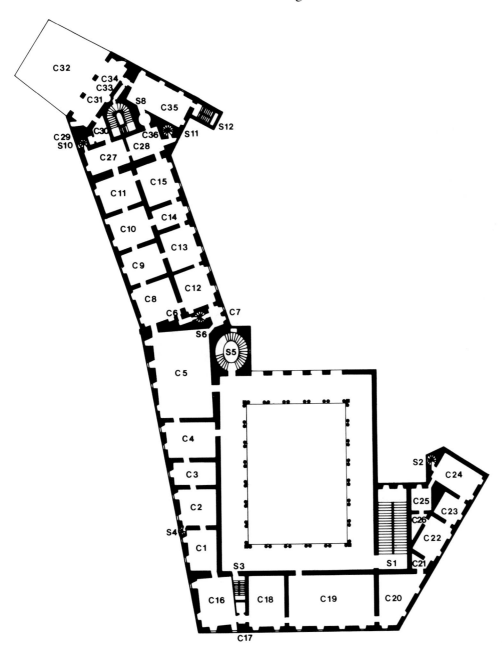

47   Palazzo Borghese, 1671–76, *piano nobile,* reconstruction (author)

well as from her first anteroom; and Giovanni Battista would have used chapel C30. As below, the *appartamento doppio* is not exploited for thermal comfort; rooms to the southwest and northeast alike have fireplaces, and it seems that both prince and princess would use their apartments during the winter.

Similar refurbishing accompanied the shifting of doorways in the rooms around the courtyard, from *salone* C5 around to the angled corner room C20.

In the apartment opening southeastward from the *salone*, room C4 is called "anticamera," and C3 is a chapel. C2, C1, and C16 followed en suite, and the apartment was now continued downward via stair S3 to a group of four intimate mezzanine rooms, B22, B21, and newly built B20 and B19 (see Fig. 44).[260] From November 1671 to 16 January 1673 (with one additional bit of work on 17 October 1673), Gaspard Dughet, Francesco Lauri, Luigi Garzi, and others were paid for their painting of landscapes and mythological scenes in the two new rooms, called simply "His Excellency's mezzanines" or the "new mezzanine."[261] Tessin, who entered the group of four rooms from stair S3, found their walls hung with red damask and gold braid.[262] Low-ceilinged and oriented to the southwest, they must have been an intimate winter apartment for Giovanni Battista.[263] The double leaves of the windows suggest that he would have slept there,[264] likely in B21 or B22, with "gallariola"[265] B20 and its painted companion as rooms for private enjoyment in their traditional position beyond the bedroom. The little apartment of private rooms would therefore contribute significantly to the usefulness of the major apartment on the *piano nobile* above, whose rooms were too few to suit a noble resident.

Tessin noted a second mezzanine apartment of four rooms opening from stair S3. These rooms, to the left of the southeast entrance to the palace, must have been those occupied in 1607 and 1608 by Francesco Borghese's butler and carver.[266]

The removal of a billiards table from the *sala grande* to the angled corner room C20 may signal the residence of the three Borghese boys in that part of the palace.[267] A single notice of two new window sashes measuring 10¼ × 5 *palmi* for "the rooms of the Signorini"[268] suggests that they had rooms on the *piano nobile* — reasonably those in the eastern part of the palace. Born in 1660, 1662, and 1663, respectively, Marcantonio III, Scipione, and Paolo were still young enough to be attended by women in 1671.[269]

On the *terzo piano* of the Ripetta wing, where Cardinal Scipione Borghese had installed his personal quarters in 1621, rooms were remodeled according to ideals of regularity and homogeneity (Fig. 48). There were two apartments, but their occupants are not noted in the document of construction. Three rooms of the "apartment toward the street," D7, D8, and D9, were refurbished with little work. The rooms toward the garden were so extensively reworked that they deserved the appellation "appartamento restaurato." The floor of the apartment was raised 1¼ *palmi* to make it level with that of the rooms toward the street, and the old steps in the doorways between the two apartments were removed. The exterior wall of rooms D11 – D14 toward the garden was raised 16½ *palmi* to bring the rooms to the height of D15 and the apartment toward the street, and an additional stretch of wall 10½ *palmi* high was raised for attic rooms above the "appartamento restaurato." Partitions between the rooms were similarly heightened. Door and window openings were shifted. New wood ceilings and window frames were made for rooms D11 – D14.[270] The ceilings were painted and gilded (in D15 as well), and friezes were painted around the newly heightened walls of D11 – D14. A proper public entrance was given to the two parallel apartments by the construction of a flight of eight steps from the large oval stair S5 to passage D5, and by the significant alignment of the door of the passage with those of the "appar-

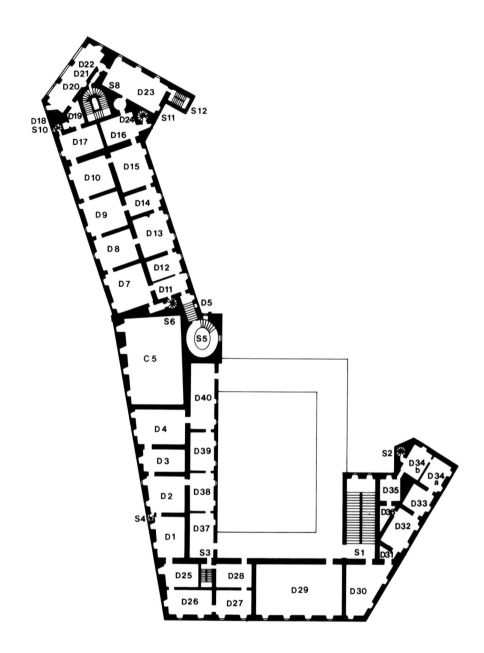

48 Palazzo Borghese, 1671–76, *terzo piano*, reconstruction (author)

tamento restaurato." The door from service stair S6 to the passage was closed, so as not to confuse service with public circulation; and a new door from S6 was opened into the first room of the apartment, D11.[271] Room D11, with doors to both the apartment toward the street and that toward the garden, was named the guard room and room D13 was called "anticamera"[272]— designations that speak of the use of these rooms for the reception of guests. Both apartments would have the public entrance, requisite number of rooms, and fine decoration appropriate for that use. They may have been alternate apartments for Giovanni Battista and Eleonora, or they may have been constructed for the eventual use of their sons, or a son and his wife.

A new women's apartment was constructed in the attic of the wing toward the Ripetta (Fig. 49). It was conveniently located with respect to Eleonora's apartments on the *piano nobile* and ground floor and connected with them by service stair S11. Seven small rooms (E15–E21) were built between the wall of the old rooftop loggia and the newly heightened wall toward the garden. These were simply finished, with sloping wood ceilings, small windows toward the garden, and doors opening to a corridor E7 constructed within the space of the old loggia.[273] Passage E22, at the top of service stair S6, contained the *rota*, or turnbox, necessary for any women's apartment.[274] At the western end of the apartment were the women's dining room and kitchen, E12 and E13. Their *sciacquatore* was salvaged from the old kitchen A15 on the ground floor.[275] A part of the adjacent attic, E14, was partitioned off and a privy installed. The modest furnishings of the women's rooms are listed in an inventory of 1693: each had a simple bed with bedding, a chair with a straw seat, another chair, perhaps a table with a single drawer, a close-stool, a chamber pot, and a devotional picture.[276]

This new apartment replaced a women's apartment in the ground-floor mezzanine rooms, which were demolished to make way for the enlarged rooms of the ground-floor apartments. The women had been using all eight mezzanine rooms (which had earlier been used by Giovanni Battista [d. 1609] and Virginia, then had been divided between women attendants and pages in 1619, and then had been taken over by Cardinal Scipione in 1621); B7, near the oval stair, had been their kitchen or dining room.[277] The turnbox for this apartment had been in the small room B1, which was taken over by the new double-ramp stair S13 in 1671 (see Fig. 44); the turnbox was salvaged and reused in the new attic apartment for women.[278]

At the same time, the women's apartment constructed in 1620 in the attic rooms on the southwest side of the courtyard was still being maintained. A corridor E6 led from the top of oval stair S5 alongside the *guardaroba* E5 to its turnbox—distinct from that of the new women's apartment toward the garden.[279]

As the Ripetta wing was expanded upward by the heightening of the walls toward the garden and the construction of the new attic apartment for women, so too it was extended downward by the excavation of new or enlarged cellars. The raising of the ground floor must have prompted this decision. The basements were vaulted and plastered and lit by small windows. The document of construction does not reveal the functions of particular basement rooms, but there are references to a reservoir for water and a basement corridor that leads to a *guardaroba*. The stair S12 constructed for Cardinal Scipione Borghese in 1626 was extended downward two more flights, or fifteen steps, to serve the basements.[280]

Stables and eight carriage rooms toward the piazza were renovated, and minor works were done in rooms of a few officers of the household, but there is no sign of the remodeling of kitchens and other offices. Their establishment in the early decades of the century, in the northeast part of the site, must have been maintained. In 1678, the four levels of the Palazzo della Famiglia

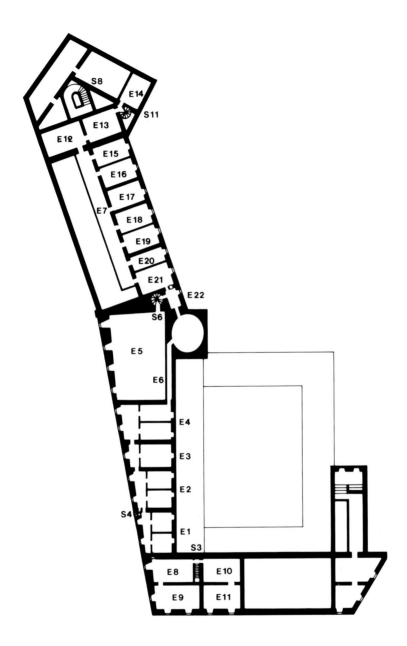

49   Palazzo Borghese, 1671–76, attic, reconstruction (author)

Borghese were ample for most of the *famiglia* of Giovanni Battista; in the palace itself there resided (besides the prince and princess and their three sons) only ten women attendants, and sixteen men, two women, and two small children; the stable master and stable boys lived as usual over the stables, and "il Sig.ʳ Simone" lived on the *piano nobile* of the house through which the *prospettiva* passed.[281]

Work must have proceeded rather quickly, for wood ceilings and windows were ready for the new third-floor and attic rooms toward the garden by 28 January 1672.[282] Yet some work continued on until 1677.[283] The prince was living in the palace during its reconstruction — both involving himself in decisions about the new work and impeding that work by his desire for quiet in the morning.[284] His pleasure in the *prospettiva,* necessitating the dismantling and reerection of scaffolding, has already been noted. He similarly wanted to show his visitors the progress on the stucco decoration of the gallery A14 (see Fig. 43).[285] He participated in approving the positioning of the two alabaster fountains in that gallery.[286] He was surely involved in other changes as well. The biggest change was the decision to enlarge gallery A14 and continue the enfilade through the palace to the neighboring building and beyond. Other changes have already been noted — the corner fountains in room A18, the number of steps from the princess's audience room down to the garden. Even the addition of the balcony on columns at the short Ripetta façade (see Figs. 16, 35, 46) may be seen as a change or addition to the design, since foundations for the balcony were not laid until 1676. Through all the changes there remained the aesthetic ideal of homogeneity and regularity, and the notion of visual continuity as the axis uniting the several rooms was only enhanced by the most important of the changes.

Hibbard, looking at the palace from the outside, has considered the Ripetta balcony as "similar to the lower story of a small Baroque church

façade," like Rainaldi's S. Maria in Campitelli, and has reluctantly forgiven its placement before the handsome portal façade of 1612–14.[287] Viewed from the inside, the balcony becomes the inevitable culmination of ever-extending vistas from within the palace, beginning with the two-story loggia looking out beyond the hanging garden in 1612–14 and continuing with the alignment of doors and the *prospettiva* of the 1670s. From the newly raised room A18 one can only look out. The palace had never had a formal entrance from the Ripetta; the portal of 1610 had led to the "Cortile della legna," and that of 1612–14 had opened to a service entrance where carriages were stored. In 1671–76 the room behind the portal was unambiguously named "rimessone." No visitors were to enter there, and the superimposition of the new shuttered balcony (a version of the *palchi* often built for the watching of public spectacles) on the large portal arch in effect canceled that sign of entry with a sign of discreet viewing. The change in exterior form was eminently consistent with the changes in interior arrangement.

The remodeling was thoroughgoing and costly. The *misura* for masonry alone amounted to 23,174.49 scudi, of which 13,153.16 scudi was for stuccoes in the rooms, gallery, and garden.[288] One can only imagine the cost of all the alabaster doorframes. In addition there were charges for carpentry, glazing, metalwork, painting, and so forth. Yet the remodeling took place entirely within the confines of the already existing structure and affected its outer appearance only by the addition of the small Ripetta balcony. Rainaldi's artistry was exercised in plan and internal arrangement. He took into account modern fashions for ground-floor apartments for works of art and long axial views, as did Chigi and Barberini architects in those same years. He developed the expansive southwest part of the palace, along the lines of Bernini's unfinished Palazzo Ludovisi-Montecitorio (see Fig. 8), centered on the *salone,* so that the duality of the old palace eventually was forgotten and the *sala vecchia* C19 abandoned and subdivided.[289] Both the finely articulated façade toward the piazza della Fontanella Borghese and the small but rich Ripetta façade were seen as termini of the now dominant long southwest façade, imposing through the in-sistence of its size and severity (see Figs. 40, 46). No new exterior image was called for. Together with its homonymous piazza and the Palazzo della Famiglia Borghese, the position of the Palazzo Borghese in the city was secure.[290]

CHAPTER TEN

Barberini Family

THE Barberini family in the later sixteenth and seventeenth centuries presents a virtual paradigm of the well-managed Roman family (Fig. 50). The Barberini recognized that the way to power and wealth lay through the Church and that the perpetuation of the family was dependent on marriage; and they accordingly consistently pursued both of those channels of family development. For several generations they were blessed with sufficient male offspring, and they managed this natural resource to the benefit of the family as a whole.[1]

The family had been settled in Florence since the fourteenth century and had enjoyed moderate prosperity in business by the time of Antonio Barberini's marriage to Camilla Barbadori in 1561. Antonio's death only ten years later left Camilla a widow with six young sons. Two of them, first-born Carlo (1562–1630) and second-youngest Maffeo (1568–1644), seemed to offer most promise and were taken as protégés by uncles — the pattern of the seventeenth century already apparent in that Carlo was groomed for a career in business by his uncle Taddeo Barberini in Ancona, and Maffeo, after studies in law at the university of Pisa, went to Rome to live with another uncle, Monsignor Francesco Barberini, Apostolic Protonotary, and to find his future in the Church. Alessandro, Nicolò, and Gian Donato died before this generation came into promi-

nence. The youngest son, Marcello (1569–1646), called Antonio after his deceased father, became an exemplary Capuchin monk. Maffeo, with the sponsorship of Monsignor Francesco, rose quickly through the ecclesiastical hierarchy to become a cardinal in 1606, in the second year of the pontificate of Paul V Borghese; and he was himself elevated to the papacy as Urban VIII on 6 August 1623. He created his younger brother Antonio cardinal in 1624. Carlo meanwhile was tending to his responsibilities in the family by advancing in business, marrying Costanza Magalotti[2] (1575–1644; eldest daughter of a respectable Florentine family) in 1595, and fathering the next generation of Barberini. Uncle Francesco died in 1600; Maffeo as Francesco's heir inherited the "Casa Grande" ai Giubbonari; and Carlo, with his widowed mother Camilla and his young family, moved to Rome to join Maffeo there.

Now established in Rome, the Barberini family continued the same pattern of family management as had been employed in Florence. Costanza Magalotti Barberini bore eight children, and the six who survived infancy were disposed according to the bifurcation of their society into ecclesiastical and secular realms. First-born Francesco lived only a year (1596–97),[3] but he was soon succeeded by a second Francesco (1597–1679),[4] who was created cardinal by his uncle Pope Urban VIII in 1623 and appointed

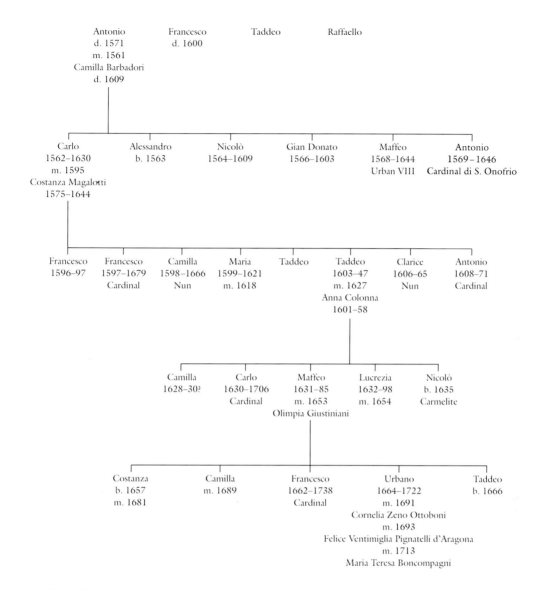

Antonio	Francesco	Taddeo	Raffaello
d. 1571	d. 1600		
m. 1561			
Camilla Barbadori			
d. 1609			

Carlo	Alessandro	Nicolò	Gian Donato	Maffeo	Antonio
1562–1630	b. 1563	1564–1609	1566–1603	1568–1644	1569–1646
m. 1595				Urban VIII	Cardinal di S. Onofrio
Costanza Magalotti					
1575–1644					

Francesco	Francesco	Camilla	Maria	Taddeo	Taddeo	Clarice	Antonio
1596–97	1597–1679	1598–1666	1599–1621		1603–47	1606–65	1608–71
	Cardinal	Nun	m. 1618		m. 1627	Nun	Cardinal
					Anna Colonna		
					1601–58		

Camilla	Carlo	Maffeo	Lucrezia	Nicolò
1628–30?	1630–1706	1631–85	1632–98	b. 1635
	Cardinal	m. 1653	m. 1654	Carmelite
		Olimpia Giustiniani		

Costanza	Camilla	Francesco	Urbano	Taddeo
b. 1657	m. 1689	1662–1738	1664–1722	b. 1666
m. 1681		Cardinal	m. 1691	
			Cornelia Zeno Ottoboni	
			m. 1693	
			Felice Ventimiglia Pignatelli d'Aragona	
			m. 1713	
			Maria Teresa Boncompagni	

50 Barberini family

vice-chancellor in November 1632; he had a long and distinguished career in the church. The youngest son, Antonio (1608–71), was made a cardinal in 1627. The responsibility for continuing the family through marriage then devolved on Taddeo (1603–47).[5] The choice of a bride was a major family and political decision, and Tad-deo naturally deferred to his father and uncle Urban VIII in the matter. Among several possibilities even a French match was considered. Urban VIII was at first reported to be disinclined to any but a Roman marriage, but eventually Anna Colonna (1601–58), daughter of the Conestabile Filippo Colonna of Naples, was chosen.

The pair were married in Castelgandolfo on 24 October 1627.[6] Taddeo became Prince of Palestrina on 26 February 1630, on the death of his father Carlo (who had acquired the territory of Palestrina and its princely title only a few weeks earlier); and on 6 August 1631 he was invested as Prefect of the City of Rome. Carlo and Costanza's three daughters were similarly divided between the Church and marriage: Camilla (1598–1666) and Clarice (1606–65) became nuns; and Maria (1599–1621) married, to die in childbirth.

In the next generation the same husbandry of family resources can be seen. Since the development of Taddeo's family is linked closely to the building of Barberini palaces, and since the birth dates of some of his five children have been in dispute,[7] it seems worthwhile to clarify the history of this generation. Taddeo and Anna's first child, Camilla (not Lucrezia), was born in the year following their marriage.[8] Her uncle Cardinal Francesco Barberini writes of the charms of this child, who died before her second birthday.[9] The eagerly awaited birth of a son, Carlo, occurred on 1 January 1630; and the second son, Maffeo, essential for the bifurcated management of the family's resources, was born on 19 August 1631. A fourth child was born in the family's new Palazzo Barberini alle Quattro Fontane and baptized in its chapel on 8 September 1632; this child has sometimes been thought to be Nicolò, but a pair of *avvisi* make clear that it was a female child and give her complete baptismal name, Maria Lucretia Anna Camilla Francesca Domenica Candida Rosa Angela.[10] Records of salary payments to her wet nurse, from 1 November 1632 until 30 November 1634, confirm that the child was Lucrezia, who married the Duke of Modena in 1654 and died only in 1698.[11] Taddeo and Anna's fifth child, Nicolò, was born somewhat later, probably in late 1635: earlier in that year, the Venetian ambassador Alvise Contarini reported that Taddeo and Anna had only two sons, "Maffeo e Carlo, piccioli figliuolini" — that is, not yet Nicolò; payments for Nicolò's wet nurse begin

on 9 January 1636.[12] As in previous generations, the sons divided family responsibilities: in 1653 Carlo gave up his primogeniture to his younger brother Maffeo and was created cardinal, and Maffeo married the twelve-year-old Olimpia Giustiniani to the end of continuing the family for yet another generation.[13] Nicolò, whose date of death remains even more obscure than his date of birth, became a Carmelite monk in 1662.[14]

As both the bipartite structure of the family and its chronological development were important for the history of Barberini palace building, so too the personalities of the main players affected what was built. The vigorous pope Urban VIII was chief among them. As cardinal (and even earlier), he sponsored construction at the "Casa Grande" ai Giubbonari; later, as pope, he lived at the Vatican and used other papal properties, but even so, the force of his personality was such that he affected what other members of his family built. First, his interest in the welfare of his family and his generosity toward its members, in terms of both money and rank, simply made possible the scale on which the Barberini built. His patronage of the arts is well known.[15] Further, his confidence in his own opinions is attested by the Venetian ambassador Alvise Contarini, who, in his characterization of Francesco as deferential to the pope, tells us that Urban did not like people who showed themselves to know more than himself.[16] Many years later, in his biography of Taddeo, Francesco speaks of Urban's involvement in Taddeo's projects: a certain design for Palazzo Barberini alle Quattro Fontane "also pleased Pope Urban, who, however, as His Holiness also had good taste in these matters, added a few embellishments and improvements which had not been foreseen [by others]"; and for Taddeo's villa of Mompecchio Urban proposed some ideas and a design for a "beautiful residence"; and Francesco alludes to the general possibility that Taddeo's work at the "Casa Grande" would have been influenced by his uncle the pope, even as he explains that it was all for Anna's sake.[17]

Francesco Barberini's position as the representative of the Church in his generation of the family was expressed in building. Most conspicuously, the bulk of his architectural patronage, as listed by his biographer Archangelo Spagna, was religious — monasteries, convents, churches, chapels.[18] At Palazzo Barberini alle Quattro Fontane (not mentioned by Spagna), the south half of the building, paid for by Francesco, was intended as his residence and was seen as the pendant of the north wing, where Taddeo would live. Francesco's scholarly interests provoked the construction of the large library at the palace, to house his extensive collection of books and manuscripts; and his passion for collecting both contemporary and antique art (together with the inheritance of his brother Antonio's collection in 1671) led to the remodeling of the palace in the 1670s.

Taddeo as steward of the secular aspect of the family was most closely connected with Barberini palace building. Like Francesco's, his residence in the bifurcated Palazzo Barberini was to be a visible sign of the nature of the family. His patronage of the arts (other than architecture) was slight, but, according to Francesco, he enjoyed miniature painting in his youth and took an active interest in building.[19] His sober, shrewd, and economical character, combined with his sense of responsibility for maintaining and improving both the image and the material substance of the family, would find expression in his many architectural projects.

Antonio, relieved of the representational responsibilities of his two older brothers, was interested more in the things that could take place in buildings than in the buildings themselves; therefore, his main contributions to building were the construction of the Barberini theater at Palazzo Barberini alle Quattro Fontane, the remodeling of the ground floor of the "Casa Grande" ai Giubbonari as an art gallery, small modifications to suit both buildings to his particular interests, and the accumulation of rich furnishings for his apartments.

CHAPTER ELEVEN

"Casa Grande" ai Giubbonari

HE Barberini family's "Casa Grande" ai Giubbonari,[1] in the heart of seventeenth-century Rome, grew over the years, not according to a distinctive controlling idea but rather in response to the changing constitution and fortunes of the family. From the beginning the owners were actively involved with the development of their building. Three generations of Barberini consulted an array of architects and builders over the course of nine decades. Sometimes the collaboration of patron and architect resulted in minor adjustments and reshuffling of elements; once there was a major revision that fundamentally changed the palace. Its form remained intimately tied to the cellular structure of urban Rome. It grew through the addition of cells, extensions upward and downward, combination, and reshaping of the preexisting masonry. At every stage in its growth, it remained in harmony with its mercantile context, and the one major change in its outward form occurred exactly in response to a major change in the plan of the neighborhood. Even today the casual shopper in the busy via dei Giubbonari is hardly aware of the existence of what was once a palatial residence (Fig. 51). Altogether, the saga of growth and change in the "Casa Grande" is characteristic of one kind of Roman architecture; and its organic development is in marked contrast to the design and construction of the family's other city palace, the Palazzo Barberini alle Quattro Fontane, within a few years' time and according to a single controlling idea.

Monsignor Francesco, 1581–1600

Monsignor Francesco Barberini bought the nucleus of the property in 1581 (Fig. 52, property 1).[2] Already called "Casa Grande" (or "Domus Magna" in the instrument of sale), the relatively small house was accompanied by four ground-floor shops opening to the via dei Giubbonari, three smaller houses, a stable, and courtyards. The purchase price was 10,000 scudi, to be paid over the course of five years; and Francesco calculated that the property could yield 583 scudi per year in income: the "Casa Grande" itself was at that time rented to Monsignor de Graffi, Bishop of Faenza, for 250 scudi, and the shops, smaller houses, and one room of the main house together would produce 333 scudi.[3] Francesco's house (Fig. 53) was bordered to the northwest, toward Campo dei Fiori, by the house of Jacopo Matei and to the southeast by a house owned by the Paperoni family. It was only two structural bays wide, subdivided on the ground floor into four shops (of unequal size, to judge by the rents charged).[4] The six mezzanine windows above the shops, smaller than the others of the eventually expanded palace, can still be identified in the façade toward via dei Giubbonari (Fig. 54; cf.

51   "Casa Grande" in via dei Giubbonari (author)

Fig. 80, far right). The entrance was not from via dei Giubbonari[5] but from a narrow L-shaped vicolo extending from the present via Arco del Monte to the southeast: a portal in a simple wall admitted visitors into a large courtyard behind the house. To the back of the courtyard lay the stable, and to the right was the entrance to the house proper; a corridor led past a kitchen to a stair and a small courtyard. The *sala* and Monsignor Francesco's "camera" were on the *piano nobile* toward the street, and his "studio" overlooked the courtyard. The *guardaroba* and its loggia were toward the street on the level above.[6] This house of only a few rooms did not provide suites for the ceremonial reception of guests or accommodations for the housing and working of a large *famiglia*. Francesco's status as apostolic protonotary did not require such an establishment. Still, it was his own house, a good investment especially with the shops below; its quality was such that it had earlier housed the Bishop of Faenza; and its *sala, camera,* and study, with service rooms below and *guardaroba* above, were certainly more luxurious than the apartment of Don Francesco Ceccarelli in the Palazzo della Famiglia Borghese in 1643 or the quarters of other gentlemen attached to large households.[7]

During the first five years of his ownership of the "Casa Grande," Francesco's architectural works were small, apparently repairs and minor adjustments, costing only a few scudi at a time and not more than 70 scudi altogether. The earliest record of work at the "Casa Grande" is dated 5 September 1581, within three months of Monsignor Francesco's purchase. It is for work on the stable, amounting to only 11.48 scudi, and signed by "Anibal Lippi architetto."[8] An up-and-coming architect in the 1570s, Annibale Lippi fell ill not long after seeing to the work at the "Casa Grande," wrote his testament on 18 November 1581, and then, it seems, died.[9] His willingness to undertake the very modest job of renovating Monsignor Francesco's stable may indicate either the client's aspirations for his property or the architect's hope that more substantial work might follow the first trial. Lippi seems to have had no successor at the "Casa Grande," for Francesco's subsequent works were conducted without reference to an architect in the surviving documentation.

In 1586, having completed the payment of 10,000 scudi, Francesco was ready to enlarge and improve his property. He bought the house immediately to the southeast in via dei Giubbonari, formerly belonging to the Paperoni but by then owned by Francesco and Galeazo Colombo, paying 2,550 scudi for it on 11 March 1586 (see Fig. 52, property 2).[10] With the master mason Bartolomeo Sala da Bibbiena he joined the new house

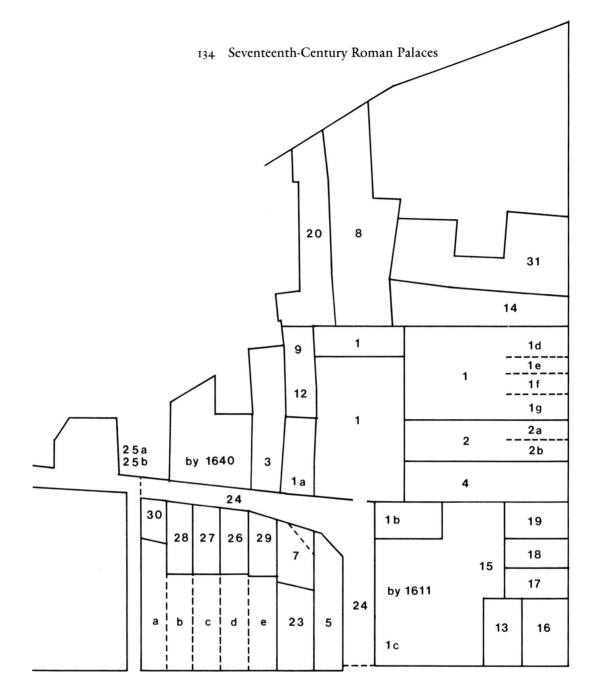

52   "Casa Grande," property acquisition (author)

I   1581, 15 June, "Casa Grande," including

　　1a   House at right of entrance, exiting courtyard

1b   House at left of entrance, exiting courtyard

1c   "Casetta attacata al fornarella ma dritta di ponte sisto"

1d "bottegha . . . in la strada de giubbonarj"

1e "bottegha attaccata alla sopra detta"

1f "bottegha attaccata alla sopradetta"

1g "bottegha attaccata alla sopradetta"

2 1588, 11 March, House with shop bought from Francesco and Galeazo Colombi (formerly belonging to H. and Fr. Paperoni)

3 1604, 31 May, House bought from S. Salvatore

4 1609, 24 August, House bought from S. Giacomo degli Incurabili

5 1611, 9 December, House bought from Jacobus De Vellis, demolished for piazzetta

6 1612, 28 May, "casa con forno," at S. Barbara, bought from S. Caterina da Siena

7 1612, 6 or 10 December, House bought from brothers de Donatij, for widening street

8 1620, 21 [month unknown], "casa con forno e suoi membrij attaccata alla Casa Grande," in vicolo della Grotta, bought from Cesare di Pasquale Cioli da Camerata

9 1620, 15 December, "casa attaccata alla stalla," bought from Ott. Lotti

10 1621, 21 August, "casetta contigua al palazzo," bought from Ippolita Brandi

11 1622, 21 March, "casa chiamata la Turricella (Torretta) in strada detta de capo di ferro," bought from Marcantonio, Paolo, and Andrea Bonigli (de Roviglia) and Collegio Angelicano [date is possibly 1621]

12 1623, 28 August, "casetta rovinata attaccata alla Casa Grande del cortile," bought from S. Salvatore Maggiore

13 1623, 22 December, House of *tinozzaro,* bought from S. Marta

14 1624, 6 April, "casetta à canto al Palazzo"

15 1624, February–March, Rooms and well, bought from six owners

16 1624, 17 July, House with shop, in via dei Giubbonari, on corner, bought from Antonio Rocci

17 1624, 30 July, House with shop, in via dei Giubbonari, bought from Orphans and Annunciation

18 1624, 30 July, House with shop, in via dei Giubbonari, bought from Purification

19 1624, 23 July, House with shop, in via dei Giubbonari, bought from S. Salvatore di S. Giovanni and Consolation

20 1624, House in vicolo dei Balestrari, bought from B. de Velli and Giulio Bonaventura

21 1634, December, or 1635, Site of houses burned at S. Barbara, purchased to leave open as a piazza

22 1638, 1 March, House in piazza S. Martinello, bought from Bonfante

23 1638, House in piazza Monte di Pietà, bordered on one side by Barberini piazzetta, bought from Lelio Parisani

24 1640, 22 August, Piazzetta and vicolo

25a 1641, 1 June, Shop with two mezzanines, in vicolo, at piazzetta, under house of Pietro Leiti, bought from Cappella Paolina in S. Maria Maggiore

25b 1641, 1 June, House in vicolo, at piazzetta, bought from Pietro Leiti

26 1641, 1 June, House in vicolo, bought from Angelo Jacobutio da Valle Cupola

27 1641, 1 June, House in vicolo, bought from heirs of Vincenzo Perini

28 1641, 14 June, House in vicolo, bought from widow of Giulio Conforti

29 1641, 14 June, House in vicolo, bought from Marc Antonio Vittori

30 before August 1642, House of Achille Martorij or Martone

31 before February 1648, House with two shops and mezzanines, in via dei Giubbonari

32 Casa contigua incorporata nel detto [Palazzo ò Casa Grande]"

33 "Casa à Capo di ferro contigua al sudetto Palazzo Incorporata come sopra"

34 "Casa à Capo di ferro contigua come sopra" (Houses 32, 33, and 34 are listed in Taddeo Barberini's inventory of 1648; they may be identical with houses above.)

a House never owned by Barberini

b–e Four houses belonging to SS^ri Fabri da Rieti, never owned by Barberini

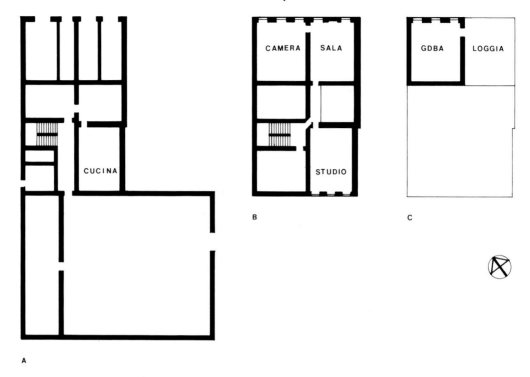

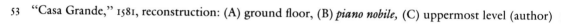

53   "Casa Grande," 1581, reconstruction: (A) ground floor, (B) *piano nobile,* (C) uppermost level (author)

to the old, transferred the *guardaroba* to the upper story of the Colombo house, added a small loggia to the *guardaroba* (in addition to the "loggia grande"), with small rooms below it toward the courtyard of the Colombo house, and built a new small chapel.[11] He then rebuilt and enlarged the northwestern file of rooms, so that the apartment on the *piano nobile* comprised three rooms beyond the *sala,* in addition to the already existing study. Another set of three rooms was built as the *secondo piano* (where previously there had been only the *guardaroba* and its loggia), and a single room was constructed over the middle of the three rooms, on a third level. On the ground floor, where there probably had earlier been a small courtyard, the "room under the *tinello*" was built; and the *tinello* found its place in the mezzanine above. Other ground-

floor and mezzanine rooms were rebuilt for the use of the *famiglia.*[12] The work therefore involved enlarging the house laterally by the purchase of the Colombo house, filling in spaces that had previously been open, and extending the house vertically by adding rooms on the *secondo piano* and attic stories (Fig. 55).

The resultant plan meant that Francesco might have had an apartment of five or six rooms en suite, but his description shows that he did not think of his enlarged living quarters in that way. The *sala* remained in its old place, now in the center of the three rooms toward the street, so that the new room to the southeast was outside the potential suite. The rooms to the northwest were so contrived that one could pass to the third by means of a windowless corridor, without going through the second. The study main-

54 "Casa Grande," extent of façade in 1581 (author)

tained its identity. One of the rooms was for sleeping — possibly the new middle room with windows to the small courtyard.[13] Francesco had gained the luxury of articulated rooms for different activities but had not felt the need for a suite of rooms for the reception of guests according to the etiquette that his nephews and grand-nephews would require in only a few years.

Francesco's nephew Maffeo Barberini, the future Urban VIII, must especially have welcomed the remodeling and enlargement. He had come to Rome to live with his uncle in 1584, finding quarters somewhere in the small "Casa Grande." It may be that the three new rooms of the *secondo piano* were for the younger churchman, since a few years later, in 1594, an account of woodwork for the palace mentions several rooms for Maffeo which seem to be on an upper level of the palace.[14]

It was not long before Monsignor Francesco was remodeling again. In 1591, without buying additional property, he enlarged his house by excavating new cellars and building above already existing walls, and he completely rearranged the circulation and sequence of rooms (Fig. 56).[15] It is perhaps a sign of increased concern with entrance and the reception of guests that he revised the main stair. He turned it so that it could be entered directly from the courtyard, and he enlarged it to fill the entire cell in the western corner of the palace, where only a few years earlier he had arranged rooms for his *famiglia* and one of the new rooms for his own apartment. Forty-six new travertine treads were about 9 *palmi* wide, both wider and lower than the thirty-nine steps of the old stair, producing a slower and more ample ascent. Beginning at the shallow courtyard loggia, they rose in a U to a vestibule measuring 30½ × 19¼ *palmi* and lit by windows to the courtyard. The thirty-nine old treads were cut and pieced together to make twenty-nine steps for the steeper ascent to the *secondo piano*.[16] The *piano nobile* was completely rearranged as an apartment of four rooms: the new room made in 1587 was joined with that toward the via dei Giubbonari to form a new, larger *sala,* and then other rooms were built — still not entirely en suite.[17] More rooms were built above, probably filling out the square of the *secondo piano,* and probably for the accommodation of Maffeo Barberini.[18] The walls of the old stable wing at the northwest end of the courtyard were heightened to allow the construction of rooms (B12) in that wing. On the lower level, the *dispensa* was fitted in under the new stair; and a kitchen with scullery, fireplace, and oven was built in the ground-floor "saletta," probably the "room under the *tinello*" of 1587. Circulation was improved by the

55   "Casa Grande," 1586, reconstruction: (A) ground floor, (B) ground-floor mezzanines, (C) *piano nobile,* (D) *secondo piano,* (E) uppermost level (author)

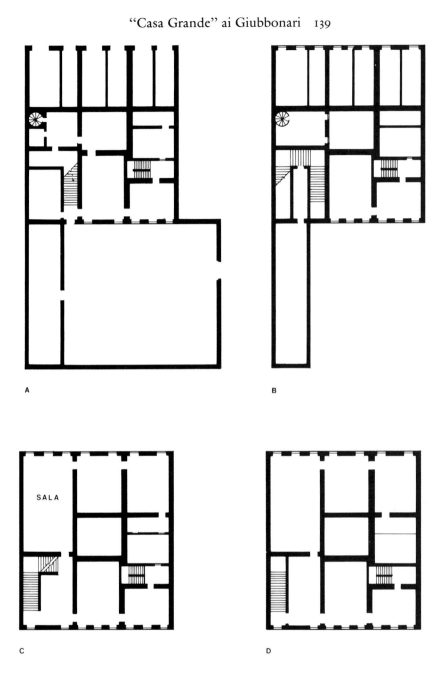

56   "Casa Grande," 1591, reconstruction: (A) ground floor, (B) mezzanines, (C) *piano nobile,* (D) *secondo piano* (author)

insertion of a spiral stair so that food could be taken from the kitchen to the mezzanine without going outside. Belowground, a new cellar and a reservoir for water were made.

Francesco also had plans for the improvement of the exterior of his palace—only partly put into effect, he reported, because of a change in the price of masonry. He had wanted to regularize the windows of the courtyard as well as the street façade, but this had to be left incomplete. As it was, he spent a total of 3,670.37 scudi, including 1,791.60 scudi for masonry, 775 scudi for woodwork, 123.90 scudi for wood, 199.87 scudi for ironwork, and 780 scudi for stonework.[19]

In the course of two decades Monsignor Francesco had considerably enlarged and improved his "Casa Grande." It had gained a structural bay through the purchase of the Colombo house and had gained an additional story in two building campaigns. New cellars had been excavated, and new rooms had been built within the existing framework. Entrance was enhanced through the construction of the ample and airy staircase. Many-roomed apartments for two ecclesiastical men filled two levels. Services were improved by the construction of the new kitchen, service stairs, and other rooms. The intense involvement of the owner is shown by his personal record of the work and the increasing amounts of money devoted to it, after the cautious financial reckoning and five-year mortgage of 1581. Still, the description of the building included in a survey of Roman palaces prepared in 1601 shows that it remained rather inconspicuous and not much changed in its relation to the city: the entrance was still from the narrow vicolo through a portal into the courtyard with the building arranged asymmetrically on two sides; and the façade toward via dei Giubbonari had no entrance to the palace, displaying instead shops, now six in number, on the ground floor and a row of eight windows above (the original six and two more due to the addition of Colombo's house).[20] Such was the "Casa Grande" inherited by the future Urban VIII on the death of his uncle Francesco Barberini in May 1600.

Maffeo Barberini, 1600–1621

Within weeks of his uncle Francesco's death, Maffeo had begun to remodel the "Casa Grande"—whether to improve things according to his own taste or to provide accommodations for his brother Carlo and Carlo's young family, who soon arrived from Florence.[21] In 1600 Carlo and Costanza's children Francesco, Camilla, and Maria were three, two, and one year old, respectively; Taddeo was to be born in Rome in 1603.[22] The two men's widowed mother Camilla Barbadori Barberini also joined the family in via dei Giubbonari. The building that had previously housed two churchmen would now have to accommodate women, children, and their nurses. At the same time, Maffeo's prominence in ecclesiastical Rome was growing, and his requirements had changed beyond those of his uncle Monsignor Francesco. He had a modest household staff, if we may judge from a payment of 25 scudi for monthly provisions for "my *famiglia,* that is, *staffieri* [*palafrenieri*], coachman, butler, groom, cook, and scullery boy."[23] The inclusion of *staffieri* (perhaps the minimum number of four) suggests a public aspect of his life, for which the palace was the setting.

Work valued at 2,598.50 scudi was completed between 8 July 1600 and 4 September 1603, the bulk of it done by May 1601. It included new construction as well as adjustments to already existing parts in the major apartments, the shops, and elsewhere in the building. More specific information is not given in the documentation, but the work took place within the confines of the property as Maffeo inherited it, without the addition of other houses. Only a few new beams of unexceptional length were required.[24] It may be that Maffeo's work involved the filling in of the old small courtyard in the middle of the palace (certainly done before the remodeling

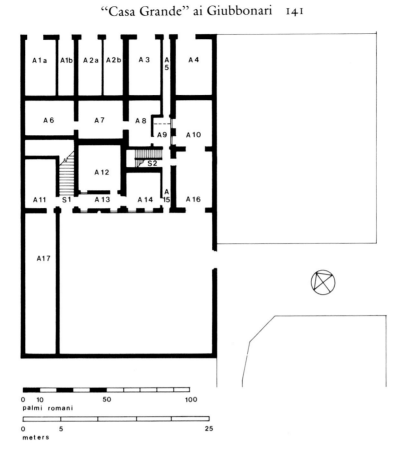

57   "Casa Grande," 1612, ground floor, reconstruction (author)

campaign of 1609), an improvement that would make possible a suite of four consecutive rooms after the *sala*.

The work was measured by the architect Flaminio Ponzio.[25] About forty years old and well established in Rome by this time, Ponzio was soon to rise to prominence with the accession of Paul V to the papacy in 1605. It is unfortunate that more cannot be said about his planning at the "Casa Grande," preceding his work at Palazzo Borghese by only a few years.[26]

The records of Maffeo's payments for the work consistently speak of "my Casa Grande where I live," and the provision of a suite of modest length, suitable for the ceremonial reception of guests, might be seen as a response to Maffeo's new needs. Yet Maffeo was often away from Rome; and, even when he was resident in the city, he left the "Casa Grande" to the construction workers and the growing family of his brother Carlo. In 1602, just after his return from his first legation in France, he rented an Aldobrandini house, probably that in the via del Pozzo delle Cornacchie; in 1607, after having been made cardinal *in absentia* the year before, he stayed in the Palazzo Salviati in piazza del Collegio Romano; somewhat later, he lived in the Palazzo di Madruzzo in the Borgo.[27]

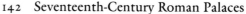

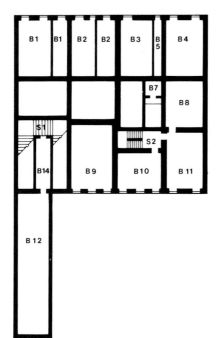

58 "Casa Grande," 1612, ground-floor
mezzanines, reconstruction (author)

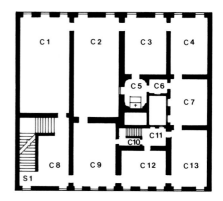

59 "Casa Grande," 1612, *piano nobile,*
reconstruction (author)

According to an *avviso* of 1607, at least part of
Maffeo's dissatisfaction with the "Casa Grande"
was due to its cramped entrance, inadequate for
the coaches that would bring visitors to the
prominent new cardinal, or even for his own
coaches.[28] He may also have found the accommodations not entirely in keeping with his rank
in society, even after the improvements in 1600–
1603.

Maffeo accordingly undertook extensive work
at the palace in 1609–12 (Figs. 57–61).[29] He
bought a house in via dei Giubbonari, to the
southeast and adjacent to his own (see Fig. 52,
property 4);[30] the rooms of this house, incorporated in the "Casa Grande," were completely rebuilt, from the foundations to the roof. The palace was enlarged upward by raising the walls 7 or
8 *palmi* above rooms D1 and D2 to create attic
rooms E2–E4.[31] Walls were straightened and
rooms squared.[32] The main apartment, on the
piano nobile (Fig. 59), was extensively remodeled
so that the *salone* at the north corner would lead
to a large anteroom C2 (formed by the removal
of a partition between two smaller rooms),
which in turn opened into two sets of three
rooms (C3, C4, C7; C9, C12, C13) wrapping
around a core of chapel, service stair, and *cortiletto.*[33] The chapel C5 was newly built, projecting
beyond the small room previously in that position; it was enriched with stuccoes and its oval
vault was painted by Passignano.[34] New stone
doorframes and fireplaces were installed, and the
beamed ceiling of at least one room (C9) was
painted.[35] The ground floor with its mezzanine
was remodeled, and a narrow passage (A5–A15)
was inserted to connect the courtyard with the
via dei Giubbonari (see Fig. 57).[36] To alleviate the
problem of the constricted entrance, Maffeo
bought two little houses in the L-shaped vicolo
(see Fig. 52, properties 5 and 7). He demolished
house 5 to provide a rectangular "piazzetta,"
about 40 × 95 *palmi,* before the portal of the palace (Fig. 62); and he cut back house 7 to ease the
turn into the vicolo.[37] In the end, the masonry
alone was evaluated at 3,296.42 scudi, several

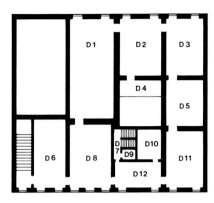

60 "Casa Grande," 1612, *secondo piano,*
reconstruction (author)

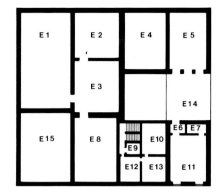

61 "Casa Grande," 1612, attic, reconstruction
(author)

hundred scudi more than preliminary estimates.[38]

The enlarged and reformed palace remained
unchanged in its relation to the surrounding
city, its shops with mezzanines toward the via dei
Giubbonari (Fig. 63), and its main entrance from
the southeast, directly into the courtyard; and
the accommodations that it provided for its
many occupants must still have been rather
cramped. (By 1609 Carlo and Costanza had six
young children.) The grand stair S1 constructed
by Monsignor Francesco in 1591 rose from the
north corner of the courtyard to the *piano nobile,*
which provided the only rooms suitable for the
reception of visitors. These were intended for
Maffeo,[39] but they were so arranged that they
might serve two persons. For Maffeo alone, the
salone and large anteroom (C1, C2) would lead to
a sequence of up to six additional rooms (C3, C4,
C7, C13, C12, C9); for a pair of residents (Maffeo
and Carlo, or Carlo and Costanza), each suite in
the bifurcated apartment would be five rooms
long—respectable but not extremely prestigious. The plan did not offer the luxury of separate apartments for winter and summer use, for
fireplaces in the coolest rooms (C4, C7) indicate
their year-round use. The chapel was properly

positioned so that the household staff might hear
mass from the large anteroom C2, through a
window, while its door opened to the second
anteroom C3. Over one-third of the volume of
the ground floor and mezzanine was given over
to the rental shops (A1a–A4, B1a–B4). Two
large rooms opening from the east corner of the
courtyard were for carriages (A10, A16); and the
two kitchens, for the Barberini and their household, respectively, were also placed on the
ground floor (A7–A8, A6). The wet nurse (the
youngest of Carlo's sons, Antonio, was born on
4 August 1608) stayed in one of the mezzanine
rooms (B10 or B13); the *auditore* occupied room
A14; and other household offices and officers
must have filled the remaining lower spaces.[40]
The shallow wing to the rear of the courtyard
(formerly the stable) contained a *dispensa* A17 on
the ground floor, adjacent to the *tinello,* which
was probably in area A11; and the mezzanine
above (B12) apparently was intended to house
Camilla's women attendants.[41] Camilla herself
used the second-floor rooms to the southeast
(D3, D5, D11; but she died in 1609, while these
were being rebuilt); and a very large room on
that floor was given over to the *guardaroba*
(D1).[42] "Il Filicaia," presumably a relative of

Costanza's by marriage, lived in an attic room.[43] Only a few other rooms on the second floor and in the attic then remained for the family.

The architect was Giovanni Maria Bonazzini. On 24 August 1610 he wrote a letter to Cardinal Maffeo Barberini, absent in Spoleto, discussing work at the palace;[44] he signed the drawing made in anticipation of the removal of the small house (property 5) to form the new piazzetta before the entrance to the palace, dated 4 February 1612 (see Fig. 62);[45] and he signed the *misura* for masonry.[46] The little-known Bonazzini may have been a relative of Ambrogio Bonazzini, who supplied woodwork for the "Casa Grande" in 1591–94 and again in 1600–1603;[47] and he must have been a kinsman of Flaminio Ponzio, the architect of Maffeo's work in 1600–1603, since Ponzio was married to Caterina Bonazzini.[48] He seems to have worked with Ponzio, assisting him at the Cappella Paolina at S. Maria Maggiore and executing the façade of S. Eligio degli Orefici after Ponzio's death in 1613 according to his design.[49] He may have worked for Maffeo Barberini again in 1621, since a bill for metalwork for the "Casa Grande" notes that four chains were weighed in the presence of "M. Giovan Maria";[50] but another Bonazzini, Angelo, joined Carlo Maderno and Filippo Breccioli in signing the *misura* for the work in 1624,[51] and Angelo Bonazzini also worked at the Barberini's palace at Monterotondo with a team of five other architects.[52] It may be that Ponzio, busy with Borghese commissions in 1609, handed Maffeo Barberini's work over to Giovanni Maria Bonazzini. His few drawings (that for the piazzetta, 1612, and two small drawings included in the letter of 1610; Figs. 62, 64, 65) show him to be a neat and capable draftsman. The letter reveals his earnestness in his attention to the cardinal's interests, his knowledge of the properties of stones and of woods to be used for window frames, and his concern with details of circulation; and it also shows that details of the plan remained to be worked out, so that the small chamber C11 can be arranged one way or another way, without any *a*

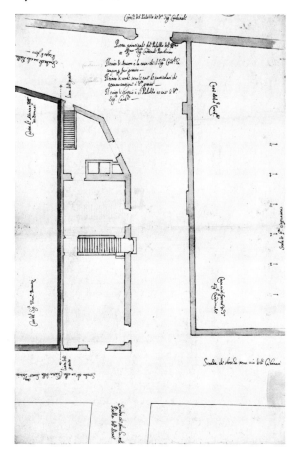

62   Vicolo and house to be demolished to form piazzetta before the entrance of the "Casa Grande," 4 February 1612 (Biblioteca Apostolica Vaticana, ABarb., Ind. III, no. 647 [1, 13], Cartella disegni barberini)

priori concern for the well-formed unit. It further reveals Maffeo's interest in the project, so that even absent in Spoleto he will exercise authority over matters of detail. As with the small part discussed in the letter, the whole plan, too, likely involves a collaboration of amenable architect and active client.

If cramped, the plan is nevertheless skillfully worked out. For the reception of guests, a stair

63   "Casa Grande," extent of façade in 1612 (author)

structures means that there is no room for subtlety in the sizes or proportions of rooms in the suite. Necessary services are provided in convenient locations. The path of public movement is clear and smooth and quite separate from private circulation. (One of Bonazzini's concerns in his letter of 24 August 1610 is precisely the control of circulation to the private rooms of the palace by means of the small stair S2.) As there was no change in the façade or outward expression of the building, the architect's art must have been expended almost entirely on plan and interior arrangement.[53]

In spite of the major addition to the palace, the reforming of its interior arrangement, and the enhancement of its entrance by the clearing of the piazzetta, Cardinal Maffeo must still have felt some dissatisfaction with his palace: only three years after the completion of this extensive work, on 2 September 1615, he was reported to be interested in selling the palace and buying another in via Giulia.[54] In the end, he kept the "Casa Grande" and set his hand to revising it again in 1621.

Maffeo, Carlo, and Taddeo, 1621–32

By around 1620 the growing wealth and power of both Carlo and Maffeo, as well as the coming of age of Carlo's three sons, must have provoked the Barberini to enlarge their compact palace. The cardinal was maintaining a *famiglia* of moderate size, considerably larger than that of 1603; in 1621 he paid wages to forty-six persons, including eighteen gentlemen and chaplains, nine *palafrenieri,* three coachmen, and a servant for his eighteen-year-old nephew Taddeo (at that time destined for an ecclesiastical career).[55] Carlo's establishment must have increased, too.

Two plans in the Archivio Barberini[56] must belong to this period and show proposals for virtually doubling the size of the palace and extending the fundamental scheme of the *piano nobile* of 1609–12, with its twin suites (Figs. 66, 67). The old palace is shown in lighter poché (but the

and an apartment of appropriate size, arrangement, and flexibility are devised. An increase in grandeur is achieved by combining two rooms to form the first large anteroom C2, but the reuse of the preexisting matrix of the cellular urban

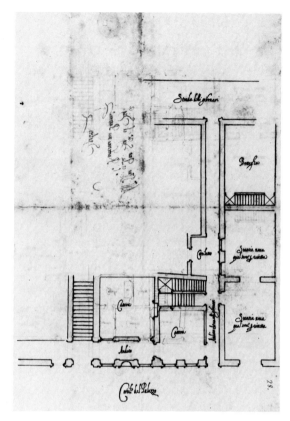

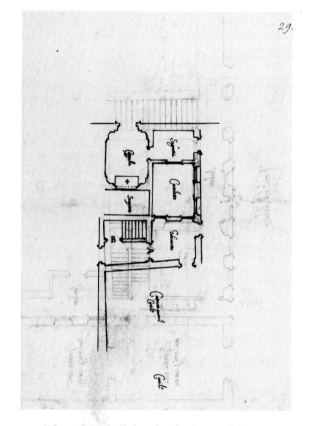

64   "Casa Grande," drawing by Bonazzini for remodeling the ground floor, 1610 (Biblioteca Apostolica Vaticana, Barb. lat. 6540, fol. 28r)

65   "Casa Grande," drawing by Bonazzini for remodeling the *piano nobile,* 1610 (Biblioteca Apostolica Vaticana, Barb. lat. 6540, fol. 29r)

staircase of 1591, in the western corner, is not drawn in). Its *sala* and first anteroom will remain, but the scale of these large rooms will be continued in the suite toward the Giubbonari, as a partition is removed and two smaller rooms combined to make a second grand anteroom (still serving the chapel of 1612). Both northeast and southwest suites are extended to the southeast (as is also the core of small courtyards, service stairs, and passages), into the block toward the Monte di Pietà. Some indication of the smaller houses that would be demolished to make way for the new construction is given by the incised lines of the underdrawing of Figure

67 (redrawn in Fig. 68). Thus, at least on the *piano nobile,* the apartments would increase in grandeur but not in number.

Neither of these plans was put into effect. Properties necessary for the expansion were not bought until after the new construction was completed: property 13 was acquired on 22 December 1623, and the houses along the via dei Giubbonari, properties 15–19, were bought only in the following summer (see Fig. 52). Instead, work in this area was kept within the confines of the property that the cardinal already owned, possibly as early as 1611 (see Fig. 62, which notes "Case del Sr Cardle" and "Casa cioè forno di do

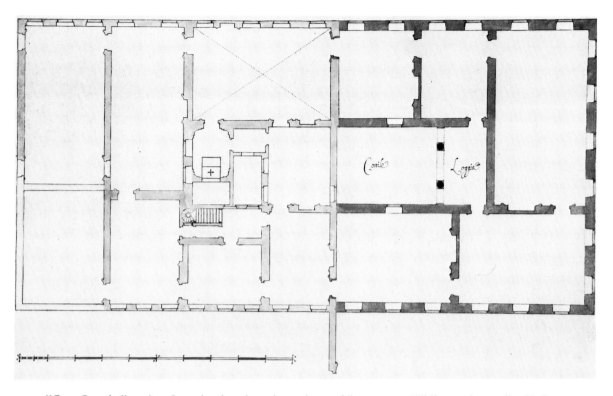

66   "Casa Grande," project for enlarging the palace, *piano nobile,* ca. 1620 (Biblioteca Apostolica Vaticana, ABarb., Ind. III, no. 647 [3, 13], Cartella disegni barberini)

Sig^r Cardinale" to the right of the courtyard portal; and Fig. 52); and the palace was further expanded to the northwest, into the recently purchased house once belonging to Pasquale Cioli (Fig. 52, property 8; Fig. 69, left), and to the southwest, in the direction of Capo di Ferro.[57]

While the plan of 1621 cannot be reconstructed, something of the scope of the work can be deduced from financial records. A bill for metalwork for the "fabrica nova" mentions a *sala* for the cardinal and another "*sala* where Sig^r Carlo lives," indicating separate major apartments for the two brothers; it lists hardware for the apartments of eleven gentlemen, whose names appear on the list of Maffeo's household in 1621, and rooms for coachmen and cleaning men *(scopatori);* and it refers to carriage rooms, a

new *tinello,* and a new small stair ("le scalette nove").[58] A bill for whitewashing "in the rooms in the new fabric attached to my palace" includes work in the rooms of six officers of the household, the *dispensa* with its inner room, and four rooms "where the nephew [Taddeo] of the Illmo Sr Cardinal lives."[59] A major payment for masonry completed between 9 November 1621 and 6 December 1623 speaks of work done "in the above-mentioned Casa Grande for stables, carriage rooms, and rooms above, and an apartment for the *famiglia* in the houses bought toward the vicolo, other repairs in the Casa Grande, and a spiral stair."[60] More work was done in the "Apartment at Capo di Ferro," in the "Apartment of rooms bought toward the [via dei] Balestrari . . . , rented to Sig^r Alessandro Roncari,"

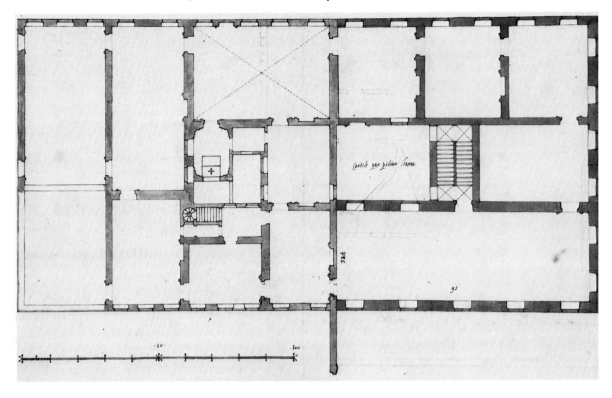

67 "Casa Grande," project for enlarging the palace, *piano nobile,* ca. 1620 (Biblioteca Apostolica Vaticana, ABarb., Ind. III, no. 647 [2, 13], Cartella disegni barberini)

and "in the Cardinal's private kitchen."[61] The two faces of the southeast wing were regularized, according to a license obtained in April 1623 and work recorded in a *misura* dated 26 July 1623.[62] In other words, the project involved not only the block of houses newly incorporated to the southeast of the old "Casa Grande" but also houses to the north and west. It provided major apartments for Maffeo and Carlo and another good-sized apartment for the young Taddeo (and, presumably, rooms for Costanza, her two youngest children, and her women attendants). There were several apartments and rooms for the habitations of gentlemen and servants, as well as a *tinello* and *dispensa* for their service and a separate kitchen for the preparation of the cardinal's

food. There were stables, several carriage rooms, and rooms for coachmen. Both the scale of the undertaking and the specific facilities included show a major shift in the prestige and consequent requirements of the family; the compact "Casa Grande" of 1603 or 1612 was no longer adequate.

However expanded and enhanced, the "Casa Grande" still maintained much of its old relationship to the surrounding neighborhood. The houses newly incorporated in the palace were not cut back so as to align their southwest wall with that of the courtyard and increase the size of the piazzetta before the portal, as proposed on the two drawings. Seven shops remained on the ground floor toward the via dei Giubbonari.[63]

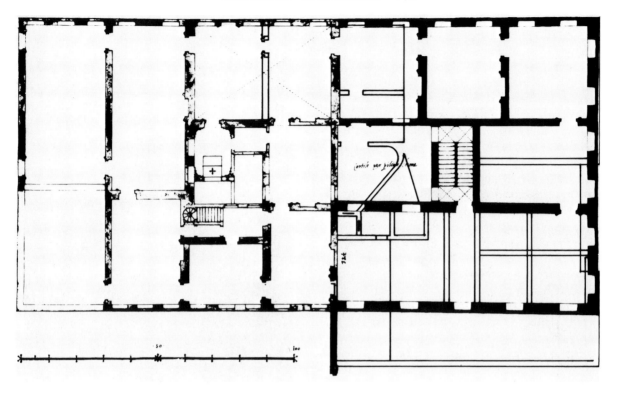

68   "Casa Grande," Fig. 67 with overdrawing to show incised lines (overdrawing, author)

Entrance was not from the Giubbonari but still from the southeast, into the angle of the L-shaped plan, and not into a vestibule but directly into the courtyard; and there was no exterior statement of the "presence" of this large palace in the neighborhood, beyond the larger scale of its newly regularized southeast wing. The Maggi map of Rome of 1625 shows the L-shaped block, barely distinguishable from its more modest neighbors (Fig. 70).

Even while this work was going on, an event occurred that dramatically altered the life of the Barberini and consequently their architectural patronage: Gregory XV Ludovisi, pope for barely two years, died and on 6 August 1623 Maffeo Barberini was elected his successor, taking the name Urban VIII. This meant that Maffeo would no longer reside in the "Casa Grande," for as pope he would live at the Vatican. Whatever personal interest he may have had in the work still under way, he promptly gave the palace to Carlo, on 22 September 1623.[64] The twin apartments of the enlarged *piano nobile,* probably intended for Carlo and Maffeo, would now accommodate Carlo and Costanza, as the modest sister-in-law of the pope would be pushed forward to receive guests as the "consort" of the pope.

The major project of enlargement and revision must have been almost finished when that momentous event occurred. Although extensive, the work had involved the economy of reused structures. Maffeo had spent 1,353.20 scudi on the work in 1622 and 1,522.43 scudi in the first seven months of 1623.[65] The bills for whitewashing and locks show that large parts of the building were virtually finished by December 1622 or January 1623.[66] The work could be completed quickly, as final *misure* for masonry, woodwork, and stonework were submitted to Carlo for payment early in 1624.[67] The work accounted for in Carlo's Libro Mastro, executed between November 1621 and December 1623, amounted to a total of 10,100.44 scudi.

Urban VIII's accession to the papacy meant that both the prestige and the financial resources of the family were greatly increased, and the family's thoughts seemed to turn immediately to yet another enlargement of the "Casa Grande."

Carlo Barberini's purchase of six properties in December 1623 and the summer of 1624 extended Barberini ownership to the easternmost corner of the block and roughly doubled the palace's frontage in via dei Giubbonari (see Fig. 52, properties 13, 15–19). Property 13, "where the tub-maker lives," was measured on 31 July 1623 (that is, before Urban's election) and bought on 22 December 1623.[68] A group of four houses, properties 16–19, all with shops on the ground floor and all "in via dei Giubbonari contiguous to the palace," was purchased from six owners. The houses were measured by Carlo Maderno on 2 May 1624, and their purchase for a total of 6,783.96 scudi followed in July.[69] The sixth parcel, property 15, included rooms and a well shared in various proportions by the same six owners; its several shares were acquired in February and March 1624.[70]

Three additional houses expanded the palace's boundaries in other directions. The small "casetta rovinata attaccata alla Casa Grande del cortile" (property 12) was bought for only 290.50 scudi on 28 August 1623; its purchase had likely been anticipated even before Urban's election.[71] The purchase of the "casetta à canto al Palazzo" was recorded on 6 April 1624; while the documentation does not specify its location, it is likely property 14, "next to the Palace," in via dei Giubbonari.[72] A house in the vicolo dei Bales-

69   Vicolo delle Grotte (vicolo dei Balestrari) 3-4-6 and 7-8, Barberini properties 8 and 20 (cf. Fig. 52) (author)

trari, probably property 20, belonging to B. de Velli and Giulio Bonaventura, was measured on 8 August 1624 (see Fig. 69, right); its owners were likely the heirs of Mutio de Belli and Marco Bonaventura, whose house was cited as bordering the original "Casa Grande" to the rear in 1581.[73]

Although Maffeo and Carlo Barberini may have had great aspirations for their "Casa Grande" even before the elevation of Maffeo to the papacy in August 1623 (and had already taken steps to purchase property 13), the fact remains

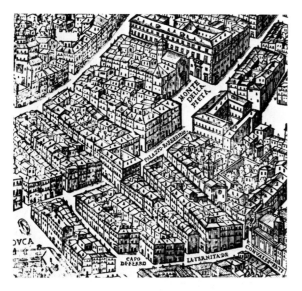

70   Maggi Map of Rome, 1625, detail with "Casa Grande," labeled "Palazzo Barberino" (Bibliotheca Hertziana, Rome)

that their campaign of enlargement in 1621–23 was completed without properties 13 and 15–19, and probably without property 14 as well. Carlo's prompt purchase of the houses along via dei Giubbonari in 1624 shows that he had no intention of abandoning the family property for some grander or more nobly situated palace; in particular, even though the Barberini were already in pursuit of the property at the Quattro Fontane as early as February 1624,[74] whatever might come to be built there would not replace the old "Casa Grande." The new purchases gave Carlo's palace a frontage of about 300 *palmi* along the via dei Giubbonari — even longer than the facade of the nearby Palazzo Farnese. The situation in the narrow street was less than ideal, but it was near Campo dei Fiori, which could provide ample parking for visitors' carriages. Carlo's purchases toward vicolo dei Balestrari suggest that he might even have been thinking of buying the northern triangle of the block and clearing away the houses to form his own piazza.

With his architect, Carlo Maderno, he must

have envisioned a monumental unified façade to replace the cacophony of small shops. A drawing in the Uffizi, A6720, traditionally associated with Palazzo Barberini alle Quattro Fontane, may better be associated with plans for the "Casa Grande" (Fig. 71).[75] The facade as drawn is 300 *palmi* in width — that is, the length of the Barberini property along via dei Giubbonari (including property 31, which was purchased at an unknown date but before 1648), and also the length along the southeast side of the property to which Taddeo Barberini would aspire in the 1640s. With the demolition of the triangle of houses in the north angle of the block, the stipulation in the caption of the drawing, that the same façade would be used for all four faces of the palace, could readily be met on the level site. Even the enigmatic addition to the drawing of two angle towers, drawn in a cruder hand on a sheet of paper pasted just above the cornices of the windows of the *secondo piano,* fits more comfortably into the context of the "Casa Grande" and its rooftop loggia to be built in 1625 (Fig. 72) than into discussions of the palace at the Quattro Fontane. Whether for via dei Giubbonari or for the Quattro Fontane, the rebuilding envisioned in Uffizi A6720 would have had to be extensive (as was that of Palazzo Chigi in piazza SS. Apostoli in the 1660s, discussed in Chapter 15, or indeed as was that undertaken but not completed at the "Casa Grande" in the 1640s): in its floor levels and its number and spacing of windows, the drawing matches neither Barberini property (cf. Figs. 71, 85, 88, 95, and 97).[76]

Carlo pursued some architectural work at the "Casa Grande" in 1624–26, spending 2,600 scudi for masonry by 12 December 1625 and an additional 537.51 scudi for wood and woodwork completed by 8 May 1626.[77] This must have included the large rooftop loggia at the southeast end of the palace block (see Fig. 72), set well back from the street façade; Francesco Barberini specifically mentions the loggia as his father Carlo's contribution to the palace,[78] and Carlo paid for the copper gutters of the "new loggia" on 2 Feb-

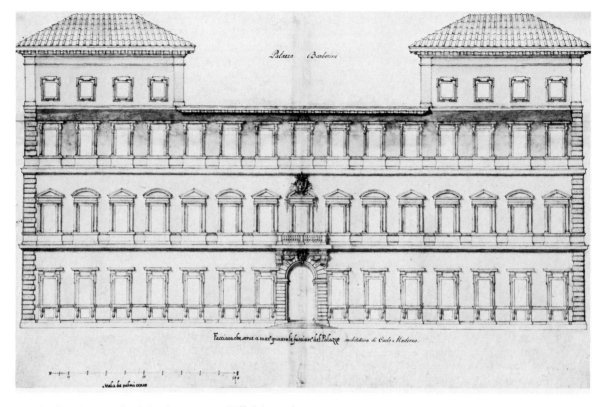

71   Design for a Barberini palace, 1620s (Uffizi A6720)

ruary 1625.[79] The quantity of the work seems modest, in the wake of the purchase of the several houses and the expectation of a major extension of the palace; soon after the summer of 1624 attention must have turned to the property at the Quattro Fontane and the prospect of building a new palace there.[80]

Meanwhile, life continued at the "Casa Grande," and Taddeo's marriage to Anna Colonna on 24 October 1627 must have prompted yet another building campaign there. Apartments had to be arranged for the couple, the children to be born of their union, and Anna's women attendants; and housing had to be found for their *famiglia*. Payments for the "new fabric" were initiated in December 1627 for both wood-

work and masonry, and the work was concluded by midsummer 1628, at a total cost of 3,050.19 scudi.[81] The "new fabric" included a "new apartment," "new kitchens," and a "new chapel," likely in the area of the houses bought in 1624.[82] The fact that more was spent for wood-work than for masonry (1,400 scudi for wood-work, 1,129 scudi for masonry) suggests that there was much refurbishing of already existing rooms. Even with its recent enlargements, the "Casa Grande" could not accommodate Taddeo's new *famiglia,* and the nearby Condulmer-Orsini-Pio palace at Campo dei Fiori was rented for the *famiglia* beginning 1 December 1627 (Figs. 73, 74, 75 [no. 636]).[83]

D'Onofrio reported that over 43,000 scudi

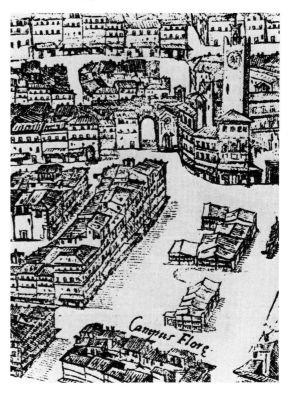

73   Tempesta Map of Rome, 1593, detail with
Palazzo Condulmer-Orsini-Pio

72   "Casa Grande" from southwest, with loggia of
1625 and piazza Monte di Pietà (author)

had been spent on the "Casa Grande" in the
years after Maffeo's accession to the papacy, but
Hibbard countered that "only a few thousand
scudi were spent on construction between 1623–
26 and even less in the succeeding years."[84] An
accurate picture of Barberini building activity at
their old family palace lies somewhere between
the two statements. Carlo's Libro Mastro A
(1623–28) indeed reports a total expenditure of
43,210.58½ scudi,[85] but this figure includes over
14,000 scudi for the acquisition of neighboring
houses and a payment of over 12,000 scudi for
outstanding debts. Actual construction falls in-

to three campaigns: 10,100.44 scudi for work
from November 1621 until the end of 1623, that
is, Maffeo's prepapal project of enlargement;
3,137.51 scudi for Carlo's work in the wake of the
purchase of the neighboring houses, only a frac-
tion of what would have been spent had the
scheme proposed above been carried through;
and 3,050.19 scudi for necessary work in 1627–
28, related to the marriage of Taddeo and Anna
and the establishment of their household, if only
for a few years, at the "Casa Grande." It seems
that the Barberini first moved vigorously toward
a major enlargement of their city palace after
1623, even after they had begun to pursue the
purchase of the Sforza property at the Quattro

74 Palazzo Condulmer-Orsini-Pio, from Campo dei Fiori (author)

Fontane; that this movement was checked, perhaps around the beginning of 1625, as the idea for a major palace on the hill at the edge of town emerged; and that specific works were undertaken in response to the needs of Taddeo and Anna in the years before their removal to the Palazzo Barberini alle Quattro Fontane.

Taddeo, 1634–44

Filled with anticipation, Taddeo moved with his family to the new Palazzo Barberini alle Quattro Fontane in the spring of 1632, and the "Casa Grande" was rented to Stefano Durazzo, the papal treasurer, for 1,000 scudi per year;[86] but, for reasons explored in Chapter 12, after only two and a half years in the still unfinished palace on the Quirinal, he returned to the via dei Giubbonari.

Taddeo's reestablishment at the "Casa Grande" in the autumn of 1634 and his eventual realization that it would be permanent must

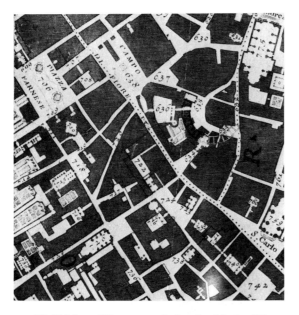

75   Nolli Map of Rome, 1748, detail with the "Casa Grande" (no. 722) and Palazzo Condulmer-Orsini-Pio (no. 636) (Bibliotheca Hertziana, Rome)

have led him to undertake major improvements there. The ideas of organization and orientation in support of an understanding of the Barberini family, which he had nurtured at the Quattro Fontane (see Chapter 12), were not relevant at the old city palace; but a coherent exterior form, a purposeful relationship between building and site, a striking and generous entrance, and well-arranged apartments, all seen at Palazzo Barberini, could also be pursued at the "Casa Grande."

A major problem of the Giubbonari property was its location in a congested neighborhood, with no possibility of a spacious and dignified setting for the palace and little room for the passage and parking of carriages. A disaster that occurred shortly after Taddeo's return to the "Casa Grande" may soon have seemed like an opportunity: on the night of 20 December 1634 a great fire destroyed three shops and houses in via dei Giubbonari, near the little church of Santa Barbara—that is, just opposite the eastern

corner of Taddeo's palace. Taddeo promptly bought the property and left it free as a small piazza (no. 634 on Nolli's map, Fig. 75). There was even the possibility of cutting a new street from the area of the burned houses to the church of S. Andrea della Valle (where the Barberini family chapel was located).[87] But this turned out to be a false start. It was not until 1637 that another opportunity presented itself, when a nearby financial institution, the Monte di Pietà, began improvements in the neighborhood. Taddeo was quick to respond with a project that effectively reoriented the palace away from the via dei Giubbonari; indeed, his scheme would have been inconceivable before the Monte's initiative.

In 1603 the Monte had acquired a palace on the southwest side of the piazza di S. Martinello, opposite the small church of S. Martino ai Pelamantelli, and in subsequent years the building was remodeled and enlarged by Carlo Maderno and, after his death, by Bartolomeo Breccioli.[88] Papal chirographs dated 21 September and 3 November 1637 signal the beginning of work for the Monte di Pietà that came to affect the "Casa Grande" ai Giubbonari: houses between the piazza and the "Casa Grande" were to be cleared away, so that the piazza would stretch northwestward to the present via dell'Arco del Monte and the Barberini's piazzetta; and the façade of the Palazzo del Monte was to be extended to complete the southwest border of the enlarged piazza (the present piazza del Monte di Pietà).[89] The Palazzo del Monte was then enlarged to include the entire city block on which it stood, in 1639–42 (cf. the Maggi map of 1625, Fig. 70, and the Falda map of 1676, Fig. 76).[90] The plans to enlarge and enhance the piazza (with S. Martino ai Pelamantelli at its eastern corner) must have been an invitation to Taddeo to bring his palace forward to share in its openness and prestige — to give his palace the public face and ample area for the circuit of carriages that it had previously lacked. His contribution to the civic improvement was the purchase of property 22, in piazza S. Martinello, on 1 March 1638.[91]

A plan accompanying a papal chirograph dated 22 August 1640 (Fig. 77)[92] clearly shows the partial outline of the newly extended Palazzo del Monte ("fabbrica nuova del Sacro Monte della Pietà") as well as the width of the piazza, in sharp contrast to the narrow street that previously opened toward the piazzetta (cf. Fig. 62, lower edge). According to the chirograph, the piazzetta before the old entrance to the palace and the short vicolo extending from it were to be given to Taddeo, to be incorporated in his palace. The text further explains that Taddeo intended to move the entrance to his palace forward to the present via dell'Arco (at the head of the newly enlarged piazza) and to enlarge his palace in an unspecified way to include some or all of the houses in the small block to the southwest of the piazzetta. The façades of the houses of that block, opposite the newly enlarged Palazzo del Monte, are shown in a drawing in the Archive of the Monte di Pietà (Fig. 78).[93] Taddeo prepared to buy house 23, on the east corner of the block (the two-bay house to the right in the elevation; cf. Fig. 52) in 1638,[94] even before the donation of the piazzetta and vicolo. In June 1641 he bought four small houses facing the vicolo (behind the four houses with uniform roofline shown in the elevation, which belonged to the signori Fabri da Rieti) and a fifth house, with a shop and two mezzanines below, on the corner of the vicolo and the piazzetta toward Capo di Ferro (see Fig. 52, houses 25a [the shop and mezzanines], 25b [the house above], 26, 27, 28, 29).[95] Before August 1642, he had also acquired house 30, on the west corner of the block.[96]

A chirograph of August 1642 (Fig. 79) shows another important aspect of Taddeo's design — the projected straightening of the façades of the palace toward both the via dei Giubbonari (Fig. 80) and the piazza and street to the southeast.[97] At last the relationship of palace to site would be

76   Falda Map of Rome, 1676, detail with "Casa Grande"

radically reformed. The building would present itself as a large, clear, unified form (at least on the northeast and southeast), with a prominent portal centered in the façade (although not centered on the piazza; the block of the building would take precedence), commanding a large open space from which one could view and appreciate the imposing structure and contemplate the prestige of the family that it housed.

Work was quickly under way, and masonry for the new entrance hall between piazza and courtyard, constructed in the area of the piazzetta between 8 July 1641 and 28 September 1642, amounted to almost 3,000 scudi.[98] One black granite column was brought from the hospital of S. Giovanni in Laterano by 21 January 1642, and the transportation of thirteen other columns was paid for on 5 April 1642.[99] The plan on the chirograph of August 1642 (see Fig. 79) shows the new entrance hall, by then already under construction. It established for the first time at this palace

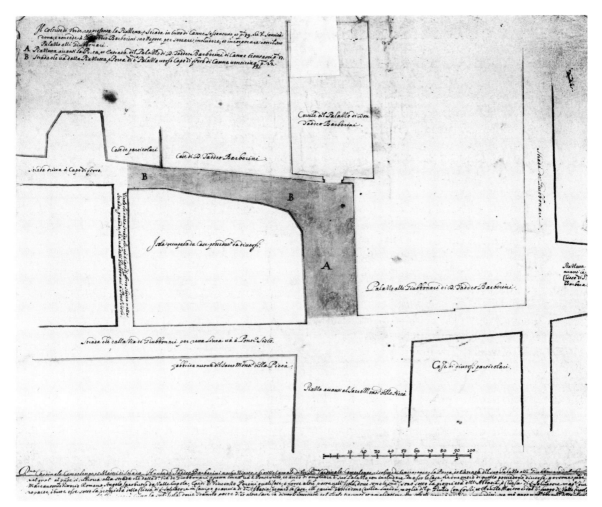

77   "Casa Grande," chirograph of 22 August 1640 (Biblioteca Apostolica Vaticana, ABarb., Ind. III, no. 647 [2], Cartella disegni barberini)

78   Block of houses south of the portal of the "Casa Grande," ca. 1734 (Rome, Archivio Storico del Monte di Pietà, vol. 572; photo, Centro di studi sulla cultura e l'immagine di Roma)

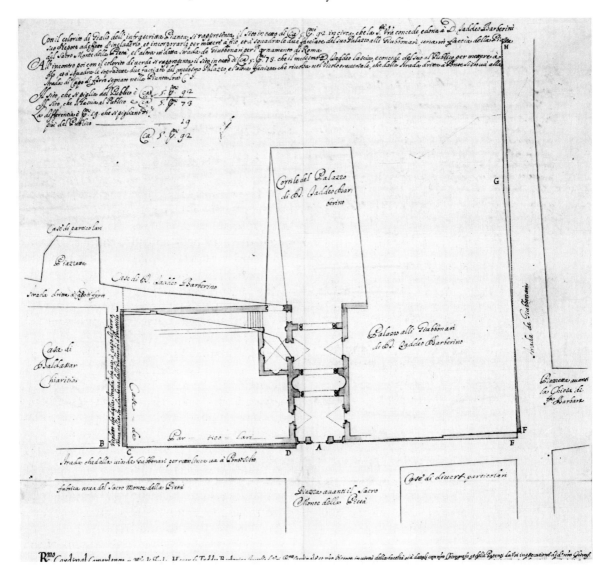

79   "Casa Grande," chirograph of August 1642 (Biblioteca Apostolica Vaticana, ABarb., Ind. III, no. 647 [3a], Cartella disegni barberini)

80   "Casa Grande" in via dei Giubbonari, extent after 1624 (author)

a central entrance with reference to whose axis the façade and courtyard were to be adjusted and regularized. Filling the entire area of the old piazzetta, it provided ample covered space for the entry, waiting, and turning of carriages.[100] Its length was broken into three sections with cross-axial accents, the divisions marked by free-standing paired columns of black granite: a squarish bay, its barrel vault interrupted by a lunette penetration from each side, was followed by a narrow bay held between big semicircular niches and then by another bay like the first. The two niches of the center bay of the entrance hall must have contained the two antique sculptures discovered during the course of excavations for the new construction.[101] The third bay not only

belonged to the ensemble of the entrance hall; it also served as a kind of loggia toward the court-yard and, on its cross axis, led to a vestibule whose cross vault and niches supported another right-angle turn to the new stair. This stair, only partially indicated in the plan, was to lie approximately in the area of the little vicolo donated to Taddeo by the chirograph of 22 August 1640 (see Fig. 77); one long flight from ground floor to *piano nobile* is suggested, and a second was probably to continue upward to the *secondo piano*.

In the next phase the kitchens were rearranged, the staff kitchen being transferred to small houses purchased in June 1641, in the area of the vicolo that had been absorbed into the palace, and the private kitchen taking the place of the old staff kitchen, likely in the extension toward via dei Balestrari; and quarters for the pages were arranged below Taddeo's apartment. This work was measured on 8 November 1642 and valued at 327.22 scudi.[102]

In 1643 and 1644 attention turned to the "new addition," or "new apartment."[103] With the re-orientation of the palace toward the piazza, and entrance from the southeast, the interior organization would also be revised. A copy of the chirograph of August 1642 (Fig. 81) was used as a base for a light pencil sketch of the *piano nobile,* barely visible in the photograph.[104] The new staircase, about 12 *palmi* wide, would rise to the *piano nobile* in a single long flight extending almost the entire length of the western addition, about 120 *palmi*. A second and somewhat narrower flight would lead on to the rooms of the upper story. Most of the new addition would be consumed by a huge *salone* about 80 *palmi* square (presumably rising through two stories) in the south angle of the palace. It would be followed by a large anteroom, about 45 × 80 *palmi*. A second anteroom, only slightly narrower than the first, might rise over the new entrance hall; it would open into a pair of apartments extending into rooms in the part of the palace constructed in the 1620s, effectively reversing their sequence. The requisite chapel might be fitted into the

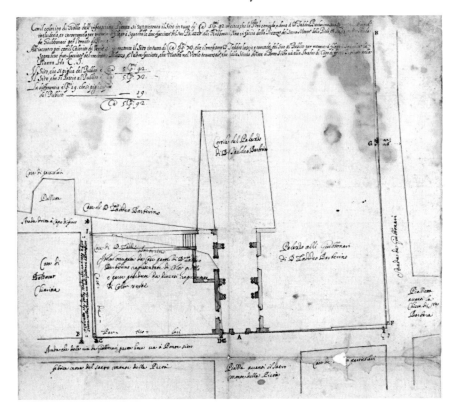

81   "Casa Grande," chirograph of August 1642 (Biblioteca Apostolica Vaticana, ABarb., Ind. III, no. 647 [2b], Cartella disegni barberini)

angle between the two anterooms, over the ground-floor landing of the stair (Fig. 82). The scale of the proposal would greatly exceed that of the older parts of the palace, whose *sala* measured about 29 × 57 *palmi* in 1612; and it would rival that of the Palazzo Barberini alle Quattro Fontane, whose *salone* measures 110½ × 65⅔ *palmi,* and whose anteroom C3 is 70 × 46¾ *palmi.* The sequence of rooms would be rather like that of Palazzo Farnese (see Fig. 5), with the *salone* behind the leftmost bays of the façade, an anteroom opening to a balcony over the portal, and apartments continuing around the right-hand angle of the building; but, unlike Palazzo Farnese, it would have the advantage of two major apartments extending from the ante-rooms. The scheme would further have the economy of reusing all the existing fabric.

The chirograph of August 1642, over which the scheme for the *piano nobile* was sketched, clearly anticipated Taddeo's ultimate ownership of the entire block of small houses and his incorporation of the property in his palace. Yet his plans were cut short in 1644, and he never came to own the four houses of the Fabri da Rieti and the corner house (see Fig. 52).[105] Only a small part of the "new addition" or "new apartment" could be completed.

According to Francesco Barberini's account of Taddeo's work at the "Casa Grande," "above [the] entrance hall is the second [main] story with its chapel and anteroom opening to four

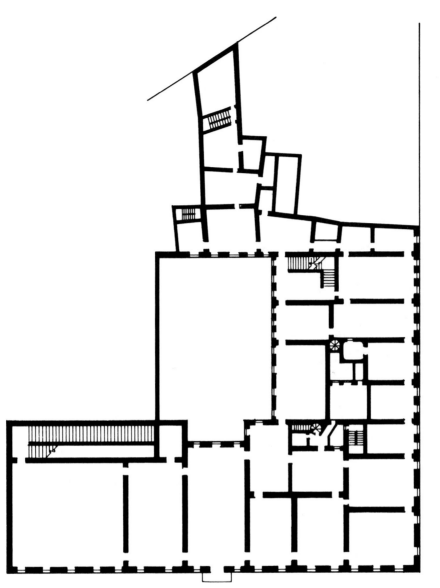

82 "Casa Grande," reconstruction of *piano nobile* of project of 1642, based on Figs. 81 and 86 (author)

apartments, which, although difficult to do, is arranged with such facility and convenience that experts in building value and esteem it highly."[106] Four fir beams, each 42 *palmi* in length, "for the fabric which is being made," were paid for on 20 October 1643.[107] These must have spanned the anteroom repeating the volume of the entrance hall below—that is, the anteroom mentioned by Francesco. Two shorter beams, only 28 *palmi* long, may have been for the new

83   "Casa Grande," entrance hall (remodeled as a theater), 1932 (*Capitolium* 8, 1932, p. 454, Fig. 3)

chapel.[108] The *salone* and first anteroom of the "new apartment" were not built — hence Francesco's omission of mention of them. Only two apartments could extend northeastward from the anteroom; the four apartments mentioned by Francesco must have included two more that were never built, on the southwest side of the palace. A document speaks of the painting of the wall opposite the windows of the new apartment — the wall of a house "where the druggist Jacomo Balloncini lives."[109] The house would have to be opposite the right half of the newly straightened façade. The five feigned painted mezzanine windows mentioned in the same document probably belong to this part of the palace too.

Francesco Barberini's evaluation of the "Casa Grande," constructed through the successive efforts of several members of the Barberini family, gives credit to Taddeo for "whatever it has of dignity [*decoro*]." In particular, he mentions the façade, newly extended and straightened and fronting on the piazza; the colonnaded entry hall, both novel and grand, and embellished by the two antique statues discovered in the excavations for the foundations; and the arrangement of the *piano nobile*, praiseworthy for its facility and convenience.[110]

Monte di Pietà, e banco pubblico

Chiesa dei SS. Teresia, e Gio. della Croce, 2. Convento dei PP. Teresiani Scalzi, già palazzo ove abbitò Urbano VIII mentre era Cardinale, 3. Casamento, ove era la Chiesa di S. Martinello.

84   Palazzo Monte di Pietà and "Casa Grande," engraving by Vasi (Biblioteca Apostolica Vaticana)

Although it has been subjected to much abuse in the past three hundred years, the gracious entrance hall still retains much of its old dignity (Fig. 83). It is distinguished not only by its freestanding paired columns but also by the arrangement of the single hall into a rhythmic sequence of spaces with cross-axial accents; by the rather complicated entry to the projected stair (again facilitated by a sequence of orthogonal axes); and by the way in which the new element at once gives order, control, and dignity to a previously irregular accretion of parts. It is different from the three-aisled, strongly directional entrance to the Palazzo Farnese; the spreading, vaulted hall of Palazzo Barberini alle Quattro Fontane (see Figs. 101, 131, 132); or the airy hall, with stair and dark apsed chamber beyond, of Palestrina (see

Figs. 180, 181). It calls to mind not earlier Roman palace architecture but church architecture[111] — especially Mascarino's nave of S. Salvatore in Lauro — and it anticipates the greater richness and complexity of G. A. De Rossi's entrance to the Palazzo d'Aste (1658). Its abstract complexity would have been enhanced by the black granite columns (now replaced by simple travertine) and the two antique statues. A bit of its original richness can still be seen in the masks of the keystones and the delicate reliefs of laurel, bees, and sun in the spandrels of the arches.

The architect was Francesco Contini, who was overseeing the installation of the Nile mosaic in the apsed chamber of the Barberini palace at Palestrina in 1641 and who would later do other

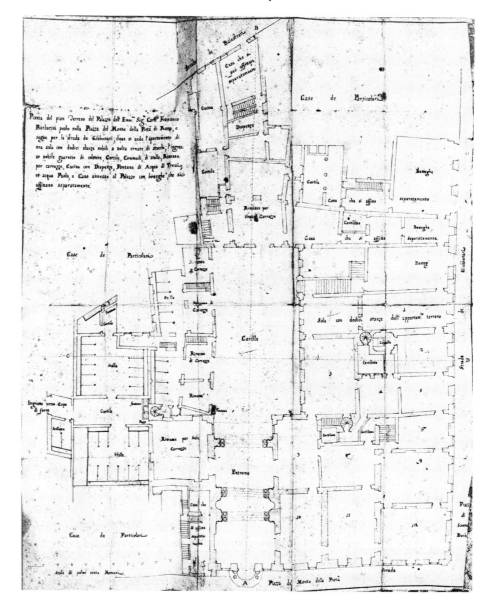

85   "Casa Grande," ground floor, ca. 1734 (Rome, Archivio Storico del Monte di Pietà, vol. 572; photo, Centro di studi sulla cultura e l'immagine di Roma)

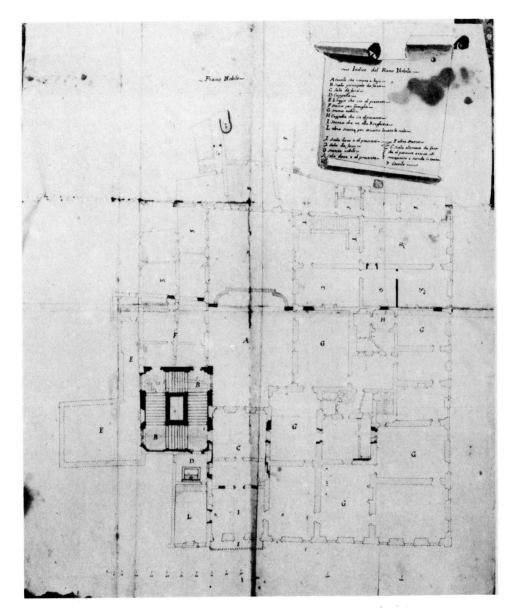

86 "Casa Grande," *piano nobile* with proposed remodeling, ca. 1734 (Rome, Archivio Storico del Monte di Pietà, vol. 572; photo, Centro di studi sulla cultura e l'immagine di Roma)

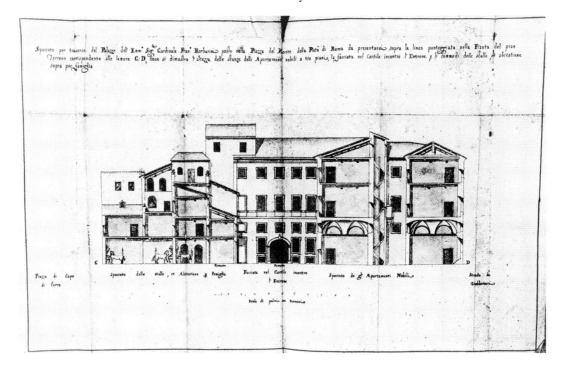

87 "Casa Grande," cross section, ca. 1734 (Rome, Archivio Storico del Monte di Pietà, vol. 572; photo, Centro di studi sulla cultura e l'immagine di Roma)

work for the Barberini family;[112] and Taddeo as patron must have been actively involved too.[113] Formal control can be expected to be due to Contini, the professional architect; but the scheme by which isolated parts can be brought together in a larger order seems to belong with the thinking of Taddeo at the Quattro Fontane, at Palestrina, and at other Barberini properties. The appreciation of the importance of entrance, here so apparent in the arresting design, and the search for inspiration beyond the precedents of palace architecture, seem a continuation of the discussions leading up to the design of Palazzo Barberini (see Chapter 12). At the Quattro Fontane, entrance was combined with exterior image, tying together old and new, secular and ecclesiastical, and even family and papacy; and the image ignored the immediate urban context for the sake of a larger relationship. At the Giub-

bonari the façade remains plain, in keeping with the usual Roman urban practice; but entrance becomes part of a dynamic sequence in plan and section, as the space of the long and bland piazza del Monte di Pietà is compressed and intensified in the hall through the cross-axial accents and the plasticity of wall and column and then is released between reentrant angles into the controlled trapezoid of the courtyard. Taddeo's particular sensitivity to context, entrance, and organization (especially, according to Francesco, on the *piano nobile*), his willingness to look beyond standard solutions, and his interest in bringing parts together into a larger whole, are apparent here as in the Palazzo Barberini alle Quattro Fontane.

In all, over 4,000 scudi was spent in 1643 and over 3,000 scudi was spent in 1644. Although there are a few payments in November and De-

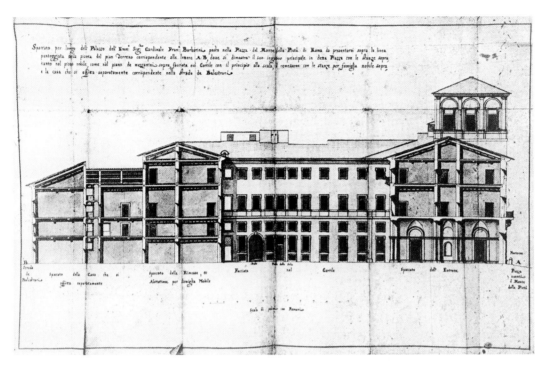

88   "Casa Grande," section through entrance hall, ca. 1734 (Rome, Archivio Storico del Monte di Pietà, vol. 572; photo, Centro di studi sulla cultura e l'immagine di Roma)

cember of 1644, work seems to have come to a stop just after the death of Urban VIII on 29 July 1644.[114] The façade was left unfinished, according to Vasi's view of the mid-eighteenth century (Fig. 84); the southern corner pilasters, although similar to those on the east corner (see Fig. 80, left), bear the *monti* of the Monte di Pietà, a later owner of the palace, instead of the Barberini bee.

The palace in 1644 stood somewhere between its state in 1638 and Taddeo's unfulfilled vision for its reformation. No plans have survived from this period, but a set of drawings in the Archive of the Monte di Pietà, dating from around 1734, give some idea of the extent and arrangement of the palace (Figs. 85–89).[115] An inventory begun on 15 February 1648,[116] in the wake of Taddeo's untimely death a few months earlier, can be correlated with the drawings of 1734 to suggest how Taddeo, Anna, and their children

arranged their lives within its walls.

The old stair of 1591 remained in use, across the irregular courtyard from the new entrance hall. It led to the old *sala* (with windows overlooking via dei Giubbonari), outfitted with the customary baldacchino and *credenza*. To the right of the *sala* opened Anna's apartment (fols. 854r–862v) — first the large anteroom and then the second anteroom toward the courtyard. The fourth room in the suite, formed (at some time) by the combination of rooms C12 and C13 (cf. Fig. 59), had four windows toward the courtyard, and the chapel apparently was reoriented to open from this room. Both the fourth and the fifth room en suite had baldacchinos, and either or both must have been used as audience rooms. The sixth room seems to have been out of suite and used for storage. The seventh room was Anna's bedroom — the *portiera* bearing the combined

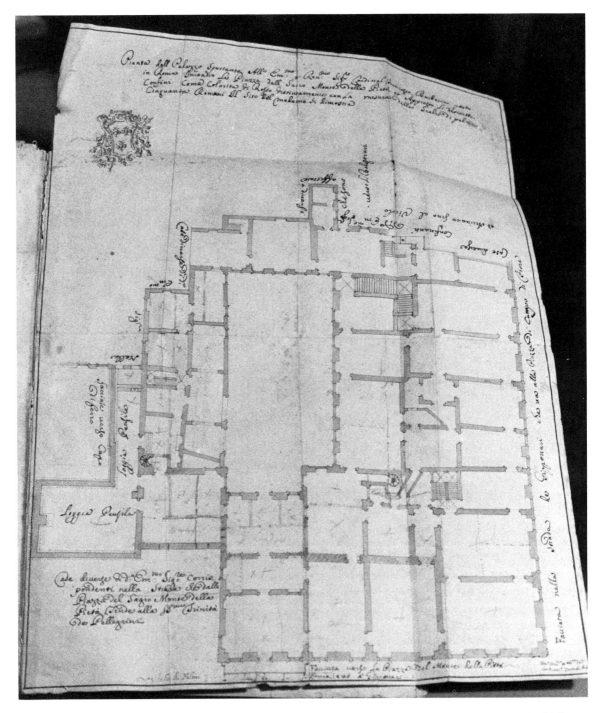

89   "Casa Grande," *piano nobile,* ca. 1734, drawing signed by Giovanni Francesco Zannoli (Rome, Archivio Storico del Monte di Pietà, vol. 572; photo, author)

Barberini and Colonna arms announcing its occupant. Hung with tapestries, it was furnished with Anna's bed, a more modest bed for her attendant, two low women's chairs, and such signs of personal use as sheets, blankets, a prie-dieu, and devotional paintings. This must have been the room toward the piazza, just next to the new room over the entrance hall. To the left (northeast) of Anna's bedroom was another woman's bedroom, likely that of her daughter Lucrezia; and behind that room, toward the *cortiletto,* was an ancillary room containing cupboards, more women's chairs, and so forth. On the other side of Anna's bedroom, in the "tenth room where there is the big balcony over the portal," were three small iron beds, presumably for Anna's three sons (aged fourteen, twelve, and eight when their great-uncle Urban VIII died in 1644), and a fourth bed for an attendant.[117] A nearby *stanzino* seems to have been for storage, as was the "room after the balcony," which must have been opened in the house bought in 1638 (see Fig. 52, property 23). The "room above the apothecary" must also have been in this area.

The sequence of the inventory then continues to the *secondo piano,* above the rooms occupied by Anna and her children (fols. 862v–865v). Here Anna's women attendants must have lived. The rooms include the "room next to the turnbox [*rota*]," the "room next to the signora's kitchen," the "upstairs kitchen," and the "room where the women used to eat"; the "room above the chamber where the signora sleeps" contained, along with bedding, chairs, and so forth, "six children's chairs for eating at table." The inventory continues still upward, to the great "loggia with nine big windows" and the adjacent rooms of the *guardaroba* (fols. 865v–878r).

Downward, but apparently still in this section of the palace, were the laundry (fol. 878r), the well-equipped apothecary (fols. 880v–881r), a small kitchen "below the apothecary," and a few more rooms.

The course of the inventory returns to the *sala* and surveys the rooms of the apartment that lay behind the façade toward via dei Giubbonari

(fols. 881r–885r). Although furnished, these rooms seem not to have been in use when the inventory was taken. The third room contained a bed, and the fifth room, "before the chapel," contained various plans and maps and two Barberini family trees. The chapel and a "windowless room" do not appear on the plan of 1734; they must have been eliminated in some successive remodeling.

Returning once again to the *sala,* the inventory notes a single room "at the head of the *sala* on the left side" (fol. 886v); it must be the room toward the street in house 14. The well-stocked armory, described just before the room to the left of the *sala* (fols. 885v–886v), might be behind that room, also opening from the *sala;* alternatively, if not very conveniently, it might be at the extremity of the suite to the right of the *sala.*

At this point the inventory descends to the carriage room "under the entrance" (to one side, and opening from the entrance?) and the "rimessa grande," containing ten coaches and various other fittings and saddles (fols. 887r–889v). Next comes the kitchen (fols. 889v–890r), and then the apartment of the "Prince and Prefect," Taddeo Barberini (fols. 890r–904v). It seems that we are now in the wing projecting toward the vicolo dei Balestrari, with the "rimessa grande" and kitchen on the ground floor and Taddeo's rooms arranged in several levels behind and above. The description of Taddeo's apartment begins at the end, in the "room where he used to sleep," likely because the inventory workers ascended from the kitchen by a private stair. From the bedroom the inventory moves to a room equipped with a richly hung bed (presumably a representational bedroom) and then to the audience room, complete with red velvet baldacchino. Three anterooms follow en suite, and a chapel is listed. It seems that this apartment opened directly from the main stair hall, without benefit of *sala,* and extended back through six major rooms into the house once belonging to Pasquale Cioli and its neighbor (see Fig. 52, properties 8 and 20). Taddeo's rooms continued upward and downward in this wing.

First were the two rooms of the "mezzanines under the apartment of His Excellency" (fols. 895v–896r); then followed two rooms of "His Excellency's lower apartment at street level" (fols. 896r–897r)—apparently a miniature painting gallery, with a marble fountain. Two porphyry vases and several small paintings were in the stair that led to the "first upper room" and three successive rooms (fols. 898r–904v). These four rooms on the *secondo piano* seem to have formed Taddeo's study. They contained various maps, plans, medals, a box of Carlo Barberini's letters, paintings, statuettes, cupboards, six "bastoni di appoggio," and so forth.

The following section of the inventory describes various service rooms, which must be on the ground floor, whether in the old part of the palace or in the rooms added to the west: *credenza*, pages' room, *bottiglieria*, "cantina nova," "torretta," staff kitchen (which was installed in the houses bought in 1641), *dispensa* and related rooms, and *tinello* (fols. 904v–911v).

The palace was thus full. Services were on the ground floor (and shops may well still have survived toward via dei Giubbonari); Anna's major apartment extended from the old *sala* along the courtyard to the new addition of 1641–44 and included rooms for her children; her women attendants were above, and her apothecary and laundry below; a second major apartment (perhaps for summer use) filled the rooms along via dei Giubbonari; and Taddeo arranged his life both horizontally and vertically in the wing toward vicolo dei Balestrari.

The "Casa Grande" after 1644

The death of Urban VIII on 29 July 1644 signaled the collapse of the Barberini's fortunes. After the election of Innocent X Pamphili, long pent-up criticism of the Barberini broke out. Urban's generosity toward his family had surpassed the norms of seventeenth-century nepotism. The tremendous increase in the wealth of

the Barberini family contrasted conspicuously with the virtual bankruptcy of the papal treasury (in part due to the disastrous war of Castro, from which the Barberini nephews were believed to have profited) and the consequent imposition of new taxes.[118] The men of the family felt it prudent to leave for France. During the night of 28–29 September 1645 Cardinal Antonio left; and a few months later, during the night of 16–17 January 1646, Francesco, Taddeo, and his four children followed to Paris.[119] Barberini properties (including the Roman palaces) were confiscated by the pope, and Anna Colonna Barberini was left in Rome to defend the interests of the family.[120] She was eventually able to travel to France, on 23 April 1646, but she returned to Rome on 23 June 1647, before the death of Taddeo, still in exile in Paris, on 14 November 1647.[121] The efforts of the King of France and his minister Mazarin on behalf of the Barberini were finally successful, and Francesco could return to Rome on 24 February 1648, where his properties were restored.

For a while Anna continued to live at the "Casa Grande," where her apartment was rented to her by Francesco, acting on behalf of Carlo as heir of Taddeo, for the sum of 300 scudi per year.[122] Excluded from affairs of the family and supported only by her youngest son Nicolò, she soon drew closer to her Colonna relatives; in 1651 and 1652 she bought houses near SS. Apostoli to form the Palazzo "dell'Olmo," or "dei Colonnesi," where she lived in a condition appropriate for her high rank from 1652 until her death there on 31 October 1658.[123]

In 1652 Carlo returned to Rome, and his uncle Antonio followed in 1653. Also in 1653 the younger generation of the family settled itself as Carlo gave up his primogeniture (including ownership of the "Casa Grande") to his younger brother Maffeo and was created a cardinal; and Maffeo, now designated continuator of the family, married the twelve-year-old Olimpia Giustiniani.[124]

Maffeo chose to live with his young bride in the Palazzo Barberini alle Quattro Fontane, but he did not neglect the old family palace in via dei Giubbonari. His uncle Francesco had already resumed the work interrupted in 1644: from January through September 1653 he spent 1,640 scudi for the "nova fabbrica" at the palace.[125] Maffeo then took up the work, spending an additional 2,980 scudi by the end of 1654.[126] The following year the palace was rented to the Cardinal d'Este, who paid for further work at the palace in lieu of rent. His contributions totaled 1,783 scudi through December 1657.[127] The work in 1655–57 (and presumably that of 1653–54) was supervised by the architect Francesco Contini, who had guided the earlier work for Taddeo. Although we have no specific information about the nature or extent of the work, it must have represented a sort of retrenchment and adaptation of the fragment of a larger scheme that Taddeo had envisioned in the early 1640s.

In 1658 Maffeo sold the "Casa Grande" ai Giubbonari to his uncle Cardinal Antonio,[128] who made further architectural adjustments according to his own needs. From 1663 to 1666 Antonio spent 2,500 scudi on work focused on the ground floor and courtyard. As he had for previous occupants of the palace, Francesco Contini served as architect.[129]

On the ground floor, where previously there had been assorted service rooms and (toward via dei Giubbonari) shops, Antonio created an apartment of twelve rooms, with a chapel, especially for the display of his large collection of paintings and sculptures — anticipating by a few years the similar ground-floor apartments at Palazzo Borghese. The plan of these rooms was probably essentially as shown in the plan of the palace in 1734 (see Fig. 85), which notes "*sala* with twelve rooms of the ground-floor apartment" (the thirteenth room having been added at some time after 1666). According to an inventory of the palace in 1671, more than three hundred paintings were installed in these rooms

90   "Casa Grande," southeast façade, from via dei Giubbonari (author)

(in addition to those in the upstairs apartments). Like the Borghese apartments, Cardinal Antonio's seems to have resembled a normal apartment while being intended only for daytime use: two rooms were arranged as audience rooms, with baldacchinos; another contained a *zampanaro* over only a daybed; there was the requisite chapel; but the inventory yields no signs of sustained occupation. Five rooms are noted as having fireplaces, so that the cardinal might enjoy his collection year-round.[130]

The second major feature of Antonio's work at

the "Casa Grande" was the "new façade of the courtyard." A note of a "frescoed landscape in the wall opposite the new window made in the room at the top of the stairs," in 1666,[131] suggests that it was at this time that the old stable wing at the far end of the courtyard was finally removed. The courtyard would then have assumed the proportions shown in the plan of 1734 (see Fig. 85), and the new window would have been opened where previously there had been the upper part of the stable wing. The "new façade of the courtyard" would be that northwest wall of the courtyard, its orderly, symmetrical design shown in the transverse section through the palace in 1734 (see Fig. 87). (The southwest side of the courtyard was surely not the recipient of the new façade, since its disorderly collection of carriage rooms and stables survived at least until 1734.)

Remembering the heated bath that he had built in the Palazzo Barberini alle Quattro Fontane in 1641,[132] Antonio also installed a "nuova stufa" at the "Casa Grande." We know neither the location nor the form of the *stufa,* but a professional attendant came to the palace and operated it for the cardinal's benefit for ten days in June 1666.[133]

The cardinal apparently found the upper floors of the palace suitable for his use. His main apartment extended through thirty-one lavishly furnished rooms and even opened to a garden, built over the low structures in the southwest part of the site (the garden is labeled "loggia" on Fig. 86 [E] and "loggia pensile" on another of the plans of 1734, Fig. 89). His winter apartment was on the *secondo piano,* as were his private rooms and the three rooms of his library.[134] He lived in the "Casa Grande"—where he had been born sixty-three years earlier—until his death in 1671 (Fig. 90).[135]

CHAPTER TWELVE

Palazzo Barberini alle Quattro Fontane

T HE impressive form of the Palazzo Barberini alle Quattro Fontane, rising imperiously on the north slope of the Quirinal hill, has attracted attention since the time of its construction (Figs. 91, 92). Its very form is a surprise, in the context of seventeenth-century Roman palaces: instead of a compact, impersonal, and homogeneous block, we see a richly articulated west façade, with a three-story, seven-bay loggia of round-headed arches framed by engaged columns or pilasters, spanning between two strongly projecting wings. Its distinctive form is visible even through the haze of modern Rome from the Gianicolo and St. Peter's on the other side of town. From the north (as Ingres would have approached from the Villa Medici in the nineteenth century), the astounding loggia is eclipsed by the projecting north wing, and the building presents itself as two parallel blocks (Fig. 93). Their façades of regularly spaced rectangular windows, the bays framed by band articulation overlapping flat rustication on the ground floor, are familiar to the Roman eye, perhaps recalling the southeast façade of the Palazzo Borghese (Fig. 94; cf. Fig. 13). The very location, not in the center of town but on the eastern edge of the inhabited part of the seventeenth-century city, must have surprised the people who watched its construction. And then, when the Barberini refused to let their new palace front on the piazza in the ordinary way

but rather kept it hemmed in by a jumble of already existing little houses, Romans and visitors to the city alike might well have wondered at the disdain of both building and family for the conventions of Roman palace building.

Without obvious precedent and without succession, this powerful structure stands outside the norms of Roman palace building. Golzio's early and valiant attempt to reconcile the design with an evolutionary explanation of the Roman palace could not succeed.[1] Nor does it seem adequate to view this large and expensive building as the heroic achievement of an architectural visionary.[2] Its exceptional qualities must be due to exceptional circumstances and exceptional intentions, both exploited by exceptional designers. To understand this design we must push aside accretions of all sorts, to try to discover the original intentions of both patrons and designers and the characteristics of the life that informed this building in the beginning. Its site, the patterns of use for which it was intended, the aspirations of its owners, and its origin in far-ranging discussions among many advisors, all entered into the design as it was shaped by the architects' craft and art.

The Sforza Palace

A large building already stood on the property that Francesco Barberini bought from Alessan-

91   Piazza Barberini and Palazzo Barberini alle Quattro Fontane, drawing by Lieven Cruyl (reversed), February 1665 (The Cleveland Museum of Art, Dudley P. Allen Fund)

dro Sforza in 1625.[3] Constructed in part on a foundation of ancient Roman masonry, its nucleus was the mid-sixteenth-century casino of Cardinal Rodolfo Pio da Carpi. Two major additions had been built by Sforza owners, in 1583 and 1612; together these formed the main part of the long, narrow palace that was to be incorporated as the north wing of the new Palazzo Barberini. Michelangelo Buonarroti the Younger describes the palace at the time of the purchase — the extent of its grounds, its imposing situation above the corner of the piazza Grimana (Barberini),

and its inadequacies for its new owners: the building was small in its entirety and in its parts, and badly arranged. Its entrance was "incomprehensible," with narrow, unroofed, poorly located stairs. The apartments were too few in number, and paths of circulation were inadequate. The unevenness of both perimeter and surface of the site was a problem with which any designer would have to grapple. The building seemed "besieged" by the blocks of small houses on all but its upper (south) side.[4]

More detailed information about the Sforza

(Ed.ⁿⁱ Alinari) P.ᵗ I.ᵒ N.ᵒ 6304. ROMA - Palazzo Barberini. (Carlo Maderno.)

92   Palazzo Barberini alle Quattro Fontane, from southwest (Alinari/Art Resource, N.Y.)

property is provided by a survey plan of 1625 (Fig. 95),[5] the description in an anonymous proposal for the palace to be built (Barb. lat. 4360),[6] and a few references in the documents of Barberini construction.[7] The main part of the long, narrow building was 60 *palmi* wide (Figs. 96, 97). Built against the north slope of the Quirinal hill, its lowest level opened to the north and contained stables, carriage rooms, and a kitchen for the household staff.[8] On the next level (the "pian terreno" of the present palace) were two small apartments whose plan provided the basis for the rooms above. They were separated by a three-bay loggia, built against the higher ground and terrace to the south and opening to the north.[9] Part of the construction of 1583, this loggia is shown schematically in Tempesta's map of 1593 (Fig. 98); it replaced an earlier painted loggia facing north from the lower level of the Pio casino.[10] The eastern rooms of the *pian terreno* contained ceiling paintings of recent date, which the Barberini would preserve.[11] The main entrance to the palace was on the *piano nobile,* in the center of the south side; it was reached from the piazza by a

93 Palazzo Barberini from north, drawing by Ingres (Hans Naef, *Ingres in Rome,* Fig. 41)

drive up the slope of the hill to a pair of court-yards, an open square-well stair, and an unroofed entrance terrace (labeled "scoperto innanzi al salone" on Fig. 95) at the level of the gardens and the *piano nobile*. Alternatively, visitors approach-ing from the south could pass directly into the south courtyard and then on up to the entrance terrace. Without benefit of vestibule or loggia, one entered directly into the *salone,* about 45 × 70 *palmi.* To the left opened an apartment of an anteroom and four small rooms arranged as an *appartamento doppio* (the Sforza addition of 1612), and to the right were three rooms en suite. These latter, with windows to both north and south, were extended by a room with a door opening onto the cross axis of an enclosed gar-den, and then by a suite of smaller rooms, to the

first of which the chapel was appended. As on the floor below, the vaults of a number of rooms on the *piano nobile* had been frescoed only a few years earlier for their Sforza owners.[12] Above were two mezzanine stories.

The planning is appropriate for a villa, and any number of country houses could be named which show a similar pattern of central *salone* flanked by apartments of only a few rooms. The Villa Aldobrandini in Frascati is especially close in that it too is a long, narrow block situated against the slope of a hill, with small apartments flanking its central *salone.* For a major palace in the city, however, the Sforza building was clearly inadequate. The apartments had too few rooms for the full-blown ritual of the reception of guests. The entrance preceding the apartments

94   Palazzo Barberini, north façade (Alinari/Art Resource, N.Y.)

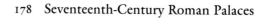

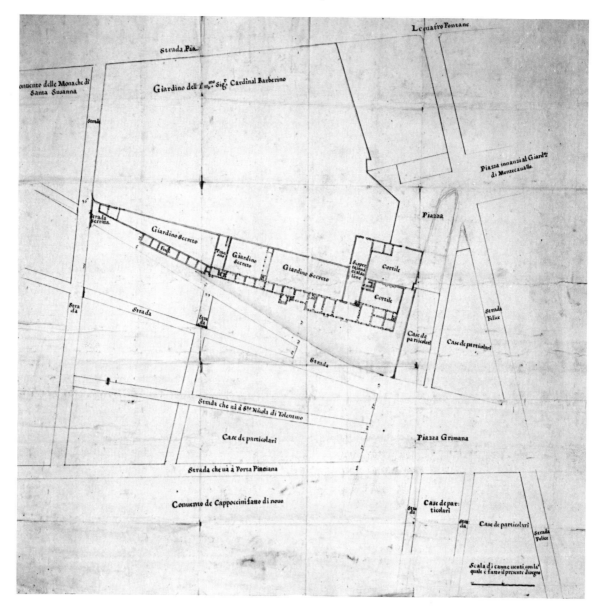

95   Palazzo Sforza-Barberini, site plan in 1625 (Biblioteca Apostolica Vaticana, ABarb., Ind. II, no. 2826 [c])

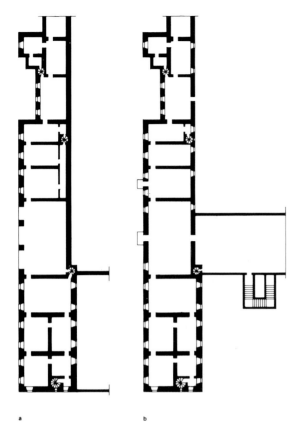

a   b

96   Palazzo Sforza in 1625, reconstruction:
(a) lower level, (b) *piano nobile* (author)

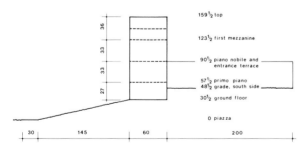

97   Palazzo Sforza in 1625, section, reconstruction
(dimensions in *palmi romani*) (author)

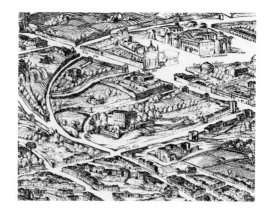

98   Tempesta Map of Rome, 1593, detail with
Palazzo Sforza (later Barberini)

did not provide for the sheltered approach of a carriage to the foot of the stair and the ascent of a distinguished guest, accompanied by the ringing of a bell, to the *salone*. For the Barberini in particular, there were simply not enough apartments for the several members of the family, in both summer and winter. A distinctive image was lacking. Still, these walls and rooms (and even much of the fresco decoration) would come to form part of the new Barberini palace. There was apparently never any thought of demolishing the structure or abandoning it to the *famiglia* and building on the clear, higher part of the large site to the south.[13] Whether considerations of economy or appreciation of some special attributes of the old palace led to its preservation, it physically conditioned what the Barberini's designers did; and it may have predisposed them to think along similar lines in their larger design.

Two Palaces

The striking form of Palazzo Barberini — two palace wings joined by an extraordinary loggia — speaks clearly of its content (Fig. 99). References throughout the document of construction

FACCIATA PRINCIPALE DEL PALAZZO BARBERINO DELL'ECC.ᵐᵒ SIG.ᵣ PRENCIPE DI PELLESTRINA CON LI DVE FIANCHI CHE LA CONPONGANO *nel monte Quirinale. Architettura del Caualier Bernino.*

99   Palazzo Barberini from west, engraving by Specchi (Biblioteca Apostolica Vaticana)

make it clear that the north half of the palace was built for Taddeo Barberini and his family and that the south half was intended for his brother Cardinal Francesco.[14] The two halves were planned according to the usages of seventeenth-century Roman palace building, as surely as their exterior forms announce their identity. The atypical center contains the only shared spaces — the deep westward portico and the grand *salone* above; and it correspondingly embodies the idea that makes of two palaces one. The discovery of what actually was built for Taddeo and Francesco, clients with both customary and particular requirements, is the first step in deciphering the meaning of the building, understanding its history, and evaluating the artistic accomplishment of its designers (Figs. 100–106).

NORTH WING

Taddeo, Prince of Palestrina in 1630 and Prefect of Rome in 1631, had apartments in the north wing on the ground floor or, if properly approached from the north, one level above the entrance (see Figs. 100, 101). His armorial devices are still to be seen in the decoration of the rooms throughout this suite. From the big northern entrance hall A8 one would ascend a broad flight of steps to the vestibule B21 just outside his apartments. The first room (B19) was his "salotto," or "sala de palafrenieri."[15] Then followed three anterooms (B20, B29, B28),[16] their number commensurate with Taddeo's high rank. The second anteroom B29 was distinguished by its vault, painted with a balustrade,

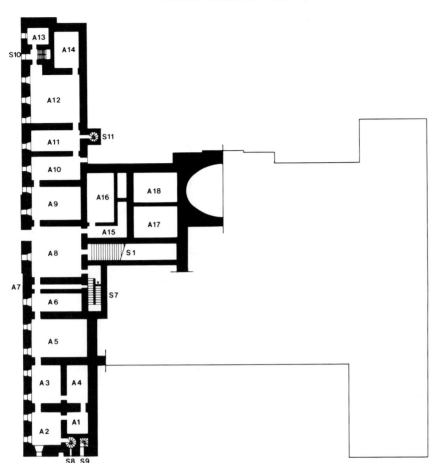

100   Palazzo Barberini, north wing, lowest level, 1628–38, reconstruction (David DiMarco)

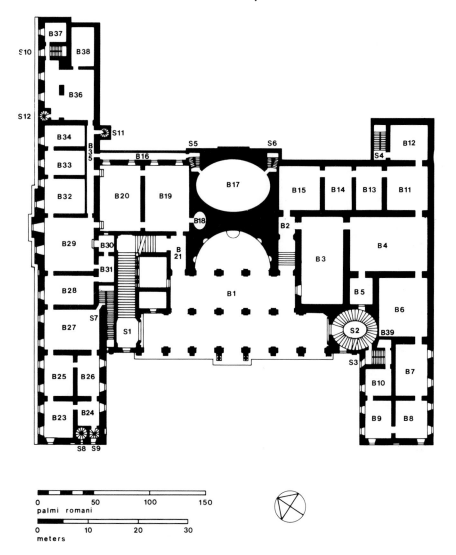

101   Palazzo Barberini, ground floor, 1628–38, reconstruction (author)

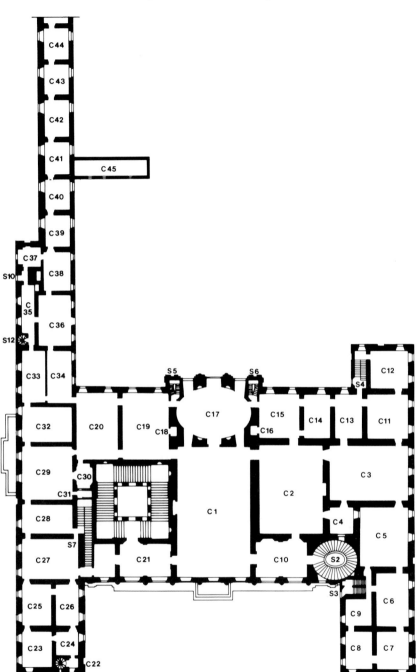

102   Palazzo Barberini, *piano nobile,* 1628–38, reconstruction (David DiMarco)

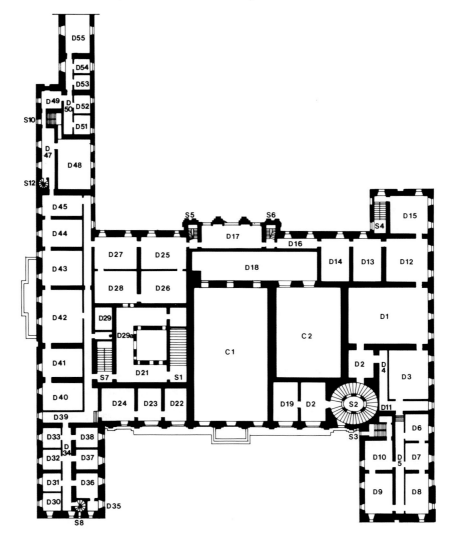

103   Palazzo Barberini, *secondo piano,* 1628–38, reconstruction (David DiMarco)

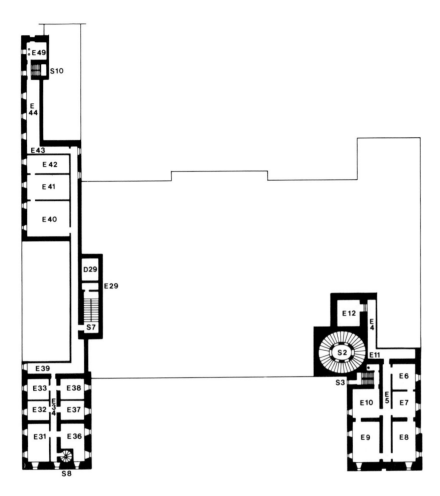

104   Palazzo Barberini, mezzanines, 1628–38, reconstruction (David DiMarco)

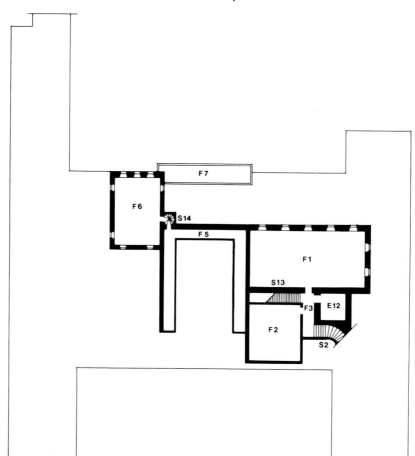

105   Palazzo Barberini, library level, 1628–38, reconstruction (author)

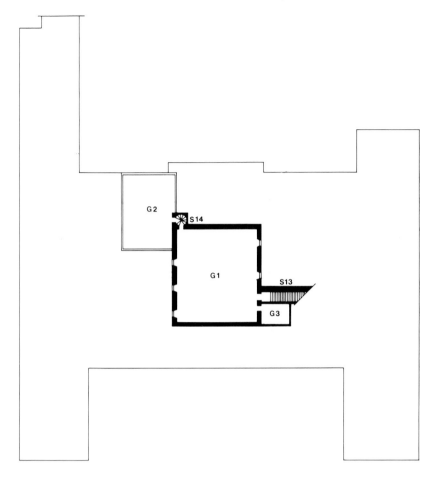

106   Palazzo Barberini, *guardaroba* level, 1628–38, reconstruction (author)

monkeys, and exotic birds, and by a fountain in the center of the room (Fig. 107).[17] The new vault of the third anteroom displayed the "Choice of Hercules," painted by Marziani.[18] Taddeo's chapel B30 was properly positioned adjacent to the second anteroom, with a little chamber next to it so that he could hear mass privately.[19] The next room in the suite, B27, its ceiling newly painted by Andrea Camassei with a scene of "Apollo on Mount Parnassus,"[20] would have been suitable for Taddeo's audience room. Beyond this room were four small private rooms. B25, with Marziani's painting of "Bellerophon Slaying the Chimaera" in its vault, might have been Taddeo's private study. The martial character of the painting[21] corresponds to Taddeo's duties as General of the Church. Later, at the "Casa Grande" ai Giubbonari, a group of four rooms on the *secondo piano* of Taddeo's apartment was outfitted as B25 may well have been, with shelves, tables, maps, plans, and other accessories to its owner's life of action.[22] B26 was likely Taddeo's bedroom; in 1644, when Antonio Barberini was occupying this apartment, it was fitted with three "bussole," or inner doors, and identified as Antonio's bedroom.[23] The nearby private stair S7 led to services below and above to the bedroom of Taddeo's wife, Anna. Beyond the bedroom was a small service room and a passage giving access to a spiral stair S9, which connected Taddeo's apartment to a private exit.[24] Small corner room B23 completed the apartment. Except for the anteroom B20, the bedroom B26, and its service room, all the rooms of this suite were equipped with fireplaces[25] — a sign that they were to be inhabited in the winter in spite of their north orientation. In 1644 Antonio used these rooms in the winter, but both Tessin and Rossini later call them a summer apartment.[26] To the right of the anteroom B29 were three rooms B32, B33, B34, without fireplaces, which would be comfortable in the summer even though they had no access to the garden to the south. Lacking proper private facilities, they would have been for daytime use

107   Palazzo Barberini, room B29 (Barbara Bini)

only. They might have been useful for entertaining a distinguished guest who might have arrived while Taddeo was giving audience to another.[27] Farther to the east, the large room B36 was not part of Taddeo's apartment. It was the *tinello* for his mother Costanza's women attendants. Sealed off from Taddeo's rooms, it was part of a vertical chain from the kitchens in the basement to Costanza's apartment above.[28]

Anna Colonna Barberini's apartments lay above those of her husband, on the *piano nobile* of the north wing (Fig. 102). Her visitors would arrive at the west façade, ascend the stair S1 to the left of the great portico, and enter the vestibule C21.[29] The grand *salone* in the center of the palace served as Anna's "sala dei palafrenieri" (Fig. 108), and her anterooms C19 and C20 followed from its northeast corner.[30] The suite continued into C29, the "Salotto della Divina Sapienza,"

108 Palazzo Barberini, *salone* C1 (I.C.C.D., Rome, ser. E, no. 33433)

its vault frescoed with Sacchi's famous painting (Fig. 109).[31] In the angle between the second anteroom and the third (the room of the "Divina Sapienza"), and directly over Taddeo's chapel, was located the chapel C30, with its little room for hearing mass privately.[32] The room of the "Divina Sapienza" would seem to be the principal antechamber to the chapel, because of the formal relationship between Sacchi's painting and the chapel's altar; but there was also a smaller door from the second anteroom C20 to the chapel, providing a potentially useful flexibility.[33] Room C28, its ceiling painted with the

"Creation of the Angels," would seem to be a fourth anteroom, leading to the audience room C27.[34] The bedroom of this suite was room C26,[35] with convenient access from Taddeo's bedroom below by the nearby private stair S7; the small room C24 and spiral stair S8 would serve the bedroom. As in Taddeo's apartment, two small rooms, C23 and C25, were available for private enjoyment. Fireplaces are documented in rooms C19, C20, C27, and C28;[36] like Taddeo's below, this apartment would be acceptable for use in the winter, if short of ideal because of its northern exposure. When Antonio Barberini

109   Palazzo Barberini, room C29, toward chapel entrance (Barbara Bini and John Beldon Scott)

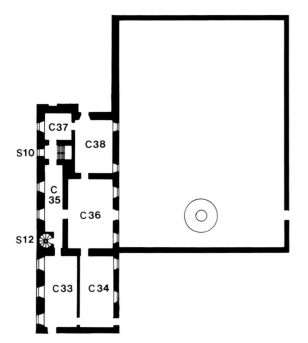

110 Palazzo Barberini, reconstruction of Anna's garden apartment, 1631–34 (David DiMarco)

moved into the palace in 1635, he recognized the summer-like character of the rooms by ordering a set of sky-blue silk revetments, "all painted with various flowers, fruits, birds, fountains, and so forth," complete with a baldacchino for room C27 and eight covers for small tables; and the pattern of use implied by the inventory of 1644 suggests that he abandoned this apartment for warmer rooms in the winter.[37]

Like Taddeo, Anna might use her major northward apartment in summer as well as winter; but she had a second apartment for warmer months. Beyond room C32, which could have served as an alternate audience room,[38] the group of six rooms C33–C38, all without fireplaces, formed a coherent apartment (Fig. 110). In 1644 room C34 was identified as the first room of the "appartamento della Conversatione,"[39] a group of small, intimate rooms centered on the "salotto" C36, whose door and two

windows opened to the enclosed garden of orange trees to the south.[40] In spite of its southern exposure, the "salotto" was shaded from the afternoon sun by the central body of the palace; still, if the room might become too warm, Anna and her companions could withdraw to the adjacent "gallarietta" C35, with windows only to the north. Room C34 was balanced by "saletta" C38, which opened to a chapel C37, surviving from the old Sforza palace. Spiral stair S12 went up to the *secondo piano* and down to the women's *tinello*, and stair S10 extended upward the full height of the north wing to the women's rooms.[41] The diminutive names of the rooms *(salotto, gallarietta, saletta)* speak of their quality; and their symmetrical composition, centered on the door to the garden, creates what amounts to a casino embedded in the mass of the palace. This was done by a small but purposeful modification of the old building, the reforming of rooms C33 and C34 by turning their dividing wall 90 degrees,[42] along with the addition of the little gallery C35 (surely provoked by the desire to create a large and homogeneous façade to the north).[43] The little apartment would have been an especial delight for Anna and her companions, whose activities were confined within the palace. Anna's children might join them as well, in the informality of the rooms and garden.[44] A secluded garden which women might enjoy was earlier recommended by the anonymous author of Barb. lat. 4360,[45] but our architect has gone further in finding a complementary "casino" within the palace.

The rooms of the little apartment were appropriately decorated for Anna's use in conjunction with the enclosed garden. Hooks for revetments were installed in rooms C33, C34, and C36.[46] For room C36, its vault to have been painted by Camassei,[47] an inventory dated 3 December 1631 lists a revetment of gilded leather, painted by Urbinese with views of gardens and palaces, and six overdoors and overwindows with arms of the House of Barberini.[48] A similar revetment was painted by the same artist for "the room before the chapel"; its three overdoors and two overwindows would fit room C38, and its scenes of

111   Palazzo Barberini, *gallarietta* C35, vault, looking east (Barbara Bini)

112   Palazzo Barberini, *gallarietta* C35, east end wall with lunette and the "Founding of Palestrina" (John Beldon Scott)

various gardens (including Castelgandolfo, the site of Anna and Taddeo's marriage) would complement the theme of this garden apartment.[49] The vault of *saletta* C38 held four landscapes still surviving from the period of Sforza ownership, new Barberini arms, and a short-lived Nativity painted by Marziani — a theme in keeping with Anna's role in the perpetuation of the Barberini family.[50] The *gallarietta* too was decorated in accord with the dual themes of garden and family: its barrel vault was painted with a symmetrical pattern of vegetal motifs, animals, and family emblems (Fig. 111); putti supporting Barberini arms filled the lunettes under the vault (that to the west repainted when the room was enlarged by the removal of the spiral stair S12 in

1677); and the upper circuit of the walls, a band 15 *palmi* high, was painted with scenes that must have included the two fragments still surviving in the room — the "Sacrifice to Juno" and the "Founding of Palestrina" (the principality purchased by the Barberini in 1630) (Figs. 112, 113, 114).[51]

The identity of this apartment was soon to be

114   Palazzo Barberini, *gallarietta* C35, "Sacrifice to Juno" (Barbara Bini)

113   Palazzo Barberini, *gallarietta* C35, "Founding of Palestrina" (Barbara Bini)

obscured, first by Antonio Barberini's extension of a suite for his paintings through the *saletta* to the small rooms to the east, and then by the revision of the gardens and light court immediately to the east of the palace in the 1670s, which destroyed the relation between casino and garden.[52]

Considered from the north, Taddeo's apartment is appropriately on the level above the entrance, and his wife's apartment is farther removed, on the floor above. Yet considered from the west, Anna has the superior position on the *piano nobile* as well as a more elaborate stair, access to the central *salone,* a string of four anterooms (in contrast to Taddeo's three), and a summer apartment with rooms turned toward the garden. Is this a sign of Taddeo's modesty and deference to his wife? Francesco's biography of his brother tries to impress both of these traits on the reader and in particular remarks that, when he was about twenty years old, Taddeo chose the worst room in the house for his own.[53] However modest Taddeo may have been, it would seem that a more pressing reason for the prominence of Anna's apartment would have been her role as "consort" of the reigning pope, obliged as Urban VIII's close female relative to receive guests on his behalf, once her mother-in-law Costanza had been relieved of that duty.[54] Since a woman's etiquette would not normally allow her to go beyond the door of her own apartment (that is, beyond the door of her first anteroom C19 into the *salone*), the larger number of anterooms would be especially useful in providing her the number of stages necessary to show her respect for differences in the ranks of her many diplomatic visitors. (In an apartment with only two anterooms Costanza had earlier been obliged to distinguish among guests by compliments and other nonarchitectural signs.)[55] The ingenious design of the palace on the slope of the hill therefore allows Anna's special prominence as female relative of the pope and at the same time her normal position with respect to her husband.

The main stair extended upward one more story, to the *secondo piano* and its more private rooms (see Fig. 103). The landing at the top of the stair D21 gave guarded access to the quarters of Anna's women attendants in the western end of the north wing.[56] Their small rooms were arranged in two levels (each with a central corridor, D34 and E34) connected by stair S8. From corridor D39 they could enter their kitchen, *tinello* (with a fireplace), and *armaria,* or storeroom (D24, D23, D22).[57] Supplies could be delivered to them through a turnbox between the landing D21 and the *armaria,* which was also called the "stanza della ruota."[58] The spiral stair S8 connected the women's rooms with the private rooms of Anna's apartment and, in the basement, with their laundry A2.[59]

Donna Costanza's apartment was to the east on this level. Having received release from her official obligations as relative of the pope, she lived a modest and secluded life—not in an apartment of splendid reception rooms as did Anna but in a few modest and sparsely furnished rooms. Her rooms were D25 and D26, just next to the kitchen D28 and *tinello* D27 of her women attendants.[60] The kitchen borrowed light from the stair through a grilled window and another window over the door; and a turnbox was installed so that food and other supplies could be passed through. Costanza's chapel—D49, over the old Sforza chapel—was somewhat removed from her apartment;[61] and her women attendants must have slept in rooms D51–D54—not so convenient a location with respect to the rooms of the woman whom they served. The other *tinello* for Costanza's women, B36, possibly more comfortable in the summer, could be reached from these rooms by the small stair S10.[62]

The organization of the rooms for Costanza and her women is not so lucid as one might expect, and they seem arranged in whatever spaces might have been available. This is probably the case, since, when the palace was designed and begun, Costanza's husband, Carlo, was still alive. Carlo and Costanza would have continued to live in appropriately splendid apartments at the "Casa Grande" ai Giubbonari. But Carlo died in 1630, while the Palazzo Barberini was under construction, and that changed everything. Costanza gained permission from her brother-in-law the pope to live in a withdrawn, convent-like manner,[63] and secluded rooms had to be found for her in Taddeo and Anna's palace. Costanza's rooms were surely not part of the original design program but rather were found within the building whose construction was already well under way.

There was room for one or two more apartments at this level, to the north, over the larger rooms of Anna's apartment. Six rooms (D40–D45) were arranged en suite, with windows to the north and a narrow corridor to the south.[64] D42, the largest, provided access from the corridor. These rather large rooms, equipped with fireplaces and convenient access from the main stair, are not specified as being for any particular person in the document of construction; but the designer might have been looking forward to the day when Taddeo and Anna's sons (not yet born when construction began in 1628) would have required apartments of their own. There is a hint that they might have been considered for Costanza, after 1630 and before more secluded rooms were decided on, in a reference to her anteroom in the upper part of the old palace.[65] By 1644 it seems that Antonio Magalotti, Costanza's brother, was living comfortably in four of them, D42—D45, with his servants in other rooms near at hand.[66]

When Taddeo and Anna moved to their new residence in May 1632, their two sons Carlo and Maffeo were toddlers and they were awaiting the birth of Lucrezia in September. These children and their respective nurses required accommodation, yet the document of construction reveals no nursery and, at least in the lower parts of the

115   Palazzo Barberini, *guardaroba* G1, with cabinets destroyed ca. 1930 (I.C.C.D., Rome, ser. E, no. 39256)

palace, no space for a nursery. Clearly these all-important members of the family could not command an identifiable apartment. A single note refers to an attic over Costanza's apartment, where the "signorini" were to have slept.[67] Pecchiai writes of Anna's devotion to her children and her sleeping near them if they were sick or had some special need;[68] yet she must have had to climb to the attic, far from her own formal quarters on the *piano nobile,* to perform this service.

Also at this level were the old *guardaroba* (D48), the "torretta" or light well (D29) over the vault of Anna's chapel, and a little room for privies (D29a), with another small room above it (accessible from the stair S7).[69] In the attic over the eastern extremity of the north wing were a few more small rooms. Somewhere here was a room for Costanza's chickens.[70] Antonio's archive D17 was fitted in over the oval *salone,* toward the garden.[71]

Taddeo's *guardaroba* G1 occupied the attic rising above the central *salone*—a spacious room measuring 79¾ × 71 *palmi*, lit by five windows to the north and south (Fig. 115). Below, a secure U-shaped corridor-like room F5 was fitted in over the cove of the *salone* vault. Spiral stair S14 connected the U-shaped room, the main room, its one-story loggia F6, and the terrace G2; but access to the *guardaroba* was by means of a stair S13 from the south half of the palace (see Figs. 105, 106).[72] The princess's *guardaroba* was separate from that of her husband, in an attic just to the north of the main *guardaroba*.[73]

Returning to the basement, whence we began (see Fig. 100), we find Taddeo's central *entrone* A8 flanked by various service rooms. Taddeo's kitchen was room A12; the bakery, with ovens, was A11; and the scullery, also intended to be used by the staff kitchen A9 until its removal from the palace, was A10.[74] Spiral stair S11 connected the kitchen with the corridor on the *pian terreno,* just outside the turnbox to the women's *tinello* B36. To the west of the *entrone* were the two rooms of the *dispensa,* A5 and A6; an old carriage door was walled up, a new door was made from the *entrone,* pavements were laid, and a counter and a lavatory were installed.[75] Anna's laundry was in corner room A2.[76] Under Taddeo's *sala* and first anteroom were reservoirs for water (A17, A18) and a room for wood storage (A16).[77]

Taddeo's palace was almost entirely filled with apartments for himself, Anna, Costanza, and the two noblewomen's attendants. No more than a few members of Taddeo's large household (143 persons, including twenty-six women, in 1633, and 163 in 1634)[78] could have been housed there. The new *dispensa* and laundry in the lowest level of the palace had displaced the stables and coachrooms of the old Sforza palace, and Taddeo's many horses and coaches would also have to be sheltered outside the palace. For these purposes Taddeo bought or rented many small nearby houses.

To the north of the palace, many already built houses were bought for the horses and coaches.[79] These were ordinary Roman row houses, with ground-floor shops and dwellings above, about 20 × 55 *palmi* in plan.[80] The large street-front openings of the shops were walled up and new doors made to the courtyard behind; the separate buildings were connected by new doorways; and some new construction was added. There were eleven carriage rooms of various sizes (the smallest holding a single carriage), grouped around a courtyard toward the piazza. The large building facing the piazza (to the left of the portal in Fig. 91) and several small houses were remodeled for coaches; and at least one large coach house was built anew.[81] The stables were farther to the east, around the large stableyard with its fountain;[82] the small houses could easily be converted to that use, with the insertion of a row of horse stalls about 14 *palmi* deep. Storage for hay, straw, and grain was in the easternmost part of the site.

According to the document of construction, several staff members lived in rooms over the coach rooms and in houses adjacent to the stables (but not over the stables).[83] More lived in houses that Taddeo rented, mostly to the north and west of the palace. About twenty-eight houses belonging to almost as many owners were rented for annual amounts ranging from 20 to 118 scudi, for a total of about 1,600 scudi.[84] Most of them are noted as being "contiguous to the palace," some more specifically facing the piazza, the vicolo, or strada Felice, one immediately next to the portal on the piazza, and one (the kennel) near S. Nicola da Tolentino. The plans of a few of them in the block just to the northwest of the palace are shown in Figure 116.[85] These ordinary Roman houses, shown before the palace in the Maggi-Maupin-Losi map of 1625 (Fig. 117) and in Lieven Cruyl's drawing of 1665 (see Fig. 91), were two or three stories high. Their renovation for members of Taddeo's staff left their modest character intact.[86] Most of the ground-floor shops were eliminated. New doorways connected their courtyards. Ground-floor

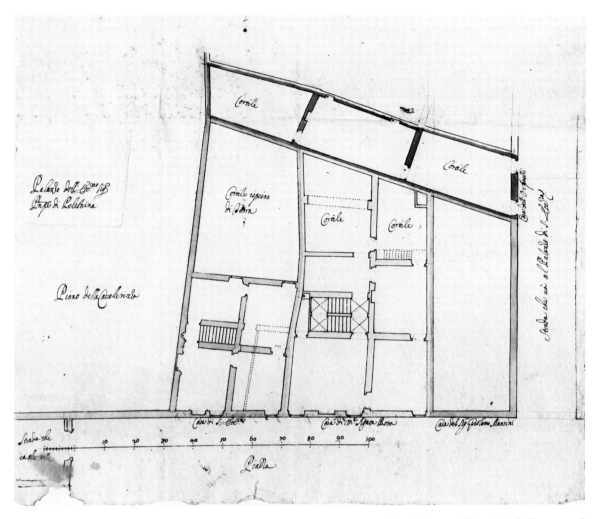

116   Houses at northwest corner of Barberini property (Biblioteca Apostolica Vaticana, ABarb., Ind. II, no. 2911)

rooms of two houses were used for storage of wood and charcoal, and another housed the infirmary. The old *cucina comune* in ground-floor room A9 of the palace having been removed, kitchens were maintained in the individual houses; but in addition a new staff kitchen was constructed, not far from the intersection of the Quattro Fontane.[87]

Stables, coach houses, and housing for the staff were so contrived that the visual texture of

the neighborhood remained essentially unchanged, although whatever commerce had once occupied the ground-floor shops was now removed.

This much of the palace and its adjacent buildings was completed when Taddeo and his family moved to the Quattro Fontane on 13 May 1632.[88] The entire north wing, taking advantage of the earlier Sforza construction and decoration, was ready. The central portion—loggia, north stair, central *salone,* rooms east of the stair, and ante-rooms C2 (where theatrical performances were given, beginning in February 1632)[89] and C3 — had been built although not entirely finished. The vault of the *salone* was finished and ready to be painted by the end of 1630, but Pietro da Cortona's painting had not yet begun.[90] The truncated form of the palace can be seen in the 1634 edition of the Greuter map (Fig. 118). Still, Taddeo could move in because the palace was complete in all its essential parts, at least for his family: façade, entrance, stairs, complete apartments, and services were ready. Just as the Palazzo Farnese and the Palazzo Deza-del Giglio (later Borghese) could be occupied for decades as fragments,[91] so too could the Palazzo Barberini. Living in the midst of a construction site would be nothing new for Taddeo, if we remember the

117   Maggi Map of Rome, 1625, detail with Palazzo Sforza-Barberini (Biblioteca Apostolica Vaticana)

118   Greuter Map of Rome, 1634, detail with Palazzo Barberini (Biblioteca Apostolica Vaticana)

frequent remodelings of his "Casa Grande" ai Giubbonari and Francesco's report of an injury sustained by Taddeo's tutor when something fell from a woodworker's scaffolding (while the future Prince of Palestrina was spared);[92] and it would actually facilitate his monitoring of work still in progress.

SOUTH WING

Attention could now turn to the construction of Francesco's half of the palace, all newly constructed, without the assistance or restriction of preexisting masonry. Francesco's apartments would be the pendants of Anna's on the *piano nobile* (see Fig. 102). Like Anna's visitors, his would approach from the west, into the first aisle of the deep portico, but they would turn to the right and ascend an elliptical stair S2 to the "loggia" C10, the counterpart of Anna's vestibule C21; and, like Anna, he would use the great central *salone* as his *sala dei palafrenieri* (see Fig. 108). From the *salone* a visitor would pass into Francesco's first anteroom, the large hall C2 (Figs. 119, 120), which became memorable as the site of the early Barberini theatrical productions, and then into the second anteroom C3, also unusually large.[93] The chapel C4 was in its accustomed position, opening from the anteroom, and to the side it had a window so that the cardinal could hear mass privately from room C5. This last-named room would have been Francesco's audience room, for it seems that Antonio gave audience here in 1644.[94] Alternatively, Francesco may have preferred to extend the sequence of anterooms and give audience in room C6.[95] It can be seen that his anterooms, fewer in number than Anna's, were impressive through size rather than number. In 1644 Antonio was using room C8 for his bedroom and C9, adjacent to the service stair S3, apparently for his attendant.[96] The small room C7, with its south and west exposures, would be for the cardinal's private enjoyment. These rooms formed the winter apartment of the south wing: the south and west exposures,

the walls hung with tapestries, and the fireplaces in all but the sleeping rooms speak of this seasonal use.[97] To the east, toward the garden, were Francesco's summer rooms (C11–C15). Their orientation, adjacency to the garden, and especially their damask wall coverings[98] all marked them as summer rooms, and so they were called in the descriptions of Rossini and Tessin, though Panciroli considered them suitable for the temperate seasons.[99] These rooms were conspicuously without fireplaces and uninhabited in April 1644.[100] An inventory of 1636 mentions a baldacchino in C11 and a bed in C12; but by 1692–1704 the bed had been moved to C13 and C12 was omitted from the suite.[101]

The large anteroom C2 rose through the height of two stories, its two high windows admitting light from a light well D18 to the east;[102] but anteroom C3 had a lower vault, allowing for a vaulted room D1 above it (see Fig. 103). This upper vaulted room, 70¼ × 47 *palmi* in plan, is called the "large hall where His Eminence [Francesco] used to have his *guardaroba* and where they dress for the comedies" in the document of construction.[103] Its use as a dressing room for theatrical productions lasted only as long as anteroom C2 was used for those performances; and Francesco's residence in the Cancelleria after 1632 robbed it of its first function as his *guardaroba*. To the east were rooms D12–D15, of unspecified function, repeating the plan of those of the *piano nobile,* with a light well D18 and corridor D16 over C15.[104] To the west was a set of smaller, low-ceilinged rooms D2–D10, each accessible from a narrow corridor.[105] Their function is not identified in the document of construction, but they could well have housed a few of the cardinal's gentlemen attendants. Above the westernmost rooms (as in the corresponding part of the north wing) there was space for a similar set of small rooms in the "piano delli mezzanini," their ceilings only 13 *palmi* high and their windows opening through the frieze of the façade (see Figs. 92, 104).[106] An inventory of paintings and sculptures in the palace in 1692–

1704 describes a "mezzanine apartment" or "studio apartment," which can be identified with these rooms.[107] They may have been intended from the beginning as a private retreat, in conjunction with the library.

The library F1 rose above rooms C2–C3 and above the roof of the main part of the palace, in the fashion of a *guardaroba* (see Fig. 105).[108] Scholars could easily ascend to the library by means of the large elliptical stair S2. It was originally constructed to measure only 100 × 47¾ *palmi* in plan, so that its south wall rose above the vault of the pair of rooms C3 and D1 — surely the occasion for the extensive reinforcement of the vaults of these two rooms with chains.[109] The library had five windows to the east (the ideal orientation for a library, according to Alberti)

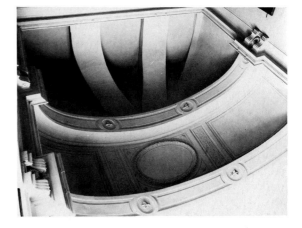

119 Palazzo Barberini, anteroom C2, vault (Barbara Bini)

120 Palazzo Barberini, anteroom C2, looking west (Barbara Bini)

121 Palazzo Barberini, east façade, reversed (Teti, 1642) (Biblioteca Apostolica Vaticana)

and two to the south but, like the great central *guardaroba,* none to the west.[110] The library was soon enlarged so that its south wall stood in line with the south wall of the palace below, whether because the cardinal needed more room for his books or because the structural precautions were found to be inadequate; it is shown in its full extent, with a projecting pier and a sixth window to the east, in Teti's engraving of 1642 (Fig. 121). Its carved wood bookcases were constructed by the joiner-architect Giovanni Battista Soria (Fig. 122).[111] The library was complemented by a smaller room F2 for manuscripts and medals to the west, and between this room and the library rose the straight stair S13 leading to the central *guardaroba.*[112]

Downstairs, on the *pian terreno,* it seems that the plan of the rooms simply supported the apartments of the *piano nobile,* without having any particular design of its own (see Fig. 101). It was only in the 1670s that these rooms were developed into a coherent apartment.[113] Meanwhile, the *credenza* was located in B3. Its built-in sink for dishwashing measured 6×2 *palmi* and was drained by a pipe leading to the main sewer of the palace. Although large ($74\frac{1}{4} \times 38\frac{1}{2}$ *palmi*), vaulted, and relatively convenient to the *sala* above, it must not have been especially dry and airy. Its main virtue may have been its security, with no windows to the outside. Adjacent B4 was simply a big room where carpenters worked during construction of the palace. To the east were "grotte," the passage B2 next to the hemicycle leading to them.[114] The rooms in the western wing came to serve various purposes.[115]

While Taddeo's service rooms, stables, and staff housing are amply documented, no such facilities appear for Francesco's part of the palace. Space was available within the palace, on the ground floor and in the mezzanine, but there was no development of this space; nor is there any record of the use of nearby houses. Surely this omission is due to the fact that Francesco never lived here. Just as construction of his part of the palace was under way, he found himself appointed vice-chancellor and therefore entitled to residence in the Cancelleria. Later, when his brother Cardinal Antonio was living alone in the palace, Taddeo's service facilities would suffice.

CONSTRUCTION

An understanding of the palace as two buildings is validated not only by the original intended pattern of occupation of the building, with Taddeo and his family to the north and Francesco to the south, but also by the course of construction and payments. The work begun in December 1628 was for Taddeo and, according to the document of construction, included the north wing and those parts of the central portion that were essential for the operation of Taddeo's palace:

122   Palazzo Barberini, shelving for the library (Moscioni; Monumenti Musei e Gallerie Ponteficie, Archivio Fotografico)

the entrance portico, the square-well stair, the central *salone,* and the anterooms to the north, with the addition of only the two large anterooms to the south.[116] Taddeo's major expenditures for construction continued until 1632.[117] The balance of the palace, to the south, was treated as a separate job, and Cardinal Francesco began large payments for the "nuovi appartamenti" in autumn 1632.[118] This work was measured and evaluated separately.[119] Several years later, in 1641, a lawsuit brought forth testimony that shows the conception of separate undertakings within one building—work for Taddeo, other work for Francesco, and (later) work for their brother Antonio.[120]

OLD PALACE, NEW PALACE

In the design of a balanced and seemingly symmetrical palace, the designers were faced not only with different functional requirements but also with different physical circumstances. Taddeo's half was constructed largely within the confines of preexisting walls, while Francesco's was totally new. Yet the seeming freedom of design in the "new palace" was tempered by the presence of the "old palace." The building demanded of the designer a full range of architectural skills.

The "old palace" was transformed for Taddeo's use with surprising economy, with a relatively small expenditure of masonry. The building was enlarged by heightening its walls several *palmi*.[121] Inside, above the *piano nobile,* there was now room for a "secondo piano" and an attic story or "mezzanino"; and outside, the new height and revised fenestration would give the appearance of three full stories, raised on a battered basement to the north and capped by an ornate frieze containing the attic windows. The outline of the building was filled in by the addition of the *gallarietta* between the main rooms and the appended chapel to the east, pulling the previously fragmented north façade into a single large form which then could be ordered by the new pattern of banded bays and windows (see Fig. 94). Stables and carriage rooms were removed from the basement to nearby small buildings, and a major entrance was inserted where those services had once been tucked away. What had been the back of the building had been turned into a front.

Inside, the space for principal apartments was considerably increased and reformed. The new design developed apartments on two levels. The Sforza palace's orientation to gardens on higher ground had meant that the two lower levels, both open to the north, were destined to be subordinate. The Barberini's new double orientation brought with it the possibility of ennobling the upper basement, as a "pian terreno" when viewed from the west and even a "piano nobile" from the north; and so it became Taddeo's, while Anna's apartments stretched through the level above. The designer filled in the Sforza loggia in the "pian terreno" rooms.[122] He added a single wall, from the foundations to the roof, dividing the former loggia, old Sforza *salone,* and similar spaces above and below into a large square room and a smaller rectangular one on each level.[123] Horizontally, this insertion made the rooms in the middle of the long block more nearly the same size; and vertically, it provided for Taddeo's entrance, a penetration through the center of the building from its lowest level. Both Taddeo's and Anna's suites were doubly enlarged by additions to the south: the new *saloni* and anterooms (B19, B20, C1, C19, C20) increased the number of rooms in each suite and also increased the scale by their size. Each apartment is formed by an appropriately graduated sequence of rooms, from a large *sala* to small private rooms. A new service stair S7 provided the proper conjugal connection between the two apartments. In Anna's rooms, the rotating of a single wall 90 degrees[124] changed the shape of her eastern apartment, to create a "garden casino" opening to the secluded garden to the south. If Anna gained a pleasure apartment within the palace, Taddeo gained a way to leave, with the addition of a little spiral stair and ground-floor exit to his private rooms. New chapels were built for both husband and wife, properly adjacent to their anterooms. Finally, Taddeo's palace came to participate in a much larger entity as it joined Francesco's palace to the south, by means of the great central construction, to form the palace of the Barberini family.

Having searched within the preexisting structure and added to it judiciously, the designer created impressive apartments where before there had been only a few rooms. Still, a critic might find some shortcomings. Taddeo really had only one apartment, rather chilly in the winter and without access to gardens for the summer. Fireplaces must work especially hard to warm his north-facing living rooms. Anna's situation was somewhat better, thanks to her "casino," but those small rooms for summer enjoyment opened to the south. The north wing, on the lower slope of the hill, seemed doomed to less than optimal exposure.

For Francesco's palace, the designer worked within fewer constraints than for Taddeo's pendant dwelling. There was to be only a single resident, the cardinal, without wife and attendant women. Accordingly, controlled connections to and separation among several apartments were not required. The site was clear, so that preexisting walls, rooms, and floor levels did not have to be dealt with. The slope of the ground meant that the lower level might be darkened, but the upper parts of the building could take advantage of east, south, and west orientation and ready access to the gardens in the upper part of the site. Even the general outline of the wing could be adjusted while still appearing to correspond to Taddeo's palace to the north. At this point Francesco's only special requirement seems to have been the inclusion of a library for his already growing collection of books and manuscripts.

The designer concentrated his efforts on the *piano nobile,* where he found plenty of room for both summer and winter apartments for the cardinal. The rooms were especially large, with correspondingly higher ceilings than could be arranged for Taddeo or Anna. While fewer in number, their vastness would make them at least as impressive as those to the north. Even the four private rooms in the western wing are more amply proportioned than the corresponding rooms in Anna's apartment, since the wing is 7 *palmi* wider. Three small stairs provide services to the private rooms. The winter rooms enjoy southern and western sunlight, and the summer rooms turn to the east and the gardens. The dark ground floor, not needed for principal apartments, can be given over to services.

Both north and south wings—prince's and cardinal's palaces—provide impressive, well-functioning apartments, well within the norms of seventeenth-century Roman society, from the foot of each grand stair to the discreet service stairs in their most remote rooms. Presented with such living quarters, any Roman prince or cardinal would happily make himself at home. The atypical aspects of the Palazzo Barberini

would seem to lie at the center, which makes of the two palaces one. The western forecourt, loggia, portico with deep fountained niche, stairs, *salone,* and oval room, and substance in place of the usual hollow of a courtyard, all set this building apart from other Roman palaces. While we can admire the skill with which the designer worked out living accommodations in both old and new palaces, we must still wonder at the art of the central part and the concept underlying the whole building.

One Palace: The Center

The progress of a visitor through a Roman apartment to its audience room is measured and linear; and the visitor's position with respect to that of his host is revealed as he proceeds up the stairs and through the *salone* and anterooms. At Palazzo Barberini the visitor's preparation for his audience begins earlier, proceeds through more stages, and has more richly developed layers of meaning than in an ordinary palace. The path to the apartments of Anna and Francesco in particular takes one through the problematic central part of the palace; accordingly, our explication of that part, which eventually gives wholeness to the bifurcated palace, will follow that path.

APPROACH

The path begins long before one draws near the palace, for its distinctive form, high on the north slope of the Quirinal, is visible from afar—from the steps of St. Peter's, or from the Gianicolo, or even from Lieven Cruyl's viewpoint as he drew the Fontana di Trevi and its piazza (Fig. 123).

Winding through the narrow streets of Rome, one's cortège would at last emerge in the piazza Barberini, a spacious trapezoid almost entirely ringed by small, ordinary buildings (see Fig. 91). Those to the east and south were the little houses purposefully maintained by the Barberini for their horses, carriages, and household staff. The presence of the palace in the neighborhood was

123   Piazza di Trevi, with Palazzo Barberini in the background, print by Lieven Cruyl, 1667 (by permission of the British Library)

unavoidable, if only because of its large scale; yet it stood aloof, ignoring the piazza. Whether the visitor sought Taddeo's north entrance or Anna and Francesco's west entrance, the way was obscured by the brood of small buildings around the base of the hill.[125]

Taddeo's visitors found a monumental portal in the southeast corner of the piazza, indicating the entrance to the palace on the hill.[126] Passing through this portal, carriages proceeded up a long drive, parallel to the north façade of the palace, then turned right onto a terrace or "piazza da basso"[127] and took visitors to the door at the base of the north wing, or even into the large squarish "entrone"[128] (Fig. 124; see also Fig. 100) to leave the guests properly at the foot of the stair to Taddeo's apartment. The *entrone* was $46 \times 44\frac{1}{2}$ *palmi* and therefore large enough for carriages to turn around.

The claim to frontality of the west façade was at least as strong as that of the north. Teti's frontispiece to *Aedes Barberinae* (Fig. 125) presents it forcefully, and Totti's early guide describes entrance into the "double portico with fountain, and double stair, which leads from the sides to the halls and the apartments." He continues, clearly describing the west front: "The façade of this unusual palace is almost in the form of a

124   Palazzo Barberini, north façade (Totti, 1638)
(Biblioteca Apostolica Vaticana)

125   Palazzo Barberini, west façade (Teti, 1642)
(Biblioteca Apostolica Vaticana)

theater." [129] To reach this entrance to the stairs leading to the apartments of Donna Anna and Cardinal Francesco, one could continue from the north terrace around the west end of the north wing to the space before the west façade, ambivalently called "piazza overo cortile grande" in the document of construction.[130] Alternatively, one might approach from the Quirinal palace or the Quattro Fontane on the ridge of the hill to the south. Visitors arriving from this direction would be met by a low wall along the east side of the strada Felice, stretching 225 *palmi* between small houses. Near the north end of this wall, opposite the opening of the strada Rasella, was a simple arched portal, not to be

compared with the elaborate forms of the portal on the piazza Barberini.[131] Beyond this was a shallow triangular courtyard separated from the space immediately before the palace by a second low wall, made of whitewashed earth and, like the outer wall, interrupted asymmetrically by a plain arched portal.[132] Totti's illustration (Fig. 126) shows the pair of walls in summary fashion. The wall along the street can be seen in Lieven Cruyl's drawing (see Fig. 91); and the plain forms of the inner wall and portal, close before the west façade of the grand palace, are shown in Piranesi's etching of the mid-eighteenth century and in Rossini's view of the early nineteenth century (Figs. 127, 128).[133] The irregular courtyard, encumbered for decades by the broken stones of the Barberini obelisk,[134] and the shallow "piazza

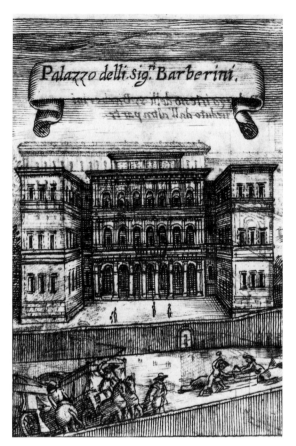

126   Palazzo Barberini, west façade (Totti, 1638)
(Biblioteca Apostolica Vaticana)

overo cortile" hardly formed an imposing approach. Both Falda (1676) and Nolli (1748) show the north and west approaches, constructed in the 1630s and enduring for decades (Figs. 129, 130). Teti's ideal view of the west façade was possible only from a distance. The reality of contrast between the palace and its immediate setting was unavoidable to the visitor.[135]

The ramped approach from the north leads to the entrance to Taddeo's apartment, on the second level behind the decorous façade. The space before this part of the palace is consistently called "piazza da basso" in the document of construction—a term that specifies its location and also its traditional function as a setting for the façade and an arena for traffic. Taddeo's entrance hall A8 is always called "Entrone," for it simply (if grandly) admits the visitor to the stairs leading to Taddeo's apartment. On the west side of the palace, terminology is not so simple, for the usual categories do not entirely explain the forms found there. The space before the west façade is smaller and more cramped than the "piazza da basso," the two wings of apartments advancing to pinch it off at the sides; and the first reference to it in the document of construction reflects the recorder's uncertainty: "la piazza overo cortile grande." It resembles the "piazza da basso" and is large enough for perhaps seventy waiting carriages;[136] but at the same time it has the sense of enclosure of a traditional palace courtyard. Even the architectural forms contribute to the ambiguity: to the west are small houses and a low wall, but to the east rises the three-story loggia, an expanded version of the courtyard elevation of Palazzo Farnese.[137] Eventually the second reading gains strength, as the space is called "cortile di sopra" and "cortile grande" in later pages of the document.[138]

ENTRANCE

The great entrance hall B1 on the *pian terreno* (see Fig. 101) is not a simple "entrone" like Taddeo's but requires a longer description: the "Portico da basso dov'è il nichione tondo con la fontana in mezzo."[139] Totti's description of 1638 and Girolamo Teti's of 1642 also speak of the "portico."[140] The big niche is further called "teatro" in the description of the construction of the walls around it,[141] because of both its semicircular shape and the inclusion of the fountain;[142] and even the portico as a whole receives that identity in the document's reference to "il portico overo teatro."[143] Immediately behind the seven open arches of the façade toward the "cortile grande," the seven bays of the portico extend to the two stairs at opposite angles of the courtyard. Like a typical courtyard loggia (a term not used in the document of construction), the bays provide

Palazzo Barberini

Piranesi. F.

127   Palazzo Barberini, from southwest, etching by Piranesi (Biblioteca Apostolica Vaticana)

covered access to the stairs for guests arriving in carriages and sheltered waiting areas for carriages and retainers alike (Fig. 131). But unlike the typical courtyard loggia, these bays are not bounded by a wall; instead, the central five are doubled by a second aisle of vaulted bays, and the central three are extended even farther under the mass of the palace in the deep semicircular "nicchione" with its fountain (Fig. 132). The first bay of the second aisle provides a secondary entrance B21 to Taddeo's apartment, presumably no more significant than the door in the fifth bay, to a passage B2 leading to service rooms. The central axis of this deep portico is contained by the curve

of the hemicycle and blocked by the fountain; paths of movement are thereby deflected from the axis to the lateral extremities. The entire portico can be considered an amplification of the normal courtyard loggia, providing greater shelter and turning area for carriages, as Borromini would later propose in his designs for Palazzo Pamphili;[144] and in conjunction with the "cortile grande" this is a reasonable functional explanation for the space. A fountain too is a fixture of many palace courtyards — as, for example, at Palazzo Mattei. Yet the deep, shaped, and shaded portico, with its hemicycle, fountain, and niches for statuary, seems more like a grotto

Veduta del Palazzo Barberini
presso sulla Strada
Architettura del Bernini

128　Palazzo Barberini, west entrance, engraving by Rossini (Bibliotheca Hertziana, Rome)

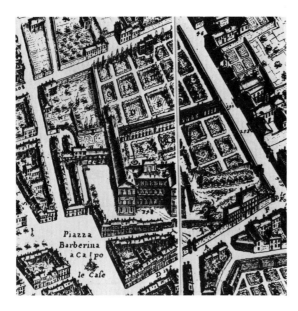

129   Falda Map of Rome, 1676, detail with Palazzo Barberini

130   Nolli Map of Rome, 1748, detail with Palazzo Barberini

131   Palazzo Barberini, portico, looking toward entrance to stair S1 (author)

132   Palazzo Barberini, portico, looking toward hemicycle (author)

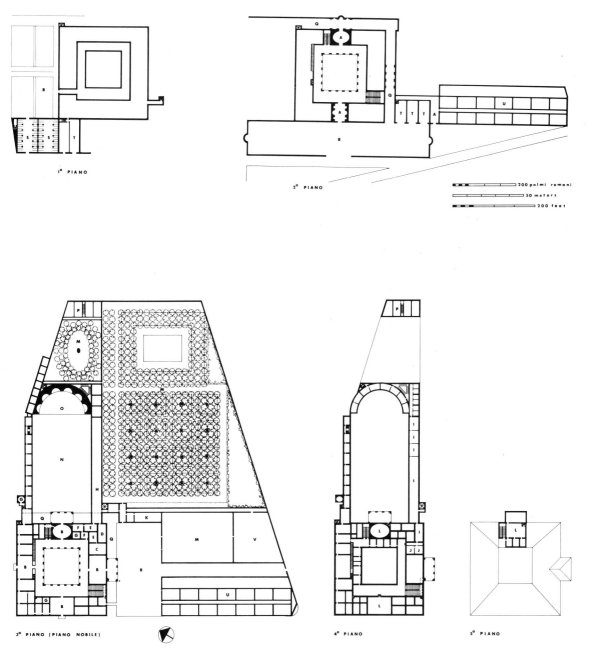

133   Barb. lat. 4360, design for Palazzo Barberini, reconstruction (author)
Key: A, *andito;* B, *salone;* C, *anticamera;* D, second *anticamera;* E, audience room; F, sleeping room; G, chapel;
H, gallery; I, library; J, librarian; K, ball court; L, *guardaroba;* M, garden; N, *giardino secreto;* O, hemicycle
(*teatro*); P, gardeners' quarters; Q, drive; R, terrace; S, stables; T, carriages; U, *famiglia;* V, casino

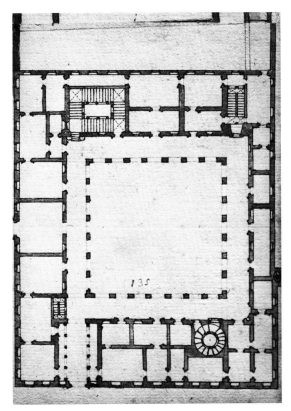

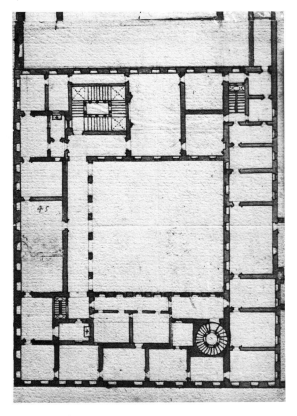

134   Design for Palazzo Barberini, ground floor (Stockholm, Nationalmuseum, CC1419d)

135   Design for Palazzo Barberini, *piano nobile* (Stockholm, Nationalmuseum, CC1419c)

than a loggia for the commerce of a palace court-yard.

The denomination "teatro" increases our associations of the portico with constructions in the gardens of contemporary villas; yet the reality of the Roman palace, with its important entrances to grand stairs, pulls us back to the sunny western courtyard. This is the façade that Pompilio Totti described as "quasi in forma di Theatro," that multivalent word conjuring up still other associations and a reading of the great three-story loggia no longer (or not only) as a loggia of a contained urban courtyard but also as an ancient theater or amphitheater façade, like that of the well-known Colosseum. The scooped-out form of the "portico overo teatro"

seems but an extension of the rectangular theater of the "piazza overo cortile grande." We see at once the concavity of the inside of an ancient Roman theater and the arcuated façade of its exterior.[145]

ASCENT

The two main staircases fall within the enigmatic central portion of the palace. The existence of two stairs is readily explained by the traditional requirement of separate stairs for separate households within a single building, as seen in Palazzo Borghese (see Fig. 20). Although symmetrical in the location of their entrances, the stairs are different in form — again, a distinction that seems normal in the context of Roman palaces. Palazzo Borghese's old switchback stair leading to Francesco's apartments is contrasted by the new elliptical stair leading to Giovanni Battista's part of the palace. The proposed design for the Barberini described in Barb. lat. 4360 included a large switchback stair at the southwest corner of the courtyard, leading to the main apartment to the south (as well as those to the west), and a smaller one at the northeast corner, serving the apartments in that part of the building (Fig. 133). Another proposal for the palace, Stockholm CC1419, shows a large rectangular stair opening from the northeast corner of the courtyard and leading to *saloni* in the north and east wings; and a circular stair in the southwest angle, leading to rooms to the south and west (Figs. 134, 135). Not only the number but the relation of the stairs to the courtyard and its loggia seems normal. The engaging qualities of the stairs emerge in the particulars of their designs.

To the right, the stair leading to apartments designed for Cardinal Francesco is elliptical in plan, and its unbroken ascent extends from the *pian terreno* to the level of Francesco's library (Figs. 136, 137). It receives light from its open well and from windows at the angle of the façade. An early plan study shows a near circle instead of the ellipse eventually built (see Fig. 146). In the document of construction the stair is always the "lumaca grande,"[146] distinct from the many smaller "lumache," or spiral service stairs, with which the building is laced. Although still somewhat unusual, the elevation of the humble service stair to graceful major stair had begun long ago in Rome, with Bramante's famous helical ramp at the Vatican. In the late sixteenth century, the ellipse appeared as an alternative for the circle, as seen in Mascarino's Quirinal casino and Ponzio's Palazzo Borghese. The circular version appears in Maderno's plan for an archpriest's palace at St. Peter's[147] and in Stockholm CC1419, the proposed plan for Palazzo Barberini, which seems to have come from Maderno's workshop (see Figs. 134, 135). Its graceful form and simplic-

ity of ascent must have appealed especially to Borromini, who later used the type in several of his buildings. In Palazzo Barberini, it has the advantage of compactness, leaving space for the large rooms of Cardinal Francesco's apartment, as well as an anticipation of the form of the elliptical salon on the *piano nobile*. The modification of the form from circle to ellipse underlines the strength of the lateral axis of the portico. The ascent is simple: two circuits to the *piano nobile,* two more to the *secondo piano,* and another to the library. Scholars coming to use the library would find a direct path, without involvement in the rest of the palace.[148]

The stair to the left, larger and considerably more complex than the elliptical stair, serves Taddeo's wing of the palace (Fig. 138). While its entrance from the portico of the *pian terreno* is the symmetrical counterpart of that of Francesco's stair, it actually begins at a lower level, at Taddeo's north *entrone*. A single broad flight rises directly to the vestibule B21 outside the door to Taddeo's apartment. At this level the stair is discontinuous, and the prince's visitors would not be tempted to ascend higher. Similarly, Anna's visitors would not use Taddeo's entrance but would arrive at the west portico and find a familiar-looking stair — three steps up to a landing, then a turn to a long straight flight (Fig. 139), portending a similar parallel flight beyond the next landing, that is, a stair like that of Palazzo Farnese, Palazzo Borghese, and any number of other Roman palaces. This simple anticipation would soon be abandoned, however, as the big square well framed by paired columns would open to the right. At the next landing, the visitor would turn into a flight rising directly over Taddeo's straight single flight. Now fully within a square-well stair (Fig. 140), the visitor would continue his ascent around the square, vaulting over the north bay of the second aisle of the portico, to arrive at the *piano nobile* not at an expected corner landing but at a landing midway in the fourth side of the square. The attraction of the vestibule C21, with its two large arched win-

136   Palazzo Barberini, elliptical stair S2 (Moscioni; Monumenti Musei e Gallerie Ponteficie, Archivio Fotografico)

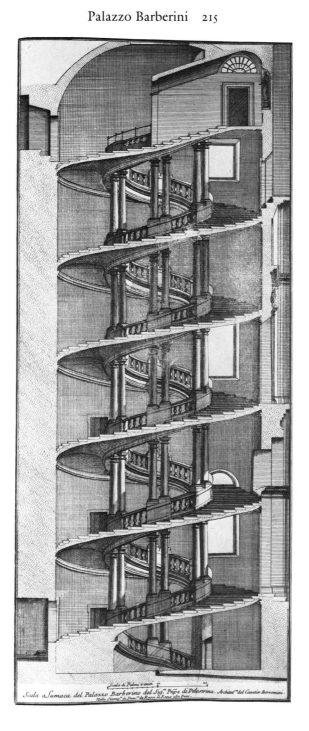

137   Palazzo Barberini, elliptical stair S2, section, engraving by Specchi (Bibliotheca Hertziana, Rome)

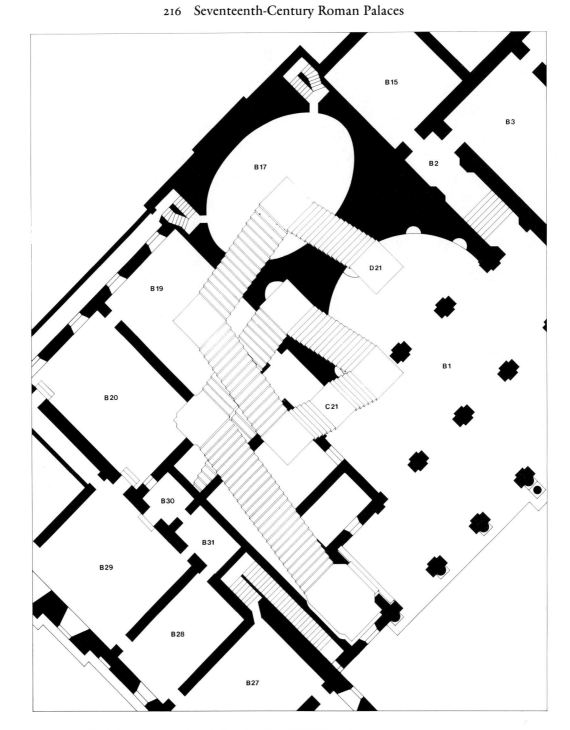

138   Palazzo Barberini, stair S1, analytical drawing (David DiMarco)

139 Palazzo Barberini, stair S1, first flight (author)

140 Palazzo Barberini, stair S1 (Alinari/Art Resource, N.Y.)

dows to the west, would be enough to draw the visitor to Anna's apartment on the *piano nobile*. But the stair stretches on, and the visitor could also continue almost a full circuit to the corridor of the *secondo piano* that leads to the north apartment D40–D45 at that level.

The complexity of this stair is overwhelming. The designer must deal with floor levels already established by the old Sforza construction, the necessity of engaging Taddeo's single flight in the heart of the building, the desire to make the entrance to the stair a pendant to Francesco's to the south, the articulation of entrances to two major and one minor apartment, and requirements of lighting. The solution involves superimposition of stairs, transformation of a familiar form into the less common square-well stair, and exit from the stair at a landing in the midst of a flight, all with apparent ease, grace, and grandeur.[149]

CENTER

Whether by north or by south stair, the visitor ascends around a colonnaded well of light to a vestibule that puts him immediately in contact again with the "piazza overo cortile grande,"

141   Palazzo Barberini, *salone* C1 (I.C.C.D., Rome, ser. E, no. 60552)

through the arches of the second story of its loggia. From either vestibule, C10 or C21, he is admitted directly into the grand *salone,* which stretches behind the central three bays of the façade loggia and served both Anna and Francesco as "sala dei palafrenieri" (Fig. 141; see also Fig. 108). This is the fulcrum around which the bipartite palace is balanced. Its vast size (110½ × 65⅔ *palmi*) is complemented by a lofty cove vault — a rather unusual feature in *saloni,* which up until this time normally had flat beamed ceilings.[150] Its vault provided the occasion for Pietro da Cortona's great fresco, "The Triumph of Divine Providence and the Accomplishment of Its Ends

through the Pontificate of Urban VIII Barberini," a composition firmly bound to its setting by the painted architectural framework, following the lines of the vault, before and beyond which its many figures move.[151] Here the visitor pauses in his progress. Although light is admitted from high windows to the east, there is no view to the gardens in that direction because of the intervening oval salon. The explicit message of the painting, in this hall opening to both secular and ecclesiastical Barberini apartments, now directs the visitor to stand within the façade of the "theater" of the palace — to look out, not at the cramped "piazza overo cortile grande" and jumble of small houses, but across the city to St. Peter's and the Vatican rising on their corresponding hill. If modern buildings now block this view from the *salone* windows, St. Peter's can still be seen clearly from the forward rooms of the north wing of the *piano nobile,* as well as from rooms D22–D24, closer to the center of the building, on the *secondo piano.* A nineteenth-century visitor to the palace remarked precisely this feature of the view.[152] A visitor to the Barberini would have seen the white, domed form of St. Peter's, with Maderno's newly completed façade, rising above the dull clutter of the city, much as Michelangelo must have envisioned it. In the same way, the clear form of Palazzo Barberini's seven-bay loggia is visible from St. Peter's.

Some sixteenth- and seventeenth-century theatrical productions explored the correspondences between audience and stage, in terms of both the form of the theater and the content of the drama.[153] On a larger scale, landscape too could be seen as a theater or amphitheater, the viewer discerning correspondences between his own vantage point and distant landmarks. Looking out from the Villa Aldobrandini at Frascati, Agucchi saw the "grandissimo teatro" of the bowl-shaped landscape, with the mountain of Viterbo fifty miles distant as the counterpart of that of Frascati; the monte di Santo Resto and montagna della Tolfa marked other points on the horizon of the theater, which included St. Peter's in its compass.[154] So too the anonymous author of a description of Palestrina wrote of the panoramic view from the theater-like Palazzo Colonna-Barberini (see Fig. 177): ". . . to the south, besides the whole territory of Palestrina which lies before it, an infinity of sea, Montefortino, Lugnano, la Colonna, Rocca Priora, Monte di Compatri, la Selva dell'Agliaro; to the east . . . Segni, Valmontone, Cavi, Pagliano, Anagni, Fiorentino, and innumerable towns and places; and to the west . . . Rome, and all the seacoast beyond."[155]

There was a fascination with distant views in

Rome, in the wake of Galileo's dramatic demonstrations of the telescope in Rome in 1611.[156] His visit to Rome in 1624 must have been the occasion for the Barberini acquisition of a telescope, the "occhialone del Galileo longo, con sua coperta di corame rosso" listed in Antonio's inventory of 1644 in the tiny room C22, appropriately in the westernmost chamber of the north wing (see Fig. 102).[157] The Quirinal hill was a good observation post: Alexander VII could watch the progress of construction of S. Maria in Via Lata and Palazzo Chigi in piazza SS. Apostoli from the Quirinal palace. Later, his nephew Cardinal Flavio Chigi could look out from a high corner room of his palace (see Fig. 206, E17) and survey the city with the aid of a telescope he kept there.[158]

The physical relationship between the Palazzo Barberini on the Quirinal hill and St. Peter's and the papal palace on the Vatican hill was enhanced by a formal relationship (Figs. 142, 143). To the right of St. Peter's was the three-story loggia of the Cortile di S. Damaso, surprisingly like Palazzo Barberini's western loggia, not only in its form but also in its ambivalent setting, both courtyard and public façade. In recent memory was the three-story Benediction Loggia begun by Pius II in 1461 and destroyed only in 1616 to make way for Maderno's nave and façade of St. Peter's, its arcaded Colosseum-like façade especially suggestive of the Barberini loggia.[159]

Both the formal reference to the two prominent Vatican loggias and the physical direction of the Barberini palace across the city are affirmations of the declaration of Divine Providence in Cortona's ceiling painting, itself a "theater" in the seventeenth-century sense of compendium.[160] The temporal and spiritual aspects of the papacy (paralleling the secular and ecclesiastical aspects of the family) are joined in their celebration of Divine Providence, which elevated a member of the Barberini family to the papacy. The form of the building speaks as loudly: two rather ordinary halves are joined by an extraordinary center (see Fig. 99). Although

142   St. Peter's and the Vatican palace, drawing by Heemskerck (Albertina, 43.837c)

Urban VIII was never intended to live there, he made the Palazzo Barberini possible and gave it its meaning.

With this sequential preparation, now impressed with the nature of the united family and the source of its status, the visitor was ready to proceed onward to the apartments.

RESTATEMENT: THE OVAL *SALONE*

Beyond the central *salone* to the east, and still within the intriguing central part of the palace, lies the oval salon C17 (Fig. 144; see also Fig. 102). (Its counterpart B17 on the *pian terreno* was simply the foundation for the room above and did not come into play as part of a spatial sequence until the remodeling of the 1670s.) The existence of some sort of room in this position seems necessary, if only to block the view from the *salone* to the garden and direct the visitor's attention westward. The room is especially intriguing because of its elliptical plan, a novelty in palaces at this date, and its classical articulation.

How was this room used? It is not part of a suite, for, as we have seen, both Anna's and Francesco's apartments are complete without it. Their first anterooms, opening from the grand *salone,* are rooms C19 and C2, respectively. The oval salon is like a gallery, or like the "study or gallery" or loggia of Maderno's extension of Palazzo Borghese (see Fig. 30, C31, C35), not for the formal ritual of the reception of guests but for private enjoyment of some sort.

Without a fireplace,[161] the oval room must have been intended for summer use only. It opened to the gardens to the east and so might have been a pleasant room in the summer, rather like the ground-floor gallery of Palazzo Borghese. Like the eastward loggia adjacent to the oval *salone* proposed in Barb. Lat. 4360 (see Fig. 133), it would be a cool and pleasant place for supper in the summer.[162] Although its doors opened to other rooms, it seems especially connected with Francesco's summer apartment. Its four crimson *portiere* matched the hangings in the "appartamento de damaschi cremesini" (C11–C15), and the order of rooms given in an inventory of 1636 suggests that it could have been the anteroom from the central *salone* to that suite.[163] More characteristic of Roman planning, however, is the order given in Antonio's inventory of 1644, in which the oval room follows the rest of the apartment, not as an anteroom but as a special gallery-like chamber.[164]

143   St. Peter's and the Vatican palaces ca. 1600 (Wolfenbüttel, Herzog August Bibliothek: Cod. Guelf. 136 Extrav.)

The oval room is set off from the others not only by its unusual form but also by its white walls and Ionic pilasters. Its cool classical articulation is in contrast to the colors of ceiling paintings and wall hangings of the apartments. Magnanimi has seen in its serenity an atmosphere conducive to the "literary exercises" that Teti says took place there.[165] It seems an especially appropriate setting for the ancient sculptures installed there by 1644.[166]

The anonymous author of Barb. lat. 4360 proposed an oval *salone* as the fourth of his four symmetrically disposed halls, in the center of the

east wing of his design (see Fig. 133), very much like that executed in its relation to the garden, its decoration with pilasters and niches for sculptures, and its pleasantness in the summer. The author further emphasizes its value as a private room for the pleasure of the patrons, conveniently provided with services from the courtyard loggia and nearby stair.[167] It differs from the Barberini's oval salon only in the addition of a loggia toward the garden.

There is a burst of interest in the ellipse as a plan form, immediately after its inclusion in the Palazzo Barberini. A plan for enlarging the Bar-

144 Palazzo Barberini, oval salon C17 (Magnanimi, *Palazzo Barberini*, p. 84)

berini casino at Mompecchio (see Fig. 183), dated 14 September 1633 and attributed to Bernini,[168] shows a slightly larger elliptical hall. Borromini would explore its use as entrance hall, courtyard, and stair in Palazzo Carpegna, and as refectory and common room in the Casa dei Filippini. Later palaces in Italy and abroad would take up the form. Its use in churches abounds in those years, beginning with Bernini's chapel of the Propaganda Fide in 1634 and Borromini's S. Carlino in 1638. Yet earlier instances, especially in secular architecture, are rare. We have seen elliptical stairs of monumental proportions, as at Palazzo Borghese. Maderno exploited the peculiar geometry of the ellipse in his small ground-floor vestibule in that palace (see Fig. 28, A22) and

used elliptical domes over the side-aisle bays at St. Peter's. Buonarroti considered something like an elliptical piazza in one of his *pensieri* for Palazzo Barberini (Fig. 145). A few Roman churches, notably Vignola's S. Andrea in via Flaminia and S. Anna dei Palafrenieri and Francesco da Volterra's S. Giacomo degli Incurabili, had longitudinal elliptical plans. The scarcity of elliptical plans, especially in palaces, makes it unlikely that the thorough but pedestrian author of Barb. lat. 4360 would have come up with the idea on his own, and his proposal may instead reflect the idea of someone else (possibly Maderno, who had previous experience with the form, or Bernini, who enjoyed its use later).

Earlier large elliptical volumes (not stairs or

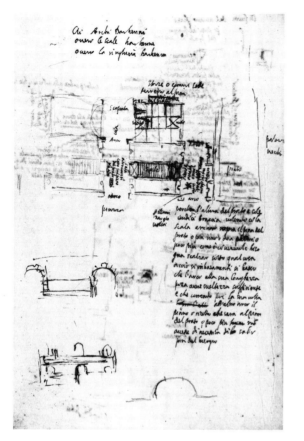

145   Michelangelo Buonarroti the Younger, study for Palazzo Barberini (Biblioteca Medicea-Laurenziana, ms. Buon. 90, fol. 70v)

Maderno's small vestibule) were all churches, and this in combination with the unusual articulation of pilasters and niches suggests the transferal of a form from ecclesiastical architecture to secular. The cross-axial disposition of the Barberini ellipse deprives the form of the focus that earlier elliptical church plans had directed to the altar. The confrontation of three doors from the *salone* with two windows and a door to the garden transforms the ellipse into something like the loggias extending from the *saloni* of any number of villas (for example, the old casino at Mompecchio, Fig. 184, or Villa Mondragone at Frascati). Doors from rooms C19 and C15 of the

apartments avoid the cross axis and the dynamism inherent in the form, to isolate its curve from the ordinary rooms to either side. In a palace dedicated to the idea of the union of both ecclesiastical and secular aspects in a single family, and on the central axis of the palace, it seems especially appropriate to discover a single room that fuses forms associated with church and dwelling, as surely as the many ramifications of "teatro" are fused in the western façade.

PALACE OR VILLA?

Several features of the central part of the palace — the absence of an internal courtyard, the great western loggia, the two westward-projecting wings, the grotto-like entrance hall, the pairing of a central *salone* with a loggia-like room, the garden setting — have suggested that the building "has something of the character of a villa,"[169] or "[ought to be regarded] as a monumentalized 'villa suburbana,'"[170] or, more explicitly, is "a kind of gargantuan villa."[171] Yet it is not a villa. The Barberini clearly were interested in a palace better suited to their newly gained prestige than was their old palace in the via dei Giubbonari. All the early documentation calls it "palazzo" and never suggests that it would be considered a villa. The author of Barb. lat. 4360 insists on the distinction in the presentation of his proposal for the new building: "I would not know what other building in Rome, or what other location could compete with the present one, which is no longer a *vigna,* as it was once called, nor is it a garden, as it is now named, but it would be a most magnificent and most commodious palace. . . . "[172] The apartments are not the abbreviated suites common to villas but the fully developed apartments of Roman palaces. There are both summer and winter apartments, and members of the Barberini family lived in the palace year-round. The loggia is not turned toward the garden, as in a villa, but is fronted by a shallow walled courtyard.[173] Indeed, the palace has a courtyard: it was so named in the document of construction, and it fulfilled the functional requirements of a normal Roman palace courtyard.

The early proposals for Palazzo Barberini as well as the executed building suggest that the Barberini were searching for a distinctive image for their new palace. Buonarroti made this explicit as he labeled one of his studies, "Gli Archi Barberini overo le scale barberine overo la ringhiera barberina" [174] (see Fig. 145, top). Simply to make the palace look like a villa would be meaningless. Taddeo's idea of representing the nature of the Barberini family — especially if developed to indicate its relation to the power of the papacy and its roots (albeit newly established) in Roman tradition — would have more appeal. The search for appropriate forms was widespread, and questions of entrance, joining new to old, establishing a relationship between palace and city, and so on, went beyond the established norms for palaces to the more varied forms of villas. Beyond villas, designers and advisors searched elsewhere in Roman architecture — in the buildings of antiquity and in ecclesiastical architecture — and even beyond Rome. The author of Barb. lat. 4344 mentions details of buildings in Genoa and Florence. Barb. lat. 4360 suggests a Venetian clock.[175] Surely the well-traveled Barberini contributed to the search, bringing descriptions if not images to their Roman architects. Urban VIII had spent many years in France as Maffeo Barberini, and he sent his nephew Francesco there for nine months in 1625. (Francesco returned home just in time to complete the purchase of the Sforza property in December 1625.) Both must have noticed the distinctive architecture of early-seventeenth-century Paris, no longer provincial but worthy of admiration alongside Italian architecture. The typical Parisian city dwelling seems to reverberate in Palazzo Barberini, with its low wall and portal toward the street, its "piazza overo cortile grande," and its tall, rich façade framed by somewhat lower and plainer side wings. In spite of the Roman vocabulary, a Frenchman would recognize the scheme of wall, *cour d'honneur, corps-de-logis,* and side wings.[176] In particular, Maffeo would have seen the unfinished Louvre before its major addition begun in 1624, and Francesco would have seen the extension under construction. Turned 90 degrees from the major road along the Seine, its rich court façade by Lescot (followed by Lemercier) faced the court bounded on the east by lower structures. The open form of Palazzo Barberini's courtyard-*teatro* might seem exotic to other Romans but reasonable to the francophile Barberini.

Structure

For the most part, the structure of this massive building follows the classical dictate that masses should stand over masses and voids over voids.[177] Even the striking contrast between the spreading, hollowed-out volume of the entrance portico on the *pian terreno* and the orthogonal pattern of walls above is reconciled by the coincidence of walls and piers — precisely shown in Borromini's plan drawings of the two levels superimposed (Figs. 146, 147). Still, there are several instances in which the rule is either violated or in need of reinforcement.

Throughout the building (see Figs. 100–106), iron chains were used to provide tensile strength where thrusts of vaults or simple weight of superimposed masonry might have been too great to have been borne by walls alone. The 8-*palmi*-thick walls of the *salone* C1 received selective reinforcing from chains placed in the walls at the corners and over doorways.[178] Two chains, each 55 *palmi* long, were installed in the adjacent oval room C17.[179] Rooms in the old palace, reformed by the insertion of a new wall from the ground to the roof, were reinforced. The Salotto della Divina Sapienza was ringed with chains, one in each of its three old walls and one in its 3-*palmi*-thick new wall;[180] and its neighbor C28 also received chains in old walls.[181] Below, the vault of Taddeo's anteroom B29 was reinforced by two chains;[182] and above, the partition between D41

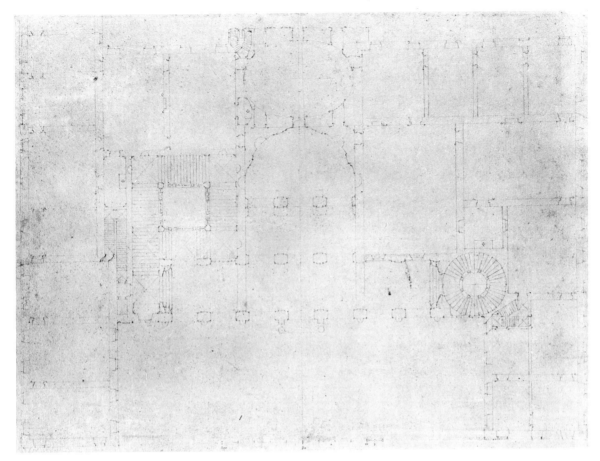

146   Palazzo Barberini, preparatory drawing by Borromini (Albertina, It.AZ Rom 957)

and D42 was similarly strengthened with a chain.[183] Another new partition at this level, between D44 and D45, was the occasion for placing a chain to reinforce the vault below.[184]

The library F1, its vault *a schifo* reinforced with five transverse chains, each 55 *palmi* long, posed a special problem for the large room D1 below it. The library's 4-*palmi*-thick south wall was designed to stand above D1's vault; accordingly, that lower room was thoroughly laced with chains: two transverse chains in its vault and one below its floor, each of 56 *palmi*, and two other chains 57 *palmi* long exposed over its vault; and three longitudinal chains, each 80 *palmi* long, two in the vault and one beneath the floor.[185] It may be that these precautions did not suffice, since by 1640 the library had been enlarged so that the south wall would stand securely over the south wall of the palace below. The situation was very similar to that essayed by Borromini at the Oratory of the Filippini only a few years later: the end wall of Oratorians' library was constructed above the vault of the oratory, its span of 53 *palmi* only slightly greater than that of room D1 in Palazzo Barberini. Perhaps encouraged by the lesson of Palazzo Barberini, Borromini confidently announced that his vault was standing sound under the weight of the library wall, only to be disappointed a few years later by the appearance of cracks which necessitated the removal of the offending wall and enlargement of the library in a way parallel to that of Palazzo Barberini.[186]

New interior partitions placed over vaults were made light and strong, of brick instead of the usual masonry, and only one brick thick — for example, walls in the small rooms on the upper levels of the west end of the south wing; the walls in Costanza's apartment separating rooms D25 and D27 from rooms D26 and D28; walls in the attic rooms at the west end of the north wing; and the new wall between rooms C33 and C34.[187]

This last example required further structural gymnastics. Two rectangular rooms on the *piano nobile* were to be removed from the old linear suite and, by effectively rotating them 90 degrees, attached to the new "casino" centered on "salotto" C36. This involved the destruction of the old bearing wall perpendicular to the façade as well as the construction of the new light brick partition. Remembering that vaults have weight, the designer contrived a single new vault to span both rooms and, just to be sure, installed chains in the new construction (in addition to the chain already mentioned, under the new wall between D44 and D45).[188]

The western wall of Taddeo's *guardaroba,* which rose over the central *salone,* posed special problems because it was an exterior wall and because it was very long. It was made 3½ *palmi* thick, and a special big brick arch was constructed under it, seven withes thick, spanning 71 *palmi* across the vault of the *salone.*[189]

Arches provided the support for another new thick wall, that which formed the Salotto della Divina Sapienza C29, Taddeo's anteroom B29 on the *pian terreno,* and his entrance hall A8 below. At that lowest level excavations were made for the construction of foundation piers for three new brick arches, which in turn sup-

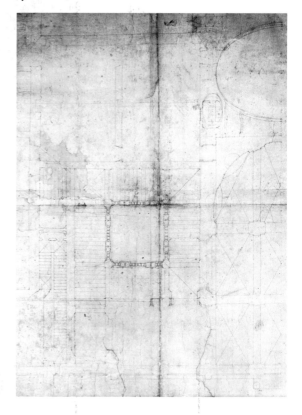

147 Palazzo Barberini, preparatory drawing by Borromini (Albertina, It.AZ Rom 966)

ported the new rising wall.[190]

The wide range of techniques for providing structural stability gives the designer freedom to shape both the interior and the exterior of the building in both plan and section. Dramatic broad spaces on lower levels can be surmounted by necessary walls above. The special "casino" can be discovered within the matrix of the masonry. Particular groups of rooms can be developed horizontally and then composed vertically through reconciling structural techniques. Rooftop structures can be separated from the dominant form of the building by holding their exterior walls away from those of the main block below. A complex and particularized form can be designed, in contrast to the simple cellular structure of the early Barberini palace ai Giubbonari, or Palazzo Borghese in 1610.

Design

Maffeo Barberini's election to the papacy on 6 August 1623 was the signal for the beginning of thinking about the design of the new palace, but five years would pass before construction would actually begin. The first decision was the selection of the site, and the Barberini seem to have spotted what they wanted by early 1624. The property was pursued. Protracted negotiations reduced the price from 120,000 scudi to the 55,100 scudi finally paid by Cardinal Francesco on 18 December 1625. Francesco promptly transferred the property to his brother Taddeo, on 30 January 1626.[191] Other smaller parcels were purchased between March 1626 and September 1632, to complete the near-rectangle of the site, although additional purchases were not so extensive as some advisors of the Barberini had anticipated.[192]

Steps were taken immediately to make the Sforza palace (see Figs. 96, 97) habitable by the Barberini — if not yet as a major residence, then as a pleasurable suburban retreat. New locks, keys, chains, gates, and so forth provided security by January 1626.[193] Virtually every room was freshened with whitewash.[194] Woodwork was refurbished.[195] Frescoes were cleaned and Barberini arms were painted in rooms of the *piano nobile*. The papal arms of Urban VIII were painted on the vault of the old *sala* (room C28–29), and three feigned doors were installed there — apparently without anticipation that the room was soon to be subdivided as part of a dramatic reformation of the palace.[196] The maintenance of the extensive gardens had to be attended to.[197] Although the family remained in residence in via dei Giubbonari, rooms in the newly acquired palace could be assigned to particular persons — for example, young Antonio Barberini's apartment was apparently on the upper floor of the palace, in the eastern half.[198] Parties could come out for the day, perhaps on special holidays, to enjoy the gardens, the view, and refreshments.[199]

By the following year, plans for the new palace were taking shape. Earth-moving in the garden began in the summer of 1627, indicating that at least basic decisions had been made about the siting of the new building. Still, much planning remained to be done, and substantial masons' work did not begin until December 1628.[200]

The genesis of Palazzo Barberini can be separated into three phases. The first — the collection and discussion of ideas and design proposals — probably extended from just after the election of Urban VIII in the fall of 1623 until 1628. The preparation of the actual design would have occurred in 1628, before the beginning of construction in December of that year. In the third phase the design was adjusted and details of ornament worked out as the building was constructed, between 1629 and 1637.

PHASE ONE: PRELIMINARY DISCUSSIONS

Between August 1623 and December 1628, discussions about the palace to be built must have been lively and far-ranging.[201] Some evidence survives in the form of drawings and memoranda, but this must represent only a fragment of the ideas and proposals from members of the Barberini circle, who included both professional architects and amateurs, technical advisors, *letterati*, and artists. Some proposals were submitted by persons who were away from Rome. Persons who had the ear of the pope or his nephews — most prominent among them, Gianlorenzo Bernini, the favored artist of Urban VIII — must have made suggestions without the formality of a drawing or description. A few proposals came early, perhaps even before the selection of the site. Others probably were responses to other submissions and ongoing discussions. Some persons were inspired by the most prestigious palaces of modern Rome and supposed that the Barberini would want something like the Palazzo Farnese, in spite of the inhospitality of the site toward that formal, regular design. Others, like Agucchi and Felice de Bianchi, extended the basic type of enclosed palace block to absurd proportions. The more practical author of Barb. lat. 4360 provided a detailed and eminently workable (albeit pedestrian) design for the site as given (see Fig. 133); others, like the author of Barb. lat. 4344, suggested only vignettes or details of the building. Occasionally a conceptual leap, like Buonarroti's suggestion of an analogy between building and manners, could carry the discussion to new levels.[202] A few themes run through the extant proposals (and the palace as constructed) so consistently that they must be considered requirements of the Barberini: the incorporation of the old Sforza building in the new palace; some new kind of entrance, in recognition of the importance of entrance in the ceremony of paying visits; a search for ideas beyond the norms of Roman palace building.

A study of the surviving early proposals for the palace — but a fragment of what must have been extended and lively discussions — yields clues as to the proper domains of the several participants.[203] As one advisor wrote, it is "almost natural for everyone to know a little about architecture";[204] anyone could be a critic, and anyone could have ideas, which could be expected to be taken seriously. Persons with varied backgrounds could augment the resources of the professional architects in the search for ideas. Features of buildings seen in Florence, Genoa, Venice, and even France might be recalled. Both texts and monuments of antiquity could be mined. Literature and manners could be called upon. Not only palaces but other building types could be consulted. Whole buildings, parts of buildings, qualities, technical details, functional requirements, ways of dealing with the site and relating the building to its neighbors, ap-

proaches to the reuse of the old Sforza palace, a distinctive image — all were suggested by Barberini advisors.

The Barberini themselves were of course major figures in the drama of design generation. As clients they set the problem; they judged and selected the solution; and they might even have crucial ideas that would come to be embodied in the final design. In the first phase, a critical member of the discussions was none other than the owner of the property, Taddeo Barberini.

Francesco's biography of his brother reveals Taddeo's importance for the design of the palace: "The Palazzo alle Quattro Fontane had its beginning in a first design made by the Prefect [Taddeo], which had one stair, which led to two large halls, to each one of which were joined one or more apartments, such that one [hall] could serve ecclesiastical persons, and the other, secular. However, when more designs were made in the light of the above-mentioned design, and not very different from that one, and when one of them was approved by the Prefect, it also pleased Pope Urban, who, however, as His Holiness also had good taste in these matters, added a few embellishments and improvements which had not been foreseen [by others]. However, one can say that the entire fabric was the work of [Taddeo's] mind, since, not only did the original intention survive, that it be a habitation for ecclesiastics and for secular persons; but there was not a day that he did not go there and see the drawings; and what was being done, if it was the idea of others, was approved and verified by him; and at least half, and perhaps more, of the expenditures for the building came from his hand."[205]

Francesco identifies the critical idea of the palace as Taddeo's: the division of the palace between ecclesiastical and secular persons, and the connection of the two halves by a common entrance. The documentation of construction has made clear that the palace was built to house Taddeo with his wife and mother in the north wing, and Francesco in the south wing, the two halves joined by entrance portico and *salone*. Francesco's insistence that "the original intention survive[d]," in spite of some modifications, only confirms our interpretation of the plan.

The idea that two persons might share a palace is nothing new. Palazzo Farnese may originally have been designed ca. 1515 as a double palace for the two sons of Cardinal Alessandro Farnese (later Paul III). Facilities for Pier Luigi Farnese would have been toward the present piazza Farnese, and his younger brother Ranuccio would have been housed in similar quarters facing a second piazza toward via Giulia — a scheme symmetrical about its transverse axis (similar to the Palazzo Strozzi in Florence). The unified block would have had two faces.[206] We have seen that the Palazzo Borghese (after 1605) was designed to house the two brothers of Paul V, with their wives (see Figs. 20–24). There were two façades, two portals into a single large courtyard, two major staircases, and, on the *piano nobile,* two large *saloni* opening to the separate quarters of the two brothers and their wives. From the outside, however, the palace presented a unified image: while the two façades had slightly different articulation, they belonged to a single block, and the inner division between Francesco's and Giovanni Battista's quarters is nowhere in evidence (see Fig. 40). It expresses its two-part occupation no more convincingly than does Palazzo Mattei, whose two façades lead to only a single stair and *salone* (see Fig. 7). Further, the Borghese palace accommodated the two secular brothers of the pope, while his nephew Cardinal Scipione Borghese lived elsewhere until 1621.[207] Later, the Chigi family would make the same distinction, Mario and Agostino Chigi, with their respective wives, living in the Palazzo Chigi in piazza Colonna, and Cardinal Flavio Chigi (son of Mario and cousin of Agostino) settling in the Palazzo Chigi in piazza SS. Apostoli.[208] The formal distinction of Palazzo Barberini is that its bipartite plan is expressed in its external form, and its further distinction is that the two parts

are identified as ecclesiastical and secular, for two brothers, according to the bipartite structure of the Barberini family.

The idea for a bifurcating plan was near at hand — as near as the old Sforza palace, which had a single stair leading to a terrace and then a single *salone,* from which branched the two small apartments of the *piano nobile* (see Fig. 96). Yet the Sforza building had no exterior expression of its symmetrical plan; and Taddeo's scheme differs from the earlier building in having two *saloni,* one for each half of the palace.

Another hillside palace must have provided the critical stimulus: the Palazzo Colonna-Barberini in nearby Palestrina (see Fig. 177). This imposing palace, built in the ruins of the ancient sanctuary of Fortuna Primigenia, was as compelling to the seventeenth-century Roman as it is to a present-day visitor. The ascent through the medieval town led to the piazza della Cortina, from which the great cavea-like flight of steps rose to the entrance (see Figs. 178, 179). In the 1620s this was a small and irregular vestibule, with a stair to a similarly small loggia on the upper floor.[209] On either level, right and left of the vestibule or loggia, there extended a large *salone,* curved according to the ancient Roman foundations beneath its walls, and then an apartment. In other words, it was exactly Taddeo's scheme — "one stair, which led to two large halls, to each one of which were joined one or more apartments" — but doubled vertically.

Not only is the palace's organization, with two *saloni* on each level, close to Taddeo's scheme for the Palazzo Barberini; Palestrina also has the virtue of expressing its bipartite plan on the exterior. The great hemicycle of the central part is framed by the projecting flat faces of the two wings of apartments. The particular form of that expression must have been especially welcome to the Barberini, since the hemicycle with its cavea-like stairs complemented the idea of a theater-like façade, which was to be developed at Palazzo Barberini. Even further, its striking image against the hillside, seen from a distance while it surveyed the countryside even as far as Rome,[210] must have been the kind of thing that the Barberini were looking for as they sought a distinctive design for their new palace on the Quirinal hill in Rome.

While everyone in Rome would have known the Colonna palace at Palestrina, Taddeo came to have a special connection with it exactly during the planning of the new Barberini palace at the Quattro Fontane. Since December 1626 the Barberini had been pursuing the purchase of the property, owned by Francesco Colonna, Prince of Palestrina.[211] Taddeo married Anna Colonna on 24 October 1627. Anna was the daughter of Filippo Colonna, head of another branch of the Colonna family and Conestabile del Regno, of Naples.[212] Both Francesco and Filippo were friendly with the Barberini. Plagued by unhappy financial affairs and courted by the Barberini, Francesco finally decided to sell the city of Palestrina (including its princely title) and other territories to Carlo Barberini, and the contract of sale was dated 16 January 1630,[213] only weeks before Carlo's death and Taddeo's inheritance of both property and title. Meanwhile, even before the Barberini acquisition of the property, almost immediately after his marriage, Taddeo had an apartment there: a document dated 18 December 1627 speaks of extensive remodeling in the rooms above Taddeo's apartment.[214] Further attention was being paid to Palestrina in these years because of the removal of the famous Nile mosaic (see Fig. 182) from the lower part of the city, sometime between September 1624 and March 1626, and its eventual deliverance into the hands of Cardinal Francesco Barberini.[215] Whatever Taddeo's interest in Palestrina in earlier years, it certainly intensified in 1627 and again in 1630.

Francesco's description of the origin of Palazzo Barberini's design continues as he writes of other designs, similar to Taddeo's idea and provoked by it. Most of the surviving early proposals cannot be related to Taddeo's scheme, even though they have multiple apartments. Only the

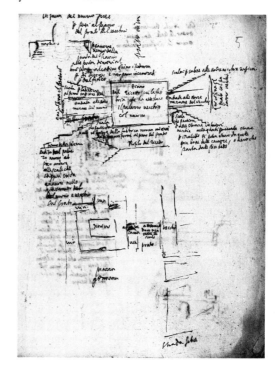

148 Michelangelo Buonarroti the Younger, study for Palazzo Barberini (Biblioteca Medicea-Laurenziana, ms. Buon. 90, fol. 70r)

ideas of Michelangelo Buonarroti the Younger can be seen as responses to Taddeo's stimulus. Buonarroti had been Maffeo Barberini's childhood friend in Florence and roommate in their student days in Pisa, and he was also on good terms with other members of the family. He was received warmly by the pope on his visit to Rome in May 1624 and again in the spring of 1629, when he was the guest of Carlo Barberini.[216] Buonarroti explores different ways of joining a "new palace" to the Sforza building, the "old palace" (terminology that was also used to describe the two-part palace at Palestrina),[217] but without ever specifying the ecclesiastical or secular nature of their inhabitants. His second scheme (Fig. 148)[218] seems especially close to Taddeo's idea, with its single broad stair leading up to a vestibule from which more stairs depart, to the *salone* in the old palace to the south and to the new palace (presumably to its *salone*) to the north. Another of his *pensieri* includes the inscription, "Gli Archi Barberini overo le scale barberine overo la ringhiera barberina" (see Fig. 145, top),[219] evidence of his search for an appropriate image for the new Barberini palace and at the same time a suggestion that his search has taken him to Palestrina, with the great arches of the lower part of the complex and the monumental stairs leading to the entrance of the palace. The convex form of the stairs of his second scheme (Fig. 148, upper left) would seem to be the reflection of the concave steps of the palace at Palestrina. Buonarroti's suggestion of *sprezzatura* — of an analogy between manners and architecture[220] — becomes relevant as it pushes discussions away from the norms of Roman palace building to a loose and articulate overall form, and to a style and details usually associated with the architecture of villas. Both of these characteristics turn up in the building as finally designed and constructed, but in forms that are different from those of Buonarroti's *pensieri*.

Other ideas now lost to us were also proposed in response to Taddeo's design, and Francesco mentions in particular the intervention of Urban VIII, "who, however, as His Holiness also had good taste in these matters, added a few embellishments and improvements which had not been foreseen [by others]." [221] In other words, he was not an originator but a critic who responded to someone else's design. The tantalizing statement does not reveal Urban's specific contribution, but it is tempting to think that he might have been responsible for the critical shift of emphasis from the division of both family and building into ecclesiastical and secular segments, to the unification of these two articulate parts, through the placement of the papacy (that is, himself) at the center. In the end, the Palazzo Barberini does not have a single stair leading to

two *saloni* with their respective apartments; rather, it has two stairs leading to a single *salone,* whence disperse the apartments; and its two separate and recognizable wings are subordinated to the unifying seven-bay loggia of the west façade. The united family has its two aspects, as the unified building has its two wings.

PHASE TWO: THE ARCHITECTS DESIGN

In spite of Francesco's silence on the matter, architects were of course involved in the design of the palace both before and after the beginning of construction. Barberini advisors acknowledged the importance of retaining a professional architect, even while believing themselves capable of giving worthy advice. The architect was recognized as a professional, a person of special expertise, who would work "within the confines of the approved design," always in consultation with the patron. His role would include the preparation of the final design, planning, architectural ornament, the design of stairs, judicious selection among alternatives, and the supervision of construction.[222]

Carlo Maderno was in charge of the actual design and, in spite of his failing health, supervised its detailed development up until the beginning of construction and his death a few weeks later.[223] His two assistants, Gianlorenzo Bernini and Francesco Borromini, may have made contributions;[224] but Maderno's sure hand can be seen especially in the plan.

Although drawings do not survive that would help us understand the genesis of Palazzo Barberini's extraordinary design, there are a few drawings that show the plan before adjustments that were effected immediately before or during construction. A precise light pencil drawing by Borromini (Albertina, It. AZ Rom 957; see Fig. 146) shows the *piano nobile* of the palace superimposed on the ground-floor portico; Thelen has dated it 1627/1628.[225] A second plan in the Albertina (It. AZ Rom 966; see Fig. 147) is a working drawing for the north half of the center

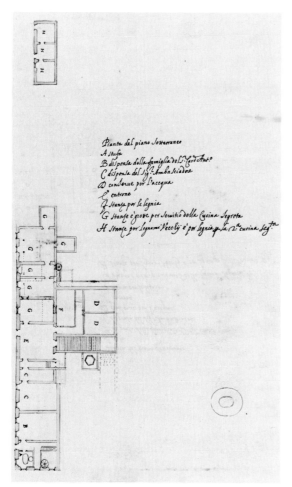

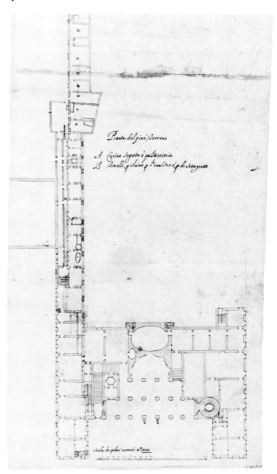

149   Palazzo Barberini, north wing, lowest level (Biblioteca Apostolica Vaticana, ABarb., Ind. II, no. 2826 [d-1])

150   Palazzo Barberini, ground floor (Biblioteca Apostolica Vaticana, ABarb., Ind. II, no. 2826 [d-2])

part of the palace, drawn to a scale of 1:48 by Borromini and dated by Thelen November 1628, or just before the beginning of construction.[226] Its meticulous detail shows the ground floor in solid lines and the *piano nobile* in broken lines; features of the plan of the north wing are indicated along its left edge. Four plans in the Archivio Barberini (ABarb., Ind. II, no. 2826 [d–1]–[d–4]; Figs. 149–153) show five levels of the palace.[227] The plan of the ground floor is signed by

Gioseppe Contelli, or Centelli (Thelen's reading), or Ceratelli (Hibbard's reading), whose delicate hand seems responsible for the basic drawings of fine ink lines and yellow wash at a scale of 1:400. These plans were probably originally made for the patron, not as working drawings (because of their small scale and lack of annotations and detail) but as an attractive presentation of the almost final design, just before the beginning of construction late in 1628. Cruder lines in

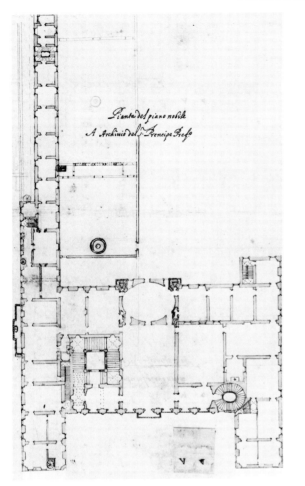

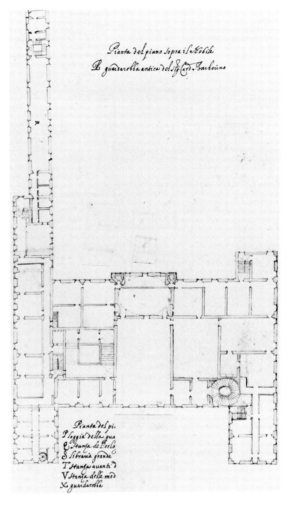

151 Palazzo Barberini, *piano nobile* (Biblioteca Apostolica Vaticana, ABarb., Ind. II, no. 2826 [d-3])

152 Palazzo Barberini, *secondo piano* (Biblioteca Apostolica Vaticana, ABarb., Ind. II, no. 2826 [d-4], flaps open)

another hand, in both pencil and ink, both ruled and freehand, show subsequent changes in the design.

The first of Borromini's drawings (see Fig. 146) shows that the designers considered removing Sforza partitions and the small spiral stair in the west end of the north wing to form two large rooms in the place of C22–C24 and C25–C26, and presumably a similar change would have been made in Taddeo's apartment below (Fig.

154; cf. Fig. 96). The rooms would have been impressive through their size and their double or even triple orientation, and it is tempting to imagine that the whole suite was to have been for the reception of guests, with sleeping and other private functions removed to the *secondo piano* so that the westernmost room of the *piano nobile* (C22–23–24) could have been an audience

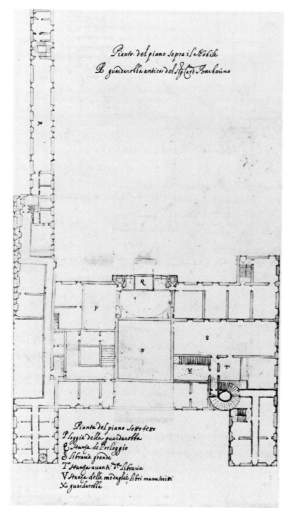

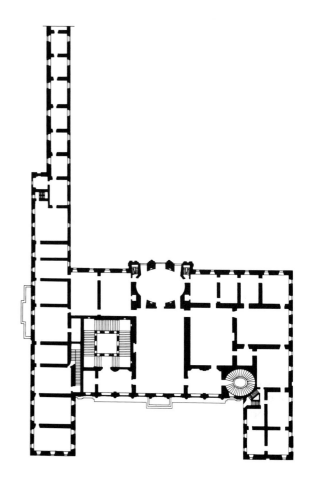

153   Palazzo Barberini, uppermost levels (Biblioteca Apostolica Vaticana, ABarb., Ind. II, no. 2826 [d-4], flaps closed)

154   Palazzo Barberini, design of 1628, *piano nobile*, reconstruction (David DiMarco)

room or gallery-like hall whose panoramic view would include St. Peter's on the western horizon.

The drawings show that the suite would also have extended to the east, uninterrupted by the garden apartment C33–C38 eventually constructed. The two drawings by Borromini show that in 1628 there was no intention to revise rooms C33–C34: the old Sforza transverse parti-

tion between the two rooms is firmly drawn. Contelli's plan of the *piano nobile* (see Fig. 151) shows a conspicuous erasure of the old wall and the crude insertion of the light partition, turned 90 degrees, as actually constructed. The wall between *gallarietta* C35 and *salotto* C36 is also a crude addition, and it seems that the earlier intention was to remove the old Sforza wall in this location and make a single large room en suite with the others of this wing. (This eastward extension of the north wing is not shown in Borromini's two drawings.)

Taddeo's suite may have been designed similarly. Contelli's drawing of the *pian terreno* (see Fig. 150), before the coarsely drawn additions of the later draftsman, showed Taddeo's suite extending through B36 (eventually constructed as the women's dining hall), possibly as far as the second room beyond the rectangular stair. A neat patch in the paper, in room B36 (very different in character from the later, crude emendations), shows that the enlargement of B36 by the removal of the old exterior wall to the north was a last-minute decision. Windows originally were drawn in the south wall of the eastward extension, suggesting that the higher gardens were to be reshaped to allow southern light into these ground-floor rooms. In that case the arrangement of the chapel B30 as shown in Contelli's plan would have made good sense. Its door would have opened to anteroom B20, and the bifurcation of east and west apartments would have occurred beyond that anteroom. As eventually constructed, the chapel door opened in the place of the window shown by Contelli, to anteroom B29, and a window was turned to the first anteroom; for Taddeo there would be only one suite, that to the west.

The *piano nobile* of the north wing, and probably the ground floor as well, would then have been conceived as a single long suite of rooms extending from west to east and entered at its midpoint from anteroom C20, a clear extension of the basic schema of bifurcation of the palace as a whole (see Fig. 154). The ample and expansive apartments would have been notable for both the number and the size of their rooms. Only room C20 would have had a fireplace, but one might imagine winter warmth in the small rooms to the east and summer coolness in the larger rooms with north exposure.

An important difference between Borromini's earlier drawing (see Fig. 146) and Contelli's plan (see Fig. 151) is the eastward extension of the south wing (on the *piano nobile*, room C12 and stair S4), shown on the latter plan as eventually

constructed in the campaign beginning in 1634. Borromini's drawing shows a perfectly reasonable summer apartment of four rooms opening from anteroom C3. The additional room is not en suite and does not offer improvement in exposure to or protection from the sun. The new stair might have been convenient, but then the apartment could have been served reasonably well by stair S6 (not yet carved out of the masonry mass in Borromini's drawing). The real advantage is not in function but in the clarification of the overall form of the building in plan and elevation: both the reading of the south wing as pendant to the north and the symmetry of the east façade are strengthened. This formal refinement, drawn in Contelli's hand, while postdating Borromini's detailed drawing, must have been decided on the eve of construction.

The diagrammatic clarity of the design (see Fig. 154) and the ampleness of the apartments (especially in the north wing) do not have parallels in Maderno's earlier palace planning. His lost scheme for remodeling and extending Palazzo Ludovisi (later Palazzo Chigi in piazza SS. Apostoli) might have provided him an opportunity to plan on a scale comparable to that of the Palazzo Barberini, but that project was barely begun when cut short by the death of Gregory XV.[228] It is only in Bernini's design for Palazzo Montecitorio (see Fig. 8), almost thirty years later, that a comparable vision is evident.

The plan nevertheless shows stylistic features of Maderno's earlier work at Palazzo Borghese and Palazzo Mattei, especially in its central part. Most prominent is the three-dimensional complexity resulting from his willingness to design different patterns or figures on the several stories of the building. The *pian terreno* is remarkable for its broad, spreading portico, hollowed out under the center and extended forward in the forecourt; the *piano nobile,* in contrast, is dominated by the strong east–west axis of the central *salone* and oval salon, laterally contained by the broad rectangular forms of the stair S1 and anteroom C2; still higher, the *guardaroba,* Fran-

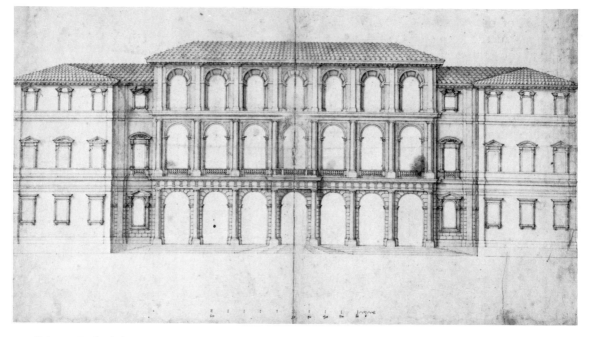

155   Palazzo Barberini, preparatory drawing for west façade (Windsor Castle, Royal Library. © 1989 Her Majesty Queen Elizabeth II)

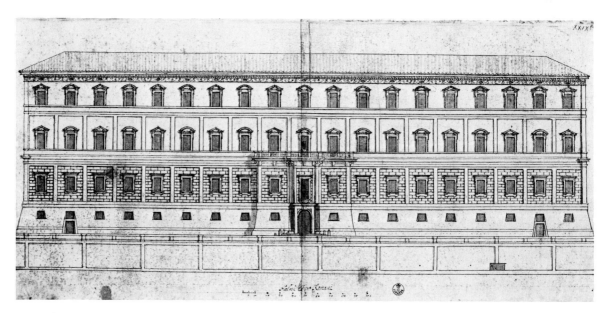

156   Palazzo Barberini, preparatory drawing for north façade (Uffizi A3533)

cesco's library, and Antonio's archive cut across the rooms of the *piano nobile*. As in Palazzo Borghese, Maderno's structural expertise comes into play, with a full range of devices invisible to the casual visitor. Maderno's real virtuosity in three-dimensional design is seen in the stair S1 (see Figs. 138, 140). Like the smaller stair S8 in his wing of Palazzo Borghese (see Fig. 32), it starts as one familiar form, transforms itself into another, and provides an exit midflight; and it is complicated by being superimposed on yet a third form, the straight stair leading to Taddeo's apartment. Further, it is undermined by the spreading portico of the *pian terreno*, whose outer bay it must leap over in its ascent to the *piano nobile*. In a larger sense, Maderno's three-dimensional imagination can be seen in the arrangement of the whole building against the hillside, providing the appearance of symmetry with the reality of the larger secular half of the building, and satisfying Anna's double role as wife of Taddeo and important female relative of the pope.[229] Maderno's insistence on regularly shaped rooms at the expense of walls of irregular thickness, as seen in Palazzo Borghese and Palazzo Mattei, is not so remarkable at Palazzo Barberini, because of the preexisting regularity of the old Sforza palace and the open site to the south; but it can be read in the central part, in the confrontation of hemicycle with oval hall and the excavation of small chambers and stairs in the thick masonry. In these same rooms can be seen another of Maderno's traits of planning, his preference for closed axes: the central axis of approach from the west is conspicuously blocked by the curve of the hemicycle and its fountain; and the oval salon remains contained and separated from the rectangular apartments to the sides by virtue of its closed cross axis. (The doors to rooms C19 and C15, while aligned with the filade through the apartments, occur at imprecise points along the perimeter of the ellipse.) While Borromini later exhibited considerable finesse in planning — including his uncle's preference for regular forms within the irregular matrix of the walls and

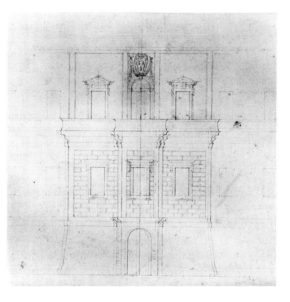

157 Palazzo Barberini, preparatory drawing by Borromini for center of north façade (Albertina, It.AZ Rom 960)

his technical skill in structure — his preference for unbroken axes is in marked contrast to Maderno's sense of containment, and his stairs, while often of unusual graceful form, are never spatially complex as are Maderno's.[230] Nor can Bernini be considered a rival in the matter of the plan of the stairs, for in his later work he consistently prefers the normal switchback stair, without spatial complications — however grand it may be.[231]

Though subject to revision during construction, the external forms of the palace were developed either by Maderno or under his supervision, and they too show his hand in many respects. In the early elevation study (Fig. 155), the north and south palace-like wings are framed simply by plain pilasters at the angles; but subsequent studies (Figs. 156, 157) show features of the final design: flat drafted masonry on the ground floor, overlaid by a band articulation which is repeated on the *piano nobile* as well. This departure from the usual Roman palace façade of plain brick or stucco (as at Maderno's Palazzo Mattei) is nevertheless familiar from the southeast façade of Palazzo Borghese, attributed to Vignola (see Fig. 13). Maderno had used the band articulation earlier in the courtyard of Palazzo Mattei. Taddeo's north entrance portal (Fig. 158) shows Maderno's characteristic superimposition of forms (for example, the east entrance of Palazzo Mattei, or the portal of S. Susanna), a development from the example of Michelangelo (for example, in the Biblioteca Laurenziana, or the Porta Pia). The specific forms here, however, are Vignolesque in their regularity, severity, and flatness, albeit perhaps Madernesque in their thickness — a combination that suggests the intervention of Borromini, who in his own work would show considerable interest in the work of Vignola as well as that of the "prince of architects," Michelangelo.[232] In the extraordinary west façade (see Fig. 89), Maderno's familiar forms are again in evidence: the columns of the *piano nobile* set into channels in the wall; columnar window frames in the side bays that recall those at St. Peter's; perspective enframements of the upper windows, like the entrance to the stair at Palazzo Mattei.[233] The breadth of the façade shows Maderno's consistent gradations of plasticity and richness of forms from the side wings through the intermediate bays to the seven-bay loggia and its centermost projecting bay, as well as hierarchical differentiations among the stories — traits especially in evidence in such church façades by Maderno as S. Susanna.

The inconsistencies between interior volumes and exterior patterns have been taken by Blunt as evidence for major changes in interior design.[234] Hibbard sees the discrepancies between inside and outside as characteristic of Maderno's oeuvre and an implied shortcoming.[235] The seventeenth-century ideal was not the modern notion of a transparent façade simply revealing interior arrangement. The much-admired Palazzo Farnese contains behind its regular three-story façade the vast two-story volume of the *salone,* rooms of normal height, and windowless mezza-

158   Palazzo Barberini, north portal (author)

nines, not to mention the sloping staircase and open light court behind the southeast façade. Maderno had earlier shown his commitment to the ideal of a regular exterior in the planning of Palazzo Mattei, whose two symmetrical façades conceal an interior organization that is anything but symmetrical; he showed it as well in his addition of a gallery wing to that palace, such that it appeared a separate building from the outside. At Palazzo Barberini it may be that the strength of the exterior expression of the building has caused modern critics to make more rigorous demands of it; yet Maderno's conception of

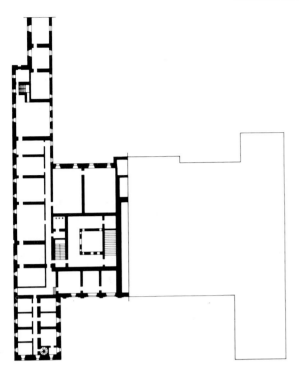

159   Palazzo Barberini, design of 1628, *secondo piano,* reconstruction (David DiMarco)

three-dimensional planning should free him from such criticism. We have seen that he discovered regular volumes and sometimes-complicated arrangements within the inarticulate matrix of Roman masonry, so that the outer form was not just incidentally but fundamentally separate from the interior. The neutral mask of Palazzo Farnese or Palazzo Mattei was set aside for a forcefully expressive external form at Palazzo Barberini.

PHASE THREE: CONSTRUCTION

In the third phase of design, after Maderno's death on 31 January 1629, Bernini was the dominant force. The building was under construction. According to Roman building practices, some details were to be designed only as work progressed.[236] The alternate curvatures and placements of the elliptical hall, sketched in pencil on Borromini's detailed working drawing (see Fig. 147), show that even a very prominent feature of the building could be subject to change during construction. Francesco reports that Taddeo followed the work closely and "approved and verified" whatever was done.[237] Padre Valerio Poggi, who had a room in the palace during construction,[238] was *soprastante,* and Bernini was the architect; and testimony given in a lawsuit of 1641 makes it very clear that ultimate authority lay with Bernini and his clients.[239]

Changes in the plan of the apartments in the north wing — both small adjustments and major revisions — must have gone hand in hand with construction and must have been due to a number of considerations.

A small but interesting change in design must have been decided early: the reduction in the size of Anna's chapel C30, the consequent shift in the location of its door, the insertion of the little room C31 for hearing mass privately, and the change in D29, the space above the chapel (cf. Figs. 102 and 154, and Figs. 103 and 159). While Anna might have heard mass from the landing of stair S7 or the doorway of either anteroom C20 or C29 (her *famiglia* gathered in the other), surely the addition of room C31 was a functional refinement. Probably more important was the relationship of the chapel to the anteroom C29. In Borromini's early drawing (see Fig. 146) the doors to the chapel and from anteroom C20 are aligned precisely with the windows opposite; in the pencil adjustment to Contelli's similar drawing (see Fig. 151), and in the actual construction (see Fig. 102), the chapel doorway is moved closer to the center of the anteroom wall. Surely considerations of the design of the whole room, involving the painter Andrea Sacchi, entered into this change. Sacchi's "Divina Sapienza" is no mere *quadro riportato* but covers the entire vault and controls the volume of the room. The painting is oriented to be viewed not as one enters the room but rather as one turns to approach the chapel, and its central figure gestures downward to the almost central chapel doorway (see Fig. 109). The decision to compress the chapel and shift its doorway must have been made in anticipation of Sacchi's fresco, very early in the period of construction, before Sacchi began painting in December 1629.[240] The new partition between the chapel and chamber C31 is already lightly sketched in Borromini's working drawing (late 1628; see Fig. 147). The change in the proportions of the chapel then opened the possibility of a domical ceiling, decorated according to Pietro da Cortona's design early in 1632 (Fig. 160); and this in turn required the light-admitting "torretta" above, in place of the privies shown by Contelli in D29 (see Figs. 103, 152). Painters and architects would seem to have been working together in the adjustment of the design of this crucial part of the palace.

The death of Carlo Barberini on 26 February 1630 must have caused some changes in the plan of the palace under construction. When it was decided that the widowed Costanza would join Taddeo and Anna at the new palace, appropriate quarters had to be arranged for her. Some changes in Contelli's drawing of the *secondo piano* record new rooms D51–D54 for Costanza's attendants and a corridor in D45 (not yet constructed in 1628–1638, according to the *misura*, fol. 182) and doorway (between D48 and D51) for passage to those rooms (see Figs. 152, 159). The removal of room B36 from Taddeo's ground-floor suite and its designation as a women's dining hall, along with the installation of the accompanying spiral stairs S11 and S12 sketched in by Contelli's corrector (see Fig. 150), may also be due to Costanza's needs.

The major revisions in the principal apartments of the north wing seem adumbrated in Contelli's drawings, which show the old Sforza partitions intact in the western part of the wing (see Figs. 150, 151). There was an obvious economy in maintaining the old walls, vaults, and even fresco decoration. The proposed large rooms may have seemed too open and unprotected for inhabitation in either summer or

160   Palazzo Barberini, chapel C30, vault (Barbara Bini)

winter. Strange as it may seem, there may have been a press for space for private functions, especially if Taddeo's apartment was to have been remodeled in this way. The service stair nearest the westernmost rooms would have been S7, accessible only from room C27. The grandness of the scheme may have stayed the hand of even the Barberini.

The formation of Anna's casino-like garden apartment — not part of the original plan — is recorded on Contelli's drawing (see Fig. 151). The second draftsman has drawn the partition between rooms C33 and C34 and the partition between the *gallarietta* and *salotto* C36 (in place of the old Sforza exterior wall); he has roughly inserted the new doorways of the *salotto* but has not bothered to change the single south window to the door flanked with windows as constructed. Outside, the enclosed garden is newly drawn by the second hand, even though it is but a modification of the old Sforza garden and could have been included by Contelli had its relevance occurred to him. The changes must have been decided on in 1629 or 1630, in order for the rooms to be ready for painters in 1631.[241] Costanza's anticipated removal to the palace and the consequent increase in the number of female inhabitants may or may not have been catalysts in the formation of this happy revision.

These changes fundamentally altered the design of the north wing. No longer simple expansive suites, the apartments became more particularized. Private rooms were included on the same level with rooms for the reception of guests. Small stairs provided better circulation for servants and women attendants. Costanza found accommodations for her modest life, and the society of two noblewomen with their attendants received a new focus in the garden apartment. The arrangements for seasonal apartments were revised, as the apartments in the northwest wing were made to serve both winter and summer needs, the rooms in the eastern part of the *piano nobile* were turned to summer use, and the eastern part of the *pian terreno* was lost to Taddeo. In the end, the north wing was less a diagram and more an articulated framework for the demanding lives of three persons.

However Madernesque these revisions may seem in their accommodation of complex functional needs and their structural virtuosity (especially in the formation of the garden apartment), they cannot reasonably be attributed to that master, since he died so soon after the beginning of construction. Taddeo, ever interested in economical and convenient arrangements, and especially attentive to the progress of the construction of his palace, may well have suggested the changes. Borromini could have provided the structural expertise. Bernini may have discovered the formal order for the garden apartment; at least, he presided over the revision of the plan which had previously been rather Berninian in its clarity.

Changes in the design of the south wing during construction were fewer in number and of lesser import than in the north wing, as recorded

in Contelli's altered drawings. A few can be seen in the *secondo piano:* the extension of corridor D4, the arrangement of privies in the space between the two stairs, and the door from mezzanine D2 to the oval stair (see Fig. 152). Since Francesco had become vice-chancellor and moved into the Cancelleria only months after the construction of his half of Palazzo Barberini had begun, it may be that he was less susceptible to changing requirements and possibilities than was his brother in the construction of the north wing.

A change in the small service stair S3 goes beyond functional necessity. The stair, adjacent to the large elliptical stair S2, has a complicated course in Contelli's plans. It begins on the *pian terreno* as a simple switchback stair. At the *piano nobile* it loses its western leg, in exchange for an angled leg fitted against the curve of the ellipse. A servant ascending the stair would have to turn left and traverse a short corridor to reach the angled flight. At the *secondo piano* the stair shifts back to its original position. The gymnastic maneuver permits a slightly larger room C9 on the *piano nobile* (shown also on Borromini's plan, Fig. 146, along with the angled flight) and a tiny chamber for latrines, E11 (the only such facility in the south half of the palace), on the upper floor. The document of construction between 1634 and 1637 records a much simpler stair, its walls and twelve straight flights moving directly from ground floor to attic, at the expense of a smaller room C9 (see Figs. 100–104).[242] The complication of the earlier stair design parallels that of Maderno's great stair S1 on the other side of the palace; the simplified stair, constructed in 1634–37, is more characteristic of the work of Bernini, who supervised its construction.

Beyond concerns of planning, documents of construction occasionally mention Bernini's specific intervention — for example, in revisions in the brick facing of the garden façade and in the prominent matter of the design of doorframes in the central *salone* — sometimes with the explicit involvement of Taddeo.[243] Other documented changes can be assumed to have been Bernini's responsibility: the walls of the landings of the square-well stair S1, shown smooth with small semicircular niches in the plans drawn by Borromini (see Figs. 146–147), were revised to receive perspective enframements (see Fig. 139).[244] Drawings attest to Bernini's working out of such details as doorframes, with the collaboration of Borromini.[245] The heightening of the building, to include a frieze for the elliptical attic windows of the side wings and a full Corinthian order for the western loggia, may also be due to Bernini. The earlier version (Fig. 161; see also Fig. 155) shows attic windows included within the pediments of the windows of the *secondo piano* and, for the loggia, pilasters without capitals or entablature, set against the plain bands enframing the bays; the whole building seems stunted by the roof and its cornice. The loggia seems a faithful response to the form of the fifteenth-century benediction loggia that had stood before St. Peter's until 1616 (Figs. 142, 143). The revision provides more generous spaces for the rooms of the upper floors (Figs. 91, 92). At the same time, the more energetic form allows a closer association of the loggia with both the Colosseum and the courtyard elevation of Palazzo Farnese (with its clusters of Corinthian pilasters). The clarification of these formal allusions enhances the complexity of meaning in the design of the façade.

While many early sources suggest Bernini's authorship of the palace,[246] they can also be taken to refer to his involvement as architect during construction. The testimony of 1641, already cited, was given in the context of determining the responsibility of Valerio Poggi, the *soprastante*, during construction. Baglione (1642 and 1649) writes of the palace as having been "raggiustato e con ornamenti abbellito dal Cav. Gio. Lorenzo Bernino"; and Martinelli, ca. 1660–62, with Borromini's annotation, also uses the term "raggiustato"—an apt characterization of Bernini's interventions after Maderno's death in 1629. Critics from the seventeenth to the twentieth century have naturally wanted to connect the extraordinary design of Palazzo Barberini

with the famous name of Bernini. He may indeed have played an undocumented role in the lively discussions preceding Maderno's actual design, but his sure contributions (always with the technical support of Borromini and the approval of Taddeo) are in the detailed shaping of the emerging construction.

Taddeo Moves In, and Out Again

Some preliminary work in the old Sforza palace and the gardens was done shortly after the purchase of the property, and major construction of the new Palazzo Barberini was under way by December 1628, only a year after Taddeo's marriage to Anna Colonna and a month or so after the birth of their first child, Camilla. The new wall extending from the ground through the Sforza *sala,* and the shaping of the resultant rooms C28–C29, were completed in time for Sacchi's painting of the "Divina Sapienza" in 1629–30.[247] The vault of the central *salone* was closed by 31 October 1630, and the structure of the façade must also have been completed by that date.[248]

The rapid pace of construction was in keeping with the pace of Taddeo's personal life: his first son Carlo was born on 1 January 1630; his father Carlo died, and Taddeo succeeded him as Prince of Palestrina, on 26 February 1630; Camilla died, apparently in the fall of 1630; on 3 August 1631 Taddeo made his solemn entry into Rome and on 6 August was invested formally as Prefect of the City; and on 19 August his second son Maffeo was born.

Now successful in establishing his young family and in gaining important titles, Taddeo was eager to be able to occupy that visible sign of his position, his new palace at the Quattro Fontane. The Florentine ambassador Niccolini reported in a letter of 21 September 1631 that Taddeo intended to move there in the following spring.[249] The opera *S. Alessio* was given at the palace during Carnival 1632, and Taddeo was hoping to move his family there during Lent of that year,[250] but his departure was delayed. The

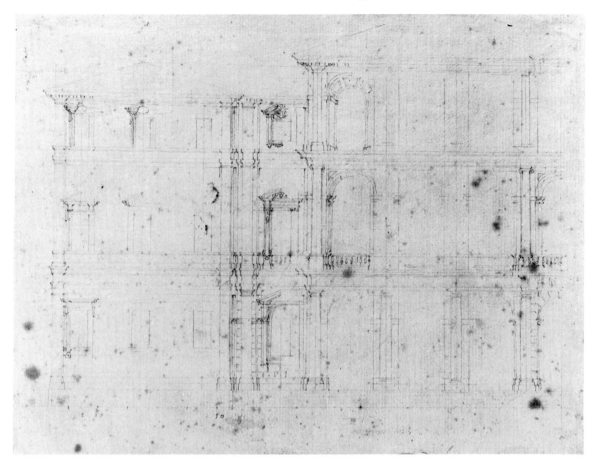

161   Palazzo Barberini, study for west façade (Albertina, It.AZ Rom 958)

actual transportation of his goods from the "Casa Grande" ai Giubbonari to the palace at the Quattro Fontane extended from 26 April until 31 May 1632,[251] but on 13 May Taddeo could finally declare himself resident in his new palace.[252] His days at the Giubbonari must have seemed behind him as he rented the old palace to Stefano Durazzo for 1,000 scudi per year.[253] The birth of his daughter Lucrezia and her baptism in the palace chapel on 8 September 1632[254] was a confirmation of the new palace's identity with the life of his family.

Meanwhile, work continued on the palace. Scaffolding for the painting of the vault of the central *salone* was finished and paid for on 9 July 1632,[255] and painting began later that year, to extend until November 1639.[256] Taddeo's payments for the construction of his part of the palace came to a conclusion during the first months of his residence there,[257] and Francesco's payments for the construction of the "novo appartamento" began on 12 October 1632.[258] Excavations for the new elliptical stair S2 were made in April 1633.[259] Work continued under Francesco's sponsorship until the end of 1636,[260] long after his appointment as vice-chancellor in November 1632 and his consequent residence in the Cancelleria.

In the spring of 1634, while the palace still stood in the unfinished state shown in Greuter's map of that year (see Fig. 118), Taddeo determined to leave the palace at the Quattro Fontane and move his family back to the old "Casa Grande" ai Giubbonari. On 27 July 1634, rental payments for the small houses for his staff at the Quattro Fontane declared that the term of rental would be concluded on 31 December 1634; and in the same month the Orsini palace in Campo dei Fiori was once again rented for the staff, for a term beginning 1 August 1634.[261] The moving of Taddeo's household goods was accomplished between 27 September and 1 December 1634.[262] An *avviso* dated 14 October 1634 reports that Taddeo, Anna, and Costanza had by then returned to live in the old palace in the via dei Giubbonari.[263]

Why did Taddeo decide to leave the splendid new palace, with whose genesis he had been so intimately involved, before it was even completely finished and only a little more than two years after he had moved there, to return to a palace which was clearly less distinguished? The reason given in the *avviso* of 14 October 1634 is that the new building was too damp.[264] Francesco Barberini recalls this reason too, while revealing another which was surely less publicized: "It was for this reason, either because [Anna] was too concerned about the safety of that air, or, having had two sons [at the Giubbonari], and having then given birth to a daughter at the Quattro Fontane, for good luck she wanted to return [to the Giubbonari] to bear the third son, that her husband's cautious judgment was at her service. . . ."[265] If Francesco is right, then Anna's superstition must have been confirmed by the birth of her third son, Nicolò, late in 1635,[266] and Taddeo must have seen that his lot was cast with the "Casa Grande" ai Giubbonari.

Early in 1635, Taddeo rented his portion of the still-unfinished Palazzo Barberini alle Quattro Fontane to his younger brother Cardinal Antonio Barberini, for 3,000 scudi per year, and Antonio also renewed the rental of the several small houses in the neighborhood for his staff.[267] With the completion of the south half of the palace, Antonio would eventually occupy the entire building. Francesco continued to maintain his library there, and the three brothers continued to sponsor theatrical performances and other special events there. By 1638, however, Pompilio Totti could report the distribution of the three brothers among three palaces: Francesco, by virtue of his office of vice-chancellor, at the Cancelleria; Taddeo in the "Casa Grande" ai Giubbonari; and Antonio in the palace at the Quattro Fontane.[268] For reasons concerning his immediate family, Taddeo was obliged to abandon the palace whose design was founded on an idea about the family in a larger sense. The Palazzo Barberini alle Quattro Fontane would never be occupied as it was originally intended.

Antonio Moves In, and Out Again

Antonio Barberini, younger brother of Francesco and Taddeo, was born on 4 August 1608 and was just fifteen years old when his uncle Maffeo became Pope Urban VIII. In spite of his youth, he was created cardinal *in petto* on 30 August 1627 and then recognized publicly on 7 February 1628. Free of the responsibilities held by his two older brothers, he could enjoy the status and corresponding wealth which his uncle's generosity afforded him. The Venetian ambassador Giovanni Pesaro focused precisely on this aspect in his brief characterization of Antonio in 1629: "He spends most generously, no less to maintain decorum than to satisfy the senses; he is little interested in the pursuit of the contemplative . . ."[269]

Francesco's appointment to the post of vice-chancellor and consequent residence in the Cancelleria, late in 1632, and Taddeo's return to the "Casa Grande" ai Giubbonari in the autumn of 1634, meant that the splendid but still unfinished palace at the Quattro Fontane was available for Antonio. He lost no time in renting the palace and its neighboring small houses. For his apartment, he chose that which had been Taddeo's, on the ground floor of the north wing, but he might take advantage of other rooms in the vast palace, as a document speaks of the room where Antonio was sleeping "in this month of July [1642]."[270] Indeed by April 1644, when an inventory was made of all his possessions in the palace, he seems to have spread himself throughout the three main apartments.[271] The ground-floor apartment of the north wing is called "His Eminence's lower apartment," and its bedroom B26 the room "where His Eminence sleeps," but the apartment on the *piano nobile* of the south wing is also called "His Eminence's principal apartment," and its western half seems much better equipped, with *portiere* and fireplace equipment, for receiving guests in April, before the seasonal shift to summer apartments (see Fig. 102). The bedroom C8, with southwest orientation, contained a wool blanket, a prie-dieu, a close-stool and a chamber pot (all missing from room B26), and the bed for an attendant in the adjacent room C9 was also supplied with wool blankets. The eastern rooms of this apartment (C11–C15), with crimson damask wall coverings, were conspicuously barren of signs of life, such as *portiere;* they were awaiting the arrival of summer. On the north side of the *piano nobile,* the "appartamento vecchio" contained some furniture bearing the arms of the cardinal, but it too seems lifeless, with its empty rods for *portiere.* Antonio had earlier ordered a set of silk revetments for seven rooms of this apartment, "sky-blue, all painted with various flowers, fruits, birds, fountains, and so forth" — a decorative scheme that recognized the suitability of these rooms for pleasurable summer occupation.[272] It is only on the floor below, in rooms B23, B25, B27, and B28, that one finds fireplace equipment and *portiere* to make the rooms comfortable for the enjoyment of the many games and musical instruments which they contained (see Fig. 101).[273]

Room B27 probably had served as Taddeo's audience room, but its ample size and its ceiling painting of "Apollo on Parnassus" made it especially appropriate for a music room. The inventory of 1644 names it the "stanza de Cimbali," and its few seats were outnumbered by six keyboard instruments and a guitar. Additional cembali were in neighboring rooms B25 and B28, and

four more were in the apartment above, in rooms C23, C29, and C39.[274] Antonio must have enjoyed billiards too, since his inventory lists four billiard tables — three of them clustered in C10, properly the passage from the oval stair to the central *salone.* The fourth was in room C11, just next to the anteroom of his main winter apartment; and room C34, in the unheated part of the palace, was noted as the room where the game "used to be played."[275] Board games were considered appropriate for gentlemen in attendance on the cardinal;[276] a backgammon set was in the small room B25, next to the music room, and another awaited the coming of warmer weather in room C36.[277]

Paintings were used throughout the *piano nobile* as overdoors and overwindows, and sculptures complemented the classicizing decor of the oval hall C17, but most of Antonio's large collection of works of art was housed in the north wing, on the ground floor and in rooms C33–C44 of the *piano nobile.*[278] Anna's garden apartment maintained part of its identity in the name "appartamento della Conversatione,"[279] but its center in *salotto* C36 was lost as the suite of rooms was extended from C33 to C44, "the last room of paintings [in the] upper [apartment]."[280] Downstairs, in the "apartment of paintings and statues,"[281] paintings covered the walls of the entire apartment. Many small paintings hung in the small westernmost rooms, and sometimes the paintings were grouped thematically — for example, thirty-six portraits in anteroom B28, twenty-eight portraits of historical and classical figures and nine tall paintings of muses in bedroom B26, and many landscapes in B32.[282] Most of the sculptures were small (from 2 to 4 *palmi* in height), and many were busts.[283] In 1644 the works of art joined musical instruments, games, and furniture in a rich setting for cultivated leisure activities; but by 1687–88, when Nicodemus Tessin visited the palace, the ground-floor apartment had no other furnishings than the sculptures and the paintings that covered its walls.[284]

During Antonio's residence in the palace, Cardinal Francesco Barberini continued to build

246 Seventeenth-Century Roman Palaces

and maintain his famous library there;[285] but Teti writes of a "private library" in the ground-floor apartment,[286] and documents suggest that Antonio had established his own library, probably in room B36, at its eastern extremity. Costanza Barberini's women attendants had used this room for their *tinello,* but, with their removal from the palace, the room became available for some other use. As Antonio seems to have developed the other rooms in this apartment for his private enjoyment (having transferred formal functions to the "appartamento nobile" in the south wing), it would be only fitting for him to locate his library here as well. A notice of small repairs speaks of "the door to the library in the lower apartment," that is, that on the ground floor of the north wing. The 1644 inventory of Antonio's paintings lists rooms in a sequence leading to "the last room, next to the library," and "the corridor before the library" (B34 and B35); the inventory of furnishings likewise proceeds through the rooms formerly occupied by Taddeo to "the room outside the gates of the library."[287] Even if overshadowed by the more famous library of his older brother, Antonio's library too could find a place in the Palazzo Barberini and then later be transferred to three rooms in Antonio's subsequent residence, the "Casa Grande" ai Giubbonari.[288]

Wherever Antonio found himself within the palace, he was surrounded with the accoutrements of wealth. The inventory of 1644 lists 575 paintings, 255 sculptures, many musical instruments, rich furnishings and wall hangings (including many tapestries), a vast quantity of silver, porcelain, crystal, and much more.[289]

Although the entire *piano nobile* and the north half of the *pian terreno* were occupied by Antonio's apartments, there was still room for several members of his household to live in the palace, especially in the upper stories (where apartments originally had been prepared for Donna Costanza and for her attendants and those of Anna Barberini). Uncle Antonio Magalotti's apartment of four rooms was conspicuous enough to be included in the inventory of 1644;

it was reached by a corridor passing the *armaria* (D22) and could well have been the four rooms D42–D45 on the *secondo piano* of the north wing.[290] His servants' rooms, also listed in the inventory, could have been in nearby small rooms. The quarters of the theologian Padre Ignazio Mignozzi were also included in the inventory.[291] Rooms of many others are noted in records of repairs and renovations and are sometimes described as being in the palace: the soprano Marcantonio Pasqualino had two rooms in the attic of the north wing; Santi Tappone, the *sottoguardaroba,* had a windowless room on the ground floor, and the Cavaliere Girolamo Pazzi's rooms were adjacent. Tomaso Valemani, the trainbearer Horatio Balsimeli, chaplains Don Marino Marini and Don Antonio, and five of the cardinal's seven coachmen had rooms; and Giovanni Braccese and Giovanni Lotti each had two rooms in the palace.[292] Still, these fourteen men made up only about 11 percent of Antonio's *famiglia,* which numbered 128 in 1642. Other members of the *famiglia* lived in the small houses around the palace, as had Taddeo's staff.[293] Andrea Sacchi lived nearby, in via Rasella, but he had rooms (B8–B9) on the ground floor of the south wing for his paintings, sculptures, and marble reliefs.[294]

Antonio's substantial addition to the palace was the building of the Barberini theater. Theatrical performances were held at the palace, still under construction, as early as Carnival 1632 (even before Taddeo and his family had moved in).[295] Francesco's *guardaroba* D1 served as dressing room, and the plays were presented in the large hall C2 on the *piano nobile,* the first anteroom to the apartments of the south wing. So memorable was this use that the document of construction (dated 1638) calls the room "the big hall where the comedies used to be given," and in 1644 it is still named "the hall where the comedies were presented."[296] Contemporary reports of the early performances consistently record that they took place in the palace.[297] Francesco's biography of Taddeo suggests both the excitement that these spectacles generated and their setting within a building still under construction: for the presentation of *Erminia sul Giordano* in 1633 he tells of crowds of people standing on the scaffolding of the masons for a glimpse of the proceedings through the windows; of the collapse of the scaffolding, sending everyone topsy-turvy; and of Taddeo's heroic calm in stilling the panic.[298]

Already by the end of 1638, when the *misura e stima* of Taddeo's construction at the palace was completed, the anteroom in the south wing of the palace could be called "the *salone* where the comedies *used to be given*"; and reports of the Barberini presentations during Carnival 1639 clearly speak of a new theater. A spacious ground-floor room, adjacent to the palace and adjoined by a small courtyard, is described, capable of holding an audience of 3,000 to 4,000. The five-hour production of *Chi soffre speri* (revised from its 1637 production) was distinguished by fine singing, rich costumes, and, especially, many elaborate sets, including one that presented a view of what actually existed just beyond the walls of the theater: the Barberini garden with its ball court and its carriage road.[299]

A memorandum dated 25 July 1637 summarizes expenditures for the new theater. The costs included 1,163.40 scudi paid by Cardinal Francesco Barberini, 2,589.63 scudi paid by Cardinal Antonio, and 1,403.45 scudi still owed to Luigi Arigucci for large beams and other wood.[300] Antonio's account books show expenditures for masonry, carting, beams, and metalwork, all for the "new large hall which is being newly built contiguous to our palace at the Quattro Fontane," extending from 13 June to 16 December 1636. Payments to Giovanni Battista Soria for woodwork in the spring of 1639 confirm the location of the theater adjacent to the palace ("nel salon delle comedie contiguo al Palazzo alle 4 fontane").[301]

The new construction took advantage of a wall and portal already built, extending from the north wing of the palace and separating the terrace below the north façade from the riding arena to the east. Borromini's drawing of a design attributed to Pietro da Cortona shows this wall, 136 *palmi* long and 30 *palmi* high, with an elaborate rusticated portal in the center and four mezzanine windows suspended from the entablature along its upper edge.[302] The record of construction describes its location, dimensions, and materials.[303] Totti's illustration in his guide to Rome (see Fig. 126), published in 1638, would seem to be slightly out of date in showing the wall alone, without the new theater which by then had absorbed the wall as part of its façade.[304] The depth of the theater, only slightly less than its width, is indicated on Contelli's plan of the *pian terreno* of the palace and is shown as a penciled addition to his plan of the *piano nobile* (see Figs. 150, 151): its two thick walls, about 118 *palmi* apart, extend from the eastern chain of granaries and service rooms. Arigucci's total bill of 1,503.45 scudi, of which only 100 scudi had been paid by 25 July 1637, included 1,360 scudi for forty-one fir beams imported from Florence,[305] an average of more than 33 scudi each. A few years later, he would furnish four beams for the new anteroom of Taddeo's "Casa Grande" ai Giubbonari, 42 *palmi* long, at a cost of 20 scudi each.[306] From the price of the beams for the theater, we can imagine that they must have been especially long, perhaps about 60 *palmi,* or half the distance between the two walls shown on the plan. While there may have been some interior piers, the *stanzione* would nevertheless have been impressive in its vastness, even larger than the central *salone* of the palace (110½ × 65⅔ *palmi*). Cortona's wall was only 30 *palmi* high, and so a second story had to be built above it to contain the great interior volume. This can be seen in the engraving published by Girolamo Teti in 1642 (see Fig. 125) and, more clearly, in Alessandro Specchi's engraving of 1699 (Fig. 162), where the theater is labeled "Teatro da Comedie." The designer of the enlarged façade placed four rectangular windows above Cortona's pendant mezzanine windows and coordinated the new upper entablature with the horizontal courses separating the ground floor and *piano nobile* of the palace.

SEGVE L'ALTRA VEDVTA PER FIANCO DEL PALAZZO VERSO LA PIAZZA DELL'Ec. SIG. PRENCIPE DI PELLESTRINA
Architettura del Caualier Bernino
1. *Facciata per fianco verso la Piazza.* 2. *Facciata Principale.* 3. *Altro fianco verso il Giardino.* 4. *Teatro da Comedie.*   *data in luce da Domenico de Rossi dalle sue Stampe in Roma alla Pace con licenza de Sup.*   18

162   Palazzo Barberini from northwest, engraving by Specchi (Bibliotheca Hertziana, Rome)

A few years later Antonio again turned his attention to the theater, attaching two rooms of normal dimensions to it. Once again he took advantage of a preexisting wall to raise a façade 65½ *palmi* long, "verso la strada," or along the carriage road leading to the garden. Behind this wall he built two rooms (40½ × 30 *palmi* and 32¼ × 28½ *palmi*) and cut a doorway from the smaller of the two through the wall of the theater to the "palco delle comedie." [307] These were presumably rooms for the use of himself and his honored guests, comparable to the rooms that normally were outfitted adjacent to grand banquets, for withdrawal and rest — surely welcome during the lengthy performances. [308] This improvement to the theater cost considerably less than the building of 1636, only 172.19½ scudi for its masonry.

The theater building survived the last of the Barberini theatrical productions and, although altered internally, stood until 1932, when it was demolished to make way for the new via Barberini, intended to link the old center of Rome with the train station. Its portals, windows, and angle rustication were preserved and incorporated in a new building on the truncated site, in a compressed but heightened version of Cortona's original wall. [309]

Another of Antonio's revisions to the palace that his brothers had built was considerably smaller than the theater but no less interesting. In 1641 he had made a heated bathing room. [310] An anonymous advisor to the Barberini had suggested the inclusion in the new palace of a bathing room with a heating system similar to that which he had observed in ancient Roman structures; but, even while recommending a bath for its salubrity, cleanliness, and pleasure, he ac-

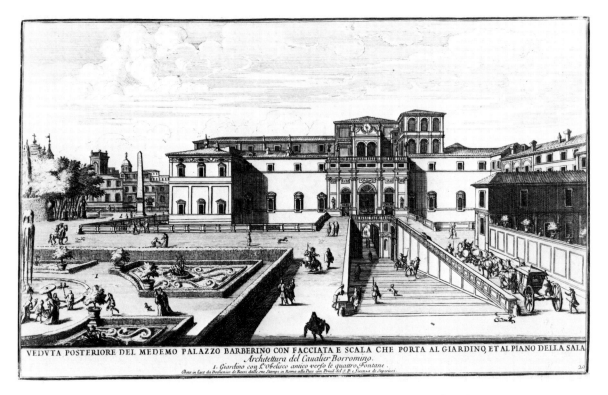

VEDVTA POSTERIORE DEL MEDEMO PALAZZO BARBERINO CON FACCIATA E SCALA CHE PORTA AL GIARDINO, ET AL PIANO DELLA SALA
Architettura del Caualier Borromino.
1. Giardino con L'Obelisco antico verso le quattro Fontane.
Data in Luce da Domenico de Rossi dalle sue Stampe in Roma alla Pace con Priuil del S.P. e Licenza de Superiori.

163   Palazzo Barberini from east, engraving by Specchi (Biblioteca Apostolica Vaticana)

knowledged that it was no longer a common practice.[311] While heated bathing rooms were not uncommon in the sixteenth century, the most recent bath in Rome that the anonymous antiquarian could have pointed to would probably have been that constructed in the Palazzo Borghese by Carlo Maderno in 1612–14.[312] The record of construction from 1628 to 1638 shows that no baths were built in the Palazzo Barberini at that time. As Antonio's thoughts turned to the benefits or pleasures of bathing, he must have noticed a room in the palace which was no longer needed, the laundry built for Donna Anna's women (see Fig. 100, A2). It was located on the lowest level of the north wing, in its northwest corner, conveniently connected to the private rooms of the two main apartments in that wing by a spiral stair S8, and already provided with running water.[313] Within the cubic volume of Anna's laundry Antonio had built two new walls

and a vault, so that his new, more intimately proportioned chamber could enjoy windows to the north and west while still allowing a passage around to the small service door in the second bay of the north façade. Inside the room, about 19 *palmi* square, were a small furnace for heating water in a caldron, a sunken elliptical tub (18 *palmi* in circumference and 4½ *palmi* deep) surrounded by a low parapet, and a tiled bench around the perimeter of the room. Antonio's "stufa" is shown as an addition to Contelli's plan of the basement (see Fig. 149, A). The inventory of the cardinal's goods in 1644 lists several copper vessels especially for the *stufa*.[314] The document of construction gives no indication of painted or stucco decoration, but, given the sybaritic connotations of warm bathing and the conspicuous luxury of Antonio's apartments, it is hard to imagine that this room would have been anything but richly decorated.

Antonio was responsible for a small but prominent addition to the varied assemblage that formed the east façade of the palace—a clock tower rising over the central bay of the central pavilion.[315] This "new loggia for the clock" was built between June 1643 and October 1644. Behind its façade of twin arches was a chamber covered by a painted vault measuring 20 × 12 *palmi,* and the clock face rose above. An elaborate carillon of thirty-eight bells was installed there; it could be played from a keyboard, or it could be made to sound automatically every quarter hour.[316] The tower was later removed, but it can be seen in Specchi's engraving of 1699 (Fig. 163). Its framing pilasters continue the vertical lines of the central bay of Maderno and Bernini's façade below, strengthening its central axis and its priority over the loggia of the *guardaroba* above and to the right.

If Antonio was able to extend his own activities through the entire *piano nobile* and the northern half of the ground floor, he found the south half of that lower level ill defined as far as use (see Fig. 101). The *credenza* remained in room B3. The large room next to the *credenza,* B4, left empty when the woodworkers moved out on the completion of the palace, was first remembered as the "big room on the ground floor where the carpenters' workshop used to be" and then simply as the "room next to the bookkeeping office," with no identity of its own.[317] The bookkeeping office itself migrated from B6 in 1641–43 to the two smaller rooms B9–B10 toward the forecourt in 1644–45.[318] This move meant that Andrea Sacchi's studio had to make way: his two rooms B8–B9 in 1641–43 shrank to only one in 1644.[319] Between Sacchi's remaining room B8 and the old bookkeeping office B6 was the cellarer's room B7, and this too could be converted: it became a kitchen in 1646.[320] The *grotte* (B11–B15) to the east must have provided rather gloomy chambers for Santi Tappone and Girolamo Pazzi.[321]

Antonio's architectural work at Palazzo Barberini appears as adjustments within an already existing structure, which recognize both the removal of previous requirements (rooms and a laundry for women) and his own special interests (the theater, bathing, music). The impact of his additions on the exterior was minimal, the clock tower enhancing an already existing axis and the theater emerging discreetly from behind Cortona's wall. The interior arrangement suited his expanded pattern of activities as well as those for whom it was first designed. He could even find within it the ideal room, already decorated, for his musical interests. It may not even be important to know who his architectural advisor was.[322] Probably the most significant thing he did was to occupy the entire palace, thereby depriving its form of the significance that Taddeo had intended it to have. The building remained impressive, as it does to this day; but without the living content of the two pendant brothers, secular and ecclesiastical, it was no longer expressive.

Having recorded the palace's contents in the two inventories of April 1644, in the last days of his uncle Urban VIII's pontificate, Antonio Barberini abandoned the palace and departed for France under cover of darkness, disguised as a barrel-maker, on the night of 28–29 September 1645.[323] On 29 April 1646, after Innocent X had confiscated Barberini properties, Cardinals de Valençay and Grimaldi entered the palace, declared that Antonio had given it to the king of France, and occupied it with French soldiers. Meanwhile, the elder Antonio Barberini, Cardinal of S. Onofrio, had maintained a small apartment in the palace, probably in upper rooms of the north wing, where he died on 11 September 1646.[324] Although the pope absolved the Barberini family on the following day, the younger Cardinal Antonio did not return to his palace but remained in France until the summer of 1653, by which time the Barberini were fully reconciled with Innocent X. Instead, the ambassador of France arrived in Rome on 24 May 1647 and went to live in the palace, repeating that Cardinal Antonio had given it to the king of France; he stayed there until the crucial summer of 1653. On his eventual return to Rome, 11 July 1653, Antonio went first to the palace at the Quattro Fontane but soon rented Palazzo Bonelli at the south end of piazza SS. Apostoli (see Fig. 211, no. 4), where he was able to display the arms of the king of France along with those of the pope and the Roman people, leaving Palazzo Barberini to the younger members of the family. Finally, in 1658, he purchased the "Casa Grande" ai Giubbonari from his nephew Maffeo, where he lived until his death in 1671.[325]

Francesco Remodels

Palazzo Barberini underwent extensive remodeling in the 1670s, work paid for by Cardinal Francesco Barberini. In the south wing, basement rooms were excavated for the installation of a new multiroom kitchen, and the ground-floor rooms were finally finished as a major apartment; apartments on both the *pian terreno* and the *piano nobile* were revised; the *pian terreno* was freed from the higher gardens to the south and east by extensive earth removal and the construction of a retaining wall; a carriage drive was pierced through the great niche of the portico and the oval room at that level and ramped upward through the gardens to the east; the bridge connecting the oval room of the *piano nobile* with the gardens was consequently rebuilt; and a new bridge, its apparently collapsing arches connected to anteroom C3 by a wooden drawbridge, was extended toward the south gardens.

Blunt dated the construction of the carriage drive and the consequent alterations to the garden façade between 1673 and 1679.[326] He cited the testimony of Nicodemus Tessin, who visited Rome in 1673 and again in 1687–88 and remarked on the latter occasion that, since his previous visit, the "Durchfarth" had been cut according to the design of Bernini.[327] Noting that Bernini died in 1680 and that Cardinal Francesco Barberini, who had traditionally been held responsible for the work, died in 1679, Blunt reasonably concluded that the work was completed by 1679. The

extent of the work was, however, much greater than he had realized, and its inception was earlier. The *misure* of the construction reveal a comprehensive remodeling and allow the dating of its several parts with greater precision.

The work may have been stimulated by the need to accommodate the rich inheritance of works of art following the death of Cardinal Antonio Barberini on 4 August 1671. His holdings are enumerated in an inventory of his possessions at the "Casa Grande" ai Giubbonari in April 1671;[328] and their sheer bulk is conveyed by the bill for moving them to the Palazzo Barberini alle Quattro Fontane in August, September, and October 1672: ninety-one cartloads of sculptures, medals, busts, figurines, pedestals, and a large harp, at a cost of 29.50 scudi, and 116 cartloads of paintings, costing 14.20 scudi.[329]

THE WORK

A comprehensive plan must have been ready before June 1672, when the architect Erigo Zuccalli was paid for having assisted in the preparation of "plans for the new fabric" at the palace at the Quattro Fontane.[330] Although work extended until Cardinal Francesco's death on 10 December 1679 and was paid for according to several distinct *misure,* nevertheless the sequence shows that the earlier work anticipated the later. Details may have remained to be worked out at the last moment, in the usual Roman fashion, but the outlines of the entire project were foreseen from the beginning.

The first step was to clear the ground floor of the south wing to make way for the new construction (see Fig. 101). Sculptures had already been moved from an old antiquarium in these rooms to a new one opposite the palace, in many days' work from 30 August to 11 October 1670.[331] The bookkeeping office (*computisteria*) had been arranged in rooms B9–B10 in 1644–45. Between 15 June 1672 and 30 June 1673, a new *computisteria* was constructed outside the main palace, in a building containing a *tinello*, a *dispensa*,

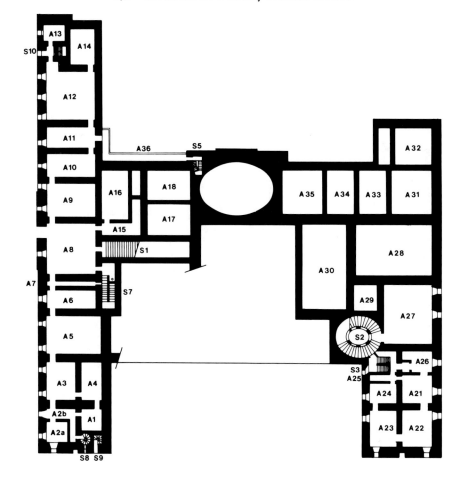

164   Palazzo Barberini, basements, 1679, reconstruction (David DiMarco)

and a bakery on its lower floor.[332] But the *credenza* in B3 could not be removed until the new *credenza* was ready in basement room A21.[333]

The first vigorous campaign lasted barely one year. The pavements of ground-floor rooms B4 and B6–B10 were removed and the earth below shaped to serve as formwork for the construction of masonry vaults; the earth was then removed to create basement rooms A21–A27 (but not yet A28; Fig. 164). By 15 August 1672, rooms B7–B10 had been finished with new pavements, plaster, stucco enframements for the central panels of their vaults, marble steps at their windows, and,

in B8, a new fireplace of cipollino marble (Fig. 165).[334] Room B6 was finished similarly by 12 January 1673, with marble frames at three newly made doors, a frieze of leaves, shells, and masks, and an especially elaborate stucco enframement for the central field of its vault, including the Barberini arms surmounted by a cardinal's hat with Maltese cross. An old fireplace was removed from B6.[335] Marble sculptures could be arranged in the rooms by 13 January 1673.[336] As yet the group of five rooms had no proper entrance, for B3 (still the *credenza*) and B4 had not yet been remodeled.

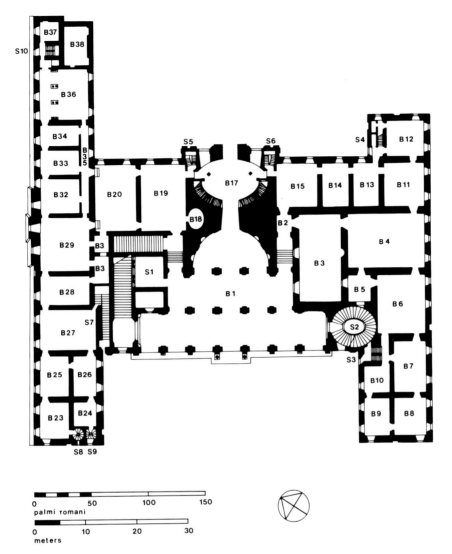

165   Palazzo Barberini, ground floor, 1679, reconstruction (David DiMarco)

At the same time, another important aspect of the remodeling was under way. By 4 July 1672 preparations had been made for the new drive that was to connect the western forecourt with the garden to the east: the old wooden bridge connecting oval salon C17 with the garden (shown by Teti; see Fig. 121) had been removed; a temporary parapet had been constructed in the doorway of room C17, where the bridge had been; and an opening had been made between the great niche of the portico and oval chamber B17.[337] The removal of earth on the east side of the palace, alongside oval chamber B17 and rooms B15–B13, by 17 June 1672, was the first step in freeing the south and east sides of the palace from the higher gardens so that light could enter the ground-floor rooms; and the *misura* specifically mentions that it prepared the way for the construction of the broad masonry bridge to the east, which would not be built until 1677.[338]

In 1673 the ambitious building project was halted. Masons' attention turned to the pressing matter of the repair of the western wall of the *guardaroba* G1, which was threatening collapse (see Figs. 99, 106). The wall was rebuilt, reinforcing chains were installed, and the roof was repaired between 2 November 1673 and 18 October 1674.[339]

In the spring of 1675, work on the major remodeling resumed. By 8 June 1675, more earth had been removed from the east side of the palace, to lower the level of the ground a few more *palmi*, and the large basement room A28 (the "cantinone"), already vaulted, had been excavated.[340] A new campaign of masons' work had begun by 2 May 1675.[341] The first part of this campaign, measured on 30 September 1676, was concentrated in the basement and ground floor of the south wing. Service stair S3, connected with the major elliptical stair S2, was extended downward to the recently excavated basement rooms, which were paved, plastered, and finished as a kitchen suite (see Fig. 164). Room A21, at the foot of the stair, was the *credenza*, with water rerouted from the old *credenza* B3. Its neighbor A22 was equipped as a scullery, with basins, running water, and a fireplace. A23, the corner room toward the forecourt, was the *bottiglieria;* it had a pair of small basins, one of which was to hold snow for cooling the wine. Small room A24 was separated from passage A25 by a new partition. Room A26 was designated the *pasticceria;* a vestibule *(bussola)* opened to it from the stair, and a new wall separated it from *credenza* A21. Drains were installed for all the rooms. A kitchen with an ample fireplace was begun in A27; not finished in time for the *misura*

of 30 September 1676, it was included in that of 26 November 1677.[342]

On the ground floor (see Fig. 165), old pavements were removed and vaults were built on the formwork provided by the earth below rooms B3 and B12 – B15, but basement rooms below the new vaults were not excavated. The passage B2, with its short flight of steps, was refurbished as an entrance to what could now be named a proper apartment. Room B3 was transformed from a *credenza* to a "sala," the first room in the newly formed ground-floor apartment. Its old basins were removed and its plaster repaired where it had been damaged by smoke. It received new pavement, plaster, a fireplace of cipollino, and a marble frame for the window to the chapel in neighboring B5. Room B4, once known only as the "big room on the ground floor where the carpenters' workshop used to be" and then as the "room next to the bookkeeping office," was now elevated to the status of "anteroom next to the *sala."* Its refurbishing included marble doorframes, an elaborate stucco enframement for the central panel of its vault, and a frieze of bees and garlands. A new door was installed from the anteroom to the chapel B5; a place for the altar was designated, and the chapel was finished with plaster, a frieze, and stucco vault ornamentation. The new *sala* and anteroom with chapel provided a proper beginning for the apartment already established in rooms B6 – B10; but following the pattern of bifurcation on the *piano nobile,* those rooms also led to a second apartment to the east. B11 (with a new fireplace of cipollino) and B12 were finished with stuccoes and marble doorframes similar to those in the other rooms. B13, B14, and B15 remained unfinished. None of the newly refurbished rooms on the *pian terreno* received hooks for wall hangings — probably an indication that the walls were intended from the beginning to be hung with the many paintings that Tessin counted there on his visit to the palace in 1688.[343] Outside, the south façade of the ground floor was freshly plastered, and grills

166   Palazzo Barberini, elliptical passage B17 (I.C.C.D., Rome, ser. E, no. 28890)

were installed at its thirteen windows.[344]

Still, the work was not done. Nineteen window frames with their interior shutters of walnut were ready by 4 March 1678, and they were glazed between 9 August 1678 and 27 March 1679.[345] Walnut doors and trim for the windows were prepared a few at a time and finally were finished by 26 November 1679.[346] The twenty-two cast-copper door handles were also ready only in 1679.[347] Sculptures and other marbles were not placed in the rooms until 1678. According to the *misure* of the work, the arduous task of moving the heavy and bulky figures was complicated by indecision as to their placement: pieces were tried in several places, and sometimes in two or three different rooms, before finally coming to rest. Sculptures were installed in rooms B4, B6, B7, and B8 by 18 May 1678; in the following months additional pieces were arranged in rooms B3, B4, B6, B12, and perhaps other rooms, and ancient paintings in room B11 were provided with protective coverings.[348] The storage of lead sheets from the roof of the oval stair S2 in the ground-floor rooms during work on the upper part of the stair, in 1678–79, is a clear sign that the new apartment was not then inhabited.[349]

167   Palazzo Barberini, east façade, central pavilion (Alinari/Art Resource, N.Y.)

Meanwhile, by 18 January 1677, things had been moved in preparation for construction of the new broad bridge from oval room C17 to the garden to the east, and by 8 March 1677 its masonry could be measured. The symmetrical curving stairs, fitted into the sides of the ground-floor oval B17 (now a passageway) and rising through the east façade to the bridge, were installed by 26 November 1677 (Figs. 166, 167).[350] At the same time, excavations and earth removal were in progress on the east side of the palace. Between 24 October 1676 and 30 June 1677, earth was cut away between the bridge and the north-

east wing of the palace, down to the level of the *pian terreno* (as had earlier been done to the south of the bridge); and three parallel drives were extended 306 *palmi* from the new bridge to the garden gate, the central drive ramping up from the newly pierced oval B17 and the vaulted space under the bridge. Four days were required to cut and remove orange trees that lay in the path of the new drive.[351] Retaining walls then were built along the central ramped drive; and another was constructed at a right angle to the northeast wing of the palace, to the level of the garden.[352] Two wings to the sides of the bridge could then be constructed and the balustrade installed along the bridge. Four sculptures were installed in the niches of the hemicycle of the portico, and several others were placed in the "facciata dell'orologio," the central pavilion of the east façade (see Fig. 163). All was ready to be measured by May 1678.[353]

In a subsequent campaign of earth removal, the axial drive was extended even farther, from the garden gate all the way to the eastern boundary of the garden, a distance of 250 *palmi*. The plan of the drive is shown by Nolli (see Fig. 130) and Letarouilly. The wooden gate was installed, and, at the terminus of the drive, excavations were made and foundations were laid for a large fountain, all by 18 May 1678.[354] In the following months, water lines and a large basin were installed. Pieces of travertine were arranged as a rocky base, their composition worked out *in situ,* and a statue of Apollo with a lyre was assembled on the *scogli,* its antique torso and newly carved head, arms, and legs hoisted and adjusted in place. The sculpture was the work of Gioseppe Giorgetti.[355] The dramatic figure of Apollo sat atop a rocky base from which springs of water flowed, his back turned to the vicolo Sterrato (now vicolo S. Nicola da Tolentino) beyond the garden wall, as shown in a nineteenth-century watercolor by Roesler-Franz (Fig. 168).[356] In 1936, the Villa Savorgnan di Brazzà was constructed in the eastern part of the garden, and the Apollo fountain was moved forward and installed in a niche in the west façade of the villa (Fig. 169), still a terminus for Palazzo Barberini's axial drive but much impoverished by its confining setting.[357]

The excavation of the area in the angle between the northeast wing of the palace and ground-floor rooms B19 and B20, by 30 June 1677, prompted revisions in that part of the palace. It was now possible to open windows in the south wall of room B36,[358] but at the same time the room above, C36, was now irrevocably cut off from the garden. The notion of a women's garden apartment centered on C36 had already been

168   Ettore Roesler-Franz, vicolo Sterrato (now vicolo S. Nicola da Tolentino) with the Barberini Apollo (Museo del Folklore di Roma)

undermined by Cardinal Antonio Barberini's occupation of the palace in the 1630s and 1640s; now the decision was taken to incorporate the rooms completely in the apartments of the *piano nobile* (see Fig. 102). Spiral stair S12, originally connecting B36, C35, and the women's rooms on the *secondo piano,* was removed for its entire length, its openings walled up, and new windows opened in the north façade of the palace.[359] *Gallarietta* C35 accordingly was lengthened and its painted decoration revised. The symmetrical design of the vault painting of 1631 was ingeniously extended westward into the area of the old spiral stair; a fine crack in the plaster still testifies to this extension (Fig. 170). The lunette under the extension was painted, presumably in emulation of the destroyed lunette. The narrow wall beneath the lunette presented greater technical problems. The fresco representing a "Sacrifice to Juno" was removed from the wall to be demolished, with the help of a specially constructed wooden frame, and then reinstalled on the new end wall of the *gallarietta* by the masons, its edges carefully plastered into the new wall surface (see Fig. 114).[360] Plaster and pavement were repaired. Enlarged doorways were cut at opposite ends of the *gallarietta,* aligned with those of rooms to the west and enframed with breccia marble (see Fig. 112), the better to insist on the relationship of the *gallarietta* to the rooms en suite instead of its old relationship to garden salon C36. The work was completed by 22 November 1677.[361]

Other rooms on the *piano nobile* of the north wing retained their form, but they too were improved in 1677. In the anterooms C19 and C20, two doorways were shifted to bring them into alignment with others.[362] Doorways in the north wing were enlarged to 6½ × 13 *palmi,* shifted if necessary to align them with others en suite, and enriched by new doorframes of breccia marble in place of the more modest travertine frames of the 1630s. First, seven doors en suite, beginning with corner room C23, were redone;[363] these would have been coordinated with the new doors of the *gallarietta* C35. Along the way, the opening of a fireplace was walled up. New doors of walnut were of course required for the enlarged openings.[364] Then other travertine doorframes in these rooms were replaced by frames of breccia — in C29, those to the chapel and the small adjacent chamber (see Fig. 109); in C27, the door to the stair S7 and that to room C26; the door between C26 and C25; and the door to C24.[365]

The removal of spiral stair S12 and the opening of two new windows were but the beginning of the remodeling of ground-floor room B36 (see Fig. 165; cf. Fig. 101). At first the dining hall for Costanza Barberini's women attendants, then probably Cardinal Antonio's library, at some

169   Palazzo Barberini, Apollo with lyre, in present location (author)

point the room had been decorated to make it deserving of the appellation "stanza dipinta."[366] An old partition between the larger rectangular portion of the room and the corridor-like portion below *gallarietta* C35 was replaced by two pairs of granite columns with marble Ionic capitals and bases. Three round arches were constructed to support the wall above the capitals, and flat arches under the round arches provided the armature for an entablature. Pilasters were placed against the east and west walls to correspond to the columns.[367] The vault of the

170   Palazzo Barberini, *gallarietta* C35, west end of vault (Barbara Bini)

kitchen A12 below was reinforced with an arch to receive the weight of the four columns.[368] Doors were remade to clarify the relationship of B36 to its neighbors: a new door was made to service corridor B35; an old door next to it, to B34 (shown on Contelli's plan, Fig. 150), was walled up; and another door to B34 (where the spiral stair S12 had formerly stood) was enlarged to align it with others in the apartment and given a travertine frame (matching the others in the suite) and a sill-step.[369] Scaffolding was built for the painters, the plaster surface was prepared, and Michelangelo Marulli Maltese painted the new parts of the vault, areas in the old vault that had been repaired, the cornice, and an architectural framework of columns, pilasters, windows, and doors corresponding to the new columns of granite. He was paid the considerable sum of 80 scudi for the work, completed by 27 July 1679.[370] Small marble columns, wood pedestals, statues,

busts, and other sculptures were brought and positioned in the room.[371] The granite columns and the painted architectural framework can be seen in an old photograph of the room (Fig. 171); but the painted landscapes, colored tile floor, and large fountain with a statue of Bacchus, all shown in the photograph, are not accounted for in the documents of 1672–79. Tessin saw granite columns, sculptures, two marble tables, and the Bacchus fountain on his visit to the palace in 1688.[372] The conspicuous fountain would surely have been mentioned in the *misure* if it had already existed or if it had been installed or at least anticipated in the work of 1677–79; it must have been added in the years immediately following the death of Cardinal Francesco in 1679. Today only the fountain, the columns, and the paving remain as reminders of the late seventeenth-century decor (Fig. 172).

Along with the removal of earth outside room B36 came the rearrangement of service passages in that area. B16, the old sunken passage along the east face of the palace between the northeast wing and stair S5, was of course removed in the excavation, but it was replaced by another at a lower level, A36, to connect kitchen A12 with stair S5 and the rooms of the *piano nobile*.[373] Stair S5 was extended correspondingly downward, and thirteen new steps were installed, to reach the new underground corridor.[374] Old spiral stair S11, with twenty-one steps, was removed from the south façade of the northeast wing, along with the window of the turnbox *(rota)* that had once served the women's dining room.[375] A new small switchback stair was built in its place, from the ground-floor rooms to the kitchen, with a new door from the ground-floor rooms, twenty-five steps, and a "camerino" over its landing.[376]

As on the *piano nobile,* so too the rooms on the *pian terreno* of the north wing were refurbished. The four windows in *sala* B19 and anteroom B20 were enlarged as a result of the excavation of the "cortile" to the east, and marble steps were installed below them.[377] In contrast to the apart-

171 Palazzo Barberini, room B36, with Bacchus fountain (I.C.C.D., Rome, ser. E, no. 28899)

ment above, the rooms of the *pian terreno* retained their old travertine doorframes (still in place today); but the occasion was taken to make various small repairs.[378] Major redecoration was reserved for the ceilings of the rooms in the western part of the apartment. The central panels of the vaults in rooms B22–B26 and B28 all were newly painted, and the stucco enframements of three were either made anew (B28) or remade (B25, B23).[379] Sculptures and paintings had to be removed from the rooms while work was in progress and then brought back. Similarly, other sculptures and paintings were moved and then replaced in rooms to the east, as the apartment was refurbished.[380]

The wing that once formed the eastern boundary of the garden of orange trees, projecting from the northeast wing of the palace, also was reformed. The garden had been greatly reduced in size as a result of the new drives and "cortili." Now designated an "armaria" (armory), its walls were raised by 13 *palmi,* a new roof and eight new windows were installed, and it was plastered inside and out (but its old pedimented portal toward the garden to the west was left intact). It apparently contained a single room, C45, mea-

172   Palazzo Barberini, room B36, in 1983 (Barbara Bini)

suring about 14 × 64¾ *palmi*.[381] Two large cabinets, measuring 18 × 18 *palmi* and 12 × 12 *palmi,* were dismantled and moved from the "armaria vechia" to the new armory.[382]

Throughout the palace many small adjustments and repairs were made and incorporated in the *misure* of the larger work. For example, adjustments were made in the princess's mezzanine rooms,[383] and hooks for revetments were installed in the corridor leading to the rooms of the "signorini," the teenage sons of Prince Maffeo and Princess Olimpia, only to be redone when their placement was found to be too high.[384] These do not seem to be parts of a comprehensive plan; rather, they show that working procedures were loose enough to allow the masons' attention to incidental requests, while they pursued the larger project.

The south wing of the palace already was separated from the earth of the higher gardens in September 1676, when the ground floor of the south façade was finished with plaster and its thirteen window grills were installed. Even before the remodeling, there had been a bridge spanning from anteroom C3 on the *piano nobile* to the south gardens at that level.[385] New excavations on the south side of the palace, completed by 28 June 1678, greatly increased and regularized the space between palace and garden,[386] and a retaining wall 36 *palmi* high, constructed in the following months, confirmed its volume (Fig. 173).[387] Along with the retaining wall, a new bridge was built from C3 to the garden (Fig. 174). Its position was shifted from that of the old bridge, so that it was aligned with the door from anteroom C2.[388] Pilasters were built against the retaining wall and that of the palace, and two granite columns, each 18½ *palmi* high, with their socles, bases, capitals, and imposts, were positioned. Then arches were made to span from columns to pilasters. The capitals were too small for the diameter of the columns, as though the bridge were an assemblage of mismatched *spoglie* (Fig. 175); and the arches were formed so as to seem ruined—that toward the garden on the verge of collapse, with displaced voussoirs, and that toward the palace already half fallen away. Thanks to reinforcing chains of metal, the masonry construction was indeed stable, but a wooden drawbridge was required to span the gap between the door of the anteroom and the firm pavement of the bridge. The mechanism for the operation of the drawbridge was installed in the wall of the anteroom.[389]

The axis of the "ruined bridge" was to have been continued farther, into the garden, by the reassembly and erection of the obelisk of Antinoos, which had lain in the outer forecourt of the palace since 1632 (see Figs. 126, 127).[390] In 1658 Cardinal Francesco had considered erecting the obelisk on a base in the form of an elephant, according to a design by Bernini, but nothing

ALTRO FIANCO DEL PALAZZO BARBERINO DELL'ECC.^{MO} SIG. PRENCIPE DI PELLESTRINA NEL MONTE QVIRINALE.
Architettura del Caualier Bernino.
1. Facciata principale con li due fianchi che lo conpongono. 2. Fianco uerso il Giardino col ponte leuatore che porta all.'Appartamenti. 3. Altro Fianco uerso la Piazza.
dato in luce da Domenico de Rossi dalle sue Stampe in Roma alla Pace con Priuil. del S.P. e licenza de Superiori.

173 Palazzo Barberini from southwest, engraving by Specchi (Bibliotheca Hertziana, Rome)

was done.[391] Finally, by 12 August 1678, a deep excavation was made for the foundation for the obelisk and the massive foundation was laid. Its top surface measured 26 × 25 *palmi,* and it extended downward 35½ *palmi* (to the level of the drive between palace and garden retaining wall).[392] The obelisk itself was 41.4 *palmi* (9.247 meters) high and 3.11 *palmi* wide at its base.[393] A base for the obelisk was designed and a large model (employing 23½ pounds of wax) was made by Gioseppe Giorgetti and his partner Lorenzo Ottone, by 28 May 1679; it was not the appealing elephant of 1658, but rather an elaborate assemblage of devices of an ancient Roman triumph — "trophies, palms, figures, elephants, a bull, a ship's rostrum, rams, clubs, sacrificial altars, bas-

tions, shields, helmets, and various other weapons."[394] Cardinal Francesco's death in December of that year must have interrupted plans for the erection of the obelisk, for it remained in the forecourt until 1773. Presumably knowing the plan of 1678–79, Specchi included the obelisk in the garden opposite the "ruined bridge" in his engravings of the palace in 1699, but he placed it on a simple classical pedestal (see Figs. 99, 163, 173).

The two main foci of the work — the ground-floor apartment in the south wing and the axial drive — then had many ramifications: the separation of the palace from the higher ground to the south and east; the two bridges; the design of the gardens; the revisions in rooms B36 and C35; ad-

174   Palazzo Barberini, "ruined bridge" (Alinari/Art Resource, N.Y.)

justments in the main apartments; and so forth. Both main foci were under construction from the beginning, in 1672, and the many overlapping *misure* show that work was pursued on several fronts simultaneously until 1679. They also show that there was always room for adjustment and modification, however coherent the plan of 1672, as work proceeded. It was probably for reasons of accounting and payment that the work was executed in several *misure,* a single *misura* containing work in diverse parts of the building, and single aspects of the design requiring work in more than one *misura.* There were changes in the contractors for the several trades in the course of the work: the masons Ferrari and Bossi were succeeded by the two Bossi brothers, and they in turn were replaced by Pietro Giacomo Patriar-

cha; the *fossarolo* Anselmi was followed by Cecchini; the woodworker Manfrini gave way to Cartone. Only the supervising architect, Angelo Torrone, and the patron, Cardinal Francesco Barberini, remained constant through the eight years of construction. Happily, the work was essentially complete (with door handles installed in the new rooms and sculptures moved into place) by the time of Cardinal Francesco's death on 10 December 1679. Only the erection of the obelisk in the south garden seems to have been prevented by his death.

THE OCCUPANTS OF THE PALACE AND THEIR APARTMENTS

By the 1670s the palace had resumed its originally

intended pattern of occupation, with secular members of the family (Prince Maffeo, his wife Olimpia Giustiniani, and their children) housed in the north wing and ecclesiastical members (Cardinals Francesco and Carlo) in the south wing, and the grand *salone* at its core; but the three-dimensional complexity of the plan of 1628 had been changed. The delicate balance between north and west entrances had been tipped in favor of the west, so that *entrone* A8 is never mentioned, whether in the extensive documentation of remodeling or in the descriptions of visitors to the palace. One approached by either the square stair or the elliptical stair to a vestibule and then to the central *salone,* according to Tessin.[395] The *piano nobile* therefore prevailed as the level of the main apartments, the "appartamenti nobili," for all major residents.

In the north wing, prince and princess shared the *piano nobile* (see Fig. 102). The apartment was unified by its new doorframes of breccia marble, aligned for its entire length; but at the same time it was divided by room C29, the room of the "Divina Sapienza" — not between summer and winter occupation, or between formal and informal uses, but between husband and wife. The room is included among those of the "Appartamento dell' Piano Nobile dell' Sig^c Principe" and is called the "Camera dell'Udienza dove e il primo Baldacchino." [396] A visitor would have to pass through it to reach the "Camera della Udienza della Sig^a Principesa," room C27.[397] The princess's audience room had a baldacchino, and she is noted as having four rooms in her *appartamento nobile* — perhaps rooms C23–C26 beyond the audience room, or perhaps the four rooms en suite after the room of the "Divina Sapienza," that is, C28, C27, C25, C23.[398] The "Anticamere della prima udienza" are mentioned among the prince's rooms[399] — presumably C19 and C20, preceding C29 (where he may have held audience). The prince's rooms must also have included those to the east of C29: gallery C35 particularly is identified as his.[400] Tessin

175   Palazzo Barberini, "ruined bridge," capitals and springing of arches (author)

describes the apartments similarly. He saw a sequence of nine rooms opening from the left-hand door of the *salone,* all with a view of the court and gardens behind the palace — that is, rooms C19, C20, C34, C36, C38–C42 — and all hung with tapestries. From the beginning of the suite of nine rooms, he writes, one can also go directly to the room painted with Sacchi's "Divina Sapienza" (C29) and thence left to five rooms where the princess lives and right to four rooms for the prince, all with a view of the piazza — the nine together admirable for the unity provided by the handsome perspective of the suite of nine rooms and by tapestries in all the rooms. For him, the most remarkable object in the rooms was the bronze model of an equestrian statue of Don Carlo Barberini as General of the Church, by Bernini.[401]

The division of the *piano nobile* between husband and wife meant that each could have only a single apartment on that level. Arrangements for seasonal comfort were therefore curtailed. Only by taking advantage of the few rooms arranged as *appartamenti doppij* (C22–C25 for the princess and C33–C38 for the prince) could Maffeo and Olimpia find natural winter warmth. Documents make no mention of rooms for sleeping, but these must have been at the extremities of the suites — hardly as convenient as the arrangement of Taddeo and Anna Barberini's bedrooms, connected by stair S7, in 1632.

There are several references to the "ground-floor apartment of the Prince" in the north wing — his summer apartment, according to visitors to the palace;[402] but, with one exception, documents of construction do not identify rooms by specific uses (see Fig. 165). The "anticamere terrene del Sigʳ Prencipe," which received enlarged windows toward the "cortile," would be rooms B19 and B20. Tessin noted these two rooms as the proper entrance from the "Vestibule" B1 to the apartment.[403] Room B36, the "large new ground-floor room in the old part of the palace in the apartment of the Prince of Palestrina,"[404] is identified repeatedly with the prince and with his ground-floor apartment, but it is assigned no particular use (see Fig. 171). Tessin came to this room directly from the prince's apartment on the *piano nobile* by way of the private stair S10; Rossini, noting the fountain, and Panciroli, identifying the room by its majolica pavement, also began their tours of the apartment here.[405] The slightly later installation of the Bacchus fountain and the landscape paintings on the walls suggest that it was a room for enjoyment in the summer, outside the basic linear apartment — a substitute for an exterior garden. No other

room on the *pian terreno* (including those that received new ceiling paintings in 1678) is assigned a particular function. When Tessin visited the palace in 1688, he found many works of art in these "Sommerzimbern" of the prince but no furniture in any of the thirteen rooms.[406] In 1644 Cardinal Antonio Barberini had filled the same apartment with works of art but had also supplied it with musical instruments, games, and furniture.[407] It seems likely that, by the time of Tessin's visit, the apartment had become an art gallery, to be enjoyed on summer days but not to be inhabited by Prince Maffeo on a regular basis.[408]

The princess had rooms on the upper floor of the palace. Stair S7 led from her audience room C27 to her "appartamento di sopra."[409] Its small mezzanine rooms cannot be identified precisely, but they must include those at the west end of the *secondo piano*.[410] A fireplace of peperino replaced one of travertine "nell'apartamento di cima della Sigᵃ Principessa"; the small rooms may have been especially comfortable in the winter.

The documents of construction make no mention of daughters Costanza and Camilla, but the "signorini" — the three teenage sons of Maffeo and Olimpia, born in 1662, 1664, and 1666 — had an apartment of at least five rooms, including mezzanine rooms, on the upper floor. A fireplace provided winter warmth.[411] There were steps in the corridor leading to "the rooms where the signorini sleep." Nearby were the latrines (D29a) and quarters for the pages.[412]

The newly finished rooms on the ground floor of the south wing (see Fig. 165) are usually called the "apartamento terreno" or the "stanze nuove terrene" in the documents of construction, but in a single instance they are identified as the "apartamento nuovo dell' Sigᵉ Cardᵉ"[413] — that is, the older cardinal, Francesco. Later, Rossini too called them "l'Appartamento terreno del Sign. Cardinal Barbarino" — by that time the younger Cardinal Francesco (1662–1738).[414] Within the apartment, the *sala* B3, "anticamera" or "anticammerone" B4, chapel B5, and "anticamera ultima" B6 are singled out in the *misure*,[415] but no more than these general indications of use are given. An inventory of paintings and sculptures in these rooms in 1692–1704 speaks of B3 as "sala" and B4 as "Prima anticamera," but the other rooms are simply "stanze."[416] To the left of B4, only two rooms (B11, B12) were finished when Tessin visited in 1688; B13 was included as the "third room newly made" in the inventory of 1692–1704 and was counted by the two later visitors, Rossini and Panciroli.[417] To the right, all four sources agree in counting five rooms (B6–B10). Only *sala* B3, B11, and corner room B8 had fireplaces, so that the apartment must have been intended for summer use, as Panciroli noted in his guide to the palace.[418] Further, the early installation of many antique sculptures suggests that this was planned as a sculpture gallery from the beginning and not as the living quarters of any person. The inventory and three visitors' accounts make it clear that the apartment was richly furnished with both sculptures and paintings, and it seems to have been designed solely for the display of these works of art. It complemented the ground floor of the north wing, so that the entire *pian terreno* of the palace was devoted to paintings and sculptures. The two apartments bear comparison to contemporaneous developments at Palazzo Borghese, where the ground-floor apartments were rebuilt as a gallery for paintings and sculptures in 1671–78, and to the slightly earlier apartments for works of art in the "Casa Grande" ai Giubbonari and Palazzo Chigi.[419]

On the *piano nobile* of the south wing, the summer and winter apartments of the 1630s remained intact. A single note in the entire documentation of construction suggests that the young Cardinal Carlo may have used them: a bridge is mentioned as entering Carlo's apartment,[420] as the "ruined bridge" to the south of the palace enters anteroom C3. Tessin recognizes the rooms as "the Cardinal's apartment"—

Cardinal Carlo by the time of his visit in 1688—as do Panciroli and Rossini.[421] The later visitors to the palace distinguish between summer rooms or rooms for intermediate seasons to the east and winter rooms to the west, just as in the 1630s.[422] Tessin observes that there were two audience rooms in the winter apartment: room C5, the "Sala d'Audienzo dei Cavallieri e Prelati," and room C6, the "andere Sale d'audience." (Similarly, he saw two audience rooms in the apartment of Cardinal Chigi in Palazzo Chigi in piazza SS. Apostoli [see Fig. 204, C11 and C14]).[423] Cardinal Francesco, as vice-chancellor, continued to live at the Cancelleria.

On the upper floor of the southwest wing, both cardinals may have had apartments of small rooms, according to an account of roof maintenance over Carlo's apartment "toward the courtyard" and over the presumably adjacent apartment of "S. Eᵃ"—that is, Francesco—in 1677 (see Fig. 104).[424] An inventory of paintings and sculptures in the palace in 1692–1704 describes a "mezzanine apartment" or "studio apartment," which can be identified with the rooms there. The first room E10, at the top of the small stair, was hung with tapestries; it was adjoined by a second room E9; a sequence of three rooms E6–E8 formed the "Studio"; and its little corridor had red hangings. The rooms held several paintings and a few small sculptures.[425] It is easy to imagine that the two cardinals might have used these rooms as private retreats, in conjunction with the library, in the 1670s, and that Carlo continued to enjoy the group of five rooms after his uncle's death.

Excepting the pages, no members of the Barberini *famiglia*—not even women attendants —are noted as living in the palace. Even offices seem greatly reduced. Kitchen A12 served the north wing, the new subterranean passage A36 facilitating service in the anterooms B19, B20, C19, or C20; the new basement kitchen A21–A27 (including *bottiglieria* and *credenza*) served the south wing; and the *guardaroba* remained in its customary place at the top of the house. The bookkeeping office, *dispensa, tinello,* and bakery were removed from the palace, and the *armaria* was shifted to the small wing projecting from the northeast wing.

THE DESIGN

The work was a major undertaking, lasting eight years and costing more than 25,000 scudi. Yet it remains difficult to isolate and assess its artistry and even more difficult to fix responsibility for that artistry.

In the shaping and disposition of rooms, the designer simply followed the pattern bequeathed to him by Maderno and his successors. In the south wing the new ground-floor apartment and basement rooms may be considered the completion of the design of 1628. In the oval passage B17, the new stairs follow the already established form of the ellipse and emerge through already existing openings. In the north wing, adjustments are made with minimal changes in the structure of the building. Even so, the designer of 1672 has considerably relaxed and clarified the complexity of the earlier arrangement. The vertical composition is much simplified, with the lowest level for kitchens (in both wings), the *pian terreno* given over to works of art, the *piano nobile* for major apartments for all principal residents, and the *secondo piano* and mezzanines for more private rooms. In the north wing, the discontinuities of the earlier design are removed and emphasis is placed on long suites and visual continuity. A similarly long cross axis is established by the shifting of doorways in C19 and C20 and the shifting of the bridge that spans from anteroom C3 to the south garden.

While the façades of the palace remained essentially intact, the relation of the building to its site was altered. The widening and regularization of the "cortile" or "stradone" on the south and east sides of the palace emphasized the independence of the building form from the struc-

tured hillside, but at the same time axes tied the two together. The new axial drive, opened through the *nicchione* of the portico and the ground-floor ellipse, extended all the way to the Apollo fountain at the eastern extremity of the site, uniting lower and upper levels, building and land, by both vision and movement. The eastern end of the axis is firmly established, and it is curious that the western end received no similar attention — especially given the haphazard form of the western forecourt. In fact, the forceful frontality of the design of 1628 is undermined both literally and figuratively by the axial drive cutting beneath the palace and revealing a vista to the garden. Similarly, a north–south axis is extended through the palace to the gardens; and again similarly, its inner end was to have been fixed by the obelisk (and possibly by other arrangements in the walled garden), while its outer end projected into space from the balcony on the north façade. Like the west forecourt, the north "piazza da basso" received virtually no attention beyond the heightening of its retaining wall by 3 *palmi.*[426] Further, with the abandonment of the north entrance (in conjunction with the abandonment of the *pian terreno* to works of art and the establishment of all major apartments on the *piano nobile*), the area before the north façade lost even the formal control provided by paths of movement. The formal dilemma of the exterior of the palace is well expressed by Specchi's engravings (see Figs. 99, 162, 163, 173): the aggressive forms of north and west façades are compromised by their formless settings, and the chaos of the east and modesty of the south façades are contrasted by the firmness of the site planning. In the end, the new axial drive made no more sense in functional terms than in formal terms, because (as Tessin observed in 1688) entrance to the palace was still by way of the two stairs rising from the portico, and because the drive conducted carriages from the entrance forecourt to the extremity of the garden — an unlikely path, since gardens were part of the private realm of the palace.[427] Perhaps the drive would have been useful for outdoor receptions or entertainments not requiring entry into the palace; but even so, the gardens lay to the south of the walled drive, not at its terminus. So, too, it is hard to imagine what noble person would use the curving stairs rising from oval passage B17 to the broad eastern bridge, just as it is hard to appreciate the stairs' rupture through the formal composition of the central pavilion of the east façade (see Figs. 166, 167).

Whatever its merits, the axial drive essentially changed Maderno's design. Originally, the hemicycle and fountain at the rear of the entrance portico contained the space, reinforced the theater-like quality of the façade, and helped visitors find their way to the lateral entrances to the stairs. Maderno's preference for closed axes seemed to serve perfectly the needs of the complex design. The new long vista is comparable to the perspectives extended through the west wing of Palazzo Borghese in exactly these years, equally in contrast to Maderno's earlier efforts at containment.

In the 1630s the whole building spoke of the bipartite nature of the family and of its relationship to the papacy. That message was not so compelling in the 1670s, three decades after the death of Urban VIII. The remodeling proposes a shift in emphasis. The approach from the west brings the visitor to the portico of the *pian terreno,* from the right and left of which open apartments filled with works of art. In the distance, on the central axis, there beckons the colossal statue of Apollo with his lyre. Only above this broad foundation rise the apartments of prince and cardinal. The lasting contribution and honor of the family is to be due to its service to the arts. The transverse axis, piercing the apartments of both prince and cardinal and passing over the ruined bridge to an Egyptian obelisk supported on the apparatus of a Roman triumph, would seem to bear yet another message. The ruined bridge composed of *spoglie* has captured the imagination of observers for three centuries — among them M. and M. Fa-

giolo dell'Arco, who have constructed a literary interpretation of the bridge, both collapsing and collapsed, in conjunction with objects in the garden; but they did this without knowledge of the intended design for the base of the obelisk or even of the date of the construction.[428]

In the end, the new arrangements of the 1670s elude any consistent explanation. In spite of a certain simplification with respect to Maderno's design, the composition remains ambiguous, a design of concatenated parts.

Designers

Who then was responsible for the design of this far-reaching modification of the palace? Blunt, following the testimony of Nicodemus Tessin in his description of the palace in 1688, has attributed the work to Bernini, but Tessin writes specifically about the new axial drive and nothing else.[429] Pinaroli, in his guide of 1703, attributes the ruined bridge (but nothing else) to Bernini,[430] and he is soon followed by Rossini[431] and myriad writers up to the present day. Yet we have seen that the project was both extensive, including much more than the drive or the bridge, and comprehensive. Further, Bernini's name appears nowhere among the documents of construction. The question of design attribution deserves more careful consideration.

On 17 June 1672 "Sr Erigo Zuccalli Architetto" is paid 15 scudi "for having helped make the plans for the new fabric at our palace of the Quattro Fontane" — that is, a bit more than the cost of moving 116 cartloads of paintings from the via dei Giubbonari to the Quattro Fontane two months later.[432] It must have been a considerable job, given the payment, but still it was limited to helping with the drawings; Zuccalli was not the designer. This is Zuccalli's only appearance in the documents of construction. Before dismissing him, however, we should note that he is distinguished by the profession "Architetto," his expertise including the ability to make working drawings for someone else's design.

All the *misure* for the new construction are signed by "Angelo Torrone Architetto," and all payments are according to the authorization of "Angelo Torrone nostro architetto." This little-known architect was in the employ of Cardinal Francesco Barberini throughout the 1670s, with responsibility for all the cardinal's building projects and building maintenance, beginning in November 1669; he was the successor to Paolo Pichetti, similarly little known, who died on 20 October 1669.[433] He oversaw repairs — for example, the stabilization and rebuilding of the west wall of the *guardaroba* at Palazzo Barberini in 1673–74; he also oversaw the construction of the façade of SS. Luca e Martina, which had been designed by Pietro da Cortona. He may or may not have designed any of the other projects sponsored by the cardinal, including the work at Palazzo Barberini. The several *misure* provide no additional clues as to his duties or the contributions of other persons to the design at Palazzo Barberini during construction, as had, for example, the *misura* of 1628–38.[434]

The *misura* for the construction of the Palazzo Barberini in 1628–38 was signed by Valerio Poggi and Giovanni Maria Bolina, and the *misura* for the construction of Francesco's half of the palace, beginning in 1634, was also signed by Valerio Poggi[435] — the *soprastante* of the work but not the designer, whether of the whole or of details devised as construction was in progress.[436] The *misure* for Palazzo Chigi in piazza SS. Apostoli were signed by Carlo Fontana — later to become Rome's leading architect but at that time explicitly following the orders of Bernini, who was responsible for the design.[437] In contrast, Carlo Rainaldi, the architect of the extensive remodeling of Palazzo Borghese in 1671–76, signed the *misure*.[438] Similarly, it seems reasonable to accept the work at the Palazzo Barberini in via dei Giubbonari in the 1640s as the design of Francesco Contini, an architect on Taddeo's monthly payroll and signer of the *misure*.[439] Angelo Torrone's signature on *misure* therefore neither precludes nor guarantees that

he was the actual designer of the work.

The third architect whose name has been connected with the work of 1672–79 is Gianlorenzo Bernini. Tessin named him as responsible for the design of the "Durchfarth," in 1688, and Pinaroli attributed to him the "ruined bridge" to the south of the palace, in 1703.[440] Neither author recognized the extent of the work of which these were but parts. In addition, drawings by Bernini have been associated with the design of the base for the Barberini obelisk, to have been erected as part of the comprehensive undertaking, but none of the drawings shows the assemblage of ancient Roman motifs described in Giorgetti's bill for the wax model of the base; indeed, the drawings must have been made for Francesco's aborted scheme of 1658 — that is, two decades before the date of the wax model. Further, the case for Bernini is doubtful because Cardinal Francesco Barberini was never a particular patron of Bernini. The artist's two biographers, Domenico Bernini and Filippo Baldinucci, write at length of the patronage and friendship of Urban VIII and then of Antonio Barberini, "who, it seems, had inherited the protection of the Cavaliere from Urban," but they say nothing about Francesco.[441] Among the many works of Bernini, neither author mentions the work at Palazzo Barberini in the 1670s, in the closing years of Bernini's long and productive life. Baldinucci's assessment of Bernini's contributions to the palace (however it might be interpreted) includes the façade, the staircase, and the *salone*, but nothing more.[442] The documents of construction make no mention whatever of Bernini. Their silence is greatly in contrast to the record of Bernini's activity at the Palazzo Chigi in piazza SS. Apostoli just a few years earlier, where he signed authorizations for payments to the builders, supervised and directed specific parts of the work, consulted with Alexander VII, made sketches, and even received explicit credit from Carlo Fontana in the preface to the *misura* of masonry.[443] Even at Palazzo Barberini in the 1630s his participation in the shaping of the building during construction is evident in both documents and drawings.[444]

An attribution on the basis of style is as difficult to make as one on the basis of documentation. Blunt writes that the attribution to Bernini is "quite plausible on stylistic grounds, for although the arrangement of the balconies is damaging to the whole effect, the detail is fine and quite in conformity with Bernini's late work"; and as an example of the detail he refers to his Plate 22c, showing one of the sun-faced brackets under the protruding balconies (Fig. 176; see also Fig. 167).[445] Yet the brackets, the depressed curve of the balconies, and the paired columns with partial entablatures set awkwardly under the curving ramps of stairs in oval B17 (see Fig. 166) seem to have nothing to do with Bernini's late work. The "damaging" arrangement of the balconies seems especially contrary to Bernini's classical sensibility in architecture. The tiny bas-reliefs seem impoverished in the fields of masonry above the arches, as the sculptures envisioned by either Maderno or Bernini, in drawings studied by Blunt, do not.[446]

The long axial drive has no close counterpart in Bernini's work. Once past the oval passage, it is essentially eventless; even the looming figure of Apollo at the end of the drive must not have been a great attraction. At St. Peter's, by contrast, Bernini devised a dynamic sequence culminating in the crucial monuments of the Baldacchino and Cathedra. The long ascent of the Scala Regia was similarly structured. At Palazzo Chigi the central axis was much shorter and also more abstract, a line around which the asymmetrical design of the palace was balanced. The simplicity of the plan of the Barberini drive seems to separate it from Bernini's work. Nor does the planning of the remodeled apartments give many clues. The extensive work in the south wing simply followed the lines already set out in 1628. On the *piano nobile,* the most important change is the extension of a long and impressive enfilade through the pair of apartments in the north wing and another at right angles, through prince's and

176   Palazzo Barberini, east façade, bracket under north balcony (author)

cardinal's apartments, out into the south garden to the obelisk to have been erected, and possibly beyond. An aesthetic choice, the desire for long enfilades nevertheless seems to be a trait shared by many architects and patrons in the 1670s.

The north–south axis contains two of the most interesting parts of the project—the "ruined" bridge and the obelisk. Both the bridge and the foundation for the obelisk were constructed only in 1678–79. A bridge of some sort must have been envisioned from the beginning, as a replacement for the old bridge, which would be rendered useless by the enlargement and regularization of the space between palace and garden and besides was misaligned with the new enfilade. Still, nothing was done about it until the second half of 1678, and it would have been in accord with normal Roman design practice to turn to the design of the bridge and the obelisk base only at that time. The sculptor Giorgetti may well have designed the obelisk base in 1679, just before making the model.[447] The conceit for the bridge may have been developed in mid-1678. The idea may have come from anyone, including Cardinal Francesco, for it is more a poetic idea, playing on ideas of antiquity, ruin, and imminent collapse, than a tectonic or especially architectural idea. The capitals and columns have the air of antique *spoglie,* not quite matching in their diameters. The pair of arches springs from a central column, without even the benefit of an impost block — a surprising departure from the norm, in the context of Bernini's architecture, but perhaps fitting in this artificial ruin.[448]

The work seems surprisingly close to that undertaken at Palazzo Borghese in the 1670s, begun just a year earlier than the Barberini project. In both cases the ground floor is given over to an impressive multiroom gallery for works of art; travertine doorframes are replaced by frames of marble (whether alabaster or breccia); long enfilades are constructed, the axes even extending beyond the limits of the buildings; awkward juxtapositions (the stairs and balconies at the east façade of Palazzo Barberini, and the stairs and balcony at the westernmost end of Palazzo Borghese) are accepted. The work at Palazzo Chigi after 1664 also includes a ground-floor sculpture gallery, colored marble doorframes, and enfilades as long as possible. Cardinal Francesco's architect was bringing his palace "up to date."

The architectural personality of Angelo Torrone is considerably more obscure than that of Bernini; however, the work at Palazzo Barberini seems well within the capabilities of a competent "house" architect and administrator of a number of architectural projects over the course of a decade, as was Torrone. For the most part, logistics and technical expertise seem especially to have been needed. Detailing does not reveal brilliance.

It would seem most likely then that it is a question of a few simple decisions on the part of the patron — Francesco Barberini, perhaps along with friends or family members. The possibility that Bernini was among these persons is not to be ruled out, but everything that happened at Palazzo Barberini in the 1670s can be explained without recourse to the participation of that prolific artist, at that time busy with important sculpture commissions. The crucial moment would have been late in 1671, when it was decided to give the ground floor over to works of art. Francesco's architect Angelo Torrone saw what that might entail. The comprehensive concatenation of revisions to the building was set in motion. The matrix earlier provided by Maderno and others proved generous enough to accept the extensive changes. The idea for the "ruined bridge" probably came only in 1678. That this small and late part of the work should be its most appealing feature seems an ironic inversion of the "vision" of Cardinal Francesco and Torrone in 1671.

CHAPTER THIRTEEN

Palazzo Colonna-Barberini at Palestrina

O SOONER was Urban VIII elected pope than a search was under way for a property that would enhance his family's newly elevated status. After preliminary consideration of other fiefs, the Barberini focused their efforts on the acquisition of the territory of Palestrina. As early as December 1626, careful negotiations were begun with the reluctant but financially troubled Francesco Colonna, Prince of Palestrina. By April 1627, the Barberini agent Nicolò Benigni was hopeful of eventual success.[1] Carlo Barberini finally concluded the purchase on 16 January 1630,[2] acquiring not only the property, including a palace built into the ruins of the ancient Roman sanctuary of Fortuna Primigenia, but also the title of Prince of Palestrina; and when he died only a few weeks later, on 26 February 1630, both property and title passed to his son Taddeo.

The dramatically situated structure (Fig. 177) has long attracted attention, whether for its intrinsic power or for its evocation of ancient Rome. In the sixteenth and seventeenth centuries many artists made reconstructions of the monumental sanctuary,[3] and its influence was felt in such modern structures as Bramante's Cortile del Belvedere.[4] The ancient remains have been the subject of much study; the fifteenth- and sixteenth-century constructions have been examined; and Fasolo has written sympathetically of the "symbiotic" relationship between those ancient and Renaissance parts.[5] This chapter will focus on the life of the palace in the seventeenth century, in the context of Roman palace building in general and Taddeo Barberini's particular architectural patronage.

The city and palace that Carlo Barberini bought are described in two memoranda preserved in the Archivio Barberini, the first probably prepared before 11 December 1629, in anticipation of the sale, and the second written by Carlo's agent Giovanni Battista Scanaroli early in 1630, when he went to take possession of the property.[6] The approach to the palace was then as it is today: from the piazza della Cortina, a double stair led to the great cavea-like stair, centered on a wellhead and expanding upward to the hemicycle of the façade (Figs. 178, 179). At the summit of the stair, a rectangular portal flanked by two windows opened to a vaulted entrance hall, described in 1629 as "un poco di aditetto," its vault supported by "three or four" columns (fol. 363), and called simply "andito" in 1630 (fol. 364v). Its small size and apparent asymmetry distinguished it from the present spacious hall. Apartments extended to left and right, and an open stair[7] led up to a colonnaded loggia ("una loggia con colonne scoperta dalle bande in poi," fol. 364v), which in turn gave access to the upper apartments. Above the loggia was a chamber inhabited by wild pigeons. To the left, or west, of the entrance hall was the major apart-

177   Palestrina, Palazzo Colonna-Barberini (I.C.C.D., Rome, ser. F, no. 7406)

ment used by the princess in 1629, a *sala* followed by six or seven rooms. One of the rooms led to the small three-bay loggia, so distinctive a feature of the façade, within which was a fountain drawing its water from a spring on the hillside above the palace. The chapel opened from the princess's *sala*.[8] Her apartment was adjoined by a little garden, with a house apparently for the "signorini." On the upper floor of the palace was a similar apartment for the prince, its "sala secreta dipinta" lying above the princess's loggia. The prince's apartment was expanded by a gallery paralleling the suite from the first room to the "sala secreta" and allowing the possibility of

dividing the rooms into two apartments. Beyond the western end of the gallery was a little courtyard, with a carriage entrance for the convenience of the prince. Both of these large apartments, turned toward the south, had splendid views extending for many miles, even as far as Rome. To the right, or east, of the entrance were two more apartments, considerably smaller than the western apartments but still "nobile." Each had a *sala* followed by only three rooms. The upper apartment is called the "appartamento vecchio," in contrast to the western "appartamento nuovo," the old apartment even having old-fashioned cross-mullion windows; and the

178 Palestrina, Palazzo Colonna-Barberini, stair (author)

earlier memorandum advises that the "palazzo vecchio," that is, the entire east side of the palace, might be enlarged, as had the west half, without much trouble or expense. Behind the eastern rooms were a small courtyard where ball games could be played, rooms for the *famiglia*, the *guardaroba*, and other services; and below were prisons. Below the long western apartments were other service rooms—kitchens, storerooms, *tinelli*, and so forth—with *cantine* at the level of the piazza della Cortina. Two stables, for a total of seventy-five horses, were somewhat removed from the palace, near the convent of S. Francesco to the northwest. There was also a "palazzetto" in the lower part of the city, at the corner of the present Corso Pier Luigi

da Palestrina and via E. Toti, where the cardinal bishop would stay on his official visits to the city, with an extensive garden on four levels to the south.[9]

Like so many Roman buildings, the Palazzo Colonna-Barberini was the product of much rebuilding and remodeling, its roots extending to the ancient Roman masonry on which it was founded. The most recent improvement found by the Barberini was probably the gallery of the upper western apartment, built, according to the memorandum of 1629, by the current prince, Francesco Colonna.[10] It seems to have replaced a loggia mentioned in an inventory of timbers and stone frames removed in the course of work in this apartment, dated 18 December 1627; accord-

179   Palestrina, Palazzo Colonna-Barberini, hemicycle and stair (author)

ing to the inventory, windows of four or five of the rooms, opposite windows facing Rome to the south, had opened to the loggia.[11]

The suite of rooms in 1627 was essentially that described in 1629: its "sala nova" was succeeded by six "stanze" with beamed ceilings, fireplaces in at least four of the rooms (the first, second, third, and fifth), and the windows already mentioned. The rebuilding of the apartment in 1627, which preceded the transformation of the loggia into the gallery, seems to have been motivated by disrepair rather than by any desire to change its form. The wood ceiling planks removed in 1627 were in such bad condition that their original

installation must have been many years earlier.[12] Still, the description of 1629 calls this apartment the "appartamento nuovo," in contrast to the "appartamento vecchio" to the east, and the inventory of 1627 names the "sala nova" in the western apartment. The "newness" of the long western wing probably has to be understood in the context of the centuries of the structure's history.

The "appartamento nuovo" must have been part of a major rebuilding of the palace effected over a century earlier, in 1498, by an earlier prince Francesco Colonna. His work is attested in the inscription over the central portal, "Vastarunt toties quod ferrum flamma vetustas Francisci instaurat cura Columnigeri 1498."[13] In this campaign, earlier fourteenth- or fifteenth-century openings were filled in and floors and ceilings raised to make larger volumes, in the east wing as well as the west wing. The cavea-like entrance stairs were rebuilt atop ancient foundations and medieval constructions, using classical spoils; and the double-ramp stair, "like that of the Palazzo del Campidoglio" according to the author of 1629 (fol. 363), was added.[14] Many elements of the present building are stylistically compatible with a date of 1498 — the three-bay façade loggia, the balustrade of the double stair, the inscribed portal, the rectangular windows, the columns and other stonework of the entrance hall.[15] The three-bay loggia lies in the extension that distinguishes the western from the eastern part of the palace — that is, in the "appartamento nuovo"; its style provides a surprisingly early date for the many-roomed suites. Although the entrance hall and interior stair are also characterized by sturdy Tuscan columns, moldings, and balustrades which speak of a date ca. 1498,[16] these spaces cannot have been built then in their present form, for the memorandum of the palace in 1629 clearly describes a smaller, irregular, entrance — not much more than a passage *(andito)* — and a stair whose course returns to the hemicycle of the façade at the upper level. The early-sixteenth-century stonework must have been reused in a remodeling after 1629. Fasolo's analysis of the several types of masonry in the building is careful to distinguish between the columns and other stonework in the vestibule (ca. 1498) and the seventeenth-century walls.[17]

Other distinctive remains of masonry and stonework speak of a mid-fifteenth-century state of the palace as rebuilt by Stefano Colonna, father of the earlier Francesco, shortly after 1444. Still earlier masonry, possibly fourteenth-century in date, survives in the easternmost part of the palace and suggests a tower, later truncated and incorporated in the fifteenth-century construction. There may have been a similar tower

180 Palestrina, Palazzo Colonna-Barberini, entrance hall (author)

on the west side, with some sort of structure for habitation built into the ancient portico of the hemicycle. Those medieval constructions, however, were so subordinated to their mighty Roman matrix that Fasolo can speak of a "true survival of the Roman monument" at that time.[18]

Taddeo Barberini could see in the palace several interesting and potentially useful things. The site and structure were steeped in venerable Roman history, with which he and his previously Florentine mercantile family would willingly be associated. His marriage to Anna Colonna on 24

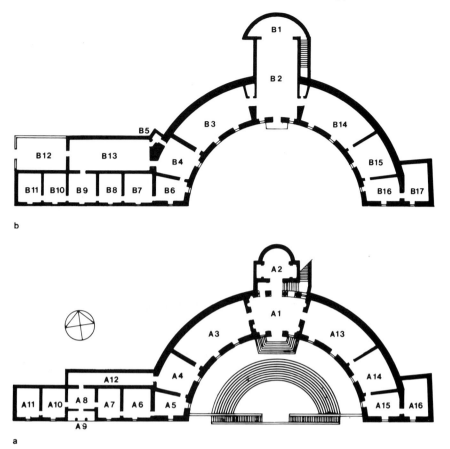

181 Palestrina, Palazzo Colonna-Barberini, plans in the 1630s, reconstruction: (a) entrance level, (b) upper level (author)

October 1627 would seem to legitimize his assumption of the territory and title of Palestrina, even though Anna's father Filippo, Conestabile of Naples, was of another branch of the Colonna family. The form of the palace, with its impressive siting against the hillside, its imposing approach, and its bifurcated plan, must have appealed to Taddeo as he sought ideas for his new palace in Rome. In a practical sense, the palace was a perfectly reasonable Roman palace, as suitable for Taddeo and Anna as it had been for Francesco Colonna and his wife, with its pair of long apartments to the west and services below.

It further held the possibility of the enlargement of the eastern "old" apartments as pendants to those to the west.

Taddeo was quick to take advantage of the opportunities of Palestrina. Almost immediately after his marriage, and even before his father had concluded the purchase of the property, Taddeo had claimed the lower western apartment: the inventory of timbers and stone frames dated 18 December 1627 documents the rebuilding of the apartment above Taddeo's, "sopra l'apratamento [sic] del Ecc^mo Sr Don Tadeo."[19] His crucial idea for the design of the new Barberini palace in Rome might have occurred at this time, or surely no later than 1628.[20] The ancestral associations of the territory were promptly exploited in a new fresco painting of the mythological founding of the city, complete with reconstruction of the ancient sanctuary in the background, in the *gallarietta* of his wife Anna's apartment in the Palazzo Barberini alle Quattro Fontane, in 1631 (see Figs. 112, 113).[21] An inventory dated 28 May 1630 shows that Taddeo occupied the palace at Palestrina very soon after he came into possession of it, by moving many furnishings there from his property at Monterotondo.[22] The inventory lists mattresses and bedding of a range of qualities suitable for persons of all ranks in his household; such necessary items as fittings for fireplaces and chamber pots; and furnishings for major apartments, including wall hangings and some paintings. The men of the family came as soon as the change in seasons allowed, and Urban VIII visited in October 1630, attended by Taddeo, the three Barberini cardinals, Cardinal Colonna, Filippo Colonna, and much public ceremony.[23] At the same time Taddeo undertook his first architectural work there, apparently refurbishing and readying the palace for his occupancy: his *giornale* lists payments totaling 1,316.67 scudi for whitewashing, woodwork, wood planks probably for roof repairs, nails, keys, glass, and masonry, in November and December 1630.[24]

Taddeo soon made substantial changes in the form of the Palazzo Colonna-Barberini. Francesco Barberini summarizes his contribution: "At Palestrina . . . since the palace was still divided such that one could not go from one apartment to another without going outdoors, by making a hall [*sala*] and enclosed stairs to go up to it, he made [the palace] more comfortable and majestic, beyond having straightened it up and adorned it."[25] Another memorandum connected with Francesco and datable 1655–56 speaks of Taddeo's construction of the *sala* and, beneath it, the apsed chamber ("gran nicchia, tribuna o absida").[26] The archaeological evi-

dence discussed by Fasolo confirms that Taddeo's efforts were concentrated in the center of the building. The small and fragmented forms reported in the memorandum of 1629 gave way to the present broad entrance hall, the stair and apsed chamber beyond, and the large *salone* on the upper floor (Figs. 180, 181). Taddeo's designer took advantage of ancient foundations to the rear; and columns, balustrades, window seats, and even stair treads from the remodeling of 1498 were reused in the enlarged vestibule. These economies of space, materials, and labor meant that the project could be done quickly and relatively inexpensively. The work was certainly finished by 1640, when the famous Nile mosaic was installed at Francesco's expense in the apsed chamber A2 on the lower level;[27] but a survey of payments recorded in Taddeo's account books of the 1630s suggests that he undertook the work much earlier, in 1631–32.[28] The significant sum of 1,710.87 scudi, paid in three installments to the *muratori* Domenico and Tomaso Damini for work at Palestrina in 1631–32, could well be for the revision of the central part of the palace.[29] There is no other comparable amount recorded between 1630 and 1640. Considering the scope of the work—with the reuse of foundations, the façade, and the stone columns, steps, and balustrades—1,710.87 scudi would be an appropriate amount. The timing would also be appropriate, as Taddeo would naturally want to improve his newly acquired property.

The major import of Taddeo's relatively small undertaking was succinctly described by Francesco. The palace became more comfortable and convenient through the enclosure of the central part, so that one would no longer have to go outdoors to pass from one apartment or floor to another. (So, too, the old Sforza palace, the nucleus of the Barberini's new palace at the Quattro Fontane in Rome, had been criticized for its open stair and entrance terrace.)[30] At the same time it became more satisfying aesthetically—more majestic, ordered, and adorned. The curve of the façade, previously fragmented by the old

182   Palestrina, Palazzo Colonna-Barberini, Nile mosaic (Soprintendenza archeologica per il Lazio)

loggia and dovecote, became unified. Taddeo maintained the simple stucco surface and stone window frames of the early sixteenth-century construction, surely understanding that the impressiveness of the façade lay in the strength of its large forms as seen from a distance. The newly inserted vestibule A1 below and the *sala* B2 on the upper floor enhanced the apartments to which they led. The broad entrance hall in itself must be more imposing than the small and asymmetrical hall that it replaced. Its spreading volume leads naturally to the ground-floor apart-

ments to the sides, and its reused columns screen the depth of the apsed chamber A2. The stair is contrived to lead the visitor to the entrance at the far end of the upper *sala*, from which he can best appreciate the vastness of the hall and the light and grand panorama to the south.

If the dramatic siting and the distinctive two-part form of the palace at Palestrina had sparked Taddeo's imagination during the planning of the new Palazzo Barberini in Rome, it was now the turn of the new design to affect the revision of the old. Taddeo's first idea for the palace in

Rome had been revised to emphasize the unity of the bifurcated family in its special relation to the papacy: the portico with its deep grotto-like niche extended laterally to the two staircases, which then led to a single *salone,* the formal and ideological center of the building. At Palestrina the new *sala* likewise provides an important focus, where previously there had been the trivia of wild pigeons. Its depth, extending back over the emplacement of the old Roman tholos against the hillside, provoked the designer to compose the lower story as a sequence of three laterally expanding but differentiated volumes: the light entrance hall, the first flight of the stair, and the apsed chamber which was eventually to contain the Nile mosaic (see Fig. 182). Not only the diagrammatic scheme but also the visual richness of the sequence from entrance to apartments brings the two Barberini palace designs together—although the import of their respective images is radically different, the palace in Rome looking across space to find its larger significance in its relation to the papacy, and the palace in Palestrina looking across time to the remembered image of Roman antiquity.

Taddeo's architect was Paolo Maruscelli. His name appears in records of payments for the work at Palestrina, and he was retained as Taddeo's architect, receiving a salary of 50 scudi every six months, at least from May 1632 until October 1637.[31]

Another distinct campaign of masons' work followed that of 1631–32, as Tomaso Damini joined with Gregorio Fossati to restore the oven and make chimneys and drains, at a cost of 313.84 scudi, by 12 November 1632.[32] Payments for woodwork in the palace in 1635–37 speak of two more improvements, new kitchens and an armory.[33] In an inventory of furnishings of the palace in 1637, both "old kitchens" and "new kitchens" are noted, the former in the west wing, apparently at the lowest level, and the latter probably behind the east wing.[34] The armory, "la sala detta Armaria" of the inventory, would seem to be the large hall A13 to the right of the

entrance hall, preceding the three rooms (A14, A15, A16) used then as a *guardaroba.*[35] The establishment of the armory at Palestrina was significant enough to merit notice in Francesco's biography of Taddeo.[36]

In 1640 another major work occurred, this time at Francesco's expense: the installation of the Nile mosaic (Fig. 182) in the apsed chamber A2 to the rear of the entrance hall. The splendid Roman mosaic had only recently been discovered, in the so-called *Sala absidata* in the lower part of the city.[37] Cardinal Andrea Peretti had removed sixteen sections of the mosaic during his tenure as bishop of Palestrina, between 16 September 1624 and 1 March 1626, and sent them to Rome, much to the displeasure of the citizens of Palestrina.[38] Peretti gave the fragments to Cardinal Lorenzo Magalotti, who in turn gave all but one of them to his nephew Cardinal Francesco Barberini. Francesco had the mosaic restored by the noted Roman mosaicist Giovanni Battista Calandra,[39] returned to Palestrina on 20 June 1640,[40] and installed in the palace, in the already existing chamber. Masons' work in the amount of 135.90 scudi (approved by the architect Francesco Contini) was required to accommodate the room to the mosaic, and a new iron gate was built before it.[41]

Francesco's involvement with the Nile mosaic is in keeping with his sustained interest in the Palestrina of antiquity. Survey drawings of Palestrina commissioned by Duke Federico Cesi in 1614 were given to Francesco by Cesi's widow in August 1631.[42] Francesco himself commissioned reconstructions of the ancient sanctuary of Pietro da Cortona—drawings which seem to have served as a basis for the view of Palestrina painted in 1631 in the *gallarietta* of Palazzo Barberini alle Quattro Fontane.[43] In 1633 Francesco had a model made of Palestrina.[44] Still later, in 1669, Francesco had made a drawing of the "Tempio della Fortuna" at Palestrina, and in 1673 he had a plan of the temple made.[45]

If Francesco's interest in Palestrina was antiquarian, Taddeo's was practical. The palace was a functioning dwelling and a visible sign of his high secular dignity. Inventories of the palace in June 1637[46] and February 1648[47] show how well it accommodated the life of the Roman nobility. On the upper floor, the *sala* B2 had a table and *scalinata* for the *credenza*. The first seven rooms of the western apartment were hung with rich revetments of either leather or fabric, and *portiere* were at the doors. The fifth room B8 contained ten low women's chairs ("10 sedie basse da donna di damasco rosso"),[48] indicating that this apartment, which had been designated for the prince's use in 1629–30, was now occupied by the princess. The seventh room B10 contained her bed, with its elaborate red damask fittings and wool blankets, a set of seven chairs, a prie-dieu, a close-stool, and a few other items. The last room in the suite, B11, seems to have been not a servant's room but rather a room for private enjoyment, with its daybed, set of chairs, and cembalo. Fireplace equipment in all but the fifth and sixth rooms[49] shows that these south-facing rooms would be used in cool weather. The sparsely furnished gallery B12 to the north—containing twenty-seven paintings, ten of which were portraits of emperors—would have been more comfortable in the summer.[50] The chapel B5, at the east end of the gallery, could be entered from either the second room or the gallery; in 1637 a large painting of St. Elizabeth Queen of Portugal hung there.[51]

The pendant lower western apartment was adorned similarly, with leather or fabric revetments on the walls of all the rooms except the painted *sala* A3 and room A8. In 1648 it was called the "Apartment of the Prelates," and a narrow corridor opening from the second room A4 allowed individual access to the others.[52] Beds were in rooms A6, A10, and (in 1648) A11, with such signs of use as blankets, chamber pots, and close-stools. Rooms A5, A6, A10, and A11 were supplied with fireplace equipment.[53]

To the east, *sala* B14 of the upper apartment contained a broken billiards table and four large tables. Room B16 was well equipped as a bed-

room and had andirons and tools for a fireplace, but the furnishings of the other rooms of this short apartment do not suggest a fully functioning suite for the reception of guests. Below, rather than follow the suggestion of the author of the memorandum of 1629 by extending the four-room apartment, Taddeo had converted it to other uses. The *sala* A13 was now the armory, its newly built *credenzoni*[54] filled with arms. The three other rooms formed the *guardaroba* in 1637, but by 1648 they too had been taken over for the armory.[55]

Several rooms were outfitted with the very simple beds and furnishings of servants. A suite of six rooms stretched below the western apartments but above the "new kitchens," at the level of the well (presumably that on which the hemicycle of the façade is centered); its first room contained benches and tables suggestive of a *tinello,* and the other five were simple bedrooms. Fourteen similar bedrooms were arranged in two stories in the vicinity of the "old kitchens," possibly behind the east wing, where there were rooms for the household, *guardaroba,* and other uses in 1629.[56] In June 1638 there were two dining halls, one for "la famiglia bassa," the other for persons of the rank of gentleman, and a "Casino delle Donne"—possibly the house for the "signorini" adjacent to the little garden that was mentioned in the description of 1629, turned to a new use.[57]

The palace would then seem well suited for the life of a noble Roman pair, with two long apartments, a house for women attendants, kitchens, storage rooms, and dining halls and bedrooms for the gentlemen and servants displaced from their normal dwellings in Rome. The high elevation of Palestrina would make even the south-facing rooms comfortable in summer, although only the shallow spaces between the sheltering hillside and the main rooms would be protected from the summer sun: the gallery to the west and, behind the eastern wing, a small courtyard where, according to the description of 1629, ball games could comfortably be played in the summer. Taddeo's adaptation of the palace for his and Anna's inhabitation was probably much like that of Francesco and Ersilia Sforza Colonna before 1630.

Over the years the palace was further adapted to serve its noble residents. An account of the visit of the ambassador of Spain on 2 July 1669[58] indicates some of the subsequent changes while showing how this building could accommodate a special occasion. The prince (now Taddeo's son Maffeo) and princess could maintain separate apartments while the best apartment, of ten rooms, was given to the honored guest; this was the uppermost western apartment, opening to the just-finished *teatro* with fountains built against the hillside by Francesco Contini.[59] Sunday dinner was served in a middle room of this apartment, taking advantage of the splendid *teatro* and, for the services of *credenza* and *bottiglieria,* an adjacent gallery. During the ambassador's visit, the princess used an apartment whose gallery was brought into service as her anteroom. Special entertainments took place in rooms reserved for those uses: a musical drama was presented in the "sala della commedia," a large ground-floor room permanently kept as a theater, presumably the remodeling of one of the old *cantine* or prisons; and a ball was held in another hall. By this date the little church of S. Rosalia, "la chiesa del Palazzo," constructed just west of the palace in 1656–60 by Francesco Contini,[60] could serve as a grand palace chapel.

CHAPTER FOURTEEN

Taddeo's Building for the Barberini Family

THE three Barberini palaces — the "Casa Grande" ai Giubbonari, the Palazzo Barberini alle Quattro Fontane, and the Palazzo Colonna-Barberini at Palestrina — differ in their urban contexts, the extent of construction, the roles that they were intended to play in the life of the family, and their architects. They nevertheless share a single significant patron in the person of Taddeo Barberini, and they share many themes which can shed light on Taddeo's intentions and accomplishments as an architectural patron.[1]

It is clear that all three palaces were eminently suited to Roman aristocratic life. Their apartments were of the basic Roman type, extraordinary only in their magnificence, and they were arranged within the building according to the relationships among the several residents. Facilities for the smooth operation of the large household were provided — from an ample *guarda-roba* to an exit for the private movements of the prince. At Palazzo Barberini alle Quattro Fontane, complex functional requirements led to a virtuosic plan in three dimensions. The palaces in via dei Giubbonari and at Palestrina are praised specifically by Francesco Barberini for the functional improvements that Taddeo had introduced: the plan "arranged with such facility and convenience that experts in building value and esteem it highly" at the palace in Rome (fol. 21r), and the greater comfort of enclosed stairs

and passage between apartments at Palestrina (fol. 16v). In this regard, the three Barberini palaces are unlike the Palazzo Borghese as left by Ponzio in 1610.

In good Roman tradition, the three buildings reused whatever preexisting structure was found. Surprisingly little demolition and new construction were required for the incorporation of the old Sforza palace in the distinctive design of the new Palazzo Barberini alle Quattro Fontane. At Palestrina the new entry and *sala* are neatly inserted within earlier Colonna and ancient Roman walls. At the "Casa Grande," already an impressive example of the Roman practice of preserving older structures, the major revision planned by Taddeo in the 1640s was largely an addition. In this regard all three palaces differ from, for example, the completely new Palazzo Laterano of Sixtus V, Bernini's design for the Palazzo Ludovisi (Montecitorio) begun on land cleared of earlier structures, or even the virtual rebuilding of the Palazzo Chigi at piazza SS. Apostoli. The economy extended to reusing columns and other stonework at Palestrina and incorporating Sforza ceiling paintings in a new Barberini scheme at the palace at the Quattro Fontane. Yet Taddeo's reuses seem qualitatively different from those of Bonazzini at the "Casa Grande" in 1610: there seems to be special ingenuity in discovering forms within those that already exist (as in the garden apartment for Anna and her attendants in the north wing of Palazzo Barberini alle Quattro Fontane), in understanding the power of an insertion to bring wholeness to what had formerly been fragments (as at Palestrina), and in designing an addition that can both reorient and magnify an earlier palace (as with the new entrance and proposed *salone* at the "Casa Grande"). In the end the buildings are not just further adjustments of old forms but are conceptually new.

Taddeo's three palaces share some features. All three have distinctive entrances that depart from the norm of Roman palace building in one way or another. That at Palazzo Barberini alle Quattro Fontane is most complex in its forms and multiple allusions, but the other two hold their own surprises. All are spacious, laterally expansive sequences, generously accommodating carriages (except of course at Palestrina). Even the unbuilt proposals for Palazzo Barberini alle Quattro Fontane present a variety of suggestions for innovative entrances—surely a result of the patron's desire for something both different and impressive, in recognition of the very great importance of the reception of guests at the palace.

All three entrances eventually admit the visitor to a grand *salone*. At the Quattro Fontane and at Palestrina, its rectangular volume is perpendicular to the façade. Not pushed aside to a corner (as at the "Casa Grande" in 1610), turned lengthwise (as at the old Sforza palace), or multiplied (as at Palestrina before Taddeo's work), these two *saloni* reinforce the axis of entry, dominate the prospect from the palace, and provide a unifying focus for the multiple apartments extending from them. The two Roman *saloni* in particular are significantly larger than the old halls they replaced.

All three designs show concern for an impressive exterior image. A great shortcoming of the old "Casa Grande" before Taddeo's work in the 1640s was that it was almost invisible within the dense fabric of the city. Its long façade on the via dei Giubbonari was undermined by shops,

and its main portal was around the corner at the back of the tiny piazzetta. Taddeo's ordering of the façade and bringing the entrance forward to the newly cleared piazza del Monte made the presence of the palace (and hence its owners) felt in the city. At Palazzo Barberini alle Quattro Fontane, the image removed the Barberini from the immediate urban context and set them in a larger context of power within Roman society; and at Palestrina the image was reinforced by the memory of history.

Two of the palaces are related in the development of their designs. The functional scheme and impressive image of the old building at Palestrina provoked discussions leading to the design of the palace at the Quattro Fontane. That plan in turn led to Palestrina's new focus in its entry and central *salone*. All three designs reached out to precedents beyond those previously established in Roman palaces. They went beyond the palace to villas, other civil architecture, and ecclesiastical architecture; beyond the seventeenth century to antiquity; beyond Rome to northern Italy and even France; and beyond architecture to literature and history.

A survey of Taddeo's other building projects, although not urban palaces, may further clarify the special qualities of his building activity. Francesco's biography of Taddeo lists work outside Rome—at Monterotondo, Palestrina, Montelibretto, S. Marinella, Mompecchio, Valmontone, Casa Corbola (Casape), Gericomio, S. Gregorio, and Falcognane—and the suburban "Giardino de' Bastoni" near St. Peter's.

In the context of the three palaces, Mompecchio (near Castelgandolfo) holds special interest, since a design for its casino has been associated with the design of the Palazzo Barberini alle Quattro Fontane (Fig. 183).[2] The plan is identified as for a casino "to be built" at Mompecchio, dated 14 September 1633, and attributed to Bernini by an inscription on the reverse.[3] It proposes a very large addition to a casino whose three stories are shown on another sheet in the same volume (Fig. 184).[4] The small rectangular

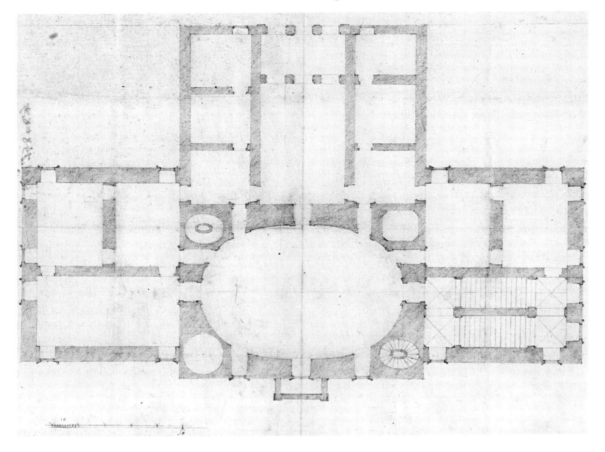

183 Mompecchio, design by Bernini for a casino, 14 September 1633 (Biblioteca Apostolica Vaticana, ABarb., Ind. II, no. 690, fol. 1)

casino measured about 95 × 68 *palmi* in plan, its modest central *salone* (45 × 32 *palmi*) preceded by a three-bay loggia and flanked by a suite of three small rooms to the right and two rooms and a stair to the left. A small elliptical stair was appended on the right. The addition envisioned by Bernini would have more than tripled the size of the casino and elaborated its shape as a T. In the new design a large elliptical hall (about 50 × 77 *palmi*) provides the focus for the plan, its crossing axes organizing orientation and paths of movement. Its short axis opens into the old casino's *salone,* and its long axis extends from one flight of a monumental switchback stair

through the ellipse to a rectangular anteroom. Two additional anterooms fill out each side of the T shape of the new design, and the small staircases of the old building are removed. The new design provides a significant shift in scale, the old casino with its small rooms becoming a mere appendage to the large forms of the addition. The apartments are enlarged, from the two or three small rooms of the old casino to a grand six-room sequence on one side and a combination of five rooms on the other.

The ellipse calls to mind the elliptical hall at Palazzo Barberini alle Quattro Fontane (see Fig. 102, C17), designed by 1628 and already complete in its basic structure by the date of the Mompec-chio plan. Surely this is one more instance of exchanges among the several Barberini palace designs. Yet, as in the other exchanges, revisions occur in the translation. In Rome the elliptical hall, in spite of its position on the central axis of the palace, was a special room outside the regular suite of the apartments; at Mompecchio it is the *salone,* the first room at the top of the stair. In Rome the long axis was blocked by paired pilasters, the openings from the apartments being at imprecise points along the curve of the ellipse; at Mompecchio the long axis accentuates the major path from stair to first anteroom. The obvious exploitation of the cross-axial structure of the ellipse seems in accord with Bernini's use of the form in his chapel at the Collegio di Propaganda Fide at about the same time, and in contrast to Maderno's deployment of the form at Palazzo Barberini.

The design with the elliptical hall, labeled as Bernini's, could well be that mentioned by Francesco, in his description of Taddeo's contributions to Mompecchio (fols. 18v–19r, Appendix 3), as having been designed by Bernini's great patron, Urban VIII: "Pope Urban had designed a beautiful residence [for Mompecchio]; however, a house already built by Monsignor Visconti turned out to be both less ambitious and more comfortable, after the Prefect [Taddeo] had built what was useful for a stay in the country . . ." This ambitious enlargement was not built, as notes for minor architectural work at Mompecchio in September 1635 make clear: among other tasks, whitewashing is to be done "in the ground-floor *sala* with the five rooms of that story [that is, the rooms shown in the plan of the old small casino], and the new wall of the chapel [its location not specified]"; and hardware is to be provided for twelve windows (only one more than the eleven per floor shown on the old plan).[5]

In spite of the abandonment of the Bernini/ Urban VIII design, the casino at Mompecchio was not to remain unimproved. Francesco writes

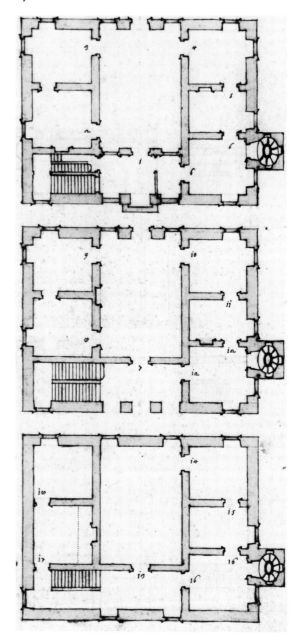

184   Mompecchio, casino, plans (Biblioteca Apostolica Vaticana, ABarb., Ind. II, no. 690, fol. 2)

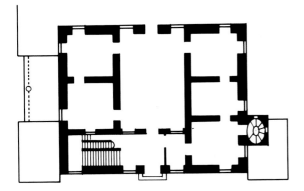

185   Mompecchio, redrawing of Fig. 184 (ground floor) showing light pencil additions (author)

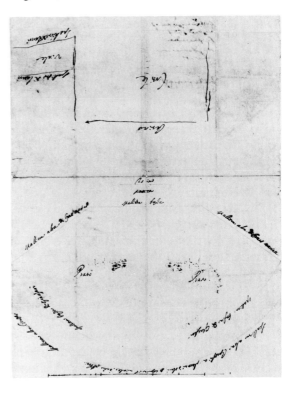

186   Mompecchio, plan of the lawn before the casino (Biblioteca Apostolica Vaticana, ABarb., Ind. II, no. 690, fol. 5)

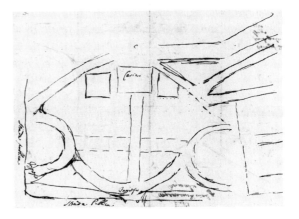

187   Mompecchio, preliminary sketch of the site (Biblioteca Apostolica Vaticana, ABarb., Ind. II, no. 690, fol. 4)

that the already existing house was made "both less ambitious and more comfortable, after [Taddeo] had built what was useful for a stay in the country, having carved many service rooms out of the substructures and strengthened the old structure by rising walls . . . [and] it no longer seemed to be a house [*casa*], but a small palace [*palazzetto*] . . ." He suggests modest works improving the stability and comfort of the house while enhancing its appearance. The provision of a chapel through the construction of a new wall (as already noted in the document of September 1635) would be one such improvement. Very light pencil pentimenti to the plans of the old casino (Fig. 185) and another simple sketch on the back of the sheet suggest the kinds of modest additions that Taddeo might make: a few small rooms and a loggia in keeping with the scale of the old rooms, the addition of which would enrich the exterior form of the building without disturbing its basic symmetry.

The wrapper for the small bundle of notes and drawings for Mompecchio gives the date 1637,[6] perhaps the year in which Taddeo's thoughts turned to improving his casino. Some work had been done in the gardens in 1633,[7] if not at the casino. Payments for an addition to the casino were made in 1643–44.[8] Francesco reports that work had to be discontinued because of "public wars and private disasters," probably the war with Castro of 1641–44 and the death of Urban VIII on 29 July 1644 and the subsequent collapse of Barberini fortunes, both events consonant with construction as late as 1643–44.

The casino or "palazzetto" did not stand in isolation, and Francesco emphasizes that much of the delightfulness of the villa was due to Taddeo's work in the gardens. He speaks of "well-ordered fenced avenues and tall borders [*spalliere*], with water piped in from many miles away . . . [and] a fine lawn which forms a semicircle before [the casino] . . . [as well as] every more curious sort of fruit, which [Taddeo] had procured from his many other properties." The villa was praiseworthy in spite of its having "neither the palaces nor the parks nor the theaters that make others famous." A further indication of the landscaping is given by the drawings showing the small arc of lawn before the casino, its enframing avenues lined by tall borders of cypress and other trees to the outside and low plantings at the edge of the lawn (Figs. 186, 187).[9]

As at Mompecchio, so too at his other properties[10] Taddeo eschewed extravagant building projects in favor of conservation, repairs, and small additions from which considerable advantage could be gained. His father had acquired Monterotondo[11] in 1626 and had begun improvements there which dealt more with practical than with formal concerns. After Taddeo's accession to the property, work was slow for several years, perhaps because Taddeo was more interested in Palestrina; but it intensified in 1637. Taddeo completed his father's project, doing what he could, according to Francesco, to correct the squat proportions *(tozzezza)* of the earlier design of Fra Michele Cappuccino. He improved the church and provided accommodations for the clergy; and he added rooms joining the palace to the church, with chambers for hearing mass privately. At the Giardino de' Bastoni,[12] acquired only in 1641, he added a loggia, a room, and a little chapel to an old *casetta,*

thereby transforming it into a well-arranged casino. At Valmontone he joined two old buildings, which had been "almost uninhabitable separately." At several properties, he stabilized and repaired old structures: Montelibretto, half in ruins and on the verge of collapse, according to Francesco, was secured and repaired; Casa Corbola (Casape) was reroofed with lead; one of the casini at Gericomio was rebuilt; the palace at S. Gregorio was conserved; several rooms of the house at Falcognane received new ceilings. Grounds were tended and fountains installed, not only at Mompecchio but also at Santa Marinella,[13] the Giardino de' Bastoni, and S. Gregorio. The economic viability of properties was improved, for example by the port, granary, and tunny snare at Santa Marinella. "There was no property that was not only conserved by him, but also improved," according to Francesco.

In short, Taddeo was intent on the stewardship of the material possessions of the family, an assessment in accord with that of the Venetian ambassadors. Already in 1629 Angelo Contarini had reported that Taddeo was like his father (who earlier had had to play a similar role in the bifurcated life of the family) "in his assiduous and attentive application to domestic affairs, and to the interests of the family." Giovanni Pesaro wrote of Taddeo's mild manner, his well-regulated life, and his accumulation of great wealth for the family. Alvise Contarini concluded that, in his opinion, Taddeo was devoted solely to the interests of the family.[14]

With few exceptions, the bipartite structure of the family, which found expression in the design of Palazzo Barberini, was further expressed in the brothers' architectural patronage. Taddeo's projects were entirely secular, the only exceptions being churches or convents closely connected with his properties at Monterotondo and Palestrina. Occasionally his ecclesiastical brothers joined him in paying for the work. Francesco made a few early payments for construction at the Palazzo Barberini alle Quattro Fontane as well as paying for construction of his half of the palace beginning in 1632; and he also paid for some of the painted decoration.[15] Francesco was responsible for the installation of the Nile mosaic in the palace at Palestrina.[16] All three brothers joined forces to pay for the new theater at Palazzo Barberini, even as they shared in sponsoring theatrical productions there.[17] Antonio had no need to build a palace for himself, for he was able to succeed his brother at both the Palazzo Barberini alle Quattro Fontane (1635) and the "Casa Grande" ai Giubbonari (1653); instead, he concentrated on furnishings within the palaces. Francesco maintained his interest in the Palazzo Barberini alle Quattro Fontane, even though his office as vice-chancellor included residence at the Cancelleria; but his major patronage was directed toward religious buildings, according to his biographer, Archangelo Spagna.[18]

Francesco's account of Taddeo's building activity not only tells what Taddeo did but also indicates what qualities in his work were especially valued. Solidity, comfort or convenience, and an implied economy of means are recurring themes. The several projects are "majestic," "elegant," "perfected," "splendid," "well arranged," "exquisite," "magnificent," "dignified," "ingenious." In the three palaces these qualities are realized in large scale, ampleness, regularity of both composition and individual forms, symmetry, richness of experience as a visitor enters and ascends to the apartments, and richness of interior decor. The qualities are not peculiar to buildings but inform all Taddeo's undertakings: "Not only in [theatrical performances] but in banquets, and in similar occasions, in liveries, the decoration of rooms, and in whatever he put his hand to, one could see perfection, splendor, and attention; . . . he did not do, and did not know how to do anything which would not be well thought out and perfected" (fols. 15v–16r). The palaces exemplify the admirable qualities that Francesco would have us see in Taddeo himself: ". . . [in these fabrics], above all, beyond his singular ingenuity

and perfect judgment, can be discerned magnificence, which was in his buildings, as generosity shines forth in all his actions" (fol. 20r).

Taddeo did not achieve his architectural ends single-handedly. The intervention of Urban VIII to some extent must always have been a possibility. We have seen that the papal uncle "added a few embellishments and improvements" to the design of the Palazzo Barberini alle Quattro Fontane (fol. 15r). He contributed ideas to Mompecchio, including the ambitious design for a "beautiful residence" which was never built (fol. 18v). He might have prompted the work at the "Casa Grande" ai Giubbonari, although Francesco assures us that in that case Taddeo had other motivation (fol. 21r). In addition, there were many other amateur advisors.

There were also architects, even though Francesco mentions only one: Fra Michele Cappuccino, whose awkward proportions at Monterotondo Taddeo did his best to improve (fol. 16r). First Carlo Maderno and then Gianlorenzo Bernini (both ably assisted by Francesco Borromini) served at the Palazzo Barberini alle Quattro Fontane. Paolo Maruscelli worked for Taddeo for many years and saw to the work at Palestrina. He was succeeded by Francesco Contini, who was architect of the improvements at the "Casa Grande" (as well as the installation of the Nile mosaic at Palestrina). After the experience of the Palazzo Barberini alle Quattro Fontane, it seems that Taddeo stayed clear of architects of the first rank and chose those who might be especially amenable to his goals of good stewardship of family properties. Joseph Connors's characterization of Maruscelli seems especially apt: "For a patron who took an active role in the design, this reliable and transparent personality was the perfect architect. He could guarantee a rational plan and solid construction at reasonable expense. . . . And yet there remains a deep-seated anonymity about Maruscelli . . ."[19] Contini too must have deferred to his clients' wishes, as can be inferred from Anna Colonna Barberini's confidence that he would execute her intentions for her monument in S. Maria Regina Coeli.[20] Yet he seemed able to go beyond the prosaic to create a work of distinction in the entrance hall to the "Casa Grande."

Whatever the particular genius of the architect, we can see Taddeo's kinds of contributions. He established consistent goals, priorities, and strategies for the works, for which the architects would design. He was open to ideas from nontraditional sources. He himself might have a critical idea, as for the Palazzo Barberini alle Quattro Fontane. He might add ideas as work progressed, and he joined with his architect in supervising and approving what was done.

CHAPTER FIFTEEN

Palazzo Chigi in Piazza SS. Apostoli

LIKE the Barberini "Casa Grande" ai Giubbonari, Palazzo Chigi is a product of growth and transformation from modest beginnings (Fig. 188).[1] Its starting point, however, was not the basic Roman row house with ground-floor shop. It may have been more like the bar-shaped house of Enea Orlandini incorporated in the west wing of Palazzo Borghese — a broad house fronting on the piazza SS. Apostoli, with a loggia to a courtyard or garden behind. So strong was the Roman tradition of the perpetuation of a cellular masonry structure that, even when the exterior of the Palazzo Chigi was radically reformed in the 1660s, the interior, equally surely redesigned, remained founded on those modest beginnings.

The Palace before 1664

A house was on the site as early as 1548. In 1562, the property was inherited by Cardinal Marcantonio Colonna, who held it until his death in 1597. He enlarged his property by the acquisition of several neighboring houses and, to the north, a garden with a tower and two stables (shown on the plan of the site ca. 1664, Fig. 189, right),[2] and he was responsible for "many improvements, and rooms both downstairs and upstairs."[3] His palace is shown in the Tempesta map of 1593 (Fig. 190) and is described in the census of Roman palaces of 1601.[4] These two sources, along with

plans made in preparation for the remodeling of 1664–67 (see Figs. 193–196), make it possible to reconstruct the general lines of the house as improved by Cardinal Marcantonio (Fig. 191). It was a U-shaped building, entered asymmetrically from the piazza. Its wings framed a courtyard measuring 28 × 24 *passi* (84 × 72 *palmi*). Tempesta's little view shows the open arcade of a loggia on only the ground floor of the entrance wing. To the right on entering were two rooms, and to the left were a carriage room and six other rooms, some large and some small. These were for services and included a *bottiglieria* and two small kitchens; dampness precluded their use as apartments. Also on the ground floor was an apartment of a "saletta" and three small rooms, from which one could enter the garden, which was apparently on a higher level; these must have formed a small summer apartment for daytime enjoyment. On the upper floor, a suite of four large rooms stretched over the service rooms to the southeast, and an apartment of "saletta" and smaller rooms repeated the pattern of those on the ground floor toward the garden. There were also a gallery and a "camera grande" adjacent to the major stair. There were only three finished attic rooms — perhaps those rising as an altana over the entrance wing in Tempesta's view.[5] This U-shaped house, eventually to form but a small part of Palazzo Chigi, was itself composed of smaller houses. The central portion, with its loggia of four or five bays, would once have been a house rather like that of Enea Orlandini, incorporated in Palazzo Borghese in 1610 (see Fig. 25).[6] The wing to the northwest, about 25 *palmi* wide, would have originated in a typical Roman row house. The thick wall of the eastern corner room suggests that it was not built at the same time as the rooms that follow it en suite. Cardinal Marcantonio's improvements would have forged the U-shaped house from the several disparate properties.

The cardinal then would have had at his disposal a house of moderate quality, with a broad (albeit asymmetrical) façade, two apartments of differing sizes and orientations on the *piano nobile,* a ground-floor summer apartment, a place for his three coaches,[7] and a few service rooms on the ground floor and in the attic. In comparison, Monsignor Francesco Barberini's "Casa Grande" in the 1590s rose an additional story, but its rooms were not arranged in suites. While Francesco's house, with its ground-floor shops, partook of the mercantile economy of via dei Giubbonari, Cardinal Marcantonio's house enjoyed gardens, a garden apartment, and an entrance from the piazza.

From 1596 to 1606, Cardinal Francisco Guzmán de Avila lived in the palace, and he agreed to improve the building in lieu of paying rent. His contribution was "the new apartment that gives onto the piazza and adjoins the garden"[8] — that is, the wing extending northwest from the north corner of the U-shaped building (Fig. 192). Since this wing is not described in the census of 1601, the cardinal's addition must date from the last five years of his tenancy. A glance at the reconstruction of the *piano nobile* shows a great leap in scale: the new apartment is a sequence of six rooms, and the rooms are larger than those of the old building. Further, there is a chapel opening from the second room of the suite, and the rooms are arranged in an *appartamento doppio,* with large rooms to the northeast and smaller rooms to the southwest. The addition is a mod-

188   Palazzo Chigi in piazza SS. Apostoli, left portion of façade built in 1664–67 (author)

ernization according to the developments outlined in Chapter 1. The façade must have become more impressive by virtue of its greater width (although we have no clues as to its articulation); and ground-floor rooms were gained for additional services. It was also during Cardinal Guzmán's tenancy, in 1604, that a row house fronting on the via del Corso was acquired by Marzio Colonna, heir of Cardinal Marcantonio (see Fig. 189, "Casa nel Corpo di d° Palazzo"; cf. Fig. 208, I);[9] this finger of building connecting the Colonna property to the Corso provided not only the possibility of a balcony on that important

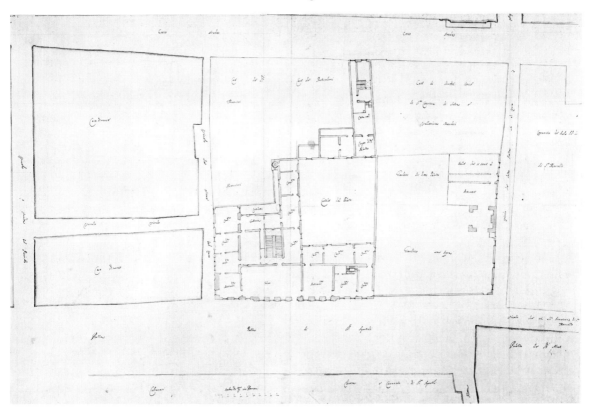

189   Palazzo Chigi, site plan, drawing by Carlo Fontana (Biblioteca Apostolica Vaticana, Chigi P.VII.10, fol. 61v–62r)

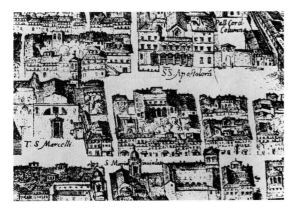

190   Tempesta Map of Rome, 1593, detail with Palazzo Colonna (later Chigi)

street[10] but also the seed of plans for expansion and even reorientation of the palace in the second half of the seventeenth century.

In 1622–23 the palace's fortunes turned again. Cardinal Ludovisi, nephew of Gregory XV, bought the palace for 39,000 scudi and began to rebuild it. His plans were cut short, however, by his appointment as vice-chancellor on 7 June 1623 and his subsequent resale of the palace to Pierfrancesco Colonna for 53,988 scudi on 17 July. Baglione reports that Carlo Maderno (Ludovisi's architect) "restored the interior of the palace, and remade the courtyard."[11] In addition, he must have intended to remodel and regularize the southwest side of the piazza, for on 10

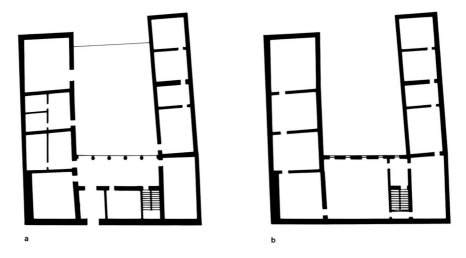

191   Palazzo Colonna (later Chigi), 1590s, reconstruction (author)

February 1623 a license was issued for the incorporation of a strip of land from the piazza, 191 *palmi* in length[12] — that is, the length of the garden wall from the north corner of the palace to the north corner of the site.

There is no direct graphic evidence for Maderno's contribution to the planning of the palace. Instead, we must work backward from a set of drawings prepared by Carlo Fontana before the work of 1664–67 (Figs. 193–196, see Fig. 189) and from documentation for that later construction (for little must have been done by Pierfrancesco Colonna and his successors at the palace until it was acquired by the Chigi). Felice della Greca's grandiose plans for enlarging the palace, sometime after 1657 (Figs. 197–199), can also be of help.

Baglione states that Maderno "remade the courtyard" of the palace. The old courtyard of the U-shaped palace must have seemed small and poorly located after the addition of the "new apartment" of 1601–6. Maderno shifted the courtyard to the space behind the new apartment and built ground-floor loggias on two sides. Although a ground-floor plan by Fontana has not survived, Felice della Greca's scheme shows a

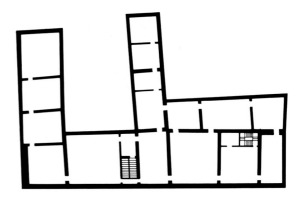

192   Palazzo Colonna (later Chigi), 1606, *piano nobile,* reconstruction (author)

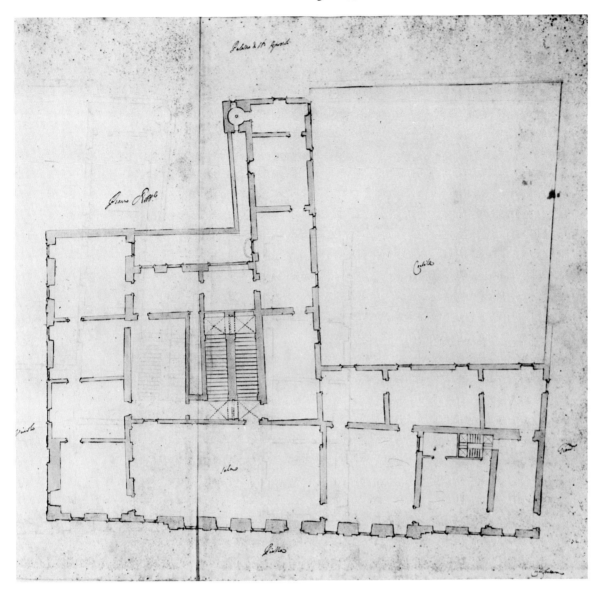

193 Palazzo Chigi before remodeling, *piano nobile* (Biblioteca Apostolica Vaticana, Chigi P.VII.10, fol. 52)

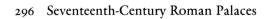

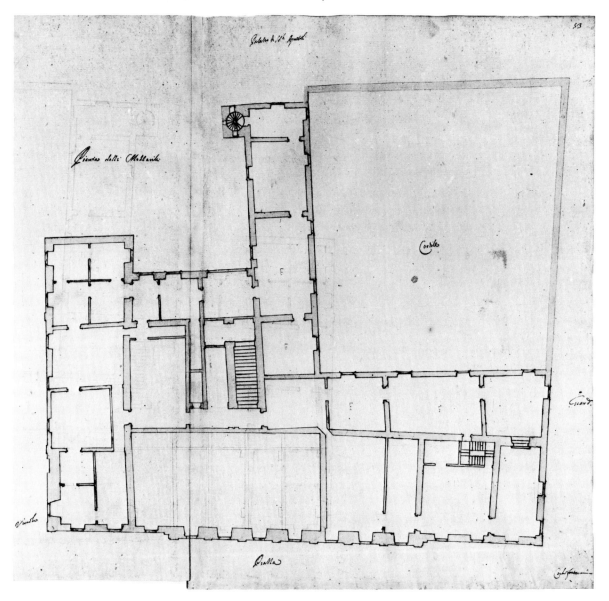

194   Palazzo Chigi before remodeling, *secondo piano* (Biblioteca Apostolica Vaticana, Chigi P.VII.10, fol. 53r)

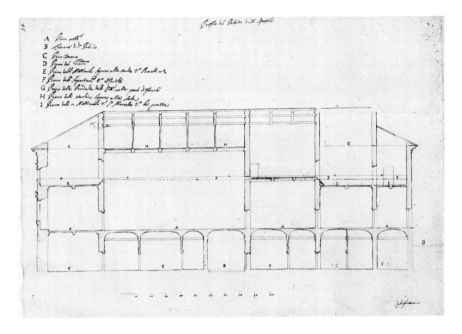

195   Palazzo Chigi before remodeling, section behind façade (Biblioteca Apostolica Vaticana, Chigi P. VII.10, fol. 54r)

196   Palazzo Chigi, southeast flank (Biblioteca Apostolica Vaticana, Chigi P.VII.10, fol. 79)

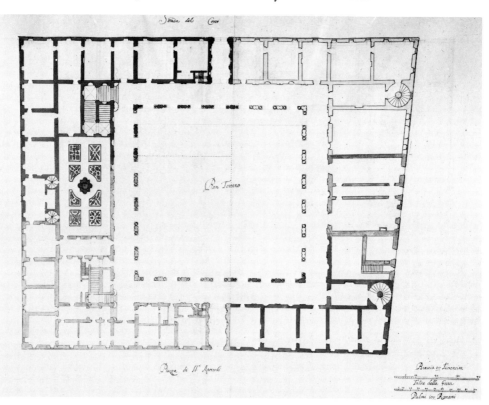

197 Felice della Greca, project for Palazzo Chigi, ground floor (Biblioteca Apostolica Vaticana, Chigi P.VII.10, fol. 62v–63r)

regularized version of Maderno's work, distinguished by the violet color of its poché from the red and yellow proposed additions (see Fig. 197). Arches supported on Tuscan columns are framed by substantial piers faced with broad pilasters (Fig. 200). On the *piano nobile,* rectangular windows with molded frames are set within a low-relief frame of blind arches and tapered channeled pilasters. The documents of construction in the 1660s make no reference whatever to the arches, columns, and pilasters of the courtyard; they must already have been in place. They were painted the color of travertine so as to distinguish the architectural membering from the ground of the wall, in 1665–68.[13] The pattern is

shown in Specchi's engraving of the palace in 1699 (see Fig. 210), even continued onto the third side of the courtyard, the upper stories of which did not exist in 1668 (cf. the view in Falda's map of 1676, Fig. 209). The four bays on the northeast side of the courtyard and the five bays to the southeast must have been only a part of a larger scheme, perhaps even anticipating the scale of della Greca's designs of thirty-five years later.[14]

The relocation of the courtyard required the shifting of the entrance to the palace, probably to the place where Fontana and Bernini found it in 1664 (see Fig. 195, B, "Entrone del Palazzo").[15] The stair was then displaced to the old courtyard,

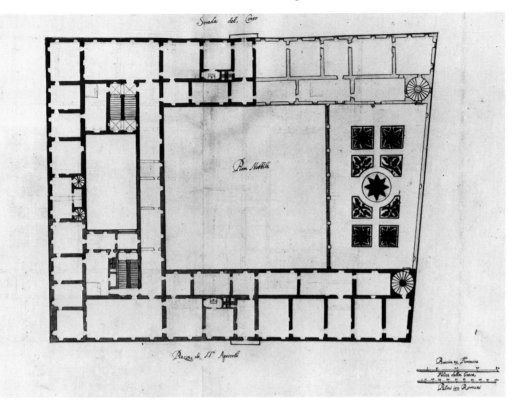

198 Felice della Greca, project for Palazzo Chigi, *piano nobile* (Biblioteca Apostolica Vaticana, Chigi P.VII.10, fol. 64v–65r)

where it could be developed at a scale compatible with that of the new.

A brief accounting of the short but vigorous campaign is provided in a memorandum of 15 July 1623 (just before the resale of the property to Pierfrancesco Colonna) and a Ludovisi ledger.[16] In all, the work amounted to almost 12,000 scudi. The accounting includes an allowance of 600 scudi for materials salvaged from the "apartment razed to the ground," consigned to the mason[17] — likely the wing to be replaced by the loggia and rooms on the southeast side of the new courtyard. New masonry amounted to almost 4,500 scudi. The work on the interior of the palace, reported by Baglione, would have in-

cluded the new entrance and stair, the rooms behind the stair (later to be remodeled as galleries B14 and C17), the large *sala* on the *piano nobile* (created by the removal of old partitions), and the new rooms above the loggia on the southeast side of the courtyard. In addition, whether in this campaign or in the work undertaken earlier by Cardinal Guzmán, walls were heightened to allow not only the lofty *salone* but also a full second story (although the walls were still considerably lower than those shown in Fig. 195). The fourteen beams mentioned in the ledger would have spanned the enlarged *salone,* above the new painted wood ceiling.[18] An expensive fireplace was carved for the *sala.*[19] More than 800

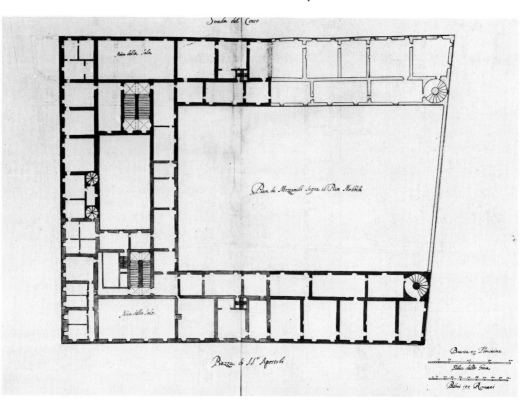

199   Felice della Greca, project for Palazzo Chigi, mezzanines (Biblioteca Apostolica Vaticana, Chigi P.VII.10, fol. 70v–71r)

scudi was spent on stucco work. The vault of the room on the *piano nobile* at the angle of the new courtyard, C12, was painted by Agostino Tassi, and his work must have included marine scenes in four lunettes of neighboring C13.[20] Only three other rooms on the *piano nobile* (C13, C14, C17) had vaulted ceilings in 1664, and the two vaults painted by Nicola Ventura in 1623 were likely those of C13 and C14, above the new loggia.[21] They may have been used as a gallery, since the account identifies the room painted by Tassi as "attached to the gallery." The substantial sum of 3,930.11 scudi was spent in two *misure* for stonework, including pieces that had not been

installed — a sign that the ambitious project was cut short.

Although but a fragment of a larger scheme, the palace nevertheless could evoke Totti's admiration in 1638, when he called it a "nobilissimo palazzo . . . ben risarcito, e di bel giardino adornato."[22]

The last in a series of renters in the palace were Mario and Agostino Chigi. Alexander VII Chigi had wanted to avoid the practice of nepotism and had been slow to summon his family from Siena to Rome after his election to the papacy (Fig. 201). By the summer of 1657, however, his older brother Mario, Mario's wife Berenice, and

200   Palazzo Chigi, courtyard (I.C.C.D., Rome, ser. F, no. 19333)

their nephew Agostino were in Rome, installed as tenants in the palace of Stefano Colonna in piazza SS. Apostoli. In July of the following year, Agostino married Virginia Borghese (see Fig. 19), and she with her women attendants joined the Chigi at the palace. By the spring of 1659, Mario and Berenice's household numbered sixty-one persons, including five women, and Agostino and Virginia supported 104 persons, including five women.[23] Not surprisingly, some architectural adjustments to the old palace were called for. According to a papal chirograph of 7 June 1657, Alexander VII authorized "repairs, restoration, and improvements" intended to make the palace "a comfortable and suitable residence" for his relatives.[24] A bill for gilding was submitted in 1657, and two bills for stonework and another for gilding were paid in 1658. Meanwhile, successive chirographs, on 11 June, 31 July, and 9 August 1658, provided for more work on the palace.[25]

On the basis of Carlo Fontana's drawings of the palace before the extensive remodeling of 1664–67 (see Figs. 193–196), we can speculate on how the four principal residents distributed themselves in the palace. Don Mario Chigi, as

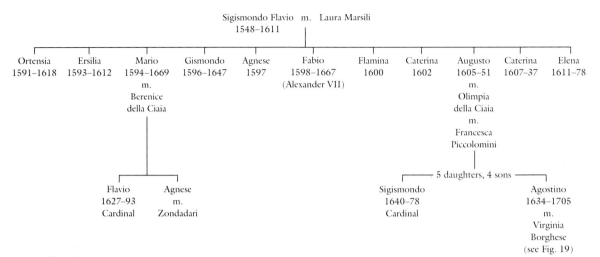

Sigismondo Flavio m. Laura Marsili
1548–1611

| Ortensia 1591–1618 | Ersilia 1593–1612 | Mario 1594–1669 m. Berenice della Ciaia | Gismondo 1596–1647 | Agnese 1597 | Fabio 1598–1667 (Alexander VII) | Flamina 1600 | Caterina 1602 | Augusto 1605–51 m. Olimpia della Ciaia m. Francesca Piccolomini | Caterina 1607–37 | Elena 1611–78 |

Flavio 1627–93 Cardinal

Agnese m. Zondadari

5 daughters, 4 sons

Sigismondo 1640–78 Cardinal

Agostino 1634–1705 m. Virginia Borghese (see Fig. 19)

201   Chigi family

senior member of the family and General of the Church, likely took the "appartamento nuovo" on the *piano nobile*. Agostino would have used the four-room apartment opening from the opposite side of the *sala*. Berenice, who would have had to receive guests not only in her husband's behalf but also in that of her brother-in-law the pope, could have used the apartment along the southeast side of the courtyard; and her women attendants could have been housed in the mezzanine rooms above. (In 1664–67, a turnbox, a necessary accessory of a women's apartment, was removed from the top of the main stair, adjacent to these rooms.)[26] Virginia, intent on maternity, might have stayed with her women in the mezzanine rooms above Agostino's apartment. A few members of the *famiglia* could have lived in attics over the "appartamento nuovo," or in lofts over their ground-floor offices, but most would have been housed outside the palace. The building was full, and it may have been at this time that Felice della Greca prepared several designs for greatly enlarging the palace (see Figs. 197–199).[27] He would have filled the entire block, so that there would be a long façade and entrance on the via del Corso as well as on piazza SS. Apostoli. The duplication of stairs, *saloni,* and many-roomed linear apartments suggests

that he envisioned a double palace for two important residents — presumably for Mario and Agostino, with their respective wives, but also conceivably for the two papal nephews, Prince Agostino and his slightly older cousin Cardinal Flavio Chigi.

On 9 December 1661 Alexander VII recorded in his diary that his nephew Cardinal Flavio Chigi had decided to buy the palace.[28] The pope authorized the sale in a chirograph dated 21 December 1661; Stefano Colonna received 25,000 scudi for the palace and the contiguous small house opening to via del Corso, on 2 January 1662; the transfer was accomplished on 21 January 1662.[29] Meanwhile, Mario and Agostino had moved to the Palazzo Aldobrandini-Chigi in piazza Colonna, which they had purchased on 25 September 1659; they were recorded as resident in the palace in the spring census of 1660.[30] The palace in piazza SS. Apostoli was turned over to an assortment of eleven persons, including Francesco Leoparducci (a gentleman in the court of Cardinal Flavio Chigi) and several young students, in 1662. In 1663, 1664, and 1665, one Gregorio Zamperini, his wife and children, and a few other persons lived in the palace. It was completely unoccupied in 1666 and 1667, during reconstruction.[31] Unlike Taddeo Barberini and

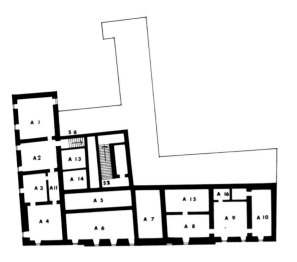

202   Palazzo Chigi, 1664–67, basement,
reconstruction (author)

203   Palazzo Chigi, 1664–67, ground floor,
reconstruction (author)

204   Palazzo Chigi, 1664–67, *piano nobile*,
reconstruction (author)

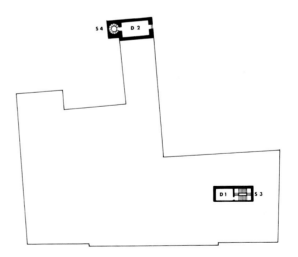

205   Palazzo Chigi, 1664–67, mezzanines,
reconstruction (author)

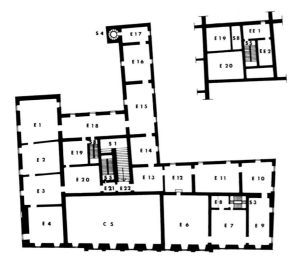

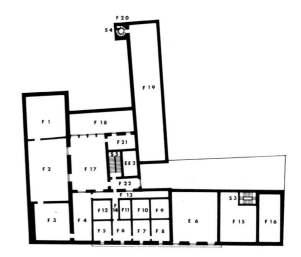

206 Palazzo Chigi, 1664–67, *secondo piano,* reconstruction (author)

207 Palazzo Chigi, 1664–67, attics, reconstruction (author)

Giovanni Battista Borghese, Flavio Chigi chose not to live in the midst of the work.

Still, the embellishment of the palace continued. Camillo Saraceni was paid on 20 November 1661 for having decorated two ceilings; Giovanni Paolo Schor, assisted by Giovanni Battista Passeri and Carlo Reimo, were paid for frescoes on 19 June 1662. On 25 January 1663, 300 scudi was paid "a buon conto" to Francesco Mola for frescoes in a room of the palace. In 1664 the Sienese painter Bernardino Mei made four large paintings for the *sala*. In addition, in August 1663 a number of marbles and statues were brought to the palace.[32]

Reconstruction, 1664–67

Some preliminary masons' work, amounting to only 115.37 scudi, was done between 7 February and 21 July 1664; it included scaffolding for the painter in room C9.[33] Major masonry construction and stonework began on 20 July 1664 and

lasted for three years, with woodwork continuing until 13 February 1669.[34] The building was extended downward and upward; its interior was extensively reformed and embellished to suit the requirements of Cardinal Flavio Chigi; it received a distinctive new façade; but its basic outlines and cellular structure remained unchanged (Figs. 202–207).

The *sala* C5 (Fig. 204), surviving from Colonna ownership, was expanded upward, refinished, and regularized. Old walls were heightened so that the *sala,* now 46½ *palmi* high, embraced five windows of the *piano nobile* and five windows of the *secondo piano* toward the piazza. A cornice was installed around the room below the new wood ceiling, which was richly carved with deep, variously shaped coffers, rosettes, leaves, and, in the middle, the cardinal's arms. Windows were shifted and doorways aligned. A marble fireplace, surely that installed by Maderno in 1623, was removed. The four large paintings by Mei, painted in 1664, were installed in wood frames each measuring 14 × 17 *palmi*. The area under the baldacchino was set off by a railing 53 *palmi* in length. Seven *cassapanchi* were newly made for the *sala*, and a *letto à credenza* for the guard was repaired. Two antique statues were set on pedestals 7½ *palmi* high.[35]

The cardinal's major apartment opened to the left from the *sala* and extended through the six rooms of the "appartamento nuovo" to those along the southeast side of the courtyard—an impressive sequence of ten rooms. In anteroom C6 and the following room C7 windows were reshaped and shifted to conform with the new façade. The chapel C8 opened from room C7, but a window connected it with anteroom C6 as well; it was newly outfitted with an altar, various cabinets, and rich stuccoes in its vault.[36] A door opened from corner room C9 to stairs descending to the garden, the landing shielded by *gelosie*.[37] Following the four anterooms (C6, C7, C9, C10) was the audience room C11, furnished with a damask baldacchino and nineteen chairs.[38]

Room C14 must have been intended as the cardinal's bedroom in 1665, when Giovanni Angelo Canini painted the vault of "the room where we [Cardinal Chigi] sleep," and Francesco Galli painted three windows with landscapes and grotesques "where we sleep";[39] there were only four vaulted rooms on the *piano nobile* (C12, C13, C14, and C17), and none at all on the *secondo piano*; and of the four, only C14 had three windows.[40] But when Tessin visited the palace in 1687–88, this room was a second audience room (in addition to C11), for the reception of women and certain knights; he saw a baldacchino here, and an undated inventory of the cardinal's palace also lists a baldacchino in C14, along with a set of eighteen chairs of crimson velvet.[41] The cardinal's bedroom presumably was moved to a more secluded location on the *secondo piano* when the following pair of rooms, C15 and C16, was completed as the culmination of the suite of reception rooms. The "alcove" C16 contained a richly furnished bed, which was not actually used for sleeping; Sebastiani's guidebook of 1683 makes it

clear that the bed "serves no other purpose than to be seen by strangers, nor is it ever used."[42] It was screened from C15, the "anteroom to the alcove," by two Corinthian columns surmounted by a broken pediment, above which two figures held an oval painting of "Diana and Endymion"—a painting for which Giovanni Battista Gaulli was paid 150 scudi on 18 June 1668. The decor also included mirrors painted by Stanchi—like those in Palazzo Borghese, according to Tessin.[43] Cardinal Chigi would have seen both representational beds and bed alcoves in many important residences on his visit to Paris in 1664. It may be that the idea to convert the small room shown in Fontana's plan into the richly decorated alcove C16 was a result of his travel abroad.

In these same years, the newly remodeled ground-floor apartments of Palazzo Borghese included rooms with representational beds for both prince and princess; and the cardinal's apartment at Palazzo Barberini, according to Tessin, had two audience rooms, the first for "knights and prelates" and the second presumably for other visitors.[44] The arrangement at Palazzo Chigi, with a very long suite, two audience rooms, and a representational bedroom, seems very much in keeping with the times.

A marble fireplace "alla francese" in anteroom C6, a fireplace of breccia in C9, and another of mischio in C15 were cleaned and polished;[45] these three seem to have been the only fireplaces in the long suite. Gentlemen in attendance in anterooms C6 and C9, to the northeast, would have welcomed the warmth of a fire in the winter; the inner rooms of the apartment, including audience rooms C11 and C14, would have been dependent on the warmth of the afternoon sun for winter comfort.

Throughout the suite, old travertine doorframes were removed and replaced with frames of more richly colored portasanta marble.[46] Friezes of landscapes and seascapes painted on canvas were installed in rooms C7, C9, C10, and C11.[47] The *indoratore* Vincenzo Corallo painted wooden ceilings in rooms C6, C7, and C9.[48] Tassi's vault painting of 1623 survived in room C12.[49] The vault of the neighboring room C13 featured a central field of gilded stucco, and that of C14 held Canini's painting of 1665, with a cornice of gilded stucco.[50] Cardinal Chigi's inventory lists matching wall hangings of damask, with overdoors and overwindows, in all the rooms of the suite; Tessin was impressed by the rich decor of gold and crimson.[51]

The rooms to the right of the *sala,* C1–C4, had formed the principal apartment for Cardinal Colonna in the late sixteenth century, but their number must have seemed modest in comparison to Cardinal Chigi's apartment in the 1660s. They were now refurbished and outfitted for the display of paintings as the "Appartamento nobile de quadri."[52] Windows were shifted in all the rooms, to bring them into order with the new façade to the southeast and (in C4) the enfilade through the *sala.* Travertine doorframes were removed and replaced with green marble. Wood ceilings were painted by Corallo. Room C4 was designated "Anticamera," and C2 resembled an audience room in that it contained a baldacchino beneath which hung a portrait of Clement IX (elected 20 June 1667, before completion of the remodeling). There was no bedroom. Only room C3 had a fireplace, and it was not allotted any equipment, according to the inventory of the palace.[53] The adjacent "stanza oscura" C18, which received only borrowed light from gallery C17, was included in the apartment. Two large battle paintings (each $14 \times 9\frac{1}{2}$ *palmi*) were installed here, but the room would seem to have been most useful as an adjunct to rooms with better light: two long *cassapanchi,* a table for the *credenza,* and three tables for meetings of the Congregazione della Segnatura were kept here, and the small chamber C23 with latrines opened from the room.[54] Tessin counted 406 paintings in this apartment in 1687–88.[55] There was no need for wall hangings, for paintings covered the walls from the ceiling downward, but damask *portiere* hung at five doorways, and the nine windows had green taffeta curtains. The works of art were joined by a work of nature, a parrot in a cage.[56]

Gallery C17 was a natural extension of the apartment for paintings and linked it with the inner rooms of the cardinal's apartment. It was formed by the removal of a partition between two smaller rooms (cf. Fig. 193). To the southwest were two extraordinarily broad arched openings, each about 24 *palmi* wide—one of which had to be cleared of an infilling wall and smaller openings; these were fitted with parapets and operable wooden frames to hold abundant glazing. On the opposite side of the narrow gallery were two large openings with fixed glazed panels, each $9\frac{3}{4} \times 11$ *palmi,* to lend light to the major stair S1; a small door topped by a window, and two additional windows, each measuring $7 \times 15\frac{1}{2}$ *palmi,* to light the "stanza oscura" C18; and still another small window to stair S8.[57] The southwest sunlight was so plentiful that crimson curtains had to be hung in the large arches as well as in the arches toward the stair.[58] Even with the many windows, there was still room for perspective paintings of flowers and fruits and, on the vault, a "Flora" with putti painted by Girolamo Troppa in 1668, and for the display of antique busts on wooden pedestals.[59]

Rooms for the cardinal's use continued on the *secondo piano* (see Fig. 206), on either side of the two-story volume of the *sala* C5. To the southeast, over the painting gallery, was an apartment possibly intended for winter use; its high elevation would allow the southern sun to reach its windows, in spite of the narrowness of the vicolo del Piombo. The partitions that had earlier subdivided rooms E1–E4 (cf. Figs. 194, 199) were removed, a new partition divided room E19 from E20, new pavements were installed, walls were plastered, and window openings were shifted. In corner room E1, a vault was removed and replaced by a wood ceiling. New wood ceilings were made for the other rooms, too, including windowless rooms E19 and E20, and all were painted by Corallo. Friezes 2 or 3 *palmi* high may have been painted around the tops of the walls in E1, E2, and E3, to judge from the description of plastering in these rooms. In E2, a fireplace opening and an opening for a storage cupboard *(armario)* were walled up; this may earlier have been the women's kitchen and dining room. Another fireplace was removed from the northwest wall of E4. A new fireplace of mischio marble was installed in E1 — apparently the only one in this apartment.[60]

Gallery E18 rose over the similar room on the *piano nobile.* Instead of large arches to the southwest, it had three windows of normal dimensions (6¼ × 12¼ *palmi*), partially covered by *gelosie* for privacy. Doors to neighboring E19 and stair S8 were surmounted by windows so that those dark spaces might receive some light. As in other rooms on this floor, Corallo painted its new wood ceiling.[61] A revetment of crimson damask enriched the walls.[62] As private rooms, this gallery and the rooms to the southeast were not seen by Tessin or Sebastiani on their visits.

The cardinal's library was in the large room E6. The northwest, northeast, and southeast walls were heightened about 20 *palmi* to make its nearly cubic volume;[63] windows were shifted and new mezzanine windows opened; an old wall was cut back to straighten it; and paving was laid. A new wood ceiling was carved by the *falegname* Antonio Chiccheri, installed, and painted by Corallo; its central field contained three figures representing Religion, Hope, and Charity — a condensation of the iconography of the slightly earlier Biblioteca Alessandrina at the Archiginnasio, where Clemente Maioli painted the "Triumph of Religion," in which the central figure is accompanied by the evangelists and the three Theological Virtues.[64] Shelving for the four walls of the library, with a wooden spiral stair to give access to the books on the upper level, was made by Chiccheri, according to the design provided by the architect. Chiccheri also provided a large table, 16½ × 7 *palmi,* for the middle of the room.[65] The library was soon expanded into neighboring room E7, and Chic-

cheri began work on its shelving on 16 September 1669.[66] This room too was refurbished: it received new paving and plaster, its wood ceiling was raised 7 *palmi* and painted, and a fireplace framed in mischio was installed.[67] The little adjacent room E8 was outfitted as a chapel, with a painted wood ceiling, an altar, a baldacchino over the altar, and a wooden *cancellata.*[68] Its floor level was raised 2¾ *palmi* and its wood ceiling raised 6 *palmi.*[69]

Visitors to the library would ascend the main stair, turn left into windowless room E13, and continue into E12, where a new door was made to the library and two steps installed. (The floor of the library was slightly higher than that of other rooms in this wing, because it rose over the high ceiling of the large anteroom C6.) Before Cardinal Chigi's remodeling, a door opening had passed diagonally from the corner of E13 to room E6, as shown in Fontana's plan and section (see Figs. 194, 195). The revisions in these rooms fill in that doorway and open the new orthogonal passage from E12 to the library.[70] A single step then led down from the library to room E7, and another step led down to E9, at the level of other rooms of the *secondo piano.*[71]

All the rooms on the *secondo piano* were refurbished, with new painted wood ceilings, doors, window frames, pavements, and plaster on the walls; but clues as to specific uses of rooms other than the library are scarce. A fireplace was specifically removed from room E14; in the rooms around the courtyard only E11 seems to have been warmed by a fireplace.[72] *Gelosie* at the two windows of room E16 provided visual privacy, possibly for sleeping;[73] however, the undated inventory of the palace notes a richly outfitted bed in room E10 and calls room E9 a *retrocamera* (with respect to either E10 or E7).[74] Just at this point, the inventory abandons its orderly room-by-room sequence and lists entirely too many pieces of furniture, revetments, tapestries, objects, sculptures, and so forth to fit into any single room — among them a writing desk and a cabinet for papers (suggesting that the cardinal's study was near the library) and "12 velvet chairs in the rooms where His Excellency sleeps." The listing of rooms then resumes with E17, containing ninety pieces of majolica as well as a writing desk, a box for papers, a set of shelves for the same purpose, and a footwarmer—indications of a private study. In this same small room, high and exposed, was a telescope, with which its owner could survey the city.[75] In sum, it seems that the rooms on the *secondo piano* around the courtyard were for the cardinal's private use, for sleeping and studying. The footwarmer in room E17 and the several bedwarmers listed in another inventory[76] would keep him warm in winter, in spite of the scarcity of fireplaces.

The ground floor of the palace (see Fig. 203), once judged too damp for anything but services, was extensively remodeled. The old offices to the left of the entrance were converted into a sculpture gallery and summer apartment[77]—the contemporary of that of Antonio Barberini at the "Casa Grande" ai Giubbonari and the precursor of those to be built by Giovanni Battista Borghese and Francesco Barberini in the 1670s. The rooms were regularized and refurbished, door and window openings shifted or walled up, a fireplace removed from B1 and a chimney from B6, the opening for a privy walled up in B4, doorframes replaced, pavements laid, and walls plastered. Vincenzo Corallo painted the perimeter of the vault of "anteroom" B6 as a balustrade supporting antique sculptures, with painted birds perching or flying overhead; his airy perspectives filled the deep jambs of the windows. He also painted the beamed ceilings of B2, B3, and B4 and the vault in corner room B1.[78] A chapel, or "cappella segreta," B26, was installed at one end of the corridor-like space alongside the anteroom, with an altar, a window toward B6, a wooden screen separating it from B5, and a wooden ceiling painted with a representation of God the Father with angels and clouds. Again, the *indoratore* Corallo was the artist.[79] (In 1669 a wall was built to separate the chapel from the corridor B5; it had a door and a window through

which the *palafrenieri* could hear mass, and another window to B6 for light.)[80] Room B15 received borrowed light only through mezzanine windows over the doors from rooms B2 and B3, but Corallo's painted decoration on its vault continued the airy theme of balustrade and birds against the sky, as in nearby B6.[81] Gallery B14 looked out onto the shallow courtyard B16, where a few sculptures and a fountain were to be seen; its painted decoration continued the allusion to openness, with a vault like a pergola and perspectives on the walls.[82] Wall hangings were of green and silver—brocade in anteroom B6 and striped taffeta in rooms B1–B4 and chapel B26. Doorframes of verde antico, installed in 1673, completed the coordinated decor.

Furnishings in the summer apartment were sparse—sixteen chairs and two *buffetti* in the anteroom, and thirty-six chairs and a daybed in the next three rooms. The main attraction was of course the collection of sculptures. Tessin counted a total of fifty-five pieces, mostly antiquities, when he visited in 1687–88, but Cardinal Chigi's inventory lists ninety-two sculptures in these rooms, along with several columns, vases, and consoles. The smaller statues were set on wood pedestals. A fountain played in the middle of the last room (B1), its large marble basin brought to the palace in 1673.[83] A small door in B1 provided a private exit to the vicolo del Piombo.[84]

On the other side of the entrance, all was business. The *dispensa* was installed in room B8, toward the courtyard. Its old door to the entry hall was walled up, but it had a door toward the courtyard and another to neighboring room B9. It was outfitted with new shelves, cupboards, tables, and a bed for the *dispensiere*.[85] The bookkeeping office was apparently in B9 and B10, with a door to the entry hall.[86] Room B12 was formed by the removal of an old partition (shown in Fontana's section, Fig. 195, and in Felice della Greca's plan, Fig. 197). A fireplace was removed, plaster repaired, and paving laid. Small room B11 was seen as an adjunct to B12, but the documents of construction give no clue to the function assigned to the pair.[87] Room B13, toward the garden, was the *bottiglieria*. In its re-modeling, many openings were walled up, but its door to the courtyard was enlarged, and a new door was opened to stair S3, which led to the cardinal's apartments above.[88] Water was piped in.[89] The furnishings of the *bottiglieria* included newly made tables, two large cupboards (one newly made), pedestals, boxes, copper vessels, linens, and two beds, for the *bottigliere* and his assistant.[90]

On the southwest side of the courtyard four carriage rooms (B19 – B22) were refurbished and mezzanines (C19 – C22) installed above. The stair in B19 was newly made, and a shallow one-story tack room B18 was added behind the car-riage rooms.[91] A new carriage room B27 was built into the last two bays of the southeast log-gia of the courtyard, under the "alcove" of the *piano nobile* and behind the statue and niche forming the terminus of the view from the en-trance.[92] A door at the foot of the new spiral stair S4 opened to this carriage room, so that the car-dinal could descend privately to his carriage.[93]

Previously kitchens had been in basement rooms A6 and A4.[94] Now the kitchens became greatly expanded, as other basement rooms were excavated and finished (see Fig. 202). Corner room A4 was the new bakery, with an oven.[95] Room A3 was the cook's pantry.[96] Room A2 was the scullery, with a well, two basins, a drain to the ground, and wooden shelves.[97] A1 was the cardi-nal's kitchen (*cucina segreta*). Earth was removed to lower the level of the floor by 2½ *palmi*. A large fireplace 10 *palmi* wide was cut into the wall. An L-shaped cooking counter (*murello*), like that shown in Scappi's illustration (see Fig. 10), was built, 37 *palmi* long, with eight arches and nine piers, and an extension of 6½ *palmi* at right angles. Wooden shelves and a rack for pots were installed. There were three beds with bedding in the *cucina segreta* — presumably for the cook and two helpers.[98] Two vaults were built under the floor of room B15 — one over an old cistern and

the other over earth; excavations under the vaults then formed rooms A13 and A14, to be used for wood and charcoal.[99] None of the basement rooms seems to have been paved. In all the base-ment rooms along the vicolo del Piombo and the piazza, windows were shifted to bring them into accord with the new façade design.[100]

In the three basement rooms to the northwest of the entrance (A8 – A10), façade windows were similarly shifted.[101] A new basement room A15 was excavated, to a depth of 12 *palmi*.[102] Cantina A9 and the small adjacent room A16 were the *credenza*, with shelves and a lavatory with water brought from a fountain in the garden.[103] In ad-dition, there were a "Cantina del Bottigliero," a "cantina de S[re] Simonelli" (a gentleman in Car-dinal Flavio's service, who was not the *botti-gliere*), and a "Cantina del Sig[re] Cardinale"; but it is not clear which designation should be as-signed to which of the basement rooms in this area.[104] A little stair went down to basement room A10, adjacent to but not identical with stair S3.[105] There were, apparently, no basement rooms under the courtyard loggia or gallery B14.

As new spaces were found by excavating base-ment rooms under the palace, so they were added by heightening the walls above (see Fig. 207). The wall of the façade was raised 23¾ *palmi*, from a little below the arches of the second tier of windows, and other walls were raised compara-ble amounts to make possible the tall *salone*, the library, and other full-height rooms on the *se-condo piano*.[106] In addition, walls over the central part of the palace (above the stair and window-less rooms that had filled in the original court-yard of Cardinal Colonna's sixteenth-century house) were raised even farther to provide an elevated *guardaroba*, F17, with many generous clerestory windows opening above the large cup-boards that lined the room.[107] F19 was a second *guardaroba*, and within a few years an open log-gia had been constructed above it.[108] Attic rooms (F1 – F3, F15, F16, F18, F19) were finished with plain pavements, low plastered walls, and dormers for light.[109] A wood-framed "galley" of small rooms (F4–F14) was constructed above the ceiling of the *salone* (see Figs. 195, 207).[110] Opening from the landing of stair S5 were two small rooms EE1 and EE2, the inner of the two containing latrines whose pipes were immured in the wall toward the courtyard.[111] Except for the *guardarobe* and latrines, specific functions of the attic rooms cannot be identified, but it is easy to imagine members of the *famiglia* installed in the "galley," if not also in other rooms.

The several levels of the cardinal's palace were laced together by an articulate set of stairs. First among them was the "scala maestra," the main stair S1, probably the work of Carlo Maderno in 1623. Its broad straight flights, 10 *palmi* wide, led from the eastern corner of the courtyard to the *piano nobile* and the *secondo piano.* Probably rather dark, it borrowed light from gallery C17 through two large glazed openings hung with crimson curtains.[112] The stair was repaired and then completely refinished, with new pavements in its landings and plaster on its walls and vaults and on the pilasters and arches of the landings.[113] The vault of its uppermost flight was raised to increase the light. The old opening for a turnbox at the top of the stair was filled in, since that appliance would not be needed in a cardinal's palace.[114] It was exchanged, in a sense, for a bell-cote, constructed above the roof of the stair, for the bell that would be rung on the arrival of important visitors. The cord for ringing the bell passed through three vaults of stair landings on its way to the *pian terreno.*[115]

A visitor to the palace would wish to see the cardinal, his sculptures, his paintings, or his library. The sculptures lay immediately to the left of the entrance, and the entrance to stair S1 was only a few paces farther. This stair would take the visitor directly to the *piano nobile* and *sala* (whence to the cardinal or his paintings) and to the *secondo piano* and the entrance to the library or, through vestibule E21–E22, the southeast apartment. It went no farther. A separate, smaller stair S5 led from the *secondo piano* to the attic rooms and the *guardaroba* F17; it provided

the only access to the *guardaroba* and, from its intermediate landing, to the latrines in EE2.[116] Two separate stairs, their shared entrance B24 under the landing of stair S1, led to the basement kitchens: S2, with twenty-one normal treads, to rooms toward the piazza; and ramped stair S6, useful for heavy deliveries by cart, to scullery A2.[117]

Other small stairs were similarly precise in providing connections among the many levels and rooms of the palace. Stair S3, the "scaletta a branchi," went from the *pian terreno* to the *secondo piano,* to serve the rooms of the apartments toward the garden. It did not descend to the basement; a separate small stair alongside did that. It had doors from the courtyard and the *bottiglieria* on the *pian terreno;* it opened to both C7 and C10 on the *piano nobile;* it rose to a little mezzanine room D1 over the chapel and then on to the second library room E7 and chapel E8 on the *secondo piano.*[118] Stair S8 connected the galleries and windowless rooms on the *pian terreno, piano nobile,* and *secondo piano;*[119] it therefore indirectly served all three south apartments. Spiral stair S4 was newly made and extended from the ground to the attic. It provided a private passage to carriage room B27 or, via the narrow courtyard B16, to room B1 with its private door to the vicolo. It connected the end of the cardinal's formal apartment with mezzanine room D2 (see Fig. 205) and his private rooms on the *secondo piano.* It also led to *guardaroba* F19. At its summit was a tiny chamber F20, with a latrine.[120] There were still other private stairs, whose form cannot be reconstructed—a spiral stair at the old kitchen A6, another near the new kitchen A1, and a straight stair near the entry hall, from the *dispensa* B8 to the basement.[121] The L-shaped courtyard loggia played an important role in the private circulation, as transfers from one stair to another could be made there.

After the remodeling, few persons lived in the palace. In place of the two married couples, there was now a single cardinal. Of his large *famiglia,* only a few members could be accommodated in

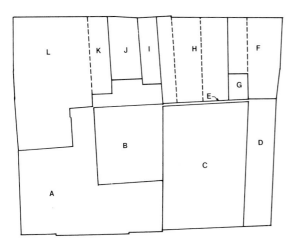

208   Palazzo Chigi. Site and adjacent properties
(author)

A   Palazzo Chigi
B   Chigi courtyard
C   Chigi garden
D   New Chigi stable
E   Corridor from courtyard to *cucina comune*
and stable
F   *Palazzetto della famiglia,* formerly Man-
dosi houses
G   *Cucina comune,* built 1667
H   Houses belonging to the Compagnia di S.
Caterina da Siena
I   Chigi house
J   *Palazzetto* or casino rented from Mancini
K   Mancini house
L   Palazzo Mancini

cific houses were members of the Chigi household.[123] Shortly before moving into his newly
rebuilt palace, Cardinal Chigi had rented two
houses from Valeriano Mandosi for use as a
guardaroba and *computisteria;* a year later, on 20
August 1667, he purchased the houses, extending
from his garden and stable westward along the
present via dei SS. Apostoli to the via del Corso,
and remodeled them as a "palazzetto della famiglia" (Fig. 208, F–G).[124] There were twenty-
eight rooms and eleven mezzanine rooms, divided into apartments of two or three rooms
each for gentlemen and a few other persons in
the cardinal's *famiglia;* the apartments generally
had fireplaces and individual privies. On the
ground floor toward the vicolo were three carriage rooms and a fourth "rimessa" for hay storage; and toward the Corso were at least three
shops.[125] There were four houses belonging to
the Compagnia di S. Caterina da Siena in via del
Corso between the "palazzetto della famiglia"
and the narrow house incorporated in the Colonna-Chigi property since 1604 (Fig. 208, H);
these were rented for members of the *famiglia*
and remodeled much as the "palazzetto" had
been. To judge by the rents paid, the four houses
varied considerably in size.[126] To the south of the
house of 1604 and also fronting on the Corso
were two houses and (at the corner of the block)
the palace of the Mancini family (Fig. 208, J, K,
L). The Mancini house (J) adjacent to the house
of 1604 was also rented for staff members; its
most important resident was D. Geronimo Mercurio, *maestro di casa* of the cardinal.[127] Other
small houses were rented in piazza SS. Apostoli,
vicolo del Piombo (to the southwest of the palace), and elsewhere.[128]

The housing of the Chigi *famiglia* seems not
to have changed the physical character of the
neighborhood, since the old, small buildings
and even their ground-floor shops were maintained. Still, even with his complete and well-defined palace, the cardinal must have desired to
possess the complete city block on which it
stood. The vision of Felice della Greca's expan-

their offices or in attic rooms. According to the
parish census, in 1668, the first year of his residence, only the cardinal with a manservant and a
porter lived in the palace; in 1669 there were an
additional eight persons, including a cook and
his two helpers; and in 1670 the same, with the
addition of four men in the stables.[122]

The cardinal followed the common practice of
housing most of his staff outside the palace, in
nearby buildings: again the parish census is helpful, in some years noting that residents of spe-

sive projects, if not their specific forms, had not been extinguished. The cardinal had purchased the Mandosi property in 1667 and rented houses from the Compagnia di S. Caterina and the Mancini; and in March 1674 it was reported that he intended to buy the Mancini property and join it to his own, with the intention of making a façade on the Corso.[129]

There was no staff kitchen or dining room in the palace. Although many members of the *famiglia* might cook in their apartments (occasionally even in a private "cucinetta"), a new "cucina comune" nevertheless was provided. It was built anew from the foundations after 15 September 1677 (Fig. 208, G). Located against the garden wall of the palace, on a corner of the property purchased in August 1667 from the Mandosi family, its two major rooms measured 34 × 43¾ *palmi* in plan. Above were two other rooms of similar dimensions and then a *guardaroba*.[130] The kitchen could be reached by a subterranean corridor (E) about 5 *palmi* wide, running along the garden wall from the corner of the courtyard of the palace to the stable;[131] or it could be entered from the stable or the houses toward the Corso. Still, there was no *tinello,* and the patrons of the kitchen would have to take their food elsewhere to eat it. The inventory of the palace includes a list of furniture and equipment in the "cucina commune"—presumably the workplace of the "coco commune," his helper, and the kitchen boy listed in the roll of the cardinal's household.[132]

New stables were built as a separate undertaking, beginning in September 1666.[133] The building formed the northwest boundary of the garden. The site plan of 1664 (see Fig. 189) shows a large squarish building toward the street, labeled "stables that are presently being used"; these were to be superseded by the new construction, a long, narrow structure measuring about 51 × 220 *palmi,* according to a plan on the license for taking narrow strips of street and piazza for the new construction, dated 5 September 1666.[134] The stable, built like a retaining wall against the

209   Falda Map of Rome, 1676, detail with Palazzo Chigi (Bibliotheca Hertziana, Rome)

higher garden to the southeast, had entrances toward both the piazza and the vicolo. Above was a loggia of fourteen arches toward the garden.[135] The new stable is shown in Falda's map of 1676 (Fig. 209).

The cardinal's need for carriage houses continued to grow. An undated inventory lists twenty-four carriages in his possession.[136] In addition to the five carriage rooms opening to the courtyard of the palace, he had three more in vicolo di S. Marcello (the modern via SS. Apostoli), on the ground floor of the "palazzetto della famiglia."[137] Another was in one of the houses rented from S. Caterina da Siena, and others were in other rented houses or were rented separately.[138] In 1683 new carriage rooms were made in the buildings to the southeast of the palace, facing the piazza. These were surmounted by a loggia, which could be reached directly from room C4 of the palace by means of a screened passage over an arched bridge (just visible at the far left of Fig. 210).[139]

The elevated walled garden to the northwest of the palace had the usual complement of fountains, statues, and orange trees. There was a sub-

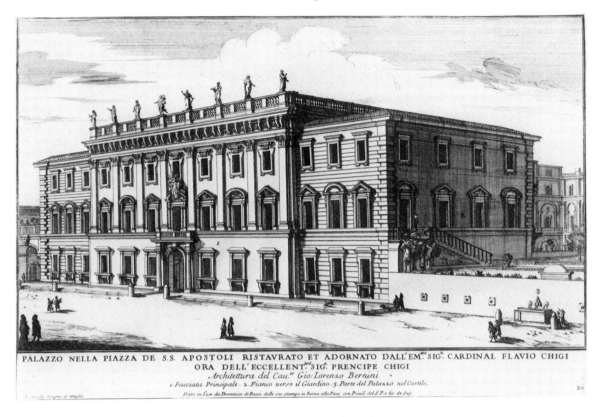

PALAZZO NELLA PIAZZA DE S.S. APOSTOLI RISTAVRATO ET ADORNATO DALL'EM.ᴼ SIG.ᴿ CARDINAL FLAVIO CHIGI
ORA DELL'ECCELLENT.ᴹᴼ SIG.ᴿ PRENCIPE CHIGI
Architettura del Cau.ᵉʳ Gio: Lorenzo Bernini
1. Facciata Principale . 2. Fianco uerso il Giardino . 3. Parte del Palazzo nel Cortile.
Dato in Luce da Domenico de Rossi dalle sue stampe in Roma alla Pace, con Priuil. del S.P.e lic. de Sup.

210   Palazzo Chigi, engraving by Specchi (Biblioteca Apostolica Vaticana)

stantial aviary in the garden, its architectural membering painted the color of travertine.[140] (Indeed, the cardinal seems to have had a special interest in birds: they abound in the painted decoration of his palace, and there was even a "stanzino dell'Ucelliera," its painted ceiling measuring $27\frac{1}{2} \times 14$ *palmi,* in the palace.[141] Birdcages were bought and installed.[142] Many birds were bought,[143] and a parrot was in attendance in the "Appartamento nobile de quadri" on the *piano nobile.*) Another feature of the garden was a "romitorio," or hermitage. There are no clues to its appearance or exact location, but it had a wood ceiling measuring 28×15 *palmi* and was furnished with two small tables, a prie-dieu, and a drum similar to the turnbox customary in women's apartments.[144] The tireless Vincenzo

Corallo worked here too, gilding and painting landscape views peopled with hermits.[145]

In front of the complex and varied assemblage of rooms of the palace, Bernini placed a façade that has long been recognized as a masterpiece (Figs. 210, 211; cf. Fig. 188). Its hierarchical organization is clear. The ground floor provides a base, above which rise the *piano nobile* and a lesser *secondo piano.* The central seven bays are set against the foil of three-bay flanking portions. Distinctions of height, relief, materials, texture, order, and ornament support the basic schema. In the center a giant order of unfluted Composite pilasters stands on the plain stuccoed base of the *pian terreno,* embraces both *piano nobile* and *secondo piano,* and supports an unbroken entablature with bracketed cornice and balustrade; the

i *Palazzo dell' Em.ᵐᵃ Sig· Card.ˡᵉ Chigi.*
2. *Chiesa et Conuento de SS.ᵗᵃ Apoſtoli de P.P.*
Conuentuali. 3 *Palazzo dell' Ecc.ᵐᵃ Sig· Conte=*
stabile Colonna .   *Gio·Batta·Falda· diſ· e fec·*

PIAZZA DE SANTI APOSTOLI.

Per Gio·Iacomo Roſſi in Roma alla Pace co Pri·del·S·P.

4 *Palazzo dell' Em.ᵐᵒ Sig· Card· Bonelli.*
5 *Cuppola della Chiesa della Madonna*
di Loreto .

4

211   Palazzo Chigi, engraving by Falda (Biblioteca Apostolica Vaticana)

verticals of the eight pilasters are continued by the sculpted figures standing against the sky. The color and fine texture of the brick wall contrast with the travertine finish of the architectural enframement. The recessive three-bay side wings are somewhat lower and set back from the plane of the central part. They have no pilasters but are finished with stucco in emulation of drafted masonry—slightly higher in relief and textured on the ground floor, and fine and crisp above the dividing string course (Fig. 212). Stuccoed quoins close the composition at the angles. The hierarchical organization continues in the windows: those on the ground floor have simple frames with brackets below (enframing basement windows) and straight hooded lintels above; the windows of the *piano nobile* are con-

structed enframements of columns or pilasters, entablatures, and triangular or segmental pediments; the *secondo piano* windows have linear enframements; and windows in all three stories in the central eight bays are more elaborate and higher in relief than their counterparts in the side bays. In the centermost bay, the arched entrance is framed by single freestanding Tuscan columns, an entablature, and a balustrade; and the window above, its columns amplified by another pair of columns set within the wall, is surmounted by a coat of arms. The number of bays and the compact proportions combine with the hierarchical distinctions in a unified, complete, and immediately comprehensible composition —virtually a paradigm of the classical ideal.[146] The extension of the façade in 1745, by the Ode-

212 Palazzo Chigi, detail of façade showing textures
of brick and stucco (author)

scalchi and their architect Nicola Salvi (Fig. 213),
only emphasizes the essential unity of Bernini's
composition.

The design represented the culmination of
decades of experimentation in search of a way to
control the broad façade, normally three stories
high, of a city palace. Variations in the spacing of
windows, large or small orders, projections both
forward and upward, contrasting textures, the
subdivision of the façade by quoins, all had been
tried—for example, in Borromini's designs for
Palazzo Carpegna and Palazzo Pamphili in piazza Navona, in the Palazzo della Famiglia
Borghese (see Fig. 38) or Palazzo del Bufalo-Ferraioli, in Bernini's own unfinished Palazzo Ludovisi-Montecitorio. To the order and authority
of the façade of Palazzo Farnese (like Bernini's
Palazzo Chigi, thirteen bays wide) were now
added unity, comprehensibility, and control.
Bernini's designs for the completion of the
Louvre were developed while Palazzo Chigi was
under construction and surely represent an extension of his thinking on the same problem. Yet
the Louvre remained a special case, if only because of its very large size. It was the model of
Palazzo Chigi that would inform palace designs

for decades, not only in Rome but throughout
Europe.[147]

Yet its originality was firmly grounded in
Roman tradition. Michelangelo's buildings on
the Campidoglio are especially important, for
the giant order, the travertine enframement
against a fine brick ground, the balustrade
against the sky, and (in the Palazzo dei Senatori)
the distinction of base and upper stories, center
and sides. Palazzo Farnese, that paragon of all
subsequent Roman palaces, provided the recognizable model for the window enframements.
Bramante's Palazzo Caprini-Raphael and other
Roman palaces of the early sixteenth century
demonstrated the mural ground floor as a base
for the order above. The regularity of the classical elements and their disposition evoked the
Roman tradition of classical antiquity.[148]

Architect and Client

Domenico Bernini wrote that his father, Gianlorenzo, "principiò, et a suo tempo ancora diè
perfezione al Palazzo del Cardinal Flavio Chigi à
SS. Apostoli," and Baldinucci concurred, writing that Bernini "edificò un palazzo dell'Emi-
nentiss. Cardinal Ghigi."[149] Giovanni Pietro
Rossini stated that he had seen the palace built
"from the foundations in the time of Alexander
VII."[150] The documents of construction 1664–
67 bear out the extent of the work, as the building was completely reformed for Cardinal Chigi.
The major *misure* show that almost twice the
cardinal's purchase price of 25,000 scudi was
spent on masonry, stonework, woodwork, and
painting and gilding alone—more than 48,000
scudi.[151] These same documents and other evidence help us understand the contributions of
both architects and clients in the major undertaking.

Between the purchase of the palace in January
1662 and the beginning of construction in July
1664, not only the cardinal but also his uncle
Alexander VII must have discussed with Bernini
the design of the palace. Cardinal Flavio was

213   Palazzo Chigi-Odescalchi, façade (I.C.C.D., Rome, ser. C, no. 4940)

away from Rome at the critical moment of the beginning of construction, as cardinal legate to Paris; he left Rome on 23 April and returned only on 9 October 1664.[152] Meanwhile, according to the diary of Alexander VII, Bernini and the pope consulted regarding the design on 29 June 1664, and a few days later, on 4 July, Bernini brought him a design for the façade.[153] The façade seems to have held primacy, for in all the surviving preliminary plans its distinctive outline is firmly drawn (see Figs. 189, 193, 194).

Only two weeks after its discussion (and in the absence of the cardinal), construction began. Payments "a buon conto" for stonework were almost twice those for masonry in the first five months of construction—an indication that almost immediate attention was given to the façade; indeed, its marble coat of arms is specifically mentioned in the payments of 29 November and 29 December 1664, and its travertine finish had been applied by 12 December 1665.[154]

The drawings prepared by Carlo Fontana (see Figs. 189, 193–196) show a combination of new and old work. The plans show the outline of the façade, the regular spacing of the windows toward the piazza, and the window of anteroom C4 aligned with the enfilade of doors just behind the façade—features that the documents of construction demonstrate to have been part of the work of 1664–67. They also show stair S4 and, behind the carriage rooms, room B18, both additions to the palace in 1664–67. At the same time, they show many things that were to be changed in Bernini's revisions: the subdivided galleries C17 and E18; the partitions in rooms E1, E3, E4, E6, and E19; the absence of stairs S5, S8, and S7; the wall in place of columns at the "alcove" C16; the angled doorway between E13 and E6; the unreformed small house toward via del Corso; and other details. The section (see Fig. 195) shows the heights of walls as they were to be extended upward, along with the profile of the entablature and cornice on the exterior walls to the side; and it shows the "galley" of small rooms to be built over the ceiling of *sala* C5. Yet the partitions in B6 and B12, the doorway in E6, the height of the ceiling in C7, and the absence of ceilings with attic rooms above in E4, E7, and E8, all belong to the state of the building before remodeling. The side elevation (see Fig. 196) shows new work in the two bays toward the façade and, to the left, the old wall height and distribution of windows. While Bernini must have had a general strategy for approaching the problem of providing specialized accommodations for the cardinal within the framework of the existing building, his actual plan was worked out after the design of the façade. The masterly proportions of the façade and the distribution of its openings were developed first — perhaps only as late as Bernini's interview with Alexander VII on 4 July 1664. Fontana's drawings then combined a careful survey of the existing interior with the features of the new design of the exterior that were essential to the working out of the plan. The early decision to add stair S4 must have been derived from the obvious desirability of a private stair in that area; the tiny addition of the "selleria" B18 must simply have filled out the property lines.

A set of quick sketches shows more of Bernini's thinking about the palace — again, it seems, in collaboration with Alexander VII (Figs. 214–216). They are on the four sides of a single folded sheet of paper, and the ideas explored in Bernini's pencil sketches are neatly summarized in Alexander VII's small hand on fol. 64r (seen in reverse, through the paper, in Fig. 214).[155] In the two plans, the outline of the building, with the distinctive projection of the façade (the one aspect of the design already established), is drawn firmly. On fol. 64v, Bernini considers the relation of the stables (begun in 1666) to the palace: the long bar-shaped building along via SS. Apostoli might be connected with the palace by a gallery or corridor along the piazza, the resultant L-shaped structure enframing the garden a formal counterpart to the L-shaped loggia of the squarish courtyard. The section of the stables is explored in fol. 67v: a one-story vaulted structure accommodating two rows of stalls along a central aisle would have a simple gabled roof (Fig. 215). A second idea is superimposed on this — a similar vaulted structure atop the stable. Fol. 64r seems to be a consideration of the plan of the stable. In fol. 67r, Bernini and the pope turn to the palace itself (Fig. 216). The regularization of the courtyard is discussed. Bernini scribbles in the piers and columns of Maderno's arcade, proposes the renovation of the carriage houses to the southwest as a counterpart to the loggias, cuts another loggia beyond the garden wall as the fourth side of the courtyard, and draws a big X to encompass the newly defined volume of the courtyard, its center now clearly established (perhaps by a fountain). The axis of entry to the palace would pass through the southeastern loggia and terminate in a wall fountain, indicated in the sketch by a heavy dot. The whole development is set within the larger context of the building, where once again the strong composition of the façade shows its primacy: its center is strongly marked; the axis of vision and movement extends from that dot to the dot representing the fountain; and that same axis becomes the fulcrum around which the whole palace is organized, the volume of the courtyard being the counterpart of the mass of the rooms to the left. Looking beyond the sketch

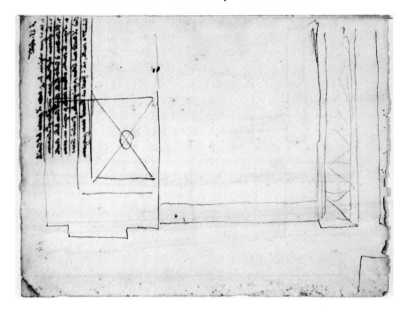

214 Palazzo Chigi, sketch by Bernini (Biblioteca Apostolica Vaticana, Chigi a.I.19, fol. 64v)

to what we have already learned of the disposition of rooms within the palace, we see that that same axis balances the cardinal's collections of art to the left against his representational life to the right, with the innermost rooms of his apartments on both *piano nobile* and *secondo piano* aligned along it. The consultation of architect and client completed, Alexander VII takes the sheet and summarizes the results of the session:

At SS. Apostoli:

1. If possible, run the portico around the entire courtyard.
2. The fountain opposite the portal, with the loss of the carriage room there.
3. The corridor or gallery from the house to the corner of the stable.
4. Above the stable, raise rooms, and cover it with a roof. Thus the courtyard will be open and larger, the house, garden, and stable will be united, and the monks [at S. Marcello] will not be able to see in so well."[156]

Ideals of containment, regularity, and visual control are interacting with use. In the end, the courtyard was not entirely surrounded by a loggia, but the carriage rooms reflected the forms of the loggia opposite; the fountain opposite the entrance portal was replaced by a statue in a niche, and the carriage room B27 in that location was not forfeited; the corridor to the stable was not built; above the stable, not rooms but a loggia open to the garden was built. The consultation must have taken place after the establishment of the façade design (July 1664) but before the beginning of construction of the stables (September 1666). Bernini was absent from Rome, on his trip to Paris to provide designs for the completion of the Louvre, from May through December 1665. The discussion may reasonably have occurred between July 1664 and May 1665, and even before Cardinal Flavio Chigi's return from Paris on 9 October 1664.

The documents of construction reveal similar concerns in the remodeling. Regularity, order, and expansiveness seem paramount. Rooms are enlarged by the removal of partitions. They are regularized by the reshaping of walls — for example, the cutting back of a wall in library E6 "to

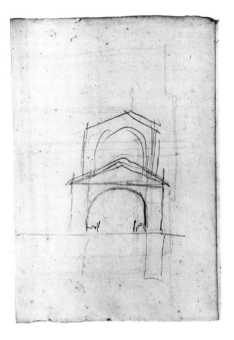

215   Palazzo Chigi, sketch for stable, by Bernini (Biblioteca Apostolica Vaticana, Chigi a.I.19, fol. 67v)

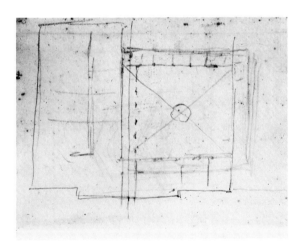

216   Palazzo Chigi, sketch by Bernini (Biblioteca Apostolica Vaticana, Chigi a.I.19, fol. 67)

straighten it."[157] Windows and doors are reshaped and shifted to align them and to provide long vistas, correspondences, and orthogonal relationships — for example, the doors of the *sala* C5 are "messe à filo"; the two doors of gallery C17 are removed and "reinstalled opposite one another"; in the courtyard the façades of the four carriage rooms are given arches, pilasters, and oval windows to correspond to those of the loggia opposite; and the entrance to library E6 is shifted from the angled passage in a corner to a proper orthogonal doorway from room E12.[158] The vista through the enfilade behind the façade on the *piano nobile* is continued through the window in the southeast wall of room C4, explicitly shifted for the purpose, to the wall of the house across the narrow vicolo del Piombo, where Vincenzo Corallo painted an enframement of Doric pilasters and architrave for a distant fluvial landscape;[159] not having the open space beyond his palace that Giovanni Battista Borghese enjoyed a few years later, the cardinal elongated his view by artificial means. Ceilings are raised in *sala* C5, library E6, E7, and even little chapel E8.[160] The floor was probably raised in E7, too, to minimize any disjunction among the rooms of the *secondo piano* while at the same time providing a more expansive anteroom (C7) below: Fontana's section (see Fig. 195) shows four steps (and a distance of about 4 *palmi*) between the floor levels of E6 and E7, but the *misura* of stonework specifies only a single stone step (that is, two risers) between E6 and E7 and another at the door of E9.[161] The basic cellular structure of the building is maintained, including its rectangular rooms and standard switchback stair. Public and private circulations are carefully controlled. Sumptuousness is achieved through the finishes of the rooms — colored marble doorframes in place of old travertine frames, painted and gilded ceilings (costing the astounding sum of 9,378.62 scudi), and rich fabric revetments.

Bernini, his assistants, and his clients attended closely to the work. From the beginning, Bernini signed the bills for the work to authorize their payment. While he was away from Rome, from May through December 1665, his brother Luigi Bernini acted in his behalf and signed the bills;[162] but Gianlorenzo's supervision resumed on his return and continued until October 1666, when Carlo Fontana began to supervise the work.[163] Even then, the introduction to the *misura* of masonry makes it clear that Fontana was conscientiously carrying out the work as prescribed by Bernini.[164] Several references in the documents of construction show that Bernini was responsible for certain decisions in the course of construction: for details of the stonework of the windows in the center part of the façade;[165] for visually monitoring the progress on the new ceiling of the *salone,* involving the repeated removal and reerection of scaffolding;[166] for providing Antonio Chiccheri with the design for the woodwork in the library.[167] Meanwhile, the cardinal too gave directions: the window toward the vicolo del Piombo was opened to complete the enfilade of doors on the *piano nobile* according to his order;[168] and a door newly made at the foot of stair S3 was walled up again at his command.[169] Alexander VII kept an eye on the progress of the work, watching from a distance, from the Quirinal palace, and also visiting the site, according to his diary, on 6, 8, 10, and 13 July 1665 (that is, during Bernini's absence from Rome); he especially noted the beginning of the roofing on 8 July and the library on 10 July.[170]

The resulting palace is a combination of the generalized and the particular. The reuse of existing structures, whatever their formal shortcomings, is typically Roman; and even Bernini, Alexander VII, and Flavio Chigi, designers and patrons with a strong sense of their own individuality, were willing to accept that matrix. The new façade, original but founded in Roman tradition, eschewed idiosyncrasy in favor of a universality that would inspire countless designs throughout Europe. In both plan and elevation Bernini employed what might be called "standard parts"—rectangular rooms, switchback stairs, normative classical orders, and so forth—in contrast, for example, to the great variety of forms that his contemporary Borromini deployed in his designs for Palazzo Carpegna. The planning accommodated the institutions and customs of aristocratic Roman life, in their most modern form—that is, very long apartments, multiple audience rooms, a representational bedroom, a ground-floor summer apartment and sculpture gallery, minimal space for the *famiglia,* and so forth. Yet at the same time the planning was so particularized that only Flavio Chigi could live there, in place of the two married couples and women attendants who had resided in the smaller palace before 1661. The approximately one hundred rooms would accommodate only one important person, and only a man, with his specialized interests in books, paintings, and sculptures, in summer and winter. His nephew lived in the "secondo appartamento nobile" in 1689,[171] but we know neither the identity of these rooms nor the rearrangements in the cardinal's pattern of life that made this intrusion possible. In the end, the formal wholeness of the masterly façade has its counterpart in the functional wholeness of the plan.

Epilogue

STRETCHING back into the sixteenth century or even to antiquity, the lives of the five palaces explored in Part II extend forward to the present day. Amenable to modification, they have repeatedly bent to changes in circumstances and uses.

Nineteenth-century plans and inventories of the Palazzo Borghese show reshaped apartments with new uses.[1] The twin apartments of the *piano nobile* in the Ripetta wing were made into a single apartment, with a new bed alcove surrounded by *retrocamere* pushing from C11 into C15. The old *salone* C19 was subdivided both horizontally and vertically. A bath was installed at C20, and a dining room at C18. Elliptical chapel A20 became a "Caffeaos" adorned with Japanese porcelain vases. Inventories describe rich French-inspired decor, in the wake of the marriage of Camillo Borghese (1775–1832) to Napoleon's sister Pauline Bonaparte (1780–1825) in 1803. Meanwhile, the ground-floor apartments and "Appartamento grande" of the *piano nobile,* attractive to Tessin and other earlier visitors because of the vast collection of paintings, were formally opened to tourists and students according to rules established on 4 August 1818: from 9:00 A.M. until 4:00 P.M. (3:00 P.M. from October through March), under the direction of the *scopatore* Vincenzo Rotati.[2]

The paintings were transferred to the Villa Borghese on the Pincio in 1891, and a decade later both villa and collections of art were sold to the State. In 1922 the *piano nobile* of the palace became the seat of the Circolo della Caccia, one of whose founding members was Francesco Borghese (1847–1926; son of Marcantonio V).[3] Today's visitor can find oriental rugs for sale in the former Galleria dei Quadri, members of the Spanish Embassy at work in the rooms above, private residents in some smaller apartments, and cars parked in the courtyard—much as carriages would have waited there in the seventeenth century.

After the death of Antonio Barberini, the "Casa Grande" ai Giubbonari fell into neglect and disrepair.[4] Eventually, in 1734, Cardinal Francesco Barberini (1662–1738; nephew of Cardinal Carlo) was able to find a purchaser for the vast block, the Discalced Carmelites of S. Teresa.[5] The monks converted the columned entrance hall to a chapel dedicated to S. Teresa and S. Giovanni della Croce (its façade noted in the caption to Vasi's engraving, Fig. 84, no. 1) before selling the palace to the Monte di Pietà only twenty-five years later, in 1759. Houses to the left of the entrance hall/chapel, which had eluded the purchase of Taddeo Barberini in the 1640s, finally were acquired to complete the uniform if undistinguished southeast façade of the block (see Fig. 90); a spacious elliptical vestibule and stair were constructed in the area of the small houses in 1759–61 under the direction of the architect Nicola Giansimoni; and offices of the Depositeria Generale della Camera Apostolica, the Banco dei Depositi, and the Archivio del Monte di Pietà were arranged in the rooms of the former Barberini palace.[6] Now belonging to the Comune di Roma, the huge palace seems completely absorbed by the city. Contini's entrance hall, later a church, was a theater in the 1930s (see Fig. 83) and now—in a deplorable state of disrepair—is a bar and gaming room. Giansimoni's vestibule leads to the Scuola Materna "Trento e Trieste" and the Istituto Magistrale "Vittoria Colonna." Children's artwork adorns the upper windows of the palace; the courtyard is fenced off as a playground. Ground-floor shops —suppressed in the later Barberini remodelings —have reasserted themselves along the busy via dei Giubbonari.

In the nineteenth century the area around Palazzo Barberini alle Quattro Fontane was much favored by foreigners. From 1822 until 1834 the Barberini theater housed the studio of the Danish sculptor Thorvaldsen. In 1856 the American sculptor William Wetmore Story and his family rented an apartment on the *secondo piano* of the north wing, with the attic rooms above, which he described in a letter to an American friend: "I never saw anything more rambling than the upper rooms above the apartment which are to be included in our lease. They are legion in number and crop out at every new visit. I should think there are some twenty at least, of every kind and shape, going oddly about, up little stairs, through curious holes, into strange lumber-rooms and then suddenly opening into large and admirable chambers."[7] When Nathaniel Hawthorne came to visit the Story family, he found Barberini retainers in the basement of the north wing and a painting gallery on the ground floor (entered near the elliptical stair); and he reported that the palace "is inhabited by a cardinal, a prince, and a duke, all belonging to the Barberini family, and each having his separate portion of the palace, while their servants have a common territory and meeting-ground in this noble hall"

(*salone* C1).[8] In 1902 the famous Barberini library and its shelving by Soria were sold to the Vatican. Today the ground floor and, in the south wing, the *piano nobile* are occupied by the Circolo delle Forze Armate; the Galleria Nazionale di Arte Antica fills the north wing of the *piano nobile* and the *secondo piano*. A visit to the gallery, however, follows a course exactly the reverse of a visit to Anna Barberini in those same rooms in 1632: the first rooms of the gallery are the innermost rooms of Anna's apartment, beginning in her former bedroom C26 and ending under Pietro da Cortona's "Divina Providenza" in the *salone* C1.

The Palazzo Colonna-Barberini in Palestrina, too, now houses a museum—the Museo Nazionale Archeologico Prenestino, whose greatest treasure is the Nile mosaic installed there by Francesco Barberini in 1640 (but now displayed on a vertical surface in the uppermost room of the building). Here the history of the structure seems almost to have come full circle: thanks to the restoration of the 1950s, its ancient state is reemerging through the palace of the sixteenth and seventeenth centuries, as Roman column bases are exposed beneath glass panels in the floor of the entrance hall and twin *sale* A3 and A13, and *opus incertum* is revealed beneath later plaster. The years of Barberini occupancy seem but a fleeting moment in the two-millennia-long history of the sanctuary of Fortuna Primigenia.

After Cardinal Flavio Chigi's death in 1693, his palace was rented to the Odescalchi family, who eventually purchased it in 1745 and greatly enlarged it, more than doubling the length of its façade. Although Bernini's forms were maintained, his compact, coherent composition was abandoned in favor of an expansive design that might be interpreted as a vindication of the vision of Felice della Greca. For fourteen years the British School in Rome was housed on the *secondo piano* of the palace.[9] Today, in what was once Cardinal Chigi's summer apartment, Corallo's airy paintings float above the high-tech installation of a photo equipment shop.

Tremendous changes in the social, economic, and political life of Rome in the past three hundred years have not rendered the five buildings obsolete. Perhaps it is enough to attribute their survival to the traditional Roman insistence on maintaining and reshaping structures for new uses — the same process that was at work in the forming of the five palaces in the seventeenth century. Nevertheless, the principle of planning that informed the buildings then — the establishment of an articulate framework within which persons could arrange their activities according to circumstances — has proved generous enough to accommodate even the diverse uses of the twentieth century. Successive designers have not been bound by a module or a preconceived geometry or been limited by exceedingly particularized forms. The subdivision of the huge palaces for disparate contemporary occupants is actually facilitated by seventeenth-century patterns of circulation and groupings of rooms into apartments, which insist on the control of access to well-defined territory.

Yet as these buildings stretch forward in time, they intersect a century of tremendously varied building activity. In the seventeenth century, even a single architect was involved with a wide range of architectural production. Carlo Maderno's practice, for example, included not only four of the five palaces studied here, but also the nave and façade of St. Peter's — the most prominent commission of his day — and the routine measurement of small houses preliminary to their sale.[10] Bernini was designing the piazza before St. Peter's even while he concerned himself with the details of Cardinal Chigi's stable. Countless architects — the likes of Giovanni Maria Bonazzini and Angelo Torrone — not only labored to fill the interstices between great monuments but also contributed in one way or another to some of Rome's major commissions. Clearly, an account of seventeenth-century Roman architecture must involve more than a simple stylistic polarity between "baroque" and "classical," with perhaps a glance at "the other side of the medal."[11] If there is an overarching theme, it is perhaps one of attitude, that then manifests itself in various modes and styles: the enthusiasm for improvisation, whether in retrofitting a row house as a stable or in reshaping the entire organization of a Palazzo Borghese, whether in making sense of various fragments and restrictions to produce the great complex of St. Peter's or in incorporating in the new entrance hall of the "Casa Grande" ai Giubbonari the antique sculptures discovered only in the excavations for its foundations. Out of circumstances comes wholeness; and in that whole there is always the possibility of further change.

Appendix 1

ASF, Medici del Principato, vol. 2658, undated but ca. 1644, unpaginated[1]

Nota de' trattamenti, soliti usarsi in Roma verso gli Ambasciatori del Serenissimo Granduca di Toscana, et di quelli, che da loro si usano verso gli altri.

Sogliono i Cardinali ricever l'Ambasciatore del Gran Duca Serenissimo dentro ò fuori della Porta dell'Appartamento, che riesce in sala. Alcuni però per l'eccesso di cortesia, vengono anche à mezza sala, et tutti quasi accompagnano vicino alla scala, senza arrivarvi, per distinguerli dalli Ambasciatori Regij. Ve ne sono però alcuni che arrivano anche alla scala, ma si deve ricever per soprabbondanza di cortesia, non per obbligo. Le famiglie dei Cardinali ricevono à capo la scala, ò fuori della sala, et accompagnano alla Carrozza.

Tutto il Collegio indifferentemente dà titolo di Eccellenza, comprendendovisi anche i Cardinali nipoti del Papa dominanti, et i Cardinali Nazionali delle Corone, essendovi questi ultimi condescesi in tempo dell'Ambasciatore Niccolini.

In casa dell'Ambasciatore di Toscana tutti i Cardinali si ricevono à capo della scala, et si accompagnano al Cocchio.

Gli Ambasciatori Regij ora ricevono, et accompagnano l'Ambasciatore di Toscana nel medesimo modo dei Cardinali, benche all'arrivo in Roma del sudetto Ambasciatore Niccolini non accompagnassero più che à mezza scala. Questi non danno titolo di Eccellenza, per spareggiarsi, et però il prefato Ambasciatore Niccolini, ha desiderato, et procurato piùtosto il trattamento in terza persona, che quello dell'Illmo, oggi comune anche à molti Cavalieri privati, come manco considerato, et di meno apparenza.

L'Ambasciatore di Toscana li riceve in casa propria al Capo della scala, et và al Cocchio, dando loro il titolo di Eccellenza.

Col duca di Bracciano, duca Caetano, come Grande di Spagna, Principe di Sulmona, et quello di Piombino, ò di Venosa, duca Sforza, Contestabile Colonna, il quale, che l'Ambasciatore Niccolini si ricordi, non è mai // entrato in casa del Granduca, si hanno à ricevere, et fare trattamenti eguali di parità, come ancora con i Nipoti secolari dei Papi viventi. A tutti questi, fuori che allj Duchi Caetano, et Sforza, si fa sonare anche la Campanella, purche siano Grandi di Spagna, perche nel resto ai Nipoti de' Papi defunti, quando non sono tali s'è levato il sudetto suono di Campana, et fù osservato col duca di Fiano, fratello di Papa Gregorio, ma non già col figlio oggi Principe di Piombino, perche è Grande di Spagna.

Al Principe di Carbognano, à quello di Gallicano, et D. Ferdinando Orsino Duca di S^to Gemini, non si arriva alla Carrozza, ma doppo di haverli ricevuti à mezza sala, si lasciano in piè di Scala, tornandosene in dietro col Maestro di Camera, doppo una breve licenza.

Nel medesimo modo si tratta anche il Duca della Cornia, et tutti questi in Casa loro, incontrano à capo della Scala, et vengono alla Carrozza, dando, et ricevendo dall'Ambasciatore titolo pari di Eccellenza.

Col Duca Altemps si diede in un'eccesso di accompagnarlo al Cocchio, et di lasciarlo partire prima di tornare in dietro, d'ordine del Sr Bali Cioli, quando il medesimo Duca tornò di Firenza con la Sra Duchessa Angelica Medici sua sposa. Si riceve però à mezza sala, come gli altri. Veggasi ora quel che paia di fare, et se sia da pigliarne qui altri ordini, ò pure continuare.

Il Duca Cesarini ha voluto sempre per sua elezione, et eccesso di cortesia, restare à capo di scala, benche l'Ambasciatore Niccolini si sia ingegnato di scender tutta la prima branca. Egli nondimeno doppo lungo contrasto l'hà necessitato di tornare in dietro, prima di volersi partire dal suddetto posto di capo della scala. Si potrebbe però, se no lo proibisse come hà fatto altre volte, scender le scale et trattarlo come Carbognano, Gallicano, et Cornia. In casa sua riceve l'Ambasciatore à capo de scala, et accompagna al Cocchio. //

Il Duca Latera, di Casa Farnese, vuole anch'egli rimanere à Capo di Scala, et si potrebbe scender la prima branca. Anche à questi si dà, e si riceve titolo pari d'Eccellenza.

Tutti i Primogeniti delle Case grandi, come Borghese, Caetano, Duca di Unano, et simili, s'hanno à lasciare à capo della scala, incontrandoli al principio della sala, con titolo d'Eccellenza, purche siano i primi à darlo all'Ambasciatore. Ma quello di Rossano non è mai comparso in casa del medesimo Ambasciatore, senza il Principe suo padre, forse per non si dispareggiare.

A secondigeniti del Duca di Bracciano, Duca Sforza, Principe di Massa, et simili, purche non siano in Prelatura, s'è data la mano, et si son ricevuti nella seconda stanza doppo la sala, et accompagnati tutta la medesima sala, con titolo d'Illustrissimo se han dato quello dell'Eccellenza all'Ambasciatore. Quando sono Prelati,

come Monsignor Sforza, Monsignor Cibo, et simili, si pigliano à man manca, usando loro nel resto tutti gli altri medesimi trattamenti. Così si è usato con Monsignor Sforza presente, con Monsignor Cesarini vivente, et con l'altro suo fratello defunto, cherico di Camera, che fù poi Cardinale, et con Monsignor Cibo ancora, al quale, entrato in Prelatura, l'Ambasciatore Niccolini fece significare, per mezzo di amico comune, prima di volerlo ricevere, di non poter continuare nel medesimo trattamento di man dritta, per l'esempio degli altri. Comparve nondimeno come prima, ricevendo la man manca, et oggi si è in questo possesso.

Al Marchese Lanti, come marito d'una zia della serenissima Granducchessa, si dà la mano con titolo di Illustrissimo ò in terza persona, come più piacerà al Sr Ambasciatore. Si riceve et si tratta come i Secondigeniti de duchi. La Sra Marchesa sua moglie è in possesso dell'Eccellenza, come zia // della prefata Serenissima.

A marchesi per ordinario non si dà la mano, come al Marchese Riario, Marchese Gualengo, Marchese Tassoni, Marchese Bentivogli Nipote del Cardinale et simili. Ai Marchesi poi Torres, Raggi, Bernardino Nari, et simili di case Romane, che possano per gentili, si fà un poco di trattamento migliore, che ai Cavalieri ordinarij, senza titolo, à elezione del Sr Ambasciatore.

Se vi fosse poi qualche Marchese di Case grandi, in questo ci vuole la distinzione, secondo la prudenza del Sr Ambasciatore sudetto.

A mandati de' Principi, come semplici loro gentiluomini, senza titolo di Residenti, non si dà la mano, et quanto al titolo di Illustrissimo si può largheggiare, secondo la condizione, et qualità della lor Casa. Con altri non tanto qualificati per lor medesimi parlar in terza persona. Così è stato trattato il Sigr di Lione mandato dal Rè Cristianissimo. Col Sigrio di Venezia Sr Girolamo Bon, et col Marchese Montecuccoli mandato dal Duca di Modana, Sigrrio Monguidi, mandato dal duca di Parma, et altri simili.

A tutti i Ministri de Duchi Serenissimi che habbino titolo di Residenti appresso S. Santità si dà la mano, si ricevono al fine della seconda stanza doppo la sala, et si accompagnano à mezza sala, ò due terzi, col titolo d'Illustrissimo.

A quelli delle corone, come Pollonia, et simili, si fanno gli stessi trattamenti, vantaggiandoli solo nell'accompagnatura di tutta la sala. Tutti questi ricevono in Casa loro l'Ambasciatore à Capo di scala, alcuni scendono qualche scaglione, et vengono alla Carrozza con trattarlo d'Eccellenza.

Quando vengono di nuovo alla Corte i sudetti Residenti, et anche gli Ambasciatori // di Bologna, et di Ferrara, si manda à complir con loro un Gentiluomo, per darli il Bene arrivato.

Li Ambasciatori di Bologna, et di Ferrara si ricevono nella prima Stanza doppo la Sala, et si accompagnano sino sopra la soglia della Porta grande della medesima Sala.

I Residenti tutti indifferentemente, ò Reggij ò ducali, et i due sudetti Ambasciatori di Bologna et di Ferrara, hanno à esser i primi à visitare, poi si restituisce loro la Visita. Mantova fà del disgustato, perche non si vuol dar titolo d'Eccellenza à suoi Ambasciatori, et però il suo Residente non venne à veder l'Ambasciatore Niccolini, benche questo mandasse à complir seco subito giunto. Non è però bene di entrare in alcuna sorte di dimostratione senz'ordine.

Alli Amici et affezzionati, et anche ai sudditi qualificati, et à dame che arrivino di nuovo à Roma, ricordarsi di mandar subito à dar loro il ben'arrivato, per termine di cortesia, et le dame andare à visitarle di persona.

Ai Patriarchi si dà la mano col titolo d'Illustrissimo, si ricevono al fine della seconda Stanza doppo la Sala, e si accompagnano tutta la Sala.

Gli Archivescovi et Vescovi tutti si ricevono à man manca nella seconda Stanza doppo la Sala, chi al principio di essa, chi al mezzo, e chi al fine, secondo le qualità loro, et si accompagnano à mezza sala. Si son trattati, quanto à titolo, chi in terza persona, et chi con l'Illustrissimo, secondo la nascita loro.

L'Archivescovo di Pisa Medici, benche ritenesse l'Ambasceria di Spagna, quando venne à Roma, per esaminarsi, fu trattato come gli altri Archivescovi, allungandosele solo l'accompagnatura fino alla Porta della Sala. //

Gli Auditori di Ruota, et Cherici di Camera si ricevono à man manca nella seconda Stanza, et si lasciano al principio della sala, dove stà il Decano de'Palafrenieri. Il Decano della medesima Ruota si tratta un poco meglio nell'accompagnatura, arrivandosi à mezza sala, et à questi da un tempo in quà si è dato l'Illustrissimo.

Gli altri Prelati tutti si ricevono, et si accompagnano come i suddetti Cherici di Camera, et Auditori di Ruota, et si trattano in terza persona, se però non siano figli di duchi, ò di nascita grande et case conspicue, come vi sono molti figli di Baroni, et titolati del Regno di Napoli, et dello stato di Milano, ai quali si è dato titolo d'Illustrissimo.

Ai Prelati destinati Nunzij non si è data mai la mano; solamente si sono accompagnati più del solito, et titolo d'Illustrissimo.

Al Nunzio destinato per Firenze, s'è data la mano per conservarsi il possesso di quel che fù in Firenze il Nunzio di S. Santità ai Cavalieri, subito che sono dichiarati Ambasciatori à Roma, che gli onora della mano. Così usò Monsignor Valieri poi Cardinale con l'Ambasciatore Niccolini, et Monsignor Giglioli, quando il sudetto Ambasciatore venne à Firenze più anni sono per suoi privati Interessi. Ai medesimi Nunzij subito dato parte, si rende la Visita.

Quando il S. Duca Salviati venne à Roma la prima volta, fù comandato di trattarlo come Parente della Casa Serenessima, et con ogni sorte di onore, con lettera patente del S. Bali Cioli. S'è usato però, di riceverlo à mezza sala, et di accompagnarlo tutta la prima branca della Scala con titolo di Eccellenza.

A tutti i Cavalieri privati sudditi, et non sudditi, la man manca, accompagnandoli secondo la qualità delle lor Case, chi tutta la seconda // Stanza doppo la sala, et chi al principio, et chi al mezzo della prima doppo la Sala allargandosi più, o meno, nel titolo d'Illustrissimo ò in terza persona. Et perche oggi ognuno par, che sfugga di havere del V.S., fuora dei sudditi, si è usato assai di parlare, come sopra in terza persona.

Tutti i Generali delle Religioni si sono ricevuti à man manca al principio della seconda stanza doppo la sala, et accompagnati sino alla porta, che và in sala, senza però uscir di essa, con titolo di Reverendissimo.

Don Ferdinando Orsino andrebbe accompagnato, et trattato al pari di Carbognano, et Gallicano, ma perche à mio credere, dubità di non esser accompagnato alla Carrozza, usa una finezza d'andar sempre à visitare l'Ambasciatore, dove l'Ambasciatore lo lascia, senza tornar più à rivederlo. Questo non si accompagna alla Carrozza, perche Capo della Casa Orsina è Don Paolo suo fratello, come il Contestabile della Colonnese; et trattandosi però nel modo suddetto, l'altre due Case di Gallicano, et Carbognano, non si può trattar questa in altra forma.

Quando l'Ambasciatore accompagna i Cardinali all'Appartamento della Ambasciatrice sua moglie, si è usato di tornare à riservirli sino alla Carrozza, quando se ne vanno. Il simile si fà anche à fratelli ò Nipoti del Papa vivente, i quali rendono in Casa propria simil termine di cortesia.

Tra Monsignor Governatore di Roma, et gli Ambasciatori, anche delle Corone, non passano Visite, perche questi tutti si cedono solamente in presenza del Papa, volendo così S. Santità. Fuori poi non intendono di voler seco neanche la parità. Ma perche in riguardo del Cerimoniale, che esercita, si hà spesso occasione di ricorrer à lui, per mezzo però di familiari di Casa, s'è usato di complir seco con un Gentiluomo et offitij di Congratulazione, quando sono assunti à quella Carica.

Il Tesauriere, et l'Auditore della Camera in tempo dell'Ambasceria del S. Giovanni Niccolini, venivano in casa del Granduca, si dava loro la mano, et si accompagnavano à capo della scala, ricevendoli nella prima Camera // doppo la sala, ò in sala medesima, ma quando andò à Roma l'Ambasciatore Francesco Niccolini, trovò che si erano messi in pretensioni più alte, et però si lasciò di praticare con loro.

Il Cardinale Colonna non si è mai visitato, doppo che il Serenissimo Granduca nostro Signore et S.r Principe Giovanni Carlo furono à Roma, per haver negato il titolo d'Altezza al suddetto S. Principe. Sarà però necessario sentir di quà quel che s'habbia à fare, e come trattar seco. Per le strade, incontrandolo l'Ambasciatore Niccolini hà sempre fermato, et egli hà corrisposto. Ma perche il Cardinale hà preteso sempre di trattar in terza persona, anche l'Ambasciatore hà fatto il simile, senza dichiarare titolo d'Eminenza, et tutto è passato sempre bene, et con reciproca cortesia.

Appendix 2

ABarb., Ind. IV, no. 598

Nota di mano di Settimio Paliani, con copia di libretto del cirimoniale, che la Sᴿᵃ D. Constanza Magalotti de Barberini praticava nel ricevere le visite.[1]

Apud Sanctam Agnesem
30 8bris 1681

L'Eccᵐᵃ Sigʳᵃ D'na Costanza Magalotti Barberini cognata della fel. Mem. di Papa Urb. VIII nel principio del pontificato, e successivamente mentre fù Capo di Casa, tenne lo stile nell'essere visitata d'incontrare et ricevere li SSʳⁱ Cardinali la prima Anticamera,[2] fermandosi, et contenendosi dentro la sogla di essa, la quale però usciva nell'incontrare li SSʳⁱ Cardinali Prencipi, procurando di giungere ivi a quel tempo punto, et li raccompagnava con l'istessa distintione la seconda Anticamera, che rispondeva sù la sala delli Parafrenieri con essibire all'EE. loro sempre la mandritta per complimento, Restandovi l'Eccᶻᵃ Sua, et procurandosi nel riceverli, come anche nel riservirli complire sempre di ringratiamento con ciascheduno di essi. Se per sorte essendo insieme non havesse complito il Cardinale Antiano à Nome di tutti.

Con li 3 Ambasciatori Regij, Venetia, Firenze, et Savoia come che nel soglo di Nostro Sigʳᵉ precedevano all'Eccᵐᵒ Sigʳᵉ Don Carlo suo marito, usava l'Eccᶻᵃ Sua di incontrarli più che à Mezo dell'Anticamera et Raccompagniarli verso la Porta della seconda due ò tre passi meno delli SSʳⁱ Cardˡⁱ con distinguere di alquanti passi l'Ambasciatori di Corona, ò Republica dall'altri due di Firenze et Savoia, si come anco poco meno di questi dua Riceveva, et Raccompagnava il Sigᶜ Contestabile Colonna, et Sigᶜ Duca di Bracciano, Prencipi di Stato, Nipoti di Papa gia [*fol. iv*] Grandi di Spagna et Titolati Eccᶻᵃ, et poco meno trattava al Sig. Contestabile Colonna, et Sig. Duca di Bracciano, et con l'istessa proportione contenendosi alquanto più nel Ricevere et accompagnare ha trattato con gl'altri Prencipi di Stato, Nepoti di Papa, Grandi di Spagna, et Titolati di Eccᶻᵃ con sola Distintione et circompettione di fare qualche cosa più verso li Capi delle famigle, che verso l'altri, Ancorche habbia titolo di Eccᶻᵃ, come particolarmente sono della famigla Colonnese et Orsina.

Alli Duca Nuovi di Titolo e di famiglia inferiori alquanto manco et tal differenza la Sua Eccᶻᵃ non teneva ogni volta con il Passo, per essere forsi insieme cercava di farlo con il complimento, et dimostratione di qualche più particolare osequie, et Affetto.

Alli Patriarchi, Archivescovi, Vescovi, Prelati, et Abbati di famiglia Principali, Officiali Maggiori di Palazzo, come Auditore, Tesoriere, Datario, Maggiordhuomo, et Maestro di Camera si è costumato di Incontrarli fuori della porta della camera dell'Audienza, et raccompagnarli tutta la prima Anticamera, uscendo et contenendosi dentro la porta di essa secondo la qualità et conditione di essi. Et con tal proportione sono stati trattati l'Ambasciatori delli nuovi Prencipi Residenti Regij et altri di titolo d'Ill^(mi) cosi li 2 et 3 Geniti delle 2 famigle et li Marchesi pur Principali parimente sono trattati nel soprascritto modo.

L'altri prelati semplici, conti, SS^(ri), et Cavalieri Romani Sua Ecc^(za) si è mossa due ò tre Passi dalla sogla, et nell'uscire et licentiarsi riaccompagnava fuori della porta della Camera dell'Audienza, et con po' di maggiore dimostrazione fatta alli gentilhuomini mandati à complire et fare Ambasciate [*fol. 2r*] per Card^(li) et Ecc^(ze), si come all'Inferiori di essi un poco manco. Nel ricevere ò complire con le dame titolate, si è osservato da Sua Ecc^(za) il ricevere fuori della porta della prima Anticamera l'Ambasciate Regie et l'Altre, che precedevano nel soglo con un poco di differenza non molto notabile fra quelle et queste, alle quali tutte sua Ecc^(za) ha data la mandritta nell'Incontrarli, introdurli sedere, et uscire, come anco ha usato di fare con l'Altre di titolo di Ecc^(za) con la sola Circomspettione avvertita di sopra con li duchi, et titolati.

Nel sedere, come che da sua Ecc^(za), che non volse mai titola, non si usa Baldacchino o Campanella, si e osservato di tenere le sedie delle dame, accostate al muro verso il prospetto della porta e fare la prima d'esse il capo, salvo però quando per commodità dell'altre titolate venute a complire, ò Necessità di sito angusto a ciò fare, si sarrà preso il Meza delle sedie per Capo, et in tal caso allontanate un palmo le sedie di sotto et di sopra puol distinguere al quanto in sito le Principali per le titolate di Ecc^(za).

Si è occorso particolarmente in occasione di buone feste, ò di qualche Congratulatione, et simili complimenti venire molte dame, si è raddoppiato et triplicato ancora se è bisognato l'ordine delle sedie delle dame. Non però quelle delle SS^(re) titolate. Alle donne compagne, damigelle serve et simili cercato di dare luogo in altra camera contigua avanti e dietro quella dell'Audienza con farla avvertire nell'entrare e uscire da un Paggo.

Il raccompagnare dell'Ecc^(me) si è fatto fin'a capo delle Scale con fermarsi sua Ecc^(za) finche quella Sig^(ra) Ambasciatrice ò Duchessa fosse stata à piedi della prima Branca d'esse, et ivi complendo di nuovo voltarsi le spalle all'E.S.; et tal forma et modo si è indifferentemente tenuto con tutte che le precedevano et per lo più con l'altre pure di titolo di Ecc^(za) subordinate sebene con l'Inferiori a questi si è usato non trattenersi ò aspettare che voltino le spalle.

[*fol. 2v*] L'Altre Ambasciatrici Mogle di Residenti, di Principi Marchesi et simili di titolo ò famiglia Ill^(ma) sono state incontrate sù la sogla ò fuori della porta della camera delle visite, ricevute alla mano sinistra con un pò di complimento et nell'uscire et licentiarle acompagnate alla porta della sala di Palafrenieri più ò meno secondo la conditione et qualità di ciascheduna et arbitrio dell'E.S. che tal volta si è compiaciuta fare qualche maggiore dimostratione con alcune Sig^(re) più sue partiali.

Le sorelle nipoti cognate et simili parenti delli SS^(ri) Cardinali o Prencipi d'Ecc^(za), come anco le contesse dame Romane più Principali sono state incontrate alla porta della Camera, et raccompagnate dentro la sogla della porta della sala, et due ò tre passi meno, si è andato facendo con le gentildonne et signore ordinarie.

Settimio Baleani Ser^(re) Obbligatissimo dell'Ecc^(ma) Casa Barberina in Eterno nel vedere la Nuova Libraria adesso aperta in Santa Agnese, osservò questo libretto manuscritto ligato con coperte dorate e vedendo, che era cosa spettante alla glor. mem. della madre della fel. Mem. dell'Em^(mo) già Card^(le) Francesco Barberini P'rone la cui Anima sia in cielo, come piamente si puol sperare, hà stimato bene copiare detto libretto in questo foglio nel medemo luogo della detta Libraria. Et quando Il Sig. Giuseppe Valuta Padrone Amorevolissimo stimasse bene farlo copiare et presentarlo all'Ill^(mo) et Ecc^(mo) Sig. Principe di Palestrina P'rone. Si rimette alla sua Prudenza.

Appendix 3

ABarb., Ind. IV, no. 1254[1]

This biography of Taddeo Barberini is an incomplete draft, with lacunae and emendations. Many internal references to other members of the family make clear that it was written by Cardinal Francesco Barberini, Taddeo's older brother, and addressed to their sister Camilla, a nun. It was composed after Taddeo's death in 1647 and Francesco's subsequent return from exile in France in 1648. It can be dated after 1653, when Taddeo's son Carlo was made cardinal (fol. 14v, "Carlo, hora Cardinale"), but before Camilla's death in 1666. It is an important early source for the life of a little-known figure, his architectural patronage, and seventeenth-century Roman society in general.

Francesco writes from memory—not surrounded by documents in Rome but in pastoral Sabina, where he was Commendatario of the abbey of Farfa. His memory is inevitably both warmed and dulled by time, and he often leaves blank spaces in the text to be filled in later. He invites his sister to "aid or correct" his memory, and it seems that she has complied by adding some notations in the broad left margin. His avowed purpose is to provide a model that younger members of the family can imitate—a model more immediate and poignant because it is drawn not from history or scripture but from their own family. He chooses Taddeo as his subject because of fraternal closeness and Taddeo's unrecognized virtues (fols. 1v–2r).

What value should be placed on this biography? Francesco is very close to his subject, having been present at his birth and having closed his eyes at the end of his life (fol. 1v). From his position within the family, he reveals many anecdotes, especially of Taddeo's accident-plagued childhood, which are not the material of public documentation. Much in Francesco's text can be corroborated by other sources: for example, for our argument, Taddeo's daughter Camilla's brief life, the sequence of operas presented in the Barberini theater in the 1630s, and the extent of his architectural patronage. At the same time, the author is very open in telling the reader that he wants to present Taddeo as an exemplar of virtue, and the tone of his words is consistently complimentary—much in contrast to Pecchiai's picture of Taddeo as a callow youth, street rowdy, and then unfeeling husband.[2]

Francesco does not mention an incident that Pecchiai makes much of. In 1626, when Taddeo was only twenty-three years old, out with two or more other men and some women, he was involved in a street fight in which one person was killed and others possibly injured.[3] Yet it is worth noting Taddeo's youth at the time of the incident; the fact that Pecchiai's evidence is a draft of a brief or motuproprio prepared several years later, when Taddeo's conscience was troubling him and when his uncle Urban VIII wished to ease his conscience and show gratitude for his devotion; and the incongruity of the incident with the rather uninteresting picture of his mildness and attention to domestic affairs consistently presented by the outspoken Venetian ambassadors.[4] Francesco could see this incident as uncharacteristic and even negated by the pope's special absolution, and therefore justifiably suppressed. He specifically states that Taddeo's thoughts and habits remained unaffected by his uncle's election to the papacy (fol. 9r), and further examples of meek behavior continue the pattern established in childhood.

An encounter between Taddeo's cortège and that of the Venetian ambassador Giovanni Pesaro (1630–32), in which precedence was at issue, is recounted by both Francesco (fols. 12r–13r) and Pecchiai.[5] Virtually all of Rome had been offended by Urban's decision that Taddeo as prefect should have precedence over ambassadors and other secular dignitaries. In the present incident, the modern author sees a sign of unjustified arrogance, while the brother describes unfortunate accidents beyond Taddeo's control. Even Pesaro's successor as ambassador, Alvise Contarini (1632–35), refuses to condemn Taddeo for this breach of very sensitive Roman etiquette: he writes of the prefect's apolitical and even asocial behavior and both the ambassadors' and Taddeo's avoidance of situations in which the issue of precedence might arise, concluding that "it is my opinion that he dislikes all the obligations of the Prefecture and that, indifferent to the princes, he is entirely concerned only with his own house."[6]

Pecchiai's third strong indictment of Taddeo concerns the rejection of Anna Colonna Barberini by her husband (as well as by the other men of the family) at a time of crisis in the early years of the papacy of Innocent X.[7] Anna's eloquent letters to her son in Paris, published by Pecchiai, are hard to ignore, but Lodispoto points to the dates of the two letters (just before and just after Anna's presentation of a memorandum in defense of Barberini interests to an assembly at the Capitoline) as an explanation for her state of mind.[8] Still, Francesco's insistence on Taddeo's attention to his wife's desires at other times (fols.

20v, 21r–v) might be read as an attempt to counter criticism of his behavior.

Francesco, the Venetian ambassadors, Pecchiai, and modern readers all look at Taddeo through different eyes. Even the same behavior can receive various interpretations. For example, in Francesco's interpretation, Taddeo's mildness and acquiescence to others' will are seen as virtues; but in the words of the Venetian ambassadors he appears boring. There is an armature of facts around which the various interpretations can play. Through Francesco's obvious enhancement of Taddeo's character, we can perceive values if not facts. The brother admires Taddeo's courage, forebearance, generosity, and submission to the demands of the family in place of any personal desires. His passive role in his own marriage and his conscientious stewardship of family properties are taken as signs of virtue.

Along the way, the narrative gives some insights into the life of a prospering Roman family, not yet of the nobility. Nurses, amusements, illnesses, education, departures of daughters to a convent, a sensible marriage, and, above all, a unified and hierarchical family all make their appearances. The prominence of architecture in both Taddeo's activities and Francesco's account is remarkable. Although much is left out (for example, the names of any architects), we nevertheless can perceive a pattern of motivations, attitudes, priorities, goals, and actions as consistent as the rather mundane and conscientious character of Taddeo Barberini.

Memorie per la vita del Sig.^{e} Prefetto, scritte da S. E.

In questo tempo che lontano dagl' affari e dallo strepito di Roma mi truovo in Sabina,[9] mi sento non solo ritornar nella memoria quello che ben spesso ho desiderato, di lasciare scritta qualche nota delli nostri passati; ma rimproverandomi l'agio et ozio che hò mi necessita. Poiche se bene non mancheranno alli nostri Nepoti esempi grandissimi da imitare cosi dalle memorie sacre come profane, tuttavia li nostri benche di non tanta eminenza forse li persuaderanno d'avantaggio, cosi per la naturalezza che porta la participation del sangue, come che ancora haveranno udito spesso i nomi de quali hora io [1v] loro rappresento l'azione, acciò non il solo nome d'Urbano, Carlo, Tadeo, in loro resti ne le sole imagini dipinte in tavola, o in muro; ma procurino di conservare in se stessi quelle qualità che resero degni di rimanere li nomi e le imagini. Comincierò da Tadeo, cosi perche l'amore più che fraterno mi strinse à lui; li nostri Nipoti sono a lui figli; mà perche havendolo visto nascere seco son vissuto, e dio ha volsuto contro delli desiderij e corso naturale, che io gl'occhij gli chiudessi. Più ancora di questo mi spinge, che havendo egli havuto, come nel discorso verrò dicendo, la fortuna meno che noi altri fratelli propitia, tanto più vivino le virtu di in lui [2r] quali ancora dalla modestia, che dirò con verità, troppa, furono assai ricoperte. Servirò à Voi questa, dilettissima Sorella,[10] perche se bene di mè posteriore di età, e separata per la santa religione dal mondo sete, tuttavia potrete aiutare, o correggere la mia memoria, e concorrere à questo benefitio, che intendo di fare à quelli che ci succedono più che di gloria à quelli che vissero; cosi perche

Illic postquam se lumine vevo etc.

E cosi non impedisce mancamento o satietà d'honori quella gloria, che mercè della divina misericordia, tengo che godino, come ancora per la rozzezza del mio dire privo de' lumi di [2v] saper ben scrivere per dar gran chiaro à quello che io mi studierò di riferire.

Nacque Tadeo di Carlo Barberini e Gostanza Magalotti Barberini in Roma nella casa paterna à Giubbonari nell' anno 1603 alli 16. di Novembre doppo la mezza notte, se io ben mi rammento; fù, come nato di casa fiorentina, battezzato à S. Giovanni de' Fiorentini da Angelo Spagnuolo.[11] Suoi compari furno [Francesco Bracciolini, e Mari Cellesi da Pistoia].[12] Era desiderato assai

cosi per esser nate doppo di me due femine V.R.ᵃ e Maria che Dio chiamò al Cielo, come ancora per non esser doppo questa, sopravissuto che poche hore un' altro Tadeo per il parto immaturo [3r] non havendo ancora toccato del nono mese. N'ra Madre per haver maggior felicità ne' parti era stata alli bagni di S. Casciano con nostro Padre, essendo appresso passati in Perugia nel borgo di S. Pietro godessimo il rimanente della state in una vita molto dolce e tranquilla. Di me posso dire che ancora in quell'età non hebbi minori in me li desiderij di havere un fratello, di quello che fosse negl' altri di casa: o perche troppo sentissi quella solitudine, o che il proprio amore mi traportasse più là dell'istesso discorso e consideratione ad havere che con subentrare alla vita travagliosa, non rendesse la mia più felice. Io mi ricordo che volsi giucare con il n'ro precettore chiamato [3v] D. Bernardino Scala, hora Vescovo di Montefeltro, e pertinacemente sostenevo, che doveva nascermi un fratello, onde ne guadagnai un par di guanti; havendo volsuto nostro Padre che io a lui pagassi quello che più avantaggio m'haverebbe vinto, se nasceva femmina. La grandezza e la faccia che Tadeo doppo hebbe, piena di venustà nell' uscire dalle materne viscere dimostrò, e cosi ancora tra le fasce crescendo; poiche particolarmente li capelli che gli nacquero di color d'oro, e ricciuti l'ornavano. Ma appena dalla nutrice divezzo essendo un giorno lasciato da una donna in l'altare della cappella di casa, ne cadde, e dà tal percossa essendogli causata febbre [4r] tanto più grande, quanto la cagione restava ignota; finche il vedersegli una costa o rotta o slogata palesò la caduta, et estorse la confessione del succerro. Fù si grave e lunga questa malattia, che lo pose in pericolo della vita, e gli fece cadere la chioma. Ne di li a pochi mesi si stette in minor paura, che la faccia e forma patisse; poiche essendo sopragiunto il vaivolo gli ricoperse di modo il volto, che restorno per più giorni chiusi gl'occhij, consolando la cecità, e l'accidente del male con sonare una picola chitarra e farsi tirare per casa con un carretto, mostrando ancora in questo caso e tenera età quella posatezza e mansuetudine, che non fù mai da lui disgiunta in tutto il resto [*4v*] della sua vita. Fù il sudetto mal del vaivolo in lui più pericoloso, come che era di complessione sanguigna e melanconica. Occorse andare à Fiorenza per mettere in monasterio V.R.ª e Maria nostra sorella, e vennevi ancora Tadeo, al quale non mancarono delle disgratie; poiche andandosi a spasso per la Città caduto egli dal cocchio, gli passo sopra la gamba una ruota, però per gran benefizio di Dio non l'offese. Tornato in Roma cominciò conforme sogliono li putti ad apprendere li primi rudimenti et elementi della lingua latina. Con tutta la sua modestia discorreva seco cosi di queste, come d'altre cose il Sigʳ Vincenzo Laurefice gentilhuomo Siracusano [*5r*] non solo buon Theologo e mathematico, dotto nella lingua greca et Hebraica, ma che quanto voleva operare come nuovo Archimede perfettionava, tratenuto perciò et amato da nostro zio; quale essendo venuto dal palazzo à S. Giacomo Scossa cavallo dove all hora habitava alla nostra casa de Giubbonari, che si fabricava, nel rientrare in carrozza preso Tadeo dal detto Sigᵉ Vincenzo in collo come se portar via lo volesse, venne dall'alto un vaso di [*blank*] urtato da un travicello di falegname, et urtando la coscia del Sigᵉ Vincenzo lo fece cadere, siche tutto indolito fù à braccia posto nella carrozza, lasciando intrepido Tadeo, e [*5v*] tutti quanti attorno erano attoniti. Quando per il monacamento di V.R.ª si tornò à Fiorenza, d'onde s'andò a Bologna dove nostro zio era legato e di la à Loreto e poi all'Avernia, per tutto dove la carrozza non poteva andare che furno più giornate, Tadeo benche piccolo, di nove in dieci Anni d'età, faceva il viaggio à cavallo. Passammo per Arezzo, e mentre con gl'altri s'usciva dalla Chiesa Cathedrale, un mattone che dall'alto della detta Chiesa cadde lo rasentò in maniera, che non senza il divin' aiuto salvolo vedemmo. Tornati à Roma seguitò Taddeo li studij della Grammatica nel Collegio Romano, dove ancora finì la filosofia. Mentre frequentò queste [*6r*] scuole si rese non tanto celebre per l'ingegno pronto, quanto per l'attentione, maturità e tenacità di quello haveva appreso; aggiustato in tutte le sue azzioni; e cosi ripieno di modestia che da tutti era ammirato, et in particolare dal Pʳᵉ Mutio Vitelleschi all'hora Generale amato e con singolarissime lodi commendato. Et in vero non havevano nè li Maestri, ne altri in che riprenderlo, cosi più dedito al silenzio che al parlare, et in questo si circonspetto, che più relegioso, che secolare appariva. Essendo ancora stato frequente nell'orationi, e nelli santissimi sagramenti senza certa affettazione, che più alla [*blank*] che alla pietà conferisce, li suoi spassi erano la ritiratezza, procurando [*6v*] di tener tutto quello che haveva ben netto e compito. Passava ancora questa sua ritiratezza col fare delle miniature, delle quali se ne vedono alcune à Castel Gandolfo e per casa in alcuni piccoli quadretti da lui illuminati in modo che paiono fatti à olio. Dell'età di quindici in sedici anni fù giudicato non havere per li costumi più bisogno di precettore. Onde venne à star in casa di nostro zio, dove più vecchio per li costumi quanto nuovo per gl'anni si portò di modo, che ne li suoi maggiori ne li mezzani, ne gl'infini havevano in cosa alcuna da dolersi di lui. Veramente io qui desiderarei poter [*7r*] ben scrivere, perche se bene questa bonta, mansuetudine piacevolezza fù costante in lui per tutta la sua vita, particolarmente spiccò fin' all'età di 20. anni in circa, che tanto haveva quando nostro Zio fù assonto al Pontificato, vivendo con libertà in una Corte, che se non era labile per il senso, poteva essere per li sentimenti di ricevere più gusti da uno, che da un'altro, e de' dispiaceri; però mai dalla sua bocca si sentì doglienza di cosa che non gli gradisce, o non gli piacesse, et atto che non fosse di persona già d'età matura, e di costumi perfetti. Egli stette per longhissimo tempo in una camera la peggiore [*7v*] di casa, forse per la suggettione dello strepito della vicina sala, ò per non darvi sole, o per non potersi affacciare. E però gliène potè venire qualche piccola indisposition; come fù una distillatione acida, che patì qualche mese, et empirsegli tutto il volto di varij bozzoletti, forse per ciò, o per il ribollimento del sangue; ma non già usci da lui alcuna querela. Alle scuole egli hebbe particolar amicitia con l'Abate Pozzobonelli figlio del Sig.ʳ Ambrogio, che morì giovane, essendo doppo alcuni accidenti di febbre, caduto in una indispositione ditisico che lo condusse à morte, essendo di grande espettatione. Haveva fatto Taddeo come uno scrittorio o stanza di tavola [*8r*] che di fuori pareva un armario, dove egli dentro studiava e teneva li suoi libri, e nella buona compostura delle cosa [*sic*] vedevasi la compositione del suo animo. Non saprei dire quali fossero li suoi divertimenti, se non era l'uscia ben di rado à giuocare al maglio, et in casa fare alcuni suoi disegni più artifitiosi per l'ingegno, e sua attentione, che per alcuna arte. Il P're Flisco che ancora vive era suo confessore dal quale io sapevo che andava ben spesso alle sue giornate assegnate, ne mai mutò confessoro, non riconosciuto (in questo ordine di dire) d'haverne bisogno. Così viveva questo giovane più come cosa inanimata [*8v*] da esser maneggiato come si voleva: però non questo negligente nell'operare, havendo anzi guadagnato in talmodo l'attentione mà di questo s'haverà più da discorrere per l'avvenire.

Pensava nostro Zio di metterci, o almeno indrizzarci in qualche stato; onde non fù difficile che havendo per lui segnato un' Abadia Papa Paolo, egli pigliasse la prima tonsura. Ma scoprendo nostro Zio che io ero alieno da pigliar moglie, non hebbe nemeno difficoltà che [*9r*] con la sua bontà Tadeo non cedesse. Seguitava però alli suoi esercitij di ballare, tirar di scherma, saltar il cavallo, e sopra tutto del cavalcare, al quale molto più il genio, che ad altro de sudetti esercitij lo tirava; mentre alto di statura e complesso di carne era necessitato à fuggire il troppo e vehemente moto. Quanto alli studij finita la filosofia sentì qualche cosa delle leggi.

Succeduta la morte di Gregorio XV. et eletto n'ro Zio Papa in lui non si vide alcuna mutatione ne di pensieri ne di costumi: solo essendo arrivato il P're D. Benedetto Castelli monaco Benedettino celebre matematico si applicò [*9v*] in modo alli studij di questa scientia, che li più difficili libri d'Euclide con non minor pianezza, che il maestro maneggiava. Del resto al suo carico di Castellano di S. Angelo, e di Capitano delle guardie era del tutto intento, eccetto quanto alla subordinatione del Padre lo conteneva, o il rispetto degl'ofitiali da quello, o da S. Stà posti, cagionava che quel più egli affaticasse. Essendo però accaduto che per l'invasione della Valtellina si dovessero far tre terzi da inviarsi à Ferrara, ad esso ne fu dato uno, acciò quel più volentieri gli altri dua fussero esercitati dal Duca Federigo Savelli, e dal Prencipe [*10r*] Francesco Colonna. Anzi restando à lui sopratutti qualche intendenza, dovendosi far' una esecutione contra un soldato, che haveva cagionato tumulto e sollevatione, quale non minore si sospettava nell'eseguire contra di quello, furono però tali li suoi buoni ordini e la di lui presenza, che à vista di tutta la soldatesca, fù sodisfatto alla giustitia, e dato il meritato castigo. Ritornato poscia egli in Roma, e parendo tempo che egli si maritasse, li fù proposto, che egli suggerisse, chi li pareva; ma tenendosi con la sua modestia senza dichiararsi, propostali D. Anna Colonna, pensandosi, come che molto di essa si era discorso, che egli perfetta contezza [*10v*] ne havesse havuto, si truovò non haverne alcuna particolar notitia; ma totalmente esser risegnato al volere di suo Zio, e di suo Padre. Si celebrarono dunque le nozze à Castel Candolfo à [*blank*] del 162[*blank*],¹³ essendosi fatti li sponsali alla presenza, e con la benedittione di Papa Urbano; e rimasero per qualche mese à Castel Candolfo ambidua li sposi.

Venuti à Roma si scoperse D. Anna gravida di Camilla. Et essendo occorso per li moti di Mantova, che il Sig.ʳ Card.ᵉ Antonio nostro fratello andasse legato, et insieme il Sigʳ D. Carlo nostro Padre portarsi à Bologna, che di lì à puochi mesi infermatosi, vi accorse ancora di volontà di n'ro Zio D. Tadeo, il quale però nonostanti le diligenze, vi giunse che di puoco era spirato. Tuttavia essendo convenuto al Sig. Card. Antonio di [*11r*] proseguire la sua legatione passare fino à Turino; rimase D. Tadeo in Bologna, dove con ogni maggior esattezza continuò à governare l'esercito non solo con sodisfattione degl' uffitiali, ma con meraviglia dell'esatta accuratezza, e vigilanza con la quale à tutto provedeva. Si era già dato principio al forte Urbano, quale cominciato sù l'argine già fatto dall'esercito romano, li Triumviri, Augusto, M. Antonio, e Lepido si spartirono l'Imperio Romano, haveva mosso l'intendente, et ingegniero à farlo di figura quadra, e conseguentemente con quattro baluardi; donde nasceva che secondo le regole communi venisse biasimato; però si pensò à togliere ancora questa difficoltà; et in tutto concorse l'ingegno, e studio di D. Tadeo, essendosi provisto con quattro mezze lune aggiunte, le quali à giuditio degl'oltramontani e di ogni più esperto Capitano, rendono [11v] la piazza più difficile ad esser espugnata, et in tempo di pace obbliga à minor presidio, di quello che bisognarebbe se di più baluardi fusse munita.

Ritornò in questo tempo il Sig. Card. Antonio, essendo entrata la peste in Bologna, e venuto à morte il Duca d'Urbino in Castel Durante a' [blank] di Aprile 1631 onde fù inviato in fretta D. Tadeo acciò in nome della Santa Sede pigliasse il possesso di quello stato, il che fece con tutta l'essattezza e puntualità e senza niun disturbo, come gl'istessi atti che si conservano negl'archivij Pontificij lo dimostrano; havendo cooperato à questa quiete, l'haver egli tenuti in sua casa per gentilhuomini e paggi varij delle migliori famiglie di quello stato, che si procurò per tal cagione venissero in Roma. E vacando per la morte del Duca la Prefettura di Roma per l'investitura di Giulio 2.do il quale secondo gl'esempij de' suoi antecessori, haveva in provedere tal dignità, volsuto esercitare l'autorità sua; cosi Papa Urbano per le [12r] fatiche da lui fatte in riunire questo stato alla Santa Chiesa, volse solo per se e per la sua casa serbare questa honorevolezza con pari, e conforme investitura, ponendola in D. Taddeo ne' suoi figli, nipoti, e pronepoti. Venuto perciò D. Taddeo à Roma non fu lasciata d'ordine dell'istesso Papa, alcuna funtione o sollennità, con la quale si riconoscesse l'honore, et

ogni prerogativa dovuta à quella dignità, cosi nell'entrata publica che egli fece, come doppo nella Cappella, ricevuta la investitura quando fù ricondotto alla sua casa.

Non lasciò la invidia di mescolare delle sue opere, e li accidenti ad accompagnarvela. Poiche tornando il Prefetto (che cosi di qui avanti lo nominarò) la sera sù l'imbrunirsi dalle visite de Cardinali, s'abbattè in Gio: da Pesaro Ambasciator Veneto, anzi intrigandosi il cocchiero del Prefetto impuntò con la carrozza. Parve però che con simile avvenimento potesse, e si dovesse ricompensare il succeduto. Ma quello che doveva accadere all'andata che faceva l'Ambasciatore all'audienza, per errore d'uno [12v] che tardò nell'avvisare, fù necessario trasferire al ritorno; il che non cosi ben successe, poiche essendosene sospettato l'Ambasciatore più si fisse nell'animo il dispiacere in vedere all'incontrare il Prefetto impuntare la sua carrozza, e per salvare il cocchiere del med.mo Ambasciatore, che non ricevesse dal padrone affronto, bisognò usare delle diligenze, che con non molta prudenza eseguite, dettero occasione alla Rep.ca di dolersi e particolarmente come qualche lancia spezzata del Palazzo Pontificio vi si fosse truovata presente, il che era stato meramente casuale, essendo da altri, che nè di Palazzo, nè della Casa del Prefetto erano, ecceduto con lo imprudenza sudetta. Che se il tutto secondo la direttione della persona à chi il Prefetto l'haveva commesso, fusse stato condotto, non vi sarebbono sopravenute quelle circostanze delle negligenze, et imprudenze sudette. Dovendosi però molto à M.r d'Avase Ambasciator del Rè Christianissimo [13r] [alla] Republica, che con la sua somma destrezza, e stima verso di Papa Urbano, condusse quel negotio à fine con gloria e gusto dell'uno, e dell'altro Prencipe.

Era venuta in Italia la Regina d'Ungheria sorella del Rè di Spagna, alla quale era stato destinato legato il Sig. Card. Antonio, ma essendo egli impedito fece questa funtione il Sig. Card. di S. Cecilia. Il Card. Poli all'hora Maggiord'huomo come suo Nuntio, presso al Monte

Argentaro presentò la Regina di quantità di rinfreschi, e la riveri, portandoli la benedittione di S.S.ᵗᵃ. Ma trattando S.M.ᵗᵃ di passare in Trieste per di li trasportarsi in Vienna, S.S.ᵗᵃ inviò il sud.ᵗᵗᵒ Card. Poli come suo Nuntio alli confini che dalla parte di Ascoli, ha la S.ᵗᵃ Sede con il Regno, et appresso ordinò che D. Taddeo per tutto servisse à S.M.ᵗᵃ come segui per quel tempo che S.M.ᵗᵃ si trattenne à Loreto [*13v*] et in Ancona, di dove non potè cosi presto partire, per attender l'armata Venetiana. Cosi nelle comparse delle livree, come nell'accompagnamento ancora di Baroni Romani non rimase cosa alcuna da desiderare, essendosi dalla Regina, che era assistita dal Duca d'Alva corrisposto con ogni dimostratione et honore, havendolo fatto coprire, e sedere. Ma la vigilanza, e prudenza di D. Taddeo fù sommamente lodata, in l'occasione d'un incendio per trascuragine delle cameriere della Regina, succeduto di notte, nella casa, e stanze dell'istessa Regina, essendovi prontamente accorso D. Taddeo, servendo S.M.ᵗᵃ in passare ad altra habitatione, essendosi estinto l'incendio, con puoco, o quasi niun detrimento delle robe di S.M.ᵗᵃ e della sua famiglia.

Non doverei toccare della morte di Camilla, poiche non ancora di due anni volò al Cielo, se non à chi scrivo. In questa fanciulla di cosi tenera età fù osservata [*14r*] tale verecundia, che dettoli dal padre, non esser conveniente, che essa uscisse delle stanze più adentro, arrivando alla porta sempre replicava, che il Padre di Camilla haveva detto che non uscisse, e si fermava. Mai fù vista ridere come fanno li figliuolini, ma con un solo volto allegro mostrava ogni maggior contento; essendo le sue maggiori fanciullezze state, il tirare li capelli ad un paggetto. Non fù giamai possibile, che essa havendo il vaivolo, che parendo cessato le replicò, si lasciasse vedere dalli medici il petto. Era ancora cosi amica della pulizia, che quando sopra una mano cadeva, o se le poneva qualche accia di seta, subito voleva, non solo che si levasse, ma essere pulita, e lavata. Non haveva, come hò detto, compito li due anni, quando puoco avanti si ammalasse, donandole

io alcune paia di guanti per regalarne le cameriere di sua madre, et havendo gliele dati scompagnati, si dolse, che non [*14v*] le potevano servire. Mi sono scappate dalla penna queste minutie, essendo non piccola gloria de padri l'indole de' figli; come maggiore l'educatione di essi. La nascita di D. Carlo hora Cardinale[14] puotè consolare la morte di D. Camilla; però quando nacque e per li travagli della madre nelle doglie, e per essersi, come dicono, addoppiato nell'uscire, si dubitò assai della di lui vita, quale, piaccia à Dio, di concedergli longa.[15]

Si era dato principio alla fabrica del palazzo alle quattro fontane,[16] secondo un primo disegno fatto dal Prefetto, che era di una scala, la quale conduceva à due gran sale, à ciscuna delle quali erano congiunti uno, o più appartamenti, come una dovesse servire per gl'Ecclesiastici, e l'altra per li secolari. Però essendosi fatti più disegni sù li lumi aperti con il sudetto disegno, e non molto varij da quello, approvatosi [*15r*] uno di essi dal Prefetto, piacque ancora à Papa Urbano, aggiungendosi però, come S.S.ᵗᵃ haveva ancora in queste cose buon gusto, alcuni abbellimenti, e perfettioni, che non erano state avvertite. Del resto si può dire tutta la fabrica essere stata opera del suo intelletto; poiche non solo restò il fine principale, che vi fosse habitazione per gl'Ecclesiastici, e secolari; ma non era giorno, che egli non vi si portasse, e con vedere gli schizzi, e ciò che si andava operando, dove era il pensiero d'altri, l'approvatione, e l'accertamento era il suo; e le spese fatte nella fabrica per la metà e forse di avantaggio uscirono dalla di lui mano. Ne lasciò di metter in opera una delle sale la minore stata adoperata per la rappresentatione di S. Alessio, facendovi il Carnovale seguente rappresentare l'Erminia sul Giordano con scene cosi varie, moti, e voli di figure, apparenze, e lontananze, con sontuosità, e vaghezza di abiti, che non solo [*15v*] non si sono viste le più belle, ma gl'istessi abiti, e machine servirno gl'anni seguenti, e per l'attione di S. Teodora, e quando di nuovo ma con maggior apparato si rappresentò il S. Alessio per la venuta del Prencipe Alessandro di Pollonia. Occorse che un di essendo piena di popolo la sala, che attendeva la sudetta tragicomedia dell'Erminia, quando un' mosso da curiosità s'era per li ponti e tavolati de' muratori traportato ad un finestrone, cadde sopra una tenda, e quella sfondando sopra il popolo à parte cadendo ancora la spada, che nella di lui caduta se gli sfoderò; talmente che li spettatori tutti sottosopra; et atterriti si commossero e andavano à precipitare et à conculcarsi, se il Prefetto mostrandosi al popolo fermo, e senza paura, non lo havesse assicurato, che non vi era pericolo alcuno. Non solo in questa festa, ma in banchetti, o in simili, nelle livree, addobamenti di stanze, et in quanto metteva mano, si vedeva [*16r*] la perfettione, splendidezza, et attentione. Siche l'accuratezza con la quale sopraintendeva alla sua casa, non solo era perche quella nelle occasioni, e convenienze maggiormente risplendesse; ma perche non faceva, ne sapeva fare cosa alcuna, che non la rendesse ben compita, e perfettionata. Onde per non tornare à parlare più di fabriche, egli non solo condusse al termine che hoggidi si truova il palazzo di Monteritondo, e la Chiesa mà procurò quanto potè di rimediare alla tozzezza la quale gli haveva dato il disegno di Frà Michele Cappuccino. Providde con esatezza li parati ordinò quadri, ripose il corpo di S. Sisto Papa nell'altar grande da lui ornato, et aumentate le rendite, fondò quelli Canonicati, e l'Archipretato di suo Iuspatronato. Aggiunse ancora le stanze per udir la messa, et altre per passare dal Palazzo à quelle. In Pelestrina ornò la porta che è detta da lui del Sole, con ispianare le strade [*16v*] le strade [*sic*] fino alla Chiesa di S. Agapito, disegnando che per quelle, la carrozza potesse andare fino nell'alto, dove stà posto il palazzo; e però avanti di quello sopra ben fondati pilastri voltò molti archi per l'istesso effetto, essendo il tutto adesso finito da D. Maffeo suo figliuolo, che ha fatto lastricare di selci tutto il cammino, con riempire e tagliare del monte dove è bisognato, facendo ancora le sponde, et altri ornamenti, che rendono molto più commoda, e vaga quella città. Essendo ancora diviso il Palazzo[17] talmente che senza andare allo scoperto, non si

poteva da un appartamento passare all'altro, con fare una sala, e scale coperte per salire à quella, lo rese più comodo e maestoso; oltre all' havendo bene adderezzato, et apparato. Vi pose quattro pezzi di cannone, et una buona armeria, mandandovi alcune spingarde prese ai Turchi dalle galere del Papa, mentre egli n'era Generale, e li stendardi furno attaccati nella Chiesa di Monteritondo. [*17r*][18] A Montelibretto havendo trovato quel Palazzo non solo mezzo rovinato, ma tutto aperto, et che minacciava prossima ruina, con havere alzato grosse, et alte pareti l'assicurò, et resarcì, se non in tutto per la maggior parte. A S.ᵗᵃ Marinella oltre al porto da lui desegnato, et che era stato condotto con tal politia e perfettione, che era à maraviglia d'ogn'uno, Nell'istesso luogo si vede da lui fabricata l'habitatione, alla quale puoco manca per compirla, un granaro assai ampio tutto coperto di lavagna, et la hosteria assai capace. Haveva in animo di fare in quel luogo fontane, e varie delitie havendo spasso per quella campagna de conigli, havendo smacchiato ancora le due[19] tenute della Catonica, et Prato Cipolloso (quale la camera hà rivoluto) in modo che dove in queste [*17v*] parti si commettevan molti ladronecci, et assassinij, adesso è libero il cammino da Roma à Civitavecchia. Haveva piantato de bei pini, de quali alcuni ancora rimangono in essere, et disegnava con settanta piante, delle quali molte haveva egli medesimo seminate, delle quali ancora alcune hora sono al giardino de bastioni.[20] Vi pose con grosse ancore una tonnara, e per non esser più lungo conchiuderò, che haveva riposto questo paese per abellirlo nella sua vecchiaia, come tra tutte le sue cose in niuna pareva, che più il suo particolare affetto havesse serbato, che al piccolo giardino de bastioni, nel quale oltre à varie piantate con aggiuntare una loggia, una stanza, et cappelletta à una casetta, che era più presto ridotto dell'hortolano, che stanza di un giardiniero, la quale [*18r*] aggiunta fa hora comparire un ben ordinato casino, quale hà per prospettiva da una parte S. Onofrio con tutta quella bella pendice del Janicolo, et in faccia la lontananza de monti, et per prospettiva tutta Roma di quà dal Tevere, con l'aspetto del fiume, e del Ponte S. Angelo frequentato dal Popolo, che abbellisce la solitudine senza turbarla; si fatti luoghi non puoco li piacevano poiche di prima haveva comprato una picciola casa et giardinetto appoggiato all'antiche mura di Roma à man dritta quando si sale à S. Pancratio posto pure in sito, et aspetto non cosi bello ma non dissimile al sudetto. Et nelli suoi beni di M.te Libretto tutto si rallegrava quando si portava à una chiesa detta la Madonna delle gratie sopra un colle vestito di quercie, et altri alberi, [18v] posto tra Ponticelli, e Nerola con di belle fontane, alle cui radici scorre il fiumicello di Coresa.

A Monpechio²¹ villa appresso à Castel Gandolfo, o nell'esecutione de pensieri di Papa Urbano, o in quello, che di propria inventione il Prefetto vi aggiunse si riconosce la di lui esquisitezza, poiche et li viali bene ordinati con le palizzate, et spalliere con l'acqua condotta di lontano più miglia parte sopra terra, e gran parte con haver cavato nell'istesso selce i condotti, fanno lodare questa villa benche non habbia, ne li palazzi, ne i parchi, ne li teatri, che altre rendono celebri; Papa Urbano haveva disegnato una bella habitatione; però, et meno ambitiosa, et più commoda è riuscita una casa già fatta da Mons.r Visconti, havendo che il Prefetto fabricato quanto per l'uso del villeggiare poteva occorrere [19r] havendo con li sostructioni cavato molti servitij et fortificato la fabrica antica per l'alzate fattevi, quali dalle guerre publiche, et dalli privati disastri fù forzato à tralasciare. Non più casa però quella comparisce; ma palazzetto con un bel prato, che forma un semicircolo postoli d'avanti. Questa casa pure egli haveva adobbata, come nella villa ogni più curiosa sorte di frutti fece piantare, il che in molti altri suoi luoghi haveva procurato. Non lascerò delli Iuspatronati, che con larghezza del suo danaro pose à Valmontone, dove con una buona fabrica haveva congiunto dua habitationi antiche quasi inhabitabili per esser separate. A Casa Corbola, che fece chiamare Casape, coprì gran parte de tetti con piombo, non bastiando li vecchij lastrichi, quali venivano dalle pioggie penetrate, cosi ancora [19v] rifondò uno de casini del Gericomio,

oltre à delle spese per la conservatione del palazzo di S. Gregorio, et fontane fatte in varij luoghi di quella montagna. Non essendo casale, ò possessione, che non solo da lui fusse conservata, ma ancora migliorata, come la casa di Falcognano con haver fatto solari, et palchi à quelle stanze. Conchiuderò con la opera et pia, et magnifica del monasterio de Palestrina, il quale oltre alla clausura, che serve ancora per muraglia della città, disegnava condurre con tal magnificenza, che il solo novitiato con le camere de publici servitij, qualche parte delle loggie è sufficiente per il servitio delle monache, quali nell'humiltà, e disprezzo del mondo emulano li fondamenti, e grossezze di mura fabricate dal Prefetto, egli per superare le ingiurie del tempo, et esse tutto quello che non sia eternità. [20r] Si vede per servitio di esse monache oltre al coro, e chiesa anteriore più che mezza fatta, non mancando che l'alzare la faccia anteriore, et ingrossare la parete à mandritta gettando la volta. Troppo mi sono steso, benche più cose m'habbia lasciato in raccontare queste fabriche, nelle quali sopra tutto si scorge oltre al singolare ingegno, e perfetto giuditio, la magnificenza, la quale fu nelle fabriche, come la generosità risplende in tutte le di lui attioni. Poiche se bene per ordinario negligentava certe apparenze valendosi di carrozze non corrispondenti alla sua famiglia, et altre spese, et non curarsi che li servitori da lui alimentati comparissero, nel numero di questi, nelle buone livree, ne trattamenti esquisiti di ciascuno nel suo grado, et ministerio, non v'era che dovitia, [20v] et liberalità, anzi eccesso particolare in ciò, che risguardava il servitio della moglie, come la larghezza nelle limosine, non havendo per oggetto il strepito, e l'applauso, mà l'istesso ben fare, soccorrere alli bisogni altrui, et beneficare à tal segno, che li donativi non solo erano spesso à centinaia, mà più d'una volta furno à migliaia. Pure nelle fabriche hò lasciato la ristauratione della casa paterna,²² nella quale benche et M.r Francesco nostro granzio, che la comprò vi havesse murato, et Papa Urbano ampliatola con case compre, et fabriche ampliatole con una piazzetta aggiunta, et l'abbellimento d'una loggia v'havesse accresciuta nostro Padre, tutta via quanto hà di decoro, tutto è opera, et ancora architettura del Prefetto, poiche non solo rifondò et aguagliò tutta la facciata verso li Giubbonari, ma estendosi verso la piazza del Monte della Pietà augumentata [*21r*] con un gettito, et vi pose la porta principale, dalla quale s'entra in un andito ornato, e sostenuto da colonne, che per la novità per la grandezza l'una e l'altra condotte con buone regole piace sommamente havendovi poste due statue antiche trovate ne vicini fondamenti, che parte erano del celebre teatro di Pompeo; sopra di questo androne il secondo ordine nobile è con sua cappella, et anticamera corrispondente à quattro appartamenti, il che, se bene per se difficile, è disposto con tal facilità, et commodità, che li esperti nelle fabriche gran conto, e stima ne fanno. A questa fabrica della casa fù non tanto portato dalla volontà sua, ò di Papa Urbano, quanto necessitato per l'offesa, che diceva la moglie ricevere dall'aria delle quattro fontane, et con non minore ansia volsutavi tornare di [*21v*] quella con la quale all'altra era andata. Fusse per questa cagione, ò per haver fatto troppo à sicurtà di quella aria, ò dove haveva hauto dua figli maschij, havendo partorito la femina alle quattro fontane, con buono augurio volesse tornare à fare il terzo, la prudenza del marito ben la servì, et questa habitatione fù da lui ridotta in qualità, che più commoda non ce n'è alcuna e à quella migliore apparenza, che fosse possibile.

Il discorso delle fabriche ne hà trasportato fuori d'ogni ordine de tempi. Adesso però tornerò à quelli, poiche essendo arrivata à Papa Urbano quella malattia, che se bene fù molto grave, nondimeno dalli concetti molto più fù ampliata à segno che come fosse vicino il conclave tutto si disponeva, egli nondimeno sempre seguì con la istessa intrepidezza ne all'hora, ne all' accidente, che pochi [*22r*] anni avanti soraprese al medesimo Papa nella Cappella si vedde alcuna mutatione nel suo volto, essendo immutabile in lui la compostura, et la modestia. Le quali non meno che la natural complessione malinconica li facevano amare la solitudine, et la retiratezza; non-

dimeno quand'era chiamato all'audienze, ò alle congregationi, era pronto, e diligente, cosi richiesto dava prontamente il suo voto et parere, et nelle conversationi non era punto tetrico, et anteponendo il gusto de gli altri ad ogni suo piacere, era con tutti facevole, benigno, e trattabile. Nelle congregationi delle acque per la soraintendenza delle anni egli era sempre chiamato, et uno della detta congreg.^ne cosi in quella che da gli Prelati, Avvocati, e Procuratori si teneva per l'azienda, et roba della casa, egli era assiduo, et attentissimo [*22v*] adoprando ancora ogni flemma; poiche se bene alcuni più là passavano in dispute legali, ò accademiche, che nelle risolutioni, altri non vi usassero tutta la diligenza, che si poteva, non era alcuno, che à torto, ò à ragione se potesse dolere d'alcun tratto, ò d'alcuna impatienza del Prefetto, ma ben stupirsi della bontà, et equanimità sua. E vero che le fatiche quali si vedono fatti di sua mano, ò in fare indici, ò summarij alle scritture, ò altre adnotationi, mostrano che egli, et le sue fatiche supplivano alli difetti di quelli, con li quali egli era non puoco indulgente, et buono.

Succedè la venuta del Duca di Parma à Roma, la quale come di gusto di quel Duca fù privata, non per li accoglimenti, che egli ricevè dal Prefetto, ne per quegli, che questo Prencipe rese, vi fù cosa da dire, sebene qualcuno osservò che il Duca non visitasse D. Anna, come si era [*23r*] da lui detto di voler fare. Però non se n'essendo ne fatta instanza, ne querela, ò non si osservò, ò non se ne fece conto. Il Duca quale più tosto nelle cerimonie haveva hauto disparer con il Card.^le Antonio, ogni lamento fece del Card.^l Francesco però generale non esprimendo cosa particolare; mà come finito che hebbe il negotio, et consumate tutte le gratie ricevute da Papa Urbano, temendo da questo di non esser [*blank*] d'una lettera simile ad un altra fatta con varie dichiarationi dal Duca Ranuccio suo Padre, in cose di stato vergognandosi dolerse del Papa tanto suo, et di fresco benefattore, si volse à farlo contro chi era secretario, et riputato conscio de pentieri, et risolutioni del Zio. Ma essendo in Papa Urbano una perpetua vigilanza per la dignità, et autorità Pontificia, et per le ragioni della [*23v*] Santa Sede dichiarò tutte le concessioni delle tratte, et altre regalie fatte dalli suoi antecessori esser da lui state rivocate; onde il D. Odoardo si pose à fortificar Castro, il che proseguì, nonostante l'ammonitione, et il divieto, si che vendendosi alle arme, tutto si trovò dal Prefetto così ben ordinato, et disposto, che se bene ne per tale esecutione parve, che apparisse un tal capo, et esecutore, e trattandosi d'una casa, quale era stata amata sommamente da Papa Urbano, come la Farnese, volentieri non adoperava più là di quello portava la necessità alcuno de suoi congiunti contro esso Duca; finita però questa speditione presto, et senza che l'aria stimato il maggior propugnacolo di Castro noiesse a alcuno stando armato il Duca Odoardo, parve al Papa d'inviar gente à Bologna, et un capo, che invigorisse tutta questa gente, [*24r*] cioè il Prefetto suo il nipote, il quale non mancò in cosa alcuna, che alla disciplina militare, et all'attentione, et vigilanza di Generale spettasse. Cadde però per l'accuratezza, e travaglio indefesso in una febre, che nel suo corpo, che altretanto era delicato quanto vigoroso, sinoltrò, mà con l'evacuatione del sangue malinconico, che in lui predominava, si rese libero da questa più pericolosa di quello si penetrò infermità. Intando parendo, che dal Duca Odoardo non ad altro si pensasse, che alla futura sedia vacante per intrare nello stato Ecclesiastico, et intanto consumarlo con le spese, et mantenimento di soldateschi; parve à Papa Urbano di voler più tosto prendere sopra di se il fastidio, che lasciarlo ad altri doppo di se; et l'esserli stato rappresentato haver li Principi preso tal gelosia [*24v*] delli avanzamenti della S.ta Sede, che ogni mossa harebbe fatto della sollevatione, cagionò, che differì S.S.ta mà non depose la risolutione; tanto più che la missione del M.se di Ghiglia inviato dal Duca di Modena per far qualche aggiustamento col Duca di Parma era riuscita di mera cerimonia, mentre non ostante, che se li fosse procurato adito con la speranza che S.S.ta harebbe usato indulgenza, di dare al Duca Odoardo tutto quello che portava seco riguardo di delitie, et che dal più potente, et che tutto haveva à sua dispositione, cominciasse dal dare, e restituire, che alle delitie era facile ad attaccare delle Terre, e delle giurisdittioni, non altro se ritrasse dal M.se di Ghiglia per ultima replica, se non che la conditione del Duca Odoardo era difficile. L'istesso di, che era stato ringratiato non [*25r*] essendosi potuto ritrarre, che ricompense, ò avanzamenti si havessero da lui volsuti, arrivando ancora, che non si sarebbe guardato à somma di denari, quando ò in Lunigiana, ò altrove havesse il Duca havuto occasione di dilatarsi, non operando per ordinario li principi, che per interesse.

Hora essendosi scoperto, che il Marchese haveva preso gran gelosia di Berselle, havendo richiesto, che si fusse potuto carcerare un prete per scoprirla, et che il sospetto fosse di intelligenza col Duca di Parma si mandò il Conte Ambrogio di Carpegna à scoprire la verità di questo, et la dispositione del Duca con instruttione da proporre delle conditioni assai avantaggiose per lui quando occorresse, e sopra tutto accertamento, che non si volevano li stati di [*25v*] Parma, e Piacenza, ma solo il disarmamento del Duca Odoardo, e sopra tutto la quiete. Trovò però tal facilità il Conte Ambrogio à suoi negotiati, che non stimò di venire à espressioni d'avantaggi per il Duca, il quale però per altra via se li procurava; come si dirà appresso, et in tanto non mancò di scoprire al G. Duca, Venetiani, et altri ogni richiesta come pescatore bramoso di pesca, non si curava di tranquillare le acque. Aggiustò dunque facilm.te il Conte Ambrogio le tappe, et di già il Prefetto haveva tutto disposto per incaminarsi quando li parve di lasciar munito lo stato donde egli si partiva, poiche se bene non lo perdeva di vista, nondimeno ancora in breve tempo potevano nascere delli accidenti, come scoperse la rivolta tramata contra Ferrara dall'istesso M.se [*26r*] di Ghiglia in Ferrara, il quale con habito di Ministro, et di persona divota era più in Roma per esplorare, che per negotiare. Haveva inviato il Prefetto à Ferrara[23]

Appendix 4

ABarb., Ind. II, no. 3112, fols. 361–385

[*fol. 361: description of the principality of Palestrina, ca. 1629*]

* * *

[*362v*] In questa piazza ha l'ingresso il Palazzo de Signori il quale [*363*] ha le sue scale di marmo in quella guisa apunto che ha il Palazzo di Campidoglio.

Salite queste scale si vede un altra scalinata tutto di marmo dentro il circuito di un gran nicchio in mezzo al quale vi è per di sotto una conserva di acqua con la sua apertura e guarnimento conforme a quello che stà nella Cisterna del Primo cortile del Palazzo Vaticano anzi è più larga e forse più bella.

Nel fine di queste scale si entra nel Palazzo per una porta con suoi conci di marmo quadra dalle bande della quale vi sono due finestre come anco per tutto il resto del nicchio, e scale sudette due altri ordini di finestre.

Entrato nella porta si trova un poco di aditetto con la volta sostenuta da 3 ò 4 colonne.

Dalla banda manca del medesimo adito si entra nella sala dove stà hoggi la Sig^{ra} Principessa e poi di essa sala in una camera, che và a terminare davanti il circuito del medesimo nicchio.

Doppo detta camera si entra in un'altra che è principio di molte e molte altre a filo che la seguitano al pari per un gran corso di stanze.

Sotto al quale apartamento vi sono altre tante stantie che servono per la cucina, et altri servitij bassi.

[*363v*] Sotto al quale, et al piano della detta Piazza della Cortina vi è la cantina con botti grossissime, freschissima con focone da cuocere il morzo et altre commodità.

S'Aggiunge che in mezzo del filo dell'appartamento della Signora Principessa vi è una loggia in mezzo della quale vi stà una fontanella dell'acqua della fonte della Madonna del Trugho soprastante al palazzo che in parte qui si descrive dalla quale fonte l'Inverno solamente deriva l'acqua in diversi altri luoghi del medesimo Palazzo.

E benche il commodo di questa acqua si ristringa al solo tempo del verno, non è per questo suo diffetto che non la dasse anco la state e tutto il resto dell'Anno, ma perche è ripiena del tartaro la forma che la conduce non si è perciò visto che in altro tempo vi sia l'acqua. Questa forma con pochissima spesa si accomodarebbe anzi dentro la medesima e si potrebbe introdure un buon capo d'acqua da derivarsi da un'altra fonte che è nel monte di Pelestrina vicino alla Rocca, mà però poco fuori di essa, chiamata formale di Stefano.

Tornando hora al Palazzo al pari dell'appartamento della sudetta signora Principessa, vi è un pochino di giardinetto, con una casa contigua che par è delli sig^{ri}.

Nella sala del medesimo apartamento vi è la

Capella da celebrare la messa.

[*364*] Sopra a questo piano delle Camere della medesima Sig.ra Principessa vi è l'appartamento simile dove stà il sig.r Prencipe e dove ogni giorno almeno una volta dà audienza a Vassalli, i quali però non resta d'intendere anco in altre occasioni.

A mezzo del quale appartamento appunto sopra la loggia detta poco fa essere nelle camere della Signora con la fontana vi è un'altra sala che chiamano la sala secreta dipinta, come anco sono dipinte l'altre due cioè dell'appartamento della Signora e Sig.r Prencipe et doppo essa altre stantie e Camere e finestre, che guardando a mezzo giorno, come anco quelle dell'appartamento della Signora e della cucina sudetta fanno bellissima vista per vedere verso mezzogiorno oltre tutto il territorio di Pelestrina che li è in faccia un'infinità di mare, Montefortino, Lugnano, la Colonna, Rocca Priora, Monte di Compatri, la Selva dell'Agliaro. Da Levante fanno vedere Segni, Valmontone, Cavi, Pagliano, Anagni, Fiorentino, et innumerabili paesi, e luoghi, e da Ponente mostrano Roma, e tutta questa marina che dopo di essa si scorge.

In questo stesso appartamento Il Sig.r Prencipe d'hoggi della parte di dietro ci ha cresciuta un poco di galeria, che come hà l'ingresso dalla prima camera del signore cosi và a terminare nella sudetta sala secreta [*364v*] et avanti a questa galleria vi è un poco di piano scoperto et in fine di esso vi è un portone che guarda verso Ponente e cosi verso Roma per il quale si può entrare con la carozza e levar li signori dalle loro stanze senza sottoporsi ad altro cielo che a quello della medesima carozza tanto è commoda la strada per andare alla detta galeria.

Per entrare a questo apartamento del signore, oltre al descritto adito del detto portone, vi è il suo ordinario che comincia in quell'andito che di sopra si desse essere avanti la sala dell'appartamento della signora salendosi per un'altra scala, che termina con il nicchio sudetto al pari di questo appartamento del Sig.r Prencipe, avanti alla cui sala vi è una loggia con colonne scoperta dalle bande in poi, che sopra di lei, vi è una Camera della medema grandezza della loggia coperta mà inhabitata dove li piccioni salvatichi, vi hanno fatto molti nidi.

La metà del Palazzo stà come si è detto l'altra parte hà l'ingresso parimente della scala del nicchio, dove è la cisterna, hà anco la sua sala al pari di quella dell'appartamento della Signora, con le sue camere al pari, mà però non tante, per essere il Palazzo vecchio de signori il quale non è stato mai cresciuto, come è stato fatto dell'altra metà gia di sopra disignata, ma può [*365*] ben crescersi, con non molta spesa.

Sopra questo appartamento al pari di quello del Sig.r Prencipe ve n'è un'altro con la sua sala nell'istessa forma di quello del Sig.r Prencipe, mà un poco meno di camere per la ragione detta, che però ancor si veggono in esso le finestre di marmo fatte a croce all'antica.

Sotto a questi due appartamenti vi sono le priggionie che vanno al paro dell'appartamento dell'altra metà del Palazzo, che si disse servire per cucina e poco delà mà però attaccato, e non sotto al Palazzo vi è il luogo dove rende audienza il governatore, e dove risiede per sua habitatione il Canceliere della Corte secolare.

Vi è da questa parte anco l'ingresso per un'altro portone verso levante, mà rare volte per esso si entra.

Dietro a questa stessa parte di Palazzo vi sono diverse stantie, che servono per la fameglia, guardarobba et altro, e nel medesimo sito, vi è un poco di cortiletto nel quale la state li signori per trattenimento giocano alla palla, senza che dal sole venghino offesi.

Tutto dunque il Palazzo cosi brevemente descritto guarda davanti a mezzo giorno, con tre ordini di finestre [*365v*] in molta quantità da man dritta, e ponente Roma e da man sinistra vede la parte di levante come s'è detto.

* * *

Poco discosto da questo convento [San Francesco delli Padri Zoccolanti], ma però prima di capitarvi si trova un'accasamento, che serve di fenile e stalla per li Cavalli delli Signori, capace di molti cavalli e fieno respettivamente.[1]

* * *

[383v] Il Palazzo del Vescovo sotto sue viscere haveva già il famoso musaico poco fà spicconato con molto disgusto di tutti li Cittadini.

* * *

Et in questa strada che va a terminare alla detta porta di San Martino li signori ci hanno un habitatione che chiamano il Palazzetto il quale per l'ordinario serve di habitatione alli Signori Cardinali Vescovi quando vanno a Pelestrina per esercitar l'officio di Pastore non servendo loro il lor Palazzo episcopale sopradetto con tanta commodità come questo havendo a sufficienza delle Camere, sale, cantina, e stalla, con buona prospettiva di finestre che riguardano verso detta strada, e dall'altra parte verso mezzogiorno tutta la Campagna di Pelestrina, con quanto si disse di sopra godersi dal Palazzo principale de Signori.

Anzi questo Palazzetto hà il suo giardino di 4 piani assai capaci et in esso si puo introdur l'acqua della botte della fontana del Borgo sudetta la qual commodità [384] monta al Palazzo già meliorato.

* * *

[to fol. 385]

[371] Palestrina . . . venduto li 16 del Genaro 1630 dal Prencipe di detta Città al Don Carlo Barberini mediante la persona del Sig.r Don Taddeo suo figliolo . . .

[372] Breve, e succincta Relatione di Pelestrina, et altri beni comprati dall'Ecc.mo Sig.r Don Carlo Barberino, fatta dal Sig. Gio. Battista Scanarolio

per sua memoria quando n'è andato à pigliare il Possesso.

* * *

Il Palazzo del Padrone fabricato nella Cima della medesima Città, sopra l'antica struttura del Tempio della Fortuna, con due Appartamenti nobili al terzo Piano, uno nell'ingresso à mano manca, che chiamano il Vecchio, che hà la Sala e tre Stanze, et è voltato à Levante, e mezzo giorno; l'altro, ch'è nuovo à mano dritta, con Sala, et Sei, ò Sette stanze divisibili commodamente da una Galleria voltate à mezzo giorno, e Ponente con la Tramontana nel modo, che viene alla Città nella quale [372v] spira di traverso, et il marino non là offende per essere impedito dalle Montagne di Rocca de Massimi, Montefortino, et altri.

Nell'ingresso al 2° piano à mano manca sotto l'Appartamento vecchio vi è un altro simile appartamento da potersi anco habitare da Padroni e sotto all'Appartamento nuovo ve n'è uno bonissimo, che si habitava commodamente dalla Principessa, Duchessa, e loro famiglie.

Vi sono poi al primo Piano per i Servitij bassi buone commodità di Cucine, Dispense, Tinelli, et altro, e Sotto Cantina Grande.

In oltre vi sono Stalle due, una per 50., l'altra per 25. cavalli con fenile sopra, e separate dal Palazzo.

Non vi è habitatione per il Governatore, nè per la Corte, e le prigioni sono mal ridotte, e poste sotto l'Appartamento vecchio sudetto.

Vi è poi un Casino, che chiamano il Palazzetto nella parte ch'è in piano della Città, con un Giardino nobile, e grande, capace di ricevere ogni sorte di delizie.

* * *

[to fol. 374]

Notes

Introduction

1. Jean Delumeau, *Vie économique et sociale de Rome dans la seconde moitié du XVIe siècle* (Bibliothèque des Ecoles françaises d'Athènes et de Rome, 184), 2 vols., Paris, 1957-59, 446.

2. Delumeau, *Vie économique,* 378–80.

3. Virgilio Spada, in 1657, clearly saw that comparisons among various architects' solutions to a given problem would reveal the respective merits of the designers; see Joseph Connors, "Virgilio Spada's Defence of Borromini," *Burlington Magazine* 131, no. 1031 (February 1989), 76–90, esp. 82 and n. 30, and 87.

1. The Apartment

1. The handbooks of etiquette and household management discussed below, nn. 3, 4, 6, 7 (chap. 1), make clear that the cardinal is the model, through their terminology and their specific prescriptions; lesser persons in the Roman hierarchy define their positions in relation to his.

2. For an illuminating discussion of the character and the roles of diplomatic ceremonial in early modern Europe, see William Roosen, "Early Modern Diplomatic Ceremonial: A Systems Approach," *Journal of Modern History* 52, no. 3 (September 1980), 452–76.

3. Francesco Sestini da Bibbiena, *Il maestro di camera,* Florence, 1621; 2d ed., "di nuovo ricorretto secondo il Ceremoniale Romano," Viterbo, 1639; and subsequent editions in 1660, 1662, 1664, 1671, 1698, and 1699. I cite the edition of 1621 unless otherwise noted.

Girolamo Lunadoro, *Relatione della Corte di Roma, e de' riti da osservarsi in essa...,* n.p., 1635, is concerned primarily with the papal court but describes the etiquette of cardinals, pp. 49–69. According to the dedication to Cardinal Medici and the preface, the book was written eighteen years earlier [1617], at the request of his mother the Grand Duch-

ess of Tuscany, on the occasion of his first going to Rome as cardinal; it had circulated in manuscript and had been partially published by someone else under the title *Maestro di camera,* but it was finally being published under the name of its rightful author. Extensive differences in presentation preclude the possibility that Sestini's volume was the illegitimate publication of Lunadoro's work. Once published, it enjoyed great popularity and many subsequent editions, with revisions.

4. F. Tantouche, *Traicte de tout ce qui s'observe en la cour de Rome, Tant par nostre sainct Père, que par Messeigneurs les Illustrissimes Cardinaux,* Paris, 1623, 5 (cf. Roosen, "Ceremonial," 465); and 23, "Si le nouveau Cardinal est plus ancien que le nepveu du Pape, (comme par exemple le Cardinal de la Valette plus ancien que le Cardinal Ludovisio,) estant sortis de l'apartement du neveu, le Cardinal de la Valette precedera comme plus ancien Cardinal . . ."; similarities between Sestini's and Tantouche's texts would seem to be due to each author's desire to give an accurate description of the same etiquette and not to any dependence of one on the other.

5. Cesare Magalotti and Cassiano dal Pozzo were in Cardinal Francesco Barberini's entourage when he went to France as legate *à latere* in 1625, and both prepared journals of the voyage, in which they recorded details of the cardinal's formal encounters with his French hosts and callers; Barb. lat. 5688 is the journal of Cassiano dal Pozzo, and Barb. lat. 5686 is by Cesare Magalotti. Cassiano dal Pozzo also accompanied Francesco Barberini on his trip to Spain as cardinal legate in 1626 and recorded the details of etiquette observed in the paying and receiving of calls in his diary of that voyage, Barb. lat. 5689, passim. See below, nn. 50, 51, 52 (chap. 1).

6. Gregorio Leti, *Itinerari della corte di Roma ò vero teatro historico, cronologico, e politico della sede apostolica...,* Valence, 1675, following Sestini very closely in many passages. For Leti's career and controversial writings, see Luigi

Fassò, *Avventurieri della penna del seicento: Gregorio Leti, Giovanni Gerolamo Arconati Lamberti, Tomaso Tomasi, Bernardo Guasconi,* Florence, 1923, xiii, 5–30.

7. E.g., Cesare Evitascandalo, *Il maestro di casa,* Viterbo, 1620, 36–39 ("cameriero"), 157–64 ("maestro di camera"). Evitascandalo first composed his text in 1585; it was published as an addendum to Cervio, *Il trinciante* (below, n. 32 [chap. 1]), in 1593; Evitascandalo revised his manuscript in 1595 and published it under his own name in 1596 (see the edition of Rome, 1598, preface, and the edition of Viterbo, 1620, 94–95). Of the several subsequent editions, I cite that of Viterbo, 1620.

8. For Taddeo Barberini, ABarb., Ind. IV, no. 1281; similarly, ABarb., Ind. I, no. 1060, is a little bundle of sixteen notes of etiquette for various persons and situations 1505–1681, which illustrate the importance of fine points of precedence. For Costanza Barberini, ABarb., Ind. IV, no. 598; transcribed in Appendix 2. For the ambassador of Tuscany, ASF, Medici del Principato, vol. 2658, ca. 1644, unpaginated; transcribed in Appendix 1.

9. Pier Bartolo Romanelli, "Etichetta e precedenze a Roma durante il soggiorno di Cristina di Svezia," *Il Giornale di Politica e di Letteratura 7,* fasc. 1–3 (January–March 1931), 1–40, esp. p. 26: the Conestabile "si ritirò immediatamente nelle sue stanze, che allora erano terrene."

10. Sestini, *Maestro di camera,* 203–5.

11. Giulio Pisano, "L'ultimo prefetto dell'urbe," *Roma 9* (1931), 159; Nicolò Barozzi and Guglielmo Berchet, *Relazioni degli stati europei lette al Senato dagli ambasciatori veneti nel secolo decimosettimo,* Ser. III, Italia, *Relazioni di Roma,* 2 vols., Venice, 1877–79, I, 370–71, and II, 33.

12. ASF, Medici del Principato, vol. 2658, unpaginated, last paragraph (Appendix 1).

13. Sestini, *Maestro di camera,* 210–11; Tantouche, *Traicte,* 83; Lunadoro, *Corte di Roma,* 1635, 56. The bell can be seen in position above the roof of the stair of the Barberini "Casa Grande" ai Giubbonari in Fig. 88 (left of center).

14. Sestini, *Maestro di camera,* 208–10; Tantouche, *Traicte,* 83–84; Lunadoro, *Corte di Roma,* 1635, 56–57, specifying that the ambassador of Tuscany would be met only one room from the audience room.

15. Sestini, *Maestro di camera,* 206–7, specifies a lowered *portiera* for cardinals' guests who are other cardinals, ambassadors, barons, or "other qualified persons"; cf. Tantouche, *Traicte,* 97–98. Lunadoro, *Corte di Roma,* 1635, 61, notes that Cardinal Aldobrandini (later Clement VIII) gave audience to women with the *portiera* raised, as did his cardinal nephews later, and commends the practice; Leti, *Itinerari,* 512, advises that the *portiera* should always be raised for women, except that it may be lowered for one's mother or sister.

16. Sestini, *Maestro di camera,* 216–18; cf. Tantouche, *Traicte,* 86–87.

17. Barb. lat. 5689, fol. 5.

18. Lunadoro, *Corte di Roma,* 1635, 58.

19. Sestini, *Maestro di camera,* 219; cf. Lunadoro, *Corte di Roma,* 59.

20. Leti, *Itinerari,* 513.

21. Sestini, *Maestro di camera,* 219–23; Tantouche, *Traicte,* 90–93; Lunadoro, *Corte di Roma,* 1635, 56–57, specifying that the ambassador of Tuscany would be accompanied only to the middle of the *sala.*

22. Sestini, *Maestro di camera,* 223–26; Tantouche, *Traicte,* 93–95.

23. ASF, Medici del Principato, vol. 2658, unpaginated; Appendix 1.

24. E.g., Sestini, *Maestro di camera,* 208, 222; and Lunadoro, *Corte di Roma,* 1635, ambassadors are to be met "in qualche stanza, conforme che in quel luogo dove riceve vi sono stanze, poche, ò assai."

25. Sestini, *Maestro di camera,* 201–2; Tantouche, *Traicte,* 97.

26. Evitascandalo, *Maestro di casa,* 101, "stanza dove il Principe mangiarà."

27. Cesare Evitascandalo, *Libro dello scalco,* Rome, 1609, 18; cf. Barb. lat. 4360, fol. 21, suggesting that supper might be served in an eastward-facing loggia on warm evenings, below, p. 220.

28. Evitascandalo, *Maestro di casa,* 99. Michel de Montaigne, *Journal du voyage de Michel de Montaigne en Italie par la Suisse et l'Allemagne en 1580 et 1581,* ed. Alessandro d'Ancona, Città di Castello, 1889, 238, observed this practice in Rome: "En certeins lieus où M. de Montaigne disna en cerimonie, les buffets ne sont pas où on disne, mais en un'autre premiere salle, et va-t-on vous y querir à boire, quand vous en demandés; et là est en parade la vesselle d'argant."

29. Cf. Barb. lat. 4360, fol. 21, recommending the use of a nearby loggia as *credenza* and *bottiglieria* when meals might be served in the oval salon.

30. Evitascandalo, *Maestro di casa,* 13.

31. Evitascandalo, *Scalco,* 5–6; *Maestro di casa,* 185.

32. Giovanni Battista Rossetti, *Dello scalco,* Ferrara, 1584, 40, assumes a kitchen 150 paces distant from the diners. See especially Vincenzo Cervio, *Il trinciante,* Rome, 1593, for a detailed description of the art of carving; and Leti, *Itinerari,* 553–68, for a detailed account of the service of meals.

Roman usages were distinct from the similarly elaborate usages of other cities and countries but might be practiced by Romans not only at home but abroad with their attendants; Cesare Evitascandalo, *Dialogo del trenciante,* Rome, 1609 (but first composed in 1576), 11–12. In Paris, on Saturday, 24 May 1625, according to the record of Cesare Magalotti, Cardinal Francesco Barberini dined with his guest the Archbishop Gondi and four other prelates: "L'Archivescovo [Gondi] fù servito dal suo coppiere senza sottocoppa, gli altri Prelati furono serviti quella mattina, e sempre all'Italiana. La sala era piena di gente curiosa di vedere, non meno S. E. [Francesco] mangiare, che Caetano trinciar le viande" (Barb. lat. 5686, fol. 231). In 1626, when in Spain, Cardinal Francesco Barberini insisted on being served "all'Italiana," in contrast to the Spanish mode of serving, as noted by Cassiano dal Pozzo (Barb. lat. 5689, fol. 68v).

33. Barozzi and Berchet, *Relazioni di Roma*, I, 261.

34. Evitascandalo, *Maestro di casa*, 7; Francesco Liberati, *Il perfetto maestro di casa*, Rome, 1658, 65.

35. Evitascandalo, *Maestro di casa*, 39.

36. ABarb., Ind. I, no. 747, unpaginated.

37. Evitascandalo, *Maestro di casa*, 33, 101.

38. This practice is attested by many references in the documentation for the palaces studied in detail in this book, e.g., pp. 188, 189, 199.

39. Tantouche, *Traicte*, 78, 82; Leti, *Itinerari*, 491–92; Lunadoro, *Corte di Roma*, 1635, 48.

40. Leti, *Itinerari*, 587.

41. Evitascandalo, *Maestro di casa*, 99–100, 172–76.

42. Ibid., 37–38, 100–101; Liberati, *Maestro di casa*, 31, 40, 66. The *maestro di camera* was never to allow "che gli staffieri si addomestichino in camera, ò che gli aiutanti, e li paggi si esercitino in sala, et altrove con la servitù bassa, abbandonando l'anticamera con danno del padrone, e nota appresso forastieri" (Liberati, *Maestro di casa*, 31).

43. Liberati, *Maestro di casa*, 65; Evitascandalo, *Maestro di casa*, 7.

44. Evitascandalo, *Maestro di casa*, 198–99.

45. Ibid., 99–100; Lunadoro, *Corte di Roma*, 49; Leti, *Itinerari*, 493–94. ABorg. 307, no. 67, 27 Sept. 1619, describes *inter alia* woodwork done for the "Salone del Palazzo novo" of Palazzo Borghese (room C5), for Prince Marcantonio, including the frame for a baldacchino 18½ × 10 *palmi*, a "Tavolone sotto detto baldacchino . . . con 3 trespidi sotto grossi straordinarij" 19 × 5½ *palmi*, and "la scalinata sopra detta tavola d'albuccio con 4 gradini" 4 *palmi* high and 18½ *palmi* long.

46. Lunadoro, *Corte di Roma*, 1635, 49; Leti, *Itinerari*, 493–94.

47. Evitascandalo, *Maestro di casa*, 100–101.

48. Ibid., 101; Lunadoro, *Corte di Roma*, 1635, 59.

49. Many inventories are cited below, chaps. 9–15. For information and illustrations of seventeenth-century furniture, see William M. Odom, *A History of Italian Furniture*, Garden City, N.Y., 1918–19, vol. 2.

50. Barb. lat. 5688, fols. 120–122v, for the cardinal's apartment; and fols. 446–446v for the etiquette followed with respect to his many visitors of various ranks. Barb. lat. 5686, fols. 226v–227v, for another description of the apartment; and fols. 228–231, for his reception of some visitors.

51. Barb. lat. 5686, fols. 232–233; and, for his visit to the queen and the queen mother, fols. 235–236v.

52. Barb. lat. 5689, including, fols. 248–248v, the protocol for the cardinal's reception of guests of various ranks in Spain. Hugh Murray Baillie, "Etiquette and the Planning of the State Apartments in Baroque Palaces," *Archaeologia* 101 (1967), 169–99, emphasizes precisely the point that different patterns of use correspond to differently planned state apartments in the four countries of his study, England, France, Germany, and Spain; he does not consider apartments in Italy.

53. Kathleen Weil-Garris and John F. D'Amico, "The Renaissance Cardinal's Ideal Palace: A Chapter from Cortesi's *De cardinalatu*," in *Studies in Italian Art History*, I, ed. Henry A. Millon, Rome, 1980, 45–123.

54. Christoph Luitpold Frommel, *Der römische Palastbau der Hochrenaissance* (Römische Forschungen der Bibliotheca Hertziana, 21), 3 vols., Tübingen, 1973, I, 66–75.

55. Evitascandalo, *Maestro di casa*, 99–101, 199. "Anticamera" continued to have two—even seemingly contradictory—meanings. The *Vocabolario degli Accademici della Crusca* of 1624 ignores what had by that time clearly become standard Roman practice and defines "anticamera" as "stanza ritirata dietro alla camera." Filippo Baldinucci (*Vocabolario toscano dell'arte del disegno*, Florence, 1681) explains "anticamera" at greater length: "Nelle case private è una stanza retirata dietro alla camera. Nelle case pubbliche anticamera è la stanza avanti a quella dell'udienza, dove si fermano, e si trattengono i concorrenti; e nelle gran Corti de' Principi sogliono essere molte le anticamere, nelle quali si scompartiscono i concorrenti secondo la diversità de' loro stati, e dignità." For Baldinucci, the differences in usages have to do with the quality of the house.

56. What follows is based on the documentation and cogent analysis of Christoph Luitpold Frommel, "La construction et la décoration du Palais Farnèse, Sangallo et Michel-Ange (1513–1550)," in *Le Palais Farnèse, Ecole française de Rome*, I, Rome, 1981, 127–224, esp. 130–59.

57. Francesco Ehrle and Enrico Stevenson, *Gli affreschi del Pinturicchio nell'appartamento Borgia del Palazzo Apostolico Vaticano*, Rome, 1897, 9–27, for the plan of the apartments of the Vatican palace and esp. 13–14 for the "camera dei paramenti." Torgil Magnuson, *Studies in Quattrocento Architecture* (*Figura*, 9, Studies edited by the Institute of Art History, University of Uppsala), Stockholm, 1958, 283–86, for the plan of the main apartment of Palazzo Venezia and its similarity to that of the Vatican palace.

58. The ceremony of papal audiences for persons of various ranks in the seventeenth century is described by Lunadoro, *Corte di Roma*, 46–47, and Leti, *Itinerari*, 481–86. The diary of Johann Burchard, papal master of ceremonies 1483–1506, reveals great concern for details of precedence, but in terms of relationships among persons—e.g., the order of persons in processions, or arrangement of persons

within the audience room—not of movements of persons with respect to architecture; see Johann Burchard, *At the Court of the Borgia,* ed. and trans. Geoffrey Parker, London, 1963, passim; and Ehrle and Stevenson, *Affreschi,* 8–27.

59.　Montaigne, *Journal du voyage,* 238: "[In Rome] Les palais ont force suite de mambres [*membri,* rooms] les uns après les autres. Vous enfilés trois et quatre salles, avant que vous soyés à la maistresse."

60.　For example, Piero Tomei, "Contributi d'archivio, un elenco dei palazzi di Roma del tempo di Clemente VIII," *Palladio* 3 (1939), 163–74, 219–30, esp. 166, no. 5, the fifteenth-century house of the Priorato dei Cavalieri di Rodi, near St. Peter's, and no. 6, the elegant Palazzo Branconio dell'Aquila ("Questa casa ha la facciata di bella architettura, ma perchè ha poche stanze è molto incomoda"); and below, p. 42, the fifteenth-century Palazzo Condulmer-Orsini.

61.　Nicodemus Tessin, *Studieresor i Danmark, Tyskland, Holland, Frankrike och Italien,* ed. Osvald Sirén, Stockholm, 1914, 169, 177.

62.　ASR, Not. A.C., 6601, 15 Feb. 1648, fols. 893–893v.

63.　Below, pp. 305, 306 (Palazzo Chigi); p. 264, 266 (Palazzo Barberini); p. 116 (Palazzo Borghese).

64.　Below, p. 169 (Casa Grande); pp. 112, 116 (Palazzo Borghese); p. 305 and Tessin, *Studieresor,* 177 (Palazzo Chigi). The alcove in which Cardinal Chigi's bed was placed would also seem to reflect French architectural models.

2. Comfort

1.　Nathaniel Hawthorne, *Passages from the French and Italian Notebooks,* 1, London, 1871, 66, 132, 152–53, 213.

2.　Johann Wolfgang von Goethe, *Italian Journey,* trans. W. H. Auden and Elizabeth Mayer, New York, 1968, 147.

3.　Ibid., 355, 360, 370.

4.　H. H. Lamb, *Climate, Present, Past and Future,* II, London and New York, 1977, 461–73. Proposed dates for the beginning of the "Little Ice Age" are ca. 1300–1310, 1430, or 1560, and its ending is set at 1700, 1850, or 1900.

5.　Emmanuel Le Roy Ladurie, *Times of Feast, Times of Famine: A History of Climate since the Year 1000,* trans. Barbara Bray, Garden City, N.Y., 1971, 58, for dates of warmer and cooler episodes; 129–226 for a careful consideration of the documentation of movements of the Alpine glaciers in particular; 227–43 for the correlation of various kinds of evidence and the development of "working hypotheses."

6.　Francesco Liberati, *Il perfetto maestro di casa,* Rome, 1658, 146.

7.　Cesare Evitascandalo, *Il maestro di casa* (Rome, 1598), Viterbo, 1620, 78.

8.　Ibid., 100.

9.　Giacinto Gigli, *Diario romano (1608–1670),* ed. Giu-

seppe Ricciotti, Rome, 1958, 201, "A di 13. di Ottobre [1641] fu la prima tramontana: et si sentì freddo"; and similar entries on 28 October 1643, 27 October 1647, 10 October 1653, and 29 October 1654, pp. 237, 306, 426, 447.

10.　Evitascandalo, *Maestro di casa,* 57–60, 8.

11.　Gigli notes winter Tiber floods on 13 November 1614, 16 December 1621, 23 December 1623, 25 December 1631, 21 February 1637, December 1647, 15 February 1648, 1, 9, and 21 January 1652, 14 October 1653, and 3 December 1654; and spring or summer floods on 17 April 1614, 19 March 1646, and 4 June 1653.

12.　Gigli, *Diario romano,* 48–49, 431, 433, 250.

13.　Ibid., 301, 406.

14.　Ibid., 400–401, 464.

15.　Ibid., 23, 269–71, 286, 290, 359–61, 377.

16.　Leon Battista Alberti, *De re aedificatoria,* V.18; trans. James Leoni, London, 1755, 110.

17.　Vitruvius, *De architectura libri decem,* I.iv.5–6.

18.　Alvise Cornaro, *Trattato d'architettura,* c. 67, in Giuseppe Fiocco, *Alvise Cornaro, il suo tempo e le sue opere* (Saggi e studi di storia dell'arte, 8), n.p., 1965, 162, "mi libero col mezzo delle mie buone stanze dalli due estremi, che sono nell'anno, cioè dal gran freddo, e dal gran caldo, nemici mortali della vecchiezza."

19.　Vincenzo Scamozzi, *L'idea dell'architettura universale,* Venice, 1615, pt. I, II.16, pp. 148–51; III.viii, p. 251.

20.　Vitruvius, VI.iv.1–2; VII.iv.4; VII.v.1.

21.　Alberti, V.3, V.7; Francesco di Giorgio Martini, *Trattati di architettura, ingegneria, e arte militare* (Trattati di architettura, 3), ed. Corrado Maltese, 2 vols., Milan, 1967, 328, 344; Scamozzi, *Idea,* pt. I, III.iii, p. 241; and others.

22.　For example, Panciroli, *Roma sacra e moderna, già descritta dal Pancirolo ed accresciuta da Francesco Posterla . . . e di nuovo con somma diligenza, e studio riordinata da Gio. Francesco Cecconi . . . ,* Rome, 1725, describes apartments in the Palazzo Barberini alle Quattro Fontane, including "l'appartamento dunque terreno abitato nell'estate" (p. 206), "l'appartamento d'Inverno di S.E." (p. 209), "l'altro appartamento di mezzo tempo" (p. 210), and "l'Appartamento festivo del Signor Principe" (p. 210); below, pp. 265–66.

23.　Vitruvius, VI.iv.1–2; Alberti, V.18; Francesco di Giorgio, *Trattati,* 328; Scamozzi, *Idea,* pt. I, III.xix, pp. 305–7.

24.　Alberti, V.18; Andrea Palladio, *I quattro libri dell'architettura,* Venice, 1570, II.2; Scamozzi, *Idea,* pt. I, III.xix, p. 305.

25.　For example, Barb. lat. 4360 repeatedly refers to the protection from winter winds that his design for Palazzo Barberini would offer.

26.　Scamozzi, *Idea,* pt. I, III.iii, p. 241, ". . . e tutto intorno alla Corte appartamenti di stanze doppie di varie grandezze, e Salotti framezo . . ."

27.　Barb. lat. 4360, fol. 3, ". . . e di fare gli appartamenti doppij, ò da loggie coperti acciòche non gli offendano il caldo, il freddo, i venti, e l'altre ingiurie dell'aria . . ."

28. Below, pp. 174–76.

29. ABarb. 4360, fol. 14, ". . . una sala con appartamenti doppij da i lati à guisa del vecchio [that is, the west part of the Sforza palace] . . ."; and fols. 5, 16, and 18 for reference to other double apartments.

30. Below, pp. 291–92.

31. Below, pp. 85–86.

32. Above, n. 27 (chap. 2).

33. Palladio, II.14, p. 53; cf. II.17, p. 77.

34. Barb. lat. 4360, fol. 15, ". . . sarà ritirata, e coperta, e buona per ogni stagione da dormire la camera posta nel cantone sù la loggia"; fol. 16, ". . . una camera coperta da ogni lato, e fresca, benche alquanto scura . . ."

35. Below, p. 199.

36. Torgil Magnuson, *Studies in Quattrocento Architecture* (*Figura*, 9, Studies edited by the Institute of Art History, University of Uppsala), Stockholm, 1958, 153–54.

37. Below, pp. 85–86.

38. Scamozzi, *Idea*, pt. I, III.iii, p. 242 (Florence); III.xix, p. 308 (Genoa); III.viii, p. 250 (Spain).

39. Scamozzi, *Idea*, pt. I, III.xix, p. 308.

40. Below, pp. 308 (Palazzo Chigi); 112–18 (Palazzo Borghese); 265–66 (Palazzo Barberini). The ground-floor apartment arranged by Cardinal Antonio Barberini in the "Casa Grande" ai Giubbonari in the 1660s (below, p. 171) is never explicitly called a summer apartment, but it should probably be included with this group; a plan of the palace in 1734 (below, n. 93 [chap. 11], drawing no. 2) identifies the rooms as summer rooms: "P. Stanze nobili per l'estate."

41. ABorg. 7504, inventory of 1693, unpaginated, "Nella sesta stanza dov'è il Zampanaro" [A13], and, in the princess's apartment, "Stanza che segue dov'è il Zampanaro" [A9].

42. For Palazzo Chigi, AChigi 702, undated inventory of Cardinal Flavio Chigi, unpaginated, "Appartamento d'abbasso del Primo Piano," lists no bed. Cf. the descriptions of Nicodemus Tessin, who visited both palaces in 1687–88, Tessin, *Studieresor i Danmark, Tyskland, Holland, Frankrike och Italien,* ed. Osvald Sirén, Stockholm, 1914, 168, 176.

Some other accounts of ground-floor apartments similarly have to do with daytime use in the summer. On 4 July 1519 Alessandro Farnese held a banquet for twenty cardinals and the pope in the north corner room of the ground floor of the unfinished Palazzo Farnese (Fig. 5a). (Christoph Luitpold Frommel, "La construction et la décoration du Palais Farnèse, Sangallo et Michel-Ange [1513–1550]," in *Le Palais Farnèse, Ecole française de Rome,* I, Rome, 1981, 134.) In Palazzo Mattei, the three ground-floor rooms with painted decorations, in the southeast angle of the building, are too few to form a complete apartment, and documents refer to them as day rooms, not bedrooms (Fig. 7a).

(Gerda Panofsky-Soergel, "Zur Geschichte des Palazzo Mattei di Giove," *Römisches Jahrbuch für Kunstgeschichte* 11 [1967–68], 109–88, esp. 130, citing documents for paintings in "la prima stanza da basso" [to the left of the eastern entrance corridor], "un'altra stanza da basso grande," also called "salotto da basso della cantonata" [the large corner room], and "salotto delle mie stantie terrene" [to the right of the southern entrance corridor].)

43. Alberti, V.18; cf. Francesco di Giorgio, *Trattati,* 328; Palladio, II.2; and Scamozzi, *Idea,* pt. I, III.iii, p. 241.

44. Lionello Neppi, *Palazzo Spada,* Rome, 1975, 137, quoting Cardinal Bernardino.

45. Scamozzi, *Idea,* pt. I, III.iii, p. 241.

46. Alberti, X.16; Francesco di Giorgio, *Trattati,* 328.

47. Alberti, X.16.

48. For Palazzo Colonna-Chigi, below, p. 291. For Palazzo Borghese, ABorg. 307, no. 67, 27 Sept. 1619, ". . . alle stantie, dove stanno li Palafrenieri . . . Per la fattura . . . di . . . dui solari rustici sopra li mattonati in dette stantie . . . alti da terra palmi 1½ per la humidità [*palmi* 33½ × 26, *palmi* 32½ × 25¾]," possibly rooms A11 and A12 (Fig. 28).

49. Scamozzi, *Idea,* pt. I, III.iii, p. 241.

50. Barb. lat. 4360, fol. 27, ". . . vi si farà un' soffitto attaccato à i travi, e di sopra un' solaro mattonato, per guardar la stanza dal caldo, e freddo, e dalle pioggie improvise."

51. Francesco di Giorgio, *Trattati,* 329.

52. Barb. lat. 4360, fol. 7.

53. Palladio, I.25; cf. Scamozzi, *Idea,* pt. I, III.xxi, p. 319.

54. Alberti, V.18.

55. Scamozzi, *Idea,* pt. I, III.iii, p. 242.

56. Alberti, V.17.

57. Cornaro, *Trattato,* ed. Fiocco, 162.

58. Scamozzi, *Idea,* pt. I, III.viii, p. 251.

59. Ibid., pt. I, III.xxi, pp. 321–22. Scamozzi describes a freestanding hearth, with a hood, about which many people can warm themselves at one time; a fireplace set entirely in front of the wall, "à Padiglione, e Francesi," used throughout most of France; a type half projecting from the wall, "à mezo Padiglione," used in Venice and Lombardy, where the walls are not so thick; a fireplace set entirely into the thickness of the wall, "alla romana"; a fireplace that transfers heat to a second room by means of a bronze plate, used in Piedmont and elsewhere beyond the Alps; and a type used in England, with a vent in the chimney that can be closed to retain heat after the fire is out.

60. In contrast to the usual Roman practice, Borromini's fireplace in the *sala di ricreazione* of the Casa dei Filippini projects strongly into the elliptical volume of the room. Its type, "a mezo Padiglione" (see the previous note) makes all the more poignant its canopied and tasseled form.

61. Evitascandalo, *Maestro di casa,* 7, 38, 99, 101, 174, 199; Liberati, *Maestro di casa,* 41, 64, 97, 104.

62. Evitascandalo, *Maestro di casa,* 100.

63. Ibid., 101, 107.

64. Barb. lat. 4360, fol. 23.

65. ABarb., Comp. 268, an inventory of the furnishings of Palazzo Barberini in April 1644, lists a "parafuoco di noce" in audience room C5 (fol. 98), a "parafuoco di taffetta" in room C28 (fol. 113), and another "parafuoco di taffetta" in the "stanza dell'audienza" C27 (fol. 114). Two firescreens in the Palazzo Colonna-Barberini in Palestrina were slatted ("parafuoco di legno di noce fatto à gelosia," in rooms B3 and B7, in an inventory of the furnishings of the palace in 1648, ASR, Not. A.C., busta 6601, fols. 939v, 941v).

66. Seventeenth-century inventories like those cited in the second part of this book give ample evidence for the blankets and warming pans. Each bed usually had one or two wool blankets—e.g., in Palazzo Barberini alle Quattro Fontane in 1644, Cardinal Antonio Barberini's bed in room C8 and that of his attendant in C9 (ABarb., Comp. 268, fols. 100, 101). The same inventory lists four *scaldaletti,* of silver or copper (doc. cit., fols. 13, 68, 93, 105); there were twelve in Palestrina in 1637 (ABarb., Ind. II, no. 3112, int. 2, unpaginated); Cardinal Flavio Chigi had nine *scaldaletti* at the Palazzo Chigi (AChigi 703, fol. 222); even Francesco Ceccarelli and his mother had four in their apartment in the Palazzo della Famiglia Borghese (ABorg. 457, Inv. 52, fols. 158v, 162; below, pp. 42–43 and n. 141 [chap. 4]). Evitascandalo, *Maestro di casa,* 39, and Liberati, *Maestro di casa,* 41, note that it is the *cameriere*'s duty to warm the bed in winter.

67. Evitascandalo, *Maestro di casa,* 54.

68. Below, chap. 15.

69. Palladio, I.27; Scamozzi, *Idea,* pt. I, III.xxi, p. 321.

70. Barb. lat. 4344, fol. 36–37.

71. Alberti, V.17.

72. Scamozzi, *Idea,* pt. I, III.xix, p. 307.

73. Palladio, II.2.

74. Barb. lat. 4360, fols. 58, 20–21.

75. Below, pp. 191–92, 199.

76. Alberti, X.16.

77. Scamozzi, *Idea,* pt. I, III.xix, p. 307.

78. E.g., for Palazzo Barberini alle Quattro Fontane, the installation of hooks is recorded in ABarb., Ind. II, no. 2888, fols. 193 (rooms C33, C34), 194 (C36), 198v (C32), 201 (C29), 203 (C28), 204 (C27), 214v (C19), 215 (C20), 239v (B19, B20, B29), and 245 (B27); and for the remodeling of Palazzo Borghese in 1671–76, a record of the installation of 850 hooks in the rooms of the *piano nobile,* in ABorg. 1476, no. 781, unpaginated, "Per haver fatto li bughi e scompartito e messo e murato n° 850 rampini nelle sudette stanze al detto pian nobile per li parati messi con il gesso messi con scomodo su le scale."

79. Below, p. 199.

80. Ursula Reinhardt, "La tapisserie feinte, un genre de décoration du maniérisme romain au XVIᵉ siècle," *Gazette des Beaux-arts* 84 (1974), 285–96, sees both tapestries and fictive tapestries as equivalent decorative enrichment, and

nothing more.

81. Evitascandalo, *Maestro di casa,* 78.

82. E.g., ABarb., Comp. 88, no. 1741, 5 Feb. 1669, "A Matteo Nuzzi festarolo scudi 33.98 mᵗᵃ per saldo d'un conto di lavori fatti per tutto li 15 Decembre prosⁱ in haver apparato in più chiesi in occasione di feste, et altro d'ordine nostro et per haver sparato d'estate, e riapparato d'Inverno le nostre stanze . . ."

83. ABorg. 1476, no. 781, unpaginated, "Stanzione del Udienza di S. Eccᶻᵃ . . . Per la mettitura in opera delle canne di piombo che portano lacqua alla fontana di argento in detto stanzione . . . ; Stanzione dell Udienza della Sigᵗᵃ Principessa . . . Per la mettitura in opera delle dui fontanelle di alabastro in detto [and their lead pipes] . . .; Stanza [A5] che segue dove e la fontana di porfido . . . Per la mettitura in opera del vaso di porfido della fontana . . . con la mettitura del vaso sopra [and its foundation and lead pipes]; Galleria [A14] . . . Per la mettitura in opera delle due fontanelle di alabastro nelle teste della galleria con tazza lon. p. 3⅔ con sotto quattro tigre alt. luno p. 3 con balaustro nel mezzo simile dove passa la canna . . . messe e levate di opera piu volte per provarle a sodisfatione delli Padroni." Cf. ABorg. 7503, an inventory of the ground-floor apartments in 1693, unpaginated, which includes the fountains among the furnishings of the four rooms.

84. ABarb., Giust. 501–625, no. 617 (fol. 262), 4 Oct. 1626, an account of the cleaning of paintings and installation of Barberini arms in rooms of the recently purchased palace, including "Nella prima stanza [C32] dopo la sala, dove è la fontana."

85. ABarb., Ind. II, no. 2888, fol. 241v, for the installation of plumbing "per la fontana" in B29, the "Camera overo Salotto dov'è dipinto la balaustrata con Scimotti Ucelli et in mezzo l'Arme del Papa"; cf. Tessin, *Studieresor,* 166.

86. Tessin, *Studieresor,* 167, and below, pp. 258–59, for room B36; and Tessin, *Studieresor,* 170, for the oval room C17, where "siehet man in der mitten vom Sal eine fontaine worinnen eine antique Venus von brontz stehet." ABarb., Comp. 348, an inventory of 1692–1704, fol. 328, identifies the bronze figure of the fountain as Galatea.

87. Tessin, *Studieresor,* 176; but this fountain is not included in the documents of construction, 1664–67.

88. *Avviso* of 22 July 1615 (Urb. lat. 1083, c. 374), published by J.A.F. Orbaan, *Documenti sul Barocco in Roma,* Rome, 1920, 234, ". . . perchè li caldi sono eccessivi ha fatta tirare una tenda sopra un cortile, che ha al pari delle stanze e fatto vi congegnare canone grande che getta acqua sopra essa tenda, la quale poi cala a basso in forma di pioggia et rinfresca assai."

89. Scamozzi, *Idea,* pt. I, III.xix, p. 307; Palladio, I.27.

90. Uffizi A1224; Gustavo Giovannoni, *Antonio da Sangallo il Giovane,* 2 vols., Rome, 1959, Fig. 312.

91. Barb. lat. 4360, fol. 21.

92. ABorg. 1476, no. 781, unpaginated, "Adi 8 giugno 1676, [*misura* of foundations, bases, and columns of the *ringhiera*, then] Per la mettitura in opera del tamburo di castagno dove sono le gelosie sopra a detta balaustrata . . ."

93. Girolamo Lunadoro, *Relatione della Corte di Roma, e de' riti da osservarsi in essa . . .* , n.p., 1635, 55, "stare in luogo ritirato, sotto Gelosia, per non esser visto." Gregorio Leti, *Itinerari della corte di Roma ò verò teatro historico, cronologico, e politico della sede apostolica . . .* , Valence, 1675, 496.

94. *Avviso* of 15 May 1610 (BAV, Urb. lat. 1078, fol. 350), published by Orbaan, *Documenti,* 170–71, "Sua Beatitudine fu veduta alle gelosie del palazzo di Cane in Borgo, hora di Borghese, dove stette a vedere passare il nuovo conservatore et sua comitiva"; and Orbaan's n. 1.

95. Barb. lat. 4360, fol. 49, ". . . onde con un poggiuolo, che alli tre lati davanti si faccia, coperto da gelosie, non saprei qual più bella vista di strade di città potesse haversi senza esser veduto."

96. Ibid., fol. 19.

97. AChigi 516, fol. 18v, for "6 sportelli alle trè finestre in detta galleria [E18], graticciati, fatti à gelosia," each *palmi* 3¼ × 3½; fol. 20v, for "4 sportelli fatti à gelosia," each *palmi* 2 × 3½, for the two windows of room E16; and fols. 46–47, for the frame and "li due sportelli alla gelosia, che guarda infaccia l'Entrone" at the garden stair. Vincenzo Golzio, *Documenti artistici sul Seicento nell'Archivio Chigi,* Rome, 1939, 68, doc. 1414, 18 March 1683, "Per haver fatto le gelosie sopra all'arco fatto di novo . . . accanto detta antiporta."

98. ABorg., 4168, 14 July 1609, "e più per quattro saliceni con suoi finimenti che hanno servito alle fenestre et alle stantie dove dormo [*sic*] il Sig.re [Giovanni Battista]."

99. ABarb., Ind. II, no. 2878, "ferri per tener le stuore alle finestre stagnati di libbre 1¼, b. 10 l'uno."

100. ABarb., Comp. 80, 14 June 1633, scudi 7.80 ". . . per n.ro 50 girelle d'ottone per le finestre delli nuovi appartamenti del palazzo alle 4 fontane per tirare le store . . ."

101. AChigi 484, unpaginated, a bill for work by Giuseppe Fornari for Cardinal Chigi in 1668, including, "Adi 15 [maggio 1668] per haver atacato a tutte le finestre del Palazzo le store numero quaranta cinque, scudi 4.50."

102. ABarb., Comp. 187, 28 Nov. 1629, scudi 8.50 to "Antonio Fabini festarolo per lavori fatti in parare, e sparare quindici stanze, e levare 35 store dalle finestre di casa mia."

103. AChigi 703, fol. 186, "Quattro bandinelle grandi . . . che riparano il sole nelle due Arcate della Galleria . . . ; Una tenda grande serve per tirare l'estate al Cortile . . ."; and a similar entry in AChigi 702, unpaginated inventory, "Nella galleria . . ."

104. ASR, CRM, Teatini, 2162, int. 216, fol. 14, ". . . la stanza dove dorme il presente mese di luglio l'Em.mo S.r Card.le Antonio Padrone . . ."

105. Above, p. 6.

106. Scamozzi, *Idea,* pt. I, III.xix, p. 308, suggests recourse to a cryptoporticus or underground room for summer use, in especially hot places. The cool three-bay loggia of the Villa Aldobrandini is described in "Relatione della Villa Belvedere," fol. 4, Archivio Aldobrandini, in Cesare d'Onofrio, *La Villa Aldobrandini di Frascati,* Rome, n.d., 82–115.

107. Michel de Montaigne, *Journal du voyage de Michel de Montaigne en Italie par la Suisse et l'Allemagne en 1580 et 1581,* ed. Alessandro d'Ancona, Città di Castello, 1889, 328–29, "Ils ont un observation ici beaucoup plus curieuse qu'ailleurs: car ils font difference aus rues, aus cartiers de la ville, voir aus departemens de leurs maisons, pour respect de la santé; et en font tel estat, qu'ils changent de habitation aus sesons, et de ceus mesmes qui les louent, qui tient deux ou trois palais de louage à fort grand despence, pour se remeuer aus sesons, selon l'ordonance de leurs medecins."

108. Alberti, V.18; Palladio, II.12.

109. Alberti, V.14; Francesco di Giorgio, *Trattati,* 327–28; Scamozzi, *Idea,* pt. I, II.16, p. 148.

110. Hawthorne, *Passages,* 83. On the stair to the apartment, Hawthorne passed an ancient bas-relief of a lion; i.e., he was ascending the stair S1 in the north wing of the palace.

111. Henry James, *William Wetmore Story and His Friends,* 2 vols., Boston, 1903, 1, 359, includes a letter from Mrs. Gaskell to Mrs. Story, remembering the "wood-fire" in the Storys' apartment.

3. Noblewomen

1. Francesco Cerasoli, "Censimento della popolazione di Roma dall'anno 1600 al 1739," *Studi e Documenti di Storia e Diritto,* 12, Rome, 1891.

2. Giovanni Battista de Luca, *Il cavaliere e la dama,* Rome, 1675. The first and by far the larger part of this book is given over to *il cavaliere;* De Luca's consideration of *la dama* begins only on p. 481. For the following description of a noblewoman's attributes and activities, see 520–45.

3. Baldassare Castiglione, *Il libro del cortegiano,* Venice, 1527, esp. Book III.

4. Letter of Christopher Wren to an unnamed friend, 1665, published in Stephen Wren, *Parentalia, or, Memoirs of the Family of the Wrens,* London, 1750, 261.

5. Barb. lat. 5686, fols. 114v–117.

6. The case of Christina of Sweden, most prominent of women in seventeenth-century Rome, is unique. Christina was an exceptional person, in whatever category one might place her. She was a crowned head but, by the time of her arrival in Rome in December 1655, was no longer wearing that crown. She was a valued convert to Catholicism, therefore worthy of special honor. And she was a woman. Special etiquette had to be devised for her reception by

Alexander VII. For instance, a specially designed chair was prepared for her, neither the stack of three or four cushions customary for women received by the pope (below, p. 28), nor the chair with arms used by kings, nor the "scabello semplice" without back or arms on which ambassadors of kings would sit (F. Tantouche, *Traicte de tout ce qui s'observe en la cour de Rome, Tant par nostre sainct Père, que par Messeigneurs les Illustrissimes Cardinaux,* Paris, 1623, 80–81; Gregorio Leti, *Itinerari della corte di Roma ò verò teatro historico, cronologico, e politico della sede apostolica . . . ,* Valence, 1675, 481–85), but something between a chair and a stool, with low arms and back (Pier Bartolo Romanelli, "Etichetta e precedenze a Roma durante il soggiorno di Cristina di Svezia," *Il Giornale di Politica e di Letteratura* 7, fasc. 1–3 [January–March 1931], 6). When she dined with the pope on the day following her formal entry into the city, again special ceremony was devised (Romanelli, "Etichetta e precedenze," 8; Georgina Masson, *Queen Christina* [London, 1968], opp. p. 320, published a drawing by Sevin showing Christina dining publicly with Clement IX at the Quirinal on 9 December 1668). Christina stayed in the Palazzo Farnese, selecting for her own use the apartment in the west angle of the *piano nobile* and receiving visitors in the "Sala delli Imperatori" (Masson, *Queen Christina,* 256–57). Later she settled in the Palazzo Riario on the Lungara. She was one of the first people on whom an ambassador or cardinal newly arrived in Rome would call: the new arrival would visit first the pope, then his cardinal patron, then the dean of the College of Cardinals, then Christina, "vice Decana e seconda Cardinalessa" (Romanelli, "Etichetta e precendenze," 11, quoting an *avviso* of 2 July 1672). The etiquette that she observed in receiving prominent guests is described by Romanelli; it followed the Roman system (below, pp. 27–28), with some adjustments for her peculiar status.

7. Massillon Rouvet, *Entrée a Rome de Charles de Gonzague, Ambassadeur du Roi de France Henri IV, d'après un comte-rendu de 1608,* Nevers, 1895, 10.

8. Giacinto Gigli, *Diario romano (1608–1670),* ed. Giuseppe Ricciotti, Rome, 1958, 383.

9. Christoph Luitpold Frommel, *Der römische Palastbau der Hochrenaissance* (Römische Forschungen der Bibliotheca Hertziana, 21), 3 vols., Tübingen, 1973, II, 109, doc. 49, 21.II.1545.

10. Alessandro Ademollo, *I teatri di Roma nel secolo decimosettimo,* Rome, 1888, 22, 26, quoting *avvisi.*

11. Pio Pecchiai, "Costanza Magalotti Barberini, cognata di Urbano VIII," *Archivi* (Rome) 16, fasc. 2 (1949), 23–24.

12. E.g., Vincenzo Cervio, *Il trinciante,* Rome, 1593, 132–36; Leti, *Itinerari,* 568; and Maria d'Angelo, *Matrimoni nel seicento romano* (Curiosità romane, ser. 1, vol. 7), Albano Laziale, 1928, 35–36. Husbands served their wives at a banquet recorded by Montaigne in 1581, in *Journal du voyage de Michel de Montaigne en Italie par la Suisse et l'Allemagne en 1580 et 1581,* ed. Alessandro d'Ancona, Città di Castello, 1889, 257. By contrast, the women and men participating in the evening discussions in the court of Urbino were to alternate positions around the circle, as far as possible, according to Castiglione, *Cortegiano,* I.6 (trans. Singleton, 1959, 18).

13. Barb. lat. 4731, "Della vita di Papa Urbano Ottavo et istoria del suo pontificato scritta da Andrea Nicoletti canonico di S. Lorenzo in Damaso, II," fols. 1440–1441.

14. ABorg. 3949, "Rolo della famiglia dell'ecce^mo s^r prin^e Borghese 1626–1632," lists twelve "donne" in 1626, presumably companions of the princess Camilla. AVR, S. Lorenzo in Lucina, Stati d'Anime, 1678, fol. 118, names ten "donne" living in Palazzo Borghese, companions of the princess Eleonora. The women included in the household of Taddeo Barberini—twenty-six in 1633 and twenty-four in 1634 (below, p. 196)—would have been divided between Donna Anna and Donna Costanza Barberini. Among the ten women named as Anna's "donne" in a household roll of 1643 were two laundresses and three servants for Anna's three young sons (ABarb., Ind. IV, no. 1282). When Costanza retired to live in a convent, in 1640, four girls went with her: her five-year-old grandniece, two maids-in-waiting, and a servant (Pecchiai, "Costanza," 27–28).

15. Some of the male staff members of Costanza Barberini, for example, are noted in documents referring to housing for the Barberini *famiglia* (ABarb., Ind. II, no. 2888, fols. 68v, 87r, 92v, 94r; and Ind. II, no. 2863, fol. 3). Seven men still received wages as members of her staff in 1643, three years after she had entered a convent (Arch. Barb., Ind. IV, no. 1282); cf. Taddeo's provisions for his mother on her entry into the convent, in a document published by Pecchiai, "Costanza," 40–41.

16. Cf., e.g., bills for clothing for several of Donna Virginia Borghese's male staff members, 1623 (ABorg. 5547, no. 25).

17. The women's kitchens are discussed below, pp. 30, 38. An example of separate accounts for the table can be seen in a summary of Borghese purchases of snow in 1623 (ABorg. 5547, no. 133).

18. E.g., ABarb., Comp. 3, fol. 6, 29 Oct. 1623, "A spese della prima carrozza del ecc^ma Sig^ra Costanza [Barberini] scudi 16.50 m^ta." When Costanza retired to the Convent of the SS. Incarnazione, her coachman Filippo was reassigned to Taddeo and his sons; Pecchiai, "Costanza," 41, publishing a document dated 8 Jan. 1642.

19. Tantouche, *Traicte,* 80; Francesco Sestini da Bibbiena, *Il maestro di camera,* Florence, 1621, 185, 234; Leti, *Itinerari,* 533.

20. ASF, Medici del Principato, vol. 2658, unpaginated (Appendix I).

21. Leti, *Itinerari,* 578, 587–88.

22. Letter of 17 October 1606, ABarb., Ind. IV, no. 580,

published by Pecchiai, "Costanza," 36–37: "So che V.S. non mancherà degl'offici continui e debiti alle ecc^me Sig^re consorti degl'ecc^mi Sig^ri fr^lli di S.Sta."

23.   ABarb., Ind. IV, no. 598 (Appendix 2).

24.   Tantouche, *Traicte*, 81; Leti, *Itinerari*, 484; Girolamo Lunadoro, *Relatione della Corte di Roma, e de' riti da osservarsi in essa* . . . , n.p., 1635, 46.

25.   That women would call on cardinals is indicated by the advice of Lunadoro, *Corte di Roma*, 61, and Leti, *Itinerari*, 512, that the *portiera* should remain up on such visits.

26.   Pecchiai, "Costanza," describes Costanza's life in a thorough and sympathetic way, drawing on documents in the Archivio Barberini.

27.   That Anna was receiving very early in her marriage, whether on behalf of her husband or on behalf of the pope, is shown by a reference to her audience room (presumably in the "Casa Grande" ai Giubbonari) in a payment recorded in ABarb., Comp. 187, 27 July 1629: ". . . spese d'un tappeto grande per la stanza dove da audiencia l'Ecc^ma S^a D. Anna . . ."

28.   Pecchiai, "Costanza," 26–28, 30.

29.   ABarb., Ind. IV, no. 598 (Appendix 2).

30.   Above, pp. 5–6.

31.   Sestini, *Maestro di casa*, 185, for visits; Leti, *Itinerari*, 514, for coaches; Leti, *Itinerari*, 568, for banquets and the limitation on yielding to women.

32.   Lunadoro, *Corte di Roma*, 1635, 61; Leti, *Itinerari*, 512.

33.   Lunadoro, *Corte di Roma*, 46; Tantouche, *Traicte*, 81; Leti, *Itinerari*, 484.

34.   The construction of these suites is described in ABorg. 1476, no. 781, unpaginated (below, pp. 112–22); the identifications of some of the rooms as given below appear in this document: for the ground-floor apartments, "Stanzione del Udienza di S. Ecc^za," "Stanza ultima dove è il Zampanaro," "Appartamento verso il giardino della sig^ra Principessa," "Prima stanza dove è il Zampanaro," "Stanzione dell Udienza della Sig^ra Principessa"; for the *piano nobile* apartments, "Anticamera," "Cammera del Udienza di S. E^za," "Galleria al Pian Nobile," "Cammera che segue verso il giardino dell'Udienza della Sig^ra Principessa," "Anticamera accanto la cappella," "Cappella," "Sala."

35.   ABorg. 7504, Inventory of 1693, pp. 1–14; Paola della Pergola, "L'inventario Borghese del 1693," *Arte antica e moderna* 26 (April–June 1964), 219–30; 28 (October–December 1964), 451–567; 30 (April–June 1965), 202–17, published the portions of this inventory listing the paintings, but omitted all references to the other furnishings.

36.   Below, pp. 85–86, 88–89, 104, 108.

37.   ABorg. 456, no. 25; ABorg. 458, Inv. 65, 18 June 1642; below, p. 109 and n. 226 (chap. 9).

38.   Below, pp. 188–89.

39.   Below, pp. 130, 189.

40.   Below, pp. 188–89 and n. 31 (chap. 12).

41.   Below, pp. 189–91, 245.

42.   Giuseppe Sacchi Lodispoto, "Anna Colonna Barberini ed il suo monumento nel Monastero di Regina Coeli," *Strenna dei romanisti* 43 (1982), 460–78, esp. 467–70.

43.   Below, p. 194.

44.   For the fireplace, ABarb., Ind. II, no. 2888, fol. 185v; for the furnishings, ABarb., Ind. IV, no. 574, fol. 115. The description may refer to rooms in either the "Casa Grande" ai Giubbonari or the Palazzo Barberini alle Quattro Fontane. The latter are listed in the inventory of the palace dated April 1644 (ABarb., Comp. 268, fols. 72–73) as the "stanze dove stava l'Ecc^ma Sig^ra"; by that time Costanza was living in the convent of the SS. Incarnazione, and the rooms were used for the storage of beds and musical instruments.

45.   Pecchiai, "Costanza," 28.

46.   Pietro Cataneo, *I quattro primi libri di architettura*, Venice, 1554, 46v.

47.   Barb. lat. 4360, fol. 62; for location of the women's apartment, fols. 18–19.

48.   Below, pp. 191–92.

49.   ABarb., Ind. II, no. 3112, fol. 363v (Appendix 4).

50.   ABorg. 307, no. 67, 26 Oct. 1620, "Alle stanze sotto tetto per le donne della Sig^ra Principessa"; 27 Sept. 1619, "Alla stantia della Rota," "Per haver fatto una rota per voltare, dove passa il mangiare per le donne di albuccio alt. p. 4½ lar. di diametro p. 4 . . ."; Arch. Borg. 4168, 27 Sept. 1619, the latrine; 4 Jan. 1623, window frames for the "cucina delle donne" and the "dispensa delle sudette donne"; and below, p. 102.

51.   ABorg. 1476, no. 781, unpaginated, describing the construction of the new "appartamento delle donne," including the corridor E7, the "scala lumaca dove tirano l'acqua le Donne" S11, the "Stanza dove mangiono le donne" E12, the seven small rooms E15–E21, the "Stanziolino dove è la rota" E22, the "cucina delle donne" E13, and other features; below, p. 124.

52.   ABorg. 7504, unpaginated, but at the end of the volume, "Mobili che stanno nell'appartamenti delle donne."

53.   ABarb., Ind. II, no. 2888, fols. 139v, 155v, 165v, 187r–188r; below, p. 194.

54.   Below, p. 194.

55.   AChigi 520, fol. 60, "Muro di una finestra rimurata in detta scala dove era la rota."

56.   See the plan of the Palazzo Del Bufalo-Ferraioli published by Gianfranco Spagnesi, "Palazzo Del Bufalo-Ferraioli e il suo architetto," in *Studi in memoria di Gino Chierici* (Società di Storia Patria di Terra di Lavoro), Caserta, 1965, 134–58, *disegni* 8 and 9.

57.   Below, chap. 12.

4. Famiglia

1.   Especially useful are handbooks for the *maestro di casa,* who oversaw the work of others, e.g., Cesare Evitascan-

dalo, *Il maestro di casa,* Rome, 1596 (I cite the edition of Viterbo, 1620); and Francesco Liberati, *Il perfetto maestro di casa,* Rome, 1658.

2. Rolls of the household, recording monthly payments to each member, were regularly kept. These confirm the practices described in handbooks of household management like those cited in the preceding note. For the following discussion, see the roll of the *famiglia* of Prince Marcantonio Borghese, ABorg. 3949, "Rolo della famiglia dell'eccemo sr prine Borghese, 1626–1632"; that of Cardinal Francesco Barberini, ABarb., Comp. 142, "Salari e Companatici della Famiglia 1637–1642" (identifiable as Cardinal Francesco's through such internal evidence as three references to the Cancelleria, contrary to Marilyn Aronberg Lavin, *Seventeenth-Century Barberini Documents and Inventories of Art,* New York, 1975, 730, who thought the volume belonged to Cardinal Antonio); the roll of the household of Cardinal Antonio Barberini, ABarb., Ind. IV, no. 176, "Rolo della famiglia dell'Eminentmo Sigr Cardinale Antonio Barberini con le loro parti, salarij, e companatici per il primo di Aprile 1642"; the roll of Taddeo Barberini's household, ABarb., Ind. IV, no. 1282, "Rolo della famiglia dell'Eccmo Sige Principe D. Taddeo nell'anno 1643"; and the roll of Cardinal Flavio Chigi, AChigi 573, "Rolo della famiglia dell'Emmo Sigr Card. Chigi Padrone per il Mese di Marzo 1666" and subsequent months until December 1675.

3. Evitascandalo, *Maestro di casa,* passim; and Liberati, *Maestro di casa,* passim.

4. Evitascandalo, *Maestro di casa,* 81–82.

5. Ibid., 66; but cf. Liberati, *Maestro di casa,* 94, who describes the dean of the *palafrenieri* as subordinate to both the *maestro di casa* and the *maestro di camera.*

6. Cesare Evitascandalo, *Libro dello scalco,* Rome, 1609, 4; idem, *Maestro di casa,* 12.

7. Evitascandalo, *Scalco,* 5; Evitascandalo, *Maestro di casa,* 42; Liberati, *Maestro di casa,* 67.

8. Liberati, *Maestro di casa,* 73–74.

9. Ibid., 11–12.

10. Evitascandalo, *Maestro di casa,* 133–34; Francesco Priscianese, *Del governo della corte d'un signore in Roma,* Rome, 1543 (republished Città di Castello, 1883), 30–31; and below, p. 44.

11. Evitascandalo, *Maestro di casa,* 79–80.

12. ABarb., Ind. IV, no. 1282 (above, n. 2 [chap. 4]).

13. Evitascandalo, *Maestro di casa,* 4, 210–11.

14. Ibid., 172–73.

15. Ibid., 21.

16. Ibid., 37.

17. E.g., Taddeo Barberini's roll in 1643 (above, n. 2 [chap. 4]), including women attendants, nurses for Carlo, Maffeo, and Nicolò Barberini, and tutors in music and drawing for the "signorini."

18. See the rolls of *famiglie* cited above, n. 2 (chap. 4).

19. Evitascandalo, *Maestro di casa,* 211.

20. Jean Delumeau, *Vie économique et sociale de Rome dans la seconde moitié du XVIᵉ siècle* (Bibliothèque des Ecoles françaises d'Athènes et de Rome, 184), 2 vols., Paris, 1957–59, 434.

21. ABarb., Comp. 37, fol. 2, "Companatici e salarij di Dicembre [1621]"; and similar lists for subsequent months throughout the volume.

22. AVR, S. Lorenzo in Lucina, Stati d'Anime, 1607–1621, fol. 73, 1621.

23. AVR, S. Susanna, Stati d'Anime, 1631–1651, 1633, fol. 2v; 1634, fol. IV.

24. ABarb., Giust. 501–625, nos. 513 (May 1626), 537 (June 1626), 558 (July 1626), 588 (Sept. 1626), 605 (Oct. 1626), 624 (Nov. 1626, for the first time listing ninety-four persons); ABarb., Comp. 142 (1637).

25. According to the rolls of *famiglie* cited above, n. 2 (chap. 4).

26. Evitascandalo, *Maestro di casa,* 67; Girolamo Lunadoro, *Relatione della corte di Roma, e de' riti da osservarsi in essa . . . ,* n.p., 1635, 6.

27. Lunadoro, *Corte di Roma,* 1635, 4–5.

28. Lunadoro, *Corte di Roma,* ed. Bracciano, 1650, 389–94.

29. Gregorio Leti, *Itinerari della corte di Roma ò verò teatro historico, cronologico, e politico della sede apostolica . . . ,* Valence, 1675, 589–90.

30. Gaetano Moroni, *Dizionario di erudizione storico-ecclesiastica,* Venice, 1843, XXIII, "Famiglia," 24–73.

31. Alessandro Ferrajoli, "Il ruolo della corte di Leone X (1514–1516)," *Archivio della R. Società Romana di storia patria* 34 (1911), 1–31.

32. Moroni, *Dizionario,* XXIII, 61–62, 66–73, including the complete roll of the household of Paul IV in July 1555.

33. Moroni, *Dizionario,* XXIII, 133–35.

34. Delumeau, *Vie économique,* 433–36, 447. For the economic situation of cardinals at the beginning of the sixteenth century, see D. S. Chambers, "The Economic Predicament of Renaissance Cardinals," in *Studies in Medieval and Renaissance History,* 3, ed. William M. Bowsky, Lincoln, Neb., 1966, 287–313; and Kathleen Weil-Garris and John F. D'Amico, "The Renaissance Cardinal's Ideal Palace: A Chapter from Cortesi's *De cardinalatu,*" in *Studies in Italian Art History,* 1, ed. Henry A. Millon, Rome, 1980, 45–123, esp. 98 n. 2.

35. Delumeau, *Vie économique,* 433–37, 447, 451–53.

36. Priscianese, *Governo della corte,* 4–5; Evitascandalo, *Maestro di casa,* 157–64.

37. Priscianese, *Governo della corte,* 5; Evitascandalo, *Maestro di casa,* 172–73.

38. Priscianese, *Governo della corte,* 4; Evitascandalo, *Maestro di casa,* 36–39.

39. Priscianese, *Governo della corte,* 72; Evitascandalo, *Maestro di casa,* 5–8.

40. Evitascandalo, *Maestro di casa,* 171–72.

41. Priscianese, *Governo della corte,* 4–5.

42. Ibid., 5, 75; Evitascandalo, *Maestro di casa,* 38.

43. Books concerned with eating are Bartolomeo Scappi, *Dell'arte del cucinare,* Venice, 1570, and later editions in 1598, 1610, and 1622; Evitascandalo, *Trenciante* manuscript, 1576; Evitascandalo, *Scalco* manuscript, 1577; Vincenzo Cervio, *Il trinciante,* Rome, 1581, and later editions in 1593 and 1610; Giovanni Battista Rossetti, *Dello scalco,* Ferrara, 1584; Cesare Evitascandalo, *Dialogo del trenciante,* Rome, 1609; and Evitascandalo, *Scalco,* 1609. Books emphasizing the "camera" are Lunadoro manuscript (ca. 1617); Francesco Sestini da Bibbiena, *Il maestro di camera,* Florence, 1621, and many subsequent editions; F. Tantouche, *Traicte de tout ce qui s'observe en la cour de Rome, Tant par nostre sainct Père, que par Messeigneurs les Illustrissimes Cardinaux,* Paris, 1623; Lunadoro, *Corte di Roma,* 1635, and many subsequent editions. Books of general household management are Priscianese, *Governo della corte,* 1543; Evitascandalo, *Maestro di casa* manuscript, 1585; Evitascandalo, *Maestro di casa,* 1593, 1596, 1598, 1606, 1620; Anselmo Adami, *Il noviziato del maestro di casa,* Rome, 1636; Liberati, *Maestro di casa,* 1658.

44. Priscianese, *Governo della corte,* 5–6; Evitascandalo, *Maestro di casa,* 57–60.

45. Priscianese, *Governo della corte,* 4, 21, 40–44.

46. Evitascandalo, *Maestro di casa,* 81–82, 210.

47. Liberati, *Maestro di casa,* 17–18, 23.

48. Ibid., 39–40.

49. AChigi 573, above, n. 2 (chap. 4).

50. Benedetto Croce, "Scrittori del pieno e del tardo Rinascimento, V: Libri sulle corti," *La Critica* 39, fasc. 4 (20 July 1941), 242–48, esp. 245–46, citing Torquato Tasso, *Il Malpiglio overo de la corte,* written 1582–83. For an English translation of Tasso's subtle dialogue, with introduction and notes, see Torquato Tasso, *Il Malpiglio: A Dialogue on the Court,* trans. Dain A. Trafton (English Literary Renaissance Supplements, 2), [Amherst, Mass., 1973].

51. Pier Bartolo Romanelli, "Etichetta e precedenze a Roma durante il soggiorno di Cristina di Svezia," *Il Giornale di Politica e di Letteratura* 7, fasc. 1–3 (January–March 1931), 1–40, esp. 28.

52. Moroni, *Dizionario,* XXIII, 139–42.

53. Ibid., 136–39; Patricia Waddy, "Palazzo Barberini: Early Proposals," Ph.D. diss., New York Univ., 1973, 160–61, with reference to documents in the archive of the Congregazione Urbana in Rome.

54. Evitascandalo, *Maestro di casa,* 172.

55. Below, pp. 86, 102.

56. Evitascandalo, *Scalco,* 5; Evitascandalo, *Maestro di casa,* 42, 99; Liberati, *Maestro di casa,* 6–7.

57. ABorg. 4173, 4 Jan. 1622, for the woodwork; ABorg. 4174, 23 Aug. 1621 for the "sciacquatore della credenza."

58. ABorg. 307, no. 67, 27 Sept. 1619, shelves, counter for cleaning silver, presses for linens and napkins, and the table; 20 Jan. 1622, for its location; ABorg. 4168, 27 Sept.

59. Below, p. 201. and, for the transfer of the *credenza* to A21 in 1676, p. 254.

60. Below, p. 309.

61. Christoph Luitpold Frommel, "La construction et la décoration du Palais Farnèse, Sangallo et Michel-Ange (1513–1550)," in *Le Palais Farnèse, Ecole française de Rome,* I, Rome, 1981, 158, citing F. C. Uginet, *Le Palais Farnèse à travers les documents financiers (1534–1612),* Rome, 1980, 76–77.

62. Evitascandalo, *Maestro di casa,* 12–17.

63. Frommel, in *Le Palais Farnèse,* I, 151, and Fig. 32 (Florence, Uffizi A952), "stanza per lo bottigliere."

64. Below, p. 309.

65. Below, pp. 250, 254.

66. Rossetti, *Scalco,* 40.

67. Christoph Luitpold Frommel, *Der römische Palastbau der Hochrenaissance* (Römische Forschungen der Bibliotheca Hertziana, 21), 3 vols., Tübingen, 1973, I, 81–82, observed this standard in sixteenth-century palaces and also noted instances of variations, especially in smaller houses and villas.

68. Evitascandalo, *Maestro di casa,* 11, 12, 54, 56; Liberati, *Maestro di casa,* 87.

69. Evitascandalo, *Scalco,* 4; *Maestro di casa,* 12, 102.

70. Barb. lat. 4360, fol. 6, describes kitchen facilities for a single prince in the south part of the ground floor and adds that rooms to the north could also be used as kitchens, "per la vicinanza degli appartamenti, ò per la divisione delle famiglie." Cf. the arrangements in Palazzo Borghese, below, p. 89.

71. Evitascandalo, *Maestro di casa,* 56.

72. Scappi, *Dell'arte del cucinare* (Venice, 1570), unnumbered plates between pp. 167 and 168, and similar illustrations in subsequent editions.

73. See the program proposed by Barb. lat. 4360, fols. 6–8.

74. Below, pp. 89, 97, 104, 137, 143, 196, 254, 309.

75. Below, pp. 89, 106.

76. Below, p. 143.

77. Below, p. 197 and n. 87 (chap. 12); p. 312.

78. Above, p. 30.

79. Evitascandalo, *Maestro di casa,* 60–66, 102; Liberati, *Maestro di casa,* 46, 67–70, 73–75.

80. ABorg. 4173, 20 Mar. 1621, woodwork, including "una bussola . . . alla porta di detta dispensa . . . e fattoci dentro un'sportello, per dare la Parte . . . e fattoci sopra un parapetto per dormire il garzone . . ." The *dispense* listed below were similarly furnished.

81. Below, p. 196; the *dispensa* was located in room A5–A6 (cf. Fig. 100).

82. Below, pp. 86, 104.

83. ABarb., Ind. II, no. 680, 7 Oct. 1609, fol. 17, "Dispensa intesta al Cortile à Pian Terreno."

84.   Below, p. 196.

85.   Below, pp. 251–52.

86.   Below, p. 308.

87.   Evitascandalo, *Maestro di casa,* 39–41. Adami, *Maestro di casa,* 8–47, gives detailed instructions for keeping books.

88.   For the furnishings of the Borghese *computisterie,* ABorg. 307, no. 67 (Prince Marcantonio), 26 Oct. 1620; and ABorg. 4173 (Cardinal Scipione), 22 Feb. 1621.

89.   Below, p. 308.

90.   Below, pp. 250, 251–52.

91.   Cf. Evitascandalo's notice that the *guardaroba* is to send soiled things to the laundress, *Maestro di casa,* 76.

92.   Adami, *Maestro di casa,* 217.

93.   ABarb., Ind. IV, no. 1282, "Donne di Sua Ecc.a," including "Livia Lavandara de panni di Casa" and "Caterina che lava panni de paggi e Tinello."

94.   ABarb., Ind. II, no. 2888, fols. 290–294v, "il lavatore di detta Sig.ra Principessa D. Anna"; fols. 2v–4, "Lavatore della S.ra D. Costanza." Cf. a similar laundry in the basement of Palazzo Borghese in 1609, below, p. 89.

95.   ABarb., Ind. II, no. 2888, fols. 67r–v, "Lavatore nel Giardino ch'era dell'Accorambono . . . lavatore per li panni fatto acanto il gioco di palla a corda gia Casa del Acorambono . . ." Its basins are built and drain installed. For the location of the property formerly belonging to Accorambono, see ABarb., Ind. II, no. 2884, a plan of the site in 1632, area labeled "B: Colorito di lava, sito del già Corambono" (Patricia Waddy, "The Design and Designers of Palazzo Barberini," *Journal of the Society of Architectural Historians* 35 [1976], 159, Fig. 8, with old collocation).

96.   Below, pp. 248–49.

97.   Wolfger A. Bulst, "Die ursprüngliche innere Aufteilung des Palazzo Medici in Florenz," *Mitteilungen des Kunsthistorischen Institutes in Florenz* 14 (1969–70), 369–92, esp. 388–90; Eugène Müntz, *Les Collections des Médicis au XVᵉ siècle, le musée, la bibliothèque, le mobilier, appendice aux Précurseurs de la Renaissance* (Bibliothèque internationale de l'art), Paris and London, 1888.

98.   William M. Odom, *A History of Italian Furniture,* Garden City, N.Y., 1918–19, I, 24, 306, 310; II, 51.

99.   Evitascandalo, *Maestro di casa,* 75–78; Barb. lat. 4360, fols. 31–34.

100.   Barb. lat. 4360, fols. 32–34.

101.   The *guardaroba*'s duties are described by the anonymous author of *Ordini et offitij alla corte del serenissimo signor duca d'Urbino,* ed. Giuseppe Ermini, Urbino, 1932, 71–74; Priscianese, *Governo della corte,* 73; Evitascandalo, *Maestro di casa,* 75–78 (describing the "aiutante di guardarobba," 9–10), and Liberati, *Maestro di casa,* 61–63.

102.   Barb. lat. 4360, fol. 33, ". . . una loggia da tendervi de panni, e godervi di una vista lontana."

103.   See below, pp. 86–87, for the construction and identification of this loggia, and for the visit of Paul V.

104.   Christian Elling, *Function and Form of the Roman Belvedere* (Det Kgl. Danske Videnskabernes Selskab, Arkaeologisk-Kunsthistoriske Meddelelser, 3, no. 4), Copenhagen, 1950, does not distinguish between open and closed "belvederes" or among the various uses of his examples; and he further clouds the question by taking "function" to mean "formal function." Frommel, *Palastbau,* 91–92, is more modest in his essay. Both authors suggest a relation to medieval towers — an appealing suggestion in light of the tower's function as stronghold — but without clearly drawing the functional and historical lines of the argument. David James Stanley II, "The Origin and Development of the Renaissance Belvedere in Central Italy," Ph.D. diss., Pennsylvania State Univ., 1978, defines "belvedere" in terms of view alone and seeks links between landscape and palace or villa, but his study is too inclusive and uncritical to be helpful.

105.   Archivio Aldobrandini, "Relatione della Villa Aldobrandini," published by Cesare d'Onofrio, *La Villa Aldobrandini di Frascati,* Rome, n.d., 82–115; for the view, fols. 4r–6v, 14v; for the *guardaroba* with its loggia, fol. 14v.

106.   Below, p. 133; for the function of the loggia, ABarb., Ind. III, no. 647, int. 25, 29 July 1582, payment "per haver messo uno travicello per distendere pani su la logia."

107.   Below, pp. 136, 169.

108.   Below, pp. 151–52, 169; ASR, Not. A.C., 6601 (the inventory of 1648), fols. 865v–869, describes the contents of the "stanza sotto alla loggia" and the "logia con nove fenestroni," along with copper vessels and "Biancaria sotto tetti," clearly a *guardaroba* with its loggia.

109.   ABarb., Ind. II, no. 55, fols. 69, 120–371.

110.   Below, p. 86.

111.   Below, p. 104.

112.   Below, p. 104.

113.   Below, pp. 195–96. ABarb., Ind. II, no. 2888, fol. 139v, "Tetto nuovo sopra la Guardarobba della Sig.ra Principessa," 41 × 51¾ *palmi*; fols. 172–172v, "Guardarobba dell'Ecc.ma S.ra Principessa D. Anna," 43 × 27 *palmi,* with a single window.

114.   ABarb., Ind. II, no. 2888, fol. 147r, "la Guardarobba Vecchia."

115.   Below, p. 199; ABarb., Comp. 80, 6 May 1633, speaks of "lavori di legname che fà nella nostra guardarobba anzi libreria del nostro Palazzo alle 4 Fontane . . ."

When Francesco moved to the older Cancelleria, he found many rooms in the upper part of the large palace for his *guardaroba,* but there was no loggia. A smaller apartment on the *piano nobile* of the Cancelleria, identified as being for his brother Cardinal Antonio, was accompanied by a two-room *guardaroba* in the attic, and this had an open loggia at the southeast corner of the building. Barb. lat. 4400, plans of the Cancelleria, from the time of Cardinal Francesco Barberini's occupancy, identify the apartment of Antonio and the two *guardarobe.*

116. Below, p. 309. A rooftop loggia is shown on Falda's engraved view of the palace, but not on Specchi's later view (Figs. 210, 211).

117. *Ordini . . . Urbino,* 36–37.

118. Bernardino Baldi, *Descrizione del Palazzo ducale d'Urbino,* Venice, 1590, 533.

119. Frommel, *Palastbau,* I, 80.

120. Priscianese, *Governo della corte,* 27; Evitascandalo, *Maestro di casa,* 107.

121. Piero Tomei, "Contributi d'archivio, un elenco dei palazzi di Roma del tempo di Clemente VIII," *Palladio* 3 (1939), 163–74, 219–30, esp. 224, no. 65; below, p. 42.

122. Below, pp. 310–11 and nn. 122, 123 (chap. 15).

123. Evitascandalo, *Maestro di casa,* 39, 101; Liberati, *Maestro di casa,* 41.

124. ABarb., Ind. I, no. 747; see above, p. 7. Francesco resided at the Cancelleria after 1632.

125. Below, p. 245.

126. Liberati, *Maestro di casa,* 67.

127. Evitascandalo, *Maestro di casa,* 56, recommends that the cook sleep in the palace, unless he be married (". . . doverà stare, e dormire in casa; et havendo moglie [che io vorrei che non l'havesse] venghi la mattina à bonissim'hora; et la sera per tempo per fare il suo servitio"); and that a bed be provided in the kitchen for the *garzone* ("Si farà dare il letto per il garzone, acciò non stia al fuoco tutta la notte").

128. ABorg. 307, no. 67, 27 Sept. 1619, "Alla Cocina segreta, Per haver fatto il solaro nel camerino, che fa palchetto per dormire il coco . . ."; "Nella dispensa, Per haver fatto una bussola nel cantone della stantia di tavole vecchie fatte per dormire . . . con il solaro sopra di robba vecchia . . ."

129. Evitascandalo, *Maestro di casa,* 168.

130. Barb. lat. 4360, fol. 42.

131. Evitascandalo, *Maestro di casa,* 96, 173.

132. Below, p. 43.

133. ABorg. 5547, no. 182, 1 June–12 Dec. 1623, repairs in the Palazzo Borghese and "in diverse Case et habitationi della famiglia," including several houses in which specific members of the *famiglia* of Prince Marcantonio Borghese were living.

134. ABarb., Comp. 3, passim, for many notices of payments of rent for such houses 1623–28.

135. Below, p. 311.

136. Cecilia Pericoli Ridolfini, *Rione VI, Parione, II* (Guide Rionali di Roma), Rome, 1971, 150–54.

137. Tomei, "Elenco," 224, no. 65.

138. Above, n. 23 (chap. 4); the twenty-six women would have lived in the main palace.

139. ABarb., Comp. 3, fol. 167, 1 Dec. 1627, "A pigione del Palazzo di Campo di Fiore che si tiene dall'Ecc^{mo} Sr Duca di Bracciano per servitio della famiglia dell'Ecc^{mo} Sr D. Taddeo scudi 624.16⅔ . . . per la piggione di 7 mesi antici-

pati . . . apigionatomi per 13 mesi per tutto l'anno 1628 a scudi 1070 l'anno, compresovi il gioco di palla à corda, la rimessa di fuori di là del lavatoro con la Grotta sotto di essa subentrata in luogo della rimessa del Cortile . . . ," and fol. 188, 15 July 1628, scudi 535 for the following six months; Comp. 187, 11 Jan. 1629, 12 July 1629, etc.; and Comp. 193, July 1634, scudi 535 to Paolo Giordano Orsini for the rental of the palace "in Campo di Fiore locatoci per servitio della Nostra famiglia," for the term 1 August 1634–31 January 1635.

140. Below, pp. 109–10.

141. ABorg. 457, Inv. 52, fols. 158–163v, "Hoc est descriptio omnium, et singolorum bonorum mobilium, repertorum in stantijs inhabitat. per D. franciscum Ceccarellum una cum D. Prudentia eius Matre in Palatio novo familia di Exc^{mi} D. Principis Burghesij ⸪ ."

142. Above, p. 41.

143. Barb. lat. 4360, fol. 54.

144. Ibid., building for courtiers, fols. 54–55; second-floor apartments for prelates, auditors, secretaries, and others, fol. 11; fourth-floor apartments, fols. 28–30; dormitories for stable boys, *palafrenieri,* and coachmen, fols. 42, 46; apartment for the *maestro di stalla,* fol. 43; women's apartment, fol. 19; gardeners' house, fol. 63.

145. Below, pp. 196–97.

146. Below, pp. 204–19.

147. ABarb., Ind. II, no. 2863, int. 1.

148. Below, p. 246.

149. *Ordini . . . Urbino,* 32. Cf. the Palazzo Colonna-Barberini in Palestrina, which had two *tinelli* for gentlemen and lower servants, respectively, according to an inventory of furnishings consigned to the palace on 21 June 1638, ABarb., Ind. II, no. 4081, int. 1: "Una credenza . . . nella stanza dove mangia la famiglia bassa," and "Una credenza . . . nella stanza dove mangiano li Gentilhomini."

150. Evitascandalo, *Maestro di casa,* 133; Liberati, *Maestro di casa,* 120.

151. Frommel, in *Le Palais Farnèse,* I, 149, Uffizi A4927.

152. Below, pp. 86, 104.

153. Priscianese, *Governo della corte,* 25–27.

154. Rossetti, *Scalco,* 10–11.

155. Evitascandalo, *Maestro di casa,* 133.

156. Barb. lat. 4360, fol. 6.

157. ABarb., Ind. II, no. 2888, fols. 287v–289v, for the "Cucina comune nel palazzo accanto l'entrone che s'è dismessa"; and below, p. 197, for the new staff kitchen. Fireplaces and/or kitchens are documented in the Barberini rented houses in ABarb., Ind. II, no. 2888, fols. 71r, 77r, 82v, 84r ("cucina nelle dette case del Soldano"), 96r, 103r, and 104r ("cucina," in the house where the *maestro di casa* was living).

158. Adami, *Maestro di casa,* 122, 179.

159. Liberati, *Maestro di casa,* 119.

160. AChigi 573 (above, n. 2 [chap. 4]) lists monthly payments in 1666 of, e.g., 10 scudi to each gentleman and

chaplain and 4.60 scudi for each *palafreniere,* while in 1655 Cardinal Francesco Barberini paid his gentlemen 3.60 scudi and his *palafrenieri* 2.60 scudi each in addition to bread, wine, and (for the gentlemen and the dean of the *palafrenieri*) brooms and candles (Barb. lat. 5635, fols. 91–93, "Rolo della famiglia dell'Em^mo Sig^re Card^le Barberino li 6 Maggio 1655"). For the Chigi "cucina comune" and the kitchens and fireplaces in the apartments of the *famiglia,* see below, pp. 311–12.

161.   Liberati, *Maestro di casa,* 119.

162.   ABarb., Ind. II, no. 3112, fol. 372v (Appendix 4); and above, n. 149 (chap. 4).

163.   Giacinto Gigli, *Diario romano (1608–1670),* ed. Giuseppe Ricciotti, Rome, 1958, 406–7.

164.   Weil-Garris and D'Amico, "Cortesi," 80–81; the gloss clarifies the meaning of the text in presenting the familiar triad, "colina cella dispensatoria et cella cenatoria," or kitchen, *dispensa,* and *tinello.*

5. Personal Cleanliness

1.   Cesare Evitascandalo, *Il maestro di casa* (Rome, 1598), Viterbo, 1620, 7, 38–39; Francesco Liberati, *Il perfetto maestro di casa,* Rome, 1658, 41, 65.

2.   ABarb., Ind. I, no. 747, unpaginated; above, p. 7.

3.   Evitascandalo, *Maestro di casa,* 7; Liberati, *Maestro di casa,* 65.

4.   Evitascandalo, *Maestro di casa,* 39; Liberati, *Maestro di casa,* 41.

5.   ABarb., Comp. 268, fol. 117, "Un cucomo di rame da barbiere senza coperchio." Below, pp. 245, 248–49, for the bath and private apartments.

6.   Evitascandalo, *Maestro di casa,* 19; Gregorio Leti, *Itinerari della corte di Roma ò verò teatro historico, cronologico, e politico della sede apostolica . . . ,* Valence, 1675, 553–54.

7.   Michel de Montaigne, *Journal du voyage de Michel de Montaigne en Italie par la Suisse et l'Allemagne en 1580 et 1581,* ed. Alessandro d'Ancona, Città di Castello, 1889, 229.

8.   ABarb., Comp. 268, fol. 66, "Quattro bocaletti di maiolica, con arme di S. Em^za per dar l'acqua alle mani; Quattro catinelle simili à costa, con arme di S. Em^za."

9.   ABarb., Comp. 268, fol. 94, "Un lavamano di legno ordinario rotto."

10.   ABarb., Ind. II, no. 4081, int. 2, unpaginated; note especially the "Stanze incontro alle cucine vecchie" and the "Appartamento di sopra alle dette stanze."

11.   ABorg. 457, Inv. 52, fol. 163, "un lavamano con la sua brocchetta di maiolica, et il suo asciugatore"; above, pp. 42–43.

12.   Alessandro Petronio da Civita Vecchia, *Del viver delli romani, et di conservar la sanità . . . ,* Rome, 1592, 312.

13.   Nancy Elizabeth Edwards, "The Renaissance 'Stufetta' in Rome: The Circle of Raphael and the Recreation of the Antique," Ph.D. diss., Univ. of Minnesota, 1983, includes a discussion of the practice of bathing and its architectural and cultural setting, and a catalogue of forty-five baths; Edwards, 71–74, remarks on the demise of bathing in the late sixteenth and seventeenth centuries. See also Christoph Luitpold Frommel, *Der römische Palastbau der Hochrenaissance* (Römische Forschungen der Bibliotheca Hertziana, 21), 3 vols., Tübingen, 1973, I, 75–78, for a discussion of particular instances of baths in sixteenth-century Rome.

14.   Barb. lat. 4344, fol. 36, "L'uso de bagni, e delle stufe è quasi dismesso à fatto, tuttavia in alcuni Palazzi se ne vede ancora hoggi, e certamente se riguardiamo l'utilità, che se ne trae per la salubrità, pulitezza et diletto, non mi par mal impiegata in essa l'opera, e la spesa principalmente dove è comodità d'acque sì come è in Roma."

15.   Vitruvius, *De architectura libri decem,* V.x.1, recommends that rooms for hot and tepid baths be oriented to the southwest or south; Alberti, *De re aedificatoria,* V.18, writes of a westward orientation for baths.

16.   The construction of the bathing room is documented in ABorg. 4168, 13 Jan. 1613, fols. 7, 7v, 8v, 10, 14, 14v, 15, 17, 18v, 23; 3 Apr. 1614, fols. 8v, 10; 13 July 1614, fol. 5; and 2 Oct. 1614.

17.   ABorg. 307, no. 67, 25 May 1619, documenting repairs.

18.   ASV, Fondo Borghese, Ser. IV, no. 73bis, fol. 156v [July 1615], "un bagno di legno."

19.   The construction of these rooms is documented in ABorg. 4168, 13 Jan. 1613, fols. 7, 17, 18v, 19v; 3 Apr. 1614, fols. 8v, 9, 9v, 10, 11; 9 July 1614, fols. 8v, 10v; 13 July 1614, fols. 4, 5.

20.   ABorg. 307, no. 67, 15 Apr. 1619, for the door to the street; ABorg. 4168, 13 Jan. 1613, fol. 7, and 3 Apr. 1614, fols. 8v, 10, for the stove. Plasterwork "attorno al labro della caldara nella stufa verso il bagno che faceva danno nel fornello" (ABorg. 5547, no. 182, 1 June–12 Dec. 1623) suggests the confusion that can arise over the use of the word "stufa" but at the same time clarifies the situation in Palazzo Borghese: there was a bathing room ("bagno," previously called "stufa") and a room for heating the water for bathing ("stufa," previously called "stanzia per servitio della stufa").

21.   ABorg. 307, no. 67, 15 Apr. 1619, refers to three two-leaf doors 5½ *palmi* high for fireplaces in these rooms.

22.   ABorg. 4168, 9 July 1614, fol. 10v, "Nel mezzanino sopra la stufa," "colla di stucco di marmo" around the walls of the room, seventy-nine hooks for revetment, and the stucco decoration of the vault.

23.   ABorg. 307, no. 67, 27 Sept. 1619, "letto à credenza per le stantie della stufa."

24.   ABorg. 1476, no. 781, unpaginated; below, p. 118.

25.   ASR, CRM, Teatini 2162, int. 202, 1 Jan.–30 Nov. 1641, fols. 2–7, is a *misura* of masonry for the construction of the "stuffa fatta di nuovo."

26. Below, pp. 232–33 and n. 227 (chap. 12), for an analysis of the drawing.

27. ABarb., Ind. II, no. 2888, fols. 290v–294v, for the construction of the laundry in 1628–38, with supply pipes and drain. Above, p. 39.

28. Vitruvius, V.x.5; cf. Francesco di Giorgio Martini, *Trattati di architettura, ingegneria, e arte militare* (Trattati di architettura, 3), ed. Corrado Maltese, 2 vols., Milan, 1967, 99–100.

29. ABarb., Comp. 268, fol. 68.

30. Ibid., fols. 122–123.

31. ABarb., Comp. 239, fol. 231, 17 June 1666, 18 scudi "allo stufarolo che stufò S.E. [Antonio] nella nuova stufa fatta nel Palazzo à Giupponari, e per haver faticato dieci giorni in custodir detta Stufa."

32. Ibid., 20 June 1666, 12 scudi "donati al Sʳ Domenico Altimanni Barbiere per haver cavato sangue à S. Emᶻᵃ."

33. Alberti, V.17.

34. Evitascandalo, *Maestro di casa*, 7.

35. ABarb., Comp. 268, fol. 100 (the cardinal's room); fol. 95 (Padre Ignazio's rooms); fols. 79–81 (the *guardaroba*).

36. ASR, Not. A.C., 6601, fols. 953, 954v, 955v, 945v, 946v, 950v.

37. ABorg., 7504, unpaginated; the first bedroom had an additional chamber pot.

38. ABarb., Ind. II, no. 4081, int. 2, unpaginated, inventory of 1637.

39. Giovanni Battista Rossetti, *Dello scalco*, Ferrara, 1584, 37; Cesare Evitascandalo, *Libro dello scalco*, Rome, 1609, 19.

40. BAV, Chigi P.VII.10, fol. 42.

41. ABorg. 7504, Inventory of 1693, unpaginated, "Nella sesta stanza dov'è il Zampanaro [A13] . . . Una seggetta à telaro . . ."

42. Francesco di Giorgio, *Trattati*, 335–37.

43. Frommel, *Palastbau*, I, 85–86.

44. Below, pp. 85, 87.

45. Barb. lat. 4360, fol. 65, "Ne già si sono commessi i luoghi comuni, e necessarij, per le quali si tengon nette le case, acciòche ve ne sien molti, e commodi, et in parti onde non si offenda il rimanente."

46. Albertina, It. AZ Rom 966, Heinrich Thelen, *Francesco Borromini: Die Handzeichnungen*, I (Veröffentlichungen der Albertina, 2), Graz, 1967, C43; the chamber is not included in Borromini's plan, It. AZ Rom 957, Thelen C40 (Fig. 146).

47. Below, pp. 239–40.

48. ABarb., Ind. II, no. 2888, fols. 144v, 154r–v; shown on the Contelli plan d-4, flap (Fig. 153), but with three places instead of the two actually constructed.

49. Ibid., fols. 165r–166r, 233r; on the Contelli plan d-4 (Fig. 152), shown in the adjacent location of the "torretta" of the chapel; see below, p. 240.

50. Ibid., fols. 247v, 284v–285.

51. Ibid., fol. 274v; the *cantera* was 13 *palmi* square.

52. Ibid., fol. 290r.

53. ASR, CRM, Teatini, busta 2200, int. 2, fols 17–17v, 19v, 20, 23v, 27, 28.

54. E.g., ABarb., Comp. 364, fol. 116, 19 Feb. 1654, 7.95 scudi to "curadestri per saldo d'un conto di dette cure fatte a detto nostro Palazzo," and similar entries on 31 July 1655, 31 May 1656, and 31 Aug. 1656.

55. ABarb., Ind. II, no. 680, fols. 2–3.

56. ABorg. 4168, 10 Sept. 1608, fol. 12 (room D6), and fol. 1, "Alla loggia nova che requadra il cortile verso il giardino e verso li lochi comuni al pian nobbile," and similar references.

57. Below, p. 92.

58. ABorg. 4168, 27 Sept. 1619, "Al Piano sotto tetto sopra il piano nobile nell'Appartamento delle Donne," a "nicchia del necessario" 6 × 3 × 1¼ *palmi* is made "nella scaletta lumacha."

59. ABorg. 1476, no. 781, "Sotto tetto sopra la galleria verso Ripetta . . . Per haver rotto il muro e fatto la nicchia del loco comune in detto sotto tetto di vano palmi 3½ × 5¾ × 2."

60. For the privy in EE2, AChigi 520, fols. 37, 55–57, 345–346; for that in C23, AChigi 516, fol. 44; for chamber F20, AChigi 520, fols. 280, 286–287, and AChigi 517, fol. 71.

61. ABarb., Ind. II, no. 2888, fols. 54v, 71r, 73v, 86v, 95r, 98v, 105r–v (including the excavation and construction of the *cantera* for the house of the *maestro di casa*), 110v–111r. AChigi 519, unpaginated, several *misure*, passim.

62. ABorg. 457, Inv. 52, fol. 162, "una cassetta con il suo vaso"; above, pp. 42–43.

6. Pleasure and Special Interests

1. Cesare Evitascandalo, *Il maestro di casa* (Rome, 1598), Viterbo, 1620, 89, 101.

2. ABarb., Comp. 268, fols. 102, 106, 134.

3. Ibid., fols. 108, 113, 116, 123–125.

4. ASR, Not. A.C., 6601 (inventory of 1648), fols. 884v, 891v.

5. Antonio Scaino da Salò, *Trattato del giuoco della palla*, Venice, 1555; Barb. lat. 4360, fol. 47.

6. Barb. lat. 4360, fol. 47; the length of 86 *palmi* is not stated, but it is implied in the author's design for a new Barberini palace.

7. Below, p. 97.

8. ABorg. 3949, "Rolo della famiglia . . . 1626–1632," listing "Palla Corda, Betto Ciarfagna."

9. Scaino, *Giuoco della palla*, 166, "Dello steccato minore da corda per il giuoco di rachetta"; 168–69, a plan of the court; 160, the cord and net; 237, the team membership.

10. ABarb., Ind. II, no. 2888, fols. 67r–67v, "Lavatore per li panni fatto acanto il giuoco di palla a corda gia Casa del Acorambono." For the location of the property, see above, n. 95 (chap. 4).

11. Alessandro Ademollo, *I teatri di Roma nel secolo decimosettimo*, Rome, 1888, 28–29, *avvisi* of 2 March and 5 March 1639, remarking on a scene including a view of "la parte del palazzo del medesimo sig. Cardinale Antonio, che guarda nel suo giardino, e dove per ordinario si giuoca alla pillotta," or, the "giardino del medemo Palazzo de sigg. Barberini con il gioco della pilotta, passaggio di carrozze, cavalli et lettighe, et cose simile . . ."

12. ABarb., Comp. 89, beginning with no. 65, 13 May 1669, and continuing passim to Comp. 90, no. 577, 11 Apr. 1673, the final payment for masonry "in refondare et assicurare il casino e gioco di pallacorda incontro a San' Nicola a Capo le Case . . . et arconi sotto il passo sotterraneo . . ."

13. Paul Letarouilly, *Edifices de Rome moderne*, Brussels, n.d., II, Pl. 181, "jeu de ballon"; Angela Negro, *Rione II: Trevi* (Guide rionali di Roma), 1980, 37–39, including an engraving by Bartolomeo Pinelli showing a game in progress in the "sferisterio," and an old photograph.

14. ABarb., Comp. 3, fol. 167, 1 Dec. 1627, "A Pigione del Palazzo di Campo di fiore che si tiene dall'Ecc^mo S^e Duca di Bracciano per servitio della famiglia dell'ecc^mo S^e D. Taddeo . . . a scudi 1070 l'anno compresovi il gioco di palla à corda, la rimessa di fuori di là dal lavatoro con la Grotta sotto di essa subentrata in luogo della rimessa del Cortile . . . ," and similar subsequent entries.

15. ABarb., Ind. II, no. 3112 (Appendix 4), fol. 365, "Dietro a questa stessa parte di Palazzo . . . vi è un poco di cortiletto nel quale la state li signori per trattenimento giocano alla palla, senza che dal sole venghino offesi."

16. ABorg. 4173, 4 Jan. 1622, "Stantia dello studio verso Ripetta."

17. ASR, Not. A.C., 6601, Inventory of 1648, fols. 898v–899, "Stanza prima di sopra . . . sette scantie di noce fatte a studiolo in due pezzi . . ."; fols. 911v–928v, "Seguitano li libri differenti conservati in sette scantie di noce, che sono nell'appartamento di sopra di S.E. [Taddeo]," a list of Taddeo's books. For the place of this room in the "Casa Grande," see below, p. 170.

18. Below, pp. 246, 172.

19. Below, pp. 200–201.

20. Pompilio Totti, *Ritratto di Roma moderna*, Rome, 1638, 273, ". . . e perche ad utile del publico possa servire, vi tiene Custodi."

21. An inventory of 1692–1704, ABarb., Comp. 348, fols. 232–235v, describes a "mezzanine apartment" or "studio apartment," which can be identified with these rooms; below, pp. 199–200.

22. Totti, *Ritratto*, 273, "Vi è la Libraria dell'Eminentissimo Cardinal Francesco di libri rari in ogni sorte di scienze, e di pretiosi manuscritti ripiena, & un nobilissimo studio di medaglie, e d'altre cose rare con gran spesa da tutte le parti del Mondo raccolte; e perche ad utile del publico possa servire, vi tiene Custodi." ASR, Cartari-Febei, 185, fols. 110–111v, quoted in Joseph Connors, *Borromini and the Roman Oratory*, New York and Cambridge, Mass., 1980, 155–56, "Si puol dunque conchiudere, che dandosi il primato, senza dubio, alla Vaticana, questa in secondo luogo sia la più bella e la più copiosa libraria di Roma."

23. Connors, *Oratory*, 49–50.

24. Barb. lat. 4360, fols. 26–28.

25. Pierre Bourdon and Robert Laurent-Vibert, "Le Palais Farnèse d'après l'inventaire de 1653," *Mélanges d'Archéologie et d'Histoire* (published by l'Ecole française de Rome), 29, Rome, 1909, 145–98, esp. 158 and Pl. XVI; Christoph Luitpold Frommel, *Der römische Palastbau der Hochrenaissance* (Römische Forschungen der Bibliotheca Hertziana, 21), Tübingen, 1973, II, 102, 116, 130, 134. Wolfgang Lotz, "Vignole et Giacomo della Porta (1550–1589)," in *Le Palais Farnèse, Ecole Française de Rome*, I, Rome, 1981, 225–41, esp. 238–39, identified a room in the northwest wing of the *secondo piano* as the library; but his evidence, a letter of Fulvio Orsini stating that the library was to the north, would fit the room to the northeast as well as that to the northwest.

26. Below, p. 307.

27. For an overview of theater and spectacle in seventeenth-century Rome, see Torgil Magnuson, *Rome in the Age of Bernini*, Stockholm, 1982–86, I, 245–52; II, 23–31. Ademollo, *Teatri*, publishes many *avvisi* and other contemporary accounts.

28. Evitascandalo, *Maestro di casa*, 18; Gregorio Leti, *Itinerari della corte di Roma ò verò teatro historico, cronologico, e politico della sede apostolica . . .*, Valence, 1675, 553–65. In France in 1624, according to Cesare Magalotti, "The *sala* was full of people curious to see not only [Cardinal Francesco Barberini] eating but Caetano [*trinciante*] carving the meats" (Barb. lat. 5686, fol. 231).

29. For a banquet in Palazzo Capranica, ". . . vi concorse la maggior parte delle Signore, et gentildonne di Roma per vedere si fatto apparecchio," a situation requiring special arrangements for crowd control, justified, however, according to Cervio, because the cardinals' table was worthy of being seen; Vincenzo Cervio, *Il trinciante*, Rome, 1593, 104–9.

30. Ademollo, *Teatri*, 36, 42.

31. Girolamo Lunadoro, *Relatione della Corte di Roma, e de' riti da osservarsi in essa . . .*, n.p., 1635, 55.

32. Leti, *Itinerari*, 496.

33. Pio Pecchiai, "Costanza Magalotti Barberini, Cognata di Urbano VIII," *Archivi* (Rome) 16, fasc. 2 (1949), 23–24.

34. ABarb., Ind. II, no. 2888 (1638), fol. 217v, "Salotto dove si faceva le Comedie"; ABarb., Comp. 268 (1644), fol. 96, "Nella sala dove si facevano le comedie." Below, pp. 199, 246–47.

35. Ademollo, *Teatri*, 21–22; Margaret Murata, *Operas for the Papal Court 1631–1698*, Ann Arbor, 1981, 256–57.

36. Below, p. 243.

37. ASR, CRM, Teatini, S. Andrea della Valle, busta

2200, int. 2, fol. 15v, "Salone dove si faceva la guardarobba di S. Em ͣ e si veste per le Comedie."

38.   ABarb., Ind. IV, no. 1254, fol. 15v (Appendix 3), describes an incident of Taddeo's heroism when an awning collapsed over the masons' scaffolding, full of onlookers outside the hall, during the presentation of *Erminia sul Giordano.*

39.   See, for example, the *avvisi* published by Ademollo, *Teatri,* 19–22, and Murata, *Operas,* 223–25, 250–51, 254–57, 260.

40.   Below, p. 247, for the documentation of the construction of the theater.

41.   Eighty-six backless benches, each 12 *palmi* long, and fifty-six benches with backs were "Nel salone delle commedie," according to an inventory of Apr. 1644, ABarb., Comp. 268, fol. 134. Both Lunadoro, *Corte di Roma,* 55, and Leti, *Itinerari,* 496, recommend that cardinals who attend performances remain behind *gelosie;* above, p. 22.

42.   ABarb., Ind. II, no. 4084, 2 July 1669, a report on the visit of the Spanish ambassador to the palace at Palestrina, including note of the presentation of a muscial drama, "Il finto amante," by the prince's brother, "con Prologo ridicoloso di Palafrenieri," and with music and dances by the pages, "alla sala della commedia, ch'è uno stanzone terreno, che non serve ad'altro, e sempre vi stà la scena."

43.   Francis Haskell and Nicholas Penny, *Taste and the Antique: The Lure of Classical Sculpture 1500–1900,* New Haven and London, 1981, chaps. 2, 4.

44.   Totti, *Ritratto,* 354, "Vi son da venti statue poste in diversi luoghi per il cortile, che oltre il valore grande, rendono a fatto detto luogo maraviglioso. Dentro poi sono stanze con ornamenti Imperiali di statue, quadri de' più rari, che siano a nostri tempi, con una galleria famosissima, et anco fontane, e giardino, e mille altre delitie."

45.   ABarb., Comp. 268, 120, "Nella scala, che scende nell'appartamento de quadri, e statue" [stair S7].

46.   ABarb., Ind. II, no. 2439 (M. A. Lavin, *Seventeenth-Century Barberini Documents and Inventories of Art,* New York, 1975, IV.inv.44), for an inventory of Antonio's holdings in 1644, room by room.

47.   Below, p. 245.

48.   Below, p. 308.

49.   Below, p. 306.

50.   Below, p. 171.

51.   Below, pp. 116–18.

52.   Below, pp. 265–66.

53.   The two ground-floor rooms of Taddeo Barberini's part of the "Casa Grande" in 1646 seem to be such an apartment in embryo (ASR, Not. A.C., 6601, fols. 896v–898; below, p. 170.

54.   Wolfram Prinz, *Die Entstehung der Galerie in Frankreich und Italien,* Berlin, 1970, for the origin of the gallery in the loggia, its early development in France, and its appearance in Italy among francophile Italians like Car-

dinal Girolamo Capodiferro in the mid-sixteenth century.

55.   Barb. lat. 4360, fol. 22, "Conviensi ad ogni gran palazzo una galleria . . ."

56.   ABarb., Ind. II, no. 4084, 2 July 1669, the ambassador of Spain called on the princess, "che l'ha ricevuto due passi fuori della Galleria che serve per anticamera."

57.   See the detail of an engraving by A. van Westerhout after a drawing by G. B. Lenardi showing the elaborate table setting in the gallery, in Anthony Blunt, *Guide to Baroque Rome,* New York, 1982, 189.

58.   Prinz, *Entstehung,* 19–22.

59.   Below, pp. 92, 105.

60.   Below, pp. 191–92.

61.   Below, pp. 306–308.

62.   Howard Hibbard, "Palazzo Borghese Studies, II: the *Galleria,*" *Burlington Magazine* 104 (1962), 9–20; and below, p. 116.

63.   See below, p. 220 and nn. 163, 164 (chap. 12), for two inventories of furnishings of the rooms that indicate these two possible readings of the sequence.

64.   Giuseppina Magnanimi, "Palazzo Barberini: La sala ovale," *Antologia di Belle Arti* 1, no. 1 (March 1977), 29–36, citing Hieronymus Tetius [Girolamo Teti], *Aedes Barberinae ad Quirinalem,* Rome, 1642, 15.

7. Coaches

1.   Jean Delumeau, *Vie économique et sociale de Rome dans la seconde moitié du XVIᵉ siècle* (Bibliothèque des Ecoles françaises d'Athènes et de Rome, 184), 2 vols., Paris, 1957–59, 443–46; Wolfgang Lotz, "Gli 883 cocchi della Roma del 1594," *Studi offerti a Giovanni Incisa della Rocchetta* (Miscellanea della Società Romana di Storia Patria, 23), Rome, 1973, 247–66; Christoph Luitpold Frommel, *Der römische Palastbau der Hochrenaissance* (Römische Forschungen der Bibliotheca Hertziana, 21), 3 vols., Tübingen, 1973, I, 88.

2.   Lotz, "883 cocchi," 248.

3.   Michel de Montaigne, *Journal du voyage de Michel de Montaigne en Italie par la Suisse et l'Allemagne en 1580 et 1581,* ed. Alessandro d'Ancona, Città di Castello, 1889, 304.

4.   John Evelyn, *Diary,* ed. E. S. de Beer, Oxford, 1955, II, 257 (19 November 1644).

5.   Gregorio Leti, *Itinerari della corte di Roma ò verò teatro historico, cronologico, e politico della sede apostolica . . . ,* Valence, 1675, 514.

6.   Leti, *Itinerari,* 513–14; Francesco Sestini da Bibbiena, *Il maestro di camera,* Florence, 1621, 242–44.

7.   Sestini, *Maestro di camera,* 220.

8.   Pio Pecchiai, *I Barberini,* Rome, 1959, 171; see below, Appendix 3.

9.   Barb. lat. 4360, fol. 46.

10.   Giacinto Gigli, *Diario romano (1608–1670),* ed. Giuseppe Ricciotti, Rome, 1958, 304.

11. Ignazio Ciampi, *Innocenzo X Pamfili e la sua corte,* Rome, 1878, 213–14.

12. Barb. lat. 4360, fols. 9–11: fol. 11, "La prima loggia . . . si farà larga palmi 33. overo 34. acciòche possano voltarvisi le carrozze, e condurre li padroni sino alle scale, e starvi in maggior numero à coperto, et acciòche riesca anche tal larghezza capace della fronte delle scale; ma l'altre tre loggie, che non hanno da usarsi per tal bisogno saranno un terzo men larghe, cioè palmi 22. o 23. ò poco più, nelle quali potranno tuttavia andare due carrozze al pari." This last dimension suggests a passage of about 11 *palmi* for a single carriage.

13. *Avviso* of 31 October 1607 (Urb. lat. 1075, c. 679), "Il cardinal Barberinj giunse in Roma, come fu scritto con le passate; alloggia nel palazzo del marchese Salviati, perchè il suo palazzo proprio è angusto d'intrata et ha poco piazza avanti, onde non ci possino star cocchi, che vengono alle visite; tuttavia si crede che non sia per starvi lungo tempo . . ."; J.A.F. Orbaan, *Documenti sul Barocco in Roma,* Rome, 1920, 86. See below, p. 141. The plan of the ground floor of the Palazzo Salviati and its piazza are shown in ASR, Notai di Acque e Strade, vol. 86 (96), 1659, c. 738, published by Richard Krautheimer, *The Rome of Alexander VII, 1655–1667,* Princeton, 1985, Fig. 64. The palace was demolished in 1659.

14. Below, pp. 155–56.

15. ABarb., Ind. III, no. 647 (2b), Cartella disegni barberini, ". . . il quale vicolo per tale relassatione restarà tanto amplo che ci potranno passare le Carrozze. Il che hoggi non possono fare."

16. Barb. lat. 4360, fol. 44 and elsewhere.

17. ABarb., Ind. II, no. 2888, fol. 257r, "Lumaca nel Cantone à detto Piano Terreno quale cala nella Porticella Secreta verso Monte Cavallo"; below, p. 188.

18. Ibid., no. 3112, fol. 364v: ". . . et avanti a questa galleria vi è un poco di piano scoperto et in fine di esso vi è un portone che guarda verso Ponente e cosi verso Roma per il quale si può entrare con la carozza e levar li signori dalle loro stanze senza sottoporsi ad altro cielo che a quello della medª carozza . . ."

19. ABorg. 306, no. 27, 22 June 1606, "Facciata della strada, per la mettitura della porta della lumaca [S4] di fuori"; Arch. Borg. 307, no. 67, 27 Sept. 1619, "la porta della scaletta [S7], ch'esce in strada."

20. Barb. lat. 6540, fol. 27v; below, pp. 142, 145.

21. AChigi 520, fol. 389, "Stanza terrena nel' Vicolo accanto Mancini dove è la Porticella Segreta [B1] . . . la porta segreta . . . che escie in strada . . ."; AChigi 516, fols. 52–52v, the wood door and its frame; AChigi 517, fol. 40v, stonework.

22. Lotz, "883 cocchi," 264.

23. Below, p. 143.

24. Below, p. 147.

25. ABarb., Comp. 3, 1 Dec. 1627, "A Pigione del Palazzo di Campo di fiore . . . compresovi il gioco di palla à corda, la rimessa di fuori di là dal lavatoro con la Grotta sotto di essa subentrata in luogo della rimessa del Cortile . . ."

26. ABarb., Ind. II, no. 2888, fols. 33v–42v.

27. ASR, Not. A.C., 6601, fols. 887–888v.

28. ABarb., Ind. IV, no. 158, inventory of 16 Sept. 1646, unpaginated.

29. ABorg. 4168, 18 Sept. 1607–12 May 1608, fol. 6, "Alle stanze vecchie dove habitava il Sigr Enea al Pian Terra, [A10] Muro di una porta remurata nella facciata denanzi per di dentro quale era la porta della rimessa [13 × 16 *palmi*] . . . [A13] Muro di una porta remurata della rimessa acanto il cortile della legna [10 × 25 *palmi*, including a part underground] . . ."

30. Ibid., fol. 36, "Nella stanza dei Palafornieri di detto pian di terra," identifiable as room A10; fol. 45, "Alle remesse nel cortile della legna verso Ripetta," identifiable as A13; 21 July 1614, unpaginated, for the remodeling of A13, the "stanza vechia acanto la fabrica nova verso la strada," including "il muro fatto dove era la porta della rimessa tra dette stanze e la cucina [A15]," and "il muro di una finestra remurata in detta stanza quale dava il lume a detta quando serviva per rimessa."

31. ABorg. 307, no. 67, 27 Sept. 1619, unpaginated, "Dove stanno le carrozze di S. Eccza nell'entrone verso Ripetta."

32. ABorg. 1476, no. 781, unpaginated, "Stanzione sopra la rimessone," newly constructed, and "Rimessone."

33. ABorg. 4168, 27 Sept. 1619, unpaginated, "Lavori fatti nelle rimesse nove," including work in four *rimesse.*

34. ABorg. 4174, 23 Aug. 1621, "Alla Casa a Piazza Nicosia . . . all porta della Rimessa . . ."

35. ABarb., Ind. II, no. 2888, fol. 281r, "Stanza dove si hà da fare la dispensa [A5], muro dove si è riservato il portone della remessa . . ."; fol. 294r, [in Anna's laundry, A2] "muro della porta della rimessa rimurata dove s'è fatto detta porta . . ."

36. Ibid., fols. 35v–42r, for the remodeling of ground-floor rooms of houses and construction of new *rimesse,* including the "Terza rimessa piccola per una carrozza solo sotto le stanze del Sre Giulio Mileti" (fol. 36v), "Rimessa nella casa del Biscontino" (fols. 39v–40v), "Rimessa fatta di novo accanto la casa del Biscontino" (fols. 40v–41r), and "Rimessa grande accanto il portone della piazza da basso" (fols. 41v–42v), the low broad building on the east side of the piazza (Fig. 91).

37. Barb. lat. 4360, fols. 40–44. For stables in the sixteenth century, see Frommel, *Palastbau,* I, 86–88.

38. A schematic plan of the stable is shown in the plan of the villa by Barrière, 1647; D'Onofrio, *Villa Aldobrandini,* Fig. 12.

39. Above, pp. 41–42.

40. ABarb., Ind. II, no. 2888, fols. 21r–33r, for the remodeling of buildings for the Barberini stables.

41. Ibid., fols. 15r–20v, for work in the "fenili." Their di-

mensions and arrangements suggest that they were first built as row houses, sometimes with shops on the ground floor.

42. Below, p. 143 and n. 41 (chap. 11).
43. Below, pp. 175, 196.
44. Below, p. 309.
45. Below, p. 312.
46. Below, pp. 317–18.

8. The Art of the Plan

1. Francesco Liberati, *Il perfetto maestro di casa,* Rome, 1658, 12, advising that the *maggiordomo* is to act "accioche tutta la Corte si muova come un corpo composto di molte membra, et inspirado da un anima sola al buon servitio del Principe."

9. Palazzo Borghese

1. Pompilio Totti, *Ritratto di Roma moderna,* Rome, 1638, 353, "La grandezza sua è maravigliosa, che più facilmente si potria giudicare un Castello, che palazzo."
2. Guglielmo de Angelis d'Ossat, "L'autore del più bel cortile di Roma barocca," *Strenna dei Romanisti,* 1958, 45–47 (republished in *Realtà dell'Architettura, Apporti alla sua storia 1933–1978,* 11, Rome, 1982, 251–55), in which the attribution of the courtyard to Martino Longhi the Elder is rejected in favor of that to Flaminio Ponzio.
3. Howard Hibbard, *The Architecture of the Palazzo Borghese,* Rome, 1962 (published simultaneously in the *Memoirs* of the American Academy in Rome, XXVII). Hibbard specifically did not deal with "the precise manner in which the palace was used and lived in at the different stages of its existence" and "the influence of such specific practical demands upon its planning" (p. xviii)—that is, the focus of the present study. Hibbard's work has provided an invaluable foundation for my own.
4. Hibbard, *Palazzo Borghese,* 4–7.
5. Ibid., 7–17 (the façade), 28–34 (the courtyard). Jack Wasserman, in a review of Hibbard's book (*Journal of the Society of Architectural Historians* 23 [1964], 116–18), argues in favor of Martino Longhi the Elder as architect of the courtyard, in 1586.
6. Hibbard, *Palazzo Borghese,* 39, 41.
7. Ibid., 47 and Text Fig. I, for the extent of the construction. The *sala* in 1610–12 is shown in Albertina 1001 (Fig. 27), and its extent can be confirmed from ABorg. 306, no. 14, 12 Mar. 1617, which documents the wood ceiling with panels of painted canvas. It was later divided into two rooms, as shown on nineteenth-century plans (ABorg. 315, published by Hibbard, *Palazzo Borghese,* Figs. 48, 49), and implied by ABorg. 457, an inventory of May 1832, list-

ing furnishings in rooms of this part of the palace.
8. Christoph Luitpold Frommel, "La construction et la décoration du Palais Farnèse, Sangallo et Michel-Ange (1513–1550)," in *Le Palais Farnèse, Ecole française de Rome,* I, Rome, 1981, 127–224, esp. 132, and below, p. 243.
9. Hibbard, *Palazzo Borghese,* 45–46.
10. For biographical information on members of the borghese family, see especially the articles in *Dizionario biografico degli Italiani,* and Nicolò Barozzi and Guglielmo Berchet, *Relazioni degli stati europei lette al Senato dagli ambasciatori veneti nel secolo decimosettimo,* Ser. III, Italia, *Relazioni di Roma,* 2 vols., Venice, 1877–79, I, 56–57, 62, 93–96. Other sources are rife with confusing errors, e.g., Nicolò Borghese, *Vita di S. Caterina da Siena . . . aggiuntovi l'elenco degli uomini illustri dell'Eccellentissima Casa Borghese,* Rome, [1869], 64–134, and Gino Borghesio, *I Borghese* (Le grandi famiglie romane, 10), Rome, 1954, 11–47.
11. Francis Haskell, *Patrons and Painters,* London, 1963, 27–28.
12. *Avvisi* reveal that Paul V stopped by the palace on several occasions; and in 1610 he ordered that neighboring properties be bought for the construction of a small palace for the use of Francesco and Ortensia when the pope should wish to stay in the main palace for a few days; below, pp. 87, 91–92, 101.
13. *Avviso* of 13 Sept. 1608, Urb. lat. 1076, fol. 660B, "Il signor G. B. Borghese ha preso il palazzo in Borgo, ove stava il già cardinal di Como per starvi questo inverno . . . ," published by J.A.F. Orbaan, *Documenti sul Barocco in Roma,* Rome, 1920, 122. For the Palazzo Giraud-Torlonia in the Borgo, previously inhabited by the cardinal of Como, see Christoph Luitpold Frommel, *Der römische Palastbau der Hochrenaissance* (Römische Forschungen der Bibliotheca Hertziana, 21), 3 vols., Tübingen, 1973, II, 207–15, and Pls. 82–85. Cf. ABorg. 4168, 13 May 1609, fol. 5, "Al Palazzo dove havitava l'Ecc.mo Sig.r Giovanni Battista in Borgo."
14. E.g., ABorg. 306, no. 27, 25 Oct. 1606, at room C4, ". . . muro del tramezzo che devide detta camera con le camere da farsi [that is, those of the second building campaign]."
15. Documents of construction consistently refer to the level above the *piano nobile* as "terzo piano" instead of the customary "secondo piano."
16. ABorg. 306, no. 27, partially published by Hibbard, *Palazzo Borghese,* docs. 12–13, 15–16.
17. The description and reconstruction of Orlandini's house (Fig. 25) are derived from the documents of construction of the new palace, ABorg. 4168.
18. ABorg. 4168, partially published by Hibbard, *Palazzo Borghese,* docs. 17–39. See also ABorg. 307, no. 67, woodwork of 1609. Foundations for the corner rooms are measured only in the third *misura* (ABorg. 4168, 10 Sept. 1608,

fol. 1; Hibbard, *Palazzo Borghese,* doc. 28), "Al cortile della legna verso Ripetta fondamenti fatti per la stanza che si ha da fare di novo che segue le stanze verso il giardino"; the rooms themselves follow in the fourth *misura* (ABorg. 4168, 20 Feb. 1609; Hibbard, *Palazzo Borghese,* doc. 31).

The ground floor of the loggia on the west side of the courtyard was originally closed on its far side, with a door in the central bay opening to the garden (see Fig. 26); its five bays were opened only in the nineteenth century; Carlo Pietrangeli, *Palazzo Borghese e la sua decorazione* (Quaderni del Circolo della Caccia, 1), Rome, 1985, 7.

19.   Hibbard, *Palazzo Borghese,* 51.

20.   According to an *avviso* of 16 July 1608, Urb. lat. 1076, fol. 527, it was thought that the irregularities in the building that displeased Paul V might be due to the desire to save the old building, for reasons of economy; Orbaan, *Documenti,* 117.

21.   ABorg. 306, no. 27, 22 June 1606, records the construction of the "muro della facciata denanzi di tevolezze" of each of rooms A1–A4, "regguagliato" from thicknesses of 6⅜ to 7½ *palmi;* and subsequent *misure* record similar shaping of other segments of the façade wall. Salone C5 has sides measuring 48½, 78, 51½, and 82 *palmi,* according to a seventeenth-century plan in the Albertina, It. AZ Rom 1001 (Fig. 27), which conforms more closely to the record of construction than do the several nineteenth-century plans.

22.   ABorg. 4168, 18 Sept. 1607–12 May 1608, fol. 12, "Muro del tramezzo fatto di novo," between C9 and C10, 62½ *palmi* high from the *piano nobile* to the attic, and 1¾ *palmi* thick; and "Muro sotto il detto sino al piano de mezanini," 14¾ *palmi* high.

23.   Ibid., 10 Sept. 1608, fol. 1, "Al cortile della legna verso Ripetta fondamenti fatti per la stanza che si ha da fare di novo che segue le stanze verso il giardino," and many subsequent entries.

24.   ABorg. 33, no. 433, inventory of 1610, unpaginated, "Corami nuovi della sala nuova . . . ," with three overdoors, four overwindows, and two "portieri in detta sala grande con arme dell'Ecc᎐ S⁻ Gio. Battista Borghese bo. me." Cf. ASV, Fondo Borghese, Ser. IV, no. 73bis, fols. 102v–103r.

25.   ABorg. 4168, 12 May 1608, furnishings made by Nettunio Roncone, including "72 scabelli di albuccio grossi, e grandi più dell'ordinario servano nella fabrica nova al piano nobile . . . , 21 scabelloni ed le spalliere corniciate per la sala del detto piano . . . , 10 buffetti d'albuccio con le testate, e tre telari . . . servano per le stanzie di detto piano."

26.   Ibid., 2 Sept. 1610, fol. 5, for the moving of two marble statues in the "sala nova"; 21 July 1614, "Per haver levato le statue che erano nel salone et portate nella stanza a canto mentre si e dipinto e poi tornate in opera statue n° sette e teste n° nove con la statua di porfido quale era dal altra testa della scala."

27.   ABorg. 33, no. 433, "Un baldacchino . . . che serve per coprire la tavola della credenza . . . ," presumably in the *sala.* A larger baldacchino and *credenza,* specifically for the *sala,* were built in 1619, and at that time an already existing balustrade was enlarged to enclose the new *credenza;* below, p. 101.

28.   Ibid.; the number of overmantels, overdoors, and overwindows of the revetments fit rooms C8, C9, and C11 but not the rooms extending to the east of the *sala;* the third room of the sequence is noted as having damask hangings. Cf. ASV, Fondo Borghese, Ser. IV, no. 73bis, fols. 104r–105v.

29.   ABorg. 4168, 18 Sept. 1607–12 May 1608, fols. 7 (the "camino vecchio" in C14), 43 (installation of new fireplaces in C12 and C13), 49 (installation of new fireplaces in C11 and C8); 20 Feb. 1609, fol. 15 (installation of new fireplace in C15).

30.   Ibid., 20 Feb. 1609, fol. 2, masonry for room C15, including "Muro remurato acanto la finestra della cappella," the earliest identification of C14 as a chapel; 22 Aug. 1609, "Per una Arme di noce dell'Ecc᎐ᵒ Sig⁻ Giovanni Battista sopra la cancellata di noce della capella al pian nobile verso il giardino."

31.   ABorg. 33, no. 433, "Nella cappella corami della medesima qualità," with three overdoors—probably C14 rather than C3 (also a chapel), because C14 has three doors and C3 only two, and because the wall hangings match those of rooms C8, C9, and C11.

32.   ABorg. 4168, 10 Sept. 1608, fol. 10, hinges installed "nelle stanze del pian nobbile dove sta l'Ecc᎐ᵒ Sig⁻ Giovanni Battista." This document indicates that Giovanni Battista had rooms on the *piano nobile,* without specifying their location; the rooms in question must be those containing his arms.

33.   Mezzanines were newly constructed over rooms A1 and A2 in 1671; below, p. 122.

34.   ABorg. 307, no. 67, 16 Oct. 1609.

35.   ABorg. 4168, 14 July [1609], ". . . per otto bandelle ordinarie che hanno servito per le stantie di mezzani dove sta il Sig⁻ᵉ, e più per quattro saliceni con suoi finimenti che hanno servito alle fenestre et alle stantie dove dormo [sic] il sig⁻ᵉ."

36.   Ibid., 4 Oct. 1609, ". . . e per haver imbiancato le fenestre de mezzanini dove habita l'ecc᎐ᵃ Sig⁻ᵃ Consorte del Sig⁻ Giovanni Battista con sette altre fenestre incima."

37.   Below, p. 86.

38.   ABorg. 4168, 4 July 1608, fol. 6, for the "sciaquatore" and "necessario" in B5, above the "scaletta che scende da detti mezzanini al pian terra."

39.   Ibid., 18 Sept. 1607–12 May 1608, fols. 53–55, including records of the erection of scaffolding for the painters in the seven rooms excluding B10, not yet constructed.

40.   Ibid., 20 Feb. 1609, fol. 16, and 11 Mar. 1609, for the fireplace in B10; 18 Sept. 1607–12 May 1608, fols. 16–17, 36–37, for the removal of fireplaces from mezzanine rooms.

41. Fireplaces are documented in rooms D7, D9, D10, and D15; ABorg. 4168, 10 Sept. 1608, fols. 12–13; 1 Oct. 1608, fols. 1–2; 2 July 1609.

42. The floors and walls of the rooms of the *terzo piano* toward the garden were raised to the level of those toward the street only in 1671; below, p. 122.

43. ABorg. 4168, 23 Feb. 1608, fol. 2, "Per giornate doi fatte in acconciare il tetto sopra l'appartamento della ecc^ma Sig^ra Virginia." Rooms D7–D10 stood under the loggia E7, and there were attic rooms over D1–D4; D11–D15 are the only rooms that fit the description.

44. Ibid., 10 Sept. 1608, fol. 5, plaster "nele tre prime stanze del 3° piano dove habita il Sig^r Giovanni Battista per far li frese lo. insieme palmi 376 alt. palmi 3"; fol. 10, "Per la fattura delli ponti per li pittori a tre stanze del terzo piano dove habita l'Ecc^mo Sig^r Giovanni Battista . . . . Per la mettitura di no° 532 cancanetti messi nelle dette tre stanze per li paramenti . . ."

45. Above, p. 27. At this time Virginia was not yet in residence in Palazzo Borghese.

46. ABorg. 4168, 9 Mar. 1609, ". . . la Capella delle Donne nelle stantie nove." This is unlikely to have been room C3; it was probably in a women's apartment on the *terzo piano* or in the attic.

47. Ibid., 7 July [1609], "a una stantia à canto alle stantie del mastro, per andar dalle Donne."

48. *Dizionario biografico degli Italiani*, "Marcantonio Borghese."

49. ABorg. 4168, 2 Sept. 1610, fol. 4, "Alla galleria delle statue," and three "stanze a piedi la lumachetta," where a statue of a seated Diogenes was placed on a pedestal and a marble table on lions' claws was set up. Hibbard, *Palazzo Borghese*, 49, 59, apparently influenced by the remodeling of the ground floor of the palace in 1671–76, thought that the sculpture gallery was a six-room suite of A4, A5, A6, A10, A11–12, A13, with doors aligned in anticipation of the *prospettiva* of 1676; but this is not consonant with a close reading of the documents of construction or those of the remodeling of 1671–76 (below, pp. 112–16).

On the development of the Borghese sculpture collection, see Lucilla de Lachenal, "La collezione di sculture antiche della famiglia Borghese e il palazzo in Campo Marzio," *Xenia* 4 (1982), 49–117.

50. ABorg. 306, no. 27, 22 June 1606, the vault in A4; 4168, 17 Oct. 1607, fols. 6–7, cornice and enframement of the central panel of the vault, and fireplace in A4; 4168, 18 Sept. 1607–12 May 1608, fol. 5 (vaults "a schifo" in A5 and A6), fol. 51 (central panel of the vaults in A5 and A6); 4 July 1608, fol. 7 (installation of fireplaces in A5 and A6); 26 July 1608, *scarpello* (two travertine fireplaces for A5 and A6).

51. ABorg. 4168, 18 Sept. 1607–12 May 1608, fol. 28, brickwork in two arches, for travertine window frames; 11 Mar. 1609, fols. 7–8, woodwork, the four windows and door of the "loggia cioè gallaria"; 19 Feb. 1609, fol. 1,

stonework, the travertine doorframe.

52. Ibid., 8 Feb. 1608, hardware "al piano da basso alla prima stanza acanto alle stanze vecchie [A1]," and "alla seconda stanza [A2] dove si fa la dispensa."

53. ABorg. 306, no. 27, Mar. 1607, "Colla fatta sopra il muro della loggia per doi bande del tinello che va nella prima stanza nova al pian terra lon. palmi 15 al. palmi 6¼ . . ." Another reference to the *tinello* would seem not to refer to room A1; it may be that there was a second *tinello*, probably in the area to the north of the courtyard. ABorg. 306, no. 27, 14 Nov. 1606, "Tinello, Per haver murato le 4. finestre di mattoni in cortello nel tinello verso la strada lo. insieme 16 alt. palmi 4."

54. ABorg. 4168, 18 Sept. 1607–12 May 1608, fol. 6, the carriage doorway was filled in; fol. 36, "stanza dei Palafornieri di detto pian di terra."

55. ABorg. 307, no. 67, "Alle stantie, dove stanno li Palafrenieri," the wood floors measured 33½ × 26 *palmi* and 32½ × 25¼ *palmi*, appropriate dimensions for rooms A11 and A12.

56. ABorg. 4168, 18 Sept. 1607–12 May 1608, fol. 45, its large doorway and paving; 11 Mar. 1609, fol. 8.

57. Ibid., 20 Aug. 1608.

58. Ibid., 18 Sept. 1607–12 May 1608, fol. 26, "Alla loggia nova sopra le stanze vecchie verso Ripetta," for the walls and arches; fol. 47 for the pilasters and other details. Hibbard, *Palazzo Borghese*, 53 and 123, believed this to be a "belvedere . . . over the old rooms toward Monte d'Oro," as shown in Greuter's engraving of 1618 (Hibbard's Fig. 63) and Specchi's engraving of the palace ca. 1704 (Fig. 46); but the forms, dimensions, and relationships specified in the documents of construction make it clear that our loggia E7 was built.

59. ABorg. 4168, 10 Sept. 1608, fol. 4, "stanza de fenestroni," masonry; 1 Oct. 1608, "loggia a tetto delli finestroni acanto la guardarobba," stonework.

60. *Avviso* of 17 July 1610, quoted by Hibbard, *Palazzo Borghese*, 54 n. 38, "Sua Santità . . . magnò in cima della casa, et si gustò d'andarla rivedendo tutta . . ."

61. ABorg. 4168, 20 Feb. 1609, fol. 20, only sixty-two steps were installed—enough to ascend only from the ground floor to the *piano nobile*, a distance of 37⅛ palmi. In comparison, service stair S6 rose to the *guardaroba* with 125 steps.

62. ABorg. 306, no. 27, 22 June 1606; 25 Oct. 1606; 23 July 1607, fols. 1, 11.

63. Ibid., 23 July 1607, fols. 3, 11.

64. These arrangements are specified in the documents of construction, ABorg. 4168, 10 Sept. 1607–12 May 1608, fols. 19, 22, 32, 34, 52, 54; 10 Sept. 1608, fols. 3, 5, 7, 8, 9, 11; 20 Feb. 1609, fols. 6, 12, 20; 4 July 1608, fols. 7, 10; 1 Oct. 1608, fols. 1, 2; 20 Aug. 1608; 12 Jan. 1609.

65. Ibid., 10 Sept. 1608, fol. 12; 20 Feb. 1609, fol. 5.

66. Ibid., fol. 1, "Alla loggia nova che requadra il cortile

verso il giardino e verso li lochi comuni al pian nobbile," and similar references.

67. ABorg. 306, no. 14, 12 Mar. 1617.

68. ABorg. 33, no. 433, inventory of 1610, "Corami nella sala dell'Appartamento vecchio." Cf. ASV, Fondo Borghese, Ser. IV, no. 73bis, fols. 106v–107r; and Arch. Borg. 7502, fol. 4.

69. ABorg. 33, no. 433, "2ª camera." Room C18, to the southwest of the *sala,* had but two windows.

70. ABorg. 456, no. 9, inventory of Francesco Borghese's goods, 25 June 1620, unpaginated, "Capella . . . Stanza dinanzi alla capella . . . Anticamera Falza . . . Nella sala vecchia . . ."

71. Below, pp. 90–91.

72. ABorg. 33, no. 433, ". . . corami dell'appartamento vecchio di sopra, Prima stanza dove habbita l'Ecc^{mo} Sr Francesco Borghese . . . [3 overdoors], Seconda stanza . . . [one overmantel], Terza stanza . . . [two overdoors], Quarta camera . . . [two overdoors]." Cf. ASV, Fondo Borghese, Ser. IV, no. 73bis, fols. 109r–110r, and ABorg. 7502, fol. 5, "Un paramento di corame per una stantia . . . et sono nella prima camera di sopra, sopra la piazza nova dove stà l'ecc^{re} Sig^{re} Francesco [D25], Un paramento di corame per una stantia . . . et sono nella seconda camera di sopra, sopra la piazza vecchia, dove stà l'ecc^{mo} Sig^{re} Francesco [D26], Un paramento di corame per una stantia . . . et sono nella terza camera di sopra come segue [D27], Un paramento di corame per una stantia . . . et sono nella quarta camera sopra la loggia di sopra dove stà l'ecc^{ma} Sig^{ra} Ortensia [D28]."

73. ABorg. 456, no. 9, 25 June 1620, unpaginated.

74. ABorg. 4168, an account of metalwork including, on 7 Aug. 1607, ". . . due catenacci piani . . . alle due porte nove dell'appartamento dell'Ecc^{mo} Sig^r Francesco cioe uno alla porta della fabrica vecchia e nova, et l'altro alla porta della fabrica vecchia nella saletta"; and, on 20 Oct. 1607, "56 bandelle stagniate per mettere alle porte e finestre delle stantie nove del Palazzo vecchio dove habita il Sig^r Francesco."

75. ABorg. 7502, fol. 6, "una tavola grande di corame . . . et stà nel anticamera dell'audientia dell'Ecc^{ma} Sig^{ra} Ortentia, un sopratavolino di corame . . . serve per il tavolino nella camera dell'audientia dell'Ecc^{ma} Sig^{ra} Ortentia."

76. Above, n. 72 (chap. 9).

77. ABorg. 4168, 28 Oct. 1607, hardware for the door "del mezzanino della fabrica vecchia dove si è fatta la credenza dell'Ecc^{mo} Sig^r Francesco."

78. Ibid., 17 Oct. 1607, fol. 1, a new partition in the *scalco's* mezzanine rooms; 7 Feb. 1608, metal reinforcements "che servono per fortificar le volte delli mezzanini della facciata vecchia sotto l'appartamento dell'ecc^{mo} Sr Francesco, dove habita il scalco di S.E."; and 3 Mar. 1608, fol. 4, a chain "nel Mezanino verso la loggia dove habita il Sig^r Scalco."

79. Ibid., 3 Mar. 1608, a partition "Al mezanino del Sig^r Trinciante verso la piazza."

80. Ibid., 22 Sept. 1607–22 Apr. 1608, fol. 1, "Alla loggia vecchia verso l'entrata principale del Palazzo, una porta di trevertino piano che va da detta loggia all'andito ò corritore che va alle stanze del Sig^r maestro di casa"; 3 Mar. 1608, "Nella loggia vecchia al pian terra," the large window to his rooms.

81. E.g., ABorg, 4168, 26 May 1608.

82. Ibid., 18 Sept. 1607–12 May 1608, fol. 36, "Nella stanza dei Palafornieri di detto pian di terra [A10] . . . Per haver remurato la canna di un camino che si era fatta nel tramezzo che divide la sala [A6] verso le dette stanze quale canna haveva da servire da il camino della cucina che si haveva da fare in cantina . . ."

83. ABorg. 306, no. 27, 14 Nov. 1606, kitchen door "nell vicolo verso il Monte doro." ABorg. 4168, 17 Oct. 1607, fols. 1–4, work in Giovanni Battista's kitchen, and fol. 5, work in Francesco's kitchen; 10 Sept. 1607–12 May 1608, fol. 3, foundation for the courtyard loggia "comenciando dal cantone verso la cucina"; 26 May 1608; 17 Dec. 1607; 22 Sept. 1607–22 Apr. 1608, fol. 8, Francesco's kitchen; 29 Apr. 1609; 13 May 1609, fols. 4–6, Giovanni Battista's kitchen, including the "bussola" in the corner; 2 Sept. 1610, fol. 7, drain passing through the "cortiletto dietro la cucina dell'ecc^{mo} sig^{re} Francesco" to the vicolo east of the palace.

84. ABorg. 4168, 13 May 1609, fols. 1–4, "Al lavatore nella cantina," including tubs, two *caldare,* and a piece of wall "verso la piazza"; and 5 May 1609, ". . . 8 sprage che hanno servito per le fornacelle delle caldare del lavatore in cantina . . ."

85. BAV, Urb. lat. 1076, fols. 287v f., quoted by Hibbard, *Palazzo Borghese,* 48–49, n. 23. This suite was on the *piano nobile,* and the report was written before the twentieth room C15 had been constructed.

86. *Avviso* of 16 July 1608 (Urb. lat. 1076, fol. 527), published by Orbaan, *Documenti,* 117.

87. ABorg. 4168, 18 Sept. 1607–12 May 1608, fol. 25, "[in C11], muro della fodera ringrossata al muro vecchio nella facciata denanzi per di dentro per riquadrare detta stanza . . ."

88. Below, p. 112 and n. 239 (chap. 9).

89. ABorg. 4168, 18 Sept. 1607–12 May 1608, fol. 35.

90. Ibid., 1 Oct. 1608, fol. 2.

91. The dimensions are from Albertina 1001 (Fig. 27); ABorg. 4168, 18 Sept. 1607–12 May 1608, fol. 34, gives the dimensions of the paving of the *sala* as 81 × 49¼ *palmi.*

92. *Avviso* of 5 December 1609 (Urb. lat. 1077, fol. 610), ". . . il Palazzo è finito et io me ne andarò"; Orbaan, *Documenti,* 159; Hibbard, *Palazzo Borghese,* 51 n. 34.

93. Hibbard, *Palazzo Borghese,* 65 and n. 13, explains that the drawing was attributed to Girolamo Rainaldi by Heinrich Thelen and Augusto Campana on the basis of

handwriting. Hibbard notes the collaboration of a number of architects in Borghese projects—in particular, that of Rainaldi and Maderno in 1609.

94. *Avvisi* of 14 July 1610 and 17 July 1610 (Urb. lat. 1078, fols. 506A–B, 508B–509, 517); Orbaan, *Documenti*, 172–74; Hibbard, *Palazzo Borghese*, 53–54 nn. 37, 38.

95. ABorg. 4168, 27 July 1608 (Hibbard, *Palazzo Borghese*, doc. 25), for the portal; 6 May 1608 (ibid., doc. 20), for the wall between the "cortile della legna" and the garden.

96. Hibbard, *Palazzo Borghese*, 63–71; Howard Hibbard, *Carlo Maderno and Roman Architecture 1580–1630* (Studies in Architecture, 10), University Park, Pa., and London, 1971, 191–92.

97. Hibbard, *Maderno*, 191.

98. The construction of this part of the palace is documented in ABorg. 4168. The first *misura* for masonry is dated 13 January 1613. The second *misura* is missing, but the third occurred on 3 April 1614, the fourth on 9 July 1614, and the fifth on 2 October 1614. Documents for woodwork and stonework are also included.

99. The space referred to as a "transito" in the first measurement (ABorg. 4168, 13 Jan. 1613, fol. 25) is later reshaped as a "cappella" (ibid., 9 July 1614, fols. 9, 10) and given decoration (ibid., 2 Oct. 1614, fols. 1v–2v).

100. Below, p. 101.

101. The two terms are used interchangeably: e.g., ABorg. 4168, 13 Jan. 1613, fol. 24v, "la galerietta ò studio" of the *piano nobile;* and, 3 Apr. 1614, fol. 1, "la galerietta o studio al piano sopra il piano nobile."

102. The loggias were at first open, and Hibbard, *Palazzo Borghese*, speculates that the glazing, framed by the striking perspective arches in the lower loggia, was not added until the eighteenth century. The upper loggia was enclosed in 1622 (below, p. 105).

103. For stair S11, ABorg. 4168, 13 Jan. 1613, fols. 25v, 26v, 28, 28v, 29v; 13 July 1613, fol. 1. For stair S10, ibid., 13 Jan. 1613, fols. 25, 27v; 9 July 1614, fols. 9, 10; 3 Apr. 1614, fol. 6. For stair S9, ibid., 13 Jan. 1613, fols. 14v–15; 3 Apr. 1614, fols. 8v, 9v–10. For stair S8, ibid., 13 Jan. 1613, passim; 3 Apr. 1614, fol. 5v.

104. For the latrine at S11, ABorg. 4168, 3 Apr. 1614, fol. 7v; 13 July 1614, fol. 2v; its pipe continued through the wall below, ibid., 13 Jan. 1613, fol. 9. For the other three latrines, ibid., 13 July 1614, fol. 1, two seats (at S8), and fol. 3 (at S10); and 3 Apr. 1614, fol. 9 (at S9).

105. Ibid., 13 Jan. 1613, fols. 3, 4, 12, 12v, 13, 15v, 17, 17v, 19, 20; 3 Apr. 1614, fol. 8v; 13 July 1614, fols. 3v, 5, 6. Cf. Barb. lat. 4360, fol. 47, where a similar ball court of dimensions 86 × 26 *palmi*, 30 *palmi* high, was recommended by an anonymous advisor of the Barberini family. For ball courts, see above, chap. 6.

106. The anonymous author of Barb. lat. 4360, fol. 47, similarly recommends that the ball court be built "in luogo quasi publico," far enough from the rooms of the *padrone*

but at the same time convenient to them; above, p. 54.

107. ABorg. 4168, 9 July 1614, fol. 12, "Per la mettitura della ramata alla finestra che dalla stanza [B17] sopra lo spogliatore guarda nel gioco con la fattura del ponte per mettere detta ramata . . ."

108. Above, pp. 48–49.

109. ABorg. 4168, 13 Jan. 1613, passim; 14 Apr. 1614, fol. 10v; 2 Aug. 1614; 2 Oct. 1614, fols. 4, 4v.

110. Ibid., 13 Jan. 1613, fols. 20v–22, "Muri dell'Entrone"; 9 July 1614, fols. 7v, 12.

111. Ibid., 13 Jan. 1613, fol. 9, for the filling in of the *rimessa* door between A13 and A14; Arch. Borg. 307, no. 67, 27 Sept. 1619, woodwork "Dove stanno le carrozze di S. Ecc.ᶻᵃ [Marcantonio] nell'entrone verso Ripetta."

112. ABorg. 4168, 13 Jan. 1613, fols. 6, 13, 13v, 18; 9 July 1614, fols. 8–8v; 13 July 1614, fol. 4v; 2 Oct. 1614, fol. 4 (two feigned doorways). This passage was called "transito," "ovato," or "cupelletta" (not "capelletta," as Hibbard, *Palazzo Borghese*, 70 n. 35, transcribed the word). ABorg. 7926, fol. 72, 4 Oct. 1613, ". . . à M. Anibale Durante Pittore scudi quaranta di moneta per haver depinto de paesi et indorato li stucchi de sei quadri nella Cupelletta à piano Terreno, che parte il Giardino del Corritore della fabrica nova così d'accordo per mezzo del Sig.ʳ Gio. Architetto di N.S. . . ."

113. ABorg. 4168, 13 Jan. 1613, fols. 16, 19v; 3 Apr. 1614, fol. 8v; 13 July 1614, fols. 3–3v.

114. Ibid., 3 Apr. 1614, fols. 7v, 12; 9 July 1614, fol. 8. There is a similar passage on the third floor, D21 and D22: ibid., 3 Apr. 1614, fols. 1, 2; 13 July 1614, fol. 2.

115. Ibid., 13 Jan. 1613, fols. 26, 26v; 3 Apr. 1614, fols. 6, 12v. There is a similar "transito tondo," D24, on the third floor: ibid., 13 Jan. 1613, fols. 27–27v, 28v, 29; 3 Apr. 1614, fol. 2; 13 July 1614, fol. 2.

116. The passage, which is accompanied by a tiny chamber C29, was at first called a "transito" (ABorg. 4168, 13 Jan. 1613, fols. 25, 26v; 13 July 1614, fol. 2v). It was then reshaped, outfitted and decorated as a chapel, with a wooden *cancellata* to separate the passage from the chapel proper (ibid., 9 July 1614, fol. 9; 2 Oct. 1614, fols. 1v–2v). There is a similar passage on the third floor (ibid., 13 Jan. 1613, fols. 27v, 28v; 3 Apr. 1614, fol. 3v; 13 July 1614, fol. 2); an intermediate mezzanine is fitted between the two main levels, over C29 and C30 (ibid., 13 Jan. 1613, fol. 26v; 3 Apr. 1614, fols. 5, 5v; 9 July 1614, fols. 9v, 10; 13 July 1614, fols. 2v–3); and all three levels are connected by the small spiral stair S10.

117. For C29, ABorg. 4168, 13 Jan. 1613, fol. 26v; for D18, ibid., 3 Apr. 1614, fol. 3v.

118. Ibid., 13 Jan. 1613, fols. 17–17v, 19.

119. Ibid., fol. 18.

120. Ibid., fol. 23v.

121. Barb. lat. 4360, fols. 26, 29.

122. Below, pp. 238–39.

123. Hibbard, *Palazzo Borghese*, 67–70.

124. ABorg. 306, no. 32, Hibbard, *Palazzo Borghese,* doc. 54; the total of 188,107.33 scudi, as given by the compiler, is considerably more than the sum of the subtotals given above. For Marcantonio's expenditures for masonry and stonework year by year, including 1613, see ABorg. 307, no. 74, Hibbard, *Palazzo Borghese,* doc. 55.

125. Not Cardinal Scipione, as stated by Hibbard, *Palazzo Borghese,* 69–70 and n. 34, in spite of the documents cited in the previous note; Hibbard cites ABorg. 7926, a volume of payments 1610–14; these are payments authorized by Scipione on behalf of Marcantonio, still a minor.

126. E.g., ABorg. 4168, 13 Jan. 1613, "Prima misura, e stima dell'opera di muro della fabrica nuova, che fa fare l'ecc^{mo} Sig^r Principe Marc'Antonio Borghese, che seguita la fabricha fatta, qual fà testa verso Ripetta . . ."

127. *Dizionario biografico degli Italiani,* "Marcantonio Borghese."

128. ABorg. 4168, 3 Apr. 1614, fol. 6, "Per haver sbusciato il muro di detta loggia per ordine del ecc^{mo} Sig^r Francesco per veder la dirittura delle porte, grosso il muro palmi 4½, et murato il vano palmi 3, et palmi 2."

129. ABorg. 307, no. 67, 27 Aug. 1615, woodwork by Giovanni Battista Soria, "Alla Cappella Nova," including "li quattro sportelli per serare detta cappella et sagrestia . . . alt. palmi 13½ lunga insiemi palmi 17½ . . ." and the cornice above it, 17½ *palmi* long, and other furnishings.

130. Hibbard, *Palazzo Borghese,* 51 n. 32, quotes a record of ironwork, ABorg. 7927, fol. 63a, 15 June 1615, ". . . per servitio della Capelletta nova fatta vicino alla scala lumaca al paro delle stantie nobile verso il Giardino, dove era prima la logetta . . ."; its roof required repair in 1619, ABorg. 307, no. 67, 7 Jan. 1619, "Per haver disfatto et rifatto un pezzo di tetto sopra la cappelletta accanto alla scala lumaca . . ."

131. Above, p. 85.

132. Paola della Pergola, "Giovan Francesco Guerrieri a Roma," *Bollettino d'Arte* ser. 4, 41 (1956), 214–37, esp. 235, doc. 79, 21 Dec. 1617, ". . . per haver disfatto il ponte del pittore nella stantia, dove era p^o la Cappella nel Pian Nobile verso il Giardino . . ."

133. Hibbard, *Palazzo Borghese,* 60 and nn. 56, 57.

134. Giovanni Baglione, *Le vite de' pittori . . . ,* Rome, 1642, 152–53.

135. *Avviso* of 16 July 1614 (Urb. lat. 1082, fol. 284), ". . . compiandosi Sua Beatitudine il dopo pranzo rimirare le pitture fattevi dal padre Castellofranco cappuccino [Piazza], riguardevoli per la brevità del tempo e quantità dell'opra fatta con securezza, con spirito, et infine per l'inventione di pingere a olio in fresco." The innovative technique was the undoing of the work, for it quickly deteriorated; Baglione, *Vite,* 151–52.

136. Della Pergola, "Guerrieri," 214–37, with extensive documentation.

137. ABorg. 306, no. 14, 12 Mar. 1617, woodwork by Giovanni Battista Soria, the frames, canvas, and installation of the twenty panels. Della Pergola, "Guerrieri," 235, doc. 79, "Per haver fatto il ponte nella Sala Vecchia per li pittori et per haver fatto un sopraponte per li Indoratori che indorano detta soffitta. . . . Per haver chiuso 4 finestre delli mezzanini della Sala Vecchia . . ."

138. ABorg. 306, no. 14, 12 Mar. 1617, the rosettes "nella stanza acanto al salone vecchio," presumably C18 and not C20, since other work in this and related documents is concentrated in the rooms to the southwest of the *sala vecchia*; della Pergola, "Guerrieri," 235, doc. 79, for the closing of the two mezzanine windows "della camera vicino alla Sala Vecchia sotto la loggia"; C20 to the northeast has no windows toward the loggia.

139. ABorg. 306, no. 14, 12 Mar. 1617, the rosettes "alli doi camerini del cantone verso la piazza"; della Pergola, "Guerrieri," 234, doc. 69, and 236, doc. 91, for the "fregio fatto in tela e messo nella Camera dell'Appartamento vecchio che fa cantone nella piazza nova e vecchia . . . ," and 235, doc. 79, for scaffolding for gilders in C16.

140. Della Pergola, "Guerrieri," 235, doc. 79, scaffolding "nella 3^a Camera che risponde nella piazza nova . . . della 4^a Camera vicino alla Ringhiera . . . della Camera che riesce nella Ringhiera [C3] . . ."

141. ABorg. 307, no. 67, 27 Sept. 1619, "Salone del Palazzo novo, Per haver fatto il telaro del baldacchino di travicelloni di castagno grosso largo straordinario per il detto baldacchino . . . palmi 18½ × 10; Per haver fatto il Tavolone, sotto detto baldacchino . . . Palmi 19 × 5½, con 3 trespidi sotto grossi straordinarij . . . Per haver fatto la scalinata sopra detta tavola . . . Per haver dato giunta al steccato denanzi a detta tavola per lunghezza palmi 9 per due teste . . ."

142. *Avviso* of 1 August 1618 (Urb. lat. 1086, fol. 296), "Il Pontefice martedì mattina, andando a prendere aria per la città, entrò nel suo palazzo vicino Ripetta e si compiacque di vedere gl'ornamenti di pitture et paramenti nuovi fattivi fare ultimamente e se ne tornò poi a pranzo a Monte Cavallo"; Orbaan, *Documenti,* 255.

143. AVR, S. Lorenzo in Lucina, Stati d'Anime, 1607–1621, 1615; unfortunately the critical page has been invaded by worms, and the numbers of men and women servants and "famiglia dell'Ecc^{mo} Sr Principe [Marcantonio]" have been eaten away.

144. *Dizionario biografico degli Italiani,* "Marcantonio Borghese." ABorg. 7502, fols. 19–27, "Argenti et altre robbe che sono al servitio dell'Ecc^{ma} Sig^{ra} Virginia Borghese, che si porti à San Lorenzo in Panisperna a dì 9 di Gen^{ro} 1610"; fol. 27, "Un parafuoco di noce . . . serve per d^o [?] adì 14. di Dec^{re} 1612," indicates that Virginia was still at the convent at that date.

145. Della Pergola, "Guerrieri," 230, doc. 21, a payment to Abelle for having painted "de paesi nella Camera seconda del Pian Nobile verso il Giardino dove habita al presente . . ."

146. *Avviso* of 16 July 1614 (Urb. lat. 1082, fol. 284),

"Lunedì mattina il Pontefice . . . se n'andò a pranzo al palazzo de signori Borghese nella piazza de signori Deza, dove mangiò nelle stanze nuove et nell'istesso tempo nelle stanze terrene desinarono il cardinal Borghese, l'eccellentissimo signor Francesco et il principe di Sulmona . . ."; Orbaan, *Documenti*, 218. The rooms of the sculpture gallery were the only suitable ground-floor rooms, the others being given over to services.

147. ABorg. 307, no. 67, 27 Sept. 1619, "Per il Giorno del Pasto per lo Sposalitio."

148. Ibid., 26 Oct. 1620, "Alle stanze sotto tetto per le donne della Sig^ra Principessa [Camilla]," wood ceilings, windows, and doors. The dimensions of the ceilings and the sequence of the description make it clear that they were installed in the subdivided rooms E1–E4.

149. ABorg. 4168, 4 Jan. 1623, "Per haver fatto tre telaretti con un sportello l'uno nella Cucina delle Donne," each 2 × 3 *palmi*, the three appropriate for the three tiny windows in E9; "Per haver dato la giunta a una finestra nella dispensa delle sudette donne . . . ," the single window in room E8. ABorg. 307, no. 67, 26 Oct. 1620, "stantia del cantone" in the women's apartment, for two "tavole alli sciacquatori in detta stantia."

150. ABorg. 307, no. 67, 27 Sept. 1619, "Alla stantia della Rota, Per haver fatto una rota per voltare, dove passa il mangiare per le donne, di albuccio alt. palmi 4½ lar. di diametro palmi 4 . . . Per haver fatto una porta d'albuccio à canto detta Rota, che entra alle stantie delle donne . . ." This *rota* was surely for Camilla's women, because the opening for a *rota* in Virginia's women's apartment was smaller in size; see below.

151. ABorg. 4168, 27 Sept. 1619, "Al Piano sotto tetto sopra il piano nobile nell'Appartamento delle Donne."

152. ABorg. 307, no. 67, 6 May 1615, "Lavori fatti nelli mezzanini sotto il piano nobbile."

153. ABorg. 4168, 27 Sept. 1619, "Mezzanini sotto al piano nobile," including "il muro di tre porte murate nel tramezzo che tramezza li mezzanini delle Donne et li mezzanini delli Paggi . . . ," the *rota,* the "nicchia del necessario fatto di novo a detti mezzanini," the "sciaquatore accanto a detto [necessario]," and the walling up of "una finestra nel gioco della palla" and "una porta . . . in cima la scaletta che sale a detti mezzanini"; ibid., 27 Aug. 1620, "Per il muro di una porta murato à capo la scala delli mezzanini dell'Appartamento delle Donne." ABorg. 307, no. 67, 27 Sept. 1619, ". . . il cancello nell'andito che va alle stanze delle donne"; there is no "andito" leading to the attic rooms of Camilla's women.

154. ABorg. 307, no. 67, 27 Sept. 1619, "Stantie delli paggi," the *credenza,* "tavola per mangiare," and twelve "sportelli." ABorg. 4168, 27 Sept. 1619, "Per la levitura di una pietra di sciaquatore nelli detti mezzanini dove habitano li paggi . . ."

155. ABorg. 3949, "Rolo della famiglia dell'ecce^mo s^r principe Borghese 1626–1632."

156. ABorg. 307, no. 67, 27 Sept. 1619, "Alle stantie, dove stanno li Palafrenieri, Per la fattura . . . di . . . dui solari rustichi sopra li mattonati in dette stantie . . . alti da terra palmi 1½ per la humidità, uno palmi 33½ × 26, l'altro palmi 32½ × 25¾ [dimensions appropriate for rooms A11 and A12]," the *necessario,* door to the street, and table 13½ × 4 *palmi,* "serve per mangiare." ABorg. 4168, 27 Sept. 1619, "Al piano terreno sotto a detti [pages' mezzanines] dove stanno li Parafrenieri," for the *sciacquatore* and fountain. ABorg. 3949, "Rolo della famiglia dell'ecce^mo s^r principe Borghese 1626–1632," for the twenty-five *palafrenieri.*

157. ABorg. 307, no. 67, 20 Jan. 1622, masonry repairs in "una casa dove habita li palafrenieri nella piazza"; ABorg. 5547, no. 182, 1 June–12 Dec. 1623, fol. 8, repairs in the "Casa alla Torretta dove habitano i Palafrenierj." For the *palafrenieri*'s work schedule, see above, p. 35.

158. ABorg. 307, no. 67, 26 Oct. 1620, woodwork by Giovanni Battista Soria, in the "Piano Nobile nell'Appartamento di S.E. [Marcantonio], Per la balaustrata della capella nuova . . . alt. tutta palmi 15 lo. palmi 21 con la porta . . . ," the two windows, and the frame for the "Baldacchino di detta capella." The dimensions of the "balaustrata" are too large to fit in chapels C7 or C30, either of which might also be called new.

159. Ibid., "Per haver disfatto un pezzo di cornicione al solaro riquadrato, nella camera dove dormiva S.E. lon. palmi 12 per guardarsi dal fuoco, e tornato a remetterlo in opera . . ."; cf. ABorg. 306, no. 14, 12 Mar. 1617, describing wooden rosettes for the "solaro requadrato" of these rooms, above, p. 101.

160. ABorg. 456, no. 9, 25 June 1620, inventory of Francesco Borghese; the numbers of overdoors and overwindows in the "Anticamera Falza" and the "Stanza dinanzi alla capella" match the numbers of doors and windows in C20 and C22.

161. ABorg. 456, no. 9, inventory of 25 June 1620, revetments in the "Prima stanza di sopra verso la loggia" (D28), "Stanza sopra la piazza vecchia" (D27), "Stanza nella cantonata sopra la piazza vecchia et nova" (D26), "Stanza sopra la piazza nova" (D25), "Altra stanza sopra la piazza nova" (D1), "Altre stanze sopra la piazza nova" (D2), "Stanza sopra la ringhiera della piazza nova" (D3), and an additional room (D4); the overdoors and overwindows match the doors and windows in the designated rooms.

162. ABorg. 4168, 27 Aug. 1620, "Per haver stuccato piu busci in n° sette stanze dove habitava la bo. me. dell'Ecc^mo Sr Francesco con calce e gesso."

163. ABorg. 307, no. 67, 26 Oct. 1620, an *armario,* 19 × 13 × 9 *palmi,* "ch'era nella stantia della Sig^ra Principessa, dove teneva le vestii, et altre cose," disassembled and reassembled "nelle stanze di S.E. nell'Appartamento di sopra," and a "soffitta . . . nella stantia dell'Armaria," 27½ × 23 *palmi.* ABorg. 5547, no. 60, 7 Nov. 1623, fol. 1v, for the identification of D1 or D25 as the "Anticamera . . . dove è l'Armario."

164. ABorg. 307, no. 67, 26 Oct. 1620, "Guardarobba nuova sopra le loggie"; the five new window frames, 10¼ × 5¼ *palmi,* and door toward the unroofed loggia would fit these rooms. Cf. the documentation of the construction of new rooms in this area in 1623, with references to the *guardaroba,* below, p. 106.

165. ABorg. 307, no. 67, 20 Feb. 1620, "l'Ecc^{mo} Sr Prencipe Borghese deve dare per li lavori di legname fatti nell'Armario per riponere le vesti dell'Ecc^{ma} S^{ra} Principessa nelle stanze sopra il piano nobile verso il Giardino nel Palazzo a Ripetta da me Giovanni Battista Soria . . . scudi 121.00."

166. Ibid., 27 Sept. 1619, "Alle stantie di sopra della Sig^{ra} Principessa," a "tavola al necessario" and two window frames with leaves "per la lumaca," presumably S11.

167. Ibid., 26 Oct. 1620, "Stanze di detta S^{ra} Virginia nel Palazzo . . . Per due impannate di castagno doppie con 8 sportelli l'una per le Vetriate, ò tele, alt. l'una palmi 10½ larg. palmi 5½ e fatto l'incastro atorno, nelle camere dove dorme . . ."

168. Ibid., "Per una soffitta di castagno alle stantie di detta Sig^{ra} [Virginia] sotto tetto . . . [*palmi* 27½ × 23]," and a window 5¼ × 4½ *palmi,* and a similar window in the next room.

169. ABorg. 4168, 27 Sept. 1619, masonry; 15 Jan. 1620, masonry; 28 Feb. 1620, woodwork, including "un armario nel cortiletto della cocina secreta per reposer dentro la carne al fresco"; 27 Aug. 1620, masonry. ABorg. 307, no. 67, 7 Jan. 1619, roofing and masonry; 27 Sept. 1619, woodwork, including the "palchetto per dormire il coco" in the *cucina segreta;* 26 Oct. 1620, woodwork, including a window frame "nella stanza de garzoni."

170. Cf. ABorg. 4168, 27 Sept. 1619, work on the "vaschetta" of Marcantonio's private kitchen, ". . con haver tagliato il muro et abbassata la canna che porta l'acqua alla cucina dell'ecc^{mo} S^{re} Francesco qual passava sopra detta vaschetta."

171. Ibid., 27 Sept. 1619, masonry; 15 Jan. 1620, masonry.

172. Ibid., 15 Jan. 1620, "Per la fattura del tetto sopra il tinello dell'Ecc^{mo} Sr Francesco . . . [*palmi* 37 × 11]."

173. Ibid., 27 Sept. 1619 and 15 Jan. 1620, masonry; ABorg. 307, no. 67, 27 Sept. 1619, woodwork, including, "Nella dispensa, Per haver fatto una bussola nel cantone della stantia di tavole vecchie fatte per dormire . . ."

174. ABorg. 4168, 27 Sept. 1619, masonry; 28 Feb. 1620, woodwork; ABorg. 307, no. 67, 27 Sept. 1619, woodwork.

175. ABorg. 307, no. 67, 27 Sept. 1619.

176. Ibid., 26 Oct. 1620.

177. ABorg. 4168, 27 Sept. 1619, masonry; ABorg. 307, no. 67, 27 Sept. 1619, woodwork at the windows of the "Stantia del Scopatore Comune" and the "tavolone per li lochi communi, incontro detta stantia."

178. ABorg. 307, no. 67, 27 Sept. 1619, woodwork. ABorg. 4168, 27 Sept. 1619, unpaginated, "Piano sotto detto," a sequence of works leading to the "guardarobba."

179. ABorg. 4168, 28 Feb. 1620 [*sic*], "Guardaroba, Per la fattura d'haver disfatto n° 9 credenzoni che erano nella guardaroba, e stanze della bo. me. dell'ecc^{mo} Sr Francesco Borghese et trasportatoli nella guardaroba di S.E. . . . e agiustatoli in doe facciate."

180. Cf., e.g., ABorg. 307, no. 67, 27 Sept. 1619, for woodwork for quarters of various persons, some obviously within the palace ("Alle Stantie del Sig^{re} Ulisse al piano dell'ultima loggia"), some obviously outside ("Nella casa acanto il S^{re} Pignattello"), and others of uncertain location.

181. *Avviso* of 11 July 1609 (Urb. lat. 1077, fol. 331) reports the Borghese interest in buying the palace. *Avviso* of 18 July 1609 (Urb. lat. 1077, fol. 359B), "Li signori Borghesi havendo comprato per 18 mila scudi il palazzo di Campeggi [Giraud-Torlonia] in Borgo, si è di già dato ordine di riddurlo a perfettione, dissegnando il cardinale Borghese habitarvi parte del tempo che 'l Papa si trova al Vaticano et darvi audientia"; Orbaan, *Documenti,* 144, 145.

182. ABorg. 4173, 22 Feb. 1621, "Per haver accommodato il ceppo della campanella acquistato, e fattoci la stanghetta, e accommodato li Billighimonta."

183. ABorg. 4174, 23 Aug. 1621, four hinges "alla Porta dove stava la Rota," and a travertine sill "alla Porta dove era la Rota."

184. ABorg. 4173, 4 Jan. 1622, woodwork in the mezzanines, "nelle stantie del Maestro di Casa verso la strada"; and "Per haver fatto una porta di castagno . . . alli mezanini verso il giardino et agiustatoci la bussola di castagno alla porta dove sta il Maestro di ceremonie [maestro di camera] di SS. Illma."

185. Ibid., "la balaustrata ò vero steccato della credenza nel salone."

186. Ibid., 20 Feb. 1621, "Per haver fatto no. 9 finestre d'albuccio scorniciate alli Mezzanini, sopra le finestre delle stanze di SS^{ria} Illma al Piano Nobile messe con gran scomodo, con la scala in aria . . . [*palmi* 4½ × 5½]."

187. Ibid., "Alla capelletta nuova nell'Appartamento di SS^{ria} Illma," the dismantling of all the fittings of the chapel, and the erection of scaffolding for painters and gilders; and the remodeling of the "porticella che và nella lumachetta [S6] in detta capella."

188. Ibid., 4 Jan. 1622, bolts for the doors "nell'appartamento di sopra dove dorme SS. Illma"; 15 Feb. 1621, "Un' Impanata di Castagno alle stanze dove dorme SS^{ria} Illma doppia, con 8 sportelli . . . [four glazed, and four with canvas, *palmi* 10¼ × 5¼]." The window dimension would be appropriate for the *piano nobile* or for the *terzo piano* toward the street.

189. Ibid., "Stantia dello studio verso Ripetta," the installation of shelving ("scanzie") from the palace in the Borgo, and scaffolding for gilders and painters; it is a question of this studio rather than C35 below, because of its adjacency to the loggia that received glazing, in the following note.

190. Ibid., "Loggia à canto detto studio [D23]," window

frames for the three arched openings, including panels "alle balaustrate," *palmi* 14 × 4¾, appropriate for loggia D20 but useless in loggia C31 below.

191. *Ibid.,* 10 Aug. 1621, "Per haver rimesso in opera la gelosia di noce nella loggia verso Ripetta . . ."; cf. 4 Jan. 1622, another reference to the "gelosia di noce alla loggia scoperta verso Ripetta . . ." Hibbard, *Palazzo Borghese,* 66–67, remarked that the false perspective arches in this loggia were later additions and concluded that both inserts and fenestration were added in 1723, the date of the Borghese-Colonna marriage commemorated in the coat of arms over the central niche within the loggia.

192. ABorg. 4173, 4 Jan. 1622, a window leaf "nell'appartamento da basso di SS. Illma."

193. Hibbard, *Palazzo Borghese,* 74.

194. Totti, *Ritratto,* 354.

195. AVR, S. Lorenzo in Lucina, Stati d'Anime, 1607–1621, fol. 73, "Palazzo dell'Illmo Sr Card^l Borghese et Prencipe di Solmone, famegli del Sr Principe 142, famegli dell'Illmo Sr Card. Borghese 224."

196. ABorg. 4174, 23 Aug. 1621; 4173, entries in 1621 and 1622.

197. ABorg. 4173, 20 Feb. 1621, ". . . la stalla del Palazo verso monte doro; . . . la stalletta delle Mule alla casa del cantone verso S. Lorenzo; . . . Stalla nova, nella casa dove è la Dogana di Ripetta [cf. 4 Jan. 1622, ". . . la stalla dove era la dogana"]; . . . stalla vecchia nel palazzo . . . la porta della stalla verso il cortile"; ABorg. 4172, 23 Aug. 1621, "All' stalla vecchia in detto Palazzo; . . . Stalla nella casa del Balduino . . ."

198. ABorg. 4174, 23 Aug. 1621, "All Casa a Piazza Nicosia . . . alla porta della Rimessa . . ."

199. ABorg. 4173, 20 Nov. 1622, "Lavori fatti nel palazzo . . . una porta alla stanza del credenziere incontro la computisteria . . ."; 4 Jan. 1622, "Stanza della Credenza di S.S. Illma . . . porta alla cucina comune di S.S. Illma."

200. *Ibid.,* 22 Feb. 1621, "cucina segreta."

201. *Ibid.,* 20 Feb. 1621, a gate "alla cantina sotto il palazzo, dove va il carbone . . . ," and another "per la cantina di SS^ria Illma dove si danno le Parti."

202. *Ibid.,* 20 Nov. 1622, "Per haver fatto la bussola nel tinello dove si tiene il vino nel gioco della palla . . . [with windows] per dare le parte . . ."

203. ABorg. 3949, Marcantonio's *rolo di famiglia* includes Betto Ciarfagna with the designation "Palla Corda."

204. ABorg. 5547, no. 182, 1 June–12 Dec. 1623, work done "per servitio dell'Ecc^mo Sig^r Principe Marcantonio Borghese . . . al Palazzo dove habita S.E. a Ripetta . . . ," including, fol. 12, "Per haver spicconato attorno al labro della caldara nella stufa verso il bagno che faceva danno nel fornello . . ."

205. ABorg. 4173, 22 Feb. 1621, ". . . nella casa del cantone, dove stà detto Mons^re Maggiordomo . . . ; Appartamento del S^re Cav^re Ansidei Casa verso fiume . . ."

206. *Ibid.,* 20 May 1623, "Lavori fatti alla casa in piazza Nicosia che si è restituita dove stavano li gentilhuomini di SS. Illma."

207. *Ibid.,* 20 Feb. 1621.

208. Hibbard, *Palazzo Borghese,* 72–73, n.5.

209. *Ibid.,* 73; cf. above, p. 100, for documentation of the cost of the stair.

210. ABorg. 5547, no. 60, 7 Sept. 1623, "Misura, et stima dell'opera di muro delle 4 stanze fatte di novo sopra la loggia in cima nel Cortile del Palazzo dell'Ecc^mo Sr Principe Marc'Antonio Borghese quali congiongono con l'Appartamento Vecchio . . ."; no. 234, 29 Dec. 1623, stone window frames and doorframes for the apartment; ABorg. 4168, 10 Oct. 1623, woodwork for windows and doors in the apartment.

211. ABorg. 5547, no. 60, fol. 3, "Colla nella sala dalla parte dove era le finestroni," 60½ *palmi* long and 23¾ *palmi* high (that is, the full height of the wall, with no frieze); fol. 5v, "Muro di una finestra murata alla prima sala dove passa la corda della campanella," 7 × 12 × 2 *palmi,* and "Per la valuta del Condotto dove passa la corda della campanella alt. palmi 28 del quale vi nè palmi 16 tagliato et murato."

212. *Ibid.,* no. 74, "Secondo fregio nella seconda camera à canto che si dice deve essere lo studio . . . longho di giro palmi 110 alto palmi 2½."

213. *Ibid.,* no. 60, fol. 5v, "Muro di un altra finestra simile murata verso la Camera dove dorme l'Inverno . . ."; the sequence of the *misura* indicates that room D2 is meant.

214. *Ibid.,* no. 60, fol. 3v, for the preparatory plaster; no. 74, 3 Oct. 1623, for the actual ". . . fregi di Pittura fatti da M. Giovanni Serodine Pittore nelle tre stanzie del'Apartamento fatto di novo dal'Ecc^mo Sr Principe Borghese, nella loggia di cima del Cortile nel Palazzo di S.E. . . ."; no. 177, Dec. 1623, a second frieze under that already painted in the "prima stanzia del'Appartamento fatto di novo, sopra le loggie al Piano di cima del Palazzo," also by Serodine; and no. 182, 1 June–12 Dec. 1623, fol. 15, the scaffolding for the painting of that second frieze. Giovanni Testori, Rudi Chiappini, and Sandro Corradini, *Serodine: L'opera completa,* Milan, 1987, does not mention Serodine's work at Palazzo Borghese. See, however, Italo Faldi, "Giovanni Serodine a Palazzo Borghese," *Strenna dei Romanisti* 49 (1988), 175–79.

215. ABorg. 5547, no. 182, fol. 12, ". . . nell'appartamento di S.E. al pian nobile . . ."; fol. 11v, ". . . le stanze di S.E. sopra il piano nobile . . ."

216. ABorg. 307, no. 67, 20 Jan. 1622, "Lavori fatti nell'Appartamento al Piano Nobile, Per haver levato li stipidi et architrave di trevertino delle tre porte in detto piano per rivoltarle di vano palmi 12 e palmi 5¾ . . ."

217. ABorg. 5547, no. 182, 1 June–12 Dec. 1623, . . . , fol. 12, "Per haver stuccato con gesso attorno alli muri di tre stanze nell'appartamento della S^ra D. Virginia . . ."

218. *Ibid.,* no. 25, 15 Jan. 1623, clothing for "li paggi dela

Sig.ra Verginia"; 16 June 1623, clothing for "li palafrinieri della S.ra Virginia"; 4 Jan. 1623, materials for clothing for "li palafarnieri e cocchiere della Sig.ra Donna Verginia" and for "li Aiutanti di Camera, li portieri, li paggi della Sig.ra Verginia et il Moretto" [probably Michelangelo Moretto, listed as *scopatore* in the roll of Marcantonio's *famiglia* in 1626, ABorg. 3949]; ABorg. 5547, no. 133, 1 June–12 Nov. 1623, a bill for snow, including 226 pounds for "[Donne] dell'Ecc.ma S.ra D. Verginia."

219. ABorg. 307, no. 67, 20 Jan. 1622.

220. Nicolò Borghese, *Vita di S. Caterina da Siena* (1869), 122, reports that Ortensia died in 1620 — the year of Francesco's death.

221. ABorg. 307, no. 67, 20 Jan. 1622, brackets installed "nella stanza dove si fa la bottiglieria al presente," in contrast to "la stanza dove si faceva prima."

222. Ibid., "Lavori fatti nel cortile del palazzo, Per il muro fatto tra la credenza et la computisteria lon. palmi 23 con la ligatura alt. palmi 20 . . ."; the height of the wall suggests the ground floor, beneath the mezzanines.

223. Ibid., "Lavori fatti nel tinello fatto di novo," including its roof and a wall toward the *cucina segreta;* cf. ABorg. 5547, no. 182, fols. 1–1v, work in the *cucina segreta,* next to the *tinello.*

224. ABorg. 5547, no. 182, 1 June–12 Dec. 1623, fols. 2v, 5, 6v–8v, 13–15v.

225. AVR, S. Lorenzo in Lucina, Stati d'Anime, 1630, "Palazzo dell'Ill.mo S.r Card.le [Scipione] Borghese e sua famiglia, Ill.mo S.r Card.le San Giorgio [Pier Maria] e sua famiglia, [Ec]c.mo Sig.r Principe Borghese e sua famiglia conforme alle liste . . ."

226. Records of a dispute over the ownership of the fittings of Pier Maria's chapel in 1642 reveal his successive use of the two apartments: ABorg. 458, Inv. 65, June 1642, "Noi infrascritti per la verità facciamo fede qualmente quando il Sig. Card.l Pier Maria Borghese di gloriosa memoria andò ad habitare nell'appartamento del Palazzo del Sig. Principe di Sulmona, nel quale è morto S.Ecc.a gliel'imprestò con tutti li paramenti, et altri mobili, come è notono à tutti, et in particolare la cappella stava parata con la sua croce, candilieri et altre cose necessarie, et come serviva di quel tempo per l'Ecc.ma Sig.ra D. Verginia madre di detto Sig. Principe, cosi hà continuato à servire per detto Sig.r Card.le." ABorg. 456, no. 25, "Inventario delle robbe della cappella dell'Ecc.mo S.r Principe di Sulmona della quale si serviva la buona memoria dell'Ecc.mo S.r Cardinal Pietro Maria Borghese. . . . Item che quando S.r Card. partì dall'appartamento nel quale habitava verso la piazza nova rilasso al Guardarobba di detto Prencipe li candelieri e paliotti della cappella di detto appartamento. . . . Item che essendo detto S.r Card.le andato ad habitare nell'appartamento verso la strada che va al Monte d'Oro s'è poi servito delli candelieri et paliotti della cappella di detto appartamento, della quale si serviva prima l'Ecc.ma S.ra D. Verginia

madre di detto S.r Prencipe . . ." (ABorg. 457, Inv. 51, fols. 193–222v, 30 June 1642, is the inventory of Pier Maria's goods, made at the order of his "sister and heir" Ortensia Borghese.)

227. Hibbard, *Palazzo Borghese,* 73–74, with reference to documents in the Archivio Borghese; Joseph Connors, *Borromini and the Roman Oratory: Style and Society,* New York and Cambridge, Mass., 1980, 19.

228. ABorg. 457, Inv. 52, 21 Apr. 1643; above, pp. 42–43.

229. Hibbard, *Palazzo Borghese,* 69 n. 33, 72.

230. ABorg. 307, no. 67, 27 Sept. 1619, *misura* for woodwork, signed by Gasparo de' Vecchi on 18 July 1620.

231. ABorg. 3949, "Rolo della famiglia dell'ecce.mo S.r Prin.e Borghese 1626–1632."

232. Hibbard, *Palazzo Borghese,* 74 nn. 9, 10.

233. Ibid., 73–74 n. 6.

234. Totti, *Ritratto,* 353.

235. Above, pp. 91–92.

236. AVR, S. Lorenzo in Lucina, Stati d'Anime, 1678, fol. 118, "Palazzo del Sig. Principe Borghese," listing Giovanni Battista, Eleonora, and their sons Marcantonio, Paolo, and Scipione; daughter Camilla was not listed.

237. ABorg. 1476, no. 781, 18 Oct. 1671, partially published by Hibbard, *Palazzo Borghese,* docs. 57, 58, 60, 61. Unfortunately this long document is unpaginated, but its arrangement is very orderly and proceeds through the palace from the roof to the cellars and then outside the palace to stables, carriage rooms, the garden, and the "Palazzetto a Ripetta dove si e fatto la veduta," to the north. See also ABorg. 1451, nos. 256 and 258, for woodwork for the remodeling. Where not otherwise noted, the reconstruction that follows is based on the *misura* of masonry in ABorg. 1476, no. 781; I will quote only especially interesting wording.

238. Mezzanines B2–B10 were gone by January 1672, according to a *misura* for the removal of their wood ceilings, ABorg. 1451, no. 258, 28 Jan. 1672.

239. ABorg. 1476, no. 781, e.g., in A9, ". . . facciata verso la stanza già misurata [A13], Per haver tagliato il muro per adrizzare la facciata . . . facciata verso il stanzione del udienza della Sig.ra Principessa, Per haver tagliato il muro in detta facciata per adrizarla . . ."; in A14–15, "Muro che si e accresciuto nel tramezzo dove si è fatto detta porta che riquadra la stanza . . ."; in A14, "Muro della fodera accanto a detta finestra [toward the street] nella testa di detta galleria dove e il specchio . . . fatta per metter in squadra la galleria." For Paul V's displeasure, above, pp. 89–90.

240. Ottavio Panciroli, *Roma sacra e moderna,* ed. Giovanni Francesco Cecconi, Rome, 1725, 283, in Palazzo Borghese, "l'Appartamento estivo a pian terreno . . ." Giovanni Pietro Rossini, *Il Mercurio errante delle grandezze di Roma, tanto antiche che moderne,* 3d ed., Rome, 1715, 40–42, "Il famoso Appartamento terreno, dove dimora il Signor Principe l'Estate. . . . Nell'Appartamento della Signora

Principessa per l'Estate . . ." Nicodemus Tessin, who visited the palace in 1687–88, spoke only of "dess Printzens Appartemens nach dhem Platz undt der Printzessin, ihre nach dem garten . . . ," without reference to seasonal use (Nicodemus Tessin, *Studieresor i Danmark, Tyskland, Holland, Frankrike och Italien,* ed. Osvald Sirén, Stockholm, 1914, 171).

Above, p. 14, for Hawthorne's discomfort.

241. ABorg. 1476, no. 781, "Scala appiedi alla porta del stanzione della Sig.ª Principessa che cala nel detto giardino, ovata . . . ," five steps, removed and replaced with six steps and a slab at the top, then undone and made a third time with nine steps and a slab.

242. Ibid., e.g., in A10, "Per haver rotto il muro e fatto il vano della porta nel tramezzo che passa nel stanzione del Udienza di S.E. per metterla a filo con le altre . . . ," and a similar entry for virtually every doorway in the apartment.

243. Ibid., "Scala segreta fatta a branchi, che dal piano de mezzanini cala al Appartamento terreno, quale scala e stata demolita per fare la nova galleria."

244. Ibid., "Cucinetta dove si è fatto la cappella e poi disfatta per fare la galleria . . ."

245. Ibid., "Stanza ovata per la cappella dove era la stanza della palla corda, dove si è fatto l'apertura della veduta"; and, near the end of the *misura,* "Lavori fatti al Palazzetto a Ripetta dove si e fatto la veduta . . ."

246. Ibid., "Stanza accanto alle stanze vecchie dove e il passo della scala segreta . . . Per haver tagliato sudetta sponda doppo che era stabilita per metterla a filo con la porta che passa nel salone del Udienza . . ."

247. Ibid., "Per haver scanzato le piane sopra li ponti della galleria sino fuori del portone dove è la fontana della veduta più e diverse volte quando venivono persone titolate per vedere detta veduta, mentre che si lavorava per perdimento di tempo delli mas.ⁱ et poi in rimettere le piane al suo loco per lavorare, scudi 2; Per haver scoperto più e diverse volte il ponte sotto la volta della galleria accio vedesse l'opera S.E.ª per il perdimento di tempo delli stuccatori, e doppo in rimettere le piane al suo loco per lavorare, scudi 2."

248. Tessin, *Studieresor,* 171–74. ABorg. 7504, Libro del Inventario, unpaginated, partially published by Paola della Pergola, "L'Inventario Borghese del 1693," *Arte antica e moderna* 26 (Apr.–June 1964), 219–30; 28 (Oct.–Dec. 1964), 451–67; 30 (Apr.–June 1965), 202–17. Della Pergola publishes only the list of paintings, room by room, with no indication that she is omitting the other furnishings of the apartments.

249. Howard Hibbard, "Palazzo Borghese Studies, II: the *Galleria,*" *Burlington Magazine* 104 (1962), 9–20.

250. Rossini, *Mercurio errante,* 41, toured the ground-floor apartments, arriving "Nella sesta stanza [A13], dove riposa Sua Eccellenza il giorno . . ."

251. Below, p. 305.

252. ABorg. 1476, no. 781, "Corritore al piano della strada dove e la fornacella della stufa." Cf. ABorg. 5677, no. 375, 15 Feb. 1672, a list of metalwork, including "per haver fatta una Caldara nuova d'ordine del Sig.ʳ Domenico Terzago Architetto peso lb. 37 per servitio della Stufa . . . scudi 11.10."

253. ABorg. 7504, Libro del Inventario, inventory of 1693, "Stanziolino sopra la stufa apparato di vecchi dipinti del Tempesta . . ."

254. ABorg. 1476, no. 781, "Stanzione sopra la rimessone," "Rimessone."

255. Tessin, *Studieresor,* 173, "Zur lincken der Chapellen ist dass zähnte zimber nembl. ein essahl mit 2:en treppen, so nach einer grossen Ringhiera hinaussgehen, welche à la Ripetta abouttiret . . ."

256. ABorg. 1476, no. 781, "Stanzione sopra la rimessone . . . lavori fatti e disfatti nelli Angoli dove si sono fatte le doi fontanelle alle scale che sallono alla ringhiera . . . ; Adi 29 Aprile 1676. Lavori fatti come si vedono al presente per le due fontanelli nelli sudetti Triangoli . . . ; Adi 8 giugno 1676, [foundations, bases, and columns of the *ringhiera,* then] Per la mettitura in opera del tamburo di castagno dove sono le gelosie sopra a detta balaustrata . . ."

257. Ibid., e.g., "Piano Nobile, Anticamera [C8] . . . Per haver tagliato il muro dalle parti per slargare et rialsare il vano di detta porta per metter al filo con le altre . . . ," and a similar entry for virtually every door in the apartments.

258. Ibid., "Cammera che segue [C11] . . . Per haver tagliato il muro dalle parti per slargare, et realsare il vano di detta porta [nel tramezzo che passa nel altro appartamento verso il giardino] rincontro alle finestre . . ."; "Cammera in volta [C27] . . . Per haver tagliato il muro dalle parti per slargare il vano di detta porta e per metterla a filo con le finestre . . ."

259. Ibid., "Scala lumaca dietro alla galleria verso il giardino, Per haver tagliato il muro per fare la centina a detta lumaca per slungarla sino al pian terreno, che restava al piano de mezzanini . . . ," with twenty-eight new steps and an opening to "il passo, che dalla galleria [A14] va a detta scala lumaca."

260. Mezzanine rooms B19 and B20 are not described in the *misura* of construction in 1671–76 (ABorg. 1476, no. 781), but they are called "mezanino nuovo" in a document for their decoration (ABorg. 1451, no. 8, 5 Dec. 1672). They were not built in 1606–7 (above, pp. 84, 85).

261. ABorg. 1450, no. 247, 23 Nov. 1671, 25 doppie [= 75 scudi] to Filippo Lauri and Gasparo Possin [Gaspard Dughet] for "le pitture che fanno nelli mezzanini dell'Ecc.ᵐᵒ P'rone," and subsequent entries in ABorg. 1450, 1451, 1452, and 1453, until 16 Jan. 1673, with one additional entry in ABorg. 1454, no. 426, 17 Oct. 1673, 20 scudi to "Luigi Garzi Pittore per le pitture da esso fatte ad una fenestra in uno delli mezzanini del Palazzo di S.E. . . ."

Other appellations for the rooms, in the series of payments to the painters, are "li mezzanini di S.E. [Giovanni Battista]," "li mezzanini del Palazzo dell'Ecc^mo P'rone," "li mezzanini per servitio di S.E.P.," "mezanino nuovo," and, for room B20, "la gallariola di detti mezzanini." Cf. Susan Jane Bandes, "The Frescoes of Gaspard Dughet," Ph.D. diss., Bryn Mawr College, 1977, 170–71 and 205–10, nn. 16–18; and Marie-Nicole Boisclair, "La décoration des deux mezzanines du palais Borghèse de Rome," *Racar* 3, no. 1 (1976), 7–27.

262. Tessin, *Studieresor,* 174.

263. Tessin notes the low ceilings and wall hangings. Bandes, "Frescoes," 183, cites *Roma moderna,* 1719, 503–5, a guidebook that describes "L'appartamento de' Mezzanini, assai commodo per l'inverno," painted by Lauri, Dughet, and others, without mentioning the occupant of the rooms. Low ceilings and orientation to the southwest are appropriate for a winter apartment (above, pp. 16, 19).

Bandes, "Frescoes," 171, citing a document for "woodwork" (actually metalwork) in May 1672 in the "appartamento di mezzo della S^ra Principessa" (ABorg. 5677, no. 407), has argued that the mezzanine apartment was painted by Dughet and others for Eleonora Boncompagni Borghese. However, the "appartamento di mezzo" is not to be confused with the "mezzanini."

ABorg. 5677, no. 407, a *misura* of metalwork beginning 20 September 1671, includes the cutting of two chains, "una nell'appartamento di mezzo della S^ra Principessa e l'altra nell'appartamento a pian terreno di detta Ecc^ma" (21 Jan. 1672), hardware for a door "nell Appartamento di mezzo" (10 Feb. 1672), and eight rods for *portiere* "per l'appartamento nobbile di mezzo" and fifteen handles for window leaves "delle fenestre verso al giardino nell appartamento di mezzo" (23 June 1672). Taken together, these entries must refer to the princess's apartment on the *piano nobile,* C12–C15 and C28, which has windows toward the garden and enough doors to make use of eight *portiere,* as the mezzanine apartment B19–B22 does not; the apartment must be "di mezzo" with respect to the princess's new ground-floor apartment and that on the *terzo piano,* both toward the garden in the Ripetta wing of the palace.

In contrast, the documents for the painting of mezzanine rooms B19 and B20, cited and transcribed by Bandes, refer consistently to "mezzanini" of "S.E." [Giovanni Battista]. Further, F. S. Baldinucci's biography of the painter Filippo Lauri specifies that the prince (not the princess) directed Lauri to paint certain subjects in the *gallariola* B20 (Francesco Saverio Baldinucci, in Bianca Riccio, "Vita di Filippo Lauri di Francesco Saverio Baldinucci," *Commentari* 10 [1959], 3–15, esp. 12, "Essendovi poi, nelle muraglie di detto stanzino [gallariola] quattro paesi di Gasparo Pussino [Dughet], volle lo stesso Principe che Filippo vi facesse le figure e gli ornati a tutto suo gusto e capriccio," cited by Bandes, "Frescoes," 183). The documentation of the remodeling of the rooms above, on the *piano nobile*

(ABorg. 1476, no. 781), mentions no specific person as resident of that apartment, of which the mezzanine rooms are logically a continuation.

Bandes's interpretation of the iconography of the decoration of the mezzanine apartment should probably be reconsidered in light of the prince's patronage and probable occupancy of the rooms.

264. ABorg. 1451, no. 256, 8 Dec. 1671, "Per haver fatti nove telari grossi d'Inpannate con sportelli e controsportelli . . . [*palmi* 5¼ × 4¼] servono alli mezanini dove dipingono li Pittori . . . Per haver fatto quattro porte . . . [*palmi* 9 × 4¼] servono alli sudetti mezzanini . . ."

265. So named in a document for its painting, ABorg. 1451, no. 18, 22 Nov. 1672.

266. Tessin, *Studieresor,* 174; above, p. 89.

267. ABorg. 1451, no. 256, 25 Oct. 1671, "Per haver levato il trucco della sala grande e portato al Biscanto che guarda nel vicolo del Monte d'oro."

268. Ibid., 20 Oct. 1671, "Per haver fatte due inbannate nove . . . servono alle stantie de' Signorini . . . palmi 10¼ × 5."

269. Ibid., 4 Dec. 1671, woodwork, including "Per haver fatto dui parafochi . . . serve dalle donne per i Signorini . . ."

270. Ibid., no. 258, 28 Jan. 1672, woodwork, "Appartamento al terzo piano verso il giardino."

271. ABorg. 1476, no. 781, "Scala che dal scalone ovato salle al terzo appartamento verso il giardino," including the eight steps, the closing of the door to S6, the vault over the stair measuring 16¼ × 10½ *palmi,* and the cutting of the wall "per largare il vano di detta porta per metterla a filo con le altre."

272. Ibid., "Stanza della guardia"; ABorg. 1451, no. 258, "Stanza della guardia," "Anti Camera."

273. ABorg. 1451, no. 258, 28 Jan. 1672, woodwork "nell'appartamento che si è rialzato dalla parte del giardino nel Palazzo dell'Ecc^mo Sig^re Principe Borghese, Sotto tetto, Appartamento delle Donne," the ceilings and windows for the seven rooms.

274. ABorg. 1476, no. 781, "Stanziolino dove è la rota"; ABorg. 1451, no. 256, 7 Dec. 1671, "Per haver accomodato la Rota delle donne, che va alla fabrica nova . . ."; no. 258, "7^a stanza [E21] . . . la finestra nel transito dove è la Rota . . ."

275. ABorg. 1476, no. 781, "Cucinetta dove si è fatto la cappella e poi disfatta per fare la galleria . . . Per haver levato di opera le lastre di travertino del labro all'altro sciacquatore . . . quali sono servite per il sciacquatore nell appartamento delle donne sotto tetto."

276. ABorg. 7504, Libro del Inventario, "Mobili che stanno nell'appartamenti delle donne."

277. ABorg. 1476, no. 781, "Mezzanini demoliti che godevono le Donne nella facciata verso il giardino e davanti per farle stanze nobile terrene," the removal of beams from eight rooms, ten doorframes, and "li conci di travertino intavolati al cammino al primo mezzanino verso il

scalone [B7] dove facevono il foco le donne." ABorg. 1451, no. 258, 28 Jan. 1672, "Piano de mezzanini che prima godevono le donne verso il giardino," the removal of four wood ceilings; "Seguono li mezzanini verso Strada," the removal of four more ceilings.

278. ABorg. 1476, no. 781, "Stanziolino dove era di prima la Rota dove si è fatto la scaletta secreta a branchi che riesce all'appartamento della Sig^ra Principessa . . . Per haver disfatto la bussola della Rota, et levato di opera li conci recinti alle due porticelle di vano palmi 2½ × 3¾ e portati nel giardino e la rota portata nell'appartamento al piano di cima delle donne verso il giardino . . ."

279. Ibid., "Seguono li lavori fatti in Cima al Scalone principale ovato nel Palazzo . . . [a wall extending] dalla spaletta della porta del coritore che va alla rota accanto la guardarobba . . . [another piece of wall] sino alla porta del stanzino dell'altra rota sopra l'Appartamento restaurato . . . [and an arch] sopra la porta che passa nel coritore della rota accanto la guardarobba . . ."

280. Ibid., "Scala che dal giardino cala in cantina."

281. AVR, S. Lorenzo in Lucina, Stati d'Anime, 1678, fols. 115v–117v, "Palazzo nuovo di Borghese [Palazzo della Famiglia Borghese]," residents of four stories; fol. 118, "Palazzo del Sig. Principe Borghese." ABorg. 1476, no. 781, "Lavori fatti nella Stalla de Muli . . . Stanza che godevono li mozzi di stalla . . . Stanze che gode il Mas° di Stalla . . ."; "Lavori fatti al Palazzetto a Ripetta dove si è fatto la veduta . . . Piano Nobile dove habita il Sig^r Simone . . ."

282. ABorg. 1451, no. 258, 28 Jan. 1672, "Misura e stima de lavori de legnami . . . nell'appartamento che si è rialzato dalla parte del giardino nel Palazzo dell'Ecc^mo Sig^re Principe Borghese."

283. Hibbard, *Palazzo Borghese,* 76.

284. ABorg. 1476, no. 781, toward the end of the *misura,* "Per le giornate di n° 10 homini cioe tre mastri e sette garzoni in spatio di quattro mesi quali hanno perso tempo tre hore per giorno per ordine di S. E^za che non voleva rumore la mattina . . . [scudi 69.30]."

285. Above, n. 247 (chap. 9).

286. ABorg. 1476, no. 781, "Per la mettitura in opera delle due fontanelle di alabastro nelle teste della galleria . . . messe e levate di opera piu volte per provarle a sodisfatione delli Padroni."

287. Hibbard, *Palazzo Borghese,* 77.

288. ABorg. 1476, no. 781, last page.

289. Above, n. 7 (chap. 9).

290. For an outline of the subsequent history of the palace and its present condition, see Pietrangeli, *Palazzo Borghese;* and for plans of the palace in the nineteenth century, see Hibbard, *Palazzo Borghese,* Figs. 47–51.

10. Barberini Family

1. For information about the Barberini family in general, see Pio Pecchiai, *I Barberini,* Rome, 1959; and articles in *Dizionario biografico degli Italiani.*

2. Pio Pecchiai, "Costanza Magalotti Barberini, Cognata di Urbano VIII," *Archivi* (Rome) 16, Fasc. 2 (1949), 11–41.

3. Pecchiai, "Costanza," 16–17.

4. An early source for Francesco's life is ABarb., Ind. I, no. 747, "Ristretto della vita dell'Em^mo Sig^r Card^l Francesco Barberino Decano del Sacro Collegio e Vicecancelliere di Santa Chiesa." Written by D. Archangelo Spagna in 1712, it was based on notes by the author's uncle Luciano Fabriani, Francesco's personal attendant for many years.

5. ABarb., Ind. IV, no. 1254, an incomplete draft of a biography of Taddeo written by his brother Cardinal Francesco, is an important source for our knowledge of Taddeo (see Appendix 3). For the first Taddeo, who lived only a few hours after his premature birth, see fols. 2v–3r. Fols. 8v–9r reveal the sorting out of the destinies of Francesco and Taddeo.

6. Ibid., fols. 10r–10v, for Taddeo's deferral to his father and uncle in the rational selection of his bride; and Nicolò Barozzi and Guglielmo Berchet, *Relazioni degli stati europei lette al Senato dagli ambasciatori veneti nel secolo decimosettimo,* Ser. III, Italia, *Relazioni di Roma,* 2 vols., Venice, 1877–79, I, 236, 266, for reports of discussions regarding the search for an appropriate match in 1625–26. For Anna Colonna, see "Anna Colonna Barberini," *Art Quarterly* (Detroit Institute of Arts) 9, no. 3 (Summer 1946), 270–73; Pecchiai, *I Barberini,* 164, 188–89; and especially Giuseppe Sacchi Lodispoto, "Anna Colonna Barberini ed il suo monumento nel monastero di Regina Coeli," *Strenna dei Romanisti* 43 (1982), 460–78.

7. Andrea Nicoletti, in the second volume of his biography of Urban VIII (Barb. lat. 4731, fols. 41bis–42), lists the five children in order of birth as Camilla (who died in infancy), Carlo, Lucretia, Maffeo, Nicolò. Pecchiai, *I Barberini,* without documentation, lists Lucrezia (1628–98), Camilla (d. 1631), Carlo (1 January 1630–1706), Maffeo (19 August 1631–1685), Nicolò Maria (September 1632); among other things, he overlooks the biological unlikelihood of three pregnancies for Anna between her marriage on 24 October 1627 and Carlo's birth on 1 January 1630. Oskar Pollak, *Die Kunsttätigkeit unter Urban VIII,* I, Vienna, 1928, 329, Reg. 928, partially published an *avviso* of 11 September 1632 indicating that the child baptized at that time was a daughter (i.e., not Nicolò).

8. ABarb., Ind. IV, no. 1254, fol. 10: Francesco writes that, when the recently married couple returned from Castelgandolfo, Anna was pregnant with Camilla ("Venuti a Roma si scoperse D. Anna gravida di Camilla . . ."). The Venetian ambassador Angelo Contarini, writing in the closing days of 1629, reported that Anna, at that moment awaiting the birth of another child [Carlo], had previously borne one daughter (Barozzi and Berchet, *Relazioni di Roma,* 1, 266).

9. ABarb., Ind. IV, no. 1254, fols. 13v–14v. Pecchiai, *I Barberini,* 259, without documentation, places Camilla's

death in September 1631, but September 1630 would better fit the contemporary evidence. According to Francesco, the birth of a son offered consolation for Camilla's death, but there is confusion as to which son: the text cites "D. Carlo hora Cardinale"; a marginal note in another hand (that of Francesco's sister Camilla, to whom the text is adressed?) remarks "fù il Sig^r D. Nicolò"; and this note is preceded by the word "anzi," in the hand of the text (fol. 14v). It is tempting to connect a payment of 6.52 scudi on 10 July 1630, for medicine for Camilla, with her fatal illness (ABarb., Comp. 187, 16 Dec. 1630, "A spese diverse scudi 6.52 . . . pagati sotto di 10 luglio presente à Stefano Saladino spetiale per saldo di un conto di robbe date per la S^{ra} D. Camilla mia figliola").

10. Two *avvisi* in a dispatch dated 11 September 1632 (Barb. lat. 6352, fols. 157, 160), only partially published by Pollak, *Kunsttätigkeit*, I, 329, Reg. 928, make clear that it was a female child: "L'Ecc^{ma} Signora Donna Anna Colonna Barberina Consorte dell' ecc^{mo} Signor Don Taddeo Barber° Prefetto di Roma Sabato notte partorì felicemente una figlia fem^a" (fol. 157); "Et il dopo pranzo di d° giorno nella cappella del nuovo palazzo de Sig^{ri} Barberini a Capo le Case fù per le mani di Monsr Scannaroli Vescovo di Sidonia fatta la cerimonia di battezzare la bambina nata all'Ecc^{mo} Sig^r Prefetto di Roma tenuta al Sac° fonte dal Sig^r Card^{le} Colonna, e gli furono posti li nomi Maria, Lucretia, Anna, Camilla, Francesca, Domenica, Candida, Rosa, et Angela" (fol. 160). Francesco in his biography of Taddeo states that Anna bore two sons [Carlo and Maffeo] at the Casa Grande and then a daughter at Palazzo Barberini (ABarb., Ind. IV, no. 1254, fol. 21v; Appendix 3). Nicolò must have been born later.

11. ABarb., Comp. 193, 4 June 1633, 19 Oct. 1633, 22 Nov. 1634: payments to "Angela Selerij balia di D.ª Lucretia Nostra figliola," at the rate of 6 scudi per month, extend from 1 November 1632 to 30 November 1634. For Lucrezia's marriage, see Giacinto Gigli, *Diario romano (1608–1670)*, ed. Giuseppe Ricciotti, Rome, 1958, 436–37.

12. Barozzi and Berchet, *Relazioni di Roma*, I, 369. Francesco's account (above, n. 10 [chap. 10]) confirms the existence of only two sons in late 1634. The services of Nicolò's wet nurse extended from 9 January 1636 to 8 May 1637 (ABarb., Comp. 194, 16 Apr. 1636, 10 Aug. 1636, 8 Jan. 1637, 21 Apr. 1637: payments to "Flavia Pompilij Ceci Balia di D. Niccolo nostro figliolo" at the rate of 6 scudi per month).

13. Gigli, *Diario romano*, 419–24.

14. Lodispoto, "Anna Colonna Barberini," 471, 476 n. 20.

15. E.g., Francis Haskell, *Patrons and Painters*, London, 1963, 24–43.

16. Barozzi and Berchet, *Relazioni di Roma*, I, 371.

17. ABarb., Ind. IV, no. 1254, fols. 15r, 18v, 21r.

18. ABarb., Ind. I, no. 747 (above, n. 4 [chap. 10]).

19. ABarb., Ind. IV, no. 1254, fols. 6v, 15r.

11. "Casa Grande" ai Giubbonari

1. The building is discussed with reference to documents in the Archivio Barberini, but from different points of view, by Bruno Maria Apollonj, "La 'Casa Grande' dei Barberini," *Capitolium* 8 (1932), 451–62; Cesare d'Onofrio, *Roma vista da Roma*, Rome, [1967], 49–63; and Howard Hibbard, *Carlo Maderno and Roman Architecture 1580–1630*, University Park, Pa., and London, 1971, 222.

2. ABarb., Ind. III, no. 647, int. 1, "Libro di memorie per la casa grande et sue coherentie dal 1581 sin'al 1596," in Francesco's small neat hand, is a chronicle of his building activities and expenditures for the house; fol. 1 records the purchase on 15 June 1581, the price, and the terms of payment. ABarb., Ind. III, no. 648, int. 5(11), is the instrument of sale of the "Domus Magna cum cortili Apothecis Cantinis et stabulo . . . ," describing its boundaries.

3. Ibid., no. 648, int. 4(37), a note in Francesco's hand listing the annual income from the property, beginning with "La Casa chiamato il palazo che ne pagha la pigione il R^{mo} Monsr de Graffi vescovo di Faenza a ragione di scudi 250 m^{ta} l'anno ma non di tutta," three houses, four shops, and a room on the ground floor of the "Casa Grande" separately rented to a baker, totaling 583 scudi.

4. Ibid., the shops were rented for 86, 40, 70, and 60 scudi per year, respectively.

5. D'Onofrio, *Roma vista da Roma*, 60, Fig. 25, mistakenly assumed that the portal spanned by an elliptical arch, visible in our Fig. 54, was the "antico ingresso" through which Maffeo Barberini's many visitors passed. This portal and the several present rectangular shop openings all post-date Barberini ownership of the property (cf. Fig. 85).

6. This schematic reconstruction is based on records of early work at the house in ABarb., Ind. III, no. 647, int. 25, unpaginated, e.g., 13 Nov. 1581, notes of the kitchen and the *guardaroba*; 29 July 1582, "per haver messo uno travicello per distendere pani su la logia," logically next to the *guardaroba*; 16 Oct. 1583, ". . . tre finestre nello studio che riesce nel cortile," and the "camera di monsig^e"; 6 Aug. 1586, ". . . il camino della sala vechia nella faciata dinanti," and the "camera acanto detta sala"; 20 Dec. 1586, "per haver alzato el solaro dello studio," 37¾ × 26¼ *palmi*; and so forth. See also Francesco's "Libro di memorie," above, n. 2, fol. 11, 10 June 1586, ". . . le finestre della guardarobba che rispondano sopra la strada"; 12 June 1586, the door from the *guardaroba* to the loggia; fol. 12, 25 Feb. 1587, below, n. 12 (chap. 11). Accounts of later renovations also reflect on the early state of the house.

7. Above, pp. 42–43.

8. ABarb., Ind. III, no. 647, int. 25, 5 Sept. 1581.

9. Glenn Merle Andres, *The Villa Medici in Rome* (Out-

standing Dissertations in the Fine Arts), New York and London, 1976, 2 vols. (originally presented as the author's Ph.D. diss., Princeton, 1970), 428–35, in an effort to identify the designers of Villa Medici, reconstructs the life and artistic personality of Annibale Lippi and concludes that he must have died in 1581.

10.   ABarb., Ind. III, no. 648, int. 4(28), the instrument of purchase. ABarb., Ind. III, no. 647, int. 1, fol. 1v, 11 Mar. 1586, a note of the purchase; and fol. 10, "A di 22 di Marzo 1586 havendo pochj di prima fatto metter mano ad incorporare la casa che fu prima di Hieron° et Fr° Paperonj, et poi di Fr° et Galeazo Colombi da quale io la comperai, con la mia Casa Grande che io comperai da Fr° Scappuccj et havendo convenuto con M° Bartolomeo Sala da Bibbiena Capo M° muratore che mi faccia tal fabbrica . . ." Cf. the instrument of purchase of the "Casa Grande" in 1581 (above, n. 2 [chap. 11]) for the location of the house to the southeast of the original purchase.

11.   ABarb., Ind. III, no. 647, int. 25, 6 Aug. 1586, for the *misura* of this work; and int. 1, fols. 10–11v, for Francesco's account.

12.   Ibid., int. 1, fol. 12, Francesco's account of the work, 25 Feb. 1587, "feci metter mano a fabbricare nella parte di verso Campo di fiore facendo l'apartamento di tre Camere alla man manca quando si entra in sala con giungendone alla che vi era et che risponde sopra la strada due altre, una cioè immediatamente et l'altra con giunta a questa mediante un corridoio serrato et sopra a quella di mezo due altre camere l'una sopra l'altra, et sopra l'altre due una per ciascuna, riformando anchora et parte di nuovo fabricando tutti membri di sotto a quellj tanto li riservatj per uso di mia famigla, quanto li altri bustj alle due botteghe che con questi si affittano, et di tutto con . . . con M° Bart° Sala da Bibbiena Capo M° muratore a tutta sua roba." Int. 25, 16 Mar. 1587 and especially Oct. 1587 contain the *misura* for this work.

13.   Ibid., int. 1, fol. 10v, 23 May 1586, nails "per rimettere il tetto alla camera la quale ho fatto tener bassa per che non impedisca il sole alla camera dove dormo." Given the orientation of the building, room C1b, with windows to the southeast, would be the only room (besides study C9) whose sunlight could be blocked by a higher part of the same building.

14.   Ibid., int. 25, 15 Aug. 1594, woodwork 17 July 1590–15 Aug. 1594, "per manifattura de tutte le palombelle andate nella facciata del'apartamento dove al presente habita mons^r R^mo Mafeo per la gronda del tetto," then his studio, the "stanze nuove dove habita mon^re R^mo Mafeo," and the "prima stanza dove habita mon^re Mafeo."

15.   Francesco describes the work in ABarb., Ind. III, no. 647, int. 1, fols. 13v–14r. The *misure* for the work are in ABarb., Ind. III, no. 647, int. 25, especially 29 Oct. 1592 (masonry) and 15 Aug. 1594 (woodwork).

16.   ABarb., Ind. III, no. 647, int. 1, fol. 13v, ". . . con vol-

tare la scala dal Cortile infino al piano della Sala per altro verso in maniera che se possa havere ingresso alle dette quattro camere nuove faccendola tutta di nuovo . . ."; Francesco describes the stair with obvious pride and speaks of the "buono ricetto avanti alla sala." Apollonj, "Casa Grande," 453, published a plan and section of the stair and vestibule at the *piano nobile*. The beginning of the stair at the *pian terreno* is shown in a drawing by Giovanni Maria Bonazzini, 24 Aug. 1610, Barb. lat. 6540, fol. 28r (Fig. 64).

17.   ABarb., Ind. III, no. 647, int. 1, fol. 13v, ". . . fabricando sopra alli mezzanini al piano della sala quattro grande camere incorporando nella prima quella che fabricai l'anno 1587 con giunta alle altre due che sonno in sala mediante un' corritore . . ."; fol. 14v, 25 May 1593, records the price of a beam to be placed over the "soffitto della Sala grande"—surely the enlarged room C1 and not the earlier sala C2, of more modest dimensions. Francesco's count of four rooms is puzzling, for surely there were rooms of some sort in area C12, in addition to rooms C1, C2, C3, and C9.

18.   Ibid., fol. 13v, Francesco writes of the construction of "altre et tante, et queste et quelle con loro porte di trivertino et fusti di albuccio," above the four major rooms of the *piano nobile*. The *misura* of woodwork cited above speaks of new rooms for Maffeo, in the vicinity of the building's cornice.

19.   Ibid., fols. 14r–15v.

20.   Piero Tomei, "Contributi d'archivio, un elenco dei palazzi di Roma del tempo di Clemente VIII," *Palladio* 3 (1939), 163–74, 219–30. The manuscript published by Tomei (Rome, Biblioteca Vittorio Emanuele, Fondo Vittorio Emanuele Mns. 721) can be dated 1601 (p. 164). The description of the "Casa Grande" is on pp. 223–24: "63. — Casa di Monsignore Barberino, s'entra per una porta ove si ritrova una facciata a man dritta et una in testa, quella a man dritta è lunga passi 32. Ha un finestrato principale di finestre otto sopra altrettante, questa facciata a man dritta ha nel terreno tutte botteghe con altre stanzotte." For the number of shops, see ABarb., Comp. 21, which records, among other notices, the rents received from six shops at six-month intervals, 1600–1604.

21.   ABarb., Comp. 21, fol. 11v, 14 Oct. 1600, "Sig. Carlo mio fratello deve avere scudi 54.60 . . . quando partij di Firenza per Roma . . ."

22.   ABarb., Ind. IV, no. 1254, fol. 2v; Appendix 3.

23.   ABarb., Comp. 21, fol. 101, 29 Dec. 1603, 25 scudi "per pagare parte a mia famiglia cioe staffierj, cocchiere, credenziere, stallone, cocho, e guattero per novembre passato."

24.   ABarb., Comp. 21, includes payments beginning 8 July 1600 and continuing to a final payment for masonry totaling 1,747 scudi on 30 August 1603; a final payment for woodwork totaling 360 scudi on 22 January 1603; a final payment for stonework totaling 305 scudi on 12 April 1603, a final payment for ironwork totaling 120 scudi on 18 Feb-

ruary 1603, and payments for wood (34.50 scudi), bronze (20 scudi), and the final *misura* (12 scudi, below, n. 25 [chap. 11]). By May 1601 payments totaled 1,779.50 scudi. The extent of the work is specified in the final payment to the mason Matteo Canevale (fol. 93v, 30 Aug. 1603), "per tutti i lavorj fatti nella mia casa grande dove io habito tanto di muri nuovi, come per ogni altro acconcime così nelli appartamenti principali come nelle botteghe, et altri attenenti a detta Casa e per ogni resto sino al presente giorno." Fol. 3, 20 July 1600, records the payment of 23 scudi for six beams; in 1643 Taddeo Barberini would pay 80 scudi for four beams each 42 *palmi* in length (below, n. 107 [chap. 11]).

25.   Ibid., fol. 93v, 4 Sept. 1603, 12 scudi "a m. Flaminio Pontij sono per intera sua provisione di tutte le misure fatte nella mia Casa Grande dove io habito . . ."

26.   Howard Hibbard, *The Architecture of the Palazzo Borghese*, Rome, 1962 (published simultaneously in the *Memoirs* of the American Academy in Rome, 27), 97–104; above, pp. 78–90.

27.   D'Onofrio, *Roma vista da Roma*, 54.

28.   Above, n. 13 (chap. 7). Maffeo himself already owned two carriages in 1594; Wolfgang Lotz, "Gli 883 cocchi della Roma del 1594," *Studi offerti a Giovanni Incisa della Rocchetta* (Miscellanea della Società Romana di Storia Patria, 23), Rome, 1973, 264.

29.   The work is anticipated in two estimates of the cost, ABarb., Ind. III, no. 647, int. 41, the first amounting to 2,215.92 scudi and the second, 2,497.10 scudi. The *misura* for masonry, ABarb., Ind. II, no. 680, records work begun 7 October 1609. The work described in these documents can be correlated to plans accompanying a letter written by the architect Bonazzini (Barb. lat. 6540, fols. 27–29, 24 Aug. 1610, to Cardinal Maffeo Barberini, below, p. 144; Figs. 64, 65) and later plans in the Archivio Barberini (below, pp. 145–46 and n. 56 [chap. 11]; Figs. 66, 67) to produce the following description and my reconstructions, Figs. 57–61.

30.   ABarb., Ind. III, no. 648, int. 4(25), instrument of purchase of the house, 24 Aug. 1609; cf. Ind. III, no. 647, int. 41 (cost estimates), which includes reference to "la casa che si ha da comprare."

31.   ABarb., Ind. II, no. 680, fols. 1, 1v, 7.

32.   Ibid., fols. 8 (room C2), 27 (room C13), 32 (the shop under C2).

33.   ABarb., Ind. III, no. 647, int. 41, anticipates the demolition of the partition ("Prima facendosi dalle doi Camere attaccata al Sala un Salotto, sarà necessario farci come segue una parte di solaro che costara scudi 41.25.") ABarb., Ind. II, no. 680, fol. 9, for the demolished partition; and fols. 8–13 for the identity and sequence of rooms. The shaping of the doorframes in drawings made before the remodeling of 1622 (ABarb., Ind. III, no. 647 [2, 13] and [3, 13], Cartella disegni barberini; Figs. 66, 67) confirms the sequence of rooms and bifurcation of the *appartamento nobile*.

34.   ABarb., Ind. III, no. 647, int. 41, anticipates this work ("La Cappella con farci il tetto, sofitto, muri, finestre, porta, et tutto il bisogno senza ornamenti costarà scudi 64.66."); and ABarb., Ind. II, no. 680, documents the construction of the chapel (fols. 32v–34), its stuccoes (fols. 34v–35v), and Passignano's work (fol. 34, "Per haver fatto il ponte due volte al Cavaliere Passignano per dipingere l'ovato in detta Capella"). At the same time (1604–16), Passignano was painting in the Barberini chapel in S. Andrea della Valle (Joan Lee Nissman, "Domenico Crespi (Il Passignano), 1559–1638: A Tuscan Painter in Florence and Rome," Ph.D. diss., Columbia Univ., 1979, 305–6).

35.   ABarb., Ind. II, no. 680, fols. 8–13v (the new stonework), 10 (scaffolding for painting the ceiling).

36.   Ibid., fol. 14: "andito fatto di novo che va alli gipponari"; Barb. lat. 6540, fol. 28r, "Andito che va alli gibonari" (Fig. 64).

37.   ABarb., Ind. III, no. 647 (1, 13), Cartella disegni barberini, 4 Feb. 1612 (Fig. 62), showing the house "che il Sig^r Card^{le} ha compro per far gettito" (house 5) and the location of the neighboring house of the de Donati (house 7); published by d'Onofrio, *Roma vista da Roma*, 52, Fig. 20. ABarb., Ind. III, no. 648, int. 4(35), instrument of purchase of the house of Jacopo de Velli (house 5), 9 Dec. 1611, the property measured Aug. 1611; and int. 4(42), copy of instrument of purchase of the house of the de Donati brothers (house 7), 6 Dec. or 10 Dec. 1612, specifically for widening the street.

38.   ABarb., Ind. II, no. 680, the main *misura* totaling 3,214.87 scudi (fol. 36v) and another smaller *misura* amounting to 81.55 scudi (fol. 38); cf. the preliminary estimates, above, n. 29 (chap. 11).

39.   Ibid., fol. 32, identifies room C2 as "l'anticamera del Sr Card^{le}," and Barb. lat. 6540, fol. 27v, speaks of "l'appartamento di V.S. Illma [Maffeo]" in this location.

40.   ABarb., Ind. II, no. 680, fols. 27v and 28, for the fireplaces; fol. 33, "Muro del fianco dove è la finestra per la famiglia," the chapel window; fols. 23–23v, 30–32v, for the shops; fols. 22v–23 (and Barb. lat. 6540, fol. 28r), for the carriage rooms; fols. 20–22v, for the "cocina comune" and "cucina segreta"; fol. 16v, for the wet nurse, who must have left before construction was complete (". . . ci habitava la Balia"); fol. 15, for the "Stantia dell'Auditore."

41.   ABarb., Ind. II, no. 680, fol. 17, for this wing, including the "Dispensa intesta al Cortile à Pian Terreno." A turnbox (a necessary fixture for a women's apartment) was installed at the entrance to the mezzanine B12 "per ord^e della bo. me. della S^{ra} Camilla e poi levata," presumably after her death, when the apartment would no longer be needed. ABarb., Ind. III, no. 647, int. 41, estimating the cost of reroofing the wing, identifies the previous location of the stable here ("Alla Gallaria con la stantia à canto verso il Cortile con la stalla sotto, e mezzanini sotto tetto il tetto costara scudi 100").

42. ABarb., Ind. II, no. 680, fol. 38, for Camilla's rooms; fols. 1, 6, 20v, 29v, for the *guardaroba*.

43. Ibid., fol. 25, for the room "dove ha da habitare il Filicaia." Costanza's younger sister Settimia married Bartolomeo Filicaia (Pio Pecchiai, "Costanza Magalotti Barberini, cognata di Urbano VIII," *Archivi* [Rome] 16, fasc. 2 [1949], 11–41, esp. 14). "S. Filicaia" is included in Maffeo's *rolo di famiglia* in 1621–22 (ABarb., Comp. 37, e.g., fol. 2, Dec. 1621); and Zenobio Filicaia accompanied Cardinal Francesco Barberini on his trip to Paris in 1625 (Barb. lat. 5688, fol. 471v).

44. Barb. lat. 6540, fols. 27–29.

45. Inscribed on the reverse, "Io Gio. Maria Bonazzini ho fatta la p'nte Pianta mano p^ria."

46. ABarb., Ind. II, no. 680, fol. 36v; and another small *misura* of masonry, doc. cit., fol. 38.

47. ABarb., Ind. III, no. 648, int. 25, 15 Aug. 1594, a *misura* of work by the *falegname* "Ambrogio Bonazini"; and Comp. 21, payments beginning 28 July 1600 (fol. 3v) and continuing until 16 August 1603 (fol. 92), to "Mastro Ambrogio Bonazini falegniame."

48. Hibbard, *Palazzo Borghese*, 103.

49. Ibid., 99, for the Cappella Paolina; and Luigi Crema, "Flaminio Ponzio, architetto milanese a Roma," *Atti del IV Convegno Nazionale di Storia dell'Architettura, Milano, 18–25 giugno 1939-XVII*, Milan, 1940, 281–308, esp. 290–92, for S. Eligio.

50. ABarb., Comp. 38, fol. 28, 1621.

51. ABarb., Ind. III, no. 647, int. 14, fol. 13.

52. Pier Nicola Pagliara, "Monterotondo," in *Storia dell'arte italiana*, pt. III, 1, *Inchieste su centri minori*, Turin, 1980, 233–78, esp. 264.

53. Carla Benocci, "Due disegni per la 'Casa Grande' dei Barberini in via dei Giubbonari," *Alma Roma* 24, no. 1–2 (January–April 1983), 1–9, has seen an elevation of a street-front of three contiguous buildings and part of a fourth, with shops on the ground floor (Fig. 78; Benocci's Fig. 1), in the Archivio del Monte di Pietà (Cassa di Risparmio di Roma) (ACR, Piante e disegni, tomo 573 [*sic:* 572], inv. 1791), and has identified it as the elevation on via dei Giubbonari of the whole Barberini complex, before 1612. It does not match the building as reconstructed here. Instead, the drawing is surely of the group of houses along the present via Arco di Monte, below, p. 156 and n. 93 (chap. 11).

54. *Avviso* of 2 September 1615 (Urb. lat. 1083, fol. 444B), published by J.A.F. Orbaan, *Documenti sul Barocco in Roma*, Rome, 1920, 237: "Monsignor Raimondo tratta di comprare il palazzo del cardinal Barberino, che all'incontro sta in prattica di comprare quello delli signori Acquaviva in strada Giulia."

55. ABarb., Comp. 37, fol. 2, "Companatici e salarij di Dicembre [1621]," and similar lists for subsequent months throughout the volume. For Taddeo's intended career in the church, see Arch. Barb., Ind. IV, no. 1254, fols. 8v–9r (Appendix 3).

56. ABarb., Ind. III, no. 647 (2, 13) and (3, 13), Cartella disegni barberini; one of these was published by D'Onofrio, *Roma vista da Roma*, 163, Fig. 79, who considered it simply "di qualche anno posteriore," with respect to one of the drawings of 1610 (Barb. lat. 6540, fol. 29r).

57. ABarb., Comp. 1, fol. 139, 22 Dec. 1627. Comp. 3, fol. 4, 12 Oct. 1623, payment of 3,100 scudi for the "Casa con forno e sua Membrij attacata alla Casa grande che risponde nel Vicolo della grotta compera dal S. Cesare del Pasquale Cioli conf^e lo strumento fatto sotto di 21 del anno 1620 [month not given] per li atti del rosciolo notaro . . ." Cf. ABarb., Ind. III, no. 648, int. 5, for location of the Cioli house adjacent to the "Casa Grande." Cf. ABarb., Ind. III, no. 647, int. 1, fols. 13v, 14r, for further indications of location. Comp. 38, fol. 33v, Nov. 1621, refers to "Lavori fatti all'Appartamento delle stanze comprate verso li Balestrari . . . quali stanze tiene à piggione Il Sig^r Alessandro Roncari," presumably in this same house. (Although today the vicolo delle Grotte and the vicolo dei Balestrari are different streets, in the seventeenth century both names were applied to the street bordering the Barberini property to the northwest; see the description of the property in an Inventory of 1648, ASR, Not. A.C., 6601, fol. 853r, "Il Palazzo . . . [bordered] di dietro col Vicolo detto de Balestrari ò della Grotta . . .")

Although properties were bought in the vicinity of Capo di Ferro, they cannot be identified precisely.

58. ABarb., Comp. 38, fols. 28–30.

59. ABarb, Comp. 37, fol. 382, including an authorization to pay for "imbiancature fatte alle stanze alla fabrica nova attacata al mio Palazzo," dated 19 December 1622.

60. ABarb., Comp. 1, fol. 47; and a similar entry in Comp. 3, fol. 16v.

61. ABarb., Comp. 38, fols. 32–33v, work done in 1621.

62. Howard Hibbard, "Di alcune licenze rilasciate dai Mastri di Strade per opere di edificazione a Roma (1586–'89, 1602–'34)," *Bollettino d'Arte* ser. 5, 52 (1967), 99–117, esp. 111, doc. 119, 11 Apr. 1623, illustrated as Fig. 51 (Archivio Storico Capitolino, Cred. IV, tomo 86, c. 283v); a copy of this license is in ABarb., Ind. III, no. 648, int. 4 (loose sheet). ABarb., Ind. III, no. 647, int. 14, fol. 3v, 26 July 1623, the *misura* of walls at the level of the *piano nobile*.

63. Cf. the document of Maffeo's donation of the palace to Carlo, 22 September 1623, published by d'Onofrio, *Roma vista da Roma*, 424: "Il Palazzo di Roma, con sette Botteghe di sotto, che riescono nella strada detta de Giubonari . . ."

64. Doc. cit. (with old collocation).

65. ABarb., Comp. 37, *passim*, payments totaling 850 scudi for masonry, 350 scudi for woodwork, 50 scudi for stonework, 90 scudi for ironwork, and 13.20 scudi for whitewashing, in 1622; Comp. 38, *passim*, payments total-

ing 950 scudi for masonry, 100 scudi for woodwork, 148.50 scudi for eighteen beams, 260 scudi for stonework, and 63.93 scudi for the locksmith.

66. Above, nn. 58, 59 (chap. 11).

67. ABarb., Comp. 1, fol. 47, 6 Dec. 1623, 2,338.83 scudi for masonry since 9 November 1621; 5 Mar. 1624, 638. 60 scudi for stonework 10 September 1622–9 January 1624; 27 Mar. 1624, 2,722.20 scudi for masonry 9 September 1622–31 December 1623; 6 Apr. 1624, 1,306.32 scudi for woodwork from 1616 until 31 January 1624; cf. similar entries in Comp. 3, fols. 16v, 33, and 37; and the second *misura* for masonry, ABarb., Ind. III, no. 647, int. 14.

68. ABarb., Ind. III, no. 648, int. 4(20), 22 Dec. 1623, the instrument of purchase from the nuns of S. Marta, which cites the *misura* of 31 July 1623. The license cited above, n. 62, notes the location of this "casa delle monache di Sta Marta dove al presente habita il Tinozaro."

69. ABarb., Ind. III, no. 648, int. 4(34), "Misura e stima delle case che vuole comprare l'Illmo et Ecc^{mo} Sig^r Don Carlo Barberini per ampliar la fabrica del suo palazzo," 2 May 1624; int. 4(3, 6, 11, 18, 31, 36), the six instruments of purchase, 17, 23, and 30 July 1624. ABarb., Comp. 1, fol. 112(19, 23, and 30 July 1624), with small preliminary payments recorded on fol. 47 (15 and 27 Mar., 6 Apr.) and fol. 112 (6 Apr.); Comp. 3, fols. 52–53 (19, 23, and 30 July 1624).

70. ABarb., Ind. III, no. 648, int. 4(10), the six instruments of purchase. ABarb., Comp. 1, 15 Mar. 1624, 27 Mar. 1624, 6 Apr. 1624.

71. ABarb., Comp. 1, fol. 47, 6 Apr. 1624. Comp. 3, fol. 4, 12 Oct. 1623, giving date of purchase as 28 August 1623.

72. ABarb., Comp. 1, fol. 47, 6 Apr. 1624. The same wording is used to describe a house in the Inventory of 1648. Property 14, shown in the plan of the palace in 1734 (Fig. 85), is otherwise unaccounted for, and the description "à canto al Palazzo" does not fit any other parcel whose identity is not known.

73. ABarb., Ind. III, no. 648, int. 4(8), the *misura* of 8 August 1624 of "una casa del Sig^r Bla . . . de Velli et Sig^r Giulio Bonaventura posta nel vicolo o strada detta de Balestrari," valued at 3,629.51 scudi; int. 5(11), the instrument of purchase of 1581, with bordering properties including "et retrobona Pasqualis Ciolli de Camerata, Mag^{ti} D. Marci Bonaventure, ac D'ni Mutie debellis . . ."

74. Patricia Waddy, "The Design and Designers of Palazzo Barberini," *Journal of the Society of Architectural Historians* 35 (1976), 151–85, esp. 154 n. 11. Francesco Niccolini, Florentine ambassador to the papal court, reported, on 3 February 1624: "Alcuni vogliono che Sua Santità habbia voglia di comprar dal Duca Sforza qualche suo luogo" (Hans Posse, "Das Deckenfresko des Pietro da Cortona im Palazzo Barberini und die Deckenmalerei in Rom," *Jahrbuch der Preuszischen Kunstsammlungen* 60 [1919], 93–118, 126–73, esp. 93, n. 1).

75. Uffizi A6720; see Heinrich Thelen, *Francesco Borro-*

mini: Die Handzeichnungen, 1 (Veröffentlichungen der Albertina, 2), Graz, 1967, C15. Thelen, 19–20, also noted the correspondence of the dimension of 300 *palmi* to the width of the palace in via dei Giubbonari as well as to that of the Barberini palace at Monterotondo. See also Patricia Waddy, "Palazzo Barberini: Early Proposals," Ph.D. diss., New York Univ., 1973, 27–48.

76. The floor heights of Uffizi A6720, scaled to the tops of the cornices dividing the façade, are 43 *palmi (pian terreno),* 39 *palmi (piano nobile),* 32 *palmi (secondo piano),* and 31 *palmi* (towers), totaling 145 *palmi.* Those of Palazzo Sforza, to be incorporated as the north wing of the Palazzo Barberini alle Quattro Fontane, are derived from Barb. lat. 4360 and are shown in Fig. 97; their interpretation is complicated by the sloping terrain. If one can judge from the section of 1734 (Fig. 88), the floor heights of the "Casa Grande" were, roughly, 35 *palmi (pian terreno),* 25 *palmi (piano nobile),* 20 *palmi (secondo piano),* 16 *palmi* (attic), 34 *palmi* (tower), totaling 130 *palmi.* The irregular spacing of the windows of the two properties, as shown in the plans, Figs. 85 and 95, is in obvious contrast to the regularity of the fifteen bays of Uffizi A6720.

77. ABarb., Comp. 3, fols. 40–118, entries dated 13 Apr. 1624–8 June 1626.

78. ABarb., Ind. IV, no. 1254, fol. 20v (Appendix 3).

79. ABarb., Comp. 1, fol. 139, 2 Feb. 1625, 97.44 scudi for "canali di rame messi alla loggia nuova et altro . . ."

80. Below, p. 227.

81. ABarb., Comp. 1, fol. 139, and Comp. 3, fols. 167–191, entries dating from 2 Dec. 1627 to 19 Aug. 1628.

82. ABarb., Comp. 1, fol. 139, "il novo appartamento [che] si fa in detta Casa"; Comp. 3, fol. 186, ironwork "per servitio di Casa mia, et part^{te} per le nuove cucine"; fol. 172, "A spese della nuova Cappella di Casa . . ."

83. ABarb., Comp. 3, fol. 167, 1 Dec. 1627, "A pigione del Palazzo di Campo di Fiore che si tiene dall'Ecc^{mo} S^e Duca di Bracciano per servitio della famiglia dell'ecc^{mo} S^e D. Taddeo . . . ," at the rate of 1,070 scudi per year; above, p. 42.

84. D'Onofrio, *Roma vista da Roma,* 53; Hibbard, *Maderno,* 222.

85. ABarb., Comp. 1, fol. 139.

86. ABarb., Comp. 192, 2 June 1632; Comp. 193, 14 June 1633.

87. Giacinto Gigli, *Diario romano (1608–1670),* ed. Giuseppe Ricciotti, Rome, 1958, 150, a report of the fire on 20 December 1634. ABarb., Ind. III, no. 648, int. 4(26), undated, "Memoria di danari dà pagarsi per le Case abbruggiate avanti S. Barbara," regarding the purchase of the burned houses, to leave the site open. Alessandro Ademollo, *I teatri di Roma nel secolo decimosettimo,* Rome, 1888, 8, *avviso* of 23 December 1634, "A Giupponari sono abbruggiate tre Case di Mercanti vicino al Principe D. Taddeo et con quest'occasione si farà piazza e s'aprirà una strada dal Palazzo del detto Principe Prefetto a Santo Andrea della

Valle." For a plan showing the course of the proposed street from the palace to S. Andrea della Valle, in the Archivio Storico del Monte di Pietà, see *Roma 1300–1875: La città degli anni santi, Atlante,* ed. Marcello Fagiolo and Maria Luisa Madonna, Milan, 1985, 52, Fig. A.1.9 (g).

88.   Hibbard, *Maderno,* 218–20, concisely summarizes the documentation as well as the scholarly literature on this building.

89.   D'Onofrio, *Roma vista da Roma,* 54 n. 11; Hibbard, *Maderno,* 219.

90.   Hibbard, *Maderno,* 220, with reference to documents; the architect was Francesco Peparelli.

91.   ABarb., Ind. III, no. 648, int. 4(8).

92.   Ibid., no. 647 (2); published by D'Onofrio, *Roma vista da Roma,* 52, Fig. 21, and 54 n. 11, in which part of the text is transcribed.

93.   Archivio Storico del Monte di Pietà (Cassa di Risparmio di Roma), Piante e disegni, vol. 572, inv. 1791, unpaginated. (The number on the spine of the volume is blurred, but the archivist states that it is catalogued as no. 572.) Benocci, "Due disegni," 1–9, first published this drawing as her Fig. 1 (giving the volume number as 573) and identified it as probably an elevation in via dei Giubbonari of the whole Barberini complex, between 1591 and 1612. Daniela Porro repeated this identification in *Roma 1300–1875,* 53, Fig. A.1.9 (m); and again in "Lo scalone del palazzo Barberini ai Giubbonari e altre opere di Nicola Giansimoni architetto," *Studi romani* 24, nos. 1–2 (1986), 95–106, esp. 97 and Pl. III, Fig. 2. In the context of the group of drawings to which the elevation belongs — surveys of the palace in anticipation of its sale in 1734 — an elevation of the building in the early seventeenth century makes no sense. Besides, it does not match any information that we have about the palace in those years. Instead, it is to be compared with the engraving by G. Vasi showing the Barberini palace at one end of the piazza Monte di Pietà (Fig. 84): the tall structure at the right edge of the elevation, set slightly behind the other houses, is the left edge of the Barberini palace; and the two-bay house just to the left is the two-bay house in the Vasi engraving. The other five houses, hidden in the Vasi engraving by the Palazzo del Monte di Pietà, are houses that the Barberini never owned: according to the documentation of Barberini purchases in this block (below, nn. 95, 96; cf. the chirograph of August 1642, Fig. 81, and Fig. 52), the four similar houses belonged to the Signori Fabri da Rieti, and the owner of the house on the corner is unknown.

The group of seven drawings to which the elevation of the block of houses belongs includes (1) a plan of the ground floor of the "Casa Grande" (Fig. 85; *Roma 1300–1875,* Fig. A.1.9[l]; Porro, "Lo scalone," Pl. I); (2) a second ground-floor plan (*Roma 1300–1875,* Fig. A.1.9[q]; Porro, "Lo scalone," Pl. V) and (3) a plan of the *piano nobile* (Fig. 86; Porro, "Lo scalone," Pl. IV), together proposing alter-

ations that would divide the building into two palaces; (4) a longitudinal section (Fig. 88; Benocci, "Due disegni," Fig. 2; *Roma 1300–1875,* Fig. A.1.9[o]; Porro, "Lo scalone," Pl. II, Fig. 1); (5) a transverse section of the palace (Fig. 87; *Roma 1300–1875,* Fig. A.1.9[p]; Porro, "Lo scalone," Pl. II, Fig. 2); and (6) a second plan of the *piano nobile* (previously unpublished; Fig. 89). This last is the only one of the group that bears a signature ("Vm.º Dev.mo et Obl.mo Ser.re Gio. Franc.º Zannoli Arch.º"), but the drawing is in a different hand (evident in the notes) and technique (pink wash instead of the gray or yellow of the other drawings) from the others. The drawings are surely among those sent to the Discalced Carmelites in 1734 in anticipation of the sale of the palace to that religious community (ABarb., Ind. III, no. 648, 27 Aug. 1734, "Sette fogli di piante con altro del fruttato furono mandati al pᵉ Geˡᵉ de Carmelitani Scalzi"). They would have passed to the Monte di Pietà when that entity bought the palace from the Carmelites in 1759. They are mentioned briefly by Mario Tosi, *Il Sacro Monte di Pietà di Roma e le sue amministrazioni,* Rome, 1937, 138; and by Cecilia Pericoli Ridolfini, *Le case romane con facciate graffite e dipinte,* Rome, 1960, 69.

94.   ABarb., Ind. III, no. 648, int. 4 (unnumbered document), a complete *misura* of the house, then owned by Lelio Parisani, dated 17 November 1638. The instrument of purchase has not been found, but a chirograph of August 1642 (Fig. 81) indicates Barberini ownership of the site by that date, and the house is listed in the Inventory of 1648, ASR, Not. A.C., 6601, fol. 853v, "Casa attacata al Portone del detto Palazzo per andare alla Trinità."

95.   ABarb., Ind. III, no. 648, int. 4(36bis), a memorandum written after the death of Taddeo, describing the six properties, naming their previous owners, and giving their prices and the dates of 1 June and 14 June 1641; cf. the text of the chirograph of 22 August 1640, which names those same owners.

96.   The chirograph of August 1642 (Fig. 81) indicates by its coloring that Taddeo owned house 30 as well as houses 28, 27, 26, 29, 7, and 23 in this block, but not properties a–e. ABarb., Ind. III, no. 648, int. 4(36bis), indicates that the previous owner was Achille Martorij.

97.   ABarb., Ind. III, no. 647(3a), Cartella disegni barberini.

98.   ABarb., Comp. 184, fol. 132, 4 Dec. 1642: ". . . scudi 2997.25 a mᵣⁱ Jacopo e Giovanni Battista Beccaria fratelli e Compagni muratori per tanti che importa una misura, e stima di lavori fatti a tutta loro robba nella fabrica dell'Androne fatta in questo nostro Palazzo alli Giubonari dalli 8. di luglio 1641 a tutto li 28. di settembre prossime, conforme alla misura, e stima fatta dal Contini nostro Architetto."

99.   Ibid., 21 Jan. 1642 and 5 Apr. 1642. Two columns framed the portal; see Fig. 85. Twelve black granite columns were still in place when the entrance hall was converted as the church of SS. Teresa e Giovanni della Croce

(Giovanni Marangoni, *Delle cose gentilesche e profane trasportate ad uso, e adornamento delle chiese,* Rome, 1744, 348–49). They were removed and sent to the Museo Pio-Clementino in 1819, for the new wing then under construction. Columns of peperino were to have been substituted, but travertine columns were used instead (Tosi, *Sacro Monte,* 142–43; A. Pasquinelli, "Alla ricerca di dodici colonne antiche," *Roma* 8 [August 1927], 378–79).

100. The piazzetta of 1612, which the new entrance hall replaced, was cleared exactly to accommodate these functions. The new construction still allowed the width of 33 or 34 *palmi* specified for the maneuvering of carriages in Barb. lat. 4360, fol. 11 (above, p. 62).

101. ABarb., Ind. IV, no. 1254, fol. 21r: ". . . havendovi [in the entrance hall] poste due statue antiche trovate ne vicini fondamenti, che parti erano del celebre teatro di Pompeo"; cf. ABarb., Comp. 196, 30 May 1643, ". . . à Francesco Contini nostro Architetto scudi 25 quali sono per doverli distribuire a suo arbitrio à Muratori, che hanno fatigato in trover e cavar fuori le due statue trovate nelli fondamenti di questo nostro Palazzo alli Giubbonari per ricognitione . . ."; and a similar entry in ABarb., Comp. 184, fol. 132, 3 June 1643.

102. ABarb., Comp. 184, fol. 132, 4 July 1643: 327.22 scudi paid to "Beccaria Muratori per una misura e stima di opere di muro, et altro fatto in trasportar la Cucina comune nelle Casette del Palazzo à Giubonari nella strada che andava à Capo di ferro, et altri rappezzi fatti sotto le stanze del nostro [Taddeo's] appartamento dove si sono messi li Paggi, e Cucina secreta trasportata dove era la comune con altri rappezzi fatti per detto Palazzo conforme alla detta misura e stima fatta li 8 di Novembre 1642 da Francesco Contini Architetto." One of the ground-floor plans in the Archivio Storico del Monte di Pietà (above, n. 93, no. 2) indicates a kitchen in the extension toward via dei Balestrari in 1734 ("7. Cocina con su dispenze"), as does the sequence of an inventory of the palace in 1648 (ASR, Not. A.C., 6601, fols. 889–890; below, p. 169).

103. ABarb., Comp. 196, 30 June 1643, roof tiles "per servitio delli tetti della fabrica nouva della giunta di quel nostro Palazzo . . ."; 7 Aug. 1643, masonry for "la fabrica del nuovo appartamento che fanno in questo nostro Palazzo alli Giubbonari"; 20 Oct. 1643, beams for the "nuova fabrica che si fa in questo nostro Palazzo alli Giubbonari . . ." (see below, n. 107 [chap. 11]).

104. ABarb., Ind. III, no. 647(2b), Cartella disegni barberini.

105. The two houses to the right, however, were rented by Cardinal Antonio Barberini in 1665; ABarb., Comp. 229, fol. 101, "scudi 20 per la Casa contigua al Palazzo di S.E. [Antonio] nella Piazza del Monte di Pietà, e scudi 5 per le stanze terrene dell'altra Casa, che segue alla sudetta, quali si continuano in locatione stante in nuovo negotio hauto con . . . con detto S. Fabri, e questi per sei mesi cominci-

anti il primo Gennaro corrente [1665]."

106. ABarb., Ind. IV, no. 1254, fol. 21r (Appendix 3).

107. ABarb., Comp. 196, 20 Oct. 1643, ". . . a Luigi Arigucci scudi 80 quali sono per il prezzo di quattro travi grossi d'abeto di lunghezza di palmi 42 l'uno dati da lui per servitio della nuova fabrica che si fa in questo nostro Palazzo alli Giubbonari . . ."; cf. a similar entry in Comp. 184, fol. 132, 2 Dec. 1643.

108. ABarb., Comp. 196, 30 Apr. 1644, 30 scudi for two beams, each 28 *palmi* long.

109. Ibid., 5 July 1644, ". . . à Marco Tullio Montagna Pittore scudi 23 quali sono per la pittura à fresco da lui fatta nel muro della casa del Sr Barg^o de Sig^{ri} dove habita Jacomo Balloncini spetiale [i.e., *not* the Palazzo del Monte di Pietà, to the southeast] incontro alle fenestre del nuovo appartamento di questo nostro Palazzo a Giubonari, è dipinto cinque mezzanini di finestre finte di vetriate nella facciata del medesimo nostro Palazzo . . ."; cf. ABarb., Comp. 184, fol. 381, 2 July 1644.

110. ABarb., Ind. IV, no. 1254, fols. 20v–21r (Appendix 3).

111. This entrance hall was indeed converted to a chapel by the religious community that bought the property in 1734 (Apollonj, "Casa Grande," 456–57). It was consecrated as the church of SS. Teresa e Giovanni della Croce in 1735 (Tosi, *Sacro Monte,* 140). It was used as a theater in the 1930s (Fig. 83) and now (in deplorable condition) is a bar and gaming room.

112. Contini's name is cited consistently in documents, e.g., above, nn. 98, 101, 102 (chap. 11). In Taddeo's *rolo della famiglia* of 1643 (ABarb., Ind. IV, no. 1282) he is listed as architect, with the salary of 15 scudi a month (considerably more than the salary of 50 scudi for six months paid to his predecessor Paolo Maruscelli, below, n. 31 [chap. 13]). For a thorough and succinct account of Contini's life and oeuvre, see the article by Helmut Hager in *Dizionario biografico degli Italiani,* XXVIII (1983), 512–15; see also Alessandro del Bufalo, *G. B. Contini e la tradizione del tardomanierismo nell'architettura tra '600 e '700,* Rome, 1982, 35–56.

113. Cf. the portrait of Taddeo as active patron in ABarb., Ind. IV, no. 1254 (Appendix 3), and below, pp. 288–90; and Patricia Waddy, "Taddeo Barberini as a Patron of Architecture," in *L'âge d'or du mécénat (1598–1661),* Paris, 1985. For the respective contributions of architect and non-professional in general, see Waddy, "Design and Designers," 178–85.

114. ABarb., Comp. 196, passim.

115. Above, n. 93 (chap. 11).

116. ASR, Not. A.C., 6601, fols. 852r–935r.

117. In the plan of the *piano nobile* and longitudinal section in the Archivio del Monte di Pietà (above, n. 93 [chap. 11]; Figs. 86, 88), this room is shown divided into three by transverse walls placed over the transverse arches of the entrance hall; but the inventory of 1648 does not suggest this

condition. The division may have been made later, when it was clear that the room would never serve as an anteroom. The balcony mentioned in the inventory is listed as part of Contini's work at the palace by Giovanni Baglione, *Le vite de' pittori* . . . , Rome, 1642, 181. It is shown in both plan and section in the drawings of 1734; but by the time of Vasi's engraving (Fig. 84) it had been removed to make way for the pedimented portal.

Pio Pecchiai, *I Barberini*, Rome, 1959, 164, remarked that Anna's devotion to her children led her to sleep near them in case of illness; this seems confirmed by the arrangement of the children's rooms next to hers at the "Casa Grande," if not at the Palazzo Barberini alle Quattro Fontane (below, p. 195).

118. Lodispoto, "Anna Colonna Barberini," 464; Pecchiai, *I Barberini*, 182; Ludwig von Pastor, *The History of the Popes from the Close of the Middle Ages*, English trans., London, 1891ff., xxx, 51–56.

119. Gigli, *Diario romano*, 272, 274–75.

120. Pecchiai, *I Barberini*, 182–87, including excerpts from Anna's eloquent and poignant letters to her eldest son Carlo; and Giuseppe Sacchi Lodispoto, "Anna Colonna Barberini ed il suo monumento nel monastero di Regina Coeli," *Strenna dei Romanisti* 43 (1982), 460–78, esp. 464–66, for the political context in which the letters were written.

121. Lodispoto, "Anna Colonna Barberini," 466; Gigli, *Diario romano*, 278, 300, for the dates of Anna's departure and return to Rome. Taddeo suffered from liver trouble, which was aggravated by the misfortunes that had befallen him. An autopsy revealed the deteriorated state of his organs; Pecchiai, *I Barberini*, 187, citing the report of the autopsy.

122. ABarb., Ind. IV, no. 58, dated 23 Apr. 1650.

123. Lodispoto, "Anna Colonna Barberini," 467–70, contrary to Pecchiai, *I Barberini*, 188–89.

124. Gigli, *Diario romano*, 419–22.

125. ABarb., Comp. 84 (Francesco's Registro de' Mandati), fols. 7 (30 Jan. 1653), 11 (10 Mar. 1653), 14v (29 Apr. 1653), and 24 (10 June 1653), payments "a buon conto" to Jacomo and Carlo Beccaria *muratori* for "la nova fabbrica che fanno nel Palazzo di S.E. [Francesco] alli Giupponari"; and fol. 19 (27 May 1653), payment "a buon conto" to the *falegname* Francesco Manfrini for "diversi lavori fatti, e da farsi da lui per servitio di S.E.," likely including work at the "Casa Grande." The accounts in the volume end on 13 September 1653.

126. ABarb., Comp. 364 (Maffeo's Libro Mastro AA), fol. 115, listing payments to Jacomo Beccaria *muratore* from 24 December 1653 through 31 December 1654, totaling 2,980 scudi, for "lavori fatti, e da fare al nostro Palazzo alli Giupponari."

127. ABarb., Comp. 378, fol. 6, 30 June 1655, "Delli denari che l'Emm^mo Sr Card. d'Este ci deve per le piggioni del Pa-

lazzo, e Case à Giubbonari, ne potrà pagare à M'ro Pietro Vitale Scarpellino scudi 133.80, quali sono per saldo di una misura di lavori di scarpello fatti dal primo Gennaro per tutto li 17. st^e per servitio di detto Palazzo, conforme alla detta misura fatta, e sottoscritta dà Francesco Contini nostro Architetto . . ."; and fols. 7–12v, thirteen additional payments to the *muratore* Beccaria and one to the *scarpellino* G. B. Borselli, from 17 September 1655 through 22 December 1657, similarly for work at the palace.

128. Apollonj, "Casa Grande," 455. In July 1653 Antonio had rented as his residence Palazzo Bonelli, at the south end of piazza SS. Apostoli (Gigli, *Diario romano*, 424), shown in Falda's engraving of the piazza (Fig. 211, no. 4).

129. ABarb., Comp. 229, fol. 73, 31 Dec. 1664, "Spese della nuova fabbrica per l'Appartamento Terreno e facciata del Cortile del Palazzo alli Giupponari . . . ," and subsequent entries on fols. 104, 122, 128, 146, 157, 182, 184, 185, 300, 373, 412, 413, recording payments totaling 2,500 scudi for work extending from 28 December 1662 through December 1666. Contini is named consistently as architect.

130. ABarb., Ind. II, no. 55, inventory of the Palazzo Barberini ai Giubbonari, begun 9 April 1671 (partially published by Marilyn Aronberg Lavin, *Seventeenth-Century Barberini Documents and Inventories of Art*, New York, 1975, IV.Inv.71), fols. 1–15, "Appartamento da basso," and fols. 414–474, the paintings in this apartment, both sections including baldacchinos in rooms C and F, a *zampanaro* over a daybed in room D, the chapel opening from room I, and fireplaces in rooms B, E, F, G, and L.

131. ABarb., Comp. 229, fol. 268, 5 July 1666, 15 scudi paid to "Giovanni Battista Laurentino Pittore d'ordine del Sr Carlo Maratti per haver dipinto al fresco un' Paese nel muro incontro la fenestra nuova fatta nella stanza à Capo le Scale del Palazzo di S.E. [Antonio]."

132. Above, p. 49, and below, pp. 248–49.

133. ABarb., Comp. 229, fol. 231, 17 June 1666, "scudi 18 m^ta donati d'ordine di S. Em^za allo stufarolo che stufò S.E. nella nuova stufa fatta nel Palazzo à Giupponari, e per haver faticato dieci giorni in custodir detta stufa." Above, p. 49.

134. ABarb., Ind. II, no. 55, fols. 17–85, for the main apartment, including, fols. 49–50, "Stanza n° 27 contigua al giardino . . . Prima stanzetta contigua al giardino . . ."; fols. 88–118 for the "Appartamento di Sopra del Inverno," including, fols. 101–103, "Primo camerino di S. Em^za," fols. 103–106, "Altro camerino dove dormiva S. Em^za," and, fols. 106–109, the three rooms of the library; fols. 476–519, the paintings in the main apartment; fols. 520–605, the paintings in the winter apartment.

135. The unhappy fortune of the palace after Antonio's death is recounted by Apollonj, "Casa Grande," 453–59, who, in contrast to d'Onofrio (*Roma vista da Roma*, 54 and 53 n. 7), recognized that the elliptical vestibule and accompanying stair, to the left of Contini's entrance hall, must

date from the mid-eighteenth century. The elliptical vestibule is not yet shown in Nolli's map of Rome in 1748 (Fig. 75). Porro, "Lo scalone," has at last identified the designer of the vestibule and stair as Nicola Giansimoni and dated the work 1759–62.

12. Palazzo Barberini alle Quattro Fontane

1. Vincenzo Golzio, *Il Palazzo Barberini e la sua galleria di pittura* (I palazzi e le case di Roma), Rome, [1925], 27–32, 36–38.

In the ever-increasing literature on this problematic building, a few key works may be singled out: Oskar Pollak, *Die Kunsttätigkeit unter Urban VIII,* I, Vienna, 1928, Reg. 851ff.; Anthony Blunt, "The Palazzo Barberini: The Contributions of Maderno, Bernini and Pietro da Cortona," *Journal of the Warburg and Courtauld Institutes* 21 (1958), 256–87; Heinrich Thelen, *Francesco Borromini: Die Handzeichnungen,* I, Graz, 1968, C15, C40–67, 17–21, 54–78; Howard Hibbard, *Carlo Maderno and Roman Architecture 1580–1630,* London, 1971, 80–84, 222–30, including a survey of the early bibliography of the palace; Patricia Waddy, "The Design and Designers of Palazzo Barberini," *Journal of the Society of Architectural Historians* 35 (1976), 151–85; Giuseppina Magnanimi, *Palazzo Barberini,* Rome, 1983.

2. E.g., Paolo Portoghesi (*Roma Barocca, The History of an Architectural Culture,* Engl. trans., [Cambridge, Mass., 1970], 60) writes of Bernini's "courageous effort to overcome the block-like Roman palace model" in the design of the central part of the palace, and (pp. 90–91) of Bernini as the executor "and author of the stairs and Grand Salon sequence that was inserted into the already-defined organism in terms of a different spatial program . . ."

3. For the purchase, see below, p. 227. For the history of the site, with references to earlier literature, see Waddy, "Design and Designers," 152–54; for the pre-Sforza *vigna,* Sabine Eiche, "Cardinal Giulio della Rovere and the Vigna Carpi," *Journal of the Society of Architectural Historians* 45 (1986), 115–33; and for the dating of the westernmost rooms of the Sforza palace, John Beldon Scott, *Images of Nepotism,* Princeton, [1990], in press.

4. Florence, Biblioteca Medicea-Laurenziana, ms. Buon. 90, fol. 67r; Patricia Waddy, "Michelangelo Buonarroti the Younger, *Sprezzatura,* and Palazzo Barberini," *Architectura* 5 (1975), 101–22.

5. ABarb., Ind. II, no. 2826(c).

6. Barb. lat. 4360, transcribed in Patricia Waddy, "Palazzo Barberini: Early Proposals," Ph.D. diss., New York Univ., 1973, 228–317, and Magnanimi, *Palazzo Barberini* (Rome, 1983), unpaginated appendix. This is a detailed proposal for the new Barberini palace to be built on the site at the Quattro Fontane, incorporating the Sforza palace. The plan once accompanying the proposal is now lost, but it is reconstructed in Waddy, "Palazzo Barberini," Figs. 23–

28, and idem, "Design and Designers," Figs. 10, 11. See Fig. 133. Magnanimi, *Palazzo Barberini,* 60–61, unconvincingly proposes that the text was composed by Cassiano dal Pozzo.

7. ABarb., Giust. 501–625, no. 595, fols. 218–219, 12 July 1626, an account of whitewashing, itemizing virtually all the rooms; no. 617, fols. 262–262v, 4 Oct. 1626, an account of painting, with information about several rooms. ABarb., Ind. II, no. 2888, the *misura* of masonry 1628–38, below, n. 14 (chap. 12).

8. ABarb., Ind. II, no. 2888, fols. 280r ("muro d'un pezzo di fondamento fatto nella stalla," for the wall between room A8 and passage A7,), 281r (in room A5, "muro dove si è riserrato il portone della remessa . . ."), 289r (room A9, "Cucina comune nel palazzo accanto l'entrone che s'è dismessa"), 294r (in room A2, "muro della porta della rimessa rimurata . . ."), and 294v (in the north façade, ". . . la porta della Stalla Vecchia . . .").

9. Ibid., fols. 246v–247r, in room B28, "Camera dov'è Ercole con la virtù e vitio . . . muro di due stracci remurati nella facciata verso la Piazza [north] dov'erano gl'archi della loggia lo. l'uno p. 19 alt. p. 19 g° il muro p. 4¾ tevᵃ se ne defalca la fenestra nova alt. p. 12 lar. p. 6; . . . muro d'un'altr'arco remurato che in mezzo vi è la fenestra l. p. 13 alt. p. 19 g° p. 4¾ tevᵃ se ne defalca per il vano della fenestra alt. p. 12 l. p. 6 . . ."; and the installation of travertine frames of three windows each 12 × 6 *palmi.* Since the room is only 25 *palmi* wide, the three arches (and later the three windows) must extend into the north wall of room B29; indeed, B28 and B29 were formed by the insertion of a new wall between them (below, pp. 203, 226). At some time before 1626 the arches must have been glazed, for the account of whitewashing includes work in this room as "alla salla granda acanto alle dette stancie [i.e., next to the rooms in the west end of the *pian terreno*]" (ABarb., Giust. 595, 12 July 1626).

10. Eiche, "Cardinal Giulio," 120–22 and 129 [Doc. I], for the Pio loggia.

11. Scott, *Images of Nepotism,* forthcoming.

12. Ibid.

13. Waddy, "Design and Designers," 162.

14. For work sponsored by Taddeo Barberini, ABarb., Ind. II, no. 2888, "A di 3 di Aprile 1629 per tutto Dicembre 1638, Misura e stima di lavori d'opera di Muratore fatti per servitio dell'Illᵐᵒ et Eccᵐᵒ Sigᵉ Principe D. Taddeo Barberino Prefetto di Roma al Palazzo delle Quattro Fontane e suo ristretto da Mʳⁱ Nicolo Scala, Tomasso Damino, e Compagni misurati e stimati da noi infrascritti . . . ," partially published by Pollak, *Kunsttätigkeit,* Reg. 886; cf. a similar volume, ASR, CRM, Teatini, busta 2162, fasc. 161, int. 194; and another volume, ASR, CRM, Teatini, busta 2200, int. 1, partially published by Giuseppina Magnanimi, "Palazzo Barberini: I documenti della costruzione," *Antologia di Belle Arti* 4, no. 15–16 (1980), 194–214, esp. 195–209. In addition, for work sponsored by Francesco Barbe-

rini, see ASR, CRM, Teatini, busta 2200, int. 2, "A di 3 Dicembre 1634, Misura e stima delli lavori d'opra di muratore fatti per servitio dell'Em^{mo} e R^{mo} Sig^{re} Card^{le} Barberino nel nuovo Appartamento del Palazzo alle 4 Fontane da m^{ri} Nicolò Scala e Tomasso Damino Compagni misurati e stimati da noi sottoscritti . . . ," partially published by Magnanimi, "Documenti," 209–14.

15.   ABarb., Ind. II, no. 2888, fol. 238v, "salotto"; Comp. 268, fol. 129, "sala de palafrenieri."

16.   The first, B20, is specifically called "anticamera" in ABarb., Ind. II, no. 2888, fol. 239r; and the second, B29, is named "la stanza dell'anticamera" in ABarb., Comp. 268, fol. 126, and "anticamera" in Ind. II, no. 2439, fol. 19.

17.   ABarb., Ind. II, no. 2888, fols. 241r–243r, "Camera overo Salotto dov'è dipinto la balaustrata con scimotti Ucelli et in mezzo l'Armi del Papa." The arms have since been changed. Cf. Nicodemus Tessin, *Studieresor i Danmark, Tyskland, Holland, Frankrike och Italien,* ed. Osvald Sirén, Stockholm, 1914, 166.

18.   ABarb., Ind. II, no. 2888, fols. 246–247, "Camera dov'è Ercole con la virtù e vitio è stata buttata à basso la pittura, Seconda Camera dipinta del Maltese il quadro nella volta . . ." For the identification of "il Maltese" as Giovanni Domenico Marziani, see Marilyn Aronberg Lavin, *Seventeenth-Century Barberini Documents and Inventories of Art,* New York, 1975, 496, and Scott, *Images of Nepotism,* forthcoming.

19.   ABarb., Ind. II, no. 2888, fols. 241r–243r, 248v–250r; the Contelli plan (Fig. 150) shows a window from B29 and door from B20, but the document of construction specifies a door from B29.

20.   ABarb., Ind. II, no. 2888, fol. 245r, "Camera d'Apollo dove sono le muse dipinte del Camasei"; Ann Sutherland Harris, "A Contribution to Andrea Camassei Studies," *Art Bulletin* 52 (1970), 49–70.

21.   Scott, *Images of Nepotism.*

22.   ASR, Not. A.C., 6601, fols. 898v–904v; above, p. 170.

23.   ABarb., Comp. 268, fols. 120–121, "Nella stanza . . . dove dorme S. Em^{za}"; below, p. 245.

24.   ABarb., Ind. II, no. 2888, fol. 257r, "Lumaca nel Cantone à detto Piano Terreno quale cala nella Porticella Secreta verso Monte Cavallo."

25.   Ibid., fols. 239r, 241r, 246r–v, 245v, for fireplaces in rooms B19, B29, B28, and B27; and Comp. 268, fol. 123, for fireplace equipment in rooms B25 and B23.

26.   Below, p. 245, for Antonio's use of the rooms. Giovanni Pietro Rossini, *Il Mercurio errante delle grandezze di Roma, tanto antiche che moderne,* 3d ed., Rome, 1715, 59, describes "l'App. dell'Estate del Sig. Principe"; and Tessin, *Studieresor,* 166, descends to "den Sommerzimbern," especially recognized by the fountain in room B29.

27.   Francesco Sestini da Bibbiena, *Il maestro di camera,* Florence, 1621, 201–2.

28.   Below, p. 194.

29.   ABarb., Ind. II, no. 2888, fol. 224r, "ricetto."

30.   Ibid.; room C19 is called "Prima anticamera accanto al Salone Grande dell'App.^{to} dell'Ecc.^{ma} Sig.^{ra} Principessa D. Anna" (fol. 213v), and her "2da Anticamera" (fol. 214v), C20, followed.

31.   The door from anteroom C20 to C29 has since been filled in, but its original construction is documented in ABarb., Ind. II, no. 2888, fol. 201 ("Per haver fatto la porta dov'era una di dette fenestre [old Sforza windows, removed] fatto le spallette e arco alt. di vano p. 13 lar. p. 6 con la mettitura in opera di conci di trevertino"), and it is shown on the Contelli plan, Fig. 151.

George Lechner, "Tommaso Campanella and Andrea Sacchi's Fresco of *Divina Sapienza* in the Palazzo Barberini," *Art Bulletin* 58 (1976), 97–108, has studied the iconography of this fresco and has suggested that Urban VIII used the room for exercises of spiritual magic conducted by Tommaso Campanella. Ann Sutherland Harris, *Andrea Sacchi,* Oxford, 1977, 8–13, considers a relationship between the fresco and the adjacent chapel but supposes that "the room must always have been used for private or semiprivate purposes" (p. 13). Neither scholar was able to recognize the room's position in a coherent suite of reception rooms, before the chapel, and, most important, in Anna's apartment. See now Scott, *Images of Nepotism.*

32.   ABarb., Ind. II, no. 2888, fol. 205r–206v.

33.   Ibid., fol. 201r for the door from the room of the "Divina Sapienza" to the chapel, 12 × 6 *palmi;* and fol. 214v for the door from anteroom C20 to the chapel, 10 × 5 *palmi.*

34.   ABarb., Comp. 268, fols. 114, 118, and Ind. II, no. 2439, fol. 7, "la stanza dell'audienza"; it contained a portrait of Urban VIII.

35.   ABarb., Comp. 268, fol. 118; it contained a bed.

36.   ABarb., Ind. II, no. 2888, fols. 214r, 215r, 202, for fireplaces in rooms C19, C20, and C28; Comp. 268 (inventory of 1644), fols. 104, 105, 114, 113, for fireplace accessories in the four rooms.

37.   ABarb., Comp. 267 (partially published by Lavin, *Documents,* Inv.IV.Dec.Arts.36–40), fols. 202v–203v, describes "Un paramento di Ormesino Celeste tutto dipinto di diversi fiori frutti ucelli fontane et altro fatto fare da S. Em^{za} per sette stanze dell'appartamento vecchio . . ."; the numbers of overdoors and overwindows listed for the sequence of seven rooms can be matched with rooms C29, C28, C27, C25, C23, C24, C26. For Antonio's neglect of these rooms in the winter, see below, p. 245. Rossini, *Il Mercurio errante* (1715), 57, and Tessin, *Studieresor,* 165, do not acknowledge any seasonal use for this apartment.

38.   ABarb., Ind. II, no. 2439, fol. 10; it had a portrait of Urban VIII.

39.   Ibid., fol. 11, the first room of the "appartamento della Conversatione," coming from the anteroom C20.

40.   ABarb., Ind. II., no. 2888, fol. 193v, "Salotto che seg^{ta} [C36] dov'è la porta che responde nel giardino secreto," in-

cluding two newly made windows toward the garden. ABarb., Comp. 268 (inventory of 1644), fol. 106, lists C36 as "la stanza che responde nel giardinetto de melangoli." The garden was the truncated "Giardino secreto" of the old Sforza palace (Fig. 95). Many orange trees were removed in 1676–77, when the garden was further truncated (below, p. 256).

41.   ABarb., Ind. II, no. 2888, fols. 191r–196v, for the "salotto," door, windows, "saletta," "gallarietta," revision of C33 and C34, and stairs; and ABarb., Comp. 268, fol. 110, for the chapel.

42.   ABarb., Ind. II, no. 2888, fols. 191–192, records the construction of the new partition and the special arrangement of vaults. The original arrangement of the two rooms is shown on the survey plan of 1625, ABarb., Ind. II, no. 2826 (c) (Fig. 95), and the erasure of the earlier partition and placement of the newly constructed one are shown on the Contelli plan. ABarb., Ind. II, no. 2826 (d-3) (Fig. 151). See below, pp. 234, 240).

43.   ABarb., Ind. II, no. 2888, fol. 194v, for the newly constructed wall, "Muro della facciata dinanzi verso la Piazza . . . ," 63 × 32¼ palmi at this level.

44.   Below, pp. 194–95, for the children's rooms.

45.   Barb. lat. 4360, fol. 54.

46.   ABarb., Ind. II, no. 2888, fols. 193, 194, for the hooks.

47.   ASR, CRM, Teatini, busta 2200, int. 2, second part (an undated misura e stima for various works in and around the palace), fol. 35v, just after an account of work in the "Gallarietta accanto la Capella Vecchia" (below, n. 51 [chap. 12]), "Per la fattura del Ponte nel Salotto dove dovea dipingere il Camasei."

48.   Barb. lat. 5635, inventory dated 3 Dec. 1631, fol. 24, "Un paramento di corame dorato depinto dall'Orbinese alto palmi 17½ cioè pezzi 4 grandi con diverse prospettive di giardini e palazzi e figure larghi palmi 14½ l'uno in circa, et altri pezzi quattro con prospettiva dell'istessa altezza larghi palmi 7 incirca e sei sopraporti e fenestre dell'istesso con diversi armi dell'Eccma Casa Barberina con angelini il tutto fatto per parare la saletta che ha l'intrata nel giardino già fatte et havute in più volte dall'Orbinese." This entry is not included in the portions of the inventory published by J.A.F. Orbaan, Documenti sul Barocco in Roma, Rome, 1920, 495–513, or by Lavin, Documents, III.Barb. lat. 5635.

49.   Barb. lat. 5635, fol. 20v, "Un pezzo di corame longo palmi diciasette alto palmi diciasette con prospettiva d'un giardino dorato in cima ci è Castel Gandolfo; un'altro pezzo simile longo palmi 22 con diversi giardini, et con laghetto; un'altro pezzo simile longo palmi 13 con giardino e palazzo e con laberinto; un'altro pezzo simile longo palmi 13 con un castello all'usanza di fiandra con fiume agiocecato con giochi, mascherate; tre sopraporti dell'istesso corame con giardini e palazzi, et dua soprafinestre simili il tutto fatto fare dal Urbinese in diverse volte per parar la stanza dove sono avanti la Capella." This entry is not included in the portions of the inventory published by Orbaan, Documenti, 495–513, or Lavin, Documents, III.Barb.lat.5635.

50.   ABarb., Giust. 501–625, no. 617 (fol. 262), 4 Oct. 1626, "Sala piccola [C38], Per quattro Arme rifatte nelle Cantonate, cioè due da Cardle et due Ducali, e ranettato 4 paesi con 3 parapetti di finestre [in the north wall, removed in the rebuilding after 1628] et ranettato una porta grande [to the garden] et un sopraporta, scudi 12." ABarb., Ind. II, no. 2888, fol. 194, "Stanza dov'è dipinto la Natività di Nostro Signore," and fol. 194v, ". . . et fatto il ponte per il Pittore e disfatto." ABarb., Giust. 1726–1792, fol. 115r, "Stanza dov'era cascato la colla del quadro della volta dove sta dipinta la Natività di N.S. del Maltese [Marziani], Per haver fatto il ponte per li pittori . . . [30 Oct. 1631?]"; John Beldon Scott provided this document and suggested a date of April 1631 for Marziani's short-lived work.

51.   ASR, CRM, Teatini, busta 2200, int. 2, second part, fol. 35v, "Gallarietta accanto la Capella Vecchia, Colla fatta per pittori per dipingere la volte e li muri lo. p. 42½ lar. p. 11½ [the dimensions of the vault as originally constructed] e più colla simile lo. p. 98 alt. p. 15 [for the walls]; Per haver fatto li ponti in detta Gallarietta in due ordini uno sopra l'altro [e.g., for the vault and for the walls]; Colla in detta Camera ordinaria intorno alto dal piano del mattonato [e.g., for the undecorated walls below the 15-palmi band; the height of this band of ordinary plaster is omitted from the entry]." The later removal of the stair S12 (below, p. 257) required an addition to the west end of the originally symmetrical design of the vault painting and the repainting of the western lunette—noticeably different in style from its eastern counterpart. A crack in the plaster marks the extension of the vault fresco. It must be the removal of the stair to which Anthony Blunt (Guide to Baroque Rome, New York, 1982, 165) refers when he writes that the "corridor" was formed from two rooms.

E. K. Waterhouse (Baroque Painting in Rome, London, 1937, 59), followed by Blunt ("Palazzo Barberini," 286), attributes the paintings to Pietro da Cortona. Giuliano Briganti (Pietro da Cortona o della pittura barocca, Florence, 1962, 204) sees that Cortona was in charge of the decoration but attributes the two wall paintings to Giovanni Francesco Romanelli; he proposes a date of 1636. Walter Vitzthum (review of Briganti, Pietro da Cortona, in Burlington Magazine 105 [1963], 213–17, esp. 215) distinguishes between the two wall paintings, giving the "Founding of Palestrina" to Romanelli and the "Sacrifice to Juno" (an inferior painting) to Gimignani, and suggests an earlier date, ca. 1632. Magnanimi (Palazzo Barberini, 100–101) accepts Waterhouse's and Blunt's attribution to Pietro da Cortona. The painting of the gallarietta can be dated 1631, according to the analysis of documents of payments by Scott, Images of Nepotism, forthcoming.

52. Below, pp. 245, 256–58.

53. ABarb., Ind. IV, no. 1254 (Appendix 3), fol. 7r–v.

54. Above, pp. 26–27.

55. Above, p. 27.

56. ABarb., Ind. II, no. 2888, fol. 165v.

57. Ibid., fols. 139v, 187r–188r.

58. Ibid., fol. 155v.

59. Ibid., fols. 289v–294v, for the laundry.

60. Ibid., fols. 184r–185r, for Costanza's rooms; and fols. 185v–186v, for the kitchen and *tinello.*

61. Ibid., fols. 174r–v.

62. Below, p. 196.

63. Above, p. 27.

64. ABarb., Ind. II, no. 2888, fols. 176r–182r.

65. ASR, CRM 2162, fasc. 161, int. 194, fol. 119, "Anticamera dell partamento dell Ecc^ma Donna Costanza nel palazzo vechio"; the rooms D25–D26 described above do not have an "anticamera" and are outside the "palazzo vecchio."

66. Below, p. 246; ABarb., Comp. 268, fols. 130–133.

67. ABarb., Ind. II, no. 2888, fol. 113r, "Per haver fatto un'Impianellato s^a un solaro rustico fatto di novo s^a al soffitto nell'App.^to della S.^ra D. Costanza che vi dovevano dormire i signorini."

68. Pio Pecchiai, *I Barberini,* Rome, 1959, 164; but cf. the more convenient arrangement in the "Casa Grande" ai Giubbonari in the 1640s, above, p. 169.

69. ABarb., Ind. II, no. 2888, fol. 147r, "la Guardarobba Vecchia"; fol. 182, "Camera che segue [D45] accanto la Guardarobba vecchia," and similar references; fol. 165r, "Torretta fatta sopra tetti per dar lume alla Cappella à detto Piano"; fols. 166r–v, "Camera tra la scaletta segreta e torretta della Cappella dove sono i luoghi comuni" (only 15 × 4½ *palmi,* but with two seats in niches), and the "camerino" above.

70. Ibid., fol. 138r, " . . . tetto . . . sopra la stanza dove tiene li Polli l'Ecc^ma S^ra D. Costanza [43¾ × 20 *palmi*] disfatto e rifatto." According to Richard A. Goldthwaite, chickens were similarly kept on the uppermost floor of Palazzo Strozzi in Florence.

71. Ibid., fols. 190r–191r.

72. Ibid., fols. 158v–161, "Guardarobba grande del Sig^r Principe e sotto tetto," "Secreta sotto la guardarobba nel fianco della volta" F5 and the straight stair S13; fols. 167v–170 for the "Loggia scoperta accanto la Guardarobba" G2 with its parapet, and the "loggia coperta dove sono li fenestroni" F6; and fols. 170–171 for the "lumaca che và in guardarobba" S14. Although a loggia of only one story is clearly described in the document of construction, a second story is shown by 1642, in the view of the east façade published by Teti (Fig. 121). Urbano Barberini, "Gli arazzi e i cartoni della serie 'Vita di Urbano VIII' della arazzaria Barberini," *Bollettino d'Arte* 53, ser. 5 (1968), 92–100, Fig. 85, reports that the monumental walnut cabinets in the *guardaroba,* in which tapestries were stored (see Fig. 115),

were destroyed ca. 1930, in the course of remodeling the room, because their large size made it impossible to move them.

73. ABarb., Ind. II, no. 2888, fol. 139v, "Tetto nuovo sopra la Guardarobba della Sig^ra Principessa," 41 × 51¾ *palmi;* fols. 172–172v, "Guardarobba dell'Ecc^ma S^ra Principessa D. Anna," 43 × 27 *palmi,* with a single window.

74. Ibid., fols. 275v–280r, for the "Cucina nova secreta al piano terreno della piazza da basso," the "Stanza che segue dopo la cucina dove si farà la pasticciaria," and the "2^a stanza che segue dove soni li sciacquatori e si lava li piatti della cocina comune"; and fols. 285v–287v for further work.

75. Ibid., fols. 281r–284r.

76. Ibid., fols. 290v–294v.

77. Ibid., fols. 252v–254v, reservoirs and "la stanza della legna."

78. AVR, S. Susanna, Stati d'Anime, 1631–1651, 1633, fol. 2v; 1634, fol. 1v.

79. ABarb., Ind. II, no. 2884 (above, n. 95 [chap. 4]), shows the extent of Barberini property by 1632. For the acquisition of the many small properties, see Waddy, "Design and Designers," 154 and n. 12.

80. Their general character can be deduced from descriptions of renovations, as recorded in ABarb., Ind. II, no. 2888, fols. 21r–42v.

81. Ibid., fols. 35v–42v, including the "rimessa fatta di novo accanto la casa del Biscontino" (fol. 40v) and the "Rimessa grande accanto il portone della piazza da basso" (fol. 41v).

82. Ibid., fols. 21v–22r, "Cortile grande delle stalle dov'è la fontana."

83. Ibid., fols. 36r (*scalco* over second *rimessa*), 36v (Giulio Mileti over third and fourth *rimessa*), 43r–45r (house for coachmen), 45v (house for horsemen), and others.

84. E.g., ABarb., Comp. 193, final payments for rental houses, 27 July 1634.

85. ABarb., Ind. II, no. 2911.

86. Ibid., no. 2888, fols. 68r–105v, for the remodelings.

87. Ibid., fol. 287v–289v, for the "Cucina comune che segue dismessa" and "Cucina comune nel palazzo accanto l'entrone che s'è dismessa [A13]"; fols. 105v–109v for the "Cucina comune nuova" and its fittings; and fol. 113r for the water supply of the *cucina comune.* A plan of the site ca. 1640, in the Archivio di Stato (published without precise citation by A. M. Colini, *L'Isola della Purificazione a Piazza Barberini,* Rome, 1977, 68, Fig. 25), shows a "cucina" to the south of the large palazzetto on strada Felice, near the Quattro Fontane; the Greuter map of 1634 (Fig. 118) shows this to be a one-story building.

88. Below, pp. 242–43.

89. Margaret Murata, *Operas for the Papal Court 1631–1698,* Ann Arbor, 1981, 20–21, and below, pp. 246–47.

90. Below, p. 243.

91. For Palazzo Farnese, Christoph Luitpold Frommel,

"La construction et la décoration du Palais Farnèse, Sangallo et Michel-Ange (1513–1550)," in *Le Palais Farnèse,
Ecole française de Rome,* I, Rome, 1981, 127–224, esp. 132–
34, 145. For Palazzo Borghese, above, pp. 74–75.

92. Arch. Barb., Ind. IV, no. 1254, fols. 5r–v (Appendix 3).

93. So much so that the document of construction speaks
of the "camerone overo antecamera," ABarb., Ind. II, no.
2888, fol. 218v.

94. ABarb., Comp. 268, fols. 97–98; its complete set of
fireplace furnishings suggests that he was actually spending
time here and not just passing through. ABarb., Ind. II,
no. 2439, fol. 2, there was a portrait of Urban VIII in this
room.

95. In 1687–88 Tessin (*Studieresor,* 168) named room C6
"der andere Sale d'audience," following C5, "die Sala
d'Audienzo dei Cavalieri e Prelati."

96. Below, p. 245.

97. ABarb., Comp. 268, fols. 96–99, lists fireplace equipment in these rooms. ASR, CRM, Teatini, busta 2200, int.
2, fol. 14v, "Per la mettitura in opera di n° 3 camini di
marmoro mischio scorniciati nelle camere del braccio verso
Strada Felice e verso le 4 Fontane [*piano nobile*]." Panciroli,
Roma sacra e moderna, Rome, 1725, 200, describes room
C5, "la prima Camera . . . ornata di tapezzaria di Fiandra
(poichè questo era l'appartamento d'Inverno di S.E. [Car-
dinal Carlo Barberini])"; Rossini, *Il Mercurio errante,* 56,
writes of "l'Appartamento d'Inverno di Sua Eminenza."

98. ABarb., Comp. 267 (1636), fols. 125v–126v (below, n.
101 [chap. 12]); Comp. 268 (1644), fols. 102–104.

99. Rossini, *Il Mercurio errante,* 56, "l'Appartamento di
sopra verso Oriente, dove Sua Eminenza da udienza
l'Estate"; Tessin, *Studieresor,* 168, "ein Sommer Appartement mit rot damasch undt goldt gallunen meubliret";
Panciroli, *Roma sacra e moderna,* 210, the "appartamento
di mezzo tempo, posto verso li Giardini."

100. Below, p. 245.

101. ABarb., Comp. 267 (1636; partially published by
Lavin, *Documents,* VI.Dec.Arts.36–40), fols. 125v–126v,
"Paramenti di Damaschi cremesini . . . per le cinque
stanze verso il giardino nell'appartamento nuovo . . .
Nella prima stanza vicino alla Stanza ovata . . . Nella
quarta Stanza dove stà il baldacchino . . . Nella quinta et
ultima Stanza dove Sta il Letto . . ." and then nine *portiere,* including five for the five rooms and four for the
"stanza ovata." ABarb., Comp. 268 (1644), fol. 103, also
identifies C12 as the "stanza contigua in cima, dove è il
letto di damasco . . ." ABarb., Comp. 348 (1692–1704),
fol. 229v, "seconda stanza dove dorme S. Em ͣ [C13]"; the
sequence is made clear by further descriptions of the palace
in fols. 258v–261, 316–318, and 326–328. Cf. another version of the inventory published by Lavin, *Documents,*
VI.Inv.92–04, fol. 204v.

102. ABarb., Ind. II, no. 2888, fol. 217, "Salotto dove si
faceva le Comedie"; its walls rose 64 *palmi* to the level of

the library floor, and two windows were in the eastern wall.
A third opening was filled in when room D14 of the apartment to the east was built (ASR, CRM, Teatini, busta
2200, int. 2, fol. 25v, "Muro d'un arcone rimurato che dava
lume al Salotto dove si fanno le Comedie lon. p. 13¼ alt. p.
20 g° p. 5½").

103. ABarb., Ind. II, no. 2888, fols. 218v–219r, documents
the construction of the two vaulted rooms, "Camerone
overo Anticamera verso il Giardino e 4 Fontane [C3]", its
vault 70 × 46¾ *palmi;* and "Camerone sopra detto sotto la
libraria [D1]", its vault 70½ × 47 *palmi.* ASR, CRM, Teatini, busta 2200, int. 2, fol. 15v, calls the upper room "Salone dove si faceva la guardarobba di S. Em ͣ e si veste per
le Comedie," with pavement 70¼ × 47 *palmi* and three
doors.

104. ASR, CRM, Teatini, busta 2200, int. 2, fols. 21v–23,
records the routine construction of their walls, and fols. 3v–
4 notes their roofs.

105. Ibid., fols. 11v–13, "Piano sopra il piano nobile,"
rooms D2–D10.

106. Ibid., fols. 9v–11v, "Piano delli mezzanini," rooms
E4–E10.

107. Below, p. 266.

108. The similarity between the library and a *guardaroba*
was acknowledged in the slight confusion in recording a
payment for woodwork by Soria "nella nostra guardarobba
anzi libreria," below, n. 111 (chap. 12).

109. The library's original size is documented in ABarb.,
Ind. II, no. 2888, fols. 219v–220r (its walls, and its vault,
101½ × 48½ *palmi,* "fatta à schifo à lunette") and ASR,
CRM, Teatini, busta 2200, int. 2, fol. 5 (plaster for the four
walls, 295½ × 23 *palmi,* and its pavement, 100 × 47¾
palmi). Two sloping fin walls extended under the sloped
roof, above the walls of room D1, from the library to the
main south wall of the palace (Arch. Barb., Ind. II, no.
2888, fol. 219r; for the roof over these walls, ASR, CRM,
Teatini, busta 2200, int. 2, fol. 3). For the reinforcement of
the vaults of rooms D1 and C3, see below, p. 225.

110. ABarb., Ind. II, no. 2888, fol. 219v, for the location
of the windows. Alberti, *De re aedificatoria,* V.xviii (trans.
Leone), "Those [rooms] which require the clearest Light,
such as the common Parlour, the Portico, and especially
the Library, should be situated full East."

111. Francesco's payments to Giovanni Battista Soria *falegname* begin on 6 May 1633 (300 scudi ". . . à buon conto
di lavori di legname che fà nella nostra guardarobba anzi
libreria del nostro Palazzo alle 4 Fontane . . ."), continue
on 14 June 1633 (300 scudi "à buon conto di lavori fatti e
da fare d'opera di falegname alla nostra libreria al Palazzo
delle 4 Fontane . . ."), and conclude on 4 April 1635,
with a payment of 920.30 scudi "per resto e saldo di scudi
5348.36 simile, che importano tre suoi conti di diversi lavori di legnami fatti cioè scudi 3623.48 alla libraria del Palazzo alle 4 Fontane scudi 1053.75 per lavori fatti alli appar-

tamenti nuovi di detto Palazzo, e scudi 671.13 per lavori fatti in diversi luoghi dentro, e fuori di Roma . . ." (ABarb., Comp. 80). Another small cluster of payments to Soria concludes on 14 March 1640 with a final payment of 542.12 scudi on a total bill of 1442.12 scudi "che importa una sua misura, e stima di lavori diversi fatti per servitio della nostra libreria al Palazzo delle 4 Fontane . . ." (ABarb., Comp. 81, no. 6937); this work probably was necessitated by the enlargement of the library.

A description of the library by Carlo Cartari, dated 31 January 1665, is published by Joseph Connors, *Borromini and the Roman Oratory,* New York and Cambridge, Mass., 1980, 155–56; Cartari gives special attention to the design of the shelving.

112.   ABarb., Ind. II, no. 2888, fols. 220r–v; ASR, CRM, Teatini, busta 2200, int. 2, fols. 6–6v.

113.   Below, pp. 252, 254–55, 265–66.

114.   ABarb., Ind. II, no. 2888, fol. 266r for the *credenza,* the "Camerone al Piano Terreno dalla parte verso le 4 Fontane dove si faceva la Bottegha del Falegname," and the "andito che và alle grotte"; and fol. 117r for the sink in the *credenza* and its drain.

115.   Below, p. 250.

116.   ABarb., Ind. II, no. 2888. The two large rooms may have been needed to stabilize the tall walls of the *salone* and Taddeo's *guardaroba* above. They were useless as anterooms until the construction of the rest of the apartments to which they belonged. The use of the larger for theatrical performances, beginning in Carnival 1632 (below, pp. 246–47), was therefore an economy of sorts.

117.   ABarb., Comp. 192, large payments until summer 1632.

118.   ABarb., Comp. 80, payments beginning 12 October 1632 (or possibly 30 September 1632).

119.   ASR, CRM, Teatini, busta 2200, int. 2 (above, n. 14).

120.   ABarb., Ind. II, no. 2889, questions 12–13, fols. 9v–10v: ". . . che nel medesimo tempo che si fabricava [when Taddeo was building] ò prima ò doppo che io non mi ricordo sono stati fatti nel medemo Palazzo alle quattro fontane si facevano nel medesimo Palazzo altra fabrica ad instanza del Sig.r Card.l Barberino . . . ; è ben vero che in detto Palazzo vi sono stati fatti altri lavori [in addition to work for Taddeo] dalli detti sig.ri Nicolò Scala et Gio. Battista Caccia per servitio però del Em.mo Sig.r Card.le Antonio Barberino et nell'istesso tempo che si fabricava ad instanze del Sig.r Principe ò poco prima ò poco doppò si faceva nel medesimo Palazzo la fabrica per l'Em.mo Sig.r Card.le Barberino dalli detti Damino et Scala . . ."

121.   Ibid., no. 2888, fols. 142v–143r, for "muri rialzati sotto al tetto sopra li muri vecchi della facciata attorno al Palazzo Vecchio," in amounts from 8¼ to 9½ *palmi;* fols. 143r–144r, for "le rialzature sopra li tramezzi maestri sotto tetto," of 6 *palmi* or more: fols. 145v–146r, for "rialzature di muri sopra la gallarietta sotto tetto," about 7 *palmi.*

122.   Above, n. 9 (chap. 12).

123.   ABarb., Ind. II, no. 2888, fols. 143v, 178v, 200, 280v.

124.   Ibid., fol. 191r, "Le due stanze fatte du una, due che confinano con la Gallarietta; muro del tramezzo che divide dette camere . . ."

125.   Gustavo Giovannoni, "Il Palazzo Barberini e la sua piazza," *Palladio* 5 (1941), 227–28, noted the expressive contrast between palace and surrounding houses ("come un signore in mezzo alla sua famiglia") without assigning it any significance.

126.   ABarb., Ind. II, no. 2888, fols. 66r–67r; attributed by Blunt, "Palazzo Barberini," 281, to Pietro da Cortona.

127.   ABarb., Ind. II, no. 2888, fols. 63r–64r, 66r, 275v, and elsewhere.

128.   Ibid., fols. 280r–281v.

129.   Pompilio Totti, *Ritratto di Roma moderna,* Rome, 1638, 272–73, "Nell'entrare hà doppio Portico con la Fontana, e doppia Scala, che da lati conduce alle sale, et a gli appartamenti. La facciata di così raro Palazzo è quasi in forma di Theatro."

130.   ABarb., Ind. II, no. 2888, fol. 222r.

131.   Ibid., fol. 114r, for the "Muro in Strada Felice che serra il sito ch'era pubblico del cantone del Casino ch'era d'Ang.o Matriciano sino al cantone della casa di Mad.a Cinthia Faiola misurato in due partite lon. insieme p. 191½ alt. dalla resega sino in cima al capello regguagliato p. 15½ g.o p. 2"; and for the "Portone in faccia à Strada Rosella," 24½ *palmi* high, with an arched opening and framing piers totaling 34 *palmi* in width.

132.   Ibid., fol. 112r, for the "Muro tra li due cortili all'entrare avanti al Palazzo dalla parte di sopra; per il muro fatto di terra tra un cortile e l'altro lo. p. 219 alt. regguagliato p. 12 g.o p. 2½ di pra' fatto di terra e arricciato di calce da due bande"; and its arched opening framed by piers 25 *palmi* high, the entire portal 34 *palmi* wide.

133.   *Raccolte di varie vedute di Roma si antica che moderna intagliate la maggior parte dal celebre Gianbattista Piranesi e da altri incisori . . . ,* Rome, 1752, c. 86v; Luigi Rossini, *I monumenti più interessanti di Roma dal decimo secolo sino al secolo decimottavo veduti in prospettiva . . . ,* Rome, 1818, f. 30.

134.   The obelisk was brought to the site in 1632, apparently with the intention of erecting it in the gardens; but its broken form lay in the courtyard before the palace for decades and can be seen in the views of both Totti (1638; Fig. 126) and Piranesi (1748; Fig. 127). Specchi's views of the palace in 1699 (Figs. 99, 163, 173) show the obelisk in the south garden, in anticipation of a placement that was never effected (below, pp. 261–62). Eventually it was taken to the Vatican and then, in 1822, erected in the center of the passeggiata del Pincio. (Cesare d'Onofrio, *Gli obelischi di Roma,* Rome, 1965; 2d ed. Rome, 1967, 230–31, 296–97.)

135.   Blunt, *Guide,* 164, asserts, "Originally the main approach was through the door next to the Quattro Fontane, which brought the visitor to the entrance on the *piano no-*

bile in the middle of the garden façade," then to the oval hall C17 and the *salone*. This supposition ignores the importance of stairs and the ringing of bells in the ritual of paying visits, as well as the documentation and other early sources cited above. His idea that the western façade "had been designed to open on a small garden" and became the main approach to the palace only in 1865–67, with the construction of the present gateway on via delle Quattro Fontane, is likewise untenable.

136.   The area is approximately 28,350 square *palmi;* in Barb. lat. 4360, fol. 46, the "piazza" to the south of the proposed palace (Fig. 133c) was to have measured 14 × 28 *canne* (= 39,200 square *palmi*) and "would accommodate more than one hundred carriages without blocking the central drive."

137.   The similarity of the form of the loggia to that of the Palazzo Farnese courtyard has been noted by, e.g., Nina Caflisch, *Carlo Maderno,* Munich, 1934, 103; Golzio, *Palazzo Barberini,* 31; and Armando Schiavo, "Palazzo Barberini e Palazzo Moroni," *L'Urbe* n.s. 38, 3–4 (May–August 1975), 1–16, esp. 5.

138.   ABarb., Ind. II, no. 2888, fols. 241r ("cortile di sopra"), 304 ("cortile grande").

139.   Ibid., fol. 258v.

140.   Totti, *Ritratto,* 272, ". . . ha doppio portico . . ."; Hieronymus Tetius [Girolamo Teti], *Aedes Barberinae ad Quirinalem,* Rome, 1642, 13, ". . . in Aream, et Porticum amplissimam."

141.   ABarb., Ind. II, no. 2888, fols. 263r–265r.

142.   Klaus Schwäger, "Kardinal Pietro Aldobrandinis Villa di Belvedere in Frascati," *Römisches Jahrbuch für Kunstgeschichte* 9–10 (1961–1962), 289–382, esp. 379–82, for some meanings of "teatro" in sixteenth- and seventeenth-century architecture.

143.   ABarb., Ind. II, no. 2888, fol. 264v, ". . . muro del tramezzo sotto quello del Salone che divide tra il Portico overo teatro e scala che và all'Appartamento dove stava il Sr Principe . . ."

144.   See plan studies of Palazzo Pamphili published by Paolo Portoghesi, *The Rome of Borromini: Architecture as Language,* trans. Barbara Luigia La Penta, New York, 1968, pls. XCVIII, C, CI.

145.   The extraordinary entrance hall, or portico, is not an "atrium" in any of the seventeenth-century senses of that Vitruvian term (Waddy, "Palazzo Barberini," 84–111, for the Vitruvian atrium and proposals for Palazzo Barberini; and Waddy, "Design and Designers," 174–76). Pollak's 1913 publication of the anonymous proposal for the new Barberini palace contained in Barb. lat. 4344 introduced the notion of an "atrium" into the discussions about the palace (Oskar Pollak, "Italienische Künstlerbriefe aus der Barockzeit," *Jahrbuch der königlich Preussischen Kunstsammlungen* 34, Beiheft [1913], 1–77). The Florentine author advocates something like the entrance hall to Palazzo

Farnese, corresponding to his reading of Vitruvius's confusing text: an ample aisled hall of specified measure and proportions, either vaulted or flat-ceiled, with niches, sculptures, and similar decoration, an evocation of ancient Rome (Barb. lat. 4344, fols. 33r–35r). Antonio da Sangallo, the designer of the Farnese entrance, shared the anonymous Florentine's understanding of Vitruvius (Per Gustav Hamberg, "G. B. da Sangallo detto il Gobbo e Vitruvio," *Palladio* n.s. 8 [1958], 15–21). The similar entrance hall of the Villa Aldobrandini in Frascati was also called "atrio" by a contemporary (probably G. B. Agucchi; published by Cesare d'Onofrio, *La Villa Aldobrandini di Frascati,* Rome, n.d., 82–115, fol. 11v). At the same time, there was considerable discussion about the form of the Roman atrium, much of it centering on the question of whether it was open to the sky or roofed. In the discussions preceding the design of Palazzo Barberini, in which the patron seemed especially interested in some innovative entrance, the suggestion of an atrium *all'antica* must have been received with interest, for atrium-like halls appear in some of the extant plans and the author of Barb. lat. 4360 (fol. 9) writes that he considered but rejected the idea. However provocative the suggestion may have been, the entrance hall of Palazzo Barberini does not look like any seventeenth-century interpretation of the Vitruvian atrium. The early documentation never applies the term to the space but instead consistently calls it "portico." Even Pollak ("Künstlerbriefe," 64) carefully avoided calling it "atrium." It remained for Golzio (*Palazzo Barberini,* 9, 36) and Blunt ("Palazzo Barberini," 261–63) to popularize the idea that the entrance be an atrium—a suggestion that, besides being unsupported by documentation, has deflected attention from the designer's unique fusion of normal forms with the unexpected.

146.   ABarb., Ind. II, no. 2888, e.g., fol. 254v.

147.   Hibbard, *Maderno,* Pl. 93a.

148.   Totti, *Ritratto,* 273, in describing Francesco's library, adds, "e perche ad utile del publico possa servire, vi tiene Custodi."

149.   The merits of the stair were not appreciated by Giovanni Battista Mola, who wrote of "quella scala non molto ben intesa per non finir bene" (1660), and "quella scala poco ben intesa" (1663; both quoted by Hibbard, *Maderno,* 229).

150.   A significant exception is the Sala Clementina, in the Vatican palace begun by Sixtus V.

151.   Scott, *Images of Nepotism,* presents a spatial understanding of the fresco.

152.   The American artist W. W. Story and his family moved into the *secondo piano* of the north wing in 1856. In a letter to Mrs. Story, her friend Mrs. Gaskell exclaims, "How I should like to [tell a certain story] to you and Mr. Story and Edith, sitting over a wood-fire and knowing that the Vatican was in sight of the windows behind!" (quoted

in Henry James, *William Wetmore Story and His Friends,* 2 vols., Boston, 1903, 359).

153.   Richard Bernheimer, "Theatrum Mundi," *Art Bulletin* 38 (1956), 225–47.

154.   D'Onofrio, *Villa Aldobrandini,* 82–115, fols. 4v–6v.

155.   Arch. Barb., Ind. II, no. 3112, fol. 364r (Appendix 4).

156.   Waddy, "Design and Designers," 171 n. 51.

157.   ABarb., Comp. 268, fol. 117.

158.   Richard Krautheimer and Roger B. S. Jones, "The Diary of Alexander VII, Notes on Art, Artists and Buildings," *Römisches Jahrbuch für Kunstgeschichte* 15 (1975), 199–225, esp. nos. 631 (20 November 1662) and 686 (27 May 1663), S. Maria in Via Lata; nos. 867 (8 July 1665) and 871 (13 July 1665), Palazzo Chigi. AChigi 702, inventory of Cardinal Flavio Chigi's goods in Palazzo Chigi, unpaginated, "Stanzino [E17] sul cantone nell'Appartamento di sopra che guarda nel Cortile de Mancini . . . Un'occhialone di longa vista . . . lon. palmi 6."

159.   Armando Schiavo, "Palazzo Barberini e Palazzo Moroni," 5, states that the Barberini arcade was inspired by the unfinished Benediction Loggia at St. Peter's, and that it also shows the influence of the courtyard of Palazzo Farnese, without, however, drawing any conclusion from these observations.

160.   Bernheimer, "Theatrum Mundi," 226. Scott, *Images of Nepotism,* for an explication of Cortona's ceiling painting as a "mirror" of papal virtues, especially in the historical context of the early seventeenth century.

161.   ABarb., Ind. II, no. 2888, fols. 211r–212v.

162.   Barb. lat. 4360, fol. 21.

163.   Above, n. 101 (chap. 12).

164.   ABarb., Comp. 268, fols. 102–104. Cf. Comp. 348 (an inventory of 1692–1704), fols. 229–231, 258v–261, 316–318, 326–328, which also lists the "Stanza dell'Ovata" at the end of the sequence of rooms of the "Appartamento d'Estate."

165.   Giuseppina Magnanimi, "Palazzo Barberini: La sala ovale," *Antologia di Belle Arti* 1, no. 1 (March 1977), 29–36, esp. 31, citing Teti, *Aedes Barberinae,* 15, "litterariae exercitationes"; and idem, *Palazzo Barberini,* 82–83.

166.   ABarb., Ind. II, no. 2439, pp. 53–54; Lavin, *Documents,* IV.Inv.44.

167.   Barb. lat. 4360, fols. 20–21.

168.   Below, pp. 284–88.

169.   Blunt, *Guide,* 163.

170.   Rudolf Wittkower, *Art and Architecture in Italy 1600–1750* (Pelican History of Art), 3d ed., Harmondsworth, 1973, 114.

171.   Hibbard, *Maderno,* 81–82.

172.   Barb. lat. 4360, fol. 66.

173.   Contrary to Blunt, *Guide,* 164, who believed that the façade "had been designed to open on a small garden."

174.   Florence, Biblioteca Medicea-Laurenziana, Buon. 90, fol. 70v; below, pp. 230–31.

175.   Barb. lat. 4344, fols. 33, 33v, 36, 39; Barb. lat. 4360, fol. 51.

176.   Eberhard Hempel, *Francesco Borromini,* Vienna, 1924, 16, and Caflisch, *Maderno,* 101–2, have suggested a similarity to French châteaux but not to hôtels.

177.   Guarino Guarini, *Architettura Civile,* ed. Bianca Tavassi LaGrecca (Trattati di architettura, 8), Milan, 1968, 104: walls are not to be built "in aria, dette dagli antichi *Interpensiva,* ma ogni vivo sia sopra il vivo, ed il muro sia sopra il muro."

178.   ABarb., Ind. II, no. 2888, fol. 217r, 161r.

179.   Ibid., fol. 211r.

180.   Ibid., fols. 199v–201r.

181.   Ibid., fol. 201v.

182.   Ibid., fol. 243.

183.   Ibid., fol. 180r.

184.   Ibid., fol. 177r.

185.   Ibid., fol. 219v; above, p. 200.

186.   Francesco Borromini and Virgilio Spada, *Opus architectonicum,* Rome, 1725, chap. 5, for the vault dimensions of 83 × 53 *palmi* and Borromini's pride in the construction of the vault. Joseph Connors, *Borromini,* 276–78, Cat. 100.

187.   ASR, CRM, Teatini, busta 2200, int. 2, fol. 8; and ABarb., Ind. II, no. 2888, fols. 184v, 186r; fol. 151v; fol. 191r.

188.   ABarb., Ind. II, no. 2888, fols. 191r–193v, "le due stanze fatte di una."

189.   Ibid., fols. 159v–160r. The *salone* vault seems to have remained secure, even when the wall of the *guardaroba* was in danger of collapse and in need of rebuilding, in 1673–74 (below, p. 254).

190.   Ibid., fol. 280v.

191.   Waddy, "Design and Designers," 154 and n. 11.

192.   Ibid., 154–55, nn. 12–14, and Fig. 8. In particular, Buonarroti and the anonymous author of Stockholm CC1419 assume purchases such that the palace could be built on the piazza.

193.   ABarb., Giust. 501–625, no. 568 (fols. 151–156), 3 Jan. 1626, "Conto delli lavori de ferramenti fatti per servitio dell'Ill.mo S.re Card.le Barbarini nel Palazzo delle quattro fontane."

194.   Ibid., no. 595 (fol. 218), 12 July 1626, a bill for whitewashing, listing work in the rooms of the *pian terreno, piano nobile,* and *secondo piano;* cf. Francesco Paolo Fiore, "Palazzo Barberini: problemi storiografici e alcuni documenti sulle vicende costruttive," in *Gianlorenzo Bernini architetto e l'architettura europea del Sei-Settecento,* 1, ed. Gianfranco Spagnesi and Marcello Fagiolo, Rome, 1983, 193–209, esp. 198 and n. 1.

195.   ABarb., Giust. 501–625, no. 569 (fols. 161–163), 7 Apr. 1626, "Misura e stima di lavori di legnami . . . nel Palazzo dell'Ill.mo et R.mo Sig.re Card.le Barberino, ch'era del S.re Duca Sforza . . ."

196.   Ibid., no. 617 (fols. 262–262v), 4 Oct. 1626, work by "Simone Lagi Pittore" in *salone* C28–29 (including "per

haver fatto 3 porte finte nell'istessa Sala, finte di legno") and eight rooms east of the *salone,* as far as C40; and "Nell'Appartamento di sopra"; cf. Fiore, "Palazzo Barberini," 198 and n. 21.

197.   ABarb., Giust. 501–625, nos. 509, 528, 529, 569, etc., all in 1626.

198.   Ibid., no. 617 (fol. 262v), "Nell'Appartamento di sopra, Per haver rifatto un Arme sopra la lumaca dell'Ecc^mo Sr Don Antonio e rifatto due Arme nel fregio della loggia con le Corone." The loggia was probably at D48 (its now-closed arches still visible on the south façade of the northeast wing of the palace), and the lumaca was just to the west; cf. Fig. 95.

199.   Ibid., fol. 228, 26 Sept. 1626, payment of 7.80 scudi for "lumini di creta" (clay lamps) for the "festa dell'Incoronatione di S.S.ta nel Palazzo à Capo le Case"; Comp. 49, fol. 223, 31 Aug. 1629, payment of 191.69 scudi "per diverse spese fatte fare Mons. nostro maggiordomo in occasione del banchetto fatto li 15 [?] Agosto pross.mo passato di nostro ordine al Palazzo à capolecase alla S^ra D. Anna, et altri . . ."; Giust. 1502–1595, fol. 77, Sept. 1631, payment of 10.24½ scudi "Per merinda al Palazzo delle 4 fontane alla famiglia per l'andata di N.S. e per Candele per li lumi alle 28 della Creatione di S.B^ne." I would like to thank John Beldon Scott for providing me with this group of documents.

200.   Pollak, *Kunsttätigkeit,* I, Reg. 856, 1160; Reg. 874ff.

201.   Waddy, "Design and Designers," for the early projects.

202.   Waddy, "Buonarroti," 107–10, 117–18.

203.   Waddy, "Design and Designers," 178–84.

204.   Barb. lat. 4344, fol. 31v, ". . . essendo quasi naturale à tutti il sapere un poco d'Architettura . . ."

205.   ABarb., Ind. IV, no. 1254, fols. 14v–15r (Appendix 3).

206.   Frommel, in *Le Palais Farnèse,* 144–45.

207.   Hibbard, *Palazzo Borghese,* 72.

208.   Below, p. 302.

209.   ABarb., Ind. II, no. 3112 (Appendix 4), fols. 363r–365v; below, p. 272.

210.   Ibid., fol. 364r; and above, p. 219.

211.   Below, p. 272.

212.   Pecchiai, *I Barberini,* 164.

213.   *Dizionario biografico degli Italiani,* "Francesco Colonna"; and below, n. 2. (chap. 13).

214.   ABarb., Ind. II, no. 4076, "sopra l'apratamento [*sic*] del Ecc^mo Sr Don Tadeo."

215.   D. Sante Pieralisi, *Osservazioni sul mosaico di Palestrina,* Rome, 1858, 6–12; and below, p. 280.

216.   Maria Giovanna Masera, *Michelangelo Buonarroti il Giovane,* Turin, 1941, 9–20, and letters from Maffeo, Carlo, and Francesco Barberini 1599–1639 in the Appendix, 84–90.

217.   Below, pp. 273–74.

218.   Waddy, "Buonarroti," 111–13.

219.   Florence, Biblioteca Medicea-Laurenziana, ms. Buon. 90, fol. 70v; Waddy, "Buonarroti," 114–15.

220.   Above, n. 202 (chap. 12).

221.   ABarb., Ind. IV, no. 1254, fol. 15r (Appendix 3).

222.   Waddy, "Design and Designers," 183–84; and Barb. lat. 4360, fol. 3.

223.   Hibbard, *Maderno,* 81; Thelen, *Borromini,* C45, façade detail drawing with annotations in Maderno's hand.

224.   While both contemporary and modern critics have been eager to associate Bernini's name with the design, Borromini's claim has found less support. It is difficult to make a stylistic argument in Borromini's favor (as tentatively attempted in Waddy, "Design and Designers," 179), because his work could well be expected to be close to that of Maderno in 1628. In 1657, according to Virgilio Spada, Cardinal Francesco Barberini attested to Borromini's importance for the design, but in words that still leave many questions as to their exact interpretation: "L'Emminentissimo Barberino mi disse pochi giorni sono che la fabrica Barberina alle 4 Fontane fù in gran parte [*cancelled:* opera sua] disegno del Borromino, e me l'haveva detto anche l'istesso Borromini mà [*cancelled:* non l'havevo creduto] gli l'havevo finito di credere" (ASR, Archivio Spada, vol. 454, cc. 463r–501r, 2–17 May 1657, fol. 11 [c. 468r]; transcribed and discussed in Joseph Connors, "Virgilio Spada's Defence of Borromini," *Burlington Magazine* 131 [February 1989], 76–90, esp. 84 and 87).

225.   Thelen, *Borromini,* C40.

226.   Ibid., C43.

227.   ABarb., Ind. II, no. 2826(d-1), plan of the lowest level of the north wing, 283 × 382 mm.; no. 2826(d-2), ground floor with a scale of 200 *palmi,* 290 × 509 mm., including a pasted-on extension of 70 mm.; no. 2826(d-3), *piano nobile,* 299 × 373 mm., with a small flap showing two mezzanine rooms A-A over the south vestibule; no. 2826(d-4), *secondo piano,* 293 × 402 mm., with several flaps to show upper levels of the building. The drawings are cited by Thelen, *Borromimi,* 70 n. 6, who names the draftsman Giuseppe Centelli and suggests that the drawings were to illustrate the document of construction; and nos. 2826(d-2) and 2826(d-3) are published by Hibbard, *Maderno,* Pls. 94b and 95b, with the draftsman's name as G. Ceratelli.

The crude hand of the second draftsman (or draftsmen) is responsible for many of the features which we know to have been constructed in the original building campaign — for example, walls and doorways of Anna's garden apartment, shown in ink, and the smaller size of her main chapel C30, sketched lightly in pencil. Other features drawn in the later hand are additions to the basic construction: the enlarged library, ca. 1639; Antonio's *stufa* on the lowest level of the north wing, 1641; and the clock pavilion toward the garden, 1643–44 (above, p. 201, and below, pp. 248–50). There are a few uncorrected differences between Contelli's fine drawing and the documented construction, for example, the location of the door and window of Taddeo's chapel B30, and the placement of privies on the *secondo piano* over the chapels, where the "torretta" was actually built to give light to Anna's chapel below. The inscriptions identifying several rooms of the palace include the "dispensa del Sig^r Ambasciadore" on sheet no. 2826(d-1), a reference to the French ambassador who was resident in the palace from May 1647 until July 1653, during the Barberini exile in France (Giacinto Gigli, *Diario romano [1608–1670]*, ed. Giuseppe Ricciotti, Rome, 1958, 298, 424). It seems that the French ambassador's friendly occupation of the palace after the Barberini's departure was the occasion for a survey of the vast building, an operation facilitated by the reuse and alteration of old plans of convenient size (Contelli's drawings).

228.   Hibbard, *Maderno*, 78, 213–14, discusses only the façade and the courtyard.

229.   Howard Hibbard, "Scipione Borghese's Garden Palace on the Quirinal," *Journal of the Society of Architectural Historians* 23 (1964), 163–92, sensed the special three-dimensional character of Maderno's architecture in the Borghese complex of palace and gardens cascading down the Quirinal: "Maderno's spatial interests show up in the curving stair-fountain that forms the entrance to the hanging garden [the uppermost level of the Borghese Garden Palace, now Palazzo Rospigliosi-Pallavicini]. The combination of curve and rectangle, the building climax of the steps moving around and over the fountain centerpiece, are characteristic of several other designs that preoccupied him at this time [1611–16]" (p. 186). Stair S8 at Palazzo Borghese (in those same years) in its shape and the square-well stair at Palazzo Barberini in its course (vaulting over part of the grotto-like entrance portico) are especially close to the stair at the Borghese Garden Palace, which in turn is evocative of the Confessio of St. Peter's or the stair to the crypt of S. Susanna.

230.   For example, see Borromini's several studies for Palazzo Carpegna, in Manfredo Tafuri, "Borromini in Palazzo Carpegna: Documenti inediti e ipotesi critiche," *Quaderni dell'Istituto di Storia dell'Architettura*, ser. 14, fasc. 79–84 (1967), 85–107.

231.   Below, p. 320.

232.   The Vignolesque themes appear early, in Borromini's garden façade and cloister of S. Carlino.

233.   Waddy, "Design and Designers," n. 73.

234.   Blunt, "Palazzo Barberini," 270, "It is almost inconceivable that any competent architect could have designed a building of which the exterior and the interior were so contradictory . . ."

235.   Hibbard, *Maderno*, 83.

236.   Waddy, "Design and Designers," 169, 179; Barb. lat. 4360, fol. 65.

237.   ABarb., Ind. II, no. 1254, fol. 15r (Appendix 3).

238.   Ibid., no. 2888, fol. 158v, ". . . la stanza sotto tetto dov'era la camera del P. Valerio . . ."

239.   Ibid., no. 2889, fol. 10; ". . . et nelle fabriche del Palazo alle quattro fontane assistente vi stava solo il detto Padre Valerio mà per Architetto Generale era il Sig^r Cavalier Bernino et io lo sò perche pratticavo in detto Palazzo, et anco per essere della professione, et non so che nelle dette fabriche ne per assistente ne per Architetto vi habbia havuto parte altri che il detto Padre Valerio et il Cavalier Bernino respettivamente"; and fol. 16v, ". . . et il detto Padre Valerio nella detta fabrica delle quattro fontane non sò che havesse sopra di se altri Superiori che gli Padroni et l'Architetto che era il Cavalier Bernino . . ."; cf. Pollak, *Kunsttätigkeit*, Reg. 866.

240.   Giovanni Incisa della Rocchetta, "Notizie inedite su Andrea Sacchi," *L'Arte* (Rivista di storia dell'arte medioevale e moderna e d'arte decorativa) 27 (1924), 60–76, esp. 63.

241.   Above, p. 192 and n. 51 (chap. 12).

242.   ASR, CRM, Teatini, S. Andrea della Valle, busta 2200, int. 2, fols. 18v–20, for construction of the twelve straight flights of stair S3, with 130 steps, the single central wall rising 121½ *palmi*, and the privy E11.

243.   ABarb., Ind. II, no. 2888, fols. 213–213v, "Muro della cortina di 4 spallette disfatte d'ordine del Sr Cavaliere . . . Muro della Cortina simile di due stipiti o membretti ch'erano fatti e buttati come sopra . . ." (cf. Fiore, "Palazzo Barberini," 203); fol. 216v, ". . . quattro mostre di diversi impresi fatte e disfatte d'ordine del Sr Principe e del Sr Cavaliere" (cf. Fiore, "Palazzo Barberini," 202).

Pollak, *Kunsttätigkeit*, 273, Reg. 886, no. 86, published a document suggesting that Bernini had been involved with revisions in a service stair, but he misread the critical abbreviation. Not "il Sr Cav^{re}" but rather "il Sr Card^{le}" (i.e., Cardinal Francesco Barberini) ordered the change in work: ABarb., Ind. II, no. 2888, fol. 134v, "Muro dell'anima della scaletta fatto e poi gettato à terra d'ordine del Signor Cardinale lo. p. 10 alt. sopra terra p. 10 g. p. 2 tev^a."

244.   Fiore, "Palazzo Barberini," 203–4; cf. ABarb., Ind. II, no. 2888, fols. 225v–238, for the full account of stucco work in the stair and its landings.

245.   Heinrich Brauer and Rudolf Wittkower, *Die Zeichnungen des Gianlorenzo Bernini* (Römische Forschungen der Bibliotheca Hertziana, 9–10), Berlin, 1931, 27–29; Thelen, *Borromini*, 62–64.

246.   Cf. Hibbard's "Survey of Attributions," *Maderno*, 228–30.

247.   Above, n. 240 (chap. 12).

248.   Fiore, "Palazzo Barberini," 198 and n. 24; 205.

249.   Hans Posse, "Das Deckenfresko des Pietro da Cortona im Palazzo Barberini und die Deckenmalerei in Rom," *Jahrbuch der Preuszischen Kunstsammlungen* 60 (1919), 93–118, 126–73, esp. 96, giving the date as 21 September 1630.

250. Murata, *Operas*, 223, an *avviso* dated 14 February 1632: "Il Signor Cardinale Barberini questo Carnevale farà fare la rapresentatione di S. Alessio nel suo Palazzo a Montecavallo dove poi si trasferirà questa Quadragesima il Signor Don Taddeo con tutta la sua famiglia, havendo affittato il suo Palazzo di Campo di Fiore a Monsignore Thesoriere per 1000. scudi."

251. ABarb., Comp. 192, payments to "Giovanni facchino . . . in trasportare le robbe al nostro Palazzo alle 4 fontane . . ." on 2 May, 11 May, 16 May, and 17 June 1632.

252. ABarb., Ind. IV, no. 13, "A di 13. Maggio 1632: Con lode d'Iddio B.^ma Vergine Madre Maria et di tutti i suoi Santi et con Protettione di nostri Angeli Custodi Venni ad habitare circa le 22 hore nel Palazzo nuovo alle quattro fontane sia con salute d'anima et di corpo et pace di tutti." This document was discovered by John Beldon Scott.

253. ABarb., Comp. 192, 2 June 1632; and above, n. 86 (chap 11).

254. Above, p. 130.

255. ABarb., Comp. 192, 9 July 1632, Taddeo.

256. Briganti, *Cortona*, 197–200; Scott, *Images of Nepotism*.

257. ABarb., Comp. 192, passim, large masonry payments ending during the summer 1632; 31 July 1632, final payment for *scarpellino* work amounting to almost 28,000 scudi, to Carlo Fancelli, Francesco Borromini, and Battista Castelli; Comp. 193, 21 Jan. and 10 Feb. 1633, final payments for woodwork; 18 Jan. 1633, final payment for metal work from 11 December 1630 to 31 December 1632.

258. ABarb., Comp. 80, 12 Oct. 1632 (". . . à buon conto del novo appartamento che fanno al nostro Palazzo delle 4 Fontane per nostro servitio . . ."); an entry dated 30 September 1632 may be the first of this series. For the *misura* of this work, see ASR, CRM, Teatini, busta 2200, int. 2, above, n. 14 (chap. 12).

259. ABarb., Comp. 80, 20 Apr. 1633, excavations "nel luogo dove si deve fare la scala à lumaca alli nuovi appartamenti della nostra fabbrica alle 4 fontane." Cf. Fiore, "Palazzo Barberini," 198 and n. 26.

260. ABarb., Comp. 80, passim; the final payment is dated 31 January 1637.

261. ABarb., Comp. 193, 27 July 1634, for the rental of the small houses "da finire per tutto Decembre prossimo futuro per il qual tempo s'intenda finita la locatione senz'altr intimazione"; and July 1634 (without a specific date), for the rental of the Orsini palace "locatoci per servitio della Nostra famiglia," for the period 1 August 1634–31 January 1635.

262. ABarb., Comp. 194, payments for moving dated 7 October, 30 October, and 6 December 1634.

263. *Avviso* of 14 October 1634, published by Alessandro Ademollo, *I teatri di Roma nel secolo decimosettimo*, Rome, 1888, 8: "L'Ecc.mo Sig. Principe Prefetto di Roma con la Ecc.ma Signora Donna Costanza sua madre et l'Ecc.ma Signora Donna Anna sua Consorte è ritornato dal suo nuovo Palazzo a Capo le Case ad habitare nell'antico di Casa sua alli Giupponari sendo per servitio et commodità delle loro famiglie stato ripreso a piggione ivi vicino al Palazzo del Signor Duca di Bracciano in Campo di Fiore."

264. Ademollo, *Teatri*, 8, without actually quoting that part of the *avviso*, speaks of "l'umidità della fabbrica non per anco ben prosciugata perchè finito di fresco."

265. ABarb., Ind. IV, no. 1254, fols. 21r–v (Appendix 3).

266. Above, p. 130.

267. ABarb., Comp. 193, 5 Feb. 1635, for the rental of the palace to Antonio, beginning 1 February 1635 (cf. ABarb., Comp. 194, 29 July 1636, Aug. 1637); and ABarb., Ind. II, no. 2863, for Antonio's rental of the small houses.

268. Totti, *Ritratto*, 222, 211, 272–73.

269. Nicolò Barozzi and Guglielmo Berchet, *Relazioni degli stati europei lette al Senato dagli ambasciatori veneti nel secolo decimosettimo*, Ser. III, Italia, *Relazioni di Roma*, 2 vols., Venice, 1877–79, I, 265–66.

270. ASR, CRM 2162, fasc. 161, int. 202, 1 Jan.–30 Nov. 1641, fol. 20, ". . . la stanza dell partamento vechio dove dorme S. Em^a al pian terreno"; int. 216, 1 Dec. 1641–31 May 1643, fol. 14, ". . . la stanza dove dorme il presente mese di luglio [1642] l'Em^mo Sr Card^le Ant^o Pr'one . . ."

271. The inventory was made in two parts: ABarb., Ind. II, no. 2439 (Lavin, *Documents*, IV.inv.44), lists paintings and sculptures, room by room; and ABarb., Comp. 268, lists other furnishings room by room as well as goods in the *guardaroba*, kitchen, and elsewhere. Specific references are as follows: Ind. II, no. 2439, fol. 18, "nell'appartamento da basso di S. Em.^za . . ."; Comp. 268, fol. 120, "Nella stanza prima dove dorme S.Em.^za"; fol. 96, "Nell'appartamento nobile di S. Em^za"; fol. 100 for the bedroom C8 and fol. 101 for the attendant's room C9; fols. 102–104 for the apartment "de Damaschi cremesini"; fols. 104–119 for the "appartamento vecchio" on the *piano nobile;* fols. 123–125 for rooms B23, B25, B27, B28.

272. ABarb., Comp. 267, fols. 202v–203v; above, p. 191 and n. 37 (chap. 12).

273. ABarb., Comp. 268, fols. 123–125.

274. Ibid., fol. 124, for room B27, the "stanza . . . de Cimbali"; and fols. 107, 112, 115, 123, 125, for other rooms with *cimbali.*

275. Ibid., fols. 134 and 102 for the billiards-like game of *trucco* in rooms C10 and C11; and fol. 106 for room C34, ". . . dove si giuocava al trucco." Cesare Evitascandalo, *Il maestro di casa* (Rome, 1598), Viterbo, 1620, 89, notes that "palamagli da tavola, ò trucchi" are good for exercise, but should be located far from the prince's chamber.

276. Evitascandalo, *Maestro di casa*, 1620, 89–90, advises that courtiers may pass time in the anticamera with such board games as *tavoliero* and *scacchi* (although playing for large amounts of money is a vice); other games are dangerous and should not be played (cf. Evitascandalo, *Maestro di casa*, 1598, 114–16).

277. ABarb., Comp. 268, fols. 106 and 123 for rooms C36 and B25, each containing a "giuoco di sbaraglino"; a third

set was in the *guardaroba* (fol. 80).

278. ABarb., Ind. II, no. 2439; cf. Teti, *Aedes Barberinae, 17.*

279. ABarb., Ind. II, no. 2439, fol. 11, room C34 is identified as the "prima stanza del'appartamento della Conversatione passata l'anticamera [C20]."

280. Ibid., fol. 17, "Nell'ultima stanza de Quadri Sup.re."

281. ABarb., Comp. 268, fol. 120, "nell'appartamento de quadri, e statue."

282. ABarb., Ind. II, no. 2439, fols. 21–22, 33–34, 36.

283. Ibid., fols. 54–70.

284. Tessin, *Studieresor,* 168; below, p. 265.

285. Totti, *Ritratto,* 273. Payments to Giovanni Battista Soria for woodwork for Francesco's library extend from May 1633 to April 1635, and a second project was completed on 20 November 1639 (above, pp. 200–201).

286. Teti, *Aedes Barberinae, 18.*

287. ASR, CRM 2162, fasc. 161, int. 235, fol. 8, ". . . la porta della libraria al partamento da basso . . ." ABarb., Ind. II, no. 2439, fols. 39–40, 68–70, "Nell'ultima stanza accanto alla libraria," and "nel corridore avanti la libraria"; and Comp. 268, fol. 128, "Nella stanza fuori de cancelli della libraria."

288. Above, p. 172.

289. In addition to the inventory of 1644, see Teti's description of the palace in *Aedes Barberinae ad Quirinalem.*

290. The *armaria* is identified in ABarb., Ind. II, no. 2888, fols. 187r–188v, and rooms D42–D45 in fols. 178r–180v. ASR, CRM 2162, fasc. 161, int. 202, fol. 28, notes the opening of "la porta nel coritore acanto l'armaria per andare alle stanze dell Sig.r Antonio Magalotti." The furnishings of Antonio Magalotti's rooms and those of his servants are in ABarb., Comp. 268, fols. 130–133.

291. ABarb., Ind. II, no. 2439, fol. 43: the "stanze del Padre Ignazio" contained one painting. Cf. ABarb., Ind. IV, no. 176, Antonio's "rolo di famiglia," which lists "P. Ignatio Mignozzi teologo" among the "Prelati e gentil-huomini."

292. ASR, CRM 2162, fasc. 161, int. 202, 1 Jan.–30 Nov. 1641, for rooms of Valemani, Balsimeli, Marini, the coachman Santi, Pazzi, and, in "la stanza scura al pian terreno," his neighbor "Santi guardaroba"; int. 216, 1 Dec. 1641–31 May 1643, fols. 3–4, for rooms of Pasqualino (". . . nel partamento vechio sotto tetto") and Lotti; int. 235, fols. 7–8, for rooms of Don Antonio and four coachmen, and fol. 10 for Braccese's rooms. Cf. ABarb., Ind. IV, no. 176, Antonio's "rolo di famiglia" in 1642, which further identifies most of these men.

293. ABarb., Ind. II, no. 2863, int. 1, "Nota delle Case che si tengono a peggione per la famiglia." Names of residents of the rented houses correspond to names in the role of Antonio's *famiglia* in 1642, ABarb., Ind. IV, no. 176.

294. G. J. Hoogewerf, "Andrea Sacchi en Carlo Maratti," *Mededeelingen van het Nederlandsch Historisch Instituut te Rome,* ser. 3, v (1947), 123–35, for Sacchi's places of residence from 1624 until his death in 1661; ASR, CRM 2162,

fasc. 161, int. 202, fol. 26, for Sacchi's two ground-floor rooms (B8, 32 × 28 *palmi;* and B9, 31 × 24 *palmi*); int. 230, for his reduced studio; and int. 225, fol. 49, for the moving of his works to make way for the "computistaria" (below, p. 250).

295. Murata, *Operas,* for Barberini theatrical productions in general, including the testimony of many *avvisi;* and, for the presentation of *S. Alessio* in 1632, pp. 19–23 and 221–26, including, p. 223, an *avviso* dated 14 February 1632 (above, n. 250 [chap. 12]).

296. ASR, CRM, Teatini, busta 2200, int. 2, fol. 15v, "Salone dove si faceva la guardarobba di S. Em.ª e si veste per le Comedie"; Arch. Barb., Ind. II, no. 2888, fol. 217v, for the "Salone dove si faceva le Comedie"; Comp. 268, fol. 96, "Nella sala dove si facevano le comedie."

297. *Avvisi* published, e.g., by Ademollo, *Teatri,* 8–22, and Murata, *Operas,* 223–25, 250–51, 254–57, 260, describe the performances as "nel palazzo." *S. Alessio* was given there in 1632 and 1634; *Erminia sul Giordano* in 1633; *S. Teodora* in 1635 and 1636; and *Chi soffre speri* in 1637.

298. ABarb., Ind. IV, no. 1254, fols. 15r–v (Appendix 3). Murata, *Operas,* 23–27, 249–52, documents the date of *Erminia* and its presentation in the palace.

299. Murata, *Operas,* 261, quoting an *avviso* of 5 March 1639; Ademollo, *Teatri,* 28–31, quoting other *avvisi;* and ABarb., Comp. 51, fol. 348, 28 Feb. 1639, "Spese della Commedia fatta recitare il presente anno al salone grande da basso al Palazzo delle 4 Fontane . . ." (Lavin, *Documents,* doc. 438). Contemporary accounts vary in their estimations of the theater's capacity. Even so, the benches listed in Antonio's inventory of 1644, ABarb., Comp. 268, fol. 134, in the "salone delle commedie," would have seated only about one-quarter of the crowd.

300. ABarb., Ind. II, no. 2895, "Nota della spesa fatta per la fabrica del nuovo Salone al Palazzo della Ill.ma Casa Barberina alle quattro fontane per tutto questo di 25 luglio 1637" (labeled on the cover, in a seventeenth-century hand, "Conto della spesa per il Stantione della Comed.ª"). Cf. ABarb., Comp. 214, fol. 150 (Lavin, *Documents,* doc. 382), for Antonio's contributions to the costs. Antonio had already paid Arigucci 100 scudi *a buon conto* for the beams (ABarb., Comp. 233, 11 Sept. 1636). Taddeo later paid a good portion of Arigucci's bill, 1,067.05 scudi (ABarb., Comp. 194, 1 Dec. 1637).

301. ABarb., Comp. 233, 13 June, 11 July, 14 July, 11 Sept., 31 Oct., 16 Dec. 1636, for the "nuovo stantione che si fabrica di nuovo contiguo al Palazzo nostro alle 4 fontane"; and 10 Apr. and 15 May 1639 to Soria for woodwork "nel teatro delle Comedie" and "nel salon delle comedie contiguo al Palazzo alle 4 font.ᵉ"

302. Vienna, Albertina, It. AZ Rom 964; Thelen, *Borromini,* C64 and 75–77.

303. ABarb., Ind. II, no. 2888, fols. 63v–64r.

304. Totti, *Ritratto,* 275.

305. ABarb., Ind. II, no. 2895.

306. Above, p. 161 and n. 107 (chap. 11).

307. ASR, CRM 2162, fasc. 161, int. 202, 1 Jan.–30 Nov. 1641, fols. 15–17, "Stanze acanto il Salone delle Comedie."

308. Above, p. 50. Just to the east of the theater and the cardinal's "stanze" was an enclosed garden planted with tulips, hyacinths, and other flowers. Visible in Falda's map of Rome (Fig. 129), it is the subject of a study by Elisabeth Blair MacDougall, "A Cardinal's Bulb Garden: A Reconstruction of a *Giardino Segreto* at the Palazzo Barberini in Rome," forthcoming.

309. Angela Negro, *Rione II, Trevi* (Guide rionali di Roma), I, Rome, 1980, 86–88, with, p. 83, an old photograph of the theater façade; Urbano Barberini, "Il 'Grande studio' del Thorvaldsen secondo la tradizione Barberini," *L'Urbe,* 27 no. 5 (1964), 1–4; Arturo Bianchi, "Attuazioni di Piano Regolatore, le nuove arterie di allacciamento con Piazza San Bernardo," *Capitolium* 6 (1930), 434–43, an enthusiastic description of work projected north of Palazzo Barberini, including the demolition of the theater.

310. ASR, CRM 2162, fasc. 161, int. 202, 1 Jan.–30 Nov. 1641, fols. 2–7, "Stufa fatta di nuovo."

311. Barb. lat. 4344, fol. 36; see above, p. 48.

312. Above, pp. 48–49, 97.

313. ABarb., Ind. II, no. 2888, fols. 290v–294v.

314. ABarb., Comp. 268, fol. 68.

315. ASR, CRM 2162, fasc. 161, int. 225, 7 June 1643–31 Oct. 1644, fols. 38–39, "Loggia fatta di nuovo per l'Horologgio." Magnanimi, *Palazzo Barberini,* 88, had suggested a date of 1651–52. Cf. the recommendation of the anonymous author of Barb. lat. 4360, fol. 51, that the Barberini include a mechanical clock with two bronze figures to strike the hour with hammers, like that in Venice; unlike the clock loggia built in 1643–44, this would have been a public clock, visible from the strada Felice as well as the palace to be built.

316. ABarb., Ind. II, no. 2903, a single sheet; four annotated drawings show the machine, with thirty-eight bells and two modes of playing.

317. ABarb., Ind. II, no. 2888, fol. 266r, "Camerone al Piano Terr° dalla parte verso le 4 Fontane dove si faceva la Bottegha del Falegname"; ASR, CRM 2162, fasc. 161, int. 216, fol. 11, 1 Dec. 1641–31 May 1643, "Stanza accanto la Computisteria"; the identity of the room is made clear by the dimensions of its vault, 70 × 47½ *palmi.*

318. ASR, CRM 2162, fasc. 161, int. 216, 1 Dec. 1641–31 May 1643, fol. 11, for the "Stanza accanto la Computisteria [B4]"; int. 230, 1 Oct. 1644–31 Jan. 1645, for the "computistaria nuovo," with its new door from the stair S2 and its pavement and plaster; int. 235, 30 Oct. 1644–30 Sept. 1646, fols. 1–2, for the "Stanze per la Computistaria," again identifiable by dimensions given for the two rooms and references to windows and doors.

319. Ibid., int. 225, 7 June 1643–31 Oct. 1644, fol. 49, "Per haver trasportato li quadri scolture e basi rilevi di marmo da una stanza per uso dell Sigʳ Andrea Sachi per

dare luoco per fare la conputistaria . . ."

320. Ibid., int. 246, "Adi 19 Giugno 1646 per haver rotto il muro per fare la porta nella stanza acanto la Computisteria già stanza della Botilieria per farvi la Cocina per il Sigʳ Abate Nicolao di ordine di Mʳᵉ fiorentile . . ."

321. Above, p. 246 and n. 292 (chap. 12).

322. Andrea Sacchi may be proposed for this office. Francis Haskell, *Patrons and Painters,* London, 1963, 55–56, discusses Antonio's special patronage of Sacchi and notes that the artist "acted as general artistic adviser to [Antonio] in the decoration of the palace." The rearrangement of two statues around a fountain in the garden was done "ordino al Sigʳ Andrea Sachi perche non facevano equal mostra alla dritura del Viale" (ASR, CRM 2162, fasc. 161, int. 235, 30 Oct. 1644–30 Sept. 1646, fol. 12).

323. This and most of the following events are chronicled by Gigli, *Diario romano,* 272, 281, 290–91, 298, 422, 424.

324. ABarb., Ind. IV, no. 158, dated 16 September 1646, is an inventory of the rooms in Palazzo Barberini "in quibus inhabitabat bon. mem. Eminᵐᵘˢ et Rᵐᵘˢ D. Cardinalis Sancti Honuphrij . . ."; the rooms named in the inventory are suggestive of the east part of the north wing, but they cannot be identified precisely.

325. Above, pp. 170–72.

326. Blunt, "Palazzo Barberini," 267.

327. Tessin, *Studieresor,* 165, "Sonsten ist auch zu observieren, dass sinter der zeijt, dass ich dass erste mahl in Rom wahr, hat man nach Cav. Bernino Dessein die Durchfarth hin auf practiciret unter den palais nach dem garten hinten, wohin man mit Kutschen anitzo fahren kan."

328. ABarb., Ind. II, no. 55, esp. fols. 414–546 for paintings and fols. 604–668 for sculptures; Lavin, *Documents,* IV.Inv.71.

329. ABarb., Giust. 11230–11305, no. 11234, fols. 34–35, bill for the moving of works of art from the Giubbonari to the Quattro Fontane, 30 August–28 October 1672.

330. ABarb., Comp. 89, no. 1423, 17 June 1672, "Al Sʳ Erigo Zuccalli Architetto scudi quindeci mᵗᵃ per haver aiutato à fare le piante della nuova fabrica al nostro Palazzo delle quattro fontane . . ."

331. ABarb., Giust. 11402–11457, no. 11407, fols. 113–114, 30 Aug.–11 Oct. 1670, "Nota delle giornate messe in levare le statue bassirilievi et altro che stavono nelle stanze terrene sotto il palazzo alle quattro fontane et portate parte con carioli e parte su le stanghe al Anticara nova nel Sito incontro il Palazzo . . ."; the summary of this and other work done by the masons Ferrari and Bossi, on fol. 22, describes the work as "fatiche e lavori fatti nel trasporto delle Statue e marmi dalla vecchia Anticaglia nel sudetto Palazzo alle Quattro Fontane alla nova incontro al medesimo Palazzo." For the payment of 45 scudi for the work, see ABarb., Comp. 90, no. 917, 30 July 1673.

332. ABarb., Giust. 11402–11457, no. 11407, fols. 51–61v, 15 June 1672, "Misura, e stima delli lavori di muro et altro fatto in fare la Computistaria nova sopra al Tinello e Can-

tina verso l'Orto nel Palazzo posto alle Quattro fontane . . ."; Giust. 11230–11305, no. 11236, fols. 40–42, 20 June 1672, "Lavori fatti di legname . . . nella nova Compotisteria nel Palazzo alle Quattro Fontane . . ." Cf. payments for masonry, 790.74 scudi, ABarb., Comp. 90, no. 917, 30 July 1673.

333. ABarb., Giust. 12235–12303, no. 12247, 30 Sept. 1676 (but payments for the work extend from 2 May 1675 until 21 May 1677; ABarb., Comp. 90, no. 2299, 2 May 1675, and many entries until Comp. 91, no. 1456, 21 May 1677), "Misura e stima delli lavori di muro fatti nel palazzo alle quattro fontane in stabellire alcune stanze nell'appartamento terreno verso il terrapieno e stanze sotterranee di sotto . . . ," including "sala" B3, formerly the *credenza,* fols. 107–108v, and the new *credenza* A21, fols. 124–124v.

334. ABarb., Giust. 11402–11457, no. 11407, fols. 63–72, 15 Aug. 1672, "Misura e stima delli lavori di muro stucco et altro fatto simile sin hora nelle stanze terrene nel' Palazzo alle quattro fontane . . . ," for the six vaults made "sopra la terra" and the finishing of rooms B7, B8, B9, and B10; and ABarb., Comp. 90, no. 917, 30 July 1673, for payment of 1,049.93 scudi for this work. ABarb., Giust. 11367–11400, no. 11394, fols. 270–271, 29 Feb. 1672, "Misura e stima della terra levata in votare le cantine sotto le stanze terrene del Palazzo alle quattro fontane . . . ," for excavation of the five basement rooms.

335. ABarb., Giust. 11402–11457, no. 11407, fols. 75–79v, 12 Jan. 1673, "Misura e stima delli lavori di muro di stucco et altro fatti nell'anticamera ultima delle stanze terrene al palazzo alle quattro fontane . . ."; and ABarb., Comp. 90, no. 917, 30 July 1673, for the payment of 457.28 scudi for this work. The "anticamera ultima" is identifiable by its dimensions, 50¼ × 43½ *palmi.*

336. ABarb., Giust. 11306–11364, no. 11358, fols. 280v–281, 13 Jan. 1673, "Per essere andato al palazzo alle 4 fontane à scanzare alcuni pili di marmo e piedystalli simili nelle stanze terrene trasportate da una stanza all'altra . . . scudi 5."

337. Ibid., fols. 277–280v, 4 July 1672, "Per haver fatto l'armatura sotto il ponte, che si è disfatto che per prima passava al Giardino et all'Ovato . . . ; Per haver rotto il muro e fatta l'apertura che passa dal'ovato terreno sotto il portico dove è la nicchia . . . che passa masso assi duro . . . ; Per il muro del parapetto fatto alla porta dell'ovato di sopra che passava dal giardino . . ."; and below, following note.

338. ABarb., Giust. 11367–11400, no. 11394, 17 June 1672, "Misura e stima della terra cavata et fatta portar via in fare il cavo attorno una parte del palazzo alle quattro fontane in faccia al ovato dove va fatto il ponte per entrare nel Ovato di sopra il piano nobile . . ."; the measurement of earth removed takes into account the space earlier spanned by the "ponte di legno demolito," only 7 *palmi* wide.

339. ABarb., Giust. 11789–11852, no. 11789, fols. 1–9, 18 Oct. 1674, *misura* ". . . per riparare la Guardarobba al Pa-

lazzo alle quattro fontane . . . Per haver sbugiato il muro della facciata che stava per cadere in doi lochi da banda a banda per potervi mettere doi arcareccie longhe . . . ," etc.; for payment, cf. ABarb., Comp. 958, no. 1047, 2 Nov. 1673 (the first in a series of payments "a buonconto"), and no. 2281, 24 Apr. 1675 (final payment of the total bill of 781.75 scudi).

340. ABarb., Giust. 11789–11852, no. 11827, fol. 175, 8 June 1675, "Per la terra cavata et portata via . . . dove si è fatto il piano avanti le stanze terrene dalla parte con li lavori . . . ," areas 4 *palmi* and 6½ *palmi* deep; "Per la terra levata et cavata nel cantinone di robba assai dura come tufarina [66¼ × 44½ × 16¼ *palmi*] . . ." Payment for this work is recorded in ABarb., Comp. 90, no. 2404, 29 June 1675.

341. ABarb., Comp. 90, no. 2299, 2 May 1675, the first payment in a series extending to Comp. 91, no. 1456, 21 May 1677.

342. ABarb., Giust. 12235–12303, no. 12247, 30 Sept. 1676, fols. 119v–128, for the service stair and basement rooms, including in the *bottiglieria,* "la vaschetta dove si tiene la neve," 2 × 2 *palmi.* Giust. 12482–12509, no. 12497, 26 Nov. 1677, fols. 227v–229, for the kitchen in A27, "quale non si era messa nel'altra misura perche non era finita."

343. ABarb., Giust. 12235–12303, no. 12247, 30 Sept. 1676, fols. 107–119v, for work in the "Sala in detto piano terreno accanto il Porticho," the "Anticammera accanto detta Sala," the "Cappella accanto detta Anticammera," the "Stanza penultima verso la Cantonata accanto il Terapieno accanto la detta anticamera [B11]," the "Stanza ultima fa cantone accanto detta che segue," the three rooms B13, B14, and B15, and the "Repiano della scala avanti la porta della sala di detto piano terreno [B2]." Giust. 12510–12555, no. 12529, fols. 181–182, 13 Oct. 1676, for marble doorframes for these rooms. Tessin, *Studieresor,* 168–69.

344. ABarb., Giust. 12235–12303, no. 12247, 30 Sept. 1676, fols. 129–129v.

345. ABarb., Giust. 12510–12555, no. 12510, fols. 1–1v, 4 Mar. 1678, ". . . 19 telari di castagno con 4 sportelli . . . alle fenestre delle stanze terrene nove con quattro contrasportelli di noce . . ."; for payment, see ABarb., Comp. 91, no. 2181, 24 Mar. 1678. For the glazing, see, ABarb., Comp. 92, no. 274, 2 June 1679, payment to Pietro Caselli *vetraro* for work 9 August 1678–27 March 1679, including 72.58 scudi "per quindici fenestre nell'Appartamento terreno del nostro Palazzo alle Quattro Fontane, e per quattro fenestre, che si sono ingrandite . . ."

346. ABarb., Giust. 12855–12865, no. 12862, fol. 255, 26 Nov. 1679, for the last of the nineteen windows and eleven doors.

347. ABarb., Comp. 92, no. 391, 19 July 1679, payment "per il prezzo e fattura di ventidue maniglie di rame gettate per servitio delle Porte dell'Appartamento terreno del nostro Palazzo alle quattro fontane . . ."

348. ABarb., Giust. 12566–12622, no. 12616, 18 May 1678,

fols. 225–231v; Giust. 12855–12865, no. 12856, fols. 67v–74v, including (fol. 74v) "Per il costo di n° 4 store poste per copritura delle piture antiche nel' muro in detta [B11]." The second long *misura* (no. 12856) is undated, but the series of payments *a buon conto* for the work begins immediately after final payment for the first (ABarb., Comp. 91, no. 2531, 27 Aug. 1678) and continues until the death of Cardinal Francesco Barberini in December 1679.

After 1679 the sculptures continued to be shifted from room to room, and new pieces were brought to the apartment. Still, in a few cases, the *misura*'s record of specific works and their placement can be coordinated with that of an inventory of 1698–1704 (ABarb., Comp. 348; cf. Lavin, *Documents,* VI.Inv.92–04) and Tessin's account of his visit in 1688 (*Studieresor,* 168)— for example, the "stattua di Marcho Aurelio di Bronzo" (probably actually Antoninus Pius) and the Narcissus in room B8, a marble Marcus Aurelius and a Consul in B6, and a bust of Hercules and a large statue of Flora (14 *palmi* high) in B4.

349.   ABarb., Giust. 12855–12865, no. 12856 [1678–1679], fol. 91v, for the storage of lead from the cupolino in "stanze terrene nel'appartamento novo."

350.   ABarb., Giust. 12482–12509, no. 12497, 18 Jan. 1677, fol. 152v, preparation for construction of bridge; Giust. 12235–12303, no. 12247, 8 Mar. 1677, fols. 141–145v, "Ponte fatto di novo"; Giust. 12482–12509, no. 12497, 26 Nov. 1677, fols. 219–223, "Scalinate sotto l'ovato fatto di novo."

351.   ABarb., Giust. 12235–12303, no. 12285, fols. 247–256, 1 Sept. 1676–30 June 1677; cf. payment in ABarb., Comp. 91, no. 1595, 2 July 1677.

352.   ABarb., Giust. 12482–12509, no. 12497, fols. 223–223v, 26 Nov. 1677.

353.   Ibid., fols. 241–246, 26 Nov. 1677, for the constructions to the sides of the bridge; Giust. 12566–12622, no. 12616, 18 May 1678, fols. 235v–236, for the balustrade and other work around the bridge; and fols. 231v–233v, for the installation of the sculptures. Giust. 12855–12865, no. 12859, 18 Dec. 1678, for the sculptor Giorgetti's *misura,* including the sculptures of the portico and the "facciata del orologio," fols. 219–223v. For Giorgetti, see Jennifer Montagu, "Antonio and Gioseppe Giorgetti: Sculptors to Cardinal Francesco Barberini," *Art Bulletin* 52 (1970), 278–98. Montagu, 294, has identified some of the sculptures and noted the disappearance of others from their positions in 1678.

354.   ABarb., Giust. 12566–12622, no. 12582, 28 June 1678, fols. 83–83v, earth removed "nel vialone di mezzo in faccia dove si deve fare la fontana lo. principando dal cancello sino dove termina palmi 250 lar. palmi 25½ al. reg. palmi 3½," and "dove si e fatto il masso della fontana . . ." Giust. 12566–12622, no. 12616, 18 May 1678, fols. 242–243v, "Lavore fatto per il fontanone da farse à capo il viale," the foundations for the fountain; and, fol. 243v,

"Per haver messo in opera il Cancello di legno atraverso il viale con due colonne piantate in terra murate calce et richiodate . . ."

355.   ABarb., Giust. 12855–12865, no. 12856, undated but 11 July 1678–Dec. 1679, fols. 117–127v, "Seguano li lavori fatti all'fontanone àcapo il vialone nel'Giardino," including a detailed account of the process of assemblage of parts taken from Giorgetti's studio. Cf. Montagu, "Antonio and Gioseppe Giorgetti," 294.

356.   A similar view is shown in the lithograph by J. D. Harding, published by Negro, *Trevi,* 1, 7; and in a drawing by Corot, published by Magnanimi, *Palazzo Barberini,* 138.

357.   Negro, *Trevi,* 1, 216.

358.   ABarb., Giust. 12482–12509, no. 12497, 26 Nov. 1677, fol. 224v, "Per haver rotto il muro duro grosso palmi 3½ e fatto il vano della finestra nella stanza dipinta [B36] al pian terreno di vano [*palmi* 5¾ × 12] . . . segue l'altra finestra accanto detta simile misura . . . ," and their travertine frames.

359.   Ibid., 22 Nov. 1677, fols. 225–226, "Per haver levato di opera n° 76 scalini di peperino lo. l'uno p. 4 della scala lumaca [S12] che cominciava in detta stanza dipinta [B36] e andava sino in cima . . . ," and other work for the removal of the stair. Giust. 12566–12622, no. 12616, 18 May 1678, fol. 235, installation of three windows in the north façade.

360.   ABarb., Giust. 12510–12555, no. 12510, 4 Mar. 1678, fol. 2v, "Per haver fatto l'armatura attorno ad una pittura levata dal muro nella Galleria e prima fatto le due sponde et coperchio sopra alt. p. 10 lar. p. 11 . . ."; Giust. 12482–12509, no. 12497, 26 Nov. 1677, fol. 226,"Per haver scalzato il muro attorno alla pittura che si è traportata imbicagliata attorno calato sopra li ponti fatti à posta dietro detta rotto il muro sopra la porta accanto detta finestra [*palmi* 11½ × 8] e messa e murato la detta pittura di muro rimurato attorno con calce e giesso fattoci il letto di giesso per di dietro messo due ferni sotto grossi che la reggono . . . con fattura de ponti, scudi 7." Magnamini, *Palazzo Barberini,* 100–101, notes that a recent restoration has revealed that the fresco had been placed here after having been detached and moved from some other location; but she did not realize that the location was simply the same room in its earlier form.

361.   ABarb., Giust. 12482–12509, no. 12497, 26 Nov. 1677, fols. 225v–226, pavement, 12 × 8¼ *palmi,* and plaster; Giust. 12566–12622, no. 12586, 9 June 1678, fol. 112, "Galariola dell Sig^e Pricp^e, Per la fattura di una porta di breccia anticha va posta in detta alla porta della stanza dove e la scaletta . . ."; and Giust. 12855–12865, no. 12856, fol. 48v, for the installation of the "porta di breccia anticha all' fondo della Galeria."

362.   ABarb., Giust. 12855–12865, no. 12856, fol. 48, two doors removed "dell'Anticamere della prima udienza et trasportatte per meterle à fillo," and then replaced; for the

363. ABarb., Giust. 12482–12509, no. 12497, 26 Nov. 1677, fols. 229–231, "Porte di mischio messe di novo nel'appartamento nobile," beginning with the "stanza fa cantone verso la strada." Giust. 12510–12555, no. 12529, 7 Aug. 1677, "Misure di M^ro Antonio Cartone Scarpellino," fol. 175, "Porte di breccia mischia poste all'Appartamento Nobbile dell'Sig^e Principe"; for payment, see Comp. 91, no. 2267, 15 Apr. 1678.

364. ABarb., Giust. 12720–12790, no. 12782, 12 July 1679, fol. 247, and Giust. 12799–12830, no. 12817, 25 Sept. 1679, fol. 78, woodwork.

365. ABarb., Giust. 12855–12865, no. 12856, fols. 50–53v.

366. ABarb., Giust. 12482–12509, no. 12497, 26 Nov. 1677, fols. 224v, 225, twice refer to the "stanza dipinta," clearly room B36. Giust. 12720–12790, no. 12782, fol. 247v, 12 July 1679, similarly speaks of the "stanza depinta dove si è aperta la fenestra nova" for which walnut window jambs were made.

367. ABarb., Giust. 12855–12865, no. 12856, [11 July 1678–10 Dec. 1679], fols. 56–60, for the installation of the columns and attendant masonry. Giust. 12566–12622, no. 12586, 9 June 1678, fol. 114, speaks of the partition that was removed: four Ionic capitals and bases are made for the granite columns "che vanno in opera nell'apartamento dell' sig^e Pricp^e nella stanza dove se levato il Tramezzo."

368. ABarb., Giust. 12566–12622, no. 12616, 18 May 1678, fol. 234v, "Per il muro dell'archo fatto in cocina per di sotto la volta dove posano le colonne della stanza di sopra . . ."

369. ABarb., Giust. 12855–12865, no. 12856, fols. 81v, 83, 83v.

370. Ibid., fol. 60, "Per haver fatti li ponti in detta [B36] per li pitori per dipingere la cornice et archi et in diversi lochi nella volta dove erano le crepatture . . . ," in two parts, 50 × 11 *palmi* and 42 × 27 *palmi*—dimensions that correspond to the two parts of the room; fol. 81, "Per haver scalzato diverse crepatture nella stanza dove si sono messe le colonne di granitto nella volta di detta et rimuratte con coccie, e giesso inzepatte con diligenza . . ."; fols. 82v–83, preparation of plaster surfaces "per potere dipingere," and "dove si e fatta detta pittura," may also refer to B26. Giust. 12720–12790 (actually continuing to no. 12798), no. 12796, fol. 282: "Si potrà fare il mandato al Sig^r Michelangelo Marulli Maltese Pittore di scudi ottanta moneta quali si fanno pagare per havere dipinto la volta con cornice attorno che ribatte con la vecchia et colonne basse capitelli fenestre et porte pilastri che rebattono le colonne di granito et ritocata la volta vecchia il tutto fatto nel stanzione novo terreno dalla parte del Palazzo vecchio nel Apartamento del Sig^r Prencipe di Pallestrina alle quattro fontane il tutto fatto con ordine del Em° Rev° Sig^r Card^e Barberino Padrone questa di 27 luglio 1679." Cf. ABarb., Comp. 92, no. 444, 18 Aug. 1679.

371. ABarb., Giust. 12855–12865, no. 12856, fols. 81–82v.

372. Tessin, *Studieresor,* 167.

373. ABarb., Giust. 12235–12303, no. 12285, 1 Sept. 1676–30 June 1677, fol. 254, earth removed "acanto il Palazzo vechio longo dal ponte sino al muro del Palazzo vechio p. 76¾ la. p. 78¼ compreso la grossezza del muro novo al. reg° p. 31 defalco dove era il corritore vechio lo. p. 74 al. p. 18 largo p. 6 . . . ," and then, "Per la terra cavata simile dove era il Corritore cavata sotto per fare l'altro corritore novo [74 × 8 × 11½ *palmi* high]." Giust. 12482–12509, no. 12497, 26 Nov. 1677, 232–232v, "Corritore," its walls, vault (pierced by three "finestrini"), plaster, and pavement. Giust. 12566–12622, no. 12616, 18 May 1678, fols. 234–234v, "Coritore nuovo sotteranio che dalla cocina segreta passa all'Appartamento nobile," its sloping pavement and drain.

374. ABarb., Giust. 12482–12509, no. 12497, 26 Nov. 1677, fols. 231v–232, "Corritore sotterraneo, Per haver tagliato il masso duro per sbassare la detta scaletta per potere andare a detto corritore . . . ," with steps, plaster, pavement at the landing, and a door to the corridor.

375. Ibid., fols. 224–224v, for the removal of the travertine frame "alla porta usciva dalla lumaca indetta facciata," the frame "della finestra della rota," and the twenty steps, and other work; and Giust. 12855–12865, no. 12856, fol. 83v, "Per il muro del' vano murato dove erra la rotta in detto coritore [B35]."

376. ABarb., Giust. 12566–12662, no. 12616, 18 May 1678, fols. 236v–241v, "Scaletta fatta di nuovo che dalla cocina segretta viene alle stanze nobile terene."

377. Ibid., no. 12621, 18 Aug. 1678, fols. 255–255v, "Per num° quattro fusti . . . alle fenestre del anticamere terrene del Sig^r Prencipe che sono le fenestre sbassate con il cortile [each *palmi* 6¼ × 13¼]." Giust. 12855–12865, no. 12856, fols. 94–94v, *scalini* at two windows in the "anticamera dell'Appartamento vechio tereno" and two windows of the "Sala."

378. E.g., ABarb., Giust. 12566–12622, no. 12616, 18 May 1678, fols. 245, 246.

379. ABarb., Giust. 12855–12865, no. 12856, fols. 84v–86v; Comp. 91, nos. 2251, 2252, and 2253 (12 May 1678), and nos. 2401, 2402, and 2403 (25 June 1678) for payments to the artists Urbano Romanelli, Giacinto Camassei, and Giuseppe Passari for the paintings. Jennifer Montagu, "Exhortatio ad virtutem: A Series of Paintings in the Barberini Palace," *Journal of the Warburg and Courtauld Institutes* 34 (1971), 366–72, partially publishes the relevant documents and offers an explanation of the iconography of the group of paintings, including the now-lost painting of "Parnassus" by Andrea Camassei, at that time on the vault of room B27.

380. ABarb., Giust. 12855–12865, no. 12856, fols. 83v–86v, a total of twelve bases with busts, two bas-reliefs, two porphyry vases, ten large paintings, eleven other paintings, two small tables, and a large table with a studiolo were re-

moved and then returned to rooms B33 and B34. Sixteen paintings in B28, thirteen paintings and two terra-cotta models in B25, nine paintings in B24, and nine paintings in B26 were removed and then returned.

381. ABarb., Giust. 12482–12509, no. 12497, 26 Nov. 1677, fols. 233–234v, "Armaria rialzata."

382. ABarb., Giust. 12510–12555, no. 12510, 4 Mar. 1678, fol. 2v.

383. ABarb., Comp. 12482–12509, no. 12497, 18 Jan. 1677, fols. 171–172v.

384. ABarb., Giust. 12855–12865, no. 12856, fols. 55v, 96.

385. Ibid., fols. 89–89v, on the façade of C3, toward the garden, a piece of cornice "fatta sotto la finestra dove erra il ponticello antico"; and the following note.

386. ABarb., Giust. 12566–12622, no. 12582, 28 June 1678, fol. 83, earth removal, first a bit opposite the east façade of the palace and then that "che rivolta con il vialone de lavori [86 × reg. 24¾ × reg. 35½ palmi high] segue l'altra partita à canto che risaltava dove era il ponte [39½ × reg. 32¾ × 35½ palmi high] segue [32 × reg. 38 × 35½ palmi high, 43 × 15½ × 35½ palmi high]."

387. ABarb., Giust. 12855–12865, no. 12856, fols. 60v–61, for the retaining wall; and fol. 110v, for the installation of its balustrade.

388. Ibid., fol. 89v, at room C3, a bit of plaster "di un pezzo di cornice fatto sotto la finestra dove erra il ponticello antico . . . ; Per il muro del' parapeto della finestra sopra detta . . . [10½ × 4¼ × 1 palmi]."

389. Ibid., fols. 61–67, for the bridge with its "archo rotto," the voussoirs in stucco, the three "catenne di ferro che fanno armatura à detti archi," the installation of the "ponte levatore di legname," the metal handrail of the bridge, and other details of its construction; fols. 88v–89, for the installation of the "arganello che tira il ponte levatore" in room C3; and no. 12862, 26 Nov. 1679, for the construction of the "ponte levatore," 17¾ × 14½ palmi, of elm and chestnut. Magnanimi, Palazzo Barberini, 88, assumes that the bridge belongs to the construction of the 1630s and is by Bernini.

390. Above, p. 206 and n. 134 (chap. 12).

391. Vincenco Golzio, Palazzi romani dalla rinascità al neoclassico (Roma cristiana, 14), Bologna, 1971, 40, publishes an excerpt from a letter of L. Agostini, Cardinal Francesco's antiquarian, to C. Strozzi, 9 February 1658: "L'Em. sig. Card. sta intorno per fare alzare il suo obelisco dinanzi al palazzo delle 4 fontane, che sarà una buone altezza, atteso che pensa ponerlo nel dorso di un grande elefante da farsi di pietra detta granito ovvero di metallo, ch'a questo proposito gli ho fatto vedere un mio piccolo di marmo, et il Sig. Cavalier Bernino ne ha fatto già un disegno, qui si pensa sempre cose nuove." Golzio notes that a drawing at Windsor, showing an obelisk supported by an elephant whose vestment bears Barberini bees, has been assumed to date from 1623–44 (Urban VIII's pontificate)

but that it could just as easily be for Cardinal Francesco in 1658.

392. ABarb., Giust. 12566–12622, no. 12618, 12 Aug. 1678, "Misura e stima del lavoro di terra levata dove si deve fare il fondamento della guglia al Palazzo alle quattro fontane . . . ," earth removed measuring 35 × 30 × 35½ palmi "dalla cima fino al piano del stradone di sotto"; Giust. 12855–12865, no. 12856, fol. 112v, "Per il muro del masso fatto per la guglia havanti à detto ponte levatore [26 × 25 × 36 palmi deep]." Magnanimi, Palazzo Barberini, 90, notes that the base still exists in the palace garden.

393. D'Onofrio, Obelischi, Fig. 3.

394. ABarb., Giust. 12855–12865, no. 12861, 28 May 1679, a misura of work by "Giuseppe Giorgetti e Lorenzo Ottone scultori compagni," including, fol. 245, "Modello della Guglia," 23½ pounds of wax and other materials, costing 3.80 scudi, "E più haver fatto il sudetto modello da quattro parte con trofei e palme figure elefanti un toro rostro di nave et ariotte e clave et are da sacrificio e face scudi elmi et altre armature differenti," valued at 10 scudi.

395. Tessin, Studieresor, 165. The newly built axial drive, he wrote, provided a way for coaches to go to the garden — i.e., not a normal entrance to the palace.

396. ABarb., Giust. 12855–12865, no. 12856, fol. 50, identifiable by its door to the chapel and smaller door to the chamber adjacent to the chapel.

397. Ibid., fol. 51, identifiable by its door to stair S7 ("Scalla dell' Camera dell'Udienza della Sig.ª Principessa che va all'Appartamento di sopra," fol. 54) and the door "che rivolta à canto detta" to room C26, as well as the door to the next room, C25.

398. Ibid., fol. 95v, ". . . quattro stanze del' appartamento nobile della Sig.ª Prip.ˢᵃ . . ."; and the installation of three bars "che mantegano il baldachino nella Camera della Udienza della Sig.ª Pricp.ˢᵃ."

399. Ibid., fol. 48, two doors were removed "dell'Anticamere della prima udienza et trasportatte per meterle à fillo," and then replaced.

400. ABarb., Giust. 12566–12622, no. 12586, fol. 112, "Galariola dell Sig.ᵉ Pricp.ᵉ"; Giust. 12855–12865, no. 12856, fol. 48v, the "Galeria" is included among the prince's rooms.

401. Tessin, Studieresor, 165; his count of the princess's rooms is hard to explain.

402. Documents of construction make no mention of the apartment's summer occupation, but Tessin, Studieresor, 166, calls it the "Sommerzimbern" of the prince; Rossini, Il Mercurio errante, writes of the "Appartamento dell'Estate del Sig. Principe," and Panciroli, Roma sacra e moderna, describes "l'Appartamento festivo del Signor Principe."

403. ABarb., Giust. 12566–12622, no. 12616, fol. 255. Tessin, Studieresor, 166.

404. ABarb., Giust. 12720–12790 (actually continuing to no. 12798), no. 12796, fol. 282, "Stanzione novo terreno

dalla parte del Palazzo vecchio nel Apartamento del Sigʳ Prencipe di Pallestrina."

405. Tessin, *Studieresor,* 166; Rossini, *Il Mercurio errante,* 59; Panciroli, *Roma sacra e moderna,* 210–11.

406. Tessin, *Studieresor,* 168: the rooms of the ground floor of the north wing "haben keine andere meubeln, mittlerweile die wände fast gantz von diesen herlichen obgemelten dingen überdecket seijndt." He counted 335 paintings, 44 statues, and 56 busts.

407. Above, p. 245.

408. Montagu, "Exhortatio ad Virtutem," 366, states that Cardinal Francesco Barberini had intended rooms B23–B28 for his own use, but there is no evidence for this. Francesco paid not only for the new paintings in the vaults of these rooms but also for the entire remodeling of the palace from 1672 to his death in 1679. The *pian terreno* rooms are certainly Maffeo's.

409. ABarb., Giust. 12855–12865, no. 12856, fol. 54, "Scalla dell'Camera dell'Udienza della Sigᵃ Principˢᵃ che va all'Appartamento di sopra."

410. ABarb., Giust. 12482–12509, no. 12497, fols. 171–172v, "Seguono li lavori nelle stanze della principessa . . . ," including a corridor, a "Stanza mezzanina" with a pavement measuring 27¼ × 16 *palmi,* a "mezzanino accanto, and a "stanza della cappella." Giust. 12855–12865, no. 12862, fol. 255v, repair "all'mezanini nel apartamento della Sigᵃ Prencipessa."

411. ABarb., Giust. 12855–12865, no. 12856, fol. 96, stucco in five rooms of the "Signorini"; Giust. 12566–12622, no. 12616, fol. 244v, ". . . porta che passa alle stanze mezanine nell'apartamento di cima delli Signorini [4¼ × 8¾ *palmi*]," and "Per il muro dell'archo dell'camino che si e sbasato."

412. ABarb., Giust. 12566–12622, no. 12568, fols. 116–116v, work at "li scalini nell' Coritore che va alle stanze dove dormano li Signorini fatto con ordine della Sigᵃ Principesa." Giust. 12855–12865, no. 12856, fol. 55v, for the installation of thirty-eight hooks, and fol. 96, for their adjustment; and fol. 55v for the latrines and pages' rooms.

413. ABarb., Giust. 12566–12622, no. 12586, fol. 112, "Appartamento nuovo dell' Sigᵉ Cardᵉ," a door of cipollino is made for the stair S4 in room B12.

414. Rossini, *Il Mercurio errante,* 53. Tessin and Panciroli do not mention a particular occupant.

415. ABarb., Giust. 11402–11457, no. 11407, fol. 75, "anticamera ultima delle stanze terrene"; Giust. 12235–12303, no. 12247, fol. 107, "Sala," fol. 108v, "Anticammera accanto detta sala," fol. 112, "Cappella accanto detta Anticamera," with the expectation that an altar would be installed; Giust. 12510–12555, no. 12529, fol. 181v, "anticammerone."

416. ABarb., Comp. 348, fols. 213, 214, 241, 242, 297, 298, 319, 319v. This document is similar to the inventory published by Lavin, *Documents,* IV.Inv.92–04, with different

pagination. Lavin believed the inventory to be of the entire palace, but it actually is for only the south half, belonging at that time to Cardinal Carlo Barberini. The "Appartamento terreno" does not include both right and left sides of the palace, as Lavin (p. 427) believed, but right and left (west and east) sides of the south wing.

417. Tessin, *Studieresor,* 168; ABarb., Comp. 348, fol. 223, "Terza stanza fatta di nuovo"; Rossini, *Il Mercurio errante,* 53–55; Panciroli, *Roma sacra e moderna,* 206–7.

418. Panciroli, *Roma sacra e moderna,* 206, "l'appartamento dunque terreno abitato nell'estate è composto di nuove stanze."

419. Above, pp. 112–18, 171; below, p. 308.

420. ABarb., Giust. 12566–12622, no. 12616, fol. 247, "Per haver fatto un pezzo d'amattonato sopra il ponte che entra nell'appartamento dell' Sigᵉ Cardᴵ Carlo . . ."

421. Tessin, *Studieresor,* 169; Rossini, *Il Mercurio errante,* 56; Panciroli, *Roma sacra e moderna,* 208, "l'appartamento superiore, in cui abitava il già Cardinal Carlo di sempre gloriosa ricordanza" (but rooms C11–C15 were an apartment "spettante all'istesso Ecc. Principe").

422. Above, p. 199.

423. Tessin, *Studieresor,* 169 (Palazzo Barberini), and below, p. 305.

424. ABarb., Giust. 12482–12509, no. 12497, 18 Jan. 1677, fols. 162v–163, "Per il tetto scopato e rivoltato sopra l'appartamento del Sigᵣ Carlo verso il cortile [78 × 37 *palmi*]"; "Per haver scopato e rivoltato il tetto sopra l'appartamento di S.Eᵃ [52 × 40 *palmi*]."

425. ABarb., Comp. 348 (above, n. 416 [chap. 12]), fols. 232–235v, 313–315.

426. ABarb., Giust. 12235–12303, no. 12247, 11 Aug. 1676, fols. 105–105v.

427. The caption of Specchi's engraving of the east façade and garden (Fig. 163) describes the "scala che porta al giardino, et al piano della sala." Tessin, *Studieresor,* 165, writes, ". . . hat man nach Cav. Bernino Dessein die Durchfarth hin auf practiciret unter den palais nach dem garten hinten, wohin man mit Kutschen anitzo fahren kan," and that the entrance to the palace is by way of the stairs from the portico. Blunt's assertion that "with the new carriage-way [the visitor] could drive straight through the main block of the palace and so reach the door leading to the oval vestibule" (in *Guide,* 164) is misleading, since C17 was never considered a vestibule, and since both formal and documentary evidence points elsewhere.

428. Maurizio and Marcello Fagiolo dell'Arco, *Bernini: Una introduzione al gran teatro del barocco,* Rome, 1967, 104–6, imagining that the obelisk would have been on the back of an elephant, like that before the church of S. Maria sopra Minerva. With ancient statues, columns, dedicatory inscriptions, porphyry vases, the broken bridge, and the obelisk, there would be virtually a "'giardino segreto' per un piccolo museo delle bizzarrie."

429. Blunt, "Palazzo Barberini," 267, further observing that "although the arrangement of the balconies is damaging to the whole effect, the detail is fine and quite in conformity with Bernini's later work"; Tessin, *Studieresor*, 165, ". . . hat man nach Cav. Bernino Dessein die Durchfahrt hin auf practiciret unter den palais nach dem garten hinten, wohin man mit Kutschen anitzo fahren kan."

430. Giacomo Pinaroli, *L'antichità di Roma, con le cose più memorabili che in essa di presente antiche e moderne si trovano . . .* , 2 vols., Rome, 1703, II, 183–84; G. P. Pinaroli, *Trattato delle cose più memorabili di Roma tanto antiche come moderne, che in esse di presente si trovano,* 3 vols., Rome, 1725, 228: "Questa Guglia haveva da esser eretta avanti al Ponte contiguo a questo Palazzo [Barberini] fatto industriosamente dal Cavalier Bernino havendolo rappresentato, che voglia rovinare con crepature che si vedono formalmente coll'occhio."

431. Rossini, *Il Mercurio errante,* 57.

432. Above, n. 330 (chap. 12), for Zuccalli; n. 329 (chap. 12) for the cost of moving the paintings.

433. ABarb., Comp. 89, payments authorized by "Paolo Picchetti nostro Architetto" until at least no. 241, 2 Aug. 1669, and by "Angelo Torrone nostro Architetto" beginning in at least no. 384, 22 Nov. 1669. Pichetti's date of death is given by Thieme-Becker, s.v.

434. Above, p. 241 and n. 243 (chap. 12). In the documentation of the work in the 1670s, there is only a single reference to the involvement of any individual: the princess directed that some steps be repaired in the corridor that goes to the rooms where the "signorini" sleep (ABarb., Giust. 12566–12622, no. 12586, fols. 116–116v)—an incidental repair rather than a design decision.

435. ABarb., Ind. II, no. 2888, fol. 310; ASR, CRM, Teatini, S. Andrea della Valle, busta 2200, int. 2, fol. 52r. Above, n. 14 (chap. 12).

436. Above, pp. 227–42.

437. AChigi, 520, 20 July 1664–30 July 1667, "Misura e stima delli lavori di muro . . . quali lavori sono stati ordinati dal Sig.r Cavall. Bernino, con l'assistenza continuata da me sottosc. Carlo Fontana in misurare le qui sotto quantità . . ."; AChigi, 516, 13 Feb. 1669, "Misura e stima de lavori di legname . . . misurati, e stimati dal S.r Carlo Fontana Architetto di S.a Em.za . . ." and similar *misure.*

438. ABorg. 1476, no. 781, 18 Oct. 1671, "Misura e stima de lavori di muro et altro . . . ," unpaginated; and ABorg. 1451, no. 258, 28 Jan. 1672, "Misura e stima de lavori di legnami . . . ," unpaginated, both signed by Carlo Rainaldi.

439. ABarb., Comp. 184, fol. 132, payment to "M.ri Jac.o e Gio. B.a Beccaria fratelli e compagni muratori per tanti che importa una misura, e stima di lavori fatti a tutta loro robba nella fabrica dell'Androne fatta inquesto nostro Palazzo alli Giubonari dalli 8. di luglio 1641 à tutto li 28. di settembre prossimo conforme alla misura e stima fatta dal Contini nostro Architetto," and similar entries.

440. Above, p. 268.

441. Domenico Bernini, *Vita del cavalier Gio. Lorenzo Bernino . . . ,* Rome, 1713, passim, and p. 99 for the quotation; Filippo Baldinucci, *Vita del Cavaliere Gio. Lorenzo Bernino: scultore, architetto, e pittore,* Rome, 1682, passim.

442. Baldinucci, *Vita,* 180.

443. Below, pp. 315–20.

444. Above, pp. 241–42.

445. Blunt, "Palazzo Barberini," 267.

446. Ibid., 264–66.

447. Montagu, "Antonio and Giuseppe Giorgetti," for a study of the range of Giorgetti's work as Francesco Barberini's sculptor.

448. Franco Borsi, *Bernini Architetto,* Milan, 1980, 258, explains this surprising "transgression" as Bernini's distinction between "invenzione" and (here) "capriccio."

13. Palazzo Colonna-Barberini at Palestrina

1. ABarb., Ind. II, no. 3104, includes some letters of 1623–24 reviewing other properties, but the bulk of the volume concerns the purchase of Palestrina. Letters dated 2 December 1626–6 February 1628, many of them in cipher (with or without decoded transcripts), show Francesco Colonna's reluctance and the persistence of the Barberini agent Nicolò Benigni. A letter datable by its position in the volume to April 1627, decoded, reports, "Di qua vedo il Principe inclinato a vendere, ma lo nasconde et cerca di far apparire l'entrate maggiori per suo vantaggio . . ."

2. ABarb., Ind. II, no. 3084, is the instrument of purchase on 16 January 1630. ABarb., Comp. 187, 7 Mar. 1630, documents the final installment of 483,000 scudi, for a total purchase price of 575,000 scudi. Cf. ABarb., Ind. II, no. 3112, fol. 371, also giving the date of the sale (Appendix 4); and Pietrantonio Petrini, *Memorie prenestine disposte in forma di annali,* Rome, 1795, 238.

3. Rudolf Wittkower, "Pietro da Cortonas Ergänzungsprojekt des Tempels in Palestrina," in *Adolf Goldschmidt zu seinem 70. Geburtstag 15. Jan. 1933,* Berlin, 1935, 137–43; translated as "Pietro da Cortona's Project for Reconstructing the Temple of Palestrina," in *Studies in the Italian Baroque,* London, 1975, 116–24, esp. 122.

4. Ludwig H. Heydenreich, "Der Palazzo Baronale der Colonna in Palestrina," in *Walter Friedlaender zum 90. Geburtstag,* Berlin, 1965, 85–91 and Pls. 20–23.

5. Furio Fasolo and Giorgio Gullini, *Il Sanctuario della Fortuna Primigenia a Palestrina,* Rome, 1953; Furio Fasolo, "Il Palazzo Colonna-Barberini di Palestrina ed alcune note sul suo restauro," *Bollettino d'Arte* ser. 4, 41 (1956), 73–81; Heydenreich, "Palazzo Baronale."

6. ABarb., Ind. II, no. 3112, fols. 361–365v, 382–385 (the description of 1629, untitled); and fols. 372–374 (the description of 1630, "Breve, e succincta Relatione di Pelestrina, et altri beni comprati dall'Ecc.mo Sig.r Don Carlo Bar-

berino, fatta dal sig. Gio. Battista Scanarolio per sua memoria quando n'è andato à pigliare il Possesso"). See Appendix 4. For the date of the earlier memorandum, see D. Sante Pieralisi, *Osservazioni sul mosaico di Palestrina,* Rome, 1858, 8–12. The description that follows is drawn from these two memoranda.

7.   The two descriptions do not specify that the stair was open, but Francesco Barberini's biography of his brother Taddeo states that Taddeo's improvements at Palestrina included "scale coperte" (ABarb., Ind. IV, no. 1254, fol. 16v [Appendix 3]). The particular form of the stair is not mentioned, but, unlike the present stair, it returned to the curve of the hemicycle at the upper level (". . . un'altra scala, che termina con il nicchio sudetto al pari di questo appartamento del Sig^r Prencipe . . . ," fol. 364v).

8.   The description ca. 1629 (fol. 363v) says that the chapel is "nella sala." An inventory of 1648 (ASR, Not. A.C., 6601; below, n. 47 [chap. 13]) fol. 952, notes the "porta che entra nella cappella vecchia" in the *sala* of the lower western apartment without further mention of the chapel.

9.   For the "palazzetto," ABarb., Ind. II, no. 3112, fols. 383v–384. An inventory of 1648, ASR, Not. A.C., 6601, fols. 977–979v, describes the small three-story building, at that time unfurnished.

10.   ABarb., Ind. II, no. 3112, fol. 364–364v, "In questo stesso appartamento Il Sig^r Prencipe d'hoggi della parte di dietro ci ha cresciuta un poco di galeria . . ."

11.   Ibid., no. 4076, "Fogli in libretto dove se inventaria li lengiami vechi delle stanze che sia da butare à terra et le pietre conecie de porte finestre camini et de altri loghi dove sonno questo dì di dicembre 18 1627," unnumbered pages, "Stanza 2ª . . . E più un'altra finestra verso la loggia con li stipiti . . . con il suo sedile da una parte . . . ; 3ª Stanza . . . Unaltra finestra che mira verso la loggia . . . ; 4ª Stanza . . . Unaltra finestra verso la loggia . . . ; 5ª Stanza . . . Una finestra verso la loggia . . . ; l'ultima stanza . . . E più finestre due . . ." There is no record, in Taddeo's Libro Mastro A, 1623–1630 (ABarb., Comp. 181), of Taddeo's having paid for any work at the palace in these years.

12.   ABarb., Ind. II, no. 4076, "Nelle retroscritte stanze non vi sono notate le tavole delle sofitte che quasi vanno tutti in pezzi quando si butava detto apatamento [*sic*]," a cancelled passage; and "Le sopra dette tavole delle sofitte tutte e andate à male."

13.   Fasolo, "Palazzo Colonna-Barberini," 74; Heydenreich, "Palazzo Baronale," 86 (suggesting a building period from 1490 to 1504), 88; Petrini, *Memorie prenestine,* 192.

14.   Fasolo, "Palazzo Colonna-Barberini," 76–77; Heydenreich, "Palazzo Baronale," 90, for a discussion of the possible influence of the Palestrina stair on the later stairs by Michelangelo at the Cortile del Belvedere and the Campidoglio in Rome.

15.   Heydenreich, "Palazzo Baronale," draws many comparisons with contemporary architecture.

16.   Heydenreich, "Palazzo Baronale," 89, misled by the early stonework, considers the stair as "one of the earliest 'monumentalized' interior staircases in the Roman ambient."

17.   Fasolo, "Palazzo Colonna-Barberini," Fig. 7.

18.   Ibid., 75–77; Heydenreich, "Palazzo Baronale," 86.

19.   ABarb., Ind. II, no. 4076, 18 Dec. 1627, "La prima stanza atacata alla sala nova, che và atessa sopra l'apratamento [*sic*] del Ecc^{mo} Sr Don Tadeo"; and above, nn. 11, 12 (chap. 13). Taddeo's apartment would have been that on the main entrance level, to the west.

20.   Above, pp. 229–30.

21.   Above, p. 192 and n. 51 (chap. 12).

22.   ABarb., Ind. II, no. 3112, fol. 646, 28 May 1630, "Inventario di tutte le robbe che sono state portate de Monte Rotondo a Pelestrina . . ."

23.   Petrini, *Memorie prenestine,* 238–39, "Vi si portarono bensì, subito che la stagione lo permise, tutti i Signori della Famiglia," and then Urban VIII's visit 19–23 October, with an account of his public activities.

24.   ABarb., Comp. 187, 15 Nov. 1630 (29.85 scudi for whitewashing and 425.82 scudi for woodwork at the palace), 16 Nov. 1630 (101.20 scudi for glass, suggesting considerable reglazing, and 505.66 scudi to the *muratori* Scala and Ferrari), and 31 Dec. 1630 (small amounts totaling 254.41 scudi for keys, nails, wood planks, etc.). Cf. an accounting of the same work in ABarb., Comp. 2, fol. 153.

25.   ABarb., Ind. IV, no. 1254, fol. 16v (Appendix 3).

26.   Below, n. 41 (chap. 13).

27.   Below, p. 280.

28.   Not 1641, and not by Francesco Contini, as earlier proposed in Patricia Waddy, "Taddeo Barberini as a Patron of Architecture," *L'âge d'or du mécénat (1598–1661),* Paris, 1985, 191–99, esp. 196–97.

29.   ABarb., Comp. 192, 3 Apr. 1631, to "m'ri Dom^{co} et Tomasso Damini moratori . . . scudi 250 . . . à bon conto delli lavori che fanno per mio servitio à Palestrina . . ."; 5 May 1631, to "m'ro Tomasso e m'ro Dom^{co} Damini muratori . . . scudi 300 . . . à buon conto delli lavori che fanno à Pelestrina . . ."; and 26 Mar. 1632, to "M'ro Dom° et Tomasso Damini muratori capomastri scudi 1060.87 m^{ta} sono per l'intiero pagamento . . . di scudi 1710.87 simili, che tanti importano tutti li lavori fatti da loro per nostro servitio in Pelestrina et Corcollo conforme al conto, e misura fatta da Paolo Maruscelli Architetto . . ."

30.   Above, p. 174.

31.   Above, n. 29 (chap. 13); and ABarb., Comp. 192, 16 May 1632, ". . . à Paolo Maruscelli nostro Architetto scudi 50 quali gli facciamo dare per sua per sua [*sic*] provisione di sei mesi anticipati cominciati al primo del corrente, e da finire per tutto ottobre . . . ," and similar entries at intervals of six months. The last record of a regular payment of 50 scudi to Maruscelli, for the period 1 May–31 October

1637, is in ABarb., Comp. 194, 13 July 1637. At the same time Maruscelli served other clients, including the Congregation of the Oratory in Rome (Joseph Connors, *Borromini and the Roman Oratory,* New York and Cambridge, Mass., 1980, 14–23, 107–12).

32.   ABarb., Comp. 192, 12 Nov. 1632, the entire payment of 313.84 scudi to "Gregorio Fossati e Tomasso Damini Muratori compagni . . . in restaure il forno fare le camine sopra li tetti del Palazzo le chiaviche per le Cisterne, et altro . . ." in Palestrina, as measured by Maruscelli.

33.   ABarb., Comp. 193, 24 Mar. 1635, ". . . à M'ro Giovanni Mandella falegname scudi 60 quali gli facciamo a dare à conto de' lavori fatti nelle Cucine nuove et credenzoni per l'armaria nel nostro Palazzo di Pelestrina . . ."; 10 July 1635, an additional 63.29 scudi to Mandella to complete the charge of 123.29 scudi; Comp. 194, 5 Dec. 1635, ". . . à m'ro Gio. Mandella falegname scudi 50 à buon conto delli credenzoni dell'Armeria et altri lavori fatti da lui nel nostro Palazzo di Pelestrina conforme alla fede de Paolo Maruscelli Architteto . . ."; 9 July 1636, an additional 30 scudi to Mandella, approved by Maruscelli; 14 Mar. 1637, an additional 150 scudi to Mandella for work at Palestrina; and 30 Dec. 1637, the final payment "à m'ro Gio. Mandella falegname costi scudi 101.24 . . . sono à compimento di scudi 331.24 dovuti per saldo, et intiero pagamento d'accordo d'una misura, e stima di lavori fatti da lui per nostro servitio in cotesto nostro palazzo et altri luoghi conforme alla detta misura, e stima saldatali di P. Valerio Poggi . . . havendo havuto altri scudi 230 con tre altri nostri mandati a buon conto . . ." This series may incidentally indicate the termination of Maruscelli's employment, between 9 July 1636 and 30 December 1637 (cf. above, n. 31 [chap. 13]).

34.   ABarb., Ind. II, no. 4081, int. 2, unnumbered pages, dated 12 June 1637, "Prima stanza sopra alle cucine nove dove è il pozzo," followed by five servants' bedrooms, a suite suggestive of the west wing of the palace; and "Stanze incontro alle cucine vecchie," "Cucina," "Stanza incontro la cucina," "Stanza sotto la cucina," and servants' bedrooms arranged in two levels, reminiscent of the rooms behind the east wing in the description of 1629, fol. 365 (Appendix 4).

35.   Ibid., 12 June 1637, "La sala detta Armaria," identifiable by its placement in the inventory.

36.   ABarb., Ind. IV, no. 1254, fol. 16v, "[At the palace at Palestrina] vi pose quattro pezzi di cannone, et una buona armeria, mandandovi alcune spingarde prese ai Turchi dalle galere del Papa, mentre egli n'era Generale . . ."

37.   For the seventeenth-century history of the mosaic, see Pieralisi, *Osservazioni,* and Helen Whitehouse, *The Dal Pozzo Copies of the Palestrina Mosaic* (British Archaeological Reports Supplementary Series 12), Oxford, 1976. For a summary of its early history and full account of its restoration in 1952, see Salvatore Aurigemma, "Il restauro di con-

solidamento del mosaico barberini, condotto nel 1952," *Rendiconti* (Atti della Pontificia Accademia Romana di Archeologia, Ser. III), 30–31 (1959), 41–98.

38.   ABarb., Ind. II, no. 3112, the description of Palestrina ca. 1629, fol. 383v, "Il Palazzo del Vescovo sotto sue viscere haveva già il famoso mosaico poco fà spicconato con molto disgusto di tutti li Cittadini . . ."

39.   Aurigemma, "Restauro," 48; Pieralisi, *Osservazioni,* 13–14. The restoration was done in Rome, but an accident in shipping the pieces to Palestrina required further work in 1640–41, as recorded in ABarb., Comp. 81, no. 7129, 24 July 1640; no. 7197, 4 Sept. 1640; and no. 7468, 30 Jan. 1641, "Gio. Battista Calandra scudi 100 à conto delli musaichi che restaura d'ordine nostro à Palestrina . . ."

40.   Pieralisi, *Osservazioni,* 8, and Whitehouse, *Dal Pozzo Copies,* 7, both quoting a notice in an inventory in the Archivio Barberini, "A dì 20 di giugno 1640. E più ho mandato a Palestrina molte casse di musaichi antichi per ordine dell'Eminentissimo e Reverendissimo Sig. Cardinale Padrone [Francesco]."

41.   A memorandum in the Archivio Barberini, undated but datable 1655/56, published by Pieralisi, *Osservazioni,* 9–10, describes the history of the mosaic and its installation in the chamber that resulted from Taddeo's construction of the large *sala* above: ". . . et havendo Taddeo Barberino tolto il semiciclo de' gradi ultimo e più interno, come è nella pianta del tempio, per l'edifitio di una sala, rimasta in quello una gran nicchia, tribuna o absida che vogliamo dire, ivi ripose il detto litostroto così ben ristaurato, che neppure una pietruccola vi manca . . ." The architectural work is documented in ABarb., Comp. 81, no. 7562, 15 Mar. 1641, 60.03 scudi for the purchase of iron, "mandato à Palestrina per la cancellata dove stà il musaico . . ."; no. 7617, 23 Apr. 1641, ". . . à m'ro Battista di Biagio muratore in Pelestrina scudi 135.90 m^ta per saldo della misura di lavori fatti alla stanza dove si è messo il musaico nel Palazzo di detto loco per tutto li 23 febbraio 1641 conforme alla detta misura e stima saldata, e liquidata seco d'acconto in detta somma da Francesco Contini Architetto"; no. 7666, 13 May 1641, "A m'ro Archangelo Cechearoni Archibuguioni in Pelestrina scudi 30 di m^ta cioè scudi 20 per libbre 300 di ferro per finire il cancello di ferro cha noi facciamo fare per il musaico di Pelestrina e scudi 10 a conto della fattura del detto cancello . . ." For the architect Francesco Contini, see above, n. 112 (chap. 11).

In the nineteenth century the mosaic was once again taken to Rome for restoration and then in 1855 brought back and installed in the floor of another room of the palace (Orazio Marucchi, *Descrizione del Museo Prenestino Barberiniano con brevi cenni sul Palazzo Baronale,* Rome, 1917, 17). After the restoration of the palace in the 1950s, the mosaic was installed in a vertical surface in Room XIV of the Museo Nazionale Archeologico Prenestino, which currently occupies the palace.

42. Wittkower, "Cortona's Project," 116 and n. 9. Drawings at Windsor would seem to be copies of Cesi's drawings, which are now lost. An inventory begun in 1631, included in Barb. lat. 5635, includes a list of maps and views, among them "Un disegno simile colorito con la pianta di Pellestrino largo palmi 3" (fol. 243, no. 31; Lavin, *Documents,* III.Barb.lat.5365, p. 120), which may have been one of Cesi's drawings.

43. Wittkower, "Cortona's Project," 122, proposed a date of 1636 for the reconstructions; but John Beldon Scott, *Images of Nepotism* (Princeton, [1990], in press), dating the painting at Palazzo Barberini alle Quattro Fontane 1631, has realized that Cortona's reconstructions must antedate the fresco. Karl Noehles, *La Chiesa dei SS. Luca e Martina nell'opera di Pietro da Cortona* (Saggi e studi di storia dell'arte, 3), Rome, 1970, 16, relates the design of Cortona's Villa del Pigneto (Sacchetti) to his interest in Palestrina; the Sacchetti were close to Francesco, and a general interest in the ancient structure among these persons in the 1630s can be inferred.

44. ABarb., Comp. 80, 15 Sept. 1633, a payment of 26 scudi to "M'ro Pietro Pauolo Bruscio . . . per saldo di un suo conto di diverse spese fatte da lui in fare il modello di Pelestrina . . ."; cf. Archivio della S. Congregazione de Propaganda Fide, Archivio della Computisteria, Quaderno de SS^ri Barberini 1633–1636, fol. 65, 22 Sept. 1633.

45. ABarb., Comp. 80, no. 288, 16 Oct. 1669, ". . . scudi 2 dati ad Agapito Pittore a buon conto del disegno che fa del Tempio della Fortuna"; no. 1127, 2 Dec. 1673, ". . . scudi 1.20 ad Agapito pittore a buon conto del disegno di una pianta del Tempio della Fortuna [at Palestrina] . . ."

46. Above, n. 34 (chap. 13).

47. ASR, Not. A.C., 6601, fols. 938–981, 21 Feb. 1648.

48. In 1648 these women's chairs were in the sixth room; ibid., fol. 942v.

49. The 1648 inventory (ibid., fol. 940) notes fireplace equipment in the second room, missing in 1637.

50. By 1648 this gallery had been enlarged to extend the whole length of the wing, and it held sixty-five paintings, including twelve portraits of emperors and thirty portraits of cardinals (ibid., fols. 947v–948).

51. The inventory of 1648 (ibid.) notes a door from the second room (B4) to the chapel (fol. 940v) and a door from the chapel to the gallery (fol. 949); by that date the painting of Elizabeth of Portugal had been moved to the sixth room (B9) in Anna's apartment (fol. 942v).

52. Ibid., fol. 951v, "Appartamento sotto al Nobile detto delli Prelati"; fol. 952, in the second room (A4), "porta che esce nell'anditetto stretto"; fol. 954, in the sixth room (A8), "porta che esce nel corritoretto stretto."

53. In 1637, fireplace equipment was in rooms 3 and 7 (A5, A10); in 1648 it was in rooms 4, 7, and 8 (A6, A10, A11) (ibid., fols. 953, 954v, 955v).

54. Above, n. 33 (chap. 13).

55. ASR, Not. A.C., 6601, fols. 963v–965v.

56. ABarb., Ind. II, no. 3112 (description of 1629), fol. 364r, "Dietro a questa stessa parte di Palazzo [i.e., the east wing] vi sono diverse stantie, che servono per la fameglia, guardarobba et altro . . ."

57. Ibid., no. 4081, int. 1, unpaginated, lists of goods consigned to the palace on 21 June 1638 and 16 October 1638, including a *credenza* "nella stanza dove mangia la famiglia bassa," and another "nella stanza dove mangiano li Gentilhomini." The inventory of 1648 (ASR, Not. A.C., 6601, fols. 955v–969v) lists many rooms for gentlemen, *palafrenieri,* and services, but the descriptions do not permit reconstruction.

58. Arch. Barb., Ind. II, no. 4084, a report on the visit of the Spanish ambassador to Palestrina, 2 July 1669, addressed to "l'Ecc^ma Sig^ra Principessa Padrona" and signed by Bastiano Casini.

59. Ibid., the apartment used by the ambassador "riesce al pari di un Teatro che appunto e restato terminato quest'anno, con Fontane . . ." ABarb., Comp. 367, fol. 495, records payments by Prince Maffeo Barberini for masonry amounting to 1,022.93 scudi "per tanti d'importa per una misura di lavori tassata dal Contini . . . in Pelestrina" on 17 June 1669, and for stonework amounting to 183.88 scudi, also measured by "Contini architetto," on 10 July 1669—most likely for the *teatro.* ABarb., Comp. 89, no. 59, June 1669, records Francesco Barberini's final payment for a new conduit for bringing water to the palace, possibly to feed the fountains of the new *teatro.* The modern restoration of the *teatro* is described in [Luigi Salerno], "Il ninfeo Barberini à Palestrina," *Palatino* 8 (1964), 257. By chance, Salerno correctly proposed Francesco Contini as the architect of the *teatro,* on the basis of Baglione's much earlier (1642) statement that Contini had executed various works for the Barberini at Palestrina. Contini died on 20 July 1669, after three decades in the service of various members of the Barberini family.

60. Alessandro del Bufalo, *G. B. Contini e la tradizione del tardomanierismo nell'architettura tra '600 e '700,* Rome, 1982, 41–43, and 56 n. 31 for the dedication of the church on 7 November 1660 as recorded in ABarb., Ind. II, no. 3302.

14. Taddeo's Building for the Barberini Family

1. Patricia Waddy, "Taddeo Barberini as a Patron of Architecture," in *L'âge d'or du mécénat (1598–1661),* Paris, 1985, 191–99.

2. ABarb., Ind. II, no. 690, fol. 1; Howard Hibbard, *Carlo Maderno and Roman Architecture 1580–1630* (Studies in Architecture, 10), University Park, Pa., and London, 1971, 83–

84 and Pl. 94a.

3. "Disegno della Pianta del Casino da farsi à Mompecchio à Castel Candolfo fatta dal Cavalier Bernini notata dal mastro di Casa con il di 14. di Settembre 1633."

4. ABarb., Ind. II, no. 690, fol. 2.

5. Ibid., no. 685, "Ordini all'Architetto di cose da farsi al Casino di Mompecchio settembre 1635 . . . Imbiancare la sala terrena con le cinque camere à detto piano, et il muro novo della Capella," and notes for window hardware and other work.

6. Ibid., no. 690, "Varij Disegni, e Piante per la Fabrica del Palazzo, et Aspettamento del Giardino, 1637."

7. ABarb., Comp. 193, 23 Sept. 1633, a payment for excavations and masonry in the "Giardino detto Mompecchio."

8. ABarb., Comp. 196, passim.

9. ABarb., Ind. II, no. 690, fols. 4 (Fig. 178, a preliminary sketch of the site), 5 (Fig. 177, with details of the plantings), and 6 (with specific dimensions).

10. Taddeo's work at other properties is described by Francesco in ABarb., Ind IV, no. 1254, fols. 16v–20r (Appendix 3).

11. Pier Nicola Pagliara, "Monterotondo," in *Storia dell'arte italiana*, pt. III, 1, *Inchieste su centri minori*, Turin, 1980, 233–78 and Pls. 321–58, with reference to documents in ABarb., Ind. III, no. 624.

12. Roberto Battaglia, "Il palazzo di Nerone e la Villa Barberini al Gianicolo," *Roma* 20, no. 10 (October 1942), 401–17; almost identical with Roberto Battaglia, *Il Palazzo di Nerone e la Villa Barberini al Gianicolo* (Quaderni del Centro Nazionale di Studi di Storia dell'Architettura, 5), Rome, 1943; L. Lotti, "La Villa Barberini al Gianicolo e il problema delle fortificazioni meridionali del Vaticano," *L'Urbe* 43, no. 2 (March–April 1980), 1–16; Alessandro del Bufalo, *G. B. Contini e la tradizione del tardomanierismo nell'architettura tra '600 e '700*, Rome, 1982, 83–84, 102–4 nn. 1–5.

13. Del Bufalo, *G. B. Contini*, 40–41, 54 n. 27, 311–19.

14. Nicolò Barozzi and Guglielmo Berchet, *Relazioni degli stati europei lette al Senato dagli ambasciatori veneti nel secolo decimosettimo*, Ser. III, Italia, *Relazioni di Roma*, 2 vols., Venice, 1877–79, I, 266, 334, 371.

15. ABarb., Ind. II, no. 2889, a memorandum summarizing early payments, including 7,600 scudi by Cardinal Francesco in 1628–29; and above, pp. 202 and 243.

16. Above, p. 280.

17. Above, p. 247 and n. 300 (chap. 12); p. 57.

18. ABarb., Ind. I, no. 747; above, p. 131.

19. Joseph Connors, *Borromini and the Roman Oratory*, New York and Cambridge, Mass., 1980, 112.

20. Giuseppe Sacchi Lodispoto, "Anna Colonna Barberini ed il suo monumento nel monastero di Regina Coeli," *Strenna dei Romanisti* 43 (1982), 460–78, esp. 471, quoting Anna's will.

15. Palazzo Chigi in Piazza SS. Apostoli

1. Thomas Ashby, "The Palazzo Odescalchi in Rome," *Papers of the British School at Rome* 8 (1916), 55–90, and "The Palazzo Odescalchi," *Papers of the British School at Rome* 9 (1920), 67–74; Vincenzo Golzio, *Documenti artistici sul Seicento nell'Archivio Chigi*, Rome, 1939, 3–78; Armando Schiavo, *La Fontana di Trevi e le altre opere di Nicola Salvi*, Rome, 1956, 239–86; Howard Hibbard, *Carlo Maderno and Roman Architecture 1580–1630* (Studies in Architecture, 10), University Park, Pa., and London, 1971, 213–14; Elisabeth Sladek, "Der Palazzo Chigi-Odescalchi an der Piazza SS. Apostoli," *Römische historische Mitteilungen* 27 (1985), 439–503.

2. Ashby, "Palazzo Odescalchi" (1920), 68.

3. Schiavo, *Fontana di Trevi*, 241, quoting a manuscript history of the building up to ca. 1606, "[Marcantonio] ha fatto in detto Palazzo vecchio molti miglioramenti, e stantie di sotto e sopra, quali si possono vedere."

4. Piero Tomei, "Contributi d'archivio, un elenco dei palazzi di Roma del tempo di Clemente VIII," *Palladio* 3 (1939), 163–74, 219–30, esp. 171, no. 29.

5. The dimension of 47 *passi* (141 *palmi*) for the left flank of the building, given in the census of 1601, corresponds to the length of the four rooms in the plans of 1664. The width of the façade, 76 *passi* (228 *palmi*) according to the census, must include the wall of the garden to the northwest; it is about 25 *palmi* shorter than the façade as shown in the drawings of 1664 (that is, its length would exclude the width of the north corner room in those drawings). The fenestration of twenty windows above mezzanine windows, described by the author of the census, seems impossible. The schematic reconstruction of Sladek, "Palazzo Chigi-Odescalchi," Fig. 20, fails to take into account the description of the interior arrangement of the rooms.

6. Above, p. 84.

7. Wolfgang Lotz, "Gli 883 cocchi della Roma del 1594," in *Studi offerti a Giovanni Incisa della Rocchetta* (Miscellanea della Società Romana di Storia Patria, 23), Rome, 1973, 247–66, esp. 255; the census of coaches in 1594, in the *rione* of Trevi, includes three coaches for "Illmo Cardinale Colonna," probably Marcantonio (1565–97) rather than Ascanio (1585–1608).

8. Schiavo, *Fontana di Trevi*, 239–42, quoting the early manuscript history of the building, ". . . e dal detto Cardinale di Avila ci fu fatto fabricare Appartamento nuovo che risponde alla Piazza, et è congiunto con il Giardino."

9. Ashby, "Palazzo Odescalchi" (1920), 69; Schiavo, *Fontana di Trevi*, 245, quoting the early manuscript history of the property. Since 1547 the property had been held *in emphiteusim ad tertiam generationem* by Sebastiano Giordano of Zagarolo and his heirs, and in 1604 Marzio Colonna acquired their rights, but not the actual ownership of the

property; the Colonna owned the house outright, however, by the time of its sale to Flavio Chigi in 1661.

10. AChigi 519, unpaginated *misure* of masonry, 1666–78, mentions "ringhiere" on the Corso façades of several houses inhabited by members of the Chigi *famiglia* in those years.

11. Giovanni Baglione, *Le vite de' pittori* . . . , Rome, 1642, 308, "E ristorò di dentro il Palagio, e rifece il Cortile de' Signori Colonnesi, poi de' Signori Ludovisi, incontro alla Basilica de' SS. Apostoli."

12. Hibbard, *Maderno*, 213, quoting the license: ". . . una striscia di sito publico et incorporarlo col nostro palazzo over Giardino desso Palazzo a linea retta . . . di longhezza palmi 191."

13. AChigi 483, 27 May 1668, unpaginated, an account of the whitewashing of the entire building, 1665–68, including "E più per havere imbiancato il Cortile Grande e poi dato il colore di doi sorte, cioè alli fondi dato il colore fino battuto à modo di gretoncini, e alli Pilastri, Cornice, et Archi, Aggetti, Requadri, et Colonne da trè parti di detto Cortile, et havere fatto li Ponti fuori delle finestre, e calato in molti luoghi le bilancie . . ." (cf. Golzio, *Documenti,* doc. 4053, 14 Nov. 1668, 48–51); the *misuratore* neglected to indicate the color of the architectural membering, but it was probably the "color di travertino" used elsewhere on the exterior.

14. Hibbard, *Maderno*, 214, curiously proposes a court-yard of 3 × 3 bays, in spite of the 4 × 5 bays actually constructed; he suggests that Maderno "rebuilt the old columnar arcades" [of Cardinal Guzmán's work?], and that "the upper facing of the court must date from the Bernini period."

15. Cf. Chigi P.VII.10, fol. 55, an earlier plan of the site, with "Entrata" marked in approximately that same position (Sladek, "Palazzo Chigi-Odescalchi," Fig. 9).

16. ASR, Notai Tribunale dell' A.C., 6340, fol. 302, discovered by Fedele, partially published by Hibbard, *Maderno*, 213–14, and fully published by Sladek, "Palazzo Chigi-Odescalchi," 496, Doc. 3; ASV, Arch. Boncompagni-Ludovisi, Libro Mastro A (1621–1623), fol. 250, cited by Hibbard, *Maderno*, 214, and published by Sladek, "Palazzo Chigi-Odescalchi," 1985, 497–98, Doc. 4.

17. Sladek, "Palazzo Chigi-Odescalchi," Doc. 4, "A dì 7 Luglio scudi 600 m.ta se ne da debito a m.ro Ant.o Bernascone murat.re che tanto fu stimato la rovina dell'appartam.to buttato a terra nel d.o Palazzo . . ."

18. Ibid., "A dì 8 detto Maggio scudi 342.30 m.ta . . . per prezzo di n.o 14 travi e n.o 650 travicelli . . . ; a dì 7 [luglio] scudi 291.98 m.ta . . . per saldo d'una misura di lavori fatti al sofitto del Salone del detto Palazzo . . . ; . . . scudi 12 m.ta li fanno buoni a Gir.o Curti Pittore per diversi colori e Pennilli compr.i per il soffitto dil Salone di detto Palazzo . . ."

19. Ibid., ". . . scudi 310 m.ta fannosi buoni à M.ro Jacopo Spagna Scarpellino per saldo d'un conto di lavori di marmo fatti in sala di d.o Palazzo per un Cammino e misurati sotto di 12 marzo pnte . . ." Hibbard, *Maderno,* 214, has associated the fireplace with a drawing by Borromini for a fireplace with Ludovisi arms (Heinrich Thelen, *Francesco Borromini: Die Handzeichnungen,* I [Veröffentlichungen der Albertina, 2], Graz, 1967, C17.)

20. Sladek, "Palazzo Chigi-Odescalchi," Doc. 4, "A dì p.mo luglio scudi 100 m.ta pagati a Agostino Tassi Pittore per haver dipinto una volta a quattro ordini in u.a stanza attaccata alla gallaria di d.o Palazzo . . ." AChigi 516, fol. 31v, "Stanza accanto detta dov'è la volta dipinta dal Tassi," identifiable from its context in the *misura* as C12. Golzio, *Documenti,* 18 and 21 n. 33, following Sebastiani, specifies four lunettes with marine scenes by Tassi, in the room followed by the audience room [C14] (see Pietro de' Sebastiani, *Viaggio curioso de' palazzi e ville più notabili di Roma,* Rome, 1683, 21, quoted by Schiavo, *Fontana di Trevi,* 271). C13 had a cross vault (AChigi 520, fol. 162) and, consequently, four lunettes.

21. Sladek, "Palazzo Chigi-Odescalchi," Doc. 3, "Nicola Ventura pitore in 2 volte, scudi 100"; Doc. 4, "devono dare scudi 124 m.ta che si fanno buoni a Nicola Venturi Indoratore per Lavori fatti in d.o Palazzo . . ." In 1664, besides the room whose vault was painted by Tassi, only three rooms on the *piano nobile* had vaulted ceilings—C13, C14, and C17; the vaults are noted in AChigi 520, fol. 162, "Stanza [C13] accanto ultima à Volta . . . colla nella volta dove fa la crociera"; fol. 165, Gallery C17, "colla sotto la volta"; fol. 358, room C15, ". . . il mattonato simile nella stanza grande nella volta dipinta," identifiable by its dimensions. Although several ground-floor rooms were vaulted, they were given over to services until the remodeling of the 1660s and were therefore unlikely to have received painted decoration in 1623.

22. Pompilio Totti, *Ritratto di Roma moderna,* Rome, 1638, 286.

23. According to the census of the parish of SS. Apostoli, the Chigi were not resident in the palace at the time of the spring census of 1657, but by spring 1658 the parish could record Don Mario Chigi, his wife Berenice, a household of forty-five persons for Mario and thirty persons (among them eight women) for Berenice, Prince Agostino Chigi, and his household of fifty-nine persons; in spring 1659, the census listed Mario and Berenice, with a *famiglia* of sixty-one persons, including five women, and Agostino "e la sua Moglie," with a *famiglia* of 104 persons, including five women. AVR, SS. 12 Apostoli, Stati d'Anime, 1652–1667, 1658, fols. 81v–82v; 1659, fols. 93–93v.

24. Golzio, *Documenti,* 22, for the text of the chirograph of 7 June 1657, ordering "risarcimenti, acconcimi, et abbellimenti . . . in modo che detto Palazzo s'è ridotto in

forma di commoda e condecente habitatione . . ."

25.   Ibid., 3, 20 n. 3, and, for the partial publication of the chirograph of 11 June 1658, 22.

26.   AChigi 520, fols. 58–60, "Repiano di cima della scala maestra . . . Muro di una finestra murata in detta scala dove era la rota [*palmi* 6½ × 4½ × 3]."

27.   BAV, Chigi P.VII.10, fols. 59, 60, 63–76. Dorothy Metzger Habel, "The Projected Palazzo Chigi al Corso and S. Maria in Via Lata: The Palace-Church Component of Alexander VII's Program for the Corso," in *Rome: Tradition, Innovation and Renewal* (Proceedings of a Canadian International Art History Conference, Rome, 8–13 June 1987), forthcoming, has proposed that Felice della Greca's even grander design in Chigi P.VII.10, fols. 67, 69, 71, 73, was intended to respond to the "fastigium" façade of S. Maria in via Lata, rising in via del Corso in 1658–63, directly opposite the similar window of appearance at the left end of the Corso façade of della Greca's palace elevation. The palace-church complex would be pierced by the thoroughfare, in the development of which Alexander VII showed great interest. In the event, the palace turned its face toward the piazza SS. Apostoli, and Flavio Chigi owned no property along the Corso (except the narrow house incorporated in the Colonna property in 1604) until he acquired the houses formerly belonging to the Mandosi family, opposite S. Maria in via Lata, in the summer of 1667 (below, p. 311).

28.   BAV, Chigi O.IV.58, fol. 422v, 9 Dec. 1661, Friday, "la sera il C. [Cardinal Chigi] ci dice di comprar il palazzo a S. Apostoli"; published by Richard Krautheimer and Roger B. S. Jones, "The Diary of Alexander VII, Notes on Art, Artists and Buildings," *Römisches Jahrbuch für Kunstgeschichte* 15 (1975), 199–225, no. 526.

29.   Golzio, *Documenti,* 22–24, for publication of the relevant documents.

30.   Renato Lefevre, *Il Palazzo degli Aldobrandini e dei Chigi,* Rome, 1964, 38.

31.   AVR, SS. Apostoli, Stati d'Anime, 1652–1667: 1661, fol. 112v; 1662, fol. 138v; 1664, fol. 149v; 1665, fol. 164; 1666, fol. 177v ("Palatium Emin^mi Ghigi in facie eccle. SS. 12 Ap. lorum in quo nemo habitat"). Stati d'Anime, 1667–1692, 1667, fol. 3. For the identity of Leoparducci, see AChigi 573, roll of the *famiglia* of Flavio Chigi, 1666–75.

32.   Golzio, *Documenti,* 5–6; 69–70, docs. 3978, 4314, 38, 786, 1105; and 77, doc. 349 (the painters' works). AChigi 457, fol. 29v, 31 Aug. 1663, 8 scudi to Giuseppe Bucamazza ". . . per il porto di n° undici statue, et altro portati al d° Palazzo di SS^ti Apostoli . . ."

33.   Golzio, *Documenti,* 6, and 25, doc. 883, noting construction "di un palco nella stanza ultima (?) verso il Corso dell'appartamento nobile per il pittore"—that is, C9.

34.   AChigi 520, *misura* for masonry, 20 July 1664–30 July 1667; AChigi 516, *misura* for woodwork until 13 February 1669; AChigi 517, *misura* for stonework, 3 August 1665–31 December 1667. AChigi 457, fol. 59v, records the beginning

of payments "a buon conto" to Giacomo Beccaria *capomastro muratore* and Gabriele Renzi *capomastro scarpellino* on 4 July 1664 (cf. Golzio, *Documenti,* 25, docs. 850 and 851, 30 June 1664), and, fol. 117v, the beginning of payments to "Antonio Chiccari Intagliatore e falegname" on 18 November 1665 (cf. Golzio, *Documenti,* 30, doc. 1639, 14 Nov. 1665).

35.   AChigi 520, fols. 17–26 for the heightening of walls; and fols. 133–140 for work in the *sala,* including the doorways "messe à filo"; AChigi 516, fols. 38v–40, woodwork, including the furnishings; and fols. 65v–67, for the elaborate wood ceiling. AChigi 457, fol. 117v, 18 Nov. 1665, notes the beginning of payments "a buon conto" to Antonio Chiccari "della soffitta della Sala, et altri lavori" for the palace (Golzio, *Documenti,* 30, doc. 1639, 14 Nov. 1665). AChigi 702, unpaginated inventory after 1667, "In Sala," lists the two sculptures, "Un'Ottavio Augusto [*palmi* 10] . . . antica restaurata di legno che finge marmo," and "Un Mario antico . . ."

36.   AChigi 520, fols. 399–401, including stuccoes in the vault; AChigi 516, fols. 33v–36v (door from C7, furnishings, window from C6); AChigi 517, fol. 47v (altar).

37.   AChigi 516, fol. 33, for the door to the garden, and fols. 46–46v, for the *gelosie.* AChigi 520, fol. 153, the door to the garden.

38.   AChigi 702, unpaginated inventory, identifying C6, C7, C9, and C10 as anterooms and C11 as the "Quinta stanza dell'Udienza," and listing the baldacchino and chairs of C11.

39.   AChigi 457, fol. 117r, 16 Nov. 1665, 150 scudi paid to Giovanni Angelo Canini Pittore for "una volta dipinta della Camera dove dormimo [Cardinal Chigi]" and some other work; and fol. 121r, 30 Nov. 1665, 20 scudi paid to Francesco Galli Pittore "per haver dipinto tre finestre con paesi, e grotteschi, dove noi dormimo . . ." (cf. Golzio, *Documenti,* 70, doc. 1632, 12 Nov. 1665; and 71, doc. 1676, 23 Nov. 1665).

40.   AChigi 702, undated inventory, identifies C14 as "Ottava stanza à volta con corniccioni di stucco dorati e quadro dipinto."

41.   Nicodemus Tessin, *Studieresor i Danmark, Tyskland, Holland, Frankrike och Italien,* ed. Osvald Sirén, Stockholm, 1914, 177, "Im ende der obgemehlten sieben zimbern wahr noch eine andere Audientz Cammer mit einem Himmel, worinnen den Damen undt particulier Cavallieren die Audience gegeben wirdt." AChigi 702, unpaginated, "Ottava stanza à volta con corniccioni di stucco dorati e quadro dipinto [C14] . . . un baldacchino di damasco . . ."

42.   Sebastiani, *Viaggio curioso,* quoted by Schiavo, *Fontana di Trevi,* 271: "La stanza del Letto, riuscirà al Curioso ammirabile nella vaghezza, et accompagnatura la quale non serve ad altro che a farsi vedere a' forestieri, né mai habitata."

43.   AChigi 520, fols. 358–369, "Ornamento dell'Alcova

dove servira per il letto di S. Em.za," including the two columns and two "contracolonne," the pediment, two statues, and scaffolding for the painter; AChigi 517, fol. 72, the stonework; AChigi 516, fols. 29v–30v, woodwork in the "Stanza dell'Alcova," with the frame for the painting and that for the *zampanaro,* or representational bed, and "Stanza che fa ricetto adetta Alcova." AChigi 702, unpaginated inventory, "Nona stanza detta l'Arcova [C15]"; "Dentro l'Arcova dove stà il letto [C16]." Golzio, *Documenti,* 74, doc. 3738, 18 June 1668, payment to Gaulli for "un quadro in figura ovata che rappresenta la favola di Endimione . . . per porre sopra le due colonne nella Stanza dell'Alcuova . . ."; cf. Robert Enggass, *The Painting of Baciccio, Giovanni Battista Gaulli 1639–1709,* University Park, Pa., 1964, 7–8, 156–57. Tessin, *Studieresor,* 177. Sebastiani, *Viaggio curioso,* in Schiavo, *Fontana di Trevi,* 271, ". . . il portico di 4 colonne di ordine Corinto . . . la pittura dell'Endimione del Bacicci, gli specchi pinti dallo Stanchi . . ."

44.　Above, pp. 112, 116, 266.

45.　AChigi 517, fols. 52, 52v, 62.

46.　AChigi 520, fols. 144, 150, 155, 159, 160, 161.

47.　AChigi 516, fol. 70v–71, for "12 telari per li fregi dipinti attorno detta stanza [C11]," and similar entries for C10, C9, and C8, the friezes to be 4½ *palmi* high. AChigi 457, fol. 232v, 5 Dec. 1667, payment of 50 scudi to "Cesare Marinelli coloraro" for "palmi quattrocento novantaquattro di tele imprimite, da lui fatte in n.° 48 telari per dipingervi fregi per servitio di quattro stanze del nostro palazzo . . ."; fol. 246v, 21 Feb. 1668, final payments on charges of 123.60 scudi to "Monsù Febo d'Artem e Monsù Triton d'Ortrect Pittori Olandesi" and 127.20 scudi to "Gio. Momper Pittore" for "fregi di stanze dipinti a guazzo" in the palace (cf. Golzio, *Documenti,* 73, doc. 3282, 5 Nov. 1667, and docs. 3504 and 3505, 20 Feb. 1668). AChigi 702, unpaginated inventory, lists friezes of painted cloth in C7 and C9 and friezes painted with landscapes and seascapes in C10 and C11.

48.　AChigi 520, fol. 402, "Per haver fatto il ponte nell'Anticamera accanto la sala [*palmi* 45¾ × 47½] per dipingere [C6]"; fol. 157, in C9, "Per haver fatto li Ponti al Pittore per dipingere il solaro simile all'altri [*palmi* 45 × 21]." AChigi 483, 18 July 1667, unpaginated *misura* of the *indoratore* Vincenzo Corallo, for the painted ceilings in C6, C7, and C9.

According to the *misure* of his work, the little-known painter and gilder Vincenzo Corallo worked throughout the palace (below, passim). Corallo lived nearby, in via del Corso (below, n. 126 [chap. 15]), and in 1673 he was busy on another project in the neighborhood, the decoration of S. Marta al Collegio Romano (Marilyn R. Dunn, "Nuns as Art Patrons: The Decoration of S. Marta al Collegio Romano," *Art Bulletin* 70 [1988], 451–77, esp. 458).

49.　Above, n. 20 (chap. 15); and AChigi 702, unpaginated inventory, "Sesta stanza della volta dipinta [C12]."

50.　AChigi 702, unpaginated inventory, "Settima stanza à volta con corniccione attorno, e quadro nel mezzo lavorati in stucco e dorati [C13]," "Ottava stanza à volta con corniccioni di stucco dorati e quadro dipinto [C14]."

51.　Ibid., unpaginated inventory, "Appartamento nobile," Tessin, *Studieresor,* 177.

52.　AChigi 702, unpaginated inventory.

53.　AChigi 520, fols. 121–132, including the reformed windows, the doorframes, and the scaffolding for the painter in each room; AChigi 517, fol. 47, the alignment of the window in C4 with the doors; AChigi 516, fols. 40v–42v, including reference to a fireplace in C3 and the frame of the baldacchino and portrait of Clement IX under the baldacchino in C2. AChigi 702, unpaginated inventory, "Nell'Appartamento nobile de quadri attacato alla sudetta galleria [C17]," the furnishings of the rooms, without fireplace equipment. AChigi 483, 18 July 1667, unpaginated *misura* of the *indoratore* Corallo, for the "Stanza acc.to detta che segue [C3] dov'è il Camino" with its painted ceiling.

54.　AChigi 516, fols. 44–45, for the tables, *cassapanchi,* and door to the "luoghi communi," all in the "Stanza accanto detta [C17] oscura, che risponde nella scalla maestra"; fol. 70 for two frames, each 14 × 9½ *palmi* "per due battaglie nella stanza oscura accanto la galleria."

55.　Tessin, *Studieresor,* 176–77. AChigi 702, unpaginated inventory, fills twenty-one pages with a list of paintings in the palace, without specifying their locations.

56.　AChigi 702, unpaginated inventory, "Nell'appartamento nobile de quadri attacato alla sudetta galleria [C17]," for the *portiere,* curtains, and a "torciere di noce . . . largo per posarvi la gabbia del Papagallo." AChigi 484, unpaginated, contains an account for the work of the *festarolo* Giuseppe Fornari in 1668, including, "Adì 12 [maggio] per haver in diversi giorni atacato quattro stantie di Quatri Grandi e Picoli quantità dalla suffita a Basso al Apartamento verso il vicolo del Piombo et messo a tutte le porte di detto Apartamento le sue portiere con arme di S. E., scudi 12."

57.　AChigi 516, fols. 42v–43v, for the wood frames at the several windows; AChigi 520, fols. 163–167, "Galleria al detto Piano [C17]," for the remodeling of this room, and fol. 406, in C18, "la finestra, che risponde nella Galleria sopra la porticella . . ."

58.　AChigi 702, unpaginated inventory, "Nella galleria, Quattro bandinelle grandi di telette ligata di follero e seta di color cremesino, che riparano il sole nelle due arcate di detta galleria di tre teli per ciascheduna [17 *palmi* high]," and similar curtains in the upper parts of the arches and in the two arches opposite, toward the stair.

59.　Sebastiani, *Viaggio curioso,* quoted by Schiavo, *Fontana di Trevi,* 271, the gallery painted with flowers and fruits, and antique portraits on wood *sgabelloni;* Tessin, *Studieresor,* 177, "eine artige perspectivisch gemahlte Gallerei mit 11 marmernen busten"; AChigi 457, fol. 296, 19 Dec. 1668, payment of 45 scudi to "Sig.r Girolamo Troppa

Pittore . . . d' haver dipinto nella Galleria del nostro Palazzo . . . la Flora con puttini e tre pezzi di Arazzi finti per servitio della nostra Guardarobba" (Golzio, *Documenti*, 18, and 74, doc. 4162, 12 Dec. 1668); AChigi 702, unpaginated inventory, "Nella galleria [C17] . . . 10 scabelli di noce torniti ricoperti di marocchino cremesino . . ."

60.   AChigi 520, fols. 62–86, and, for the scaffolding for the painters, fols. 408–409. AChigi 516, fols. 13–17, woodwork, including new ceilings. AChigi 483, 18 July 1667, unpaginated *misura* of the *indoratore* Corallo, for the painting and gilding of the ceilings, doors, and window embrasures.

61.   AChigi 520, fols. 87–90; AChigi 516, fols. 18v–19, including the ceiling, the three windows, and the "6 sportelli alli trè finestre in detta galleria, graticciati, fatti à gelosia [each 3¼ × 3½ *palmi*]." AChigi 483, 18 July 1667, unpaginated *misura* of the *indoratore* Corallo, for the painting and gilding of the ceiling.

62.   AChigi 702, unpaginated inventory, "Ultimo Appartamento nobile di sopra, Galleria . . ."

63.   AChigi 520, fols. 17 (the façade wall) and 19–21 (the southeast and northwest walls).

64.   Ibid., fols. 115–119 (masonry) and fol. 409 (scaffolding for the painter); AChigi 516, fol. 28 (windows, doors, and wood ceiling). AChigi 483, 18 July 1667, unpaginated *misura* of the *indoratore* Corallo for the painting of the ceiling, including the figures of *Religione, Speranza,* and *Carità;* for the ceiling of the Biblioteca Alessandrina, see John Beldon Scott, "S. Ivo alla Sapienza and Borromini's Symbolic Language," *Journal of the Society of Architectural Historians* 41 (1982), 294–317, esp. 313–14.

65.   AChigi 516, fols. 77–81, works "fatti in conformità del disegno consignatoli dall'Architetto secondo il modello principiato per mostra, con alcuni altri lavori acresciutovi, di più del Disegno stabilito . . ." On 4 August 1666 Chicheri received his first payment "a buon conto dei lavori che fa per la libraria del nostro palazzo ai SS^ti Apostoli" (AChigi 457, fol. 162r; cf. Golzio, *Documenti*, 34, doc. 2288, 3 Aug. 1666).

66.   AChigi 516, a single folded sheet at the end of the volume, 16 Sept. 1669, "Misura e stima delli lavori di legniame fatti da M° Antonio Chicheri falegniame, in fare la nova libreriola bianca nella stanza accanto la libreria grande di noce nel Palazzo dell'E^mo Sig^e Card^le Chigi posto alla Piazza di SS^ti Apostoli."

67.   AChigi 520, fols. 106–111, and, for scaffolding for the painter, fol. 409. AChigi 483, 18 July 1667, unpaginated *misura* of the *indoratore* Corallo, for the painting of the ceiling.

68.   AChigi 520, fols. 12–14 and, for scaffolding for painting, fol. 409; AChigi 483, 18 July 1667, unpaginated *misura* of the *indoratore* Corallo, for the painting of the "soffittino" of the "Cappelletta"; AChigi 517, fols. 33–33v, including its marble altar; AChigi 516, fols. 68–69, "Cappella

di Cima," including "il fusto della cancellata, che tramezza la cappella . . . [12½ × 12 *palmi*]; AChigi 702, unpaginated inventory, "Nella cappelletta [E8] contigua alla detta stantia . . . un baldacchino sopra l'altare della detta cappella . . . [11 × 6 *palmi*]."

69.   AChigi 520, fol. 114.

70.   Ibid., fols. 95–99, "Stanza accanto escie alle scale [E13] . . . Muro di una porta murata nel Cantone, che da detta stanza andava alla libraria . . . ; Stanza accanto revolta verso il cortile, e và alla libraria [E12] . . . Per haver rotto il muro e fatto la porta, che passa alla libraria [and the two steps at the door]."

71.   AChigi 517, fol. 43, in E6, "il scalino della porticella accanto la camera infacciata verso la scaletta," and in E9, a step at the door.

72.   AChigi 520, fol. 95, in room E14, "Muro di un vano di camino murato . . ."; AChigi 517, fol. 45, apparently in E11, "Per haver relustrato, è rotato di novo il Camino nella detta Stanza di marmo . . ."

73.   AChigi 516, fol. 21v, in E16, "4 sportelli fatti à gelosia," each 2 × 3½ *palmi*.

74.   AChigi 702, unpaginated inventory, "Retro Camera verso la Piazza de SS. Apostoli," E9, containing only a crimson and gold revetment and a *portiera;* and "Stantia contigua alla sudetta verso il Cortile [E10], Vi è un letto di tabbino à onde cremesino con bandinelle n° sei con il cielo e cascate doppie . . . con la sua coperta di detto drappo . . . e con il suo tornaletto . . ."

75.   Ibid., "Stanzino sul Cantone nell'Appartamento di sopra che guarda nel Cortile de Mancini," E17, including the box and shelves "da tenere scritture," the "cassetta di noce da tener il foco sotto i piedi," and the "occhialone di longa vista . . . lon. pm. 6."

76.   AChigi 703, "Inventario del Palazzo a SS^ti Apostoli, S. Card. Flavio Chigi," fol. 222, "9 scaldaletti."

77.   Sebastiani, *Viaggio curioso,* quoted by Schiavo, *Fontana di Trevi,* 272, "Appartamento pian terreno habitabile per la state"; Tessin, *Studieresor,* 176, "die sommerzimber."

78.   AChigi 520, fols. 170–190, including scaffolding for the painter in B2, B3, and B4, and fol. 276 for scaffolding "alla stanza al pian terreno verso il vicolo, accanto Mancini dove è la volta [40½ × 35¾ *palmi*]." AChigi 516, fols. 52–53, windows and doors. AChigi 517, fols. 38–38v, stonework. AChigi 483, 18 July 1667, unpaginated *misura* of the *indoratore* Corallo, "Stanza accanto detta à volta infacciata [B6], Per haver dipinto la Volta sudetta long. palmi 66½ larg. palmi 27 con una balaustrata che incorne per 4 faccie con cimasa, e basa, diversi Pilastri, che risaltano, requadrati con n° 6 figure del Naturale, sopradetta di Chiaroscuro con n° 4 busti sopradetti con n° 6 Vasi grandi, intagliati e lumeggiati d'oro, con diverse fiori dentro con Aria con diverse Ucellami con bassi rilievi nelli Pilastri, e Mascare, scudi 140," and a gilded cornice at the impost of the vault, and three window embrasures with perspectives (il-

lustrations of these last paintings are in Schiavo, *Fontana di Trevi,* 272–73, Figs. 168, 169; Schiavo's suggestion that the paintings might be by Francesco Galli must now be abandoned); "Stanza terrena à volta verso il Vicolo [B1]," chiaroscuro painting on vault; and painted wood ceilings in B2, B3, and B4 (illustrated in Schiavo, *Fontana di Trevi,* 276–78, Figs. 170–72).

79. AChigi 517, fol. 134v, "Cappella segreta al Piano terreno, che riesce all'Entrone," the altar. AChigi 516, fols. 53–54, "Cappelletta a detto piano terreno," including doors, an *armario,* the wood ceiling, 15½ × 12 *palmi,* and "il fusto di noce che serra il corritore della cappella," 11 × 14 *palmi.* AChigi 702, unpaginated inventory, in room B6, "una soprafinestra e sottofinestra della cappella." AChigi 457, fol. 325, 7 June 1669, final payment to Vincenzo Corallo on a total bill of 2,479.95 scudi, for painting and gilding 15 April–30 December 1668, including the ceiling of the ground-floor chapel (as described in the *giustificazione,* AChigi 484, unpaginated), 15 April 1668–30 December 1668, "dipintoci lo Spirito Santo con Cherubini, et nuvole, quale fù guasto, et dipintoci di novo il Dio Padre con Gloria di Angeli, Cherubini, e nuvole in detto long. p. 16, largo p. 13¼ colorito" (cf. Golzio, *Documenti,* 75, doc. 228, 6 June 1669). AChigi 520, fol. 353, the scaffolding "per l'indoratore per indorare la cappelletta [19 × 12 *palmi*]."

80. AChigi 519, unpaginated *misura* of masonry, 30 June 1669, "Muro che divide il Corritore [B5] di detta Cappelletta [B26] . . . Per haver rotto il muro, e fatto il vano della finestra per ascoltare la Messa alli Palafrenieri in detta facciata . . . Per haver rotto il muro, e fatto il vano della finestra nel muro del tramezzo, che divide la stanza infacciata [B5] per dare il lume à detta cappella della detta stanza . . ."

81. AChigi 520, fols. 194–198; AChigi 516, fol. 52v, the two windows over doors from adjacent rooms. AChigi 483, 18 July 1667, unpaginated *misura* of the *indoratore* Corallo, "Stanza oscura [B15] accanto la Galleria, Per havere dipinto la volta della detta stanza con un'ornamento d'Architettura che fa la balaustrata, con pilastri simile, con balaustri e parapetto di ferro con diverse Ucellami nell'Aria . . . [52 × 28¾ *palmi*]."

82. Tessin, *Studieresor,* 176; AChigi 702, unpaginated inventory, "Nel cortiletto," listing the sculptures. AChigi 520, fols. 168–170, the construction of the courtyard B16. AChigi 517, fol. 41, "Cortiletto della Fontana al piano di detto verso Mancini." AChigi 483, 18 July 1667, unpaginated *misura* of the *indoratore* Corallo, "Galleria Terrena verso il Cortile, Per haver dipinto la volta della detta Galleria [dimensions left blank] dipinto ad uso di pergolata . . . ," with fruits, birds, vases, flowers, feigned architecture, bells, putti, etc.

83. AChigi 702, unpaginated inventory, "Appartamento d'abbasso," the revetments, furniture, and *scabelli,* and, toward the end of the inventory, the sculptures and other

objects of stone in each room. Golzio, *Documenti,* 18 and 65, doc. 714, 13 June 1673, "un Conto di lavori delle Porte e Nicchie di Verde Antico et altro da lui fatto per servitio dell'appartamento nobile a pian terreno del Palazzo di S.E. a SS.ti Apostoli . . ." AChigi 516, fols. 55–55v, "piedestalli che servono sotto le statue dell'Appartamento terreno che attacca con li SS^{ri} Mancini," listing many pedestals of various sizes. Golzio, *Documenti,* 14 and 65, doc. 684, 5 May 1673, payment for "un sasso rustico di marmo bigio fatto venire da Carrara per servitio di una fontana che si fa nell'appartamento nobile del pian terreno del nostro Palazzo a SS.ti Apostoli . . ." Sebastiani, *Viaggio curioso,* quoted in Schiavo, *Fontana di Trevi,* 272, "Stanza della fontana, vasca di pietra Egittia, che dà acqua ad arbitrio." Tessin, *Studieresor,* 176, noting that, in B1, "in der mitten wahr eine grosse cuve mit einer fontaine."

84. AChigi 520, fol. 389, "Stanza terrena nel'Vicolo accanto Mancini dove è la Porticella Segreta . . . la porta segreta . . . che escie in strada . . ." AChigi 516, fols. 52–52v, the door. AChigi 517, fol. 40v, "Porticella segreta verso il Vicolo."

85. AChigi 520, fol. 347, in the Entrone B7, "Muro del vano di una porta murata in dispensa," with plaster over it; fols. 382–384, "Stanze terrene dove e la Dispensa," including the door to the portico and "Muro della porta murata che da detta stanza usciva nel Entrone." AChigi 516, fols. 57–57v, including the shelving and the door "che da detta passa alla stanza dove al presente si fà la computisteria [B9]." AChigi 702, unpaginated inventory, "Mobili et altre robbe esistenti in Dispensa," listing *credenzoni,* tables, and other furnishings, including "Letto del Dispensiere," with its mattress, sheets, and blanket.

86. AChigi 520, fols. 208–212, describes these rooms, with their pavings, windows, and doors. AChigi 516, fol. 57 (see previous note), identifies the rooms next to the *dispensa* (B8) as the *computisteria,* at least at the time of the *misura.*

87. AChigi 520, fols. 204–206, for their remodeling.

88. AChigi 520, fols. 199–201 for the remodeling of this room, without its identification as *bottiglieria.* AChigi 516, fol. 57v, on the ground floor, "Bottigliaria," including its window toward the garden. AChigi 517, fol. 58v, stair S3, including "porta che si è aperta di novo alla Bottigliaria al repiano della scala."

89. AChigi 522, unpaginated, 10 Jan.–31 Dec. 1689, "Per haver rotto e guasto la selciata nel pian terreno dove è il Portico per d'avanti la bottiglieria e dispensa . . . [to repair the] condotto che porta l'acqua in credenza [A9?] e bottiglieria . . ."

90. AChigi 516, fol. 57v, for the new tables and *credenzone.* AChigi 702, unpaginated inventory, "Mobili et altre robbe esistenti in Bottiglieria," for a list of furnishings, including the two beds with bedding, one of them "per il giovane."

91. AChigi 520, fols. 224–229 (the *rimesse*), 374–382

("Mezzanini novi sopra le rimesse," with the new stair); fols. 392–396 (including the new "Selleria dietro la Rimessa accanto"). AChigi 517, fols. 73–74, "Remesse resarcite di novo che stanno nel sudetto Cortile." AChigi 516, fols. 62–65, woodwork, including the new wood floors for the mezzanines, the "Appartamento detta la Sellaria [entered] sopra la quarta rimessa."

92. AChigi 520, fols. 384–385, "Remessa sotto l'Appartamento verso il Cortile dove è la scala lumaca [S4], confina con portico." AChigi 517, fol. 74v, "Rimessa in faccia l'Entrone, dietro alla Statua," its door; and fol. 126v, "Rimessa fatta di novo sotto l'Alcova." AChigi 483, unpaginated *misura* of whitewashing 1664–68, including "E più per havere imbiancato la Remessa grande a volta a mano manca nel Cortile grande a volta" (cf. Golzio, *Documenti,* 49, doc. 4053). AChigi 519, unpaginated *misura* of masonry, 30 June 1669, "Rimessa sotto l'Alcova" (a reinforcing arch and a new door to the courtyard). For the statue, see AChigi 520, fol. 337, "la statua, che sta a capo l'Entrone," and fols. 370–374, "Ornamento attorno alla Statua in faccia l'Entrone del Palazzo."

93. AChigi 520, fol. 281, "Per haver rotto il muro à piedi detta scala fatto il vano della porta che escie alle rimesse di vano [9 × 3½ × 2 *palmi*]."

94. Ibid., fols. 237–238, "Cantina del cantone che seg. dette dove erano le cucine vecchie hoggi la Pasticciaria [A4]"; fol. 240, "Cantina accanto dove era la cucina in faccia [A6]."

95. Ibid., fols. 252–253, "Cantina nel cantone verso la piazza per Pasticciaria," including the "fornello"; and fol. 269. AChigi 517, fol. 60, door of the "Pasticciaria."

96. Ibid., fols. 253–255, "Andito [A11] avanti detta cucina e dove è la dispensa per il Coco" (distinct from the *dispensa* in room B8). AChigi 517, fol. 60, door for the "Dispensa del Coco."

97. AChigi 520, fols. 256–258, "Cantina accanto dove è il pozzo"; fols. 266–269, for the basins and drain; and fol. 386, for the plumbing. AChigi 516, fols. 61–61v, for woodwork including the shelves.

98. AChigi 520, fols. 258–262 and 265, excavation, "murello delle pile," fireplace. AChigi 516, fols. 60–61, doors, windows, shelves, and rack for pots. AChigi 702, unpaginated inventory, "Robbe e mobili esistenti nella cucina secreta," including pots, utensils, and three beds.

99. AChigi 520, fol. 196, vaults over A13 (the old cistern) and A14, and excavation 10 *palmi* deep in A14; fol. 264, excavation in A13, 7½ *palmi* deep. AChigi 516, fol. 61v, "il cancello, dove stà il carbone," and the door to the "stanza della legna."

100. AChigi 520, fols. 232–246.

101. Ibid., fols. 243–246.

102. Ibid., fol. 351, "Per haver cavato la terra nella cantina sotto la dispensa [B8] . . . [44 × 23 (*ragguagliato*) × 12 (*ragguagliato*) *palmi*]."

103. AChigi 516, fols. 59–59v, in the basement, "Credenza accanto detta [Cantina del Sig.re Cardinale]," shelves, *sciacquatore,* "porticella, che va al stanzino." AChigi 522, unpaginated, 10 June 1688–31 Dec. 1688, "Giardino incontro SS. Apostoli," a pipe from a fountain that carries water to the *credenza* and *bottiglieria;* and 10 Jan. 1689–31 Dec. 1689, repair to the "condotto che porta l'acqua in credenza e bottiglieria."

104. AChigi 520, fol. 353, "Cantina del Bottigliero." AChigi 516, fol. 58, ". . . la cantina de S.re Simonelli," and "Cantina del Sig.re Cardinale," next to the *credenza.* AChigi 573, the roll of the cardinal's *famiglia* 1666–75, lists Nicolò Simonelli among the gentlemen; the *bottigliere* was Gioacchino Marij.

105. AChigi 520, fol. 352, "Scaletta che scende in cantina accanto la scala à branchi [S3]," including a door to the "cantina à mezze scale," perhaps a mezzanine under S3. AChigi 516, fol. 58, "Scaletta, che cala in cantina sotto la bottigliaria."

106. AChigi 520, fols. 17–26, the *misura* of the heightened walls.

107. Ibid., fols. 36–37, "Muri rialzati sopra la Guardaroba"; fols. 43–49, "Guardaroba al detto piano." AChigi 516, fols. 8v–11, "Guardaroba," including five *credenzoni,* the largest measuring 38 × 9¾ *palmi,* with sixteen doors.

108. AChigi 517, fol. 67v, "Porta della Guardaroba sopra le Stanze dell'Appartamento di Cima," from stair S4. Golzio, *Documenti,* 67, doc. 2266, 15 Jan. 1672–31 May 1675, *misura* of masonry including "Loggia scoperta fatta di nuovo sopra il tetto vecchio del Palazzo a capo la scala lumaca." A rooftop loggia is shown on Falda's engraved view of the palace, but not on Specchi's later view (Figs. 210, 211).

109. AChigi 520, fols. 27–31, 33–35.

110. AChigi 516, fols. 4v–8v, "Galera sopra la Sala." AChigi 520, fols. 32 and 40–43, their plaster and paving.

111. AChigi 520, fols. 55–57, "Stanzino dietro li luoghi comuni a mezza detta scaletta" and "Luoghi comuni accanto"; fol. 346, installation in the wall of stair S1, "2 condotti delli luoghi comuni," 46 *palmi* in length.

112. AChigi 516, fol. 43v, in gallery C17, "2 telari . . . che dà lume alla scala maestra . . . senza sportelli [each *palmi* 9¾ × 11, and glazed]." AChigi 702, unpaginated inventory, "Nella galleria [C17] . . . altre due bandinelle della medesima robba che ricoprano l'altre due arcate di contro verso la scala di teli 2½ per ciascheduna . . . [12½ *palmi* long]."

113. AChigi 520, fols. 215–223, "Scala maestra comincia al Piano Nobile sino al pian Terreno, Rapezzi fatti avanti che s'incollassi tutta . . . Seguono li lavori fatti doppo in detta scala per incollarla tutta . . ."

114. Ibid., fols. 58–60, "Repiano di cima della scala maestra," including "Muro di una finestra murata in detta scala dove era la rota [6½ × 4½ × 3 *palmi*]."

115.   Ibid., fol. 343, "In cima la scala maestra sopra tetto, Muro rialzato sopra la scala maestra in cima sopra tetto, che fà il campaniletto per la campana," and the installation of the bell; fol. 345, "Per haver rotto le num° 3 volte sopra il Repiano della Scala, e messo e murato li 3 canali dove passa la corda della campanella, con suo muro attorno." AChigi 457, fol. 212v, 22 June 1667, payment to the founder Jacomo Pucci "per una campana del peso di libbre 123" for the palace (cf. Golzio, *Documenti*, 41, doc. 2971, 20 June 1667).

116.   AChigi 520, fols. 50–52, "Scaletta che cala a basso avanti detta porta [the door of the *guardaroba* F17]," with twenty-four treads, each 5 *palmi* wide, in two flights.

117.   Ibid., fols. 247–252, "Scala, che dal Portico và in cucina vecchia in facciata, e cantine accanto [S2]," with the landing B24 and neighboring "sottoscala" B23; fols. 262–263, "Passo [S6] che dalla cucina sbocca à capo la scala nova sudetta [S2], che và alle cucine vecchie in facciata," built over part of an old cistern (above, p. 309 and n. 99 [chap. 15]), with twelve "cordoni" and eleven passages of ordinary pavement between them to form the ramped stair.

118.   AChigi 483, unpaginated *misura* for whitewashing 1664–68, including "Per haver imbiancato la scala a branchetti, che và dal detto Piano [secondo piano] al Piano terreno dalla parte del Giardino con doi stanziole in detta Scala, e la detta Scala in Cima, e alta dove viene il Lume in Cima sopra alli tetti . . . (cf. Golzio, *Documenti*, 49, doc. 4053). AChigi 516, fol. 56v, in B13, "porticella che và alla scaletta à branchi [S3] . . . segue un'altra simile che và alla cantina . . ." AChigi 520, fol. 352, "Scaletta che scende in cantina accanto la scala à branchi [S3]."

119.   AChigi 483, unpaginated *misura* for whitewashing 1664–68, including "E più per haver imbiancato la scala, che va dalla detta Galleria [E18], alla Galleria a Piano terreno . . ." (cf. Golzio, *Documenti*, 48, doc. 4053). AChigi 520, fols. 66, 89, 167, and AChigi 517, fols. 44v, 51, for doors to the stair.

120.   AChigi 520, fols. 278–287, "Scala lumaca nova verso Mancini," the construction of the stair, seventy pieces of pipe for its latrine, the door to the carriage room, the door to the courtyard B16, room D2 over the alcove, and the "luogo comune à cima detta scala." AChigi 517, fols. 70v–71v, stonework including the eighty-four steps and five sills. AChigi 516, fol. 49, three doors.

121.   AChigi 520, fol. 388, for the stair at A6. AChigi 517, fol. 61, "Scala segreta della Cucina." AChigi 520, fols. 213–214, "Scaletta segreta dietro dette stanze [B9, B10], che escie all'Entrone nel' Cortile," a stair that "cala in cantina."

122.   AVR, SS. 12 Apostoli, Stati d'Anime, 1667–1692, fol. 16, 1668; fol. 40, 1669; fol. 70v, 1670.

123.   AVR, SS. 12 Apostoli, Stati d'Anime, 1667–1692, e.g., 1669, members of the Chigi *famiglia* lived in houses 112, 213, 214, and 266; 1676, members of the Chigi *famiglia* lived in houses 194, 213, 220, 242, 284, 300, 302, 305, and 310; 1677, members of the Chigi *famiglia* lived in houses 164, 171, 174, 182, 250, 252, 255, 257, 258, 260, and 264.

124.   AChigi 457, fol. 136v, 27 Feb. 1666, 110 scudi paid to Valeriano Mandosio "per la piggione di due case contigue al Giardino del nostro Palazzo a SS^ti Apostoli cioè la prima a canto detto Giardino a ragione di scudi 130, e l'altra susseguente a ragione di scudi 90 l'anno prese per servitio della nostra Guardarobba, e questi per sei mesi da finire l'6 giugno prossimo" (cf. AChigi 483, unpaginated *misura* for whitewashing 1664–68, including, the third entry, "E più per haver imbiancato nel Vicolo le Case dove si fà la Guardarobba, e la Computisteria sono stanze intutto ventidoi," and more work in the two houses); AChigi 457, fol. 217, 16 July 1667, payment for expenses "nella lite fatta contro i SS^ri Mandosi nella causa della compra delle Case contigue al nostro Palazzo a SS^ti Apostoli . . . ," and fol. 222, 20 Aug. 1667, 14,286.92½ scudi paid to "SS^ri Archangelo, Prospero, et Ottavio fratelli de Mandosij" for "case contigue al nostro Palazzo a SS^ti Apostoli . . . in strada del Corso, che fanno angolo incontro la chiesa di Sta Maria in via lata et nell'Vicolo che da detta strada del Corso va alla Piazza di SS^ti Apostoli appresso da una banda le nostre stalle e dall'altra li beni della Chiesa e Compagnia di Sta Caterina di Siena . . ."

125.   AChigi 483, unpaginated *misura* for whitewashing and painting, 1664–68, including, in the "casa ch'era de' Mendosi tutti l'Appartamenti sono in tutto la detta Casa n° 28 stanze con n° 4 coritori . . . undici mezzanili con un corritore . . . 3 Rimesse nel Vicolo . . . l'Intrada incontro a Sta Maria Inviolata grande à Volta grande con la scala à lumaga sino in Cima . . ." AChigi 519, unpaginated, *misure* for masonry 1666–78, including, 15 Sept. 1667–31 Dec. 1671, ". . . Rapezzi fatti nel Palazzetto della famiglia di Sua Eminenza . . . comprata da SS^ri Mandosij," detailing the division of the house into apartments for specific persons in the cardinal's household, and including work in the *rimesse* toward the vicolo, the shops, and the "scala lumaca maestra di detto Palazzetto." Plans of the ground floor and *piano nobile* of a palace on the site of the Mandosi property are in the Archivio Chigi (Chigi P.VII.10, fols. 59, 60), but the details specified in the documents (e.g., the "scala lumaca maestra") do not match the drawings.

126.   AChigi 483, unpaginated, 3 July 1668, 289.30 scudi paid to the "Ven. Compagnia di S^a Caterina di Siena di Roma . . . per la piggione di tre Case di essa Compagnia poste nel' Corso incontro quasi la Chiesa di S^a M^a in Via Lata prese in affitto da detta per servitio della famiglia di S. Em^za per annua piggione di scudi 335 l'anno per anni tre cominc. cioè per una di dette case già habitata dal' Sig. Curtio Gallucci a ragione di scudi 100 l'anno li 25 Nov^re pros., et per le altre due cioe una già habitata dalla Sig^ra Flavia Contini a ragione di scudi 190, e l'altra habitata già dalla Sig^ra Caterina Dattoli a ragione di scudi 45 l'anno dal

giorno della consegna delle chiavi . . ."; AChigi 484, unpaginated, 6 June 1669, 200.84 scudi paid to the "Compagnia di S. Catherina da Siena . . . sono per saldo e final pagamento della piggione delle Case al Corso che tenemo per la famiglia di S. Em^za Padrone e questi per sei mesi finiti à tutti li 24 maggio prossimo cioè delle tre prime case che pagano scudi 335 l'anno e dell'altra casa ultimamente presa che paga scudi 50 l'anno e questa per sei mesi finiti nel sudetto giorno 24 maggio." AChigi 519, unpaginated *misure* of masonry 1666–78, including remodeling and repairs for apartments similar to those of the "palazzetto"; apparently next to the "palazzetto" was the "Bottega sotto la Casa di S. Caterina di Siena dove habita il Sr Coralli Indoratore," who was responsible for extensive painting and gilding in the palace.

127.   AChigi 519, unpaginated *misura,* 30 June 1669, ". . . il Palazzino dell'Em^mo Mancini dove habita il Sr Cav^e S. Piero, e Sr D. Geronimo Mercurij Maestro di Casa di Sua Em^za . . ."; 12 Apr. 1670, "Casino dell'Em^mo Mancini dove habita il Sig^r D. Gironimo Mercurio . . ."; 15 Apr. 1671, the same house, its roof 55 *palmi* wide—i.e., the width of room B18, which must have stood behind the house; and other references in this document. For Palazzo Mancini, see Armando Schiavo, *Palazzo Mancini,* Palermo, 1969; p. 114 documents the "casa grande" at the corner of the block and the two other houses, in 1651.

128.   Many separate houses are mentioned in the same *misura* of masonry cited above, AChigi 519, and other accounts of work; and rental payments are recorded, e.g., in AChigi 457, fol. 255v.

129.   Schiavo, *Palazzo Mancini,* 121, citing *avvisi* of 17 March 1674 and 31 March 1674.

130.   The construction is documented in AChigi 519, unpaginated *misura,* 15 Sept. 1667–31 Dec. 1671; other references to the kitchen are in the same manuscript, passim.

131.   AChigi 519, unpaginated *misura,* 15 Sept. 1667–31 Dec. 1671, "Corritore sotterraneo," for the construction of the corridor; AChigi 483, unpaginated *misura,* for the whitewashing of "il Corritore, che passa dal Cortile grande alla cucina communa longo à Volta"; AChigi 516, fol. 64, ". . . la porticella in testa il corritore, che va alla cucina comune . . ."

132.   AChigi 702, unpaginated inventory, "Robbe e mobili esistenti in Cucina commune," including "Letto" and "Letto per il garzone." AChigi 573, "Rolo della famiglia . . . ," 1666–1675, including "Pietro Pulciani Coco Com^e, Innocentio Bandoni Aiut^e, Gio. Lannini Garzone."

133.   AChigi 457, fol. 169r, 25 Sept. 1666, the first in a series of payments "a buon conto" to Antonio Cantalupi and Giovanni Maria Sorrisi, *muratori,* for "la nuova stalla che si fà per servitio del nostro Palazzo a SS^ti Apostoli" (cf. Golzio, *Documenti,* 66–67, doc. 2266); fol. 193r, 18 Feb. 1667, the first payment "a buon conto" to Ambrosio Appiani *scarpellino* for "la nuova stalla contigua al nostro Palazzo a SS^ti Apostoli."

134.   Chigi P.VII.13, fol. 2, 5 Sept. 1666, "Sito dove và fabricato la stalla nuova che fà fare Sua Emin^za."

135.   AChigi 519, unpaginated but toward the end of the volume, 8 Oct. 1666–2 Mar. 1668, *misura* for masonry for "il novo Stallone nella Piazza di SS^ti Apostoli," with the loggia above, the work amounting to 8,991.66 scudi. Chigi P.VII.10, fol. 81, shows a plan, section, and partial elevation of the "Primo pensiero della stalla non fù fatto e si fece come al presente."

136.   AChigi 703, fols. 243–248.

137.   AChigi 519, unpaginated, 15 Sept. 1667–31 Dec. 1671, "Lavori fatti nelle Rimesse nel vicolo di S. Marcello sotto detto Palazzetto [della famiglia]," itemizing work in the three *rimesse* (and a fourth small room used for hay); AChigi 483, unpaginated *misura* of whitewashing 1664–68, in "la casa ch'era de' Mendosi," "E più per havere imbiancato 3 Rimesse nel Vicolo" (cf. Golzio, *Documenti,* 66, doc. 2266, and 50, doc. 4053).

138.   AChigi 519, unpaginated *misura,* 15 Apr. 1671, "rimessa sotto la casa di S. Caterina di Siena per le Carrozze nobili," and another "Rimessa delle Carrozze nel Corso"; 12 Apr. 1670, in the "Casino di S. Jacomo dell'Incurabili posto nella Piazza di SS^ti Apostoli, che Sua Emin^za tiene à pigione per li Sig^ri Cav^ri et Altri," a "Rimessa sotto il detto Casino verso la Piazza de SS^ti Apostoli," which had formerly been a shop. AChigi 483, unpaginated, 18 Mar. 1668, a *rimessa* rented from "Mons^re Illmo Gavotti"; 28 July 1668, a *rimessa* behind a "stalla con fenile posta nel vicolo de fenili per andare alla Chiesa di Sta Maria in Via," both rented from the Cistercians of S. Croce in Gerusalemme; 30 July 1668, "rimessa posta nella strada da Trevi à S. Nicola," rented.

139.   Golzio, *Documenti,* 68–69, docs. 1414–2412; and 76, doc. 2240, for a bit of painting "nella muraglia della casa della Sig.a Cibbi per la veduta della Logietta fatta di novo," 13 June 1684. The building before remodeling (but with the bridge across the vicolo del Piombo) is shown in three plans, Chigi P.VII.10, fols. 56–58.

140.   AChigi 483, unpaginated *misura* of whitewashing 1664–68, "E più per haver dato il Colore di travertino all'Ucelliera à tutti li pilastri, Cornice, e requadri e intorno all'Altezza di doi piani, e dato il bianco di sopra." AChigi 484, unpaginated, another small bill for whitewashing, paid 14 February 1669, including "E più per haver dato il color dentro all'Uccelliera al Giardino . . ."

141.   For painted birds, AChigi 483, 18 July 1667, unpaginated *misura* of the *indoratore* Vincenzo Corallo, passim. In the same *misura,* "Stanzino dell'Ucelliera, Per havere dipinto il Solaretto sopradetto Stanzino long. palmi 27½ larg. palmi 14 . . ."; its position in the *misura* suggests a room in the upper part of the palace, possibly D2, which is the right size and is otherwise unaccounted for in the comprehensive *misura.*

142.   E.g., AChigi 457, 197v, 21 Mar. 1667, "A spese per la nuova fabrica del nostro Palazzo a SS^ti Apostoli scudi

25.10 . . . a Domenico Massimi Ramaro per il prezzo d'una Ucelliera col suo telaro di ferro fatta per detto nostro Palazzo"; AChigi 484, unpaginated, a bill for metalwork by Carlo Mattei Spadaro in 1668, "E più per haver limato e indorato 3 ferri lunghi palmi 14 l'uno che tengono le Gabbie dell'Ucelli all'appartamento di sopra . . ."

143. AChigi 457, passim.

144. AChigi 516, fol. 49, "Stanza detto il Romitorio," in the garden, to judge from the location of the entry in the *misura,* its wood ceiling of 28 × 15 *palmi;* fols. 73–73v, "Stanzino del Romitorio," the two tables, the prie-dieu, and the "tamburro di noce fatto à telaro con 4 sportelli in faccia, e nelli fianchi longo il vano palmi 3⅔ × 4¼ × 1¾ . . ."

145. AChigi 483, 18 July 1667, unpaginated *misura* of the *indoratore* Corallo, "Per havere dipinto un quadro nella Porta della stanza del Romitorio, con sua cornice indorata, e dipintovi un'Eremita con paesino, e diverse Vedute; Per havere dipinto il quadro sopra la porta d. il Romitorio con molte vedute di paesi, et una figurina che esprime un Eremita con sua cornice indorata attorno."

146. The construction of the façade toward the piazza and the sides of the palace is recorded in AChigi 520, fols. 288–336; it includes (fol. 302) "Per il muro della Cortina di mattoni rotati, con acqua murati in calce sottile log. p. 95¾ alt. p. 44½. Difalco per le fenestre n° 7 al pian di cima alt. l'una p. 17 lag. p. 8½ seg. n° 6 altre del pian' nobile log. p. 10½ alt. p. 17 segue quella di mezzo log. p. 14 alt. p. 17 inf. scudi 58.20," and (fol. 305) "Colla nella facciata log. p. 120 al. p. 26 da sotto il Dado del piano nobile à basso Difalco le finestre . . ." (i.e., the stucco of the ground floor, below the "cortina" of bricks of the two upper stories). The stonework is recorded in AChigi 517, fols. 1–37 (partially published by Golzio, *Documenti,* 55–56, doc. 233). AChigi 483, unpaginated *misura* of the *imbiancatore* Antonio Martignani (partially published by Golzio, *Documenti,* 48–51, doc. 4053, esp. p. 50) makes clear the original distinctions of color, texture, and material in the façade.

147. Sladek, "Palazzo Chigi-Odescalchi," 483, curiously states that the façade was exceptional in Rome and had no successor there.

148. For a cogent discussion of Bernini's possible debt to Michelangelo or Palladio, in Palazzo Chigi and other works, see Christof Thoenes, "Bernini architetto tra Palladio e Michelangelo," in *Gian Lorenzo Bernini Architetto e l'architettura europea del Sei-Settecento,* Rome, 1983, I, 105–34.

149. Domenico Bernini, *Vita del cavalier Gio. Lorenzo Bernino . . . ,* Rome, 1713, 108; Filippo Baldinucci, *Vita del Cavaliere Gio. Lorenzo Bernino: scultore, architetto, e pittore,* Rome, 1682, 39.

150. Giovanni Pietro Rossini, *Il Mercurio errante delle grandezze di Roma, tanto antiche che moderne,* 3d ed., Rome, 1715, 43, "Questo grandissimo Palazzo io l'ho veduto fabricare da' fondamenti al tempo d'Alessandro VII . . ."

151. AChigi 457, fol. 324, 29 May 1669, final payment to the *muratori* Jacomo and Carlo Beccaria, for *muratura* 1664–67 valued at 15,103.98 scudi; fol. 325v, 7 June 1669, final payment to the *scarpellino* Gabrielle Renzi for stonework 1664–69 valued at 10,640.47 scudi; fol. 288v, 27 Oct. 1668, final payment to Vincenzo Corallo *indoratore* for work 1666–68 valued at 6,898.67 scudi, and fol. 325, 7 June 1669, for further work 15 April–30 December 1668 valued at 2,479.95 scudi. AChigi 516, *misura* of work by the *falegname* Antonio Chiccheri 1665–69 valued at 13,308.39½ scudi. Total, 48,431.46½ scudi. Cf. Golzio, *Documenti,* 53–54 (doc. 226), 55–56 (doc. 233), 74 (doc. 4035), 75 (doc. 228), 59–61 (doc. 462).

152. Ludwig von Pastor, *The History of the Popes from the Close of the Middle Ages,* English trans., London, 1891ff., XXXI, 111–13.

153. Krautheimer and Jones, "Diary," 221, nos. 762 and 763, 29 June 1664, Sunday, "parliamo co Bernino sul disegno della fabrica del Palazzo SS. Apostoli"; 4 July 1664, Friday, "è da noi il Cav. Bernino col disegno della facciata del palazzo del C. Chi[gi] davanti SS. Apostoli" (Chigi O.IV.58, fols. 622v, 623r).

154. AChigi 457, fol. 59v, 4 July 1664, the first payments "a buon conto" to Gabrielle Renzi *scarpellino* and Jacomo Beccaria *muratore,* for the palace. By the end of December 1664, payments to Renzi amounted to 1,750 scudi, while Beccaria had received only 900 scudi. Renzi's payments on 29 November and 29 December 1664 were for "lavori di travertino et Arme di marmo che fà" for the palace (AChigi 457, fols. 70v, 74v). AChigi 483, unpaginated *misura* of whitewashing 1664–68, begins with a summary of the four payments received "a buon conto"; the first of these is "1665 Adi 12 Decembre à buonconto dell'imbiancatura, e colori di travertino dato nella facciata, e stanze del Palazzo à SSᵗⁱ Apostoli, scudi 50."

155. Chigi a.I.19, fols. 64r–v, 67r–v. The attribution of the drawings to "Fabio Chigi (Alessandro VII) ?" in *Bernini in Vaticano,* Rome, 1981, 190–91, must be due to the presence of notes in Alexander VII's hand; it ignores Bernini's distinctive sketching style, as shown in many other drawings in the same volume.

156. Chigi a.I.19, fol. 64r:

A S.S. Apostoli

1. Se si puo rigirar da per tutto il portico del Cortile
2. La fontana infaccia alla porta con perder quella rimessa
3. Il corritoro, ò Galeria dalla Casa al Canto della stalla
4. Sopra la stalla alzare stanze, e coprir con tetto
   Cosi il cortile sarà libero, è piu grande, s'unirà
   Casa giardino e stalla, nè i frati così haveranno tanto
   prospetto.

157. AChigi 520, fol. 116, in the library E6, "Per haver tagliato il muro di una di dette facciate di detta libraria per adrizzarlo [47½ × 37½ *palmi*] taglio p. ¼."

158. Ibid., fol. 134, doorframes in C5 are removed and

then reinstalled "e messe à filo"; fol. 163, the doorframes in C17 are removed "e rimessi in opera in faccia"; fol. 220, "Facciata di fuori di dette rimesse verso il cortile"; fols. 97–98, "Muro di una porta murata nel Cantone, che da detta stanza [E13] andava alla libraria . . . Per haver rotto il muro e fatto la porta, che passa alla libraria [from E12]."

159. AChigi 517, fol. 47, "[in C4], finestra che si è aperta di novo in faccia al filo delle porte di detto piano Nobile, che responde nel Vicolo . . ." AChigi 483, 18 July 1667, unpaginated *misura* of the *indoratore* Vincenzo Corallo, in room C4, "Per haver dipinto a fresco il Muro incontro detta finestra [toward the vicolo] sopra la casa di S. Giacomo dell'incurabile dipintoci, un ordine d'architettura con doi Pilastri dorici dalle parti con sua basa, Capitello, con Cornice Architravata sopra con doi risalti che termina il Vano dov'è il Paese dipinto con suo piedistallo sotto con cimasa, e basa con havere s . . . to finto attorno le due finestre e dipintovi à una l'impannata finta e dipintovi il Paese à fresco colorito con distanze, arbori, boscaglie, e figurine barche, e fiumi il quale ornamento è longo palmi 25 alt. reguagliato palmi 24, scudi 30."

160. AChigi 520, fol. 17, the upward extension of the façade wall begins "sino palmi 2 sotto l'arco della seconda finestra della sala"—i.e., the old *sala* ceiling was at least 10 *palmi* lower than the new; fol. 115, in E6, plastered walls are 37½ *palmi* high—i.e., in the area of the newly raised walls; fol. 106, in E7, "Per haver alsalto il solaro di detta stanza . . . alzato palmi 7"; fol. 114, in E8, "Per haver rialzato li doi solari in detto stanzino uno sotto, et l'altro sopra quello di sopra alzato palmi 6 et quello di sotto palmi 2¼."

161. AChigi 517, fol. 43. Cf. preceding note for the raising of the floor in adjacent E8 (that is, the ceiling in D1).

162. Golzio, *Documenti*, 27–30, docs. 1260–1759 (8 May–20 Dec. 1665); Domenico Bernini, *Vita* (1713), 150.

163. Golzio, *Documenti*, 35, doc. 2460, for the earliest *giustificazione* signed by Fontana, 16 Oct. 1666; some bills continue to be signed by Bernini, until December 1666. Fontana was involved with the work even earlier: the drawings of 1664 bear his signature, and on 8 August 1665 and again on 15 January 1666 he was paid 25 scudi "per recognitione delle fatiche fatte in assistere a detta fabrica" (AChigi 457, fols. 105v, 129v).

164. AChigi 520, fol. 1,". . . quali lavori sono stati ordinati dal Sig.r Cavall. Bernino, con l'assistenza continuata da me sottoscritto Carlo Fontana in misurare le qui sotto quantità . . ."

165. AChigi 517, fol. 23, ". . . lavori fatti di poi delle suddette fenestre nove [in the center part of the façade], come qui sotto secondo l'ordine del Sig.r Cavaliere."

166. AChigi 516, fol. 67v, regarding the ceiling of the *sala*, "Per la fattura del Ponte sotto detto, disfatto, e rifatto diverse volte per sodisfare la vista del S.re Architetto e disfatto la soffitta vecchia, scudi 45."

167. Ibid., fol. 77, Chiccheri's work "fatti in conformità del disegno consignatoli dall'Architetto . . ."

168. AChigi 517, fol. 47, "Appartamento Nobile in facciata verso la Piazza e prima finestra che si è aperta di novo in faccia al filo delle porte di detto piano Nobile, che responde nel Vicolo che s'apri d'ordine di S.E. [i.e., the cardinal]."

169. AChigi 520, fol. 348, at stair S3, "Per haver murato il vano di detta porta [just made] con ordine di S.Em.za . . ."

170. Krautheimer and Jones, "Diary," 223–24, nos. 865, 867, 868, 871.

171. AChigi 522, unpaginated, 10 Jan.–31 Dec. 1689, itemizing miscellaneous repairs, including "Nel 2° appartamento nobbile Hab.a il Nepote di S.a Em.za P.rone," work at the altar "della cappella dove si dice messa."

Epilogue

1. See nineteenth-century plans published by Howard Hibbard, *The Architecture of the Palazzo Borghese,* Rome, 1962 (published simultaneously in the *Memoirs* of the American Academy in Rome, 27), Figs. 47–51 (ABorg. 315), and other plans in ABorg. 315 and ABorg. 8611; an inventory in ABorg. 457, inv. 35 (1832); and other inventories in ABorg. 458, inv. 64 (1759), inv. 72 (1839), and an unnumbered inventory (1809).

2. ABorg. 310, no. 181, 4 Aug. 1818. In the same document, responsibility for other apartments in the palace and other Borghese properties is assigned to other Borghese officials. Two years earlier, Camillo Borghese had been legally separated from Pauline and had moved to Florence.

3. Carlo Pietrangeli, *Palazzo Borghese e la sua decorazione* (Quaderni del Circolo della Caccia, 1), Rome, 1985, 7.

4. ABarb., Ind. III, no. 647, int. 3, is an inventory of repairs needed in the derelict palace in 1713.

5. Ibid., no. 648, int. 6, records the sale of the palace to the Carmelitani Scalzi di S. Teresa, 12 October 1734. Earlier attempts to sell the palace are documented in int. 7 (to Cardinal Pallavicini, 1717 and 1720) and int. 8 (to the Tribunale del Governo, 1726).

6. Daniela Porro, "Lo scalone del palazzo Barberini ai Giubbonari e altre opere di Nicola Giansimoni architetto," *Studi Romani* 24, nos. 1–2 (1986), 95–106.

7. W. W. Story, letter to Charles Eliot Norton, 21 May 1857, quoted in Henry Janes, *William Wetmore Story and His Friends,* 2 vols., Boston, 1903, I, 351–52.

8. Nathaniel Hawthorne, *Passages from the French and Italian Notebooks,* London, 1871, I, 68, 83, 168–69.

9. Thomas Ashby, "The Palazzo Odescalchi in Rome," *Papers of the British School at Rome* 8 (1916), 55–90, esp. 55.

10. E.g., a house in Trastevere, valued at only 700 scudi, 14 January 1611 (Getty Center, no. 850314; my thanks to Gene Waddell for bringing this *misura* to my attention),

and, less surprisingly, houses in via dei Giubbonari purchased by Carlo Barberini in 1624 (ABarb., Comp. 1, fols. 47 and 112).

11.   Anthony Blunt, "Roman Baroque Architecture: The Other Side of the Medal," *Art History* 3 (1980), 61–80.

Appendix 1

1.   This document was discovered by Joseph Connors. I am very grateful to him for recognizing its importance and suggesting that I include it in this book.

Appendix 2

1.   Note on cover.
2.   Immediately preceding the audience room.

Appendix 3

1.   I would like to thank Irving Lavin for drawing this manuscript to my attention, when he realized its relevance for my interpretation of the plan of Palazzo Barberini alle Quattro Fontane.
2.   Pio Pecchiai, *I Barberini,* Rome, 1959, 159–63, 182–87.
3.   Ibid., 161–63.
4.   Nicolò Barozzi and Guglielmo Berchet, *Relazioni degli stati europei lette al Senato dagli ambasciatori ʋeneti nel secolo decimosettimo,* Ser. III, Italia, *Relazioni di Roma,* 2 vols., Venice, 1877–79, I, 266 (1629), ". . . gentiluomo veramente modesto che con la soavità de' costumi attrae a se l'animo di tutta la Corte," like his father in his "assidua accurata applicazione alle cose domestiche, et negli interessi famigliari"; 334 (1632), "non posso riferire che bontà di costumi, placidezza e fiacchezza di spirito, educato humilmente, vive ristretto in ogni maggior regola et economia, accumula per tutti li mezzi immensità d'oro e d'aquisto, et il Pontefice e la Casa tutta acconsente al suo accrescimento"; 370 (1635), a similar report; II, 33 (1640), a similar report.

5.   Pecchiai, *I Barberini,* 171–74; see also Giulio Pisano, "L'ultimo prefetto dell'urbe," *Roma* 9 (1931), 103–20, 155–64, esp. 113–17; and Giacinto Gigli, *Diario romano (1608–1670),* ed. Giuseppe Ricciotti, Rome, 1958, 122–24.
6.   Barozzi and Berchet, *Relazioni di Roma,* I, 371.
7.   Pecchiai, *I Barberini,* 182–87.
8.   Giuseppe Sacchi Lodispoto, "Anna Colonna Barberini ed il suo monumento nel monastero di Regina Coeli," *Strenna dei Romanisti* 43 (1982), 460–78, esp. 464–66.
9.   Francesco was Commendatario of the Abbey of Farfa in Sabina.
10.   Camilla Barberini, 1598–1666.
11.   The name is written in the left margin, replacing the cancelled passage, "un buon sacerdote chiamato D. Magno Perneo da Anagni, quale morì Parochiano di S. Nicolò alli Cesarini."
12.   Written in a space left in the text, in another hand (that of Francesco's sister Camilla?).
13.   24 October 1627.
14.   Written in left margin, in another hand, "fù il Sig.ʳ D. Nicolò"; and, preceding this, in the hand of the text, the word "anzi."
15.   Written in left margin, "Qui và posto quanto si è raccontato della Prefettura," a reminder of a passage that was not written.
16.   Palazzo Barberini alle Quattro Fontane.
17.   Palazzo Colonna-Barberini at Palestrina; above, chap. 13.
18.   At this point another, clearer, hand begins.
19.   Written above, "tre"; and in the left margin, "Campo Leone."
20.   Villa Barberini alli Bastoni, near St. Peter's in Rome.
21.   Mompecchio, near Castelgandolfo; above, pp. 284–88.
22.   "Casa Grande" ai Giubbonari; above, chap. 11.
23.   The text ends in the fifth line of the page.

Appendix 4

1.   Other materials, including the description of 1630 given below, p. 344, are bound in as fols. 366–381v.

List of Documents Consulted

Abbreviations

ABarb.	Archivio Barberini	BAV	Biblioteca Apostolica Vaticana, Vatican City
ABorg.	Archivio Borghese		
AChigi	Archivio Chigi	Comp.	Computisteria
ASF	Archivio di Stato, Florence	CRM	Congregazioni religiose maschili
ASR	Archivio di Stato, Rome	Gior.	Giornale
ASV	Archivio Segreto Vaticano	Giust.	Giustificazioni
AVR	Archivio del Vicariato, Rome	LM	Libro mastro
		Reg.Mand.	Registro de mandati

Biblioteca Apostolica Vaticana

Barb. lat. 1926   Int. 2, De obelisco extra urbem via Labicana (sive de obelisco Barberino)

Barb. lat. 4344   Discorso sopra la Fabrica del Palazzo

Barb. lat. 4360   Pianta del sito degli Ecc^{mi} SS^{ri} Barberini à piazza Grimana, overo quattro fontane

Barb. lat. 4731   Della vita di Papa Urbano Ottavo . . . , vol. 2

Barb. lat. 5635   Inventario . . . Ecc^{ma} Casa Barberini . . . 1631; Ruolo della famiglia dell'E^{mo} Sig. Card. Francesco Barberini

Barb. lat. 6352   [avvisi]

Barb. lat. 5686   Viaggio in Francia . . . Francesco Barberini [Cesare Magalotti]

Barb. lat. 5688   Legatione del Sig^{re} Cardinale Barberino in Francia descritta dal commend^{re} Cassiano dal Pozzo

Barb. lat. 5689   Legatione del Sig^r Cardinal Barberino in Spagna [Cassiano dal Pozzo]

Barb. lat. 6540   [various Barberini letters and memoranda]

Chigi a.I.19

Chigi O.IV.58

Chigi P.VII. 10

Chigi P.VII. 13

Urb. lat. 1075   [avvisi]

Biblioteca Apostolica Vaticana, Archivio Barberini

CARLO (1562–1630)

Comp. 1   LM A, 1623–1628

Comp. 2   LM B, 1629–1630

Comp. 3   Gior., 1623–1628

MAFFEO (1563–1644)

Comp. 21   Gior., 1600–1604

Comp. 37   Spese, 1621–1622

Comp. 38   Spese, 1622–1623

FRANCESCO (1597–1679)

Comp. 51   LM C, 1635–1640

Comp. 80   Reg.Mand., 1630–1636

Comp. 81   Reg.Mand., 1637–1641

Comp. 84   Reg.Mand., 1653

Comp. 88   Reg.Mand., 1666–1669

Comp. 89   Reg.Mand., 1669–1672

Comp. 90   Reg.Mand., 1672–1675

Comp. 91   Reg.Mand., 1675–1678

Comp. 92   Reg.Mand., 1679–1680

Comp. 142   Salari e companatici, 1633–1637

TADDEO (1603–1647)

Comp. 181   LM A, 1623–1630

Comp. 184   LM I, 1642–1644

Comp. 187   Gior., 1623–1630

Comp. 192   Reg.Mand. B, 1630–1633

Comp. 193   Reg.Mand. D, 1633–1635

Comp. 194   Reg.Mand. E, 1636–1637

Comp. 196   Reg.Mand., 1643–1644

ANTONIO (1608–1671)

Comp. 214   LM bianco C, 1636–1644

Comp. 229   Gior. G, 1664–1667

Comp. 233   Reg.Mand. C, 1636–1644

Comp. 267   Inventario di guardarobba 1636–1640

Comp. 268   Inventario generale della guardarobba
1644

CARLO (1630–1706)

Comp. 348   Copia dell'inventario della guardarobba,
1704

MAFFEO (1631–1685)

Comp. 364   LM AA, 1653–1657

Comp. 367   LM DD, 1665–1670

Comp. 378   Reg.Mand., 1654–1680

Giust. 501–625, Francesco, 1626

Giust. 11230–11305, Francesco, 1672

Giust. 11306–11364, Francesco, 1672–1673

Giust. 11367–11400, Francesco, 1672–1673

Giust. 11402–11457, Francesco, 1673

Giust. 11789–11852, Francesco, 1674–1675

Giust. 12235–12303, Francesco, 1677

Giust. 12415–12443, Francesco, 1678

Giust. 12482–12509, Francesco, 1677–1678

Giust. 12510–12555, Francesco, 1678

Giust. 12566 [sic: 12556]–12662, Francesco, 1678

Giust. 12720–12790 [sic: 12798], Francesco, 1678–1679

Giust. 12799–12830, Francesco, 1679

Giust. 12855–12865, Francesco, 1678–1679

Ind. I, no. 747   Ristretto della vita del Card.
Francesco Senior . . .

Ind. II, no. 55   Inventario della
guardarobba . . . Antonio
Barberini 1653

Ind. II, no. 680   Misura e stima dei lavori
fatti . . . nel Palazzo del Sig.e
Card. Maffeo
Barberino . . . 1609

Ind. II, no. 685   Ordini all'Architetto di cose da
farsi al Casino di Mompecchio
Settembre 1635

Ind. II, no. 690   Varij Disegni e Piante per la
Fabrica del Palazzo
[Mompecchio] . . . 1637

Ind. II, no. 2439   Inventario delli quadri e
statue . . . Antonio
[Barberini] . . . 1644

Ind. II, no. 2826   Piante del palazzo alle Quattro
Fontane

Ind. II, no. 2863   Iuxa diversa parvi momenti, 1628
[Antonio, rented houses]

Ind. II, no. 2884   Pianta con discorso degli
architetti de siti del Palazzo alle
Quattro Fontane [containing
only the site plan of 1625]

Ind. II, no. 2878   Tre libretti continenti
conventioni e patti con diversi
Artisti della fabrica del Palazzo

alle Quattro Fontane [dal 1629 al 1634]

Ind. II, no. 2888 Libro contenente le misure, e stima de' lavori del Palazzo alle Quattro Fontane da Aprile 1629 a tutto il 1638

Ind. II, no. 2889 Nota delli denari pagati alli Muratori, Falegnami, Ferraro, ed altri per li lavori della nuova fabrica al Palazzo delle Quattro Fontane . . . [1628–1640] con diverse altre simile [sic] scritture

Ind. II, no. 2895 Conto della spesa dello Stanzione della Comedia 1637

Ind. II, no. 2903 Disegno del Gariglione posto sulla Torre dell'Orologio verso il Giardino del Palazzo Barberini

Ind. II, no. 2911 Pianta delle case d'Agata Rosa, e del Mancini, con altre scritture 1655

Ind. II, no. 3084 Istromento di Compra della Città di Palestrina . . . 1630

Ind. II, no. 3104 Lettere di negoziato per la compra di Palestrina . . . 1626–1628

Ind. II, no. 3112 Diverse scritture appartenenti a detta Città [Palestrina] . . .

Ind. II, no. 3302 Istromento aut° della Benedizione della Chiesa di Sᵃ Rosalia

Ind. II, no. 4076 Libretto ed inventario de' legnami vecchi delle stanze che si hanno da buttare a terra . . . [Palestrina] . . . 1627

Ind. II, no. 4081 Inventario di tutte le robbe del Palazzo Baronale di [Palestrina] . . . 1637

Ind. II, no. 4084 Relazione dell'alloggio fatto nella Città di Palestrina . . . al Sigᵉ Ambasciator di Spagna . . . 1669

Ind. III, no. 624 Beni già appartenenti all'Eccᵐᵃ Casa . . . Monte Rotondo

Ind. III, no. 647 Beni già appartenenti all'Eccᵐᵃ Casa . . . Palazzo ai Giupponari

Ind. III, no. 648 Beni già appartenenti all'Eccᵐᵃ Casa . . . Palazzo ai Giupponari

Ind. IV, no. 13 Libro contenente diversi mandati della Sigᵃ Dᵃ Anna

Ind. IV, no. 58 Copia di poliza privata di locazione dell'appartamento del Palazzo de' Giupponari, fatta all'Eccᵐᵃ Sigᵃ Dᵃ Anna

Ind. IV, no. 158 Inventario de' mobili, ed altro esistenti nel Palazzo Barberini alle Quattro Fontane nell'Appartamento abitato del Card. Antonio Seniore detto di S. Onofrio . . . 1646

Ind. IV, no. 176 Ruollo della Famiglia . . . Antonio Barberini . . . 1642

Ind. IV, no. 574 Vita della Sigᵃ Dᵃ Costanza Barberini . . .

Ind. IV, no. 580 Lettera di Urbano VIII quando era Cardinale alla Sigᵃ D. Costanza

Ind. IV, no. 598 Copia del cerimoniale, che la Sigᵃ Dᵃ Costanza de' Barberini Magalotti praticava nel ricevere le visite

Ind. IV, no. 1254 Descrittione della vita del Sigᵉ D. Taddeo Barberino . . .

Ind. IV, no. 1268 Ruolo della Famiglia dell'Eccᵐᵒ Sigᵉ Principe di Palestrina 1630

Ind. IV, no. 1281 Relazione delle forme colle quali il Sigᵉ Principe D. Taddeo doveva andare incontro al Sigᵉ Duca di Mantova . . .

Ind. IV, no. 1282 Ruolo della famiglia . . . Taddeo . . . 1643

Biblioteca Apostolica Vaticana, Archivio Chigi

FLAVIO CHIGI

AChigi 457 Gior. B, 1663–1670

AChigi 483 Giust., 1668

AChigi 484 Giust., 1669

AChigi 516	Conti di Antonio Chiccari falegname [1669]
AChigi 517	Conti di Gabriello Renzi scarpellino [1665–1667]
AChigi 519	[*misure*, masonry, 1667–1678]
AChigi 520	Iacopo e Carlo Beccheria capimaestri muratori [1664–1667]
AChigi 521	Iacopo e Carlo Beccheria capimaestri muratori [1669]
AChigi 522	[*misure*, masonry, 1687–1689]
AChigi 573	Ruolo della famiglia del Card. Flavio I Chigi, 1666–1675
AChigi 702	Inventario del palazzo a' SS.ti Apostoli, Giardino alle 4 Fontane, Ariccia . . . Sr Card. Flavio Chigi
AChigi 703	Inventario del palazzo a' SS.ti Apostoli, Sr Card. Flavio Chigi

Archivio Segreto Vaticano, Archivio Borghese

ABorg. 33, no. 433	[inventory Giovanni Battista Borghese 1610]
ABorg. 306	[*misure*, Palazzo Borghese, 1606–1617, and memorandum of expenditures for Palazzo Borghese]
ABorg. 307	[*misure*, Palazzo Borghese, 1609–1621]
ABorg. 310	[regulations for Borghese properties, 1818]
ABorg. 315	[19th-century plans]
ABorg. 456	[Borghese inventories]
ABorg. 457	[Borghese inventories]
ABorg. 458	[Borghese inventories]
ABorg. 1450	[payments, 1671]
ABorg. 1451	[payments, 1671–1672; *misura, legnami*]
ABorg. 1452	[payments, 1672]
ABorg. 1453	[payments, 1673]
ABorg. 1454	[payments, 1673]
ABorg. 1476, no. 781	[*misura*, masonry, 1671–1676]
ABorg. 3949	Rolo della famiglia dell'eccemo sr principe Borghese 1626–1632
ABorg. 4168	1605–1623 Fabbrica del Palazzo Borghese in Roma [*misure*]

ABorg. 4172	[1621]
ABorg. 4173	[*misure, falegnami, cavaterra, fornaciari*, many Borghese buildings, 1607–1623]
ABorg. 4174	1608–1623 Conti saldati dei lavori ad uso di scarpellino [Cardinal Scipione Borghese, diverse buildings]
ABorg. 5547	[*misure*, 1623]
ABorg. 5677	[*misure*]
ABorg. 6095	Inventario dopo la morte del Card. Scip. Borghese 1634
ABorg. 7502	Inventari di Robbe in Roma e nei Castelli 1622 [including Francesco Borghese 1610 and other inventories]
ABorg. 7504	Libro del Inventario [1693]
ABorg. 7926	Registro dei Mandati, 1610–1614 [Marcantonio]
ABorg. 8611, Cartella VI	Carte del Palazzo Borghese . . . [19th-century plans]

Archivio Segreto Vaticano, Fondo Borghese

Serie IV, no. 73bis inventory 1615

Archivio di Stato, Rome

CRM, Teatini, S. Andrea della Valle, busta 2162, fasc. 161, various *misure* for Palazzo Barberini alle Quattro Fontane

CRM, Teatini, S. Andrea della Valle, busta 2200, various *misure* for Palazzo Barberini alle Quattro Fontane

Not. A.C., 6601, fols. 852ff., inventory of the estate of Taddeo Barberini, 1648

Archivio del Vicariato, Rome

S. Susanna, Stati d'anime, 1631–1651

SS. 12 Apostoli, Stati d'anime, 1652–1667, 1667–1692

S. Maria in Via Lata, Stati d'anime, 1672–1685

S. Lorenzo in Lucina, Stati d'anime, 1607–1621, 1625, 1630, 1678

Archivio della S. Congregazione de Propaganda Fide

Archivio della Computisteria, Depot, Quaderno de' Sig^ri Barberini, 1633–1636

Archivio di Stato, Florence

Medici del Principato, vol. 2658

Biblioteca Medicea-Laurenziana

Buonarroti 90

Cassa di Risparmio di Roma, Archivio Storico del Monte di Pietà

Piante e disegni, vol. 572, inv. 1791

Bibliography

Adami, Anselmo. *Il novitiato del maestro di casa . . . ,* Rome, 1636.

Ademollo, Alessandro. *I teatri di Roma nel secolo decimosettimo,* Rome, 1888.

Alberti, Leon Battista. *De re aedificatoria,* trans. James Leoni (1726), ed. Joseph Rykwert, London, 1965.

Andres, Glenn Merle. *The Villa Medici in Rome* (Outstanding Dissertations in the Fine Arts), 2 vols., New York and London, 1976.

"Anna Colonna Barberini," *The Art Quarterly* (Detroit Institute of Arts) 9, no. 3 (Summer 1946), 271–73.

Apollonj, Bruno Maria. "La 'Casa Grande' dei Barberini," *Capitolium* 8 (1932), 451–62.

Ashby, Thomas. "The Palazzo Odescalchi in Rome," *Papers of the British School at Rome* 8 (1916), 55–90.

——. "The Palazzo Odescalchi," *Papers of the British School at Rome* 9 (1920), 67–74.

Aurigemma, Salvatore. "Il restauro di consolidamento del mosaico barberini, condotto nel 1952," *Rendiconti* (Atti della Pontificia Accademia Romana di Archeologia, Ser. III) 30–31 (1959), 41–98.

Baglione, Giovanni. *Le vite de' pittori . . . ,* Rome, 1642.

Baldi, Bernardino. *Descrizione del Palazzo ducale d'Urbino,* Venice, 1590.

Baldinucci, Filippo. *Vita del Cavaliere Gio. Lorenzo Bernino: scultore, architetto, e pittore,* Rome, 1682.

——. *Vocabolario toscano dell'arte del disegno . . . ,* Florence, 1681.

Bandes, Susan Jane. "The Frescoes of Gaspard Dughet," Ph.D. diss., Bryn Mawr College, 1977.

Barberini, Urbano. "Gli arazzi e i cartoni della serie 'Vita di Urbano VIII' della arazzaria Barberini," *Bollettino d'Arte* 53, Ser. 5 (1968), 92–100.

——. "Il 'Grande studio' del Thorvaldsen secondo la tradizione Barberini," *L'Urbe* 27, no. 5 (1964), 1–4.

Barozzi, Nicolò, and Guglielmo Berchet, *Relazioni degli stati europei lette al Senato dagli ambasciatori veneti nel secolo decimosettimo,* Ser. III, Italia, *Relazioni di Roma,* 2 vols., Venice, 1877–79.

Battaglia, Roberto. "Il palazzo di Nerone e la Villa Barberini al Gianicolo," *Roma* 20, no. 10 (October 1942), 401–17; almost identical with Roberto Battaglia, *Il Palazzo di Nerone e la Villa Barberini al Gianicolo* (Quaderni del Centro Nazionale di Studi di Storia dell'Architettura, 5), Rome, 1943.

Benocci, Carla. "Due disegni per la 'Casa Grande' dei Barberini in via dei Giubbonari," *Alma Roma* 24, no. 1–2 (January–April 1983), 1–9.

Bernheimer, Richard. "Theatrum Mundi," *Art Bulletin* 38 (1956), 225–47.

Bernini, Domenico. *Vita del cavalier Gio. Lorenzo Bernino . . . ,* Rome, 1713.

Bernini in Vaticano, Rome, 1981.

Bianchi, Arturo. "Attuazioni di Piano Regolatore, le nuove arterie di allacciamento con Piazza San Bernardo," *Capitolium* 6 (1930), 434–43.

Blunt, Anthony. *Guide to Baroque Rome,* New York, 1982.

———. "The Palazzo Barberini: The Contributions of Maderno, Bernini and Pietro da Cortona," *Journal of the Warburg and Courtauld Institutes* 21 (1958), 256–87.

———. "Roman Baroque Architecture: The Other Side of the Medal," *Art History* 3 (1980), 61–80.

Boisclair, Marie-Nicole. "La décoration des deux mezzanines du palais Borghese de Rome," *Racar* 3, no. 1 (1976), 7–27.

Borghese, Nicolò. *Vita di S. Caterina da Siena . . . aggiuntovi l'elenco degli uomini illustri dell'Eccellentissima Casa Borghese,* Rome, [1869].

Borghesio, Gino. *I Borghese* (Le grandi famiglie romane, 10), Rome, 1954.

Borromini, Francesco, and Virgilio Spada. *Opus architectonicum,* Rome, 1725.

Borsi, Franco. *Bernini architetto,* Milan, 1980.

Bourdon, Pierre, and Robert Laurent-Vibert. "Le Palais Farnèse d'après l'inventaire de 1653," *Mélanges d'Archéologie et d'Histoire* (L'Ecole française de Rome) 29, Rome, 1909, 145–98 and 4 plates.

Brauer, Heinrich, and Rudolf Wittkower. *Die Zeichnungen des Gianlorenzo Bernini,* 2 vols., Berlin, 1931.

Briganti, Giuliano. *Pietro da Cortona o della pittura barocca,* Florence, 1962.

Bulst, Wolfger A. "Die ursprüngliche innere Aufteilung des Palazzo Medici in Florenz," *Mitteilungen des Kunsthistorischen Institutes in Florenz* 13 (1969–70), 369–92.

Caflisch, Nina. *Carlo Maderno,* Munich, 1934.

Castiglione, Baldassare. *Il libro del cortegiano,* Venice, 1527.

Cataneo, Pietro. *I quattro primi libri di architettura,* Venice, 1554.

Cerasoli, Francesco. "Censimento della popolazione di Roma dall'anno 1600 al 1739," *Studi e Documenti di Storia e Diritto* 12, Rome, 1891.

Cervio, Vincenzo. *Il trinciante,* Rome, 1593.

Chambers, D. S. "The Economic Predicament of Renaissance Cardinals," in *Studies in Medieval and Renaissance History,* III, ed. William Bowsky, Lincoln, Neb., 1966, 287–313.

Ciampi, Ignazio. *Innocenzo X Pamfili e la sua corte,* Rome, 1878.

Colini, A. M. *L'Isola della Purificazione a Piazza Barberini,* Rome, 1977.

Connors, Joseph. *Borromini and the Roman Oratory,* New York and Cambridge, Mass., 1980.

———. "Virgilio Spada's Defence of Borromini," *The Burlington Magazine* 131 (February 1989), 76–90.

Crema, Luigi. "Flaminio Ponzio, architetto milanese a Roma," in *Atti del IV Convegno Nazionale di Storia dell'Architettura, Milano, 18–25 giugno 1939–XVII,* Milan, 1940, 281–308.

Croce, Benedetto. "Scrittori del pieno e del tardo Rinascimentò, V: Libri sulle corti," *La Critica* 39, fasc. 4 (20 July 1941), 242–48.

D'Angelo, Maria. *Matrimoni nel seicento romano* (Curiosità romane, ser. 1, vol. 7), Albano Laziale, 1928.

De Angelis d'Ossat, Guglielmo. "L'autore del più bel cortile di Roma barocca" [first published in *Strenna dei Romanisti,* 1958, 45–47], in *Realtà dell'Architettura, Apporti alla sua storia 1933–1978,* II, Rome, 1982, 251–55.

De Lachenal, Lucilla. "La collezione di sculture antiche della famiglia Borghese e il palazzo in Campo Marzio," *Xenia* 4 (1982), 49–117.

Del Bufalo, Alessandro. *G. B. Contini e la tradizione del tardomanierismo nell'architettura tra '600 e '700,* Rome, 1982.

Della Casa, Giovanni. *Il Galateo . . . overo trattato de' costumi, e modi che si debbono tenere, ò schifare nella comune conversatione . . . ,* Florence, 1561.

Della Pergola, Paola. "Giovan Francesco Guerrieri a Roma," *Bollettino d'Arte,* Ser. 4, 41 (1956), 214–37.

———. "L'Inventario Borghese del 1693," *Arte antica e moderna* 26 (April–June 1964), 219–30; 28 (October–December 1964), 451–67; 30 (April–June 1965), 202–17.

De Luca, Giovanni Battista. *Il cavaliere e la dama,* Rome, 1675.

Delumeau, Jean. *Vie économique et sociale de Rome dans la seconde moitié du XVIᵉ siècle* (Bibliothèque des Ecoles françaises d'Athènes et de Rome, 184),

2 vols., Paris, 1957–59.

Dizionario biografico degli Italiani.

D'Onofrio, Cesare. *Gli obelischi di Roma,* Rome, 1965; 2d ed., Rome, 1967.

——. *Roma vista da Roma,* Rome, [1967].

——. *La Villa Aldobrandini di Frascati,* Rome, n.d.

Dunn, Marilyn R. "Nuns as Art Patrons: The Decoration of S. Marta al Collegio Romano," *Art Bulletin* 70 (1988), 451–77.

Edwards, Nancy Elizabeth. "The Renaissance 'Stufetta' in Rome: The Circle of Raphael and the Recreation of the Antique," Ph.D. diss., University of Minnesota, 1983.

Ehrle, Francesco, and Enrico Stevenson, *Gli affreschi del Pinturicchio nell'appartamento Borgia del Palazzo Apostolico Vaticano,* Rome, 1897.

Eiche, Sabine. "Cardinal Giulio della Rovere and the Vigna Carpi," *Journal of the Society of Architectural Historians* 45 (1986), 115–33.

Elling, Christian. *Function and Form of the Roman Belvedere* (Det Kgl. Danske Videnskabernes Selskab, Arkaeologisk-Kunsthistoriske Meddelelser, 3, no. 4), Copenhagen, 1950.

Enggass, Robert. *The Painting of Baciccio, Giovanni Battista Gaulli 1639–1709,* University Park, Pa., 1964.

Evelyn, John. *Diary,* ed. E. S. de Beer, Oxford, 1955.

Evitascandalo, Cesare. *Dialogo del trenciante,* Rome, 1609.

——. *Il maestro di casa,* Rome, 1598; Viterbo, 1620; and subsequent editions.

——. *Libro dello scalco,* Rome, 1609.

Fagiolo dell'Arco, Maurizio and Marcello. *Bernini: Una introduzione al gran teatro del barocco,* Rome, 1967.

Faldi, Italo. "Giovanni Serodine a Palazzo Borghese," *Strenna dei Romanisti* 49 (1988), 175–79.

Fasolo, Furio. "Il Palazzo Colonna-Barberini di Palestrina ed alcune note sul suo restauro," *Bollettino d'Arte* Ser. 4, 41 (1956), 73–81.

Fasolo, Furio, and Giorgio Gullini. *Il Sanctuario della Fortuna Primigenia a Palestrina,* Rome, 1953.

Fassò, Luigi. *Avventurieri della penna del seicento: Gregorio Leti, Giovanni Gerolamo Arconati Lamberti, Tomaso Tomasi, Bernardo Guasconi,* Florence, 1923.

Ferrajoli, Alessandro. "Il ruolo della corte di Leone X (1514–1516)," *Archivio della R. Società Romana di storia patria* 34 (1911), 1–31.

Fiocco, Giuseppe. *Alvise Cornaro, il suo tempo e le sue opere* (Saggi e studi di storia dell'arte, 8), n.p., 1965.

Fiore, Francesco Paolo. "Palazzo Barberini: problemi storiografici e alcuni documenti sulle vicende costruttive," in *Gianlorenzo Bernini architetto e l'architettura europea del Sei–Settecento,* 1, ed. Gianfranco Spagnesi and Marcello Fagiolo, Rome, 1983, 193–209.

Francesco di Giorgio Martini. *Trattati di architettura, ingegneria, e arte militare* (Trattati di architettura, 3), ed. Corrado Maltese, 2 vols., Milan, 1967.

Frommel, Christoph Luitpold. "La construction et la décoration du Palais Farnèse, Sangallo et Michel-Ange (1513–1550)," in *Le Palais Farnèse, Ecole française de Rome,* 1, Rome, 1981, 127–224.

——. *Der römische Palastbau der Hochrenaissance* (Römische Forschungen der Bibliotheca Hertziana, 21), 3 vols., Tübingen, 1973.

Gigli, Giacinto. *Diario romano (1608–1670),* ed. Giuseppe Ricciotti, Rome, 1958.

Giovannoni, Gustavo. *Antonio da Sangallo il Giovane,* 2 vols., Rome, 1959.

——. "Il Palazzo Barberini e la sua piazza," *Palladio* 5 (1941), 227–28.

Goethe, Johann Wolfgang von. *Italian Journey,* trans. W. H. Auden and Elizabeth Mayer, New York, 1968.

Golzio, Vincenzo. *Documenti artistici sul Seicento nell'Archivio Chigi,* Rome, 1939.

——. *Il Palazzo Barberini e la sua galleria di pittura* (I palazzi e le case di Roma), Rome, [1925].

——. *Palazzi romani dalla rinascità al neoclassico* (Roma cristiana, 14), Bologna, 1971.

Guarini, Guarino. *Architettura Civile,* ed. Bianca Tavassi LaGrecca (Trattati di architettura, 8), Milan, 1968.

Habel, Dorothy Metzger. "The Projected Palazzo Chigi al Corso and S. Maria in Via Lata: The Palace-Church Component of Alexander VII's

Program for the Corso," in *Rome: Tradition, Innovation and Renewal* (Proceedings of a Canadian International Art History Conference, Rome, 8–13 June 1987), forthcoming.

Hamberg, Per Gustav. "G. B. da Sangallo detto il Gobbo e Vitruvio," *Palladio* n.s. 8 (1958), 15–21.

Harris, Ann Sutherland. *Andrea Sacchi,* Oxford, 1977.

——. "A Contribution to Andrea Camassei Studies," *Art Bulletin* 52 (1970), 49–70.

Haskell, Francis. *Patrons and Painters,* London, 1963.

Haskell, Francis, and Nicholas Penny, *Taste and the Antique: The Lure of Classical Sculpture 1500–1900,* New Haven and London, 1981.

Hawthorne, Nathaniel. *Passages from the French and Italian Notebooks,* I, London, 1871.

Hempel, Eberhard. *Francesco Borromini,* Vienna, 1924.

Heydenreich, Ludwig H. "Der Palazzo Baronale der Colonna in Palestrina," in *Walter Friedlaender zum 90. Geburtstag,* Berlin, 1965, 85–91 and plates 20–23.

Hibbard, Howard. "Di alcune licenze rilasciate dai Mastri di Strade per opere di edificazione a Roma (1586–'89, 1602–'34)," *Bollettino d'Arte* Ser. 5, 52 (1967), 99–117.

——. *The Architecture of the Palazzo Borghese,* Rome, 1962 (published simultaneously in the *Memoirs* of the American Academy in Rome, 27).

——. *Carlo Maderno and Roman Architecture 1580–1630* (Studies in Architecture, 10), University Park, Pa., and London, 1971.

——. "Palazzo Borghese Studies, II: the *Galleria,*" *The Burlington Magazine* 104 (1962), 9–20.

——. "Scipione Borghese's Garden Palace on the Quirinal," *Journal of the Society of Architectural Historians* 23 (1964), 163–92.

Hoogewerf, G. J. "Andrea Sacchi en Carlo Maratti," *Mededeelingen van het Nederlandsch Historisch Institut te Rome* Ser. 3, v (1947), 123–35.

Incisa della Rocchetta, Giovanni. "Notizie inedite su Andrea Sacchi," *L'Arte* (Rivista di storia dell'arte medioevale e moderna e d'arte decorativa) 27 (1924), 60–76.

James, Henry. *William Wetmore Story and His Friends,* 2 vols., Boston, 1903.

Krautheimer, Richard. *The Rome of Alexander VII, 1655–1667,* Princeton, 1985.

Krautheimer, Richard, and Roger B. S. Jones. "The Diary of Alexander VII, Notes on Art, Artists and Buildings," *Römisches Jahrbuch für Kunstgeschichte* 15 (1975), 199–225.

Lamb, H. H. *Climate, Present, Past and Future,* II, London and New York, 1977.

Lavin, Marilyn Aronberg. *Seventeenth-Century Barberini Documents and Inventories of Art,* New York, [1975].

Lechner, George. "Tommaso Campanella and Andrea Sacchi's Fresco of *Divina Sapienza* in the Palazzo Barberini," *Art Bulletin* 58 (1976), 97–108.

Lefevre, Renato. *Il Palazzo degli Aldobrandini e dei Chigi,* Rome, 1964.

Le Roy Ladurie, Emmanuel. *Times of Feast, Times of Famine: A History of Climate since the Year 1000,* trans. Barbara Bray, Garden City, N.Y., 1971.

Letarouilly, Paul. *Edifices de Rome moderne,* Brussels, n.d.

Leti, Gregorio. *Itinerari della corte di Roma ò verò teatro historico, cronologico, e politico della sede apostolica . . . ,* Valence, 1675.

Liberati, Francesco. *Il perfetto maestro di casa,* Rome, 1658.

Lodispoto, Giuseppe Sacchi. "Anna Colonna Barberini ed il suo monumento nel monastero di Regina Coeli," *Strenna dei Romanisti* 43 (1982), 460–78.

Lotti, L. "La Villa Barberini al Gianicolo e il problema delle fortificazioni meridionali del Vaticano," *L'Urbe* 43, no. 2 (March–April 1980), 1–16.

Lotz, Wolfgang. "Gli 883 cocchi della Roma del 1594," in *Studi offerti a Giovanni Incisa della Rocchetta* (Miscellanea della Società Romana di Storia Patria, 23), Rome, 1973, 247–66.

——. "Vignole et Giacomo della Porta (1550–1589)," in *Le Palais Farnèse, Ecole Française de Rome,* I, Rome, 1981, 225–41.

Lunadoro, Girolamo. *Relatione della Corte di Roma, e de' riti da osservarsi in essa . . . ,* n.p., 1635.

Magnanimi, Giuseppina. *Palazzo Barberini,* Rome, 1983.

——. "Palazzo Barberini: I documenti della costruzione," *Antologia di Belle Arti* 4, no. 15–16 (1980), 194–214.

——. "Palazzo Barberini: La sala ovale," *Antologia di Belle Arti* 1, no. 1 (March 1977), 29–36.

Magnuson, Torgil. *Rome in the Age of Bernini*, 2 vols., Stockholm, 1982–86.

——. *Studies in Quattrocento Architecture* (*Figura*, 9, Studies edited by the Institute of Art History, University of Uppsala), Stockholm, 1958.

Marangoni, Giovanni. *Delle cose gentilesche e profane trasportate ad uso, e adornamento delle chiese*, Rome, 1744.

Marucchi, Orazio. *Descrizione del Museo Prenestino Barberiniano con brevi cenni sul Palazzo Baronale*, Rome, 1917.

Masera, Maria Giovanna. *Michelangelo Buonarroti il Giovane*, Turin, 1941.

Masson, Georgina. *Queen Christina*, London, 1968.

Montagu, Jennifer. "Antonio and Giuseppe Giorgetti: Sculptors to Cardinal Francesco Barberini," *Art Bulletin* 52 (1970), 278–98.

——. "Exhortatio ad virtutem: A Series of Paintings in the Barberini Palace," *Journal of the Warburg and Courtauld Institutes* 34 (1971), 366–72.

Montaigne, Michel de. *Journal du voyage de Michel de Montaigne en Italie par la Suisse et l'Allemagne en 1580 et 1581*, ed. Alessandro d'Ancona, Città di Castello, 1889.

Moroni, Gaetano. *Dizionario di erudizione storico-ecclesiastica*, 103 vols., Venice, 1840–61.

Müntz, Eugène. *Les Collections des Médicis au XVᵉ siècle, le musée, la bibliothèque, le mobilier, appendice aux Précurseurs de la Renaissance* (Bibliothèque internationale de l'art), Paris and London, 1888.

Murata, Margaret. *Operas for the Papal Court 1631–1698*, Ann Arbor, 1981.

Negro, Angela. *Rione II, Trevi* (Guide rionali di Roma), 1, Rome, 1980.

Neppi, Lionello. *Palazzo Spada*, Rome, 1975.

Noehles, Karl. *La Chiesa dei SS. Luca e Martina nell'opera di Pietro da Cortona* (Saggi e studi di storia dell'arte, 3), Rome, 1970.

Odom, William M. *A History of Italian Furniture*, 2 vols., Garden City, New York, 1918–19.

Orbaan, J.A.F. *Documenti sul Barocco in Roma*, Rome, 1920.

Ordini et offitij alla corte del serenissimo signor duca d'Urbino, ed. Giuseppe Ermini, Urbino, 1932.

Pagliara, Pier Nicola. "Monterotondo," in *Storia dell'arte italiana*, pt. III, 1, *Inchieste su centri minori*, Turin, 1980, 233–78.

Palladio, Andrea. *I Quattro libri dell'architettura*, Venice, 1570.

Panciroli, Ottavio. *Roma sacra e moderna, già descritta dal Pancirolo ed accresciuta da Francesco Posterla . . . e di nuovo con somma diligenza, e studio riordinata da Gio. Francesco Cecconi . . .*, Rome, 1725.

Panofsky-Soergel, Gerda. "Zur Geschichte des Palazzo Mattei di Giove," *Römisches Jahrbuch für Kunstgeschichte* 11 (1967–1968), 109–88.

Pasquinelli, A. "Alla ricerca di dodici colonne antiche," *Roma* 8 (August 1927), 378–79.

Pastor, Ludwig von. *The History of the Popes from the Close of the Middle Ages*, English trans., London, 1891ff.

Pecchiai, Pio. *I Barberini*, Rome, 1959.

——. "Costanza Magalotti Barberini, Cognata di Urbano VIII," *Archivi* (Rome) 16, fasc. 2 (1949), 11–41.

Pericoli Ridolfini, Cecilia. *Le case romane con facciate graffite e dipinte*, Rome, 1960.

——. *Rione VI, Parione, II* (Guide Rionali di Roma), Rome, 1971.

Petrini, Pietrantonio. *Memorie prenestine disposte in forma di annali*, Rome, 1795.

Petronio da Civita Vecchia, Alessandro. *Del viver delli romani, et di conservar la sanità . . .*, Rome, 1592.

Pieralisi, D. Sante. *Osservazioni sul mosaico di Palestrina*, Rome, 1858.

Pietrangeli, Carlo. *Palazzo Borghese e la sua decorazione* (Quaderni del Circolo della Caccia, 1), Rome, 1985.

Pinaroli, Giacomo. *L'antichità di Roma con le cose più memorabili che in essa di presente antiche e moderne si trovano . . .*, 2 vols., Rome, 1703;

[G.P. Pinaroli] *Trattato delle cose più memorabili di Roma tanto antiche come moderne, che in esse di presente si trovano . . . ,* 3 vols., Rome, 1725.

[Piranesi, Giovanni Battista]. *Raccolte di varie vedute di Roma si antica che moderna intagliate la maggior parte dal celebre Gianbattista Piranesi e da altri incisori . . . ,* Rome, 1752.

Pisano, Giulio. "L'ultimo prefetto dell'urbe," *Roma* 9 (1931), 103–20, 155–64.

Pollak, Oskar. "Italienische Künstlerbriefe aus der Barockzeit," *Jahrbuch der Königlich Preuszischen Kunstsammlungen* 34, Beiheft (1913), 1–77.

Pollak, Oskar. *Die Kunsttätigkeit unter Urban VIII,* 1, Vienna, 1928.

Porro, Daniela. "Lo scalone del palazzo Barberini ai Giubbonari e altre opere di Nicola Giansimoni architetto," *Studi romani* 24, nos. 1–2 (1986), 95–106.

Portoghesi, Paolo. *Roma Barocca: The History of an Architectonic Culture,* Engl. trans., [Cambridge, Mass., 1970].

——— . *The Rome of Borromini: Architecture as Language,* trans. Barbara Luigia La Penta, New York, 1968.

Posse, Hans. "Das Deckenfresko des Pietro da Cortona im Palazzo Barberini und die Deckenmalerei in Rom," *Jahrbuch der Preuszischen Kunstsammlungen* 60 (1919), 93–118, 126–73.

Prinz, Wolfram. *Die Entstehung der Galerie in Frankreich und Italien,* Berlin, 1970.

Priscianese, Francesco. *Del governo della corte d'un signore in Roma,* Rome, 1543 (republished Città di Castello, 1883).

Reinhardt, Ursula. "La tapisserie feinte, un genre de décoration du manierisme romain au XVIe siècle," *Gazette des Beaux-arts* 84 (1974), 285–96.

Roma 1300–1875: La città degli anni santi, Atlante, ed. Marcello Fagiolo and Maria Luisa Madonna, Milan, 1985.

Romanelli, Pier Bartolo. "Etichetta e precedenze a Roma durante il soggiorno di Cristina di Svezia," *Il Giornale di Politica e di Letteratura* 7, fasc. 1–3 (January–March 1931), 1–40.

Roosen, William. "Early Modern Diplomatic Ceremonial: A Systems Approach," *Journal of Modern History* 52, no. 3 (September 1980), 452–76.

Rossetti, Giovanni Battista. *Dello scalco,* Ferrara, 1584.

Rossini, Giovanni Pietro. *Il Mercurio errante delle grandezze di Roma, tanto antiche che moderne,* 3rd ed., Rome, 1715.

Rossini, Luigi. *I monumenti più interessanti di Roma dal decimo secolo sino al secolo decimottavo veduti in prospettiva . . . ,* Rome, 1818.

Rouvet, Massillon. *Entrée a Rome de Charles de Gonzague, Ambassadeur du Roi de France Henri IV, d'après un comte-rendu de 1608,* Nevers, 1895.

[Salerno, Luigi]. "Il ninfeo Barberini à Palestrina," *Palatino* 8 (1964), 257.

Scaino da Salò, Antonio. *Trattato del giuoco della palla,* Venice, 1555.

Scamozzi, Vincenzo. *L'idea dell'architettura universale,* Venice, 1615.

Scappi, Bartolomeo. *Dell'arte del cucinare,* Venice, 1570.

Schiavo, Armando. *La Fontana di Trevi e le altre opere di Nicola Salvi,* Rome, 1956.

——— . "Palazzo Barberini e Palazzo Moroni," *L'Urbe* n.s. 38, no. 3–4 (May–August 1975), 1–16.

——— . *Palazzo Mancini,* Palermo, 1969.

Schwäger, Klaus. "Kardinal Pietro Aldobrandinis Villa di Belvedere in Frascati," *Römisches Jahrbuch für Kunstgeschichte* 9–10 (1961–62), 289–382.

Scott, John Beldon. *Images of Nepotism,* Princeton, in press.

——— . "S. Ivo alla Sapienza and Borromini's Symbolic Language," *Journal of the Society of Architectural Historians* 41 (1982), 294–317.

Sebastiani, Pietro de'. *Viaggio curioso de' palazzi e ville più notabili di Roma,* Rome, 1683.

Sestini da Bibbiena, Francesco. *Il maestro di camera,* Florence, 1621; 2d ed., "di nuovo ricorretto secondo il Ceremoniale Romano," Viterbo, 1639; and many subsequent editions.

Sladek, Elisabeth. "Der Palazzo Chigi-Odescalchi an der Piazza SS. Apostoli," *Römische historische Mitteilungen* 27 (1985), 439–503.

Spagnesi, Gianfranco. "Palazzo Del Bufalo-Ferraioli e il suo architetto," in *Studi in memoria di Gino*

Chierici (Società di Storia Patria di Terra di Lavoro), Caserta, 1965.

Specchi, Alessandro. *Il quarto libro del nuovo teatro delli palazzi in prospettiva di Roma moderna . . . ,* Rome, 1699.

Stanley, David J., II. "The Origin and Development of the Renaissance Belvedere in Central Italy," Ph.D. diss., Pennsylvania State University, 1978.

Tafuri, Manfredo. "Borromini in Palazzo Carpegna: Documenti inediti e ipotesi critiche," *Quaderni dell'Istituto di Storia dell'Architettura* Ser. 14, fasc. 79–84 (1967), 85–107.

Tantouche, F. *Traicte de tout ce qui s'observe en la cour de Rome, Tant par nostre sainct Père, que par Messeigneurs les Illustrissimes Cardinaux,* Paris, 1623.

Tasso, Torquato. *Il Malpiglio: A Dialogue on the Court,* trans. Dain A. Trafton (English Literary Renaissance Supplements, 2), [Amherst, Mass., 1973].

Tessin, Nicodemus. *Studieresor i Danmark, Tyskland, Holland, Frankrike och Italien,* ed. Osvald Sirén, Stockholm, [1914].

Testori, Giovanni, Rudi Chiappini, and Sandro Corradini. *Serodine: L'opera completa,* Milan, 1987.

Tetius, Hieronymus [Girolamo Teti]. *Aedes Barberinae ad Quirinalem,* Rome, 1642.

Thelen, Heinrich. *Francesco Borromini: Die Handzeichnungen,* I (Veröffentlichungen der Albertina, 2), Graz, 1967.

Thoenes, Christof. "Bernini architetto tra Palladio e Michelangelo," in *Gian Lorenzo Benini Architetto e l'architettura europea del Sei–Settecento,* I, Rome, 1983, 105–34.

Tomei, Piero. "Contributi d'archivio, un elenco dei palazzi di Roma del tempo di Clemente VIII," *Palladio* 3 (1939), 163–74, 219–30.

Tosi, Mario. *Il Sacro Monte di Pietà di Roma e le sue amministrazioni,* Rome, 1937.

Totti, Pompilio. *Ritratto di Roma moderna,* Rome, 1638.

Vitruvius. *De architectura libri decem.*

Vitzthum, Walter. Review of Giuliano Briganti, *Pietro da Cortona o della pittura barocca,* in *The Burlington Magazine* 105 (1963), 213–17.

Waddy, Patricia. "The Design and Designers of Palazzo Barberini," *Journal of the Society of Architectural Historians* 35 (1976), 151–85.

——. "Michelangelo Buonarroti the Younger, *Sprezzatura,* and Palazzo Barberini," *Architectura* 5 (1975), 101–22.

——. "Palazzo Barberini: Early Proposals," Ph.D. diss., New York University, 1973.

——. "Taddeo Barberini as a Patron of Architecture," in *L'âge d'or du mécénat (1598–1661),* Paris, 1985, 191–99.

Waterhouse, E. K. *Baroque Painting in Rome,* London, 1937.

Weil-Garris, Kathleen, and John F. D'Amico, "The Renaissance Cardinal's Ideal Palace: A Chapter from Cortesi's *De cardinalatu,*" in *Studies in Italian Art History,* I, ed. Henry A. Millon, Rome, 1980, 45–123.

Whitehouse, Helen. *The Dal Pozzo Copies of the Palestrina Mosaic* (British Archaeological Reports Supplementary Series 12), Oxford, 1976.

Wittkower, Rudolf. *Art and Architecture in Italy 1600–1750* (Pelican History of Art), 3d ed., Harmondsworth, 1973.

——. "Pietro da Cortonas Ergänzungsprojekt des Tempels in Palestrina," in *Adolf Goldschmidt zu seinem 70. Geburtstag 15. Jan. 1933,* Berlin, 1935, 137–43; translated as "Pietro da Cortona's Project for Reconstructing the Temple of Palestrina," in *Studies in the Italian Baroque,* London, 1975, 116–24.

Wren, Stephen. *Parentalia, or, Memoirs of the Family of the Wrens,* London, 1750.

Index

Numbers in italics refer to figures. Buildings are in Rome unless otherwise indicated.